Fundamentals of Organizational Behavior

3 EDITION

Andrew J. DuBrin

Professor of Management
College of Business
Rochester Institute of Technology

THOMSON

SOUTH-WESTERN

Australia · Canada · Mexico · Singapore · Spain · United Kingdom · United States

FUNDAMENTALS OF ORGANIZATIONAL BEHAVIOR, 3E

Andrew J. DuBrin

VP/Editorial Director:
Jack W. Calhoun

VP/Editor-in-Chief:
Michael P. Roche

Publisher:
Melissa S. Acuña

Executive Editor:
John Szilagyi

Senior Developmental Editor:
Judith O'Neill

Marketing Manager:
Jacquelyn Carrillo

Production Editor:
Starratt E. Alexander

Manufacturing Coordinator:
Rhonda Utley

Technology Project Editor:
Kristen Meere

Media Editor:
Karen L. Schaffer

Design Project Manager:
Rik Moore

Production House:
Buuji, Inc.

Cover and Internal Design:
Tin Box Studio

Cover Image:
© Eyewire, Inc.

Printer:
Transcontinental Printing, Inc.
Louiseville, QC

For permission to use material from this
text or product, submit a request online
at http://www.thomsonrights.com. Any
additional questions about permissions
can be submitted by email to
thomsonrights@thomson.com.

For more information
contact South-Western,
5191 Natorp Boulevard,
Mason, Ohio, 45040.
Or you can visit our Internet site at:
http://www.swlearning.com

Brief contents

Contents

Preface

Welcome to the third and slightly expanded edition of *Fundamentals of Organizational Behavior*. This book is designed for courses in organizational behavior and management that focus on the application of organizational behavior knowledge to achieve enhanced productivity and satisfaction in the workplace.

Organizational behavior is about human behavior on the job. Knowledge of organizational behavior is, therefore, an important repository for any manager to draw on. The same information that can propel a manager to excel can also assist individual organizational contributors in becoming more adaptive and effective. Non-managerial professionals, technology workers, sales representatives, and service providers benefit from the insight and analysis that organizational behavior provides, just as do managers and prospective managers. All are welcome under its umbrella.

Organizational behavior, because of its key contributions in driving workforce productivity, is a standard part of the curriculum in schools and colleges of business, management, and public administration. As a result, a proliferation of research and writing permeates the field. To provide just an overview of this vast amount of information, many introductory texts are quite lengthy, easily spilling over onto 800 or more pages. To soften the impact of such encyclopaedic approaches to the study of organizational behavior, many of these texts also lavishly layer figures and photographs onto their extended narratives. *Fundamentals of Organizational Behavior* takes a takes a briefer, more focused, and more applied approach to learning about the field. Instead of trying to dazzle with a baffling array of concepts, research findings, theories, and news clippings, this text judiciously concentrates on only the most useful ideas. It blends clear and thoughtful exposition of traditional topics, such as motivation, with topics of more recent origin, such as creativity, self-managing teams, knowledge management, and diversity.

And although each chapter packs in a lot of information, chapters consistently emphasize the essential and the practical. A major strategy was to omit elaborate theories and findings that are no longer the subject of active research, practice, or training programs. However, we did not permit a concern for brevity to strip the text down to a sterile outline devoid of human interest, examples, and useful applications. Most of the brief texts in organizational behavior sacrifice cases, self-quizzes, discussion questions, and in-action inserts, but *Fundamentals of Organizational Behavior* successfully manages to inject all of these elements into its pages and still stay concise.

The size and scope of this book are well suited to college courses that supplement a core textbook with journal articles, major projects, speciality texts, or other instructional media. The comprehensiveness of *Fundamentals of Organizational Behavior,* combined with its brevity, make it suitable for organizational training programs about human behavior in the workplace as well. The student who masters this text will not only acquire an overview of and appreciation for organizational behavior research, literature, theory, and opinion but will also develop a feel for managing and influencing others through the application of systematic knowledge about human behavior.

THE FEATURES

In addition to summarizing and synthesizing relevant information about essential organizational behavior topics and providing concrete examples of theories in action, *Fundamentals of Organizational Behavior* incorporates many useful features to make the material more accessible, collaborative, and incisive. It also works hard to be technologically relevant. Internet addresses are integrated into every chapter where appropriate, including in an end-of-chapter problem set, Organizational Behavior Online, which highlights a useful set of relevant sites for bookmarking. New videos, available for viewing online at **http://dubrin.swlearning.com**, demonstrate the usefulness of organizational behavior knowledge at a diverse range of organizations, from the Buffalo Zoo to General Motors to architectural firm Machado and Silvetti. And a new InfoTrac® integration feature—in every chapter—identifies passages in the text where related information on a specific topic is available online using the Gale Group's InfoTrac extensive database.

- *Learning Objectives* introduce the major themes of each chapter and provide a framework for study.
- *Definitions* of boldfaced key terms are highlighted in the text and are reinforced at the end of each chapter and in an end-of-book glossary.
- *Opening Vignettes* explore real organizational issues, highlighting the stake all types of organizations have in using human capital well. Each vignette concludes with a pointed Now-Ask-Yourself question, ensuring that *Fundamentals of Organizational Behavior* addresses the usefulness of organizational behavior ideas, not just the ideas themselves.
- *Organizational Behavior in Action* boxes describe the actions of managers and professionals in dealing effectively with the human aspects of management, making visible the connection between theory and practice.
- *Self-Assessments and Skill-Development Exercises* support self-directed learning while driving the connections between research, theory, and practice down to the personal level. They not only provide a point of departure for students in understanding and valuing their own individual attitudes and behaviors but also serve to create an ongoing dialogue as each assessment and exercise can be returned to many times over the course of a semester.
- *InfoTrac Examples* appear in the margin alongside text passages where additional, contrasting, or current news stories can be searched for and read online from a database of over 5,000 journals.
- *Video* selections are cued to places in the text where they have particular applicability.
- *Implications for Managerial Practice* boxes, located near the end of each chapter, set off several smart suggestions for applying organizational behavior information in a managerial context.

- *End-of-chapter Summaries of Key Points* integrate all key topics and concepts into several cogent paragraphs and link them with the chapter's stated learning objectives.
- *Key Terms and Phrases* provide a useful review of each chapter's terminology.
- *End-of-chapter Discussion Questions and Activities* are suitable for individual or group analysis.
- *Organizational Behavior On-line* combines "To Do" exercises and "To Bookmark" resources.
- *End-of-chapter Case Problems* illustrate major themes of the chapter and are suitable for individual or group analysis. Case Problems are uniquely designed to complement this text and include relevant follow-up discussion questions and links to related Web sites when appropriate.

THE FRAMEWORK

Fundamentals of Organizational Behavior is a blend of description, skill development, insight, and prescription. Divided into four parts, it moves from the micro to the macro, beginning with a brief introduction to the discipline. It then progresses to an exploration of the individual, to a discussion of groups and intergroup dynamics, to an examination of organizational systems.

As just noted, Part 1 provides an introduction to organizational behavior. Chapter 1 focuses on the nature and scope of organizational behavior and provides the foundation for what is to come.

Part 2 includes seven chapters that deal with the individual in the organization. Chapter 2 describes fundamental aspects of understanding individuals in terms of individual differences, diversity, mental ability, and personality. Chapter 3 describes individuals from the standpoint of learning, perception, and attributions. Chapter 4 describes attitudes, values, and ethics as they relate to behavior in organizations. Chapter 5 is about individual decision-making and creativity. Chapter 6 presents basic concepts of motivation and Chapter 7 discusses techniques for enhancing motivation. Chapter 8 describes the nature and management of conflict and stress.

Part 3, about groups and intergroup relations, contains four chapters. Chapter 9 is about interpersonal communications, and Chapter 10 covers group dynamics and teamwork. Chapter 11 deals with leadership, a cornerstone topic in organizational behavior and management. Chapter 12 extends the study of leadership by describing power, politics, and influence.

Part 4, about the organizational system and the global environment, contains four chapters covering macro issues in organizational behavior. Chapter 13 deals with organizational structure and design. Chapter 14 is about organizational culture and change. Chapter 15 covers a contemporary topic of major importance: organizational learning and knowledge management. Chapter 16 covers cultural diversity and international organizational behavior.

THE FACTS—THE THIRD EDITION, NEW AND EXPANDED

The third edition expands and thoroughly updates the second edition, with particular attention paid to refueling special features. Meatier end-of-chapter case problems, new critical-thinking questions appended to boxed inserts on organizational behavior in action, and more applied research enrich this edition. All chapter-opening vignettes as well as Organizational Behavior in Action boxes are new, 13 of the 16 case problems are new, and new research findings can be found in every chapter. Major additions and new or enhanced topical coverage are listed here, chapter by chapter:

Chapter 1: Additional information on the history of organizational behavior and management; refinement of skill-development in organizational behavior.

Chapter 2: Expanded coverage of Myers-Briggs psychological types; updating of emotional intelligence.

Chapter 3: Description of e-learning as an important new type of organizational learning; expanded coverage of the four learning orientations; and expanded coverage of Kelly's theory of attributing causes.

Chapter 4: New chapter allowed for expanded coverage of attitude, values, and ethics; more information about attitudes and organizational behavior.

Chapter 5: Analysis of NASA officials' decision making in relation to the *Columbia* crash in 2003; creative self-efficacy as a contributor to creativity; how mood influences creativity.

Chapter 6: Explanation of how affect can influence components of expectancy theory; explanation of the link between personality and motivation.

Chapter 7: Report of recent research on job crafting as a form of job enrichment.

Chapter 8: Research on accuracy of perceptions about sexual harassment, including a table of the behaviors surveyed; techniques managers use to resolve conflict between two or more other people; dealing with difficult people.

Chapter 9: E-mail time-management suggestions; expanded coverage of impact of computer-mediated communication on behavior.

Chapter 10: How to achieve teamwork in a virtual group; importance of team efficacy for an effective work group.

Chapter 11: Self-assessment about behavior and attitudes of trustworthy leader; more about trust and leadership.

Chapter 12: More explicit information about networking as a career-advancement strategy; unethical practice of boss stealing credit for employee ideas

Chapter 13: Product-service departmentalization at GE Capital; nine criteria for an effective organization design.

Chapter 14: Cultural dimension of innovativeness; sampling of organizational cultures of well-known companies.

Chapter 15: Expanded coverage of action learning; just-in-time method of knowledge management.

Chapter 16: Data about diversity initiatives at major firms; U.S. Postal Service data on positive consequences of cultural diversity; insights into dealing with blind people.

THE RESOURCES

Fundamentals of Organizational Behavior is supported by comprehensive instructional and learning support materials:

InfoTrac® College Edition Packaged free with every new copy of *Fundamentals of Organizational Behavior* is a four-month subscription to InfoTrac College Edition, an online research database that amasses over 5 million full-text articles from nearly 5,000 scholarly and popular periodicals. With InfoTrac, your students have anytime, anywhere access to journals like *Business Week, Fast Company, Fortune, Harvard Business Review,* and *Newsweek,* to name a few. If you routinely incorporate extra readings or research assignments into your course outline, directing your students to log on to InfoTrac to access particular articles or to conduct their own searches provides a quick and convenient way to gain a comprehensive view of the business environment from the most influential journals from around the world. For more information on InfoTrac, visit **http://www .infotrac-college.com**.

Interactive Self-Assessments (ISBN 0-324-23535-6) If your course includes a self-assessment component designed to get your students to start thinking about the skills they have acquired to date or to evaluate their strengths and developmental needs, a series of online self-assessments is available for free for use in conjunction with *Fundamentals*. During a quick visit to **http://selfassessments .swlearning.com**, instructors may register and tour the site. Place your order using the designated ISBN (0-324-23535-6), and *Fundamentals of Organizational Behavior* will ship to your bookstore with pre-assigned passcodes for entering the site. For additional details contact your South-Western/Thomson sales representative (800-423-0563).

Instructor's Manual with Test Bank (ISBN 0-324-28825-5) Available in print or for download at **http://dubrin.swlearning.com**, this author-generated manual includes an comprehensive array of instructional resources, all geared to offering instructors insights into how course content might be taught. Each chapter includes an outline along with key lecture notes; answers to end-of-chapter discussion questions and activities, usually in the form of a comment rather than an absolute dictation; and notes about the self-assessments and skill-building exercises. An examination for each chapter is also included, with 25 multiple-choice questions, 25 true/false questions, and three or four essays. Appendix A contains suggestions for using Computer-Assisted Scenario Analysis (CASA). Especially designed to help students develop a contingency point of view, CASA is a user-friendly technique that can be used with any word-processing software. It allows the student to insert a new scenario into case problems and then answer questions based on the new scenario. CASA helps to develop an awareness of the contingency factor in making decisions. A briefer version of CASA was published in the October 1992 issue of the *Journal of Management Education*. Transparency masters, which duplicate key figures from the text, are also rolled into the manual, as well as background information on available videos.

PowerPoint™ Slides (ISBN 0-324-28826-3) Over 250 slides to supplement course content are available for download at **http://dubrin.swlearning.com**. A duplicate set can also be found on the Instructor's Resource CD-ROM. For use by students as note-taking guides and by instructors to enhance lectures, these full-color images were designed to help you get the most out of your experience with *Fundamentals of Organizational Behavior*. Taken together, many students have found these slides to be an effective study guide.

ExamView Testing Software (ISBN 0–324–28827–1) ExamView, South-Western's computerized testing program, contains all the questions in the printed Test Bank and is available on the Instructor's Resource CD-ROM to instructors who adopt *Fundamentals of Organizational Behavior.* This easy-to-use test-creation program is compatible with both Microsoft® Windows and Macintosh systems and enables instructors to create printed tests, Internet tests, and LAN-based tests quickly. Blackboard– and WebCT-ready versions of *Fundamental's* Test Bank are also available to qualified instructors. Contact your South-Western/Thomson sales representative for more information.

Video A range of videos featuring a diverse group of businesses (from Cannondale to On-Target Supply to the Buffalo Zoo) are available for viewing at **http://dubrin.swlearning.com** via streaming media. These high-interest video assets provide an inside look at how companies address organizational behavior issues everyday, showing managers—at all levels of an organization—in action. All videos are also available to instructors on VHS cassette (ISBN 0–324–28829–8), excluding one short CNN segment on the Terra Cross, a GM concept.

Product Support Site The dedicated *Fundamentals of Organizational Behavior* site provides broad online support. Visit **http://dubrin.swlearning.com** to view available video, download supplements, take a quiz, and find links to and repositories of related resources.

Instructor's Resource CD-ROM (ISBN 0–324–28828–X) This CD-ROM contains the Microsoft Office application files of various teaching resources (the Instructor's Manual with Test Bank and the PowerPoint slides), along with our ExamView testing program and test files.

ALSO AVAILABLE FROM THE PUBLISHER

eCoursepacks Create a tailor-fitted, easy-to-use online companion for your organizational behavior course with eCoursepacks, from Thomson businesses South-Western and Gale. eCoursepacks give educators access to current content from thousands of popular, professional, and academic periodicals, from NACRA and Darden cases, and from the Gale Group's business and industry data. eCoursepacks also give you the ability to easily add your own material—even collecting a royalty if you choose. Permission to reprint all eCoursepack content has already been secured, saving you time in securing rights and the worry.

Online publishing tools from eCourspacks allow you to search our content databases and make selections quickly, to organize your selections, and to publish a final online product in a clear, uniform, and full-color format. To learn more visit **http://ecoursepacks.swlearning.com** or contact your South-Western/ Thomson sales representative (800–423–0563).

ACKNOWLEDGMENTS

The final topical content and organization of this text were heavily influenced by the results of a survey of professors who expressed interest in using a shorter, more concise text. Instructors from 50 colleges provided their opinions on what subjects form the foundation of their courses. They also provided feedback on the types of pedagogical activities and features that provide real value to the introductory organizational behavior course. My writing also benefited from the suggestions of numerous reviewers, some of whom, for reasons of confidentiality, must remain anonymous. Grateful acknowledgment is made to

David C. Baldridge—Rochester Institute of Technology
Talya N. Bauer—Portland State University
Neil S. Bucklew—West Virginia University
Mary Humphrys—University of Toledo
Avis L. Johnson—University of Akron
Marianne W. Lewis—University of Cincinnati
Jalane M. Meloun—Kent State University
Regina M. O'Neill—Suffolk University
Douglas Palmer—Trinity College
James Smas—Kent State University
Mary Anne Watson—University of Tampa

Thanks also to the staff at South-Western who worked with me to publish this new edition of *Fundamentals of Organizational Behavior:* acquisitions editor Joe Sabatino, developmental editor Judy O'Neill, marketing manager Jacque Carrillo, production editor Starratt Alexander, and designer Rik Moore. My special thanks also go to Professors Douglas Benton of Colorado State University, Terri Scandura of the University of Miami, and Ann Welsh of the University of Cincinnati, who read the entire first-edition manuscript and made many valuable suggestions that continue to inform my work.

Finally, writing without loved ones would be a lonely task. My thanks therefore go to my family: Drew, Douglas, Gizella, Melanie, Rosie, Clare, and Camila.

Andrew J. DuBrin

ABOUT THE AUTHOR

Andrew J. DuBrin is professor of management in the College of Business at the Rochester Institute of Technology, where he teaches courses and conducts research in management, organizational behavior, leadership, and career management. He has served the college as chairman of the management department and as team leader. He received his Ph.D. in industrial psychology from Michigan State University. His business experience is in human resource management and he consults with organizations and with individuals. His specialties include leadership and career management.

Professor DuBrin is an established author of both textbooks and trade titles. He also writes for professional journals, magazines, and newspapers. He has written textbooks on the principles of management (including *Essentials of Management,* now in its sixth edition for South-Western/Thomson Learning), leadership, organizational behavior, industrial psychology, and human relations. His trade titles cover many current issues, including reengineering, team play, office politics, coping with adversity, and overcoming career self-sabotage.

Chapter 1

The Nature and Scope of Organizational Behavior

A research team led by Franklin Becker, director of the Cornell University International Workplace Studies Program (IWSP), investigated the relative advantages of closed offices, open workspaces, and cubicles. Becker—along with colleague William Sims and their graduate students—interviewed, surveyed, and observed 229 employees of eight small technology firms.

A major finding was that open workspaces fostered more employee productivity, learning, and camaraderie than closed offices or cubicles, which were also more expensive to construct. In fact, high-paneled cubicles appeared to undermine worker productivity the most, with closed offices having a particularly isolating effect.

Although many of the surveyed workers—particularly the older ones—initially said they preferred closed offices for privacy and concentration reasons, they often switched their top choice to open workspaces, claiming that increased access to coworkers improved communication. Many said that open spaces allowed employees to better read the cues of coworkers: when a coworker appeared busy, others stayed away and waited for a better time to interrupt. By comparison, offices and cubicles hid employees, which meant others interrupted at inconvenient times more often.

Cubicles created the illusion of privacy so that some employees felt free to have long, loud phone or face-to-face conversations that distracted others. In open offices, out of consideration for others, interactions tended to be shorter and often stayed focused on work matters. The result was efficient, impromptu idea generation and decision making, and less need for delayed formal meetings. "What might not have happened until tomorrow at 2 happens today," said Becker. "The whole process is speeded up—productivity improves."

Becker quickly conceded that no office environment was perfect. A good solution would give workers a choice of work environments to fit the demands of different tasks. "The point is to flip the predominant office thinking so that employees spend most of their time together as a team and less of their time going off to work alone," said Becker. "The open office is a tremendous opportunity to share knowledge and learn by osmosis."

The full results of the IWSP study appear in a report available on the Web at **http://iwsp.human.cornell.edu.**

Source: Adapted from Bridget Murray, "There's Nothing Good about Working in a Cubicle, Study Finds," *Monitor on Psychology*, May 2002, p.11.

OBJECTIVES

After reading and studying this chapter and doing the exercises, you should be able to:

1 Explain what organizational behavior means.

2 Summarize the research methods of organizational behavior.

3 Identify the potential advantages of organizational behavior knowledge.

4 Explain key events in the history of organizational behavior.

5 Understand how a person develops organizational behavior skills.

NOW ASK YOURSELF: How do the research findings just reported illustrate how organizational behavior knowledge can contribute to organizational effectiveness? A company about to invest in new office space, or in redesigning existing space, would have some useful data suggesting that open offices foster more productivity and teamwork.

The purpose of this book is to present systematic knowledge about people and organizations that can be used to enhance individual and organizational effectiveness. Managers and potential managers are the most likely to apply this information. Yet the same information is important for other workers, including professionals, sales representatives, customer service specialists, and technical specialists.

In the modern organization, workers at every level do some of the work that was formerly the sole preserve of managers. Team members, for example, are often expected to motivate and train each other. One reason organizations get by with fewer managers than previously is that workers themselves are now expected to manage themselves to some extent. Self-management of this type includes the team scheduling its own work and making recommendations for quality improvement.

In this chapter, we introduce organizational behavior from several perspectives. We will explain the meaning of the term, see why organizational behavior is useful, and take a brief glance at its history. After describing how to develop skills in organizational behavior, we present a framework for understanding the field. An important goal in studying organizational behavior is to be able to make sense of any organization in which you are placed. For example, you might be able to answer the question, "What is going on here from a human standpoint?"

THE MEANING AND RESEARCH METHODS OF ORGANIZATIONAL BEHAVIOR

1

Explain what organizational behavior means.

A starting point in understanding the potential contribution of organizational behavior is to know the meaning of the term. It is also important to be familiar with how information about organizational behavior is acquired.

The Meaning of Organizational Behavior

Organizational behavior (OB) is the study of human behavior in the workplace, the interaction between people and the organization, and the organization itself.[1] The major goals of organizational behavior are to explain, predict, and control behavior.

Explanation refers to describing the underlying reasons or process by which phenomena occur. For example, an understanding of leadership theory would explain why one person is a more effective leader than another. The same theory would help predict which people (such as those having charismatic qualities) are likely to be effective as leaders. Leadership theory could also be useful in controlling (or influencing) people. One leadership theory, for example, contends that to influence group members, a leader should help them remove barriers to goal attainment.

Data Collection and Research Methods in Organizational Behavior

2

Summarize the research methods of organizational behavior.

To explain, predict, and control behavior, organizational behavior specialists must collect information systematically and conduct research. The purpose of collecting data is to conduct research.

Methods of Data Collection

Three frequently used methods of collecting data in organizational behavior are surveys, interviews, and direct observation of behavior. The *survey questionnaire* used by a specialist in organizational behavior is prepared rigorously. Before preparing a final questionnaire, a scientist collects relevant facts and generates hypotheses (educated guesses) about important issues to explore. The questionnaire is carefully designed to measure relevant issues about the topic under survey. Among the surveys included in this text is the Creative Personality Test in Chapter 5.

Research about human behavior in the workplace relies heavily upon the *interview* as a method of data collection. Even when a questionnaire is the primary method of data collection, interviews are usually used to obtain ideas for survey questions. Interviews are also helpful in uncovering explanations about phenomena and furnishing leads for further inquiry. Another advantage of interviews is that a skilled interviewer can probe for additional information. One disadvantage of the interview method is that skilled interviewers are required.

Observers placing themselves in the work environment collect much information about organizational behavior. *Systematic observations* are then made about the phenomena under study. One concern about this method is that the people under observation may perform atypically when they know they are being observed. A variation of systematic observation is *participant observation*. The observer becomes a member of the group about which he or she collects information. For example, to study stress experienced by customer service representatives, a researcher might work temporarily in a customer service center.

Research Methods

Four widely used research methods of organizational behavior are case studies, laboratory experiments, field experiments (or studies), and meta-analysis. Although *cases* are a popular teaching method, they are often looked upon negatively as a method of conducting research. Case information is usually collected by an observer recording impressions in his or her mind or on a notepad. People have a tendency to attend to information specifically related to their own interests or needs. Despite this subjective element in the case method, cases provide a wealth of information that can be used to explain what is happening in a given situation.

An *experiment* is the most rigorous research method. The essence of conducting an experiment is making sure that the variable being modified (the independent variable) influences the results. The independent variable (such as a motivational technique) is thought to influence the dependent variable (such as productivity). The dependent variable is also known as the *criterion* (or measure).

A major characteristic of the *laboratory experiment* is that the conditions are supposedly under the experimenter's control. A group of people might be brought into a room to study the effects of stress on problem-solving ability. The stressor the experiment introduces is an electronic beeping noise. In a field setting, assuming the experiment was permitted, the experimenter might be unaware of what other stressors the subjects faced at that time. A key concern about laboratory experiments, however, is that their results might not apply to the outside world.

Field experiments (or studies) attempt to apply the experimental method to real-life situations. Variables can be controlled more readily in the laboratory than in the field, but information obtained in the field is often more relevant. An example of a field experiment would be investigating whether giving employees more power would have an effect on their ability to produce high-quality work. The

4

independent variable would be empowerment, while the dependent variable would be quality of work.

A widely used approach to reaching conclusions about behavior is to combine the results of a large number of studies. A **meta-analysis** is a quantitative or statistical review of the literature on a particular subject, and is also an examination of a range of studies for the purpose of reaching a combined result or best estimate. A meta-analysis is therefore a review of studies, combining their quantitative information. You can also view meta-analysis as a quantitative review of the literature on a particular subject. For example, a researcher might want to combine the results of 100 different studies about the job performance consequences of stress before reaching a conclusion. Many of the research findings presented throughout this text are based on meta-analysis rather than the results of a single study.

An important use of meta-analysis in organizational behavior is to understand how certain factors referred to as *moderator variables* influence the results of studies.[2] For example, in the experiment mentioned previously about stress and problem-solving ability, a moderator variable might be the amount of stress a study participant faces in personal life. Individuals who enter the experiment already stressed might be more negatively influenced by the electronic beeping noise.

Meta-analysis gives the impression of being scientific and reliable because so much information is assimilated, using sophisticated statistical tools. One might argue, however, that it is better to perform one rigorous study than to analyze many poorly conducted studies.

3 HOW YOU CAN BENEFIT FROM STUDYING ORGANIZATIONAL BEHAVIOR

Identify the potential advantages of organizational behavior knowledge.

Studying organizational behavior can enhance your effectiveness as a manager or professional. Yet the benefits from studying organizational behavior are not as immediately apparent as those derived from the study of functional fields such as accounting, marketing, purchasing, or information systems. Such fields constitute the *content* of managerial and professional work. Organizational behavior, in contrast, relates to the *process* of conducting such work. An exception may be seen with organizational behavior specialists whose content, or functional knowledge, deals with organizational behavior concepts and methods.

Visualize an information systems specialist who has extremely limited interpersonal skills in communicating, motivating, and resolving conflict. She will have a difficult time applying her technical expertise to organizational problems. She will therefore fail in serving her clients because she lacks the ability to use effective interpersonal processes. In contrast, if the same information systems specialist had solid interpersonal skills, she could do a better job of serving her clients. (She would probably also hold onto her job longer.)

Studying and learning about organizational behavior offers four key advantages: (1) skill development, (2) personal growth, (3) enhancement of organizational effectiveness, and (4) sharpening and refinement of common sense.

Skill Development

An essential requirement for entering into, surviving, and succeeding in the modern workplace is to have appropriate skills. A person needs both skills related to his or her discipline and generic skills such as problem solving and dealing with people. The study of organizational behavior contributes directly to these generic skills. Later in this chapter, we provide details about how one develops skills related to organizational behavior.

Organizational behavior skills have gained in importance in the modern workplace. According to executive search consultant Millington F. McCoy, continual rapid change in organizations has altered the mix of skills that top managers (as well as other managers) need. "Because organizations are less hierarchical, and more global, executives must be able to work effectively in teams that bring together diverse people, skills, and talents. That requires greater strength in the soft characteristics—not just a great résumé, but a cultural fit with my client organization. The brilliant person who lacks basic interpersonal skills can quickly become isolated—and therefore ineffective."[3]

The distinction between *soft* skills and *hard* skills is relevant for understanding the importance of skill development in organizational behavior (see the InfoTrac sidebar). Soft skills are generally interpersonal skills such as motivating others, communicating, and adapting to people of different cultures. Hard skills are generally technical skills, such as information technology and job design. Some skills, such as those involved with decision making, have a mixture of soft and hard components. To make good decisions you have to be creative and imaginative (perhaps a soft skill), yet you also have to weigh evidence carefully (most likely a hard skill).

Personal Growth through Insight into Human Behavior

As explained by Robert P. Vecchio, an important reason for studying organizational behavior is the personal fulfillment gained from understanding others.[4] Understanding fellow human beings can also lead to enhanced self-knowledge and self-insight. For example, while studying what motivates others, you may gain an understanding of what motivates you. Participating in the experiential exercises and self-assessments included in this text provides another vehicle for personal growth. A case in point is the study of leadership in Chapter 11. You will be invited to take a self-quiz about readiness to assume a leadership role. Taking the test and reviewing the results will give you insight into the types of attitudes and behaviors you need to function as a leader.

Personal growth, through understanding others and self-insight, is meritorious in and of itself, and it also has practical applications. Managerial and professional positions require sharp insights into the minds of others for such tasks as selecting people for jobs and assignments, communicating, and motivating. Sales representatives who can size up the needs of prospects and customers have a competitive advantage.

Enhancement of Organizational Effectiveness

A major benefit from studying organizational behavior is that it provides information that can be applied to organizational problems. An important goal of organizational behavior is to improve **organizational effectiveness**—the extent to which an organization is productive and satisfies the demands of its interested parties. Each chapter of this text contains information that is applied directly or indirectly by many organizations. One visible example is the widespread use of teams in the workplace. Certainly organizational behavior specialists did not invent teams. We suspect even prehistoric people organized some of their hunting forays by teams. Nevertheless, the conclusions of OB researchers facilitated the shift to teams in organizations.

5

If you're not sure about the distinctions today's managers make between hard and soft skills, it may be helpful to review a selection of press pieces related to this topic. Log on to InfoTrac® College Edition at **http://www.infotrac-college.com** and perform a title or key word search on "soft skills." Find out what specific skills employers are looking for in "well-rounded" job applicants. Technology workers who have not expanded their horizons beyond the lastest advances in wi-fi may be stunned by the lack of job offers they receive.

Over 45 years ago, organizational behavior specialists began to conduct formal research about the functioning of teams. A general finding of this research was that team members are happier and achieve higher productivity when given substantial responsibility.[5] The accumulation of this knowledge has strengthened and inspired attempts by many organizations to organize into teams.

Substantial evidence has accumulated emphasizing that the human factor increases productivity and gives a firm a competitive advantage. Jeffrey Pfeffer examined the evidence from hundreds of studies about the influence of people-oriented management practices on economic performance. (The application of people-oriented management practices is a way of using organizational behavior knowledge.) For example, a review of 131 field studies dealing with a change in management practices demonstrated that showing greater concern for people resulted in economic improvements took place three-fourths of the time. Furthermore, a study of nearly 200 banks found that better human resource practices are associated with substantial growth in financial performance.[6]

Why does paying more attention to the human element improve business performance? One explanation Pfeffer offers is that people work harder when they have greater control over their work environment and when they are encouraged by peer pressure from teammates. Even more advantage comes from people working smarter. People-oriented management practices enable workers to use their wisdom and to receive appropriate training. Another contribution to improved performance stems from eliminating positions that focus primarily on watching and controlling workers. Much of organizational behavior deals with people-oriented management practices. Many of these practices will be described in later chapters.

Understanding organizational behavior also improves organizational effectiveness because it uncovers factors that contribute to or hinder effective performance. Among these many factors are employee motivation, personality factors, and communication barriers. Furthermore, an advanced understanding of people is a major contributor to managerial success. This is especially true because so much of a manager's job involves accomplishing tasks through people.

Sharpening and Refining Common Sense

A manager commented after reading through several chapters of an organizational behavior text, "Why should I study this field? It's just common sense. My job involves dealing with people, and you can't learn that through a book." Many other students of organizational behavior share the sentiments expressed by this manager. However logical such an opinion might sound, common sense is not an adequate substitute for OB knowledge. Knowledge of organizational behavior sharpens and enlarges the domain for common sense. It markedly reduces the amount of time necessary to learn important behavior knowledge and skills, much as law school reduces the amount of time that a person in a previous era would have had to spend as a law apprentice.

You may know through common sense that giving recognition to people is generally an effective method of motivating them toward higher performance. By studying organizational behavior, however, you might learn that recognition should be given frequently but not every time somebody attains high performance. (You specifically learn about intermittent rewards in your study of motivation.) Formal knowledge thus enhances your effectiveness.

Organizational behavior knowledge also refines common sense by challenging you to reexamine generally accepted ideas that may be only partially true. One such idea is that inactivity is an effective way to reduce stress from a hectic schedule. In reality, some hard-driving people find inactivity more stressful than activity. For them, lying on a beach for a week might trigger intense chest pains. For these people, diversionary activity—such as doing yard work—is more relaxing than inactivity.

A BRIEF HISTORY OF ORGANIZATIONAL BEHAVIOR

The history of organizational behavior is rooted in the **behavioral approach to management,** or the belief that specific attention to workers' needs creates greater satisfaction and productivity. In contrast to the largely technical emphasis of scientific management, a common theme of the behavioral approach is the need to focus on people. Scientific management did not ignore people altogether, and in some ways contributed to organizational behavior. For example, scientific management heavily emphasized financial incentives to increase productivity. Yet the general thrust centered on performing work in a highly efficient manner.

Organizational behavior is also heavily influenced by sociology in its study of group behavior, organization structure, diversity, and culture. In addition, the insights of cultural anthropologists contribute to an understanding of organizational culture (the values and customs of a firm). In recent years, several companies have hired anthropologists to help them cultivate the right organizational culture. Organizational behavior also gains insights from political science toward understanding of the distribution of power in organizations.

Four key developments in the history of organizational behavior are the classical approach to management, the Hawthorne studies, the human relations movement, and the contingency approach to management and leadership.

The Classical Approach to Management

The study of management became more systematized and formalized as a by-product of the Industrial Revolution that took place from the 1700s through the 1900s. The classical approach to management encompassed scientific management and administrative management, and contributed some insights into understanding workplace behavior.

The focus of **scientific management** was the application of scientific methods to increase an individual worker's productivity. An example would be assembling a lawn mower with the least number of wasted motions and steps. Frederick W. Taylor, considered the father of scientific management, was an engineer by background. He used scientific analysis and experiments to increase worker output. Other key contributors to scientific management were Henry Gantt and Frank and Lillian Gilbreth. (Gantt charts for scheduling activities are still used today.)

Taylor tackled the dilemma of management wanting to maximize profits, and workers wanting to maximize possible wages. Disputes between management and labor centered on what each side saw as incompatible goals. Taylor believed that his system of scientific management could help both sides attain their goals, providing each would undergo a "mental revolution." Each side had to conquer its antagonistic view of the other. Taylor believed that management and labor should regard profit as the result of cooperation between the two parties. Management and labor both needed each other to attain their goals.[7]

7

4

Explain key events in the history of organizational behavior.

Scientific management is based on four principles, all of which direct behavior in the workplace:[8]

- Careful study of the jobs to develop standard work practices, with standardization of the tools workers use in their jobs.
- Selection of each worker using scientific principles of personnel selection.
- Obtainment of cooperation between management and workers to ensure that work is accomplished according to standard procedures.
- Plans and task assignments developed by managers, which workers should carry out.

According to these principles of scientific management, there is a division of work between managers and workers. Managers plan and design work, assign tasks, set performance goals, and make time schedules. Managers also select and train workers to do the tasks according to standard procedures, and give the workers feedback about their performance. Workers are rewarded with financial incentives when they increase their productivity.[9]

Administrative management was concerned primarily with the management and structure of organizations. The French businessman Henri Fayol and the German scholar Max Weber were the main contributors to administrative management. Based on his practical experience, Fayol developed fourteen management principles through which management engaged in planning, organizing, commanding, coordinating, and controlling. Weber suggested that bureaucracy is the best form or organization because it makes highly efficient management practices possible.

The core of management knowledge lies within the classical school. Its key contributions come from studying management from the framework of planning, organizing, leading, and controlling. The classical school provides a systematic way of measuring people and work; this is the major strength that has proven useful over time. Its major limitation is that it sometimes ignores differences among people and situations. In addition, some of the classical principles for developing an organization are not well suited to fast-changing situations.

The Hawthorne Studies

Many scholars pinpoint the Hawthorne studies as the true beginnings of the behavioral approach to management.[10] Without the insights gleaned from these studies, organizational behavior might not have emerged as a discipline. The purpose of the first study conducted at the Hawthorne plant of Western Electric (an AT&T subsidiary) was to determine the effect of changes in lighting on productivity. In this study, workers were divided into an experimental group and a control group. Lighting conditions for the experimental group varied in intensity from 24 to 46 to 70 foot-candles. The lighting for the control group remained constant.

As expected, the experimental group's output increased with each increase in light intensity. But unexpectedly, the performance of the control group also changed. The production of the control group increased at about the same rate as that of the experimental group. Later, the lighting in the experimental group's work area was reduced. This group's output continued to increase, as did that of the control group. A decline in the productivity of the control group finally did occur, but only when the intensity of the light was roughly the same as moonlight. Clearly, the researchers reasoned, something other than illumination caused the changes in productivity.

The relay assembly test room produced similar results over a 6-year period. In this case, relationships among rest, fatigue, and productivity were examined. First, normal productivity was established with no formal rest periods and a 48-hour week. Rest periods of varying length and frequency were then introduced. Productivity increased as the frequency and length of rest periods increased. Finally, the original conditions were reinstated. The return to the original conditions, however, did not result in the expected productivity drop. Instead, productivity remained at its usual high level.

One interpretation of these results was that the workers involved in the experiment enjoyed being the center of attention. Workers reacted positively because management cared about them. The phenomenon is referred to as the **Hawthorne effect.** It is the tendency of people to behave differently when they receive attention because they respond to the demands of the situation. In a research setting, this could mean that the people in an experimental group perform better simply because they are participating in an experiment. In a work setting, this could mean that employees perform better when they are part of any program—whether or not that program is valuable.

The Hawthorne studies also produced other findings that served as the foundation for the human relations movement. Although many of these findings may seem obvious today, documenting them reinforced what many managers believed to be true. Key findings included the following:

1. Economic incentives are less potent than generally believed in influencing workers to achieve high levels of output.
2. Dealing with human problems is complicated and challenging.
3. Leadership practices and work-group pressures profoundly influence employee satisfaction and performance.
4. Personal problems can strongly influence worker productivity.
5. Effective communication with workers is critical to managerial success.
6. Any factor influencing employee behavior is embedded in a social system. (For instance, to understand the impact of pay on performance, you have to understand the climate in the work group and the leadership style of the manager.)

Despite the contributions of the Hawthorne studies, they have been criticized as lacking scientific rigor. The most interesting criticism contends that the workers in the control group were receiving feedback on their performance. Simultaneously, they were being paid more as they produced more. The dual impact of feedback and differential rewards produced the surprising results—not the Hawthorne effect.[11]

The Human Relations Movement

The **human relations movement** is based on the belief that there is an important link between managerial practices, morale, and productivity. Workers bring various social needs to the job. In performing their jobs, workers typically become members of several work groups. Often these groups provide satisfaction of some of the workers' needs. Satisfied workers, it was argued, would be more productive workers. The challenge for managers was to recognize workers' needs and the powerful influence that work groups can have on individual and organizational productivity.

A second major theme of the human relations movement is a strong belief in workers' capabilities. Given the proper working environment, virtually all workers would be highly productive. Significant amounts of cooperation between workers and managers prove critical to achieving high levels of productivity. A cornerstone of the human relations movement is Douglas McGregor's analysis of the assumptions managers make about human nature, delineated in two theories.[12] Theory X is a set of traditional assumptions about people. Managers who hold these assumptions are pessimistic about workers' capabilities. They believe that people dislike work, seek to avoid responsibility, are not ambitious, and must be supervised closely. McGregor urged managers to challenge these assumptions about human nature because they may be untrue in most circumstances.

Theory Y is an alternative, and optimistic, set of assumptions. These assumptions include the idea that people do accept responsibility, can exercise self-control, have the capacity to innovate, and consider work to be as natural as rest or play. McGregor argued that these assumptions accurately describe human nature in far more situations than most managers believe. He therefore proposed that these assumptions should guide managerial practice.

The Contingency Approach

Beginning in the early 1960s, organizational behavior specialists emphasized the difficulties in finding universal principles of managing people that can be applied in all situations. To make effective use of knowledge about human behavior, one must understand which factors in a particular situation are most influential. The **contingency approach to management** emphasizes that there is no one best way to manage people or work. A method that leads to high productivity or morale in one situation may not achieve the same results in another. The contingency approach is derived from the study of leadership styles. Experienced managers and leaders know that not all workers respond in the exact same way to identical leadership initiatives. A recurring example is that well-motivated, competent team members require less supervision than those who are poorly motivated and less competent. In Chapter 11, we present more information about the contingency approach to leadership.

The strength of the contingency approach is that it encourages managers and professionals to examine individual and situational differences before deciding on a course of action. Its major problem is that it is often used as an excuse for not acquiring formal knowledge about organizational behavior and management. If management depends on the situation, why study organizational behavior or management? The answer, of course, is that a formal study of management helps a manager decide which factors are relevant in particular situations. In the leadership example just cited, the relevant factors are the skills and motivation of the group members.

5

Understand how a person develops organizational behavior skills.

SKILL DEVELOPMENT IN ORGANIZATIONAL BEHAVIOR

Developing skills in organizational behavior means learning to work effectively with individuals, groups, and organizational forces. The greater one's responsibility, the more one is expected to work well at these three levels.

The distinction between hard skills and soft skills mentioned previously is not necessarily the distinction between difficult and easy. Hard skills are not better than soft skills and vice versa. A company president may have a difficult job, yet she uses mostly *soft* skills such as leading others and bringing about organizational change. In contrast, an entry-level financial analyst might use *hard* skills in preparing an analysis. His job, however, might be considered easier than the company president's. Notice also that possessing soft skills often helps a person earn hard money.

Developing most organizational behavior skills is more complex than developing a structured skill such as conducting a physical inventory or arranging an e-mail address book. Nevertheless, you can develop organizational behavior skills by reading this text and doing the exercises. The text follows a general learning model:

1. *Conceptual knowledge and behavioral guidelines.* Each chapter in this text presents research-based information about organizational behavior, including a section titled Implications for Managerial Practice.
2. *Conceptual information and examples.* These include brief descriptions of organizational behavior in action, generally featuring managers and leaders.
3. *Experiential exercises.* The text provides an opportunity for practice and personalization through cases and self-assessment exercises. Self-quizzes are included because they are an effective method of helping you personalize the information, assisting you in linking conceptual information to your own situation. For example, you will read about creative problem solving and also complete a quiz about creativity.
4. *Feedback on skill utilization, or performance, from others.* Feedback exercises appear at several places in the text. Implementing OB skills outside of the classroom will provide additional opportunities for feedback.
5. *Frequent practice.* Readers who look for opportunities to practice organizational behavior skills outside the classroom will acquire skills more quickly. An important example is the development of creative thinking skills. The person who looks for imaginative solutions to problems regularly is much more likely to become a more creative thinker, and be ready to think creatively at a given moment. Contrast this to the individual who participates in a creative-thinking exercise once, and then attempts the skill a year later when the need is urgent. As in any field, frequently practicing a skill the right way leads to skill improvement.

As you work through the text, keep the five-part learning model in mind. To help visualize this basic learning model, refer to Exhibit 1-1.

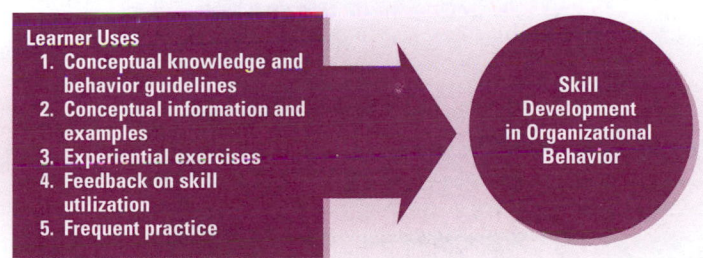

Learner Uses
1. **Conceptual knowledge and behavior guidelines**
2. **Conceptual information and examples**
3. **Experiential exercises**
4. **Feedback on skill utilization**
5. **Frequent practice**

Skill Development in Organizational Behavior

Exhibit 1-1

A Model for Developing Organizational Behavior Skills

Organizational behavior skills can be developed by using a systematic approach.

A FRAMEWORK FOR STUDYING ORGANIZATIONAL BEHAVIOR

A challenge in studying organizational behavior is that it lacks the clear-cut boundaries of subjects like cell biology or French. Some writers in the field consider organizational behavior to be the entire practice of management. ==Others focus organizational behavior much more on the human element and its interplay with the total organization.== Such is the orientation of this text. Exhibit 1-2 presents a basic framework for studying organizational behavior. The framework is simultaneously a listing of the contents of Chapters 2 through 16.

One can see, proceeding from left to right, that the foundation of organizational behavior is the study of individual behavior, presented in Chapters 2 though 8. No group or organization is so powerful that the qualities of individual members do not count. Visualize a famous athletic team with a winning history. Many fans contend that the spirit and tradition of the team, rather than individual capabilities, carry it through to victories against tough opponents. Yet if the team has a couple of poor recruiting years or loses a key coach, it may lose more frequently.

Key factors in understanding how individuals function include individual differences, mental ability and personality, learning, perception, attitudes, values, attribution and ethics. It is also important to understand individual decision making, creativity, foundation concepts of motivation, motivational programs, conflict, stress, and well-being.

As suggested by the arrows in Exhibit 1-2, the various levels of study are interconnected. Understanding how individuals behave contributes to an understanding of groups and interpersonal relations, the second level of the framework. This will be studied in Chapters 9 through 12. The topics include communication, group dynamics (how groups operate) and teamwork, and leadership. Although leadership relates directly to interpersonal relationships, top-level leaders are also

Exhibit 1-2

A Framework for Studying Organizational Behavior

To better understand organizational behavior, recognize that behavior at the individual, group, organizational system, and global environment levels are all linked to one another.

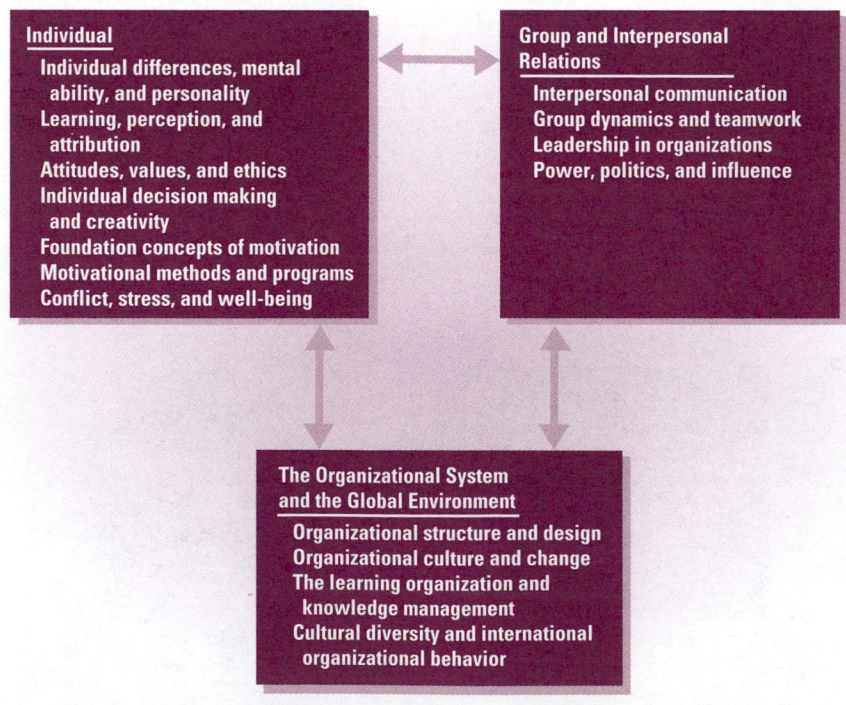

IMPLICATIONS FOR MANAGERIAL PRACTICE

Each of the following chapters includes a brief section explaining how managers and professionals can use selected information to enhance managerial practice. Our first lesson is the most comprehensive and perhaps the most important: Managers should raise their level of awareness about the availability of organizational behavior information. Before making decisions in dealing with people in a given situation, pause to search for systematic information about people and organizations. For example, if you need to resolve conflict, first review information about conflict resolution, such as that presented in Chapter 8. The payoff could be improved management of conflict.

---

concerned with influencing the entire organization. The study of power, politics, and influence is closely related to leadership.

Finally, the third level of analysis in the study of organizational behavior is the organizational system and the global environment, as presented in Chapters 13 through 16. Components of the organizational and environmental level studied here include organizational structure and design, organizational culture and change, the learning organization and knowledge management, cultural diversity, and international (or cross-cultural) organizational behavior. International organizational behavior could just as well have been studied before the other topics. Our position, however, is that everything else a person learns about organizational behavior contributes to an understanding of cross-cultural relations in organizations.

The connecting arrows in Exhibit 1-2 emphasize the interrelatedness of processes and topics at the three levels. Motivation provides a clear example. A person's motivational level is dependent upon his or her individual makeup as well as work-group influences and the organizational culture. Some work groups and organizational cultures energize new members because of their highly charged atmospheres. The arrows also run in the other direction. Highly motivated workers, for example, improve work group performance, contribute to effective interpersonal relationships, and enhance the organizational culture.

SUMMARY OF KEY POINTS

1 **Explain what organizational behavior means.**
Organizational behavior is the study of human behavior in the workplace, the interaction between people and the organization, and the organization itself. Organizational behavior relates to the process, rather than the content, of managerial work.

2 **Summarize the research methods of organizational behavior.**
Three frequently used methods of collecting data on organizational behavior are surveys (typically questionnaires), interviews, and direct observation of behavior. Four widely used research methods are case studies, laboratory experiments, field experiments, and meta-analysis. The essence of conducting an experiment is to make sure that the independent variable influences the results.

3 **Identify the potential advantages of organizational behavior knowledge.**
Knowledge about organizational behavior offers four key advantages: skill development, personal growth, the enhancement of organizational effectiveness, and sharpening and refining of common sense. Substantial evidence has accumulated which substantiates that emphasizing the human factor increases productivity and gives a firm a competitive advantage. Organizational behavior skills have increased in importance in the modern workplace, partly because of the prevalence of diverse teams.

4 **Explain key events in the history of organizational behavior.**

The history of organizational behavior parallels the behavioral approach to management, including contributions from classical management. The classical approach to management encompasses both scientific and administrative management, and contributed some insights into understanding workplace behavior. The behavioral approach formally began with the Hawthorne studies. Among the major implications of these studies were that leadership practices and work-group pressures profoundly influence employee satisfaction and performance.

The human relations movement and the contingency approach to management are also key developments in the history of organizational behavior. The human relations movement was based on the belief that there is an important link among managerial practices, morale, and productivity. Analysis of Theory X versus Theory Y (pessimistic versus optimistic assumptions about people) is a key aspect of the movement. The contingency approach emphasizes taking into account individual and situational differences in managing people.

5 **Understand how a person develops organizational behavior skills.**

Organizational behavior skills can be developed by following a general learning model that includes the use of conceptual knowledge and behavioral guidelines, experiential exercises, feedback on skill utilization, and frequent practice.

The framework for studying organizational behavior in the text emphasizes the interconnectedness of three levels of information: individuals, groups and interpersonal relations, and the organizational system and the global environment.

KEY TERMS AND PHRASES

Organizational Behavior, *2*
The study of human behavior in the workplace, the interaction between people and the organization, and the organization itself.

Meta-analysis, *4*
A quantitative or statistical review of the literature on a particular subject; an examination of a range of studies for the purpose of reaching a combined result or best estimate.

Organizational Effectiveness, *5*
The extent to which an organization is productive and satisfies the demands of its interested parties.

Behavioral Approach to Management, *7*
The belief that specific attention to the workers' needs creates greater satisfaction and productivity.

Scientific Management, *7*
The application of scientific methods to increase worker's productivity.

Administrative Management, *8*
A school of management thought concerned primarily with how organizations should be structured and managed.

Hawthorne Effect, *9*
The tendency of people to behave differently when they receive attention because they respond to the demands of the situation.

Human Relations Movement, *9*
An approach to dealing with workers based on the belief that there is an important link among managerial practices, morale, and productivity.

Contingency Approach to Management, *10*
The viewpoint that there is no one best way to manage people or work but that the best way depends on certain situational factors.

DISCUSSION QUESTIONS AND ACTIVITIES

1. The study about workspace reported in the chapter opener was conducted in small technology firms. How might the setting of the study (including the workers involved) have influenced the favorable results for open workspaces, and more negative results for private offices and cubicles?

2. What contributions might organizational behavior knowledge make in the Internet age?

3. What does it mean to say that organizational behavior relates to the *process*—as opposed to the *content*—of a manager's job?

4. Give a possible explanation why meta-analysis is considered so important in evaluating the effectiveness of prescription drugs.

5. **COLLABORATE** Work by yourself, or form a small brainstorming group, to furnish an example from physical science in which common sense proves to be untrue.

6. Have you ever worked for a manager who held Theory X assumptions about people? What was the impact of his or her assumptions on your motivation and satisfaction?

7. How might a person obtain feedback on the effectiveness of his or her organizational behavior skills?

ORGANIZATIONAL BEHAVIOR ONLINE

TO DO

Focusing on People Pays Dividends

The purpose of this exercise is to find some evidence that emphasizing the human element benefits a company, such as by increasing productivity, quality, or profits. Find evidence from Internet sources that can be located through free search engines instead of databases paid for by libraries or companies. The difference is a subtle one. Library databases often point you to printed sources available in libraries, such as the professional journals included in many of the references in this text. In other words, a library database brings the library to you. (However, the same database will sometimes locate unpublished and unprinted information.)

Use the Internet to find sources not already in print, such as unpublished research or comments by an executive or a consultant. In this way, you are developing the skills to find information through the Internet that is not available elsewhere. A good starting point is to use a search engine that searches other search engines such as http://www

.metacrawler.com. You might also use the most popular search engine, google.com. Because this type of Internet search requires such a high skill level, you may want to work in teams, each trying several different search terms such as "payoff from a people orientation" or "return on human resources emphasis."

TO BOOKMARK

Organizational Behavior Research Methods

http://www.nsf.gov/home/sbe/start.htm

Historical Perspectives on Organizational Behavior

http://web.cba.neu.edu/~ewertheim/introd/history.htm

Interpersonal Skills

http://www.medknowlogy.com/skill.htm
http://www.eno.com/catalog/intskills.html (Contains demonstration package.)

CASE PROBLEM: The Hands-On CEO of JetBlue

The first thing you notice when getting on board is the new-car smell. "No wonder," says the flight attendant, hearing your remark. She points to a metal plaque on the doorway rim that says the Airbus A320 was delivered one month ago. Then there are the blue potato chips from naturally blue potatoes. Other notable features are the free cable on your personal video screen, and the leather seats. Flight attendants are trained on how to give service with a retro flair. All attendants have to learn how to strut proudly, as if there were an imaginary string between their chin and belly button.

JetBlue attendants have a sense of fun about their jobs, and the can-do pilot informs over the p.a. system that yes, there's a major storm coming into the New York City area but that we'll get there on time anyway. And the plane and passengers do.

So the traveler wonders. Is this for real? Or maybe the right question is, "How long can they keep up this nonsense?" Just as discontent with airlines was mounting in 2000, JetBlue Airlines came into being with a new attitude, new planes and a new concept of service. What perfect takeoff timing for a carrier that is trying to bring pleasure and even style back to flying. JetBlue is low-price and all-coach, like Southwest Airlines, yet hip and sassy, like Virgin Atlantic. In the air, JetBlue offers the plush seats and satellite TV; on the ground it offers hyperefficiency and—are you ready? —candor about delays. You could call it the anti-airline.

JetBlue has been achieving an impressive profit picture. In June 2001, the company became the most ambitious start-up in U.S. aviation history when it ordered 320 jetliners to accompany 68 planes on the way and 15 in service. Of the hundreds of start-ups since the industry was deregulated in

1978, only America West has grown into a major company—and it has flown in and out of Chapter 11 bankruptcy.

Credit CEO David Neeleman, who founded the firm at age 41, for piloting JetBlue past the early disasters that typically befall fledgling carriers. For starters, Neeleman raised $160 million from investors—almost triple what other new airline entrants have managed to obtain. The hefty sum is insurance against any unforeseen cash crunch.

Consumers are usually concerned about the safety issue with "new" airlines that fly 25-year-old planes. JetBlue flies only factory-fresh, state of-the-art A320s. Neeleman has fitted each with 162 seats—versus the A320's 180-seat maximum. Flyers are ecstatic about the so-called JetBlue experience. It begins with pricing, which is competitive and doesn't torture consumers with requirements like Saturday-night stays. JetBlue is attracting business travelers, the industry's most valuable passengers and the source of up to 50 percent of its profits. Christopher Hayes, the chief investment officer at Rulison & Co. says "We were starved for an airline like this."

A JetBlue spokesperson said, "We see our customers as the same ones who can afford more but shop at Target because their stuff is hip but inexpensive." That kind of thinking drove decisions like JetBlue's choice of leather seats instead of less expensive cloth. "It's a nicer look, a better feel," says Neeleman, in full salesman mode.

Neeleman has raided rivals for employee-focused top executives. For his human resources director, Neeleman lured Ann Rhoades, who helped develop the airline industry's happiest employee group at Southwest. In 1994, Rhoades had pink-slipped Neeleman after Southwest bought Morris Air, another low-price airline he had started.

Neeleman obsesses over keeping employees happy, and with good reason. Airline watchers say JetBlue's ability to stay union-free is critical to its survival as a low-cost carrier. The industry's labor-relations record is weak. "But if there is anyone who realizes the importance of treating their employees right, it's the management team at JetBlue," says airline analyst Holly Hegeman.

Neeleman is obsessed with controlling costs. Like Southwest, JetBlue flies only one type of aircraft, which holds down training and maintenance expenses. With flight attendants and even executives chipping in to help clean the jets even before they have landed, turnaround times average just 35 minutes, as fast as industry leader Southwest. Despite the emphasis on cost control, JetBlue has some costs other airlines have avoided. For example, it has configured its planes with emergency equipment such as life rafts and beacons for flying over water, thus allowing its flights to swing out over the ocean to avoid congestion on crowded East Coast routes.

Neeleman is one of seven siblings, and has nine children of his own. He has been dreaming about airplanes since he saw a red one on his second birthday cake. A serial travel entrepreneur, he has launched four airlines, including Morris Air and Canada's WestJet Airlines, with each one being more successful than the last. Neeleman, with a strong interest in information technology, developed the computer system that became the basis for e-ticketing.

Southwest founder Herb Kelleher regards Neeleman as a genius. When Neeleman sold Morris Air to Southwest, he signed a five-year non-compete agreement. During the interim, he planned every detail of his dream airline. JetBlue's CFO says dealing with Neeleman is "like trying to put a bridle on a wild mustang." Neeleman admits that some of his ideas won't work, such as serving pizza on planes.

"I am very proud of JetBlue's performance in our sixth consecutive profitable quarter," said David Neeleman in a press release. "These strong results demonstrate JetBlue's ability to offer profitably a superior travel experience at low fares."

Case Questions

1. In what way does Neeleman demonstrate an understanding of organizational behavior?
2. Even though this text has not yet covered leadership, in what way is Neeleman a *hands-on leader* (one who gets directly involved in the details of an operation)?
3. How else might Neeleman make use of OB knowledge to improve the chances of JetBlue Airlines staying successful?

Source: Sally B. Donnelly, "Blue Skies: Is Jet Blue the Next Great Airline—Or Just a Little Too Good to Be True?", July 30, 2001 *Time,* pp. 24–27; Eric Gillin, "JetBlue Soars Past Profit Targets," *TheStreet .com,* July 25, 2002; (http://www.thestreet.com/pf/tech/earnings /10034305.html); Rosemary Pollock, "LDS Businessman's JetBlue Is New Model for Discount Airlines," *Mormon News,* March 25, 2001 (http://www.mormonstoday.com/010323/B4Dneeleman01.shtml).

ENDNOTES

1. Gregory Morehead and Ricky W. Griffin, *Organizational Behavior: Managing People and Organizations,* 4th ed. (Boston: Houghton Mifflin, 1995), p. 3.
2. Piers D. Steel and John D. Kammeyer-Mueller, "Comparing Meta-Analytic Techniques Under Realistic Conditions," *Journal of Applied Psychology,* February 2002, p. 107.
3. David Stauffer, "With Today's Global Reach and Team Approach, Soft Skills Are Crucial," *Marriott Executive Memo,* Number 8, 1997, p. 4.
4. Robert P. Vecchio, *Organizational Behavior: Core Concepts, 6th ed.* (Mason, OH: South-Western/Thomson Learning, 2003), pp. 5–6.
5. An example of such research is Rajiv D. Banker, Joy M. Field, Roger C. Schroeder, and Kingshuk K. Sinha, "Impact of Work Teams on Manufacturing Performance: A Longitudinal Field Study," *Academy of Management Journal,* August 1996, pp. 867–890.
6. Jeffrey Pfeffer, *The Human Equation* (Boston: Harvard Business School Press, 1998), p. 59; Barry A. Macy and Hiroaki Izumi, "Organizational Change, Design, and Work Innovation: A Meta-Analysis of 131 North American Field Studies, 1961–1991," in W. A. Passmore and R. W. Woodman, eds. *Research in Organizational Change and Development,* Vol. 7 (Greenwich, CT: JAI Press, 1993), pp. 235–313.
7. Joseph E. Champoux, *Organizational Behavior: Essential Tenets* (Mason, OH: South-Western/Thomson Learning, 2003), pp. 11–12.
8. Frederick W. Taylor, *Principles of Scientific Management* (New York: W. W. Norton & Company, Inc., 1911), p. 9.
9. Champoux, *Organizational Behavior,* p. 12.
10. E. J. Roethlisberger and W. J. Dickson, *Management and the Worker* (Cambridge, MA: Harvard University Press, 1939).
11. H. McIlvaine Parsons, "What Caused the Hawthorne Effect? A Scientific Detective Story," *Administration & Society,* November 1978, pp. 259–283.
12. Douglas McGregor, *The Human Side of Enterprise* (New York: McGraw-Hill, 1960), pp. 33–57.

Chapter 2

Individual Differences, Mental Ability, and Personality

In 2001, General Motors' new dream team looked like poster boys for the AARP (American Association for Retired People). GM CEO and President Rick Wagoner hired 69-year-old Robert Lutz—who also held top jobs at Ford and Chrysler—to be head of product development and vice chairman. Lutz was the third recycled executive to join Wagoner's inner circle, following Steve Harris, 55, who exited Chrysler, and former Ford executive John Devine, 57, who became chief financial officer and vice chairman. "Wagoner is getting people who don't have to be taught what a car is," says a longtime GM watcher. "They know the competition and hit the ground running."

Hiring Lutz is Wagoner's clearest signal to date that he wants to shake up GM's ingrained risk-averse culture—something he has already started by streamlining the company's engineering organization and pulling the plug on the Oldsmobile. A movie-star handsome *Uber*male, Lutz is as famous for battling bosses like Ford's Red Poling and Lee Iacocca as he is for creating the hairy-chested Viper roadster. Nobody should mistake Lutz's white hair and advanced age for lack of energy. He rides a motorcycle and flies his own jet fighter.

OBJECTIVES

After reading and studying this chapter and doing the exercises, you should be able to:

1 Explain how individual differences influence the behavior of people in organizations.

2 Describe key factors contributing to demographic diversity.

3 Explain how mental ability relates to job performance.

4 Identify major personality variables that influence job performance.

5 Explain how emotional intelligence is an important part of organizational behavior.

Source: Alex Taylor III, "GM's Over-The-Hill Gang," *Fortune,* September 3, 2001, p. 38.

NOW ASK YOURSELF: What does this story about General Motors' "over-the-hill gang" tell us about organizational behavior? For one, it illustrates several key points about differences among people and their abilities. At times, the experience and wisdom accumulated during a challenging career can be a distinct asset in solving organizational problems. This story also illustrates that yielding to negative stereotypes about a demographic group (in this case, senior citizens) can block managers from selecting the most qualified person for a job.

The purpose of this chapter is to explain how individual differences affect performance. In addition, we describe key sources of individual differences: demographic diversity, mental ability, and personality. In Chapters 3 and 4 we will consider other sources of individual differences that influence behavior in organizations: learning, perception, attributions, attitudes, values, and ethics. Although our focus in this chapter is on individual differences, we also describe principles of human behavior that apply to everyone. For example, everyone has different components to his or her intelligence. We all have some capacity to deal with numbers, words, and abstract reasoning.

1. INDIVIDUAL DIFFERENCES

Explain how individual differences influence the behavior of people in organizations.

People show substantial **individual differences,** or variations in how they respond to the same situation based on personal characteristics. An extroverted production planner might attempt to influence a plant superintendent by taking him to lunch and making an oral presentation of her ideas. In the same situation, an introverted planner might attempt to influence the superintendent by sending him an elaborate report. Understanding individual differences helps to explain human behavior, but environmental influences are also important.[1]

A basic proposition of psychology states that behavior is a function of a person interacting with his or her environment.[2] The equation reads $B = f(P \times E)$. B stands for behavior, P stands for the person, and E represents the environment. A key implication of this equation is that the effects of the individual and the environment on each other determine a person's behavior. For example, working for a firm that requires many levels of approval on a decision might trigger a person's tendencies toward impatience. The same person working in a flatter organization (one that requires fewer layers of approval) might be more patient. Have you ever noticed that some environments, and some people, bring out your best traits? Or your worst traits?

Another way of understanding the impact of individual differences in the workplace is to say that these differences *moderate* how people respond to situations. Ninety-five percent of field sales representatives assigned laptop computers might access data about inventory as instructed. The 5 percent of the sales force who dislike high-tech devices (and prefer human contact) might telephone the warehouse about inventory status.

Individual differences affect most aspects of behavior on the job. Here we identify eight consequences of individual differences that have a major impact on managing people.

1. *People differ in productivity.* A comprehensive analysis of individual differences illustrates the magnitude of human variation in job performance. The researchers synthesized studies involving over 10,000 workers. They found that as jobs become more complex, individual differences have a bigger impact on work output.[3] An outstanding industrial sales representative might produce 100 times as much sales revenue as a mediocre one. In contrast, an outstand-

ing production specialist might produce only twice as much as a mediocre one. (An industrial sales position is more complex than the job of production specialist. Industrial selling involves a variety of activities, including persuading others, analyzing problems, and mining data via a computer.)

2. *People differ in ability and talent.* Factors such as motivation, self-confidence, a favorable appearance, and political astuteness are not sufficient for work accomplishment. People also need the right abilities and talents to perform the job well. Ability is a major source of individual differences that influences job performance. For certain job types, employers have difficulty finding enough job candidates with sufficient talent to perform the job satisfactorily. An American Management Association report of 1,627 firms found that more than a third of job applicants tested in reading and math lacked the basic skills to perform the job they sought. The firms included in the survey tested an average of 278 job applicants and rejected 95 for insufficient skills.[4]

3. *People vary in their propensity for achieving high-quality results.* Some people take naturally to striving for high quality because they are conscientious, have a good capacity for precision, and take pride in their work. Workers who are less conscientious, less precise, and have little pride will have more difficulty achieving quality targets.

4. *People differ in how much they want to be empowered and involved.* A major thrust of the modern workplace is to grant workers more authority to make decisions by themselves and to involve them in suggesting improvements. Many workers welcome such empowerment and enrichment because they seek self-fulfillment on the job. However, many other workers are not looking for more responsibility and job involvement. They prefer jobs that require a minimum of mental involvement and responsibility.

5. *People differ in the style of leadership they prefer and need.* Many individuals prefer as much freedom as possible on the job and can function well under such leadership. Other individuals want to be supervised closely by their manager. People also vary with respect to the amount of supervision they require. In general, less competent, less motivated, and less experienced workers need more supervision. One of the biggest headaches facing a manager is to supervise people who need close supervision yet resent it when it is administered.

6. *People differ in their need for contact with other people.* As a by-product of their personality traits and occupational interests, people vary widely in how much human contact they need to keep them satisfied. Some people can work alone all day and remain highly productive. Others become restless unless they are engaged in business or social conversation with another employee. Some workers will often drop by the work area of other workers just to chat. Sometimes a business luncheon is scheduled more out of a manager's need for social contact than a need for discussing job problems.

7. *People differ in their commitment and loyalty to the firm.* Some employees are so committed to their employers that they act as if they are part-owners of the firm. As a consequence, committed and loyal employees are highly concerned about producing high-quality goods and services. They also maintain excellent records of attendance and punctuality, which helps reduce the cost of doing business. At the other extreme, some employees feel little commitment or loyalty toward their employer. They feel no pangs of guilt when they produce scrap or when they miss work for trivial reasons.

8. *Workers vary in their level of self-esteem, which, in turn, influences their productivity and capacity to take on additional responsibilities.* People with high self-esteem

20

believe that they can cope with the basic challenges of life (self-efficacy) and also that they are worthy of happiness (self-respect). According to Nathaniel Branden, people with low self-esteem and who are not confident of their thinking ability are likely to fear decision making, lack negotiation and interpersonal skills, and be reluctant or unable to change.[5] A group of economists found that self-esteem, as measured by a personality test, had a big impact on the wages of young workers. The researchers found that human capital—schooling, basic skills, and work experience—predictably had a significant impact on wages. Yet 10 percent of this effect was really attributable to self-esteem, which highly correlated with human capital. It was also found that differences in productivity, as measured by comparative wages, related more to differences in self-esteem than to differences in human capital.[6]

The sampling of individual differences cited are usually attributed to a combination of genetic make-up and environmental influences. Some workers are more productive because they have inherited better problem-solving ability and have lived since childhood in environments that encourage the acquisition of knowledge and skills. Experimentation with mice has given more support to the position that genetics play a major role in determining mental ability. Neuroscientists created a supermouse by altering the DNA structure of its forebears in ways that changed the reactions between neurons deep within its cranium. (A supermouse, for example, navigates a maze to find food much more quickly than its ordinary cousins.) The scientists concluded, "Our results suggest that the genetic enhancement of mental and cognitive attributes such as intelligence and memory in mammals is feasible."[7] Many other personality traits, such as introversion, also are partially inherited.

Despite the importance of heredity, a person's environment—including the workplace—still plays a significant role in influencing job behavior. The manager must therefore strive to create a positive environment in which workers can perform toward their best.

DEMOGRAPHIC DIVERSITY

2

Describe key factors contributing to demographic diversity.

Workers vary widely with respect to background, or demographic characteristics, and these differences sometimes affect job performance and behavior. **Demographic diversity** refers to the differences in background factors relating to the workforce that help shape worker attitudes and behavior. Key sources of demographic diversity include gender, age, ethnicity, and physical status. As is well known, the U.S. workforce is becoming increasingly diverse. Understanding demographic differences among workers can help the manager both capitalize on diversity and avoid negative stereotyping. For example, some managers still hold the stereotype that single people are less conscientious than married people.

Sex and Gender Differences

A topic of intense debate and continuing interest is whether men and women differ in aspects of behavior related to job performance. (Sex differences refer to actual biological differences, such as the average height of men versus women. Gender differences refer to differences in the perception of male and female roles.) A series of studies suggest that gender differences in personality exist. These findings include the following:

- Women are better able to understand nonverbal communication.
- Women are more expressive of emotion.
- The average woman is more trusting and more nurturing than the average man.[8]

More closely related to job behavior, much has been written about the different styles and communication patterns of men and women. Chapter 9 presents more details about male–female differences in communication patterns. A major finding is that men more typically communicate to convey information or establish status. Men also tend to emphasize immediate goals and communicate to exchange facts and ideas. Women are more likely to communicate to establish rapport and solve problems.

Men are generally more aggressive than women and therefore less sensitive to the feelings of others. Women, according to this generalization, tend to be more courteous and polite. Another gender difference, according to James Q. Wilson, is that men are more likely to value equity, whereas women value equality. Equity refers to people being treated fairly, such as people in a department get the salary increases they deserve. Equality refers to people sharing equally, such as when all people in a department receiving an identical salary increase.[9]

Despite the existence of these gender differences, the overall evidence suggests that there are few differences between men and women in such factors as ability and motivation that will affect job performance.[10] Furthermore, a review of the evidence about gender differences suggests that the similarities between men and women far outweigh the differences.[11]

Age and Experienced-Based Differences

Potential differences in productivity and job behavior based on age are topical. According to demographic trends, many baby boomers will retire around 2010. Because the next generation is smaller than its predecessor, workers with the skills and experience needed to fill positions left open by retiring boomers may be in short supply. A potential solution would be to encourage many people to keep working longer and to employ a larger number of older people in general.[12] Another factor keeping more seniors in the workforce was the downturn in the stock market at the turn of the century and its aftermath. With retirement funds having shrunk in value, many seniors elected to postpone retirement until their funds appreciated substantially.

In order for older people to gain prominence in the workforce, however, both subtle and overt forms of job discrimination must be reduced. The American Association of Retired Persons dispatched pairs of "testers," one 57 and one 32, to apply for 102 entry-level sales or management positions. Although they presented equal credentials, the older applicants received less favorable responses over 41 percent of the time.[13] Yet for the handful of people who have risen to the very top of their fields, such as major corporation executives or economists, age discrimination is less likely to take place. The automotive executives described at the outset of the chapter are a case in point.

The research evidence about job-related consequences of age is mixed. One study of 24,000 federal workers found that age was barely related to performance. Not surprisingly, both age and experience predicted performance better for high-complexity jobs than for other, less complicated jobs.[14] A review of articles spanning 22 years studying the relationship between age and performance (involving almost 40,000 workers) found that age and job performance were generally unrelated. However, among workers in the 17- to 21-year-old category, the 21-year-olds tended to be more productive than the 17-year-olds.[15]

Even if being older and more experienced does not always contribute to job performance, older workers do have notable attributes. In contrast to younger workers, they have lower absenteeism, illness, and accident rates; higher job satisfaction; and more positive work values.[16]

Ethnic and Cultural Differences

Differences in job performance and behavior are sometimes attributed to ethnic group differences. However, these differences are usually more attributable to culture than to ethnicity itself. For example, it is part of the culture of European countries to taker long lunch breaks. An Italian manager working in an Italian subsidiary might take a two-hour lunch break, while her American counterpart might take a 45-minute break. The Italian manager's behavior reflects cultural values rather than the fact of being Italian. Chapter 16 presents more details about cross-cultural differences in job behavior.

The accompanying Organizational Behavior in Action box illustrates how some ethnic groups gravitate toward (or specialize in) a particular line of work. These occupational preferences are probably a mixture of custom and natural predisposition.

Disability Status

Another key source of diversity is whether a person is able-bodied or physically disabled. Mental disability is also gaining attention as a source of workforce diversity. The Americans with Disabilities Act (ADA) of 1991 has alerted managers to the importance of understanding how disabilities might affect job performance. The act is designed to protect people with disabilities from discrimination in employment, public accommodations, transportation, and telecommunications. The ADA defines **disability** as a physical or mental condition that substantially limits an individual's major life activities. According to the Equal Employment Opportunity Commission (EEOC), major life activities are learning, thinking, concentrating, interacting with others, caring for oneself, speaking, performing manual tasks, working, and sleeping. All of these activities can be considered job related. For example, sleep deprivation interferes with job performance.

The ADA requires companies with at least twenty-five employees to avoid hiring practices that discriminate against people with disabilities. If an employee can perform the essential functions of a job, the employee should be considered qualified. The person is qualified even is he or she must perform certain tasks differently than someone who is not disabled, or must use equipment different from the equipment ordinarily used. Despite the advances attributed to the ADA, the employment picture among disabled people is still grim. Among the 54 million people with disabilities in the United States, more than 70 percent are unemployed. Furthermore, only 32 percent of disabled people of working age work full or part time, compared to 81 percent of the non-disabled population. Two-thirds of disabled people not working say they would prefer to be working.[17]

Making the appropriate accommodations increases the chances that a physically disabled person will perform as well as an able-bodied person. In general, employers have found that the presence of a physical disability does not adversely affect job performance.[18] Pizza Hut has employed thousands of individuals

Organizational Behavior *in Action*

Building Industry Capitalizes on Skill of Sure-Footed Mohawks

Mohawk ironworkers built Manhattan's skyline, including raising the World Trade Center Twin Towers. For more than 80 years, these paladins of high-rise have performed dizzying feats to give the city its mighty landmarks. The Mohawk Native American ironworkers lead a transient lifestyle, traveling from their reservations in upstate New York and southern Quebec to do structural steel work on skyscrapers, power plants, stadiums, arenas and bridges in New York City and elsewhere.

Starting in 1916, Mohawks have worked on every major building project in New York City, including the George Washington Bridge, the Empire State Building, the United Nations, and Madison Square Garden. Hundreds of Mohawks worked on the World Trade Center from 1966 to 1974, using rivets and bolts to assemble the frame. A younger generation was toiling at building sites when two hijacked airliners sliced into the Twin Towers on September 11, 2001.

Among Mohawks who built the 1,360-foot towers, their destruction and the deaths of more than 2,800 people evoke sadness and bewilderment. David Rice, 52, who got his start there as an ironworker apprentice in 1969, says he averted his gaze from the smoky void on the skyline after the attack. "I didn't even want to look," he says. "I still don't like to think about it." Rice has an arresting photo himself standing atop the South Tower in 1971—exactly 30 years before the disaster. He is balanced on a 10-inch girder at the 110th floor, empty space all around him.

Like his grandfather and father before him, Rice learned to "walk iron" without the safety harnesses and nets that are now standard on high-rise jobs. He disputes the legend that Mohawks are unafraid of working high up. "I'm scared of heights," says the stocky, plainspoken Rice, who left the trade after a coronary bypass. "The way I was taught, you put one foot in front of the other, look straight ahead and never look down."

Ironworkers operate in pairs in all kinds of weather at the windy heights above the city. Heavy beams and other structural materials are hoisted into place by towering cranes, then bolted together by the ironworkers. It's a dangerous job requiring teamwork. "Your partner watches your back and you watch his back. You need that trust," Rice says. Nets are strung on the exterior frame to catch falling objects, and every other floor is planked to stop falls.

Mohawks got their start in ironworking in 1886 when the St. Lawrence River was bridged on tribal land in Quebec. Foremen noticed that Mohawks were surefooted on the span and trained some as helpers. They quickly gained a reputation for reliability and courage.

Historians say ironworking is reminiscent of the tribal tradition of building longhouses. High wages are another attraction. Unionized workers earn $36 an hour and the equivalent in benefits, says Kanatakta, 47, executive director of the Kahnawake Mohawk reservation cultural center. From 600 to 800 of Kahnawake adult males are ironworkers, he says—about a quarter of the community's work force.

Kanatakta, who comes from a family of ironworkers, says aspiring Mohawks can attend ironworker training programs at the reservation. Most start out working with close relatives to foster their confidence and skills. Fatal accidents or serious injuries are constant concerns. "Every Mohawk family has known the anguish of having loved ones seriously hurt or lost on the job."

Questions

1. Based on this article, and your opinion, evaluate the roles of both culture and heredity in contributing to the Mohawks' skill as ironworkers.
2. What prevents more Mohawk women from learning the ironworking trade?

Source: John Pitcher, "Mohawk Ironworkers Helped the New York City Skyline Climb," Rochester, (NY) *Democrat and Chronicle,* August 18, 2002.

with physical and mental disabilities during the last 15 years. Turnover among these employees is negligible, leading to a savings of millions of dollars in employment costs. Pizza Hut has also received millions of dollars in tax credits for hiring people with disabilities, many of whom are developmentally disabled (mentally retarded).[19]

Recent U.S. Supreme Court rulings suggest that disabilities that can be compensated for feasibly do not interfere with job performance. In *Sutton v. United Air Lines,* nearsighted pilots, who also happen to be twins, claimed that the airline violated the ADA by denying them jobs on that basis because their vision is correctable with glasses or contact lenses. The court agreed that an individual cannot be considered "disabled" if his or her condition is correctable with assistive devices.[20]

As will be described in Chapter 16, demographic diversity will often give an organization a competitive advantage. Diversity also affects employee behavior and attitudes. A study of almost 1,600 insurance company employees found that an individual's demographic similarity to his or her work group positively influenced the individual's perception of group productivity and commitment to the work group. (The demographic characteristics studied were race and ethnicity.) Another key finding was that the greater the similarity between an individual's demographic characteristics and others in the work group, the more positive the individual's perceptions of advancement opportunities would be.[21] In short, job satisfaction tends to be higher for employees when others of similar demographic characteristics are present in the workplace.

MENTAL ABILITY (COGNITIVE INTELLIGENCE)

3

Explain how mental ability relates to job performance.

Mental ability, or intelligence, is a major source of individual differences that affect job performance and behavior. **Intelligence** is the capacity to acquire and apply knowledge, including solving problems. Intelligent workers can best solve abstract problems. More than 100 years of consistent research findings indicate that intelligence, as measured by mental ability tests, is positively related to job performance.[22]

Few people seriously doubt that mental ability is related to job performance. Controversy does abound, however, about two aspects of intelligence. One is how accurately and fairly intelligence can be measured. It is argued, for example, that intelligence tests discriminate against environmentally disadvantaged people. The second controversial aspect is the relative influence of heredity and environment on intelligence. Some people believe that intelligence is mostly the product of genes, while others believe that upbringing is the key factor.

The late Hans J. Eysenck, a leading authority in the field of intelligence and personality, concluded that a large component of mental ability is inheritable. Evidence for the genetic contributor to scores in intelligence tests has been reinforced by the twin and adoption studies demonstrating that monozygotic (or identical) twins, whether reared apart or together, exhibit relatively high correlations in intelligence. In contrast, dyzgotic (or fraternal) twins, whether reared apart or together, have correlations that are substantially lower.[23]

The argument that environment is the major contributor to intelligence centers on evidence that many people, if placed in an enriched environment, are able to elevate their intelligence test scores. Related to this argument is the fact that IQs have been steadily rising worldwide, with each successive generation having an average IQ higher than the previous one. Possible explanations for gains in mental ability (as measured by IQ tests) include better nutrition, more training in mental tasks, and more sophistication in taking tests. All of these reasons indicate that environment heavily influences intelligence.[24] (If it is true that mental ability can be improved by a stimulating environment, giving employees ample opportunity to stretch themselves mentally will help them improve their intellectual skills.)

Based on hundreds of studies, it appears that heredity and environment contribute about equally to intelligence.[25] This finding does not mean that a person with extremely limited mental capacity can be made superintelligent through specialized training. Nor does it mean that a naturally brilliant person does not need a mentally stimulating environment.

Here we describe several aspects of mental ability that have implications for organizational behavior: the components of intelligence, the triarchic theory of intelligence that features practical intelligence, and multiple intelligences. Emotional intelligence is described under the category of personality.

Components of Intelligence

Intelligence consists of multiple components. A component of intelligence is much like a separate mental aptitude. A standard theory of intelligence explains that intelligence consists of a *g* (general) factor along with *s* (special) factors that contribute to problem-solving ability. Another way of describing *g* is that it represents a general cognitive factor that pervades almost all kinds of mental ability. Scores on tests of almost any type (such as math or creative ability) are influenced by *g*. High scores on *g* are associated with good scholastic performance. In the workplace, *g* is the best predictor of success in job training, job performance, occupational prestige, and accomplishment within occupations. Also, *g* is related to many social outcomes including early death due to vehicular accidents.[26] The *g* factor helps explain why some people perform so well in many different mental tasks—they have the *right stuff*.

Various researchers have identified different *s* factors contributing to overall mental aptitude. Exhibit 2-1 lists and defines seven factors that have been consistently noted. Being strong in any mental aptitude often leads to enjoyment of work associated with that aptitude. Conversely, enjoyment of an activity might lead to the development of an aptitude for that activity.

Exhibit 2-1

Special Factors Contributing to Overall Mental Aptitude

- **Verbal comprehension:** The ability to understand the meanings of words and their relationship to one another, and to comprehend written and spoken information.
- **Word fluency:** The ability to use words quickly and easily, without an emphasis on verbal comprehension.
- **Numerical:** The ability to handle numbers, engage in mathematical analysis, and do arithmetic calculations.
- **Spatial:** The ability to visualize forms in space and manipulate objects mentally, particularly in three dimensions.
- **Memory:** Having a good rote recall for symbols, words, and lists of numbers, along with other associations.

- **Perceptual speed:** The ability to perceive visual details, to pick out similarities and differences, and to perform tasks requiring visual perception.
- **Inductive reasoning:** The ability to discover a rule or principle and apply it in solving a problem, and to make judgments and decisions that are logically sound.

Source: These seven factors stem from the pioneering work of L. L. Thurstone, *Primary Mental Abilities*, Psychometric Monographs, 1 (1938).

26

Kinko's founder Paul Orfalea seems an unlikely person to have succeeded in any venture, yet the copy business he founded in 1970 now operates more than 1,000 service centers around the world and has annual sales over the $2 billion mark. Early diagnosed as severely dyslexic, Orfalea finally graduated from high school after flunking two grades, finishing eighth from the bottom in a class of 1,500. Learn how Orfalea and others weigh their street smarts against more conventional notions of intelligence by logging on to InfoTrac College Edition at **http://www.infotrac -college.com.** Perform a subject or key word search on "Kinko's" or "Paul Orfalea." You might be surprised how far persistence and grace under pressure can get you.

The Triarchic Theory of Intelligence (Emphasis on Practical Intelligence)

Many people, including specialists in organizational behavior, are concerned that the traditional way of understanding intelligence inadequately describes mental ability. An unfortunate implication of intelligence testing is that intelligence as traditionally calculated consists largely of the ability to perform tasks related to scholastic work. Thus, a person who scored high on an intelligence test could follow a complicated instruction manual but not have street smarts; which would, for example, be needed to run a successful small business.

To overcome the limited idea that intelligence mostly involves the ability to solve abstract problems, the **triarchic theory of intelligence** has been proposed, as presented in Exhibit 2-2. The theory holds that intelligence is composed of three different subtypes: analytical, creative, and practical. The *analytical* subtype is the traditional type of intelligence needed for solving difficult problems in abstract reasoning. Analytical intelligence is required to perform well in most school subjects. The *creative* subtype is the type of intelligence required for imagination and combining things in novel ways. The *practical* subtype is the type of intelligence required for adapting to an environment to suit an individual's needs. Practical intelligence is a major contributor to being street smart.[27]

The idea of practical intelligence helps explain why a person who has a difficult time getting through school can still be a successful businessperson, politician, or visual artist (see the InfoTrac sidebar). Practical intelligence incorporates the ideas of common sense, wisdom, and street smarts. One reservation about practical intelligence is the implication that people who are highly intelligent in the analytical sense are not practical thinkers. In truth, most executives and other high-level workers score quite well on tests of mental ability. These tests usually measure analytical intelligence.[28]

An important implication for organizations about practical intelligence centers around problem-solving ability and age. Analytical intelligence may decline from early to late adulthood. However, the ability to solve problems of a practical nature is maintained or increased through late adulthood. As people become older, they compensate well for declining raw mental energy by focusing on things they do well. In job situations calling for wisdom, such as resolving conflicts, age and experience may be an advantage. The chapter opener about the experienced "car guys" is relevant here.

Multiple Intelligences

Another approach to understanding the diverse nature of mental ability is the theory of **multiple intelligences,** developed by Howard Gardner. According to Gardner's theory, people know and understand the world in distinctly different ways, or look at it through different lenses. Individuals possess the eight intelligences, (or faculties), listed here in varying degrees.

1. *Linguistic:* Enables people to communicate through language, including reading, writing, and speaking.
2. *Logical-Mathematical:* Enables individuals to see relationships between objects and solve problems such as in calculus and statistics.
3. *Musical:* Gives people the capacity to create and understand meanings made out of sounds, and to enjoy different types of music.
4. *Spatial:* Enables people to perceive and manipulate images in their brain and to recreate them from memory, such as in making graphic designs.

Exhibit 2-2

The Triarchic Theory of Intelligence

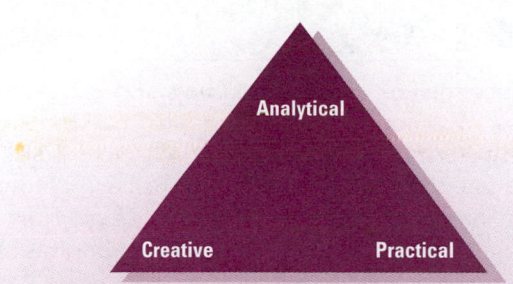

Three managers took a mental ability test as part of a career counseling program.

Analytical. Manager A scored well on mental ability tests and was good at both test taking and analytical thinking. He exemplifies the analytical aspect of intelligence and has excellent skills in budgeting.

Creative. Manager B had mediocre test scores, but she was a creative thinker and insightful in sizing up people and business situations. She exemplifies the creative aspect of intelligence and has achieved good success as a branch manager.

Practical. Manager C also had mediocre test scores, but he had street smarts and understood how to manipulate his environment in a variety of contexts. Before becoming a manager, he was an excellent sales representative.

Source: Based on information in Robert J. Trotter, "Three Heads Are Better than One," *Psychology Today*, August 1986, pp. 56–62; modified and updated with information from Robert J. Sternberg, book review in *Personnel Psychology*, Summer 1999, pp. 471–476.

5. *Bodily/kinesthetic:* Enables people to use their body and perceptual and motor systems in skilled ways such as dancing, playing sports, and expressing emotion through facial expressions.
6. *Intrapersonal:* Enables people to distinguish among their own feelings and acquire accurate self-knowledge.
7. *Interpersonal:* Makes it possible for individuals to recognize and make distinctions among the feelings, motives, and intentions of others, as in managing and parenting.
8. *Naturalist:* Enables individuals to differentiate among, classify, and utilize various features of the physical external environment.

Your profile of intelligences influences how you will best learn, and for which types of jobs you are best suited. Gardner believes that it is possible to develop these separate intelligences through concentrated effort. Another consideration is that any of these intelligences will fade if not used.[29] These separate types of intelligences might also be perceived as different talents or abilities. Having high general problem-solving ability would therefore contribute to high standing on each one of the eight intelligences.

A concern about the theory of multiple intelligences is that it is not as well documented as theories of intelligence that emphasize general cognitive ability. Should evidence be collected to support the existence of multiple intelligences, the theory could be applied to improve productivity. Workers could be assigned positions that best fit their profile of intelligences. A person who was not strong in linguistic intelligence or logical–mathematical intelligence might have high enough interpersonal intelligence to be effective as a customer service representative.

PERSONALITY DIFFERENCES

Personality characteristics such as conscientiousness and extroversion contribute to success in many jobs. Most job failures are not attributed to a person's intelligence or technical competence but to personality characteristics. The subject of personality is therefore important in organizational behavior. However, considerable controversy centers on the concept of personality. There is disagreement as to whether personality can be accurately measured and whether it is influenced more by heredity or environment.

Personality refers to the persistent and enduring behavior patterns of an individual that are expressed in a wide variety of situations. Your personality is the combination of attributes, traits, and characteristics that makes you unique. Your walk, talk, appearance, speech, and creativity all contribute to your personality. Personality can therefore be regarded as the core of who you are.[30]

We approach the topic of personality by first describing seven key personality traits related to job performance and behavior, including an example of relevant research. We then describe psychological types related to cognitive styles. Two experiential activities related to personality will also be presented.

Seven Major Personality Factors and Traits

According to the Five Factor Model of personality the basic structure of human personality is represented by five broad factors: neuroticism, extraversion, openness to experience, agreeableness, and conscientiousness. Although the Five Factor Model of personality is well documented, other aspects of personality still have merit. We therefore also present two other factors of particular significance to job behavior: behavior self-monitoring and risk taking and thrill seeking. People develop all seven factors to different degrees, partially from growing up in a particular environment. For example, a person might have a natural tendency to be agreeable. An environment in which agreeableness was encouraged would help him or her become even more agreeable.

All seven factors have a substantial impact on job behavior and performance; some of this evidence is presented here. The interpretation and meaning of these factors provide useful information because they help you to pinpoint areas for personal development. Although these factors are partially inherited, most people can improve their development in them.

1. *Neuroticism.* This trait reflects neuroticism versus emotional stability. People with high neuroticism are prone to psychological distress and coping with problems in unproductive ways. Traits associated with this personality factor include being anxious, insecure, angry, embarrassed, and worried. A person of low neuroticism—or high emotional stability—is calm and confident, and usually in control.
2. *Extraversion.* Traits associated with extraversion include being social, gregarious, assertive, talkative, and active. An outgoing person is often described as extraverted, whereas a shy person is described as introverted. Many successful leaders are extraverted, yet some effective leaders are introverted because they rely on other factors such as giving feedback and encouraging others. (Note that *extraversion* in everyday language is spelled *extroversion*.)
3. *Openness to experience.* People who score high with openness have well-developed intellects. Traits associated with this factor include being imaginative, cultured, curious, original, broad-minded, intelligent, and artistically sensitive.

Many successful managers and professionals search printed information and the Internet for useful ideas. Also, many top-level executives support the arts.

4. *Agreeableness.* This factor reflects the quality of a person's interpersonal orientation. An agreeable person is friendly and cooperative. Traits associated with the agreeableness factor include being courteous, flexible, trusting, good natured, cooperative, forgiving, softhearted, and tolerant. Agreeableness is a plus for customer service positions, such as the greeters at Wal-Mart.

5. *Conscientiousness.* A variety of meanings have been attached to the conscientious factor, but it generally implies dependability. Traits associated with conscientiousness include being careful, thorough, responsible, organized, and a good planner. Other related traits include being hardworking, achievement oriented, and persevering. Being conscientious to the extreme, however, can lead to workaholism and perfectionism.

6. *Self-monitoring behavior.* The self-monitoring trait refers to the process of observing and controlling how we appear to others. High self-monitors are pragmatic and are even chameleon-like actors in social groups. They often say what others want to hear. Low self-monitors avoid situations that require them to adopt different outer images. In this way, their outer behavior adheres to their inner values. Low self-monitoring can often lead to inflexibility. People who are skilled at office politics usually score high on the self-monitoring factor.

7. *Risk taking and thrill seeking.* Some people crave constant excitement on the job and are willing to risk their lives to achieve thrills. The willingness to take risks and pursue thrills is a personality trait that has grown in importance in the high-technology era. Many people work for employers, start businesses, and purchase stocks with uncertain futures. Both the search for giant payoffs and daily thrills motivate these individuals. A strong craving for thrills may have some positive consequences for the organization, including the willingness to perform dangerous feats such as setting explosives, capping an oil well, controlling a radiation leak, and introducing a product in a highly competitive environment. However, extreme risk takers and thrill seekers can create problems such as involvement in a disproportionate number of vehicular accidents and imprudent investments. Take the Self-Assessment that follows to measure your tendency toward risk taking.

Evidence for the relevance of the Five Factor Model of personality in understanding human behavior comes from a cross-cultural study involving 7,134 individuals. The five-factor structure of the American personality was also found to hold true for German, Portuguese, Hebrew, Chinese, Korean, and Japanese samples when the personality test questions were translated into each of these languages. Based on this extensive study, it was concluded that personality structure is universal,[31] much like the structure of the brain or the body.

Depending on the job, any one of the seven personality factors mentioned previously can be important for good job performance. The most consistent finding is that conscientiousness is positively related to job performance for a variety of occupations. Furthermore, the combination of intelligence ("can do") with conscientiousness ("will do") is especially important for job performance. In a study of ninety-one sales representatives for an appliance manufacturer, the combination of intelligence and conscientiousness made accurate predictions of job success. Representatives who scored high on intelligence and conscientiousness tended to sell more appliances and receive better performance ratings from their supervisors. In a related study with the same sales representatives, extraversion was

SELF-ASSESSMENT

The Risk-Taking Scale

Can you look at a person and tell whether he or she is a risk taker? "I've never been able to do it, and I've studied them for more than 30 years," says Frank Farley, a psychologist at Temple University. "You have to scratch the surface and get to know them." Still, there are many clues when you meet them; for example, some risk takers have high energy levels and display impulsiveness. How can you size up your capacity for risk? Here's an informal quiz. Although some of the questions seem obvious, your final score reflects the range of risk that you are comfortable with, not just whether you like taking risks or not. Answer true or false:

		True	False
1.	I don't like my opinions being challenged.	❏	❏
2.	I would rather be an accountant than a TV anchor.	❏	❏
3.	I believe that I can control my destiny.	❏	❏
4.	I am a highly creative person.	❏	❏
5.	I like a lot of varied romantic partners.	❏	❏
6.	I don't like trying exotic foods.	❏	❏
7.	I would choose bonds over growth stocks.	❏	❏
8.	Friends would call me a thrill seeker.	❏	❏
9.	I like to challenge authority.	❏	❏
10.	I prefer familiar things to new things.	❏	❏
11.	I'm known for my curiosity.	❏	❏
12.	I wouldn't like to be an entrepreneur.	❏	❏
13.	I'd rather not travel abroad.	❏	❏
14.	I'm easily bored.	❏	❏
15.	I wouldn't like to be a stand-up comedian.	❏	❏
16.	I've never gotten speeding tickets.	❏	❏
17.	I'm extremely adventurous.	❏	❏
18.	I need a lot of stimulation in my life.	❏	❏
19.	I would rather work for a salary than a commission.	❏	❏
20.	Making my own decisions is very important to me.	❏	❏

Give yourself 1 point each time your answer agrees with the key. If you score 16–20: You are probably a high risk taker. 10–15: You're a moderate risk taker. 5–9: You are cautious. 0–4: You are a very low risk taker.

1) F	6) F	11) T	16) F
2) F	7) F	12) F	17) T
3) T	8) T	13) F	18) T
4) T	9) T	14) T	19) F
5) T	10) F	15) F	20) T

Source: © 1999 by Frank Farley, Ph.D., all rights reserved. The interpretation here is modified from the original.

a good predictor of job performance.[32] A meta-analysis of seventy-three studies demonstrated a relationship between the Five Factor Model and the two criteria of leadership effectiveness, and stepping forth as a leader. Extraversion was the factor most frequently associated with the two leadership criteria.[33]

Self-monitoring is another personality factor whose relationship to job behavior has been supported by extensive research. Meta-analyses were conducted for 136 samples and over 23,000 employees to understand the relationship between work-related behaviors and self-monitoring. It was found that high self-monitors tend to receive better performance ratings and more promotions than low self-monitors. High self–monitors were also more likely to emerge as leaders.[34] In short, it pays to tell people what they want to hear if you want to succeed in business.

Research has also documented the importance of personality factors for performance as a team member. George A. Neuman and Julie Wright studied seventy–nine four–person, human resource work teams with respect to how general cognitive ability, job-specific skills, and personality traits were related to job performance. For individuals, agreeableness and conscientiousness predicted coworker ratings of team member performance, even after cognitive ability and skills were taken into account. Measures were also taken of group cognitive ability, skills, and personality by using the lowest score for any individual as the team value. (A chain is only as strong as its weakest link.) For groups, both agreeableness and conscientiousness were useful predictors of work-team performance, such as amount of work completed and supervisor ratings of team performance.[35]

In general, favorable results when using personality measures to predict job performance are more likely to occur when the job requirements are carefully analyzed. For example, agreeableness is more important for an airline reservations assistant than a Web designer.

Psychological Types and Cognitive Styles (Myers-Briggs)

Personality also influences a person's **cognitive style,** or the mental processes used to perceive and make judgments from information. Knowledge of these cognitive styles can help you relate better to people because you can better appreciate how they make decisions. According to the famous psychoanalyst Carl Jung, how people gather and evaluate information determines their cognitive style. Jung's analysis became the basis for a widely used test of personality and cognitive style called the Myers–Briggs Type Indicator. Jung reasoned that there are four dimensions of psychological functioning:

1. *Introverted versus Extroverted.* Introverts are oriented toward the inner world of ideas and feelings, whereas extroverts are oriented toward the outer world of people and objects.
2. *Thinking versus Feeling.* Thinkers prefer to make decisions logically based on facts and figures, whereas feelers base decisions on subjective information.
3. *Sensing versus Intuiting.* Sensing individuals prefer to concentrate on details, whereas intuitive individuals prefer to focus on broad issues (the Big Picture).
4. *Judging versus Perceiving.* Judging types seek to resolve issues, whereas as perceiving types are relatively flexible and search for additional information.

Combining the four types with each other in different combinations results in 16 personality types, as measured by the Myers-Briggs Type Indicator. Exhibit 2-3 presents the personal characteristics associated with four of the sixteen types of cognitive styles. The Myers–Briggs has become one of the most widely used personality tests in business and school settings. Many readers of this book will have already take the Myers-Briggs Type Indicator in a school or work setting.

Research evidence for the Myers-Briggs Type Indicator is generally positive with respect to the sixteen types, and the fact that people with different cognitive styles prefer different occupations. For example, the ENTP cognitive type is labeled the "conceptualizer." He or she is passionate about new opportunities and dislikes routine, and is more likely to be an entrepreneur than a corporate manager. The ISTJ cognitive type is labeled the "traditionalist," and will often become an accountant or financial analyst. The INTJ type is labeled the "visionary." Although

Exhibit 2-3

Four Cognitive Styles of the Myers-Briggs Typology

ENTP (Conceptualizer)	ISTJ (Traditionalist)	INTJ (Visionary)	ESTJ (Organizer)
Quick, ingenious, will argue either side of issue for fun, may neglect routine assignments. (Good for creative work where deadlines are not crucial.)	Serious, quiet, practical, logical, dependable. (Good for work requiring careful attention to detail such as accountant or auditor.)	Skeptical, critical, independent, determined, original. (Good for major leadership role such as CEO.)	Practical, realistic, has a natural mind for business or mechanics, likes to organize and run activities. (Good for plant superintendent.)

Note: I = Introvert, E = Extrovert, T = Thinking, F = Feeling, S = Sensing, N = Intuitive, J = Judging, and P = Perceiving.

Source: The personality descriptions are based on information from *Meyers-Briggs Type Indicator* by Katharine C. Briggs and Isabel Briggs Myers. Copyright 1983 by Consulting Psychologists Press, Inc. All rights reserved.

a small proportion of the population, these individuals are often chief executives of business firms. One of the most common types among managers, as well as people in general, is the ESTJ, labeled the "organizer."[36]

Many people who use the Myers-Briggs are not aware that it is an approximate measure, and not a definitive scale such as a measure of physical weight. The most reliable dimension appears to be sensing versus intuiting, which is similar to reflecting about details versus jumping to a quick decision based on feeling and experience, or being reflective versus impulsive.[37]

The role plays, in the Skill-Development Exercise that follows, give you an opportunity to practice managing for individual differences in personality. Remember that a role player is an extemporaneous actor. Put yourself in the shoes of the character you play and visualize how he or she would act. Because you are given only the general idea of a script, use your imagination to fill in the details.

5

Explain how emotional intelligence is an important part of organizational behavior.

EMOTIONAL INTELLIGENCE

Research into the functioning of the human brain has combined personality factors with practical intelligence, indicating that how effectively people use their emotions has a major impact on their success. The topmost layers of the brain govern componential intelligence functions, such as analytical problem solving. The innermost areas of the brain govern emotional functions, such as dealing with anger when being criticized by a customer.

Emotional intelligence refers to qualities such as understanding one's own feelings, empathy for others, and the regulation of emotion to enhance living. As the concept of emotional intelligence has gained in popularity, many definitions have been proposed and more and more behavior has been incorporated into emotional intelligence.

Emotional intelligence has to do with the ability to connect with people and understand their emotions. A worker with high emotional intelligence can engage in behaviors such as sizing up, pleasing, and influencing people. Based on research in dozens of companies, Daniel Goleman discovered that the most effective leaders are alike in one essential way: They all have a high degree of emotional intelligence. Without a high degree of emotional intelligence, a person can have excellent training, superior analytical skills, and many innovative suggestions. However, he or she will still not make a great leader. According to a recent con-

SKILL-DEVELOPMENT EXERCISE

COLLABORATE

Personality Role Plays

Run each role play for about 7 minutes. The people not involved in the role play will observe and then provide feedback when the role play is completed.

1. *The Extravert*. One student assumes the role of a successful outside sales representative who has just signed a $3 million order for the company. The elated sales rep returns to the office. Another student assumes the role of the sales manager. He or she decides that this is a splendid opportunity to build a good relationship with the triumphant sales rep.
2. *Openness*. One student plays the role of an experienced worker in the department who is told to spend some time showing around a new co-op

student. It appears that this worker is open to experience. Another student plays the role of the co-op student, who is also open to experience and eager to be successful in this new position.

3. *Sensing versus Intuiting Types*. One student plays the role of a sensing type individual who is responsible for reviewing the company expense accounts. Another student plays the role of a manager in whose department many expense account abuses (such as lack of documentation and high expenses) have been uncovered. The person in charge of the accounts is visiting the manager in the latter's office to discuss this problem. The manager is an intuiting type.

---

ceptualization by Goleman and his associates, the four key factors included in emotional intelligence are as follows:

1. *Self-awareness.* The ability to understand one's own emotions is the most essential of the four emotional intelligence competencies. Having high self-awareness allows people to know their strengths and limitations and have high self-esteem. Effective leaders use self-awareness to accurately measure their own moods, and to intuitively understand how their moods affect others. Effective managers seek feedback to see how well their actions are received by others. A manager with good self-awareness would recognize factors such as whether or he she was liked, or was exerting the right amount of pressure on people.
2. *Self-management.* The ability to control one's emotions and act with honesty and integrity in a consistent and adaptable manner. The right degree of self-management helps prevent a person from throwing temper tantrums when activities do not go as planned. Effective workers do not let their occasional bad moods ruin their day. If they cannot overcome the bad mood, they let work associates know of the problem and how long it might last. A manager with high self-management would not suddenly decide to fire a group member because of one difference of opinion.
3. *Social awareness.* Includes having empathy for others and having intuition about organizational problems. Socially aware leaders go beyond sensing the emotions of others by showing that they care. In addition, they accurately size up political forces in the office. A team leader with social awareness, or empathy, would be able to assess whether a team member has enough enthusiasm for a project to assign him to that project. A CEO who has empathy for a labor union's demands might be able to negotiate successfully with the head of the labor union to avoid a costly strike.
4. *Relationship management.* Includes the interpersonal skills of being able to communicate clearly and convincingly, disarm conflicts, and build strong personal bonds. Effective leaders use relationship management skills to spread their enthusiasm and solve disagreements, often with kindness and humor. A

leader with good relationship management skills would not burn bridges and would continue to enlarge his or her network of people to win support when support is needed.[38]

Many training programs are designed to improve emotional intelligence, but the earlier that people develop skills in handling emotional reactions the better. This is because the key to emotional intelligence lies in the way the brain is programmed in childhood. People learn most of their emotional habits when they are young, but can still learn to improve inappropriate responses later in life.[39]

Among the many practical outcomes of having high emotional intelligence is the ability to cope better with setbacks. A review of many studies concluded that low emotional intelligence employees are more likely than their high emotional intelligence counterparts to experience negative emotional reactions to job insecurity, such as high tension. Furthermore, workers with low emotional intelligence are more likely to engage in negative coping behaviors, such as expressing anger and verbally abusing a immediate supervisor for the organization failing to provide job security.[40]

Tests of emotional intelligence typically ask you to respond to questions on a 1-to-5 scale (never, rarely, sometimes, often, cosistently). For example, indicate how frequently you demonstrate the following behaviors:

I can laugh at myself.	1 2 3 4 5
I help others grow and develop.	1 2 3 4 5
I watch carefully the nonverbal communication of others.	1 2 3 4 5

Emotional intelligence underscores the importance of being practical minded and having effective interpersonal skills to succeed in organizational life. Many topics included in the study of organizational behavior, such as communication, conflict resolution, and power and politics, are components of emotional intelligence. The message is an old one: Both cognitive and non-cognitive skills are required for success!

IMPLICATIONS FOR MANAGERIAL PRACTICE

A major implication of individual differences in personality and abilities is that these factors have a major impact on the selection, placement, job assignment, training, and development of employees. When faced with such decisions, the manager should seek answers to such questions as:

- Is this employee intelligent enough to handle the job and deal with out-of-the-ordinary problems?
- Is this employee too intelligent for the assignment? Will he or she become bored quickly?
- Is this employee's personality suited to the assignment? For instance, is the employee con-

scientious enough? Is the employee open to new learning?

Many employees perform below standard not because they are not motivated but because their abilities and personality traits are not suited to the job. For instance, an employee who prepares garbled reports may be doing so because of below-average verbal comprehension, not low motivation. Training programs and coaching can be useful in making up for deficits that appear on the surface to be motivational problems.

SUMMARY OF KEY POINTS

1 **Explain how individual differences influence the behavior of people in organizations.**

Understanding individual differences helps to explain human behavior. Nevertheless, behavior is a function of the person interacting with the environment, as expressed by the equation $B = f(P \times E)$.

Individual differences impact on managing people because people differ in: (1) productivity, (2) ability and talent, (3) propensity for achieving quality results, (4) desire for empowerment and involvement, (5) style of leadership preferred and needed, (6) need for people contact, (7) commitment and loyalty to the firm, and (8) self-esteem.

2 **Describe key factors contributing to demographic diversity.**

Understanding demographic differences among workers can help the manager capitalize on diversity and avoid negative stereotyping. Key sources of demographic diversity include sex and gender, age and experience, ethnicity and culture, and disability status.

3 **Explain how mental ability relates to job performance.**

Mental ability, or intelligence, is one of the major sources of individual differences that affect job performance and behavior. Intelligence consists of many components. One perspective is that intelligence includes a general factor (g) along with special factors (s) that contribute to problem-solving ability. A related perspective is that intelligence consists of seven components including verbal and numerical comprehension.

To overcome the limited idea that intelligence involves mostly the ability to solve abstract problems, the triarchic theory of intelligence has been proposed. Its three component types of intelligence are analytical, creative, and practical (adapting to your environment to suit your needs).

Another approach to understanding the diverse nature of mental ability is the theory of multiple intelligences. According to this theory, people possess eight intelligences, or faculties: linguistic, logical-mathematical, musical, spatial, bodily/kinesthetic, intrapersonal, interpersonal, and naturalist.

4 **Identify major personality variables that influence job performance.**

Personality is one of the major sources of individual differences. Seven major personality factors are neuroticism, extroversion, openness, agreeableness, conscientiousness, self-monitoring, and risk taking and thrill seeking. Depending on the job, any one of these personality factors can be important for success.

Personality also influences a person's cognitive style, or the mental process used to perceive and make judgments from information. Four dimensions of psychological functioning are: (a) introverted versus extroverted, (b) thinking versus feeling, (c) sensing versus intuiting, and (d) judging versus perceiving. The four dimensions combined with each other result in sixteen personality types or cognitive styles.

5 **Explain how emotional intelligence is an important part of organizational behavior.**

The concept of emotional intelligence helps explain how emotions and personality factors contribute to success. A worker with high emotional intelligence would be able to engage in such behaviors as sizing up, pleasing, and influencing people. The components of emotional intelligence are self-awareness, self-management, social awareness, and relationship management.

KEY TERMS AND PHRASES

Individual Differences, *18*
Variations in how people respond to the same situation based on personal characteristics.

Demographic Diversity, *20*
Differences in background factors about the workforce that help shape worker attitudes and behavior.

Disability, *22*
A physical or mental condition that substantially limits an individual's major life activities.

Intelligence, *24*
The capacity to acquire and apply knowledge, including solving problems.

g (general) factor, *25*
A major component of intelligence that contributes to problem-solving ability.

s (special) factors, *25*
Components of intelligence that contribute to problem-solving ability.

Triarchic Theory of Intelligence, *26*
The theory that intelligence is composed of three different types of intelligence: analytical, creative, and practical.

Multiple Intelligences, *26*
A theory that proposes that people know and understand the world in distinctly different ways according to the varying

degrees to which they possess eight faculties: linguistic, logical-mathematical, musical, spatial, bodily/kinesthetic, intrapersonal, interpersonal, and naturalist.

Personality, *28*
The persistent and enduring behavior patterns of an individual that are expressed in a wide variety of situations.

Cognitive Style, *31*
The mental processes used to perceive and make judgments from information.

Emotional Intelligence, *32*
Qualities such as understanding one's own feelings, empathy for others, and the regulation of emotion to enhance living.

DISCUSSION QUESTIONS AND ACTIVITIES

1. Give an example from your own life of how $B = f(P \times E)$.
2. Ten years into the future, your classmates will show wide variations in terms of their career achievements. How might individual differences explain some of these differences in accomplishment?
3. ![collaborate icon] Work together in a small discussion group to uncover several positive demographic stereotypes about workers. Give examples of how these stereotypes might be used in selecting new hires or in making work assignments for present employees.
4. Suppose you or a family member required brain surgery. Would you let a neurosurgeon operate on you who claims she has good practical intelligence, even though

she has below-average analytical intelligence? Explain your reasoning.
5. Which of the personality traits described in this chapter do you think are particularly important for managers who would conduct their work in a highly ethical manner? Explain.
6. Why does having high self-esteem contribute to being more productive and earning a higher income?
7. Evaluate the President of the United States in terms of the various aspects of emotional intelligence, and justify your answer. In which area does the President need the most improvement?

ORGANIZATIONAL BEHAVIOR ONLINE

TO DO

Gaining Self-Insight
The Internet can be used to enhance your self-insight and obtain a measure of your emotional intelligence. To test your emotional IQ, go to http://www.utne.com/interact/test_ig.html. Web sites do not last forever, so if this site is no longer in operation, search for another site that offers a measure of emotional intelligence.

TO BOOKMARK

Online Tests and Quizzes
http://www.wizardrealm.com/tests
http://www.queendom.com

Discrimination Laws
http://www.eeoc.gov/small/index.html

CASE PROBLEM: "Treat Me Like Anybody Else"

When Paul D'Addario first started working at an association almost 17 years ago, his managers focused on his potential, what he might actually do for the firm. Now he's afraid he has to prove that he can be trusted to do what he's been doing for years.

D'Addario, the database manager at the American Society for Industrial Security in Alexandria, has gradually been losing his eyesight. As his disability has increased, he believes that his responsibilities at work have decreased. And as much as he hopes this isn't related to his disability, he can't be sure.

"They've done a lot of good things for me," he said. "But when you feel your supervisor has a different expectation level, it hurts."

D'Addario believes he has to prove himself more than colleagues without disabilities. Most recently, D'Addario's supervisor nixed D'Addario's trip to a convention, one he has gone to for years. When this sort of thing happens,

D'Addario said, "I don't know how to think about how they are thinking of me."

D'Addario's thinking went back and forth. He figured his manager was doing what the management plan called for, but then he worried that his vision might have something to do with the decision. In the end, D'Addario sent a two-page memo to his supervisor explaining why he should be there.

"It's not been difficult to convince people that I can do my current job. It's difficult to convince them of what my potential is," he said.

After some serious back-and-forth, D'Addario and his supervisor agreed there was nothing personal in the decision and smoothed things over. As D'Addario said, frustrations are common around workplaces everywhere.

D'Addario pointed out that he frequently suffers frustrations off the job also. Strangers on the street often shout directions to him as he takes his daily walk home from the

Metro, as though a problem with vision might somehow have spread to his hearing and intelligence.

D'Addario understands because he used to do that sort of thing as well. "I think there is almost a built-in expectation level that people have when they see someone who is in a wheelchair, blind, deaf or whatever. I think the expectation level is quite low," he said.

Cancellation of his trip was a one-time frustration, but D'Addario knows that he has to dispel some myths. One myth concerning him dealt with the cost of making accommodations for his disability. The potential problem arose when he first needed special software so he could read e-mail and do computer work.

"It was not easy to ask," D'Addario said, when about five years into his job, he told a manager what he needed because of his failing sight. His manager told him to order whatever he needed, which only made things worse when the

equipment he bought wasn't worth what it cost. D'Addario felt guilty and worried that he had to be a little more careful about purchases in the future.

Case Questions

1. What does this case illustrate about disability and job performance?
2. How fairly is company management treating D'Addario?
3. What should management be doing for D'Addario that they are not doing?
4. What should D'Addario be doing himself to advance his cause that he is not doing?

Source: Adapted from Amy Joyce, "The Thought Counts—But Does It Fit? Disabled Workers Desire to Be Recognized, But Not for the Wrong Reasons," *Washington Post*, August 25, 2002, p. H6.

ENDNOTES

1. For a full explanation of individual differences and job behavior, see Kevin R. Murphy (ed.), *Individual Differences and Behavior in Organizations* (San Francisco: Jossey-Bass, 1996).
2. Kurt Lewin, *A Dynamic Theory of Personality* (New York: McGraw-Hill, 1935).
3. John E. Hunter, Frank L. Schmidt, and Michael E. Judiesch, "Individual Differences in Output Variability as a Function of Job Complexity," *Journal of Applied Psychology*, February 1990), pp. 28–42.
4. Study reported in "Job Applicants Often Lack Basics," *Rochester, (NY) Democrat and Chronicle*, May 20, 2001, p. 1G.
5. Nathaniel Branden, *Self-Esteem at Work: How Confident People Make Powerful Companies* (San Francisco: Jossey-Bass, 1998).
6. "The Vital Role of Self-Esteem: It Boosts Productivity and Earnings," *Business Week*, February 2, 1998, p. 26.
7. Michael D. Lemonick, "Smart Genes?," *Time*, September 13, 1999, p. 54.
8. A brief review of the literature is presented in Leonard Sax, "Maybe Men and Women are Different," *American Psychologist*, June/July 2002, p. 444.
9. James Q. Wilson, *The Moral Sense* (New York: The Free Press, 1993).
10. Gary N. Powell, "One More Time: Do Female and Male Managers Differ?" *Academy of Management Executive*, August 1990, p. 74; Daniel J. Canary and Kathryn Dindia, *Sex Differences and Similarities in Communication* (Mahwah, NJ: Erlbaum, 1998).
11. Daniel J. Canary and Tara M. Emmers-Sommer, *Sex and Gender Differences in Personal Relationships* (New York: Guilford Press, 1997).
12. Allison Kindelan, "Older Workers Can Alleviate Labor Shortages," *HR Magazine*, September 1998, p. 200.
13. George J. Church, "Unmasking Age Bias," *Time*, September 7, 1998, p. H4.
14. Bruce J. Avolio, David A. Waldman, and Michael A. McDaniel, "Age and Work Performance in Nonmanagerial Jobs: The Effects of Experience and Occupational Type," *Academy of Management Journal*, June 1990, pp. 407–422.
15. Glen M. McEvoy and Wayne F. Cascio, "Cumulative Evidence of the Relationship between Employee Age and Job Performance," *Journal of Applied Psychology*, February 1989, pp. 11–17.
16. Susan R. Rhodes, "Age-Related Differences in Work Attitudes and Behavior: A Review and Conceptual Analysis," *Psychological Bulletin*, March 1983, pp. 328–367.

17. Susan J. Wells, "Is the ADA Working?" *HR Magazine*, April 2001, p. 40.
18. John P. Fernandez, *Managing the Diverse Work Force* (Lexington, MA: Lexington Books, 1991).
19. Todd Raphael, "Disabling Some Old Stereotypes," *Workforce*, August 2002, p. 88.
20. Carole O'Blenes, "Legal Intelligence: ADA Lessons From the Front Lines," *Management Review*, September 1999, p. 60.
21. Christine M. Riordan and Lynn McFarlane Shore, "Demographic Diversity and Employee Attitudes: An Empirical Examination of Relational Demography within Work Units," *Journal of Applied Psychology*, June 1997, pp. 342–358.
22. Orlando Behling, "Employee Selection: Will Intelligence and Conscientiousness Do the Job?" *Academy of Management Executive*, February 1998, p. 78.
23. Hans J. Eysenck, *Intelligence: A New Look* (New Brunswick, NJ: Transaction, 1998).
24. James R. Flynn, "The Discovery of IQ Gains Over Time," *American Psychologist*, January 1999, pp. 5–20.
25. Saul Kassin, *Psychology*, 3rd ed. (Upper Saddle River, NJ: Prentice Hall, 2001), p. 467; Eysenck, *Intelligence: A New Look*.
26. Arthur R. Jensen, *The g Factor: The Science of Mental Ability* (Westport, CT: Praeger, 1998).
27. Robert J. Sternberg, *Beyond IQ: A Triarchic Theory of Human Intelligence* (New York: Cambridge University Press, 1995); Bridget Murray, "Sparking Interest in Psychology Class," *APA Monitor*, October 1996, p. 51.
28. Richard K. Wagner, "Intelligence, Training, and Employment," *American Psychologist*, October 1997, pp. 1059–1069.
29. Howard Gardner, *Leading Minds: An Anatomy of Leadership* (New York: Basic Books, 1996); Thalia Zepatos, "6 Other Ways to Judge IQ," *USA Weekend*, March 13–15, 1998, p. 18; http://www.funderstanding.com/multiple_intelligence.cfm.
30. "From 'Character' to 'Personality,'" *APA Monitor*, December 1999, p. 22.
31. Robert R. McCrae and Paul T. Costa, Jr. "Personality Trait Structure as a Human Universal," *American Psychologist*, May 1997, pp. 509–516.
32. These studies and similar ones are reviewed in Leonard D. Goodstein and Richard I. Lanyon, "Applications of Personality Assessment to the Workplace: A Review," *Journal of Business and Psychology*, Spring 1999, pp. 293–298.

33. Timothy A. Judge, Joyce E. Bono, Remus Ilies, and Megan W. Gerhardt, "Personality and Leadership: A Quantitative and Qualitative Review," *Journal of Applied Psychology,* August 2002, pp. 765–780.

34. David B. Day, Deidra J. Schleicher, Amy L. Unckless, and Nathan J. Hiller, "Self-Monitoring Personality at Work: A Meta-Analytic Investigation of Construct Validity," *Journal of Applied Psychology,* April 2002, pp. 390–401.

35. George A. Neuman and Julie Wright, "Team Effectiveness: Beyond Skills and Cognitive Ability," *Journal of Applied Psychology,* June 1999, pp. 376–389.

36. The Consulting Psychological Press, Inc., Palo Alto, CA 94306, publishes the Myers-Briggs Type Indicator. Much of our discussion is based on the formulation of Robert P. Vecchio, *Organizational Behavior: Core Concepts,* 4th ed. (Fort Worth, TX: The Dryden Press, 2000), pp. 44–45. See also John W. Slocum and Donald Hellriegel, "A Look at How Managers' Minds Work," *Business Horizons,* Winter 1983, pp. 58–68.

37. Robert J. Sternberg and Elena J. Grigorenko, "Are Cognitive Styles Still in Style?" *American Psychologist,* July 1997, p. 703.

38. Daniel Goleman, Richard Boyatzis, and Annie McKee, "Primal Leadership: The Hidden Driver of Great Performance," *Harvard Business Review,* December 2001, pp. 42–51.

39. Patrick A. McGuire, "Teach Your Children Well—and Early, Goleman Says," *APA Monitor,* October 1998, p. 15.

40. Peter J. Jordan, Neal M. Ashkanasy, and Charmine E. J. Hartel, "Emotional Intelligence as a Moderator of Emotional and Behavioral Reactions to Job Insecurity," *Academy of Management Review,* July 2002, pp. 361–372.

Chapter 3

Learning, Perception, and Attribution

For two consecutive years stockbroker Edward Jones, based in St. Louis, Missouri, was ranked number one among the *Fortune* 100 Best Companies to Work For. Jones has over $2 billion in annual revenues. The company spends 3.8 percent of its payroll on training, with an average of 146 hours for every employee. New brokers at the 7,781 branches get four times that much training. [Edward] Jones has a reason for investing so much in its people. "In order to grow, you have to be trained," says managing partner John Bachmann, "or you get trapped in the present."

At a time period when Wall Street firms were contracting, this Main Street firm was still hiring. The company is owned by employees (25% of them have partnership stakes), and perhaps that's why they care enough to have serious profit sharing and no layoffs. Says one administrative assistant: "I have never experienced working for a company that has so many satisfied employees."

OBJECTIVES

After reading and studying this chapter and doing the exercises, you should be able to:

1 Explain the basics of modeling and shaping, cognitive learning, and e-learning.

2 Describe how learning styles influence workplace learning.

3 Describe key aspects of the perceptual process, along with common perceptual problems.

4 Describe how attribution theory contributes to an understanding of human behavior in the workplace.

Source: Adapted from Robert Levering and Milton Moskowitz, "100 Best Companies to Work for," *Fortune,* January 20, 2003, p. 128. Ann Harrington prepared the information about Edward Jones in the article.

NOW ASK YOURSELF: What is the relevance of employee learning to the welfare of a firm? For one, it's hard to argue that on-the-job training doesn't affect a firm's financial position or employee morale when confronted with the convincing evidence represented by Edwards Jones, whose managers attribute much of the company's success to its well-trained employees. In this chapter, we describe three aspects of individual functioning: learning, perception, and attributions. Understanding these aspects of behavior helps managers deal more effectively with people. Understanding these aspects of behavior should also make job seekers realize that technical aptitude alone is not enough to survive in today's information-age economy.

TWO KEY LEARNING PROCESSES AND E-LEARNING

1

Explain the basics of modeling and shaping, cognitive learning and e-learning.

Given that most organizations emphasize continuous learning, it is useful to understand how people learn. **Learning** is a relatively permanent change in behavior based on practice or experience. A curiosity about learning is that it is possible to learn something and store it in your mind without changing your behavior.[1] For example, you might read that if you press "F12" in any current version of Windows you open the "Save As" function. You keep it in mind, but do not use the command yet. The new knowledge is stored in your upper brain, but is not yet put into action.

A person does not learn how to grow physically, digest food, hear sounds, or see light. These are innate, inborn patterns of behavior. But a person does learn how to conduct a performance appraisal, use a computer network to access information, or prepare a report. Unless learning takes place, few employees would be able to perform their jobs satisfactorily.

Our concern here is with two methods of learning complex material: (1) modeling and shaping, and (2) cognitive learning, including informal learning. We also describe a growing method of delivering material for learning, e-learning. In recognition of the fact that people learn in different ways, we will also discuss learning styles.

Modeling and Shaping

When you acquire a complicated skill such as coaching a team member, you experience much more than the acquisition of a few habits. You learn a large number of habits, and you learn how to put them together in a cohesive, smooth-flowing pattern. Two important processes that help in learning complicated skills are modeling and shaping.

Modeling (or imitation) occurs when you learn a skill by observing another person perform that skill. Many sales representatives acquire sales skills by observing a competent sales representative in action. Videos are widely used to facilitate modeling of such skills as interviewing, resolving conflict, and conducting a meeting. Modeling often brings forth behaviors that people did not previously seem to have in their repertoire. To model effectively, one must carefully observe the demonstration and then attempt the new skill shortly thereafter. Although modeling is an effective learning method, the learner must have the proper capabilities and motivation.

Shaping occurs when a person learns through the reinforcement or rewarding of small steps that build up to the final or desired behavior. It is another way in which complicated skills are learned. At each successful step of the way, the learner receives positive reinforcement. As the learner improves his or her ability to perform the task, more skill is required to receive the reward.

A clerical worker might be shaped into an inside sales representative (taking telephone and computer orders). He acquires a series of small skills, beginning with learning the computerized inventory system. He receives a series of rewards as he moves along the path from a support specialist to an inside sales representative who can understand and satisfy customer requirements. Among the forms of positive reinforcement he receives are approval for his new skills, incremental pay increases, and the feeling of pride as new small skills are learned. Among the punishments he receives to assist learning are negative statements from customers when he fills an order incorrectly.

Cognitive Learning

Cognitive learning theory emphasizes that learning takes place in a complicated manner involving much more than acquiring habits and small skills. Learners also strive to learn, develop hunches, and have flashes of insight. Furthermore, they use many aspects of their personality (such as openness to experience) in acquiring knowledge. Suppose that a safety and health specialist discovers the cause underlying a mysterious rash on the skin of many employees. Cognitive learning theory would emphasize that the specialist may have reached the conclusion by acquiring bits of information that formed a cohesive pattern. The theory would also emphasize the goal orientation of the safety and health specialist, along with the person's reasoning and analytical skills. Dedication to the cause and problem-solving ability would also contribute to the learning.

Another type of learning in organizations that fits a cognitive theory explanation is **informal learning.** This is defined as any learning that occurs in which the organization does not determine or design the learning process.[2] The central premise of such learning is that employees acquire some important information outside of a formal learning situation. The employees capitalize upon a learning situation outside of a formal structure, in which the rewards stemming from the learning situation are not explicit. Informal learning can be regarded as a variation of **implicit learning,** or learning that take place unconsciously and without an intention to learn.[3]

Informal learning can be spontaneous—such as receiving a suggestion on how to calculate the value of an American dollar in terms of a euro, and vice versa, while having lunch in a company cafeteria. Or the company might organize the work to encourage such informal learning. The company might provide common areas such as an atrium or food and beverage lounges that encourage employee interaction. Sometimes these common work areas are furnished with white boards and markers to facilitate exchanging ideas.

Research conducted by the Center for Workforce Development indicated that up to 70 percent of learning takes place informally. Informal learning frequently does not have an expressed goal.[4] For example, informal learning might take place when a coworker shows a new employee how to use the company Intranet rather than acquiring the skill through a classroom presentation. According to the study in question, informal learning can be divided into four types:

- *Practical skills:* Examples include job-specific skills and knowledge, and technical competence.
- *Intrapersonal skills:* Examples include problem solving, critical thinking, exploring boundaries for risk taking, and stress management.

- *Interpersonal skills:* Examples include peer-to-peer communications, presentations skills, and conflict resolution.
- *Cultural awareness:* Examples include professional awareness, professional advancement, social norms, understanding company goals, quality standards, and company expectations and priorities.

An important implication of informal learning for managers is that knowledgeable and well-motivated employees can help one another with learning. However, the manager must still be on guard against misinformed and poorly motivated employees that would create negative learning. Classroom training is helpful in increasing the chances that the right type of learning takes place.

A factor influencing how much cognitive learning takes place is the orientation of the learner. A *mastery orientation* relates to a dedication to increasing one's competence with a task. These learners are eager to improve their ability with tasks. For example, a person might want to learn how to make more effective oral presentations so he or she could better enjoy presenting at meetings. With a *performance orientation,* learners focus on how well they perform a task and make comparisons with others.

Learners with a performance orientation are keenly interested in displaying their ability to (or performing for) others. Evidence has been collected from college students that a mastery orientation is associated with greater effort and more complex learning strategies. (An example of a complex learning strategy would be paraphrasing and generating questions with answers.) In contrast, performance orientation is associated with less effort devoted to the task and less frequent use of complex learning strategies.[5]

E-LEARNING

Important innovations in learning have taken place in both schools and industry through the use of distance learning, technology-based learning, and e-learning. Here, the learner studies independently outside of a classroom setting, and interacts with a computer in addition to studying course material. **E-learning** is a Web-based form of computer-based training. Many learning programs are computer-based without being delivered over the Internet. For example, the tutorials included in many software packages are a form of computer-based training. An e-learning course usually is carefully structured, with specific lessons plans for the student. E-learning is more of a method of delivering content than a method of learning, yet the process helps us understand more about learning.

Although e-learning is technologically different from more traditional forms of learning, it still is based on basic methods of learning. For example, the learner will often need reinforcement to keep going. Trainers at GE Capital found that when managers gave reinforcement to employees on attendance, made them feel important, and tracked their progress, they were more likely to complete the course.[6]

Another relevant aspect of e-learning here is that its success depends on cognitive processes of the learner, particularly self-motivation and self-discipline. Self-motivation is important because an assignment to take an e-learning course by the company is often not motivation enough to work independently. Self-discipline is necessary to create a regular time for performing class work, and prevents distractions by work or home activities. In educational settings, successful distance learning also requires high motivation. Some students may not take e-learning seriously. Corporate e-learning programs have a high dropout rate; most students need the structure of a face-to-face instructor, a classroom, and other students to keep them focused on the course.[7]

Research about E-Learning Outcomes

A study about computer-based training further supported the idea that individual differences in effort influence knowledge gain. The participants in the study were seventy-eight technical employees of a *Fortune 500* manufacturing firm who participated in a computer-based problem-solving course at the corporate training facility. Almost all the students were college graduates, and several held graduate degrees. Technicians on the waiting list for the instructor-based version of the course were allowed to volunteer for the computer version. The course taught a standardized problem-solving process that is an essential component of the company's design and manufacturing process. Course materials included text, graphics, and interactive activities for practice.

Analysis of the data revealed a substantial range of time invested in the computer-based training. Individual effort was associated with differences in knowledge gain. Participants who elected to skip materials or move quickly through the program reduced their knowledge gain. The employees who learned the most from computer-based training were those who: (a) completed more of the practice opportunities, and (b) took more time to complete the courses. In short, time and effort invested in studying helps, even with the assistance of computers.[8] (Few readers will be shocked by the results of this study, even though a handful might be disappointed.)

The most successful e-learning experiences combine features of technology-based learning with the emotional support possible in a classroom. At the Penn State World Campus, the distance education division of Pennsylvania State University, a particular online course completion rate was 95 percent. The director of the program says that students benefit from frequent interaction with faculty and each other. Bulletin-board discussion and e-mail messages are used extensively. The instructor monitors participation and sends e-mails to students who are not participating or falling behind.[9]

The accompanying Organizational Behavior in Action describes an extensive application of e-learning by a company that owns one of America's best-known brands.

LEARNING STYLES

Another important concept in understanding learning is **learning style, the fact that people learn best in different ways.** For example, some people acquire new material best through passive learning. Such people quickly acquire information through studying texts, manuals, and magazine articles. They can juggle images in their mind as they read about abstract concepts such as supply and demand, cultural diversity, or customer service. Others learn best by doing rather than by studying—for example, learning hands-on about customer service by dealing with customers in many situations.

Another key dimension of learning styles is whether a person learns best by working alone or cooperatively, such as in a study group. Learning by oneself allows for more intense concentration, and one can proceed at one's own pace. Learning in groups and through classroom discussion allows people to exchange viewpoints and perspectives. Considerable evidence has been accumulated that

2

Describe how learning styles influence workplace learning.

Organizational Behavior *in Action*

Anheuser-Busch Brews Up E-Learning to Enhance Skills

Not long ago, the training department at Anheuser-Busch, the beer brewer based in St. Louis, Missouri, introduced Wholesaler Integrated Learning (WIL). (Budweiser is an Anheuser-Busch product.) The targeted groups were the company's 700 independently owned distributors and their employees, as well as 13 company-owned branch operations and 12 breweries. "Prior to 1997, all training was live instructor-led classroom training at headquarters, in hotels or at wholesalers nationwide," explains Tom Nolan, WIL director.

An employee can access the WIL Web site from anywhere and take a test that measures his proficiency in areas deemed important for his job description. The test is scored instantly, and the employee sees the gaps between his abilities and those required for his position. The system then offers suggestions—classroom training, online courses, books and on-the-job activities—on how to close those gaps. "The plan report is linked to a list of available resources and then to the enrollment system," says Nolan.

Anheuser-Busch has expanded training and development opportunities to include several methods of delivery, such as interactive satellite—almost all of it available at each employee's workplace. "WIL has grown from reaching 3,500 students to more than 32,000 distributor employees," says Nolan. "Currently, more than 20,000 users have completed competency assessments and are working on their assignments."

The Logistics

To create WIL, Anheuser-Busch spent more than a year collecting information about job skills, knowledge and attributes to create a job competency database. "Core competencies are the same for everyone in the organization. And although every employee has specific competencies unique to their position, most competencies can be used for more than one job description," explains Scott Mathews, vice president of market at Maritz Learning, which helped Anheuser-Busch create its program.

"Creating competency assessments is like a bunch of LEGO blocks," Matthew continues.

"Once you have the database of all the skills, qualities, and knowledge that employees need, you assemble them to create unique job descriptions. If you create a new role or if an existing role changes, you don't have to recreate the system from scratch. Instead, you can assign a value to a competency from the pool and build a new job description. For example, although a marketing employee and a sales employee each require Microsoft PowerPoint skills, the sales rep may need a lower level of proficiency than the marketing person.

"Once the organization take the time and effort to build a competency model, it will have 70 percent to 90 percent of all the skills and competencies needed within the organization. It may only need to tweak or customize this database for the 10 percent to 30 percent," says Matthews. Anheuser-Busch has about 200 different roles and almost 400 different competencies.

To avoid getting bogged down in too many roles, Rosenberg suggests consolidating job titles into general roles and letting employees and their managers do the fine-tuning. "Focus on the most critical elements. Look at top performers, and determine the skills and knowledge that set them apart," recommends Brian Carlin, president of Maritz.

Establishing this type of e-learning system can be done in several weeks if the company starts with off-the-shelf-competency models. A completely customized job can take three to six months or more to complete the process.

Questions

1. Why might dividing jobs into small competencies be well suited for e-learning?
2. In what way does the e-learning system implemented at Anheuser-Busch blend traditional learning with online learning?
3. Why do you think a brewer would take employee learning so seriously?

Source: Kathryn Tyler, "Take e-Learning to the Next Step," *HR Magazine,* February 2002, pp. 57–58, A73.

peer tutoring and cooperative learning are effective for acquiring knowledge.[10] Another advantage of cooperative learning is that it is more likely to lead to changes in behavior. Assume that a manager holds group discussions about the importance of achieving high customer satisfaction. Employees participating in these group discussions are more likely to assertively pursue high customer satisfaction on the job than those who only read about the topic.

Learning styles have also been studied more scientifically. Some researchers have divided learning styles into four orientations, based on four stages of the learning process.[11] As shown in Exhibit 3-1, learning can be regarded as a four-stage cycle: (1) concrete experience is followed by (2) observation and reflections, which lead to (3) the formation of abstractions and generalizations, followed by (4) hypotheses to be tested in future actions, which in turn lead to new experiences. People may not be aware these four stages are taking place as they acquire new information. Three points about this model are especially important.

First, according to this model of the learning process, the learning cycle operates continuously. People continue to test their concepts through experience and modify them as a result of their observations of the experience. For example, a person might learn that the euro is worth less than the U.S. dollar (which may be true during a given time period). However, as the person reads the business pages regularly, he or she learns that the euro is often worth more than the American dollar. So the person modifies his or her original knowledge, recognizing that currency values fluctuate.

Second, a person's internal needs and goals controls the direction that learning takes. People seek experiences that are related to their goals, and interpret these experiences in light of their goals. Simultaneously, the person would test implications of the concept that are relevant to these needs and goals. Returning to our previous example the person seeking to learn more about the American dollar versus the euro would search for information on this topic. Here, the person might test the implication that the values of currencies change too rapidly to make definitive statements about their relative value.

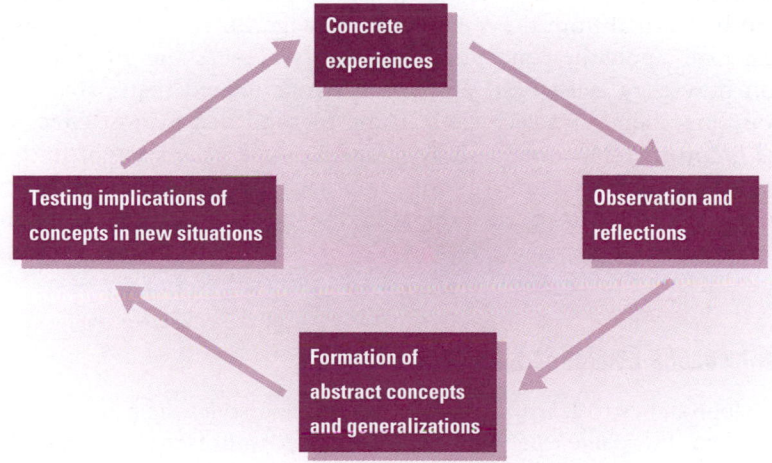

Exhibit 3-1

The Learning Process

Source: Joyce S. Osland, David A. Kolb, and Irwin M. Rubin, *Organizational Behavior: An Experiental Approach*, 7th ed. (Upper Saddle River, NJ: Prentice Hall, 2001), p. 43. Reprinted by permission of Pearson Education, Inc. Upper Saddle River, NJ.

Third, because the learning process is directed by a person's needs and goals, learning style is individualistic in both direction and process. A production manager might favor concrete experience, whereas a research and development scientist might favor abstract conceptualization.

The four learning orientations (or styles) stemming from this information are as follows:

1. An *orientation toward concrete experiences* emphasizes involvement in experiences and dealing with human interactions in a personal way. The person with this orientation is more intuitive and artistic than systematic and scientific.
2. An *orientation toward observation and reflections* emphasizes understanding the meanings of ideas, situations, and things; and describing them in an unbiased way. The person with this orientation is predisposed to reflection rather than action, and to look at situations from different perspectives and appreciate different points of view.
3. An *orientation toward formation of abstract concepts and generalizations* emphasizes applying logic, ideas, and concepts. The person prefers thinking as opposed to feeling, and has a scientific rather than an artistic approach to problems.
4. An *orientation toward testing implications of concepts in new situations* emphasizes actively influencing people and changing situations. The person with this orientation prefers practical applications as opposed to reflective understanding, with an emphasis on doing rather than observing.

Considerable practice would be required to develop such a four-barreled approach to learning. Yet the payoff would be substantial in terms of learning complex activities such as motivating people or developing business strategy. A person with an attention deficit disorder would usually prefer the orientation toward concrete experiences because he or she lacks the patience required for the three other orientations.

People tend to develop a learning style that has both strong points and weak points, instead of making good use of the four stages of learning. A person might benefit from concrete experiences (stage 1), yet not profit fully from reflecting on the lessons to be learned from these experiences (stage 2).

A manager can apply the concept of learning styles by asking group members to reflect on how they learn best. When new work-related material has to be learned, group members can select the learning method that is most effective for them. Some group members might study manuals, while others might find work in study groups valuable. A more cautious approach to capitalizing on learning styles is to encourage learners to use more than one mode of learning. They should invest some time in individual study and also interact with others to enhance learning (see the InfoTrac sidebar).

Individual Differences Related to Skill Acquisition

The various approaches to learning, including learning styles, help us understand how people learn. How *much* people learn is another important consideration in understanding learning in the workplace. In general, people with higher mental ability and personality traits that allow them to concentrate better (such as emotional stability and conscientiousness) acquire knowledge and skills more readily.

A large-scale research study supports the idea that cognitive skills and personality traits contribute to a person profiting from training, and then using the acquired information to enhance job performance. The sample consisted of 9,793

Delve a little bit deeper into the issue of workplace learning by logging on to InfoTrac at **http://www .infotrac-college.com** and searching for articles about the knowing–doing gap. The phenomenon of knowing too much and doing too little is all too common in many firms, and has important implications both for managerial practice and firm performance. What are some of the reasons why knowledgeable employees fail to follow through? You might want to come back to this question after you work your way through Chapters 6 and 7 on motivation.

trainees accepted into the FAA (Federal Aeronautics Association) training program for air traffic controllers. The average age of the trainee was 26 years; 84 percent were male, and 16 percent were female. Trainees took a cognitive skill test when applying for the program, whereas the personality test was administered as part of the medical examination of the air traffic control selection process.

The study found that air traffic controllers who rate high on general cognitive ability demonstrated greater skills acquisition than controllers who rate lower on general cognitive ability. A combination of personality traits, known as *Factor A (warmth),* proved useful in predicting skill acquisition. High Factor A people are warm, outgoing, attentive to others, cooperative, generous, and trusting. *Warmth* predicted skill acquisition, particularly when training was based on group work. The study also demonstrated that trainees who performed well in the training program were more likely to achieve full performance status when employed as an air traffic controller.[12]

PERCEPTION

Most of us interpret what is going on in the world around us as we perceive it—not as it really is. This tendency is much more pronounced when interpreting meanings rather than tangible physical phenomena. Five members of a team might give varying interpretations to receiving a 4 percent salary increase for the upcoming year. Yet the same five people would share the same accurate perception that an office tower is under construction across the street. **Perception** deals with the various ways in which people interpret things in the outside world and how they act on the basis of these perceptions.

Perceptions on the job are important. Many studies, for example, have investigated the consequence of employee job perceptions. The results show that employees who perceive their job to be challenging and interesting have high job satisfaction and motivation. In addition, these favorable perceptions lead to better job performance.[13] Our concern here is with two aspects of perception of most concern to managerial workers: (1) perceptual distortions and problems, and (2) how people attribute causes to events.

> Describe key aspects of the perceptual process, along with common perceptual problems.

Perceptual Distortions and Problems

Under ideal circumstances, people perceive information as it is intended to be communicated or as it exists in reality. For example, it is hoped that a home office executive assigned to a task force at a company division will perceive the assignment as a compliment. Yet the executive given such an assignment may perceive it as a way of being eased out the door. As shown in Exhibit 3-2, both characteristics of the stimulus and people's perceptual processes can lead to perceptual distortions. Chris Argyris has observed that people are unaware of how they form perceptions; moreover, they are unaware that they are unaware.[14] So studying perception may help reduce some of the mystery.

Characteristics of the Stimulus

As implied in the previous section, perceptual problems are most likely encountered when a stimulus or cue affects the emotional status of the perceiver. If you have strong attitudes about the issue at stake, you are most likely to misperceive the event. The perception of a stimulus or an event depends on the emotions, needs, attitudes, and motives of a person. Imagine that an irate customer writes a letter to a CEO complaining about shabby service received when asking for a

Exhibit 3-2

*Contributors to Perceptual
Distortions*

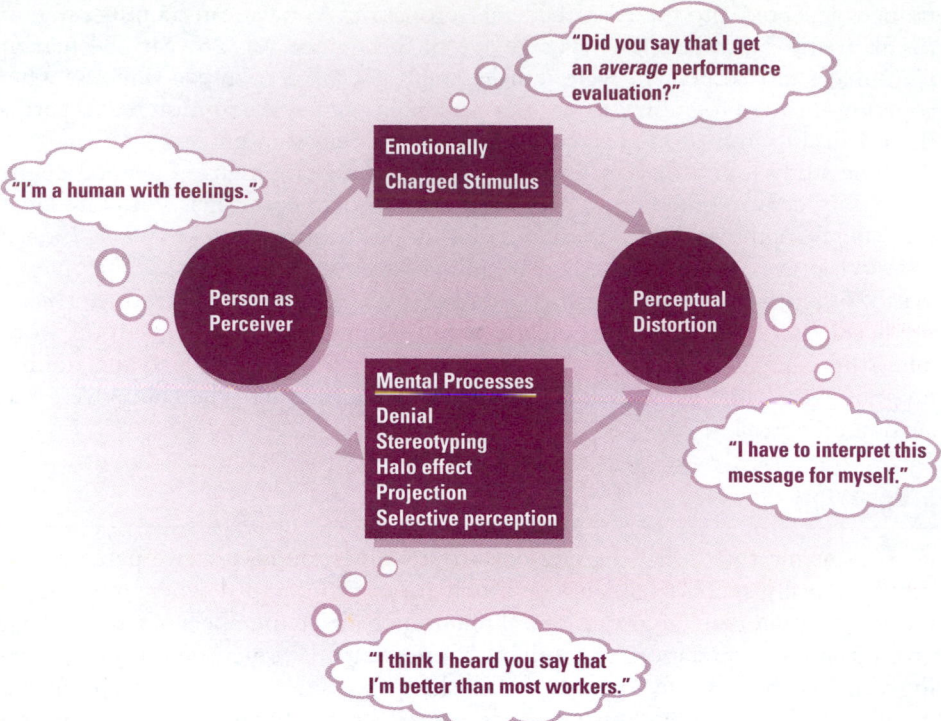

refund on a defective product. The CEO widely distributes this letter on e-mail. Among the possible perceptions of this event are the following:

Interpretation by customer service manager: "*I'm really in trouble now.* It's my job to ensure top-quality service throughout the organization. The CEO thinks I've messed up big time."

Interpretation by customer service specialist immediately involved with the case: "It's nice to have a laugh once in a while. One customer out of 2,000 I've dealt with last year is upset. The other 99.9 percent have no gripe, so why worry?"

Interpretation by merchandising manager: "It's obvious the big boss is upset with the customer service group. I don't blame him. We get no complaints about the quality of merchandise. I hope those customer service reps can get their act together."

Mental Processes of People

The devices people use to deal with sensory information play a major role in creating perceptual problems. The general purpose of these perceptual shortcuts is usually to make the reality of a situation less painful or disturbing. As such, these mental processes are types of defensive behavior.

Denial If the sensory information at hand is particularly painful to us, we often deny to ourselves and others that the information even exists. A purchasing agent was confronted by her manager with the accusation that a supplier entertained her so lavishly that it was tantamount to a kickback. The purchasing agent replied that she thought the company was only concerned about sales incentives involving tangible goods or money. Yet the agent had been on a committee six months previously that formulated the new regulations on kickbacks. Another frequently seen example of denial in organizations is when a manager ignores hints that he is falling out of favor and thus may soon lose his job. He then loses any advantage by not conducting a job search until he has been terminated.

The implication for the managerial worker is to stand ready for a message to be distorted by the receiver if the issue is emotional. Be prepared to clarify and repeat messages and to solicit feedback to ensure that the message was received as intended. Chapter 9 deals at length with the topic of overcoming communication barriers.

Stereotyping   A common shortcut to the perceptual process is to evaluate an individual based on the group or class to which he or she belongs. Stereotypes reduce tension in an unusual way. Encountering a person who does not fit our stereotype of that person's group can be painful to our ego. We lessen the discomfort by looking for behavior that conforms to the stereotype. Assume that you believe that Asian workers are meticulous. When you meet an Asian on the job, you might have a tendency to search for evidence of meticulousness.

Halo Effect   A tendency exists to color everything that we know about a person because of one recognizable favorable or unfavorable trait. When a company does not insist on the use of objective measures of performance, it is not uncommon for a supervisor to give favorable performance ratings to persons who dress well or smile frequently. The fine appearance or warm smile of these people has created a halo around them. Group members often create a positive halo about one member who is articulate and witty. In reality, the person's professional competence may be average.

Projection   Another shortcut in the perceptual process is to project our own faults onto others instead of making an objective appraisal of the situation. A manager might be asked to recommend a group member for a difficult troubleshooting assignment out of town. The manager might hesitate, saying, "Most of the people in my group do not handle pressure well." In reality, handling pressure poorly is the manager's key weakness.

Selective Perception   People use this mechanism when they draw an unjustified conclusion from an unclear situation. A feedback letter from the manager might be interpreted as a letter of documentation to help the company build a case for firing the individual. Selective perception can have negative consequences when it leads to self-deception about potentially bad news.

Many workers have succumbed to heart attacks because they denied symptoms that their general knowledge and common sense told them were warnings of trouble. For example, one manager was at a company retreat. He suffered shooting pains in his left arm and left side of the chest. When a roommate at the retreat asked if he was ill, the manager claimed he was just having indigestion. He suffered a near-fatal heart attack the next morning.

What can managerial workers do with knowledge about perceptual distortions? If it appears that a work associate is making obvious use of a perceptual distortion, one should gently confront the person about the discrepancy in his or her thinking. In the heart attack situation, the roommate might have said, "Look, I claim no medical training, but I insist we get you to a doctor right away, just in case you are suffering from more than indigestion."

ATTRIBUTION THEORY

4

Describe how attribution theory contributes to an understanding of human behavior in the workplace.

Another important aspect of perception is how people perceive the causes of behavior in themselves and others. **Attribution theory** is the process by which people ascribe causes to the behavior they perceive. Two attribution errors are quite common. The **fundamental attribution error** is the tendency to attribute behavior to internal causes when focusing on someone else's behavior. We might therefore think that a vice president achieved that position because of his or her ambition and talent. The other error, **self-serving bias**, takes place when focusing on one's own behavior. People tend to attribute their achievements to good inner qualities, whereas they attribute failure to adverse factors within the environment. A manager thus would attribute increased productivity to his or her superior leadership skills but blame low productivity on poor support from the organization. (The self-serving bias takes place more frequently than the fundamental attribution error.)

According to attribution theory as developed by Harold H. Kelley, people attribute causes after gathering information about three dimensions of behavior: consensus, consistency, and distinctiveness.[15]

- *Consensus* relates to comparing a person's behavior with that of peers. High consensus exists when a person acts similarly to others in the group and low consensus exists when the person acts differently. If others cannot perform the same feat you can, your feat will be attributed to your internal qualities.
- *Consistency* is determined by assessing whether a person's performance on a given task is consistent or not over time. If you are consistent over time, people will attribute your accomplishment to your internal qualities.
- *Distinctiveness* is a function of comparing a person's behavior on one task with that person's behavior on other tasks. High distinctiveness means that the person has performed the task in question quite differently from other tasks. Low distinctiveness refers to stable performance or quality from one task to another. If you turn in high quality performance on many tasks, your internal characteristics will receive credit.

Observe that consensus relates to other people, consistency involves time, and distinctiveness relates to other tasks. The combination of these factors leads to attribution of causes. People attribute behavior to external (or environmental) causes when they perceive high consensus, low consistency, and high distinctiveness. People attribute behavior to internal (or personal) factors when they perceive low consensus, high consistency, and low distinctiveness.

What might this approach to attribution theory mean in practice? A manager would attribute poor-quality work to external factors, such as poor equipment and resources, under these conditions: All workers are producing low-quality work (high consensus), the low quality occurs only one or two times (low consistency), and the low quality occurs on only one of several tasks (high distinctiveness). In contrast, the manager will attribute low quality to personal characteristics of the workers under these conditions: Only one person is performing poorly (low consensus), the low-quality work has persisted over time (high consistency), and the low-quality work occurs for several tasks (low distinctiveness). Exhibit 3-3 presents another example of this complicated attribution process.

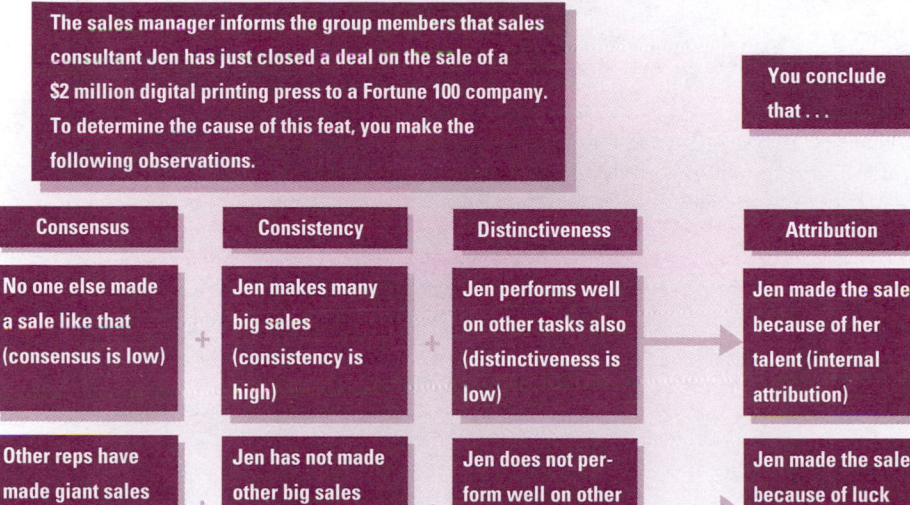

Exhibit 3-3

Kelley's Theory of Attributing Causes—an Example

51

Locus of Control

A logical extension of attribution theory is the concept of **locus of control**—the way in which people look at causation in their lives. Some people have an internal locus of control because they perceive their outcomes as being controlled internally. As a result, they feel generally in control of their lives. Some people have an external locus of control because they perceive much of what happens to them as being controlled by circumstances.[17] People with an internal locus of control feel that they create their own opportunities in life, while those with an external locus attribute much of their success and failure to luck.

Workers with an internal locus of control are generally more mature, self-reliant, and responsible. In one study of 900 employees in a public utility, it was found that employees with an internal locus of control had higher levels of job satisfaction. Also, they were more attuned to a participative management style.[18]

Attribution theory, including the locus of control theory, has another important implication for organizational behavior aside from those already mentioned. People search for causes of events and alter their behavior because of these perceptions. Managers should therefore invest time in explaining the causes of events to workers, to avoid misperceptions and counterproductive behavior.

SUMMARY OF KEY POINTS

 Explain the basics of modeling and shaping, cognitive learning, and e-learning.

Modeling and shaping, and cognitive learning are two ways of learning complex material. Modeling involves imitating another person performing the task correctly, then repeating the task. Shaping occurs when a person learns through the reinforcement of small steps that build up to the final or desired behavior.

In cognitive learning, learners strive to learn, develop hunches, have flashes of insight, and use

IMPLICATIONS FOR MANAGERIAL PRACTICE

In addition to the suggestions made for applying information throughout this chapter (as is done in all chapters of this book), here we make a few additional practical suggestions. The first two suggestions are from Kenneth Neal, e-learning solutions practice leader with KPGM Consulting in New York:[16]

1. With e-training, the structure should be three-step: show me, let me practice, and watch me do it. A good course has quizzes throughout. You also need cases and business simulations where participants get a chance to practice what they have learned. Exams are also needed to provide feedback and enhance learner motivation.

2. Not all subject matter and skills are suitable for e-learning. For example, if employees are taught teamwork skills or how to make presentations, underlying concepts can be taught online. However, the trainees also need instructor-led class where employees actually give presentations.

3. Assume that you want to teach a new skill to one or more people, such as explaining a new benefits package to employees. You have no funds available for the training program, so you must do the job inexpensively, but properly. Under these circumstances, your best tactic would be to use modeling as a learning method. The trainees could observe you in action and follow up with question-and-answer sessions.

4. Be aware of the pervasive effect of selective perception in organizational behavior. Many of the perceptions that people have, for example, are based on their needs at the time. A manager who has to fill a position by a tight deadline may overevaluate the qualifications of applicants. The judgment of a second party, who is not facing the same need, can be helpful in arriving at an objective judgment.

---

many aspects of personality. Cognitive learning includes informal learning, which occurs outside of a formal learning situation.

An important innovation in learning is e-learning, whereby the learner studies independently outside of a classroom setting, and interacts with a computer in addition to studying course material. E-learning is a Web-based form of computer-based training. Although e-learning is different from traditional forms of learning, it still is based on basic methods of learning. Self-motivation and self-discipline are required for successful e-learning. The most successful e-learning experiences combine features of technology-based learning with the emotional support possible in the classroom.

2 Describe how learning styles influence learning workplace learning.

People learn best in different ways, for example some people acquire information best through passive learning. A preference for working alone versus cooperatively is another difference in learning style. Learning styles have also been classified based on the four stages in the learning process. The styles are orientations toward: (a) concrete experiences, (b) reflective observation, (c) abstract conceptualization, and (d) active experimentation.

3 Describe key aspects of the perceptual process, along with common perceptual problems.

Perception deals with the various ways in which people interpret things in the outside world and how they act on the basis of these perceptions. Perceptual problems are most likely encountered when the stimulus or cue to be perceived affects the emotional status of the perceiver.

The devices people use to deal with sensory information play a major role in creating perceptual problems. Among these devices are denial, stereotyping, the halo effect, projection, and selective perception.

4 Describe how attribution theory contributes to an understanding of human behavior in the workplace.

Attribution theory is the process by which people ascribe causes to the behavior they perceive. The fundamental attribution error is to attribute behavior to internal causes when focusing on the behavior of others. The self-serving bias leads us to attribute good results to ourselves, and poor results to the environment.

People attribute causes after gathering information about consensus (comparison among people), distinctiveness (comparison across tasks), and consistency (task stability over time).

KEY TERMS AND PHRASES

Learning, *40*
A relatively permanent change in behavior based on practice or experience.

Modeling, *40*
Imitation; learning a skill by observing another person performing that skill.

Shaping, *40*
Learning through the reinforcement or rewarding of small steps to build to the final or desired behavior.

Cognitive Learning Theory, *41*
A theory emphasizing that learning takes place in a complicated manner involving much more than acquiring habits and small skills.

Informal Learning, *41*
A planned learning that occurs in a setting without a formal classroom, lesson plan, instructor, or examination.

Implicit Learning, *41*
Learning that takes place unconsciously and without an intention to learn.

E-learning, *42*
A Web-based form of computer-based training.

Learning Style, *43*
A person's particular way of learning, reflecting the fact that people learn best in different ways.

Perception, *47*
The various ways in which people interpret things in the outside world and how they act on the basis of these interpretations.

Attribution Theory, *50*
The process by which people ascribe causes to the behavior they perceive.

Fundamental Attribution Error, *50*
The tendency to attribute behavior to internal causes when focusing on someone else's behavior.

Self-serving Bias, *50*
An attribution error whereby people tend to attribute their achievements to good inner qualities, whereas they attribute their failure to adverse factors within the environment.

Locus of Control, *52*
The way in which people look at causation in their lives.

DISCUSSION QUESTIONS AND ACTIVITIES

1. Give an example from your own life in which you have learned through modeling.
2. What relatively inexpensive steps might a company take to promote informal learning among employees?
3. If e-learning is so effective, why haven't most colleges and universities shifted almost entirely to distance learning?
4. What implications might e-learning have for assisting customers with problems involving information technology-based products, including business hardware, software, and consumer electronics?
5. How can a person capitalize upon the halo effect in managing his or her career?
6. What implications might attribution theory have for performance appraisals in which managers evaluate the performance of group members?
7. Create a scenario in which, according to attribution theory, most people would agree that a person's success was caused by his or her inner qualities.

ORGANIZATIONAL BEHAVIOR ONLINE

TO DO

One of many companies offering e-learning to business is SkillSoft: The e-Learning Solutions Company. A visit to the SkillSoft Web site (http://www.skillsoft.com) will explain what it perceives to be the potential advantages of e-learning. For example, SkillSoft provides a system for training employees before, during, and after a product launch. How does this framework coincide with the model of the learning process depicted in Exhibit 3-1? While visiting the site, be sure to demo a course for an informative and entertaining explanation of the SkillSoft approach to e-Learning.

TO BOOKMARK

E-learning
http://www.elementk.com

Perception
http://www.visualexpert.com

CASE PROBLEM: The Stunning Plaque

A magazine reporter asked Paul Anderson, a human resources director, for his opinion of Generation X managers. Anderson explained that, based on his observations, most Gen X managers emphasized a team style of management. The journalist thanked Anderson for his comments. About six months later, the journalist's article containing a one-line quote from Anderson appeared in *Entrepreneur* magazine. Anderson was pleased to be quoted in a national magazine, and appreciated the courtesy of *Entrepreneur* sending him a copy of the magazine in which he was quoted. About 30 days after the article appeared, Anderson received the following letter on high-quality stationary at his office:

State License Documentation
22817 Ventura Blvd. Section 858
Woodland Hills, CA 91364

Dear Mr. Anderson,
Congratulations! Your write-up in *Entrepreneur* magazine is most impressive. You are among a select few that have had the privilege of being published in a major publication. Accomplishments like yours should be displayed proudly. At State License Documentation we do exactly that. We professionally mount your article in a museum quality plaque preserving your feature for a lifetime. It can then be displayed in your home, office or conference room. However, your plaque is more than a decoration . . . it connotes respect and credibility.

State License Documentation has earned a reputation of producing the highest quality plaques in the industry today. Our plaques have been made for *Fortune 500* companies, government dignitaries, celebrities, most medical and law universities, and numerous corporate executives.

Enclosed please find information on how you can receive a free graphic rendering of your own custom plaque. The rendering allows you to preview your plaque before you order. Order risk free. All plaques are sold on a 100% satisfaction guarantee basis. We look forward to hearing from you and preparing your free custom layout.
Warmest Regards,
R. W.
Robert B. West
Executive Vice President

The accompanying sheet to the letter includes the following information:
YES!!!

• Send me my FREE complimentary graphic layout of what my article/write-up would look like plaqued in a museum quality wall display.

Please provide us with the information requested so we can FAX or mail your custom layout to you. The layout includes a graphic rendering with the plaque's dimensions, color trim combinations, pricing, shipping, and ordering information. SLD is not affiliated nor endorsed by any newspaper, journal, magazine, or any other publication.

Case Questions

1. What perceptions are most people likely to have when they receive an envelope with "State License Documentation" given in the return address?
2. What might be a more accurate name to give the firm selling the plaques?
3. What is the true nature of the business of SLD? (What business are they really in?)

ENDNOTES

1. John W. Donahoe and David C. Palmer, *Learning and Complex Behavior* (Boston: Allyn & Bacon, 1994), p. 2.
2. Nancy Day, "Informal Learning Gets Results," *Workforce*, June 1998, p. 31.
3. Michael A. Stadler and Peter A. Frensch (eds.), *Handbook of Implicit Learning* (Thousands Oaks, CA: Sage, 1998).
4. Day, "Informal Learning," pp. 31–32.
5. Sandra L. Fisher and J. Kevin Ford, "Differential Effects of Learner Effort and Goal Orientation on Two Learning Outcomes," *Personnel Psychology*, Summer 1998, pp. 397–420.
6. Karen Frankola, "Why Online Learners Drop Out," *Workforce*, October 2001, p. 54.
7. "Assessing Online Learning: Defining the Efficacy of Online Learning," *Keying In*, March 2001, p. 3.
8. Kenneth G. Brown, "Using Computers to Deliver Training: Which Employees Learn and Why?", *Personnel Psychology*, Summer 2001, pp. 271–296.
9. Frankola, "Why Online Learners Drop Out," p. 54.
10. Wanda L. Stitt-Gohdes, "Chapter 1—Teaching and Learning Styles: Implications for Business Teacher Education," in *The 21st Century: Meeting the Challenges to Business Education* (Reston, VA: National Business Education Association, 1999), p. 10.
11. Joyce S. Osland, David A. Kolb, and Irwin M. Rubin, *Organizational Behavior: An Experiential Approach*, 7th ed. (Upper Saddle River, NJ: Prentice Hall, 2001), pp. 43–44.
12. David W. Oakes, et al., "Cognitive Ability and Personality Predictors of Training Program Skill Acquisition and Job Performance," *Journal of Business and Psychology*, Summer 2001, pp. 523–548.
13. Ricky W. Griffin, "Effects of Work Redesign on Employee Perceptions, Attitudes, and Behaviors: A Long-Term Investigation," *Academy of Management Journal*, June 1991, p. 426.
14. Chris Argyris, *On Organizational Learning* (Oxford, England: Blackwell, 1994), p. 7.
15. Harold H. Kelley, "The Process of Causal Attribution," *American Psychologist*, February 1973, pp. 107–128.
16. Cited in Eilene Zimmerman, "Better Training Is Just a Click Away," *Workforce*, January 2001, p. 38.
17. Julian P. Rotter, "Generalized Expectancies for Internal vs. External Control of Reinforcement," *Psychological Monographs* 80 (1966), pp. 1–28.
18. Terence R. Mitchell, Charles M. Smyser, and Stan E. Weed, "Locus of Control: Supervision and Work Satisfaction," *Academy of Management Journal*, September 1975, pp. 623–631.

Chapter 4

Attitudes, Values, and Ethics

Most folks know Buffalo, NY is famous for its chicken wings, but in the airline business Buffalo is famous for ferocious winter storms that bring air travel—and sometimes all travel—to a frozen halt. That's what happened in December 2001 when Buffalo was buried under 7 feet of snow. Southwest Airlines, with its lean scheduling system, was hit harder than most. One of its planes got stuck so long it came due for a routine maintenance check. Without it, the plane wouldn't be allowed to fly—and that would cost Southwest tens of thousands of dollars in lost revenue. What to do?

Johnny Bomaster, 38, had an idea. A certified maintenance–check mechanic for Southwest, he lived just seven miles from the Buffalo airport but couldn't reach it over roads clotted with snow. So he tossed his toolbox onto the back of a snowmobile and zoomed through the drifts to the stranded plane. By next morning, when the runways had been plowed and passengers were streaming through the terminal, Bomaster had thoroughly checked the plane and allowed it to take off fully loaded. (A new storm then stranded him at the airport for an additional 24 hours.)

Bomaster and workers like him are a big part of the reason that amid record losses by its competitors, Southwest stands as the only profitable U.S. airline among the top eight. On occasion pilots have even pitched in to help ground crews move luggage—a step virtually unheard of at Southwest's bigger rivals.

Management is working to maintain the airline's trademark high morale and good customer service, in large part, through careful recruitment and training. The airline received 200,000 résumés last year but hired only 6,000 workers—making it more selective than Harvard. "Attitude is critical; skills are not," says Lorraine Grubbs–West, director at the People Department. (Southwest doesn't use the word employee.)

OBJECTIVES

After reading and studying this chapter and doing the exercises, you should be able to:

1 Describe the importance of attitudes and emotions to behavior in organizations.

2 Describe how organizational citizenship behavior contributes to individual and organizational effectiveness.

3 Summarize why values are an important part of organizational behavior.

4 Describe three ethical decision-making criteria, along with several explanations for the existence of ethical problems.

5 Describe what organizations can do to enhance ethical and socially responsible behavior.

Source: Excerpted from Sally B. Donnelly, "One Airline's Magic," *Time*, October 28, 2002, pp. 45–46.

NOW ASK YOURSELF: What does the attitude of one Southwest Airlines mechanic tell us about the drive to perform in a superior manner? Referred to as *organizational citizenship behavior,* the type of attitude exhibited by Southwest mechanic Bomaster is one topic presented in this chapter about attitudes and emotions, values, and ethics. Understanding these aspects of behavior helps managers deal more effectively with people and also guide their own behavior toward high performance.

ATTITUDES AND EMOTIONS

1

Describe the importance of attitudes and emotions to behavior in organizations

"You've got an attitude," said the supervisor to the store associate, thus emphasizing the importance of attitude to job performance. For mysterious reasons, the term *attitude* in colloquial language often connotes a *negative* attitude. More accurately, an **attitude** is a predisposition to respond that exerts an influence on a person's response to a person, a thing, an idea, or a situation. Attitudes are an important part of organizational behavior because they are linked with perception, learning, emotions, and motivation. For example, your attitude toward a coworker influences your perception of how favorably you evaluate his or her work. Also, emotions such as joy and anger contribute to attitude formation. First we examine the components of attitudes and their relationship to organizational behavior, and then explain how emotions influence behavior in the workplace.

Components of Attitudes

Attitudes are complex, having three components. The *cognitive* component refers to the knowledge or intellectual beliefs an individual might have about an object (an idea, a person, a thing, or a situation). A market researcher might have accumulated considerable factual information about statistics (such as sampling procedures) and software for running data. The researcher might therefore have a positive attitude toward statistics.

The feeling or *affective* component refers to the emotion connected with an object or a task. The market researcher mentioned might basically like statistical analysis due to some pleasant experiences in college associated with statistics.

The *behavioral* component refers to how a person acts. The market researcher might make positive statements about statistical methods or emphasize them in his or her reports.

The cognitive, affective, and behavioral aspects of attitudes are interrelated. A change in one of the components will set in motion a change in one or more of the others. If you have more facts about an object or process (cognitive), you form the basis for a more positive emotional response to the object (affective). In turn, your behavior toward that object would probably become more favorable. For example, if you have considerable information about the contribution of feedback to personal development, you might have a positive feeling toward feedback. When receiving feedback, therefore, you would act favorably.

At times, people do not experience the type of consistency just described and feel compelled to search for consistency. **Cognitive dissonance** is the situation in which the pieces of knowledge, information, attitudes, or beliefs held by an individual are contradictory. When a person experiences cognitive dissonance, the relationship between attitudes and behaviors is altered. People search for ways to reduce internal conflicts when they experience a clash between the information they receive and their actions or attitudes. The same process is used when a person has to resolve two inconsistent sets of information.

A typical example of cognitive dissonance on the job might occur when a worker believes that the report she submits to team members is of high quality; her teammates, however, tell her the report is flawed and requires substantial revisions. To reduce the dissonance, the worker might conveniently ignore the criticism. Or the worker might reason that she is the resident expert on the topic of the report, and her teammates are therefore not qualified to judge the merits of her report.

Emotions in the Workplace

A traditional viewpoint contends that emotions in the workplace should be minimized, and decisions should be based on rational analysis. Nevertheless, the importance of emotion in influencing job behavior has long been recognized. For example, customer-contact workers need training to deal with angry customers; and supervisors have been trained how to give emotional support to a distressed group member. The widespread use of horizontal networks and teamwork has also fostered the recognition of emotions in the workplace because both approaches emphasize flexible and spontaneous behavior.[1]

In Chapter 2, we described the importance now attached to having emotional intelligence. An **emotion** is a feeling—such as anger, fear, joy, or surprise—that underlies behavior. Emotions might lead an employee who has just solved a difficult problem to shout "Yes!" and punch his or her fist into the air. Unfortunately, intense negative emotion might trigger an employee to stab another employee with a knife.

Similar to an attitude, an emotion consists of three interacting components: (1) internal physiological arousal, (2) expressive behavior in the face or body, and (3) a cognitive appraisal.[2] Imagine that a production worker has just been informed that he has won a $50,000 award for a suggestion that will save the company millions of dollars. The worker will experience a surge of physiological arousal, such as an accelerated pulse or an elevated breathing rate. His facial expressions will most likely communicate joy and surprise. The cognitive appraisal deals with quick thoughts, such as saying to himself, "Now, I will get the respect I deserve," and "Here's my chance to buy something great for my family and invest a little money also."

Neal M. Ashkany and Catherine S. Daus regard emotion in the workplace as the new challenge facing managers. Given that every worker, top executives included, is an organism governed partly by emotion, constructive use should be made of emotion. Two suggestions by Ashkany and Daus provide practical starting points in managing emotions well. First, the manager should create a friendly emotional climate by setting a positive example. Managers might serve as a model of healthy emotional expression that includes being emotionally perceptive. ("Kelly, I notice that you are quite anxious about the credit-card processing unit possibly being outsourced. How can I help you with your concerns?") Warm and sincere expression of positive emotion is usually effective, as is appropriate expression of negative emotion. The leader might indicate, for example, that he or she is also worried about a downturn in sales that could lead to cutbacks.

Another recommendation is to include a positive attitude as one factor in selecting individuals and teams. A candidate might be evaluated in part based on his or her emotional skills demonstrated during a job interview, and by reference checking. Within the organization, teams might be selected for key assignments in part based on their cheerful outlook.[3] Positive attitudes contribute to organizational health, whereas consistently negative attitudes create an unfavorable work climate.

Another aspect of emotional behavior in the workplace receiving recent attention is the problem of faking emotions. Alicia Grandey defines **emotional labor** as the process of regulating both feelings and expressions to meet organizational goals. Emotional labor involves both surface acting and deep acting. Surface acting means faking expressions such as smiling, whereas deep acting involves controlling feelings, such as suppressing anger toward a customer whom you perceive to be uncivil. Sales workers and customer service representatives carry the biggest emotional labor among all workers because so often they have to take on facial expressions and feelings to please customers.[4]

Emotional dissonance is a key aspect of emotional labor, referring to the mismatch between felt and expressed emotions. The greater the gap between actual and expressed feelings, the more frequently workers report feeling emotional exhaustion, dissatisfaction with their jobs, and cynicism toward customers.[5]

One implication of emotional labor is that managers need to take into account job characteristics in creating rules for display of emotion. Rules that conflict with job characteristics may trigger unhealthy levels of tension. For instance, asking cashiers to be overly polite to customers may conflict with a fast work pace. Cashiers facing a long line of impatient customers may need to decrease displays of courtesy to avoid having customers wait even longer. (It takes more time to be polite and conversational.)[6]

Attitudes and Job Satisfaction

Another reason attitudes are important in the study of organizational behavior is that they form the basis for how satisfied people are with their jobs. **Job satisfaction** is the amount of pleasure or contentment associated with a job. Workers will have high job satisfaction when they have positive attitudes toward such job factors as the work itself, recognition, and opportunity for advancement. The two-factor theory of job motivation described in Chapter 6 provides more details about the contributors to job satisfaction and dissatisfaction. Exhibit 4–1 provides a sampling of issues that influence employee attitudes.

A practical view of job satisfaction is that it centers on employees having fun on the job. *Fun* can be anything from doing exciting work to engaging in sports during the lunch break. During the dot-com revolution, traditional companies scrambled to provide a more fun atmosphere, such as allowing employees to dec-

Exhibit 4-1

Specific Issues That Influence Employee Satisfaction

Answers to the following questions measure employee attitudes vital to job satisfaction, increased productivity, and improved customer service.

- "**Do I know** what my boss expects of me?"
- "**Do I have** what I need to do my work properly?"
- "**Am I allowed** to do what I do best every day?"
- "**Has anyone praised** or recognized my work in the past week?"
- "**Does anyone encourage** my career growth?"
- "**Does my manager** respect my opinion?"
- "**Are my coworkers** dedicated to producing quality work?"
- "**Have I learned** something new in the past year?"

Employees who answer "Yes" to all questions are likely to stay with their firm for the long haul.

Source: *Supervisor's Guide to Employment Practices*, Clement Communications Inc., 10 LaCrue Ave., Concordville, PA 19331.

orate their own office and permitting them to play video games during working hours. After the dot-com bust, many companies still looked for ways to create a pleasant working environment in order to enhance job satisfaction. Companies today are more likely to provide a working environment that provides key satisfying elements such as casual dress, flexible working hours, and telecommuting. Gone, however, are many of the dot-com excesses such as massages at the desk, concierge services, and welcoming animal companions (the politically correct term for *pets*) in the office.[7]

Managers are concerned about maintaining high levels of job satisfaction because of its consequences, which include the following:

- High productivity when the work involves people contact.
- A stronger tendency to achieve customer loyalty.
- Loyalty to the company.
- Low absenteeism and turnover.
- Less job stress and burnout.
- Better safety performance.
- Better life satisfaction.[8]

The job satisfaction consequence of loyalty is especially important because it enhances employee retention (keeping valuable employees). Employee turnover is particularly expensive, involving such costs as recruitment, selection, training, and lost productivity while the replacement is trained. Management consultant Diane Arthur observes that if employees feel loyal to a company, they are likely to be more productive and make an extra effort for the employer. They are also likely to stay with the company, keeping the firm stable and allowing management to concentrate on sales, operations, and earnings, not hiring replacement workers.[9] An observer of worker commitment has found that a 5 percent increase in employee retention can yield profit increases of 25 percent or more.[10]

Many of the methods and techniques described in this text, such as empowerment and modified work schedules, are aimed at sustaining job satisfaction. Almost any positive management practice, however, might be linked to improving job satisfaction.

Organizational Citizenship Behavior

A broader consequence of job satisfaction is that it contributes to **organizational citizenship behavior (OCB), or the willingness to work for the good of the organization even without the promise of a specific reward.** Five important components of organizational citizenship behavior are conscientiousness, altruism, civic virtue, courtesy, and sportsmanship. A good organizational citizen would engage in such behaviors as assisting a person with a computer problem outside his or her team or department, or picking up a broken bottle on the company lawn. People who are good organizational citizens are likely to achieve some of the consequences of job satisfaction, including higher customer loyalty, higher productivity, and better safety performance.

According to George A. Neuman and Jill R. Kickul, organizational citizenship behavior has received increased theoretical attention as organizations face the challenge of global competition and the need for continuous innovation. The good organizational citizen goes "above and beyond the call of duty," or engages in *extra-role* behavior.[11]

Although organizational citizenship behavior is often a consequence of job satisfaction, personality factors are sometimes linked to OCB. Workers may be

2

Describe how organizational citizenship behavior contributes to individual and organizational effectiveness.

predisposed to being good, or poor, organizational citizens. A study with customer-contact workers supports the personality–OCB link. The employee-disposition (or personality) factors of service orientation and empathy were found to be related to engaging in good citizenship behavior in relation to customers. Four examples of service-oriented OCBs are when a person does the following:

- Encourages friends and family to use firm's products and services.
- Follows up in a timely manner to customer requests and problems.
- Contributes many ideas for customer promotions and communication.
- Frequently presents creative solutions to customer problems[12]

Similar to job satisfaction, organizational citizenship behavior has been linked to voluntary turnover. A study conducted in eleven companies in China found that employees rated low in organizational citizenship behavior by their supervisors were more likely to quit than those who were rated as exhibiting high levels of such behavior.[13]

A concern about the construct (similar to a concept) of organizational citizenship behavior is that some employees may perceive going beyond their job description as part of their job. An employee might think, for example, "I'm paid a good salary to do whatever it takes to make my company successful, whether or not it is strictly my job." In a study of master of business administration students and their supervisors, four OCB behaviors were generally perceived to be *inrole* (part of the job) if workers felt they were working for a just and fair organization. The four specific behaviors are as follows:

- Interpersonal helping (helping coworkers on their job when needed).
- Individual initiative (communications designed to improve individual and group performance).
- Personal industry (performing tasks in a way that goes above and beyond the call of duty).
- Loyalty boosterism (promoting the organization to outsiders).[14]

One implication of this study is that when workers perceive their organization to be fair and just, they are more likely to believe that OCB is part of their job. So the organization can facilitate good citizenship behavior by being just and fair.

3

Summarize why values are an important part of organizational behavior.

VALUES

Another key factor influencing behavior in organizations is the values and beliefs of people. A **value** refers to the importance a person attaches to something that serves as a guide to action. Values are also tied in with enduring beliefs that one's mode of conduct is better than the opposite mode of conduct. One person may highly value quantitative analysis and will look down on people who present a position without providing quantitative evidence.

The topic of values has received much publicity in recent years, as baby boomers are compared to younger people in Generations X and Y (also referred to as the Net Generation). With baby boomers being more conservative and respectful of authority and hierarchy, the differences in values between the generations can cause job conflict. As with other group stereotypes, generation differences are often exaggerated. Exhibit 4-2 outlines several generational differences in values. Understanding generational differences is critical to managing people effectively.[15] For example, the oldest employees in an organization may prefer adhering closely to policies and procedures, whereas the youngest employees might prefer

Exhibit 4-2

Value Stereotypes for Several Generations of Workers

61

Baby Boomers (1946–1964)	Generation X (1965–1977)	Generation Y (1978–1984)
Uses technology as necessary tool	Techno-savvy	Techno-savvy
Tolerates teams but values independent work	Teamwork very important	Teamwork very important
Appreciates hierarchy	Dislikes hierarchy	Dislikes hierarchy
Strong career orientation	Strives for work/life balance but will work long hours for now	Strives for work/life balance but will work long hours for now
More loyalty to organization	Loyalty to own career and profession	Wants to strike it rich quickly
Favors diplomacy	Candid in conversation	Ultra-candid in conversation
Favors old economy	Appreciates old and new economy	Prefers the new economy
Expects a bonus based on performance	Would appreciate a signing bonus	Expected a signing bonus before tthe dot-com crash
Believes that issues should be formally discussed	Believes that feedback can be administered informally	Believes that feedback can be given informally, even on the fly

Source: Several of the ideas in this table are from Robert McGarvey, "The Coming of Gen X Bosses," *Entrepreneur,* November 1999, pp. 60–64; Joanne M. Glenn, "Teaching the Net Generation," *Business Education Forum,* February 2000, pp. 6–14; Anita Bruzzese, "There Needn't Be a Generation Gap," Gannett News Service, April 22, 2002.

to improvise when faced with a problem. The manager may have to intervene to resolve these differences. The accompanying Organizational Behavior in Action box illustrates further the effective management of generational differences.

We discuss values from three standpoints: how they are learned, how they are clarified, and the mesh between individual and organizational values. Values will be mentioned again in the discussion of ethics because values are the foundation of ethics.

How Values Are Learned

People are not born with a particular set of values. Rather, values are learned in the process of growing up; many values are learned by age four. One important way we acquire values is through modeling. Often a person who takes considerable pride in work was reared around people who had a strong work ethic. Models can be parents, teachers, friends, siblings, and even public figures. If we identify with a particular person, the probability is high that we will develop some of his or her major values.

Communication of attitudes is another major way in which values are learned. The attitudes we hear expressed directly or indirectly help shape our values. Assume that using credit to purchase goods and services was talked about as an undesirable practice among your family and friends. You might therefore hold negative values about installment purchases.

Unstated but implied attitudes may also shape values. If key people in your life showed no enthusiasm when you talked about work accomplishment, you might not place a high value on achieving outstanding results. In contrast, if your family

Organizational Behavior *in Action*

Reverse Mentoring Capitalizes on Intergenerational Differences in Values

One of the most valuable things Judy Kirpich has learned is that some of the best ideas come from people who were barely born when she started in marketing 23 years ago. "I routinely get technology information from younger employees who have grown up on computers," says the 49-year-old CEO and co-founder of Grafik Marketing Communications Inc. in Alexandria, Virginia.

What Kirpich is doing is reverse mentoring—matching younger employees who know a lot about the Internet, wireless commerce or some other field with senior managers who aren't so up on the latest digital domains. Joining youthful insight with elder influence can have long-lasting benefits. Kirpirch says she was cool to technology in the 1980s, but invested in computers at the urg-

ing of the younger set in her company. "If I hadn't listened to the younger people," says Kirpirchk, "we'd be out of business."

Questions

1. What does this case example tell us about how intergenerational differences based on values can be managed at work?

2. What are the younger people described in this incident receiving in exchange for their helping older workers with information technology?

Source: Reprinted with permission of Entrepreneur, www .entrepreneur.com. "Kids These Days," Entrepreneur, May 2002, p. 71.

and friends centered their lives on their careers, you might develop similar values. (Or you might rebel against such a value because it interfered with a more relaxed lifestyle.)

Many key values are also learned through religion and thus become the basis for society's morals. A basic example is that all religions emphasize treating other people fairly and kindly. Members of the clergy teach many ethics courses and seminars because it is often assumed that a religious person has special expertise with constructive values.

Clarifying Values

The values you develop early in life are directly related to the kind of person you are now and will be, and the quality of relationships that you form.[16] Recognizing this fact has led to exercises designed to help people clarify and understand some of their own values. Value-clarification exercises ask you to compare the relative importance you attach to different objects and activities. The Self-Assessment on page 63 gives you an opportunity to clarify your values.

The Mesh between Individual and Organizational Values

Under the best of circumstances, the values of employees mesh with those required of the job and organization. When this state of congruence exists, job performance is likely to be higher. A national survey of managers investigated the fit between the values of managers and their firms. (One such mesh would be a highly ethical person working for a highly ethical firm.) A major finding was that managers who experienced a good fit were more successful and more likely to believe that they could reach their career goals. They were also more confident about remaining with their present firm and more willing to work long hours.[17]

SELF-ASSESSMENT

Clarifying Your Values

Directions: Rank from 1 to 21 the importance of the following values to you. The most important value on the list receives a rank of 1, the least important a rank of 21. Use the space next to the two "Other" blanks to include important values of yours not on the list.

____ Having my own place to live	____ Being a religious person
____ Performing high-quality work	____ Helping people less fortunate than myself
____ Having one or more children	____ Loving and being loved by another person
____ Having an interesting job and career	____ Having physical intimacy with another person
____ Owning a detached house, condominium, or apartment	____ Earning an above-average income
____ Having good relationships with coworkers	____ Being in good physical condition
____ Having good health	____ Being a knowledgeable, informed person
____ Watching my favorite television shows	____ Leading a Net lifestyle, including having up-to-date high-technology devices
____ Participating in sports or other pastimes	____ Other
____ Being neat, clean, and orderly	____ Other
____ Being active in a professional society in my field	

1. Discuss and compare your ranking of these values with the person next to you.
2. Perhaps your class, assisted by your instructor, can arrive at a class average on each of these values. How does your ranking compare to the class ranking? What evidence will you need before you conclude that a given rank is representative of the class?
3. Are there any surprises in the class ranking? Which values did you think would be the highest and lowest?
4. How do you think average ranks for these values would be influenced by a person's culture?

The values stated by Eastman Kodak Company represent the type of values many business firms express in their written documents:

- Respect for individual dignity.
- Uncompromising integrity.
- Trust.
- Credibility.
- Continuous improvement and personal renewal.

Not every business firm claiming to have such values carries them out in practice. As a result, problems are created for some employees. When the demands made by the organization or a manager clash with the basic values of the individual, that person suffers from **person–role conflict.** The employee wants to obey orders but does not want to perform an act that seems inconsistent with his or her values. A situation of this type might occur when an employee is asked to help produce a product or service that he or she feels is unsafe or of no value to society. Unfortunately, both safety and value to society are not easy to specify objectively. A food manufacturer was indicted for superimposing tuna fish labels on a large batch of unsold dog food, and then selling it wholesale as tuna fish for human consumption. He contended that nobody would be harmed by such actions. One could argue that any product or service is of value to society because it creates employment for somebody.

What constitutes a good fit between personal values and organizational values may change at different stages of a person's career because of a change in values. At one point in a person's career, he or she may think that founding a business is important because the new firm might create employment. At another stage of the same person's career, he or she might believe that working for the nonprofit sector is more meritorious.

A starting point in finding a good fit between individual and organizational values is to identify what type of work would be the most meaningful. Po Bronson writes that people "thrive by focusing on the question of who they really are—and connecting to work that they truly love (and, in so doing, unleashing a productive and creative power that they never imagined)."[18] After identifying your passion in terms of work, you would then seek an employment opportunity that provides such work. For example, a manager might discover that helping young people learn useful job skills brings her the most professional excitement. She might then seek an opportunity to manage a manufacturing apprenticeship program in her company.

ETHICS

4

Describe three ethical decision-making criteria, along with several explanations for the existence of ethical problems.

Our last key factor for understanding individuals in organizations is **ethics,** which are the set of the moral choices—based on what he or she ought to do—a person makes. Ethics is based on an individual's beliefs about what is right and wrong or good and bad. Ethics can also be regarded as the vehicle that converts values into action. You might value a clean environment; the corresponding ethical behavior is not to place a television set or computer in a landfill. Ethics is a major consideration in studying the actions of managerial workers and the functioning of organizations. The prominent financial scandals in business during the first two years of the new century have intensified recognition of the importance of ethics. We will therefore refer to ethics at various places in the text.

The ethical behavior of organizational members, whether individual contributors (nonmanagers) or managers, exerts a major force on how a firm will be perceived by outsiders and insiders. If the behavior of one or more organizational members is outrageously unethical, it may violate the law, thus leading to outside intervention. The former CEO of a major corporation was engaged in such behavior:

> U.S. Technologies Inc. Chief Executive Officer C. Gregory Earls was charged with misusing $15 million entrusted to him by investors, allegedly funneling some of the money into a trust fund for his children. A federal grand jury handed up a 22-count indictment charging Earls, 58, with multiple counts of securities, mail and wire fraud. The indictment says Earls controlled an investment company called USV Partners, saying he would use investors' money to buy shares of U.S. Technologies—but instead he used it for the trust fund to repay investors from other business ventures. It also says Earl stole $1.3 million from investors, saying he would finance an Internet company, but pocketing the money for himself.
>
> Earls was released at the time on $500,000 bail and returned to his home in Washington. His attorney, Thomas Green, had called the charges "overblown and substantially embellished."[19]

Here we approach ethics as it relates to individuals from four perspectives. First we look at three somewhat philosophical criteria for making ethical decisions. Second, we describe major causes of ethical problems. Third, we present an eight–part guide to ethical decision making. Fourth, we describe the role of organizations in promoting ethical and socially responsible behavior.

Ethical Decision-Making Criteria

A standard way of understanding ethical decision making is to understand the philosophical basis for making these decisions. When attempting to decide what is right and wrong, people can focus on (1) consequences; (2) duties, obligations, and principles; or (3) integrity.[20]

Focus on Consequences

When attempting to decide what is right and wrong, people sometimes focus on the consequences of their decision or action. According to this criterion, if nobody gets hurt, the decision is ethical. Focusing on consequences is often referred to as *utilitarianism*. The decision maker is concerned with the utility of the decision. What really counts is the net balance of good consequences over bad.

To focus on consequences, the decision maker would have to be aware of all the good and bad consequences of a given decision. A financial vice president might decide that if all travel expense reimbursements were delayed by ten days, the company could earn $1,000,000 per year nationwide. The earnings would stem from holding on to money longer, thus collecting interest. How would this vice president know how many family arguments and how much job stress would be created by these delayed reimbursements? How many good performers would quit in disgust?

Focus on Duties, Obligations, and Principles

Another approach to making an ethical decision is to examine one's duties in making the decision. The theories underlying this approach are referred to as *deontological,* from the Greek word *deon* (or duty). The deontological approach is based on universal principles such as honesty, fairness, justice, and respect for persons and property. Rights, such as the right to privacy and safety, are also important. From a deontological perspective, the principles are more important than the consequences. If a given decision violates one of these universal principles, it is automatically unethical, even if nobody gets hurt.

The financial vice president pondering whether to defer payments on travel expenses would not have to spend much time with deontology. She would say to herself, "Delaying these payments may earn the company another $1,000,000 per year, but it is neither honest, fair, nor just. Furthermore, employees have a right to prompt payment."

Focus on Integrity (Virtue Ethics)

The third criterion for determining the ethics of behavior focuses on the character of the person involved in the decision or action. If the person in question has good character and genuine motivation and intentions, he or she will be judged to have behaved ethically. The criteria for good character will often include the two other ethical criteria. For example, one might judge a person to have good character if he or she follows the right principles and respects the rights of others.

Trustworthiness has emerged as a virtue of major importance for managers and professionals in recent years, in part because of many well-publicized incidents of executives being untrustworthy. The name Enron has become almost synonymous with untrustworthy behavior. A prominent example is that Kenneth Lay, the former chairman and CEO of Enron, received $152.7 million in payments in the year leading up the company's collapse, during revelations that Enron hid debt and inflated profits for years. Research suggests that trust makes a major contribution to organizational effectiveness. Two major contributors to trust are consistent

65

Enron, only one in a series of recent corporate meltdowns, provides an especially compelling slant on ethical decision making. Log on to InfoTrac at **http://www.infotrac -college.com** and search for articles that reveal the choices made by some of the business world's now-disgraced executives (e.g., Kenneth Lay or Jeffrey Skilling of Enron, or L. Dennis Kozlowski of Tyco). Do the articles focus more on the consequences of the executives' actions or on their character? Now consider your own opinion about the ethics of swapping music online. How would you evaluate the ethical decision making of the most brazen of file sharers, who swap hundreds of songs in a week, versus those who have downloaded only one or two unauthorized copies?

behavior and clear communication. Any act of bad management is likely to engender distrust. At the top of the list are inconsistent messages from top management and inconsistent standards.[21] For example, Kenneth Lay's severance package was 11,000 times the maximum amount paid to laid-off Enron employees.

The decision maker's environment, or community, helps define what integrity means. You might have more lenient ethical standards for a person selling you investment derivatives than you would for a bank vice president who accepted your cash deposit. (Derivatives are high-risk investments used to hedge other investments, with their value derived from the existence of other securities.)

The virtue ethics of managers and professionals who belong to professional societies may be readily inferred. Business-related professions having codes of ethics include accountants, purchasing managers, and certified financial planners. To the extent that the person abides by the tenets of the code, he or she behaves ethically. An example of such a tenet would be for a financial planner to be explicit about any commissions he or she stands to gain from a client accepting the advice.

Major Causes of Ethical Problems

Individuals, organizations, and society must share some of the blame for the prevalence of unethical behavior in the workplace. Major contributors to unethical behavior are an *individual's greed and gluttony,* or the desire to maximize self-gain at the expense of others. Federal Reserve Chairman (and economist) Alan Greenspan commented publicly on the problem of executive greed. He said that "an infectious greed" had contaminated the business community in the late 1990s, as one executive after another manipulated earning or resorted to fraudulent accounting to capitalize on soaring stock prices.[22]

Another key contributor to a person's ethics and morality is his or her *level of moral development.*[23] Some workers are morally advanced, while others are morally challenged—a condition that often develops early in life. People progress through three developmental levels in their moral reasoning. At the *pre-conventional level,* a person is concerned primarily with receiving external rewards and avoiding punishments. A manager at this level of development might falsify earnings statements for the primary purpose of gaining a large bonus.

At the *conventional level,* people learn to conform to the expectations of good behavior as defined by key people in their environment, as well as societal norms. A manager at this level might be moral enough just to look good, such as being fair with salary increases and encouraging contributions to the United Way campaign. At the *post-conventional level,* people are guided by an internalized set of principles based on universal, abstract principles that may even transcend the laws of a particular society. A manager at the post-conventional level of moral behavior would be concerned with doing the most good for the most people, whether or not such behavior brought him or her recognition and fortune. If the manager just described wanted to direct an apprenticeship program, he or she might also be at the post-conventional level of moral behavior.

Another major contributor to unethical behavior is an *organizational atmosphere that condones such behavior.* If leaders at the top of the organization take imprudent, quasi-legal risks, other leaders throughout the firm might be prompted to behave similarly. Many believed the risk-taking culture at Enron contributed to leaders in the firm engaging in questionable financial transactions, such as creating false profit statements. An analysis by business professors and consultants included the following observation:

Enron didn't fail just because of improper accounting or alleged corruption at the top. It also failed because of its entrepreneurial culture—the very reason Enron attracted so much attention and acclaim. The unrelenting emphasis on earnings growth and individual initiatives, coupled with a shocking absence of the usual corporate checks and balances, tipped the culture from one that rewarded aggressive strategy to one that increasingly relied on unethical corner-cutting.[24]

Unethical behavior is often triggered by *pressure from higher management to achieve goals*. One study found that 56 percent of all workers feel some pressure to act unethically or illegally. Forty-eight percent of workers surveyed admitted they had engaged in one or more unethical or illegal actions during the year. Among the most common ethical violations were: (1) cutting corners on quality, (2) covering up incidents that would make them look bad, (3) deceiving customers, (4) lying to a supervisor or group member, and (5) taking credit for a coworker's idea.[25]

A new explanation for the cause of unethical behavior emphasizes the *strength of relationships among people* as a major factor.[26] Assume that two people have close ties to each other, such as having worked together for a long time, or knowing each other both on and off the job. As a consequence, they are likely to behave ethically toward each other on the job. In contrast, if a weak relationship exists between the two people, either party is more likely to engage in an unethical relationship. Executives who do not feel that they have a personal relationship with employees well below them in the hierarchy are more likely to behave unethically toward them than if a bond had been formed.

An Eight-Step Guide to Ethical Decision Making

Linda K. Treviño and Katherine A. Nelson have developed a guide to ethical decision making that incorporates the basic ideas found in other ethical tests.[27] After studying this guide, you will be asked to ethically screen a decision. The eight steps to sound ethical decision making are described here.

1. *Gather the facts.* When making an important business decision, it is necessary to gather relevant facts. Ask yourself such questions as, "Are there any legal issues involved here?" "Is there a precedent in our firm with respect to this type of decision?" "Do I have the authority to make this decision?" "Are there company rules and regulations governing such a decision?"

2. *Define the ethical issues.* The ethical issues in a given decision are often more complicated than first glance suggests. When faced with a complex decision, it may be helpful to talk over the ethical issues with another person. The ethical issues might involve common ethical problems such as:

   - Lying to customers.
   - Job discrimination.
   - Sexual harassment.
   - Offering or accepting bribes or kickbacks.
   - Overstatement of the capability of a product or service.
   - Use of corporate resources for personal gain.

3. *Identify the affected parties.* When faced with a complex ethical decision, it is important to identify those who will feel the impact of the decision. Brainstorming may be helpful to identify all of the parties affected by a given decision. Major corporate decisions can affect thousands of people. If a

company decides to shut down a plant and move manufacturing to a low-wage country, thousands of individuals and many different parties are affected. Workers lose their jobs, suppliers lose their customers, the local government loses out on tax revenues, and local merchants lose many of their customers.

The people affected by the decision to delay expense account reimbursements include the workers owed the money and their families. In some instances, the creditors of the workers owed money may also receive late payments.

4. *Identify the consequences.* After you have identified the parties affected by the decision, the next step is to predict the consequences for each party. It may not be necessary to identify every consequence. Yet it is important to identify the consequences with the highest probability of occurring and those with the most negative outcomes.

Both short-term and long-term consequences should be specified. The company closing a plant might create considerable short-term turmoil, but might be healthier in the long term. A healthy company would then be able to provide for more workers. The short-term consequences of delaying expense reimbursements might be a few grumbles; ill will probably will be created for the long term.

The symbolic consequences of an action are important. Every action and decision sends a message (the message is a symbol of something). If a company moves manufacturing out of a community to save on labor costs, it means that the short-term welfare of domestic employees is less important than the welfare of shareholders. Delaying expense account reimbursements symbolizes more concern about optimizing cash flow than treating employees fairly.

5. *Identify the obligations.* When making a complex decision, identify the obligations and the reason for each one. A manufacturer of automotive brakes has an obligation to produce and sell only brakes that meet high safety standards. The obligation is to the auto manufacturer who purchases the brakes, and more importantly to the ultimate consumer whose safety depends on effective brakes. The ultimate reason for the obligation to make safe brakes is that lives are at stake.

6. *Consider your character and integrity.* A core consideration when faced with an ethical dilemma is to consider how relevant people would judge your character and integrity. What would your family, friends, significant others, teachers, and coworkers think of your actions? How would you feel if your actions were publicly disclosed in the local newspaper or through e-mail? If you would be proud for others to know what decision you made when you faced an ethical dilemma, you are probably making the right decision.

7. *Think creatively about potential actions.* When faced with an ethical dilemma, put yourself in a creative-thinking mode. Stretch your imagination to invent several options rather than thinking you only have two choices—to do or not to do something. Creative thinking may point toward a third choice, or even more alternatives. Visualize the ethical dilemma of a purchasing agent who is told by a sales rep that he will receive a Palm™ handheld as a token of appreciation if his company signs a contract. The agent says to himself, "I think we should award the contract to the firm, but I cannot accept the gift. Yet if I turn down the gift, I will be forfeiting a valuable possession that the company simply regards as a cost of doing business."

By thinking creatively, the agent finds another alternative. He tells the sales rep, "We will grant the contract to your firm because your product fits our requirements. I thank you for the offer of the Palm, but instead please give it to the Jordan Street Youth Center in my name."

8. *Check your intuition.* So far we have emphasized the rational side of ethical decision making. Another effective way of conducting an ethics screen is to rely on intuition. How does the contemplated decision feel, taste, and smell? Would you be proud of yourself or would you be disgusted with yourself if you made the decision? Do you wonder how the businessperson who relabeled the dog food as tuna fish felt? Of course, if a person lacks a conscience, checking intuition is not effective.

Another type of decision that often requires an ethical test is choosing between two rights (rather than right versus wrong). Joseph L. Badaracco, Jr., refers to these situations as *defining moments,* because such decisions over time form the basis of a person's character. The defining moment challenges a person by asking him or her to choose between two ideals in which he or she deeply believes.[28] Suppose a blind worker in the group has personal problems so great that her job performance suffers. She is offered counseling but does not follow through seriously. Other members of the team complain about the blind worker's performance because it interferes with the group achieving its goals. If the blind worker is dismissed, she may suffer severe financial consequences. (She is the only wage earner in the family.) However, if she is retained, the group will suffer consequences of its own. The manager must now choose between two rights, or the lesser of two evils.

The Skill-Development Exercise on page 70 gives you an opportunity to practice the eight-part guide to ethical decision making.

Organizational Approaches to Enhancing Ethical and Socially Responsible Behavior

Establishing an ethical and socially responsible workplace is not simply a matter of luck and common sense. Top-level managers, assisted by other managers and professionals, can develop strategies and programs to enhance ethical and socially responsible attitudes and behavior. **Social responsibility** is the idea that firms have obligations to society beyond their economic obligations to owners or stockholders, and also beyond those prescribed by law or contract. Both ethics and social responsibility relate to the goodness or morality of a firm. However, social responsibility is broader than ethics because it relates to an organization's impact on society beyond doing what is ethical. The accompanying Organizational Behavior in Action box presents a representative example of social responsibility. We turn now to initiatives executive leadership can take to help create an ethical and socially responsible culture.

Describe what organizations can do to enhance ethical and socially responsible behavior.

Leadership by Example

A high-powered approach to enhancing ethics and social responsibility is for corporate leaders to behave in such a manner themselves. If people throughout the firm believe that behaving ethically is "in" and behaving unethically is "out," ethical behavior will prevail. Colgate-Palmolive is often cited by business analysts as being a model of ethical behavior for a large company. Much of the reputation is based on the ethical behavior of its long-time CEO Reuben Mark. Although well compensated, he shuns the role of an imperial executive. Instead, he flies on commercial airplanes during his frequent flights and does not bring about radical moves (such as purchasing a competitor) just to please Wall Street analysts.[29]

69

COLLABORATE

SKILL-DEVELOPMENT EXERCISE

Ethical Decision Making

Working in small groups, take one or both of the ethical dilemmas presented in this exercise through the eight steps for an ethical screening of contemplated decisions. Compare your answers for the various steps with other groups in the class.

Scenario 1: The Job Applicants with a Past. A state/provincial government official approaches your employer, a bank, asking you to hire three people soon to be released from prison. All were found guilty of fraudulently altering a bank's computer records for personal gain. The official says that the men have paid their debt to society and that they need jobs. Your bank has three openings for computer specialists. All three men have obviously good computer skills. Your group is wondering whether to hire these people.

Scenario 2: The High-Profit Toys. You are a toy company executive starting to plan your holiday season line. You anticipate that the season's hottest item will be Robo-Woman, a battery-operated crime fighter and superheroine. Robo-Woman should have a wholesale price of $18.50 and a retail price of $38.00. Your company anticipates a gross profit of $10 per unit. You receive a sales call from a manufacturing broker who says he can produce any toy you want for one-third of your present manufacturing cost. He admits that the manufacturer he represents uses prison labor in China but that his business arrangement violates no law. You estimate that your firm can earn a gross profit of $14 per unit if you do business with the manufacturing broker. The decision you face is whether to do business with him.

Written Codes of Ethical Conduct

Many organizations use written codes of conduct as guidelines for ethical and socially responsible behavior. Such guidelines continue to grow in importance because workers in self-managing teams have less leadership than previously. Some general aspects of these codes require people to conduct themselves with integrity and candor. Here is a statement of this type from the Johnson & Johnson (medical and health supplies) code of ethics:

> We believe our first responsibility is to the doctors, nurses, and patients, to mothers and fathers and all others who use our products and services. In meeting these needs everything we do must be of high quality.[30]

Formal Mechanisms for Dealing with Ethical Problems

Large organizations frequently establish ethics committees to help ensure ethical and socially responsible behavior. Committee members generally include a top management representative plus other managers throughout the organization. An ethics and social responsibility specialist from the human resources department might also join the group. The committee establishes policies about ethics and social responsibility, and may conduct an ethical audit of the firm's activities. In addition, committee members might review complaints about ethical problems.

Accepting Whistle Blowers

A **whistle blower** is an employee who discloses organizational wrongdoing to parties who can take action. It was a whistle blower who began the process of exposing the scandalous financial practices at Enron, such as hiding losses. Enron vice president Sherron Watkins wrote a one-page anonymous letter exposing unsound, if not dishonest, financial reporting. Enron had booked profits for two entities that had no assets. She dropped the letter off at company headquarters the next day. A well-publicized whistle blower in the public sector is Coleen Rowley, an FBI agent based in Minneapolis. She sent a letter to FBI director Robert

Organizational Behavior *in Action*

Social Responsibility at Tiffany & Co. or Clever Marketing Ploy?

Mixing comfortably with more than 100 invited patrons of the Detroit Zoo, Liz Klos makes sure that people have enough to drink and eat at this Tuesday night fund-raiser at Tiffany & Co.'s three-level store in Troy, Michigan.

Using a soft marketing approach, Klos, director of the Tiffany store, helps the zoo raise $3,000 and expands Tiffany's outreach to a new group of potential purchasers. Tiffany coordinates everything from mailing invitations to providing food. Guests leave with samples of cologne and an updated catalog. Subtle, targeted sales efforts such as this have helped the New York-based chain of jewelers stay ahead of the national average for improvement in retail sales.

"Liz is a very successful, very creative store director. She understands how to use philanthropic marketing to benefit charities and her organization. We wish other stores that size would provide similar events, but they seldom do," said Steve Horn, chief operating office of the Detroit Zoo.

For Klos, the outreach comes naturally. She anguished over a decision to work in nonprofit organizations or high-end jewelry because she thoroughly enjoyed both ends of the spectrum. She took a pay cut 10 years ago to leave the Detroit Historical Society for a job wrapping packages and handling support duties at Tiffany. Her career moved up rapidly. Two years ago she was promoted to director. She vowed to expand the charitable outreach.

Zoo patrons attended the cocktail party for free. They bought $10 keys to a large lucite box filled with hand-wrapped gifts from Tiffany with more than $3,000 in proceeds going to the zoo. Other in-store charity events have included benefits for the junior league of Birmingham (Michigan), Juvenile Diabetes, Midwest AIDS Partnership, and Gleaners Food Bank.

Bringing couples to the store, such as zoo patrons, helps Tiffany expand its newest marketing sector, according to Klos. Male customers represent an emerging market, which they are tapping with Swiss-made watches that cost more than $1,000 apiece, and appeals for men to buy family gifts.

Questions

1. What ethical problems (if any) do you see with using a fund-raiser as a marketing tool?
2. In what way are Liz Klos and Tiffany being socially responsible?

Source: Maureen McDonald, "Retailer Finds Charity Efforts Benefit Business," *The Detroit News,* December 5, 2002.

Mueller in May 2002. Rowley was concerned that top management in her office ignored her pleas in the weeks before the September 11 attacks to aggressively investigate Zacarias Moussaoui, who was later charged as a co-conspirator in the attacks.[31]

Whistle blowers are often ostracized and humiliated by the companies they hope to improve, by such means as halting promotions or giving poor performance evaluations. More than half the time, the pleas of whistle blowers are ignored. It is important for leaders at all levels to create a comfortable climate for legitimate whistle blowing. The manager needs the insight to sort out the difference between a troublemaker and a true whistle blower. Careful investigation is required.

Training in Ethics and Social Responsibility

Many companies train managerial workers about ethics. Forms of training include messages about ethics and social responsibility from company leadership, classes on ethics at colleges, and exercises in ethics. These training programs reinforce the idea that ethically and socially responsible behavior is both morally right and good for business. Much of the content of this chapter reflects the type of information communicated in such programs.

Awareness of Cross-Cultural Influences on Ethics

A key part of encouraging ethical behavior is to know what constitutes good ethics. The answer is not so easy to ascertain in dealing with companies from other countries, which vary in what they consider to be ethical and socially responsible behavior. For example, both the United States and China make extensive use of prison labor—an activity some countries would consider highly unethical. Bribes to foreign officials to conduct business with their country are usually considered unethical and illegal. Yet, these bribes, reclassified as *offsets,* are widespread in the armaments industry. An offset is presenting a lavish package to a foreign government for the right to do business in their country.

Offsets can be any form of financial or non-financial aids such as direct investments, agreements to help countries export their goods, agreements to use more foreign components in the weapons sold, and even outsourcing production jobs overseas. Military contractors have been brokers for imported figs, tomato paste, and wine. For years, McDonnell Douglas (now part of Boeing) provided holiday hams to employees under a fighter jet offset deal with Denmark.

Offsets, of course, are controversial. Liberal economist Robert E. Scott says, "It's a tragedy, and a race to the bottom. The best way to avoid these kinds of competitive and disruptive games is to outlaw the practice."[32]

The initiatives for ethics and social responsibility just described can benefit the organization. Research evidence suggests that high ethics and social responsibility are related to good financial performance. According to the International Business Ethics Institute, socially responsible behavior does enhance profits. The overall financial performance of the 2001 list of the 100 Best Firms was significantly better than the remaining companies in the S&P 500, according to the research of Elizabeth Murphy and Curtis C. Verschoor. The study took into account measures of responsibility, reflecting quality service to seven stakeholder entities: the community, minorities, women, employees, the environment, foreign stakeholders, and customers.[33]

The relationship between social responsibility and profits can also work in two directions. More profitable firms can better afford to invest in social responsibility initiatives, and these initiatives can in turn lead to more profits. Sandra A. Waddock and Samuel B. Graves conducted a large-scale study that supports the two-way conclusion. The researchers analyzed the relationship between corporate social performance and corporate financial performance for 469 firms, spanning 13 industries, for a 2-year period. Many different measures of social and financial performance were used. An example of social performance would be helping to re-develop a poor community.

Researchers found that levels of corporate social performance were influenced by prior financial success. The results suggest that financial success creates enough money left over to invest in corporate social performance. The study also found that good corporate social performance contributes to improved financial performance as measured by a company's return on assets and return on sales. Waddock and Graves concluded that the relationship between social and financial performance may be a **virtuous circle,** meaning that corporate social performance and corporate financial performance feed and reinforce each other.[34]

Being ethical also helps avoid the costs of paying huge fines for being unethical, including charges of discrimination and class action lawsuits because of improper financial reporting. Charges of age discrimination and sex discrimination are the two leading sources of lawsuits against companies.

IMPLICATIONS FOR MANAGERIAL PRACTICE

In addition to the suggestions made for applying information throughout this chapter (as is done in all chapters of this book), here we make a few additional practical suggestions:

1. Recognize emotion in the workplace as a potentially constructive force rather than a human condition to be ignored or suppressed. For example, enthusiasm and joy should be encouraged because they are symptoms of feelings of accomplishment and high job satisfaction. Also, anger can be a constructive force if directed toward overcoming problems.

2. An important interpersonal skill in the workplace is to recognize both generational and individual values, and then make some concession to satisfying the reasonable job demands stemming from these values. For example, to appeal to the value system of the stereotypical member of Generation Y, you would grant that person flexibility in choosing methods of work and working hours, frequent feedback, and meaningful projects. Also, if you were working with a member of the veteran generation (born between 1922 and 1943), you would make concessions to his or her interest in abiding by rules and regulations.

3. When facing a major decision, you will want to use many of the guidelines for problem solving and decision making presented in the next chapter. In addition, major decisions should be subject to the eight-step guide for ethical decision making presented here. For a quick check on the ethical soundness of your decisions, use steps 6 (consider your character and integrity) and 8 (check your intuition).

SUMMARY OF KEY POINTS

1 Discuss the importance of attitudes and emotions to behavior in organizations.

Attitudes influence organizational behavior in many ways. The three components of attitudes are cognitive, affective, and behavioral. A state of cognitive dissonance leads people to reduce their internal conflict when they experience a clash between the information they receive and their actions or attitudes. Attitudes are especially important because they are the basis for job satisfaction, which is linked to important consequences such as absenteeism and turnover, and job stress. An emotion consists of three interacting components: internal physiological arousal, expressive behavior, and a cognitive appraisal. Managers should make good use of emotions. Two key steps are to establish a friendly emotional climate, and to include a positive attitude as one factor in selecting individuals and teams.

2 Describe how organizational citizenship behavior contributes to individual and organizational effectiveness.

Job satisfaction also contributes to organizational citizenship behavior. The good organization citizen goes above and beyond the call or duty, or engages in extra-role behavior. Personality factors, such as service orientation and empathy, contribute to organizational citizenship behavior. Low organizational citizenship behavior has been linked to turnover. When workers perceive their organization to be fair and just, they are more likely to believe that OCB is part of their job.

3 Summarize why values are an important part of organizational behavior.

A value refers to the importance a person attaches to something that serves as a guide to action. Many values are acquired early in life, often through modeling. The values a person develops early in life are directly related to the kind of person he or she is now and will be, as well as the quality of his or her personal relationships. Job performance tends to be higher when there is congruence between individual and organizational values. A person suffers from person–role conflict when the demands made by the organization or a manager clash with the basic values of the individual.

4 Describe three ethical decision-making criteria, along with several explanations for the existence of ethical problems.

A philosophical approach to understanding ethics gives three possible focuses: on consequences; on duties, obligations, and principles; or on integrity. When focusing on consequences, the decision maker is concerned with the utility, or net balance of good consequences, of a decision. The deontological approach is based on universal principles such as honesty, fairness, justice, and respect for persons and property. The integrity, or virtue, criterion focuses on the character of the ethical action.

An eight-step guide to ethical decision making follows these steps: (1) gather the facts, (2) define the ethical issues, (3) identify the affected parties, (4) identify the consequences, (5) identify the obligations,

(6) consider your character and integrity, (7) think creatively about potential actions, and (8) check your intuition. Choosing between two rights, or defining moments, may require an ethical test.

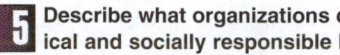 **Describe what organizations can do to enhance ethical and socially responsible behavior.**
Managers can develop strategies and programs to enhance ethical and socially responsible attitudes and

behaviors. Among these approaches are: leading by example, establishing written codes of ethical conduct, and formal mechanisms for dealing with ethical problems, accepting whistle blowers, giving training in ethics and social responsibility, and gaining awareness of cross-cultural influences on ethics.

KEY TERMS AND PHRASES

Attitude, *56*
A predisposition to respond that exerts an influence on a person's response to a person, a thing, an idea, or a situation.

Cognitive Dissonance, *56*
The situation in which the pieces of knowledge, information, attitudes, or beliefs held by an individual are contradictory.

Emotion, *57*
A feeling such as anger, fear, joy, or surprise that underlies behavior.

Emotional Labor, *58*
The process of regulating both feelings and expressions to meet organizational goals.

Job Satisfaction, *58*
The amount of pleasure or contentment associated with a job.

Organizational Citizenship Behavior, *59*
Behaviors that express a willingness to work for the good of an organization even without the promise of a specific reward.

Value, *60*
The importance a person attaches to something that serves as a guide to action.

Person–Role Conflict, *63*
A condition that occurs when the demands made by the organization or a manager clash with the basic values of the individual.

Ethics, *64*
An individual's moral beliefs about what is right and wrong or good and bad.

Social Responsibility, *69*
The idea that firms have an obligation to society beyond their economic obligations to owners or stockholder and also beyond those prescribed by law or contract.

Whistle Blower, *70*
An employee who discloses organizational wrongdoing to parties who can take action.

Virtuous Circle, *72*
The idea that corporate social performance and corporate financial performance feed and reinforce each other.

DISCUSSION QUESTIONS AND ACTIVITIES

1. One study showed that more intelligent workers are more likely to experience job satisfaction. How might you explain this relationship between intelligence and job satisfaction?
2. Some workers perceive *organizational citizenship behavior* to be part of their job. What do they really mean?
3. Give an example of a situation in which you would most likely experience person–role conflict within an organization.
4. What can a manager do to teach the right values to employees?
5. What can business schools do to increase the probability that business graduates will behave ethically on the job?
6. If one of the tests for ethical decision making is simply to use one's intuition to evaluate a decision, why should managers study ethics?
7. The Vice Fund (**http://www.vicefund.com**) bills itself as a "socially irresponsible fund" because it puts investor's assets into four industry sectors: tobacco, gambling, liquor, and defense. What is your opinion of: (a) the ethics of the founders of the fund, and (b) the advisability of investing money in such a fund?

ORGANIZATIONAL BEHAVIOR ONLINE

TO DO

Values-Based Business: Avoiding Conflicts by Discovering Your Core Values

According to http://www.mediate.com, unbalanced values and unconscious habits are potentially harmful in business. You can avoid many ethical conflicts by discovering your core values and unconscious habits, and learn to make conscious decisions about how to react in difficult situations. Visit http://www.mediate.com, and register. You will then have the opportunity to answer questions, and receive information about minimizing ethical conflicts.

TO BOOKMARK

Job Attitudes Survey

http://www.3dgroup.org/what_em.htm/ (Comprehensive approach to measuring employee attitudes)

Values in Business

http://www.character-ethics.org/articles/August2002.pdf

Business Ethics

http://ecampus.bentley.edu/dept/cbe/aboutcbe/vtour.html (Bentley College, Center for Business Ethics)
http://www.visualexpert.com

CASE PROBLEM: The "Big Squeeze" Distributor

Oil-Dri Corp. of America finally drew the line with its longtime grocery distributor: It refused to ship any more cat litter. Oil-Dri complained that when its distributor, Fleming Cos., paid its bills, it arbitrarily deducted large sums for things such as product placement or early bill payment, even it if was actually paying late. "There are hundreds of thousands of dollars of erroneous deductions that need to be cleared off our account," the company wrote to Fleming.

Deducting a little bit from a bill, usually for reasons such as incomplete or damaged orders, is a time-honored practice of wholesalers and retailers. Suppliers usually accept this annoyance as a cost of keeping the customer. But dozens of suppliers and ex-employees of Fleming say the company—the country's largest grocery distributor and one with considerable power over customers—has pushed the practice to extremes.

Some suppliers temporarily stopped shipping to the distributor one year until a deduction dispute was resolved. In other cases, when they complained, Fleming threatened to halt or reduce its purchases from them. Fleming's "relationship with vendors is ugly," says a food-industry consultant who has worked for Fleming and for a competitor. "They deduct and deduct until a vendor cuts them off, then they pay. Then they start deducting again."

Fleming denies it has ratcheted up its deductions or takes more of them than competitors. It says its deductions may simply appear to have grown lately because it has been putting them all on one bill. "The fees look different because they're all aggregated," says Fleming's chief executive, Mark Hansen.

For thousands of food-product suppliers and independent supermarket chains, the issue of Fleming's deductions is crucial. Suppliers can gain access to these independent and smaller grocers only through their distributors. And the grocers rely on their distributors for most of their merchandise, unlike giant chains such as Safeway Inc. and Wal-Mart Stores Inc. that buy direct. The situation puts Fleming in a powerful gatekeeper position, with the clout to unilaterally lower what it pays suppliers for their product.

Fleming is under its own marketplace pressure. Its big customer, Kmart, continues to struggle after declaring bankruptcy in 2002. More broadly, the independent grocers that Fleming serves are dwindling in a world of retail behemoths with great purchasing power. Fleming has about 10 percent of the market, in a slow-growth, low-margin business.

As suppliers give direct-buying giants such as Wal-Mart deals unavailable to independent grocers, Fleming says, deductions become important as a way for distributors that serve the independents to fight back. "We are still 'David' battling 'Goliath,'" says Hansen. Fleming maintains that its annual deductions are in line with industry averages of about 5% of purchases.

Reports to the contrary come in part from former Fleming employees. One former Fleming executive says he started hearing complaints from suppliers about nuisance deductions two-and-one-half years ago. He says he shrugged them off until the complaints grew more vociferous and began involving large sums from prominent companies.

The executive says he had his staff do an informal tally. It found that at that time, suppliers were disputing $100 million of deductions Fleming had taken from their bills. Fleming executives say the disputed figure is less than $100 million, and that the company takes about $800 million in deductions each year.

Shared Savings

Fleming recently imposed a deduction called Shared Savings. The distributor invited food suppliers to become Preferred Vendors, promising that it would then "eliminate nonproductive activities such as deductions" and provide quick resolution "on any deduction, invoice and or administrative errors." Fleming asked suppliers to pay a $75,000 fee for this status, a fee it said it deserved because it was saving suppliers money through a new central procurement system.

When most suppliers balked, Fleming told them in August 2001 it was taking automatic 3% deductions from what it owed them. The idea was that the suppliers saved money by using the new procurement system, and the deduction let them "share" their savings with Fleming.

The new deduction, retroactive for 12 weeks, surprised and irritated some suppliers. An Agrilink Foods Inc. official told Fleming he wasn't seeing any "shared savings" at all. "Frankly the cost of doing business with Fleming has gone up as our representatives seem to need to spend more time purchasing unauthorized deductions than building our mutual business," said a letter from an Agrilink official. Hansen says Fleming has stopped taking Shared Savings deductions, and has resolved all disputes over these deductions in some cases by canceling them.

Several former Fleming employees say Fleming also played games with "slotting allowances." These are deductions taken for the trouble of adding new products to inventory. Two former Fleming executives claim the distributor sometimes charged slotting fees for items it never actually put into distribution.

More Deductions

Fleming later developed another new deduction, the *off-shore funding equalization* deduction. Fleming informed suppliers that they weren't providing the same level of promotional discounts for food retailers in Hawaii and the Caribbean as for retailers on the U.S. mainland. So in order to provide more promotional discounts to these offshore retailers, Fleming said it was deducting some money from what it owed suppliers. A Kellogg executive wrote to Fleming stating that this deduction was unjustified and violated the preferred vendor agreement.

Jim McCaffery, who owns four supermarkets in the Northeast, felt his stores weren't receiving their full allotment of promotional discounts that suppliers provided. So McCaffery switched to a rival distributor, and says that since then his stores have seen $700,000 more in marketing discounts than the year before. Fleming denies ever failing to pass along promotional discounts provided by the supplier.

In March 2003, Fleming Cos. ended its supplier relationship with Kmart Corp, and filed for Chapter 11 bankruptcy protection one month later. Fleming listed assets of $4.2 billion and debt of $3.5 billion.

Case Questions

1. What is your evaluation of the ethical behavior of Fleming Cos.?

2. Run the Shared Savings program through the guide to ethical decision making, and reach a conclusion about the program's ethics.

3. What suggestions might you offer the Fleming Cos. so that it can still survive financially yet improve its ethical image among suppliers?

4. What is your opinion of the ethics of Fleming Cos. filing for bankruptcy protection when it had $700 million dollars more in assets than liabilities?

Source: Ann Zimmerman, "Grocery Distributor Squeezes Suppliers at Bill-Paying Time," *The Wall Street Journal*, September 5, 2002, pp. A1, A10; "Food Supplier in Chapter 11," The Associated Press, April 2, 2003.

ENDNOTES

1. Neal M. Ashkanasy, Charmine E. J. Härtel, and Wilfred J. Zerbe (eds.), Emotions in the Workplace: Research, Theory, and Practice (Westport, CT: Quorum Books/Greenwood, 2000), p. 19.

2. Saul Kassin, Psychology, 3rd ed. (Upper Saddle River, NJ: Prentice-Hall, 2001), p. 330.

3. Neal M. Ashkanasy and Catherine S. Daus, "Emotion in the Workplace: The New Challenge for Managers," *The Academy of Management Executive*, February 2002, pp. 82-83.

4. Alicia A. Grandey, "Emotion Regulation in the Workplace: A New Way to Conceptualize Emotional Labor," *Journal of Occupational Health Psychology* 5, no. 1, 2000, pp. 95–110; Alicia A. Grandey, "When the 'Show Must Go On': Surface Acting and Deep Acting as Determinants of Emotional Exhaustion and Peer-Related Service Delivery," *Academy of Management Journal*, February 2003, pp. 86–96.

5. Reported in review of Ashkanasy, Härtel, and Zerbe, *Emotions in the Workplace*, in *Contemporary Psychology*, April 2002, p. 165.

6. Ibid.

7. Matthew Boyle, "Beware the Killjoy: Does the Death of the Dotcoms Mean No One Will Ever Have Fun at Work Again?," *Fortune*, July 23, 2001, pp. 265–266.

8. Arthur P. Brief, *Attitudes in and around Organizations* (Thousand Oaks, CA: Sage, 1998), Chapter 2; "Employee Retention . . . Attitudes to Make Them Stay," *Managers Edge*, November 1999, p. 8; Wendy Cole, "Suddenly Loyalty Is Back in Business," *Time*, December 2001, pp. Y13–Y16.

9. "Success Linked to Worker Loyalty," The Associated Press, May 13, 2002.

10. "Suddenly, Loyalty Is Back in Business," p. Y14.

11. George A. Neuman and Jill R. Kickul, "Organizational Citizenship Behaviors: Achievement Orientation and Personality," *Journal of Business and Psychology*, Winter 1998, pp. 263–264.

12. Lance A. Bettencourt, Kevin P. Gwinner, and Matthew L. Meuter, "A Comparison of Attitude, Personality, and Knowledge Predictors of Service-Oriented Organizational Citizenship Behaviors," *Journal of Applied Psychology*, February 2001, pp. 29–41.

13. Xiao-Ping Chen, Chun Hui, and Douglas J. Sego, "The Role of Organizational Citizenship Behavior in Turnover: Conceptualization and Preliminary Tests of Key Hypotheses," *Journal of Applied Psychology*, December 1998, pp. 922–931.

14. Bennett J. Tepper, Daniel Lockhart, and Jenny Hoobler, "Justice, Citizenship, and Role Definition Effects," *Journal of Applied Psychology*, August 2001, pp. 789–796.

15. Ron Zemke, "Generation Veneration," in *Business: The Ultimate Resource*™ (Cambridge, MA: Peresus Books Group, 2002), pp. 39–40.

16. David C. McClelland, "How Motives, Skills, and Values Determine What People Do," *American Psychologist*, July 1985, p. 815.

17. John B. Miner, *Organizational Behavior: Performance and Productivity* (New York: Random House, 1988), p. 83.

18. Po Bronson, "What Should I Do With My Life?" *Fast Company*, January 2003, p. 72.

19. "CEO Charged with Misusing Investor Funds," Associated Press, March 25, 2003. Reprinted with permission of The Associated Press.

20. Linda K. Treviño and Katherine A. Nelson, *Managing Business Ethics: Straight Talk about How to Do It Right* (New York: Wiley, 1995), pp. 66–70.

21. Robert Galford and Anne Seibold, "The Enemies of Trust," *Harvard Business Review*, February 2003, pp. 88–95.

22. "Fed Chief Points to Cautious Recovery," Gannett News Service, July 17, 2002.

23. Research synthesized in Richard L. Daft, *Leadership: Theory and Practice* (Mason, OH: South Western/Thomson Learning, 2003), pp. 369-370.

24. John A. Byrne, reported in "The Betrayed Investor," *Business Week*, February 25, 2002, p. 118.

25. Samuel Greengard, "50% of Your Employees Are Lying, Cheating, and Stealing," *Workforce*, October 1997, p. 46.

26. Daniel J. Brass, Kenneth D. Butterfield, and Bruce C. Skaggs, "Relationships and Unethical Behavior: A Social Network Perspective," *The Academy of Management Review*, January 1998, pp. 14–31.

27. Treviño and Nelson, *Managing Business Ethics,* pp. 71–75.

28. Joseph L. Badaracco, Jr., "The Discipline of Building Character," *Harvard Business Review,* March–April 1998, pp. 114–124.

29. Nanette Byrnes, "The Good CEO," *Business Week*, September 23, 2002, p. 83.

30. Excerpted from http://www.jnj.com/our_company/our_credo/index .htm.

31. Erin McClam, "*Time* Names Whistleblowers Persons of Year," Associated Press, December 23, 2002.

32. Leslie Wayne, "Foreigners Exact Trade-Offs From U.S. Contractors," *New York Times,* February 16, 2003.

33. Study reported in http://www.business-ethics.org, and cited in Deb Koen, "Ethical Conduct Is Good for Business," *Rochester* (NY), *Democrat and Chronicle,* June 16, 2002, p. 4E.

34. Sandra A. Waddock and Samuel B. Graves, "The Corporate Social Performance-Financial Performance Link," *Strategic Management Journal,* Spring 1997, pp. 303–319.

Chapter 5

Individual Decision Making and Creativity

OBJECTIVES

After reading and studying this chapter and doing the exercises, you should be able to:

1 Work through the classical/behavioral decision-making model when faced with a major decision.

2 Identify and describe factors that influence the effectiveness of decision making.

3 Understand the nature of creative decision making in organizations.

4 Enhance your creative problem-solving ability.

A growing trend in banking is for people to take out *reverse* mortgages. These are loans that let homeowners who are 62 or older take cash from their home equity and pay nothing back—not a cent—until they move out or die. Some reverse mortgages guarantee a fixed monthly payment for life (an annuity).

Reverse mortgage payouts come in three forms: a monthly payment for as long as you or your spouse lives (the annuity), a lump sum, or a line of credit. You can combine these options. There is no credit or income requirement. The amount you can obtain depends mostly on the value of your house but also on your age. The older you are, the more you can get, but loan caps usually range from $155,000 in rural areas to $281,000 in metropolitan areas.

The lenders who dreamed up reverse mortgages figured the annuity option would be the most popular, since it gives the homeowners a chance to beat the bank (if they live longer than expected). Instead, two-thirds take the line of credit, figuring to use only as much as they need and preserve the rest. Any unused portion of the credit line grows with inflation.

When the homeowner moves out or dies, the amount must be paid back in the sum of payouts plus interest as well as any fees financed as part of the loan. Typical costs include an origination fee, mortgage insurance, other finance costs, and servicing fees. The total is approximately $15,000 on a $175,000 lump sum or line of credit. Live in the house longer than the bank expects, and you are ahead. Live (or die) much sooner, and you have paid too much.

Source: Facts from Jean Chatzky, "The Backwards Loan," *Time,* February 17, 2003, p. 99.

NOW ASK YOURSELF: Why should this story about reverse mortgages interest students of organizational behavior? A reverse mortgage may not suit every older person's taste or best interests but the concept illustrates an important point about problem solving. Going beyond traditional thinking sometimes leads to breakthrough ideas. The traditional thinking here is that in a mortgage, a homeowner borrows money from a financial institution to pay for living quarters, and then repays the institution in regular (often monthly) payments. With a reverse mortgage, the homeowner receives monthly payments or a lump sum from the financial institution and then pays it back in a lump sum in the future, instead of making regular payments.

To be an effective decision maker, a person must think creatively. In this chapter, we study creativity in the context of individual decision making in organizations. First, we describe a model of the decision-making process; then we examine key influences on decision making, followed by a careful look at the nature and development of creativity. We return to the study of decision making in Chapter 10 with a description of group decision making. The steps in ethical decision making have already been described in Chapter 4.

TYPES OF DECISIONS

A **decision** takes place when a person chooses among two or more alternatives in order to solve a problem. People attempt to solve problems because a **problem** is a discrepancy between the ideal and the real. The ability to make good decisions is enormously valuable for a person's career and job performance. Choosing the right career will most likely mean more job satisfaction, less stress, and a longer life. (Stress-related disorders often shorten life.) Making good business decisions is more complex and difficult than most people recognize. The research of Paul C. Nutt suggests that one-half the decisions made in organizations fail—meaning that the decisions were not fully used after two years. His conclusions stem from a database of more than 400 decisions made by top-level managers in a variety of firms in the United States, Canada, and Europe. The typical reason for failure is that managers employ poor decision-making tactics, such as taking shortcuts when faced with time pressures. Managers will often grab the first possible solution without analyzing the possible causes of problems and their remedies.[1]

Programmed versus Non-Programmed Decisions

Managerial workers sometimes face routine, uncomplicated problems involving alternatives that are specified in advance. The standard responses to these uncomplicated problems are called **programmed** (or **routine**) **decisions.** Procedures already exist for how to appropriately handle the problem. Examples of programmed decisions include the procedures for accepting a check or whether to grant an employee a day of personal leave.

Managerial workers frequently face complex, nonrecurring problems where the alternatives are not specified in advance. The unique responses to these complex problems are called **non-programmed** (or **non-routine**) **decisions**. Making a non-programmed decision requires imaginative or creative thinking. Higher-level managers spend more of their time making non-programmed decisions, while lower-level managers face a higher proportion of programmed decisions.

Degree of Risk and Uncertainty Associated with Decisions

Another useful way of classifying decisions is by dividing the degree of risk and uncertainty associated with them into three categories: certainty, risk, and uncertainty. A condition of *certainty* exists when the facts are well known and the outcome can be predicted accurately. A retail store manager might predict with certainty that more hours of operation will lead to more sales. (It might be uncertain, however, whether the increased sales would cover the increased expenses.) Problem solving and decision making are easiest under conditions of certainty, but few major decisions are easy to make. In other words, few business decisions are truly "no brainers."

A condition of *risk* involves incomplete certainty regarding the outcomes of various alternative courses of action. Nevertheless, there is some awareness of the probability associated with the alternatives. Based on past experience, predictions can be made about the various outcomes. An executive might be able to estimate how employees will react to an early retirement program based on previous company experience.

A condition of *uncertainty* exists when a decision must be based on limited or no factual information. In this type of decision environment, the decision maker is unable to assign probabilities to the problem-solving alternatives. When faced with a condition of uncertainty, managers rely on intuition. Michael Dell, the founder of Dell Computer, founded his company in an uncertain business environment. He predicted intuitively that enough demand existed for purchasing personal computers by telephone. His intuition proved to be eminently correct.

Another important perspective on risk taking in decision making depends upon whether the person frames the decision in terms of winning or losing. The economic model called *prospect theory* includes the idea that most people have an aversion to loss. Experiments have shown, for example, that when subjects were asked to hypothetically decide what procedure to undergo to cure a disease, most preferred a procedure that saved 80 percent of patients to one that killed 20 percent.[2]

The implication for managerial practice is that if you frame negotiations in terms of winning, you are more likely to take a chance on an outcome of potential value. If you frame the risk negatively, you are less likely to take the risk. For example, if a manager calculates that a training program has a 75 percent chance of increasing productivity, she might sign up for the program. In contrast, if the manager thinks that the program has a 25 percent chance of not improving, or decreasing, productivity, she will nix the program.

A CLASSICAL/BEHAVIORAL DECISION-MAKING MODEL

1

Work through the classical/ behavioral decision-making model when faced with a major decision.

Two different versions of how managerial workers make decisions are widely studied. The **classical decision model** views the manager's environment as certain and stable and the manager as rational. Many economists view decision making in this manner. The **behavioral decision model,** in contrast, points out that decision makers have cognitive limitations and act only in terms of what they perceive in a given situation.[3] Furthermore, decision making is influenced by many emotional and personal factors. According to the behavioral model, decision making has a messy side. For example, job performance alone may not decide who obtains big promotions in a family-controlled business.

The decision-making model described here blends the classical and behavioral decision models. Managers may make decisions in a generally rational framework. Nevertheless, at various points in the model (such as choosing creative alternatives), intuition and judgment come into play. Furthermore, the discussion in the following section about influences on decision making is based heavily on the behavioral decision model.

The seven steps in the decision-making process, reflecting both the classical and behavioral models, are outlined in Exhibit 5-1 and described in the following paragraphs. The model is useful for making non-programmed decisions of both a personal and an organizational nature. You therefore might want to use the model in purchasing a car, choosing a career, or deciding whether to drop a product line.

Identify and Diagnose the Problem

Problem solving and decision making begin with the awareness that a problem exists. In other words, the first step in problem solving and decision making is identifying a gap between desired and actual conditions. A problem occurs when something has gone wrong or has deviated from the norm.[4] Problem finding may be the key to managerial success. The more emphasis that is placed on problem finding, the less is needed for finding alternative solutions and implementation. This is especially true when lower-ranking employees are invited to participate in the problem-finding phase. Less time is required for implementation when lower-

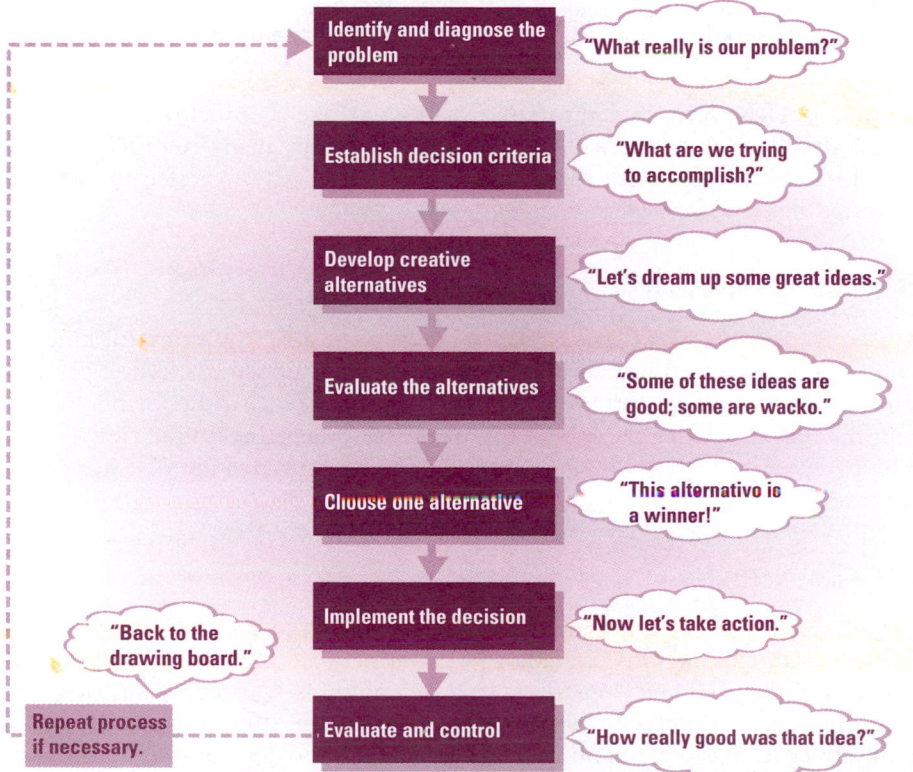

Exhibit 5-1

The Decision-Making Process

ranking workers participate from the beginning in finding and defining the problem and participating in choosing alternatives.[5]

At times, a problem is imposed on a manager, such as a demand from upper management to increase e-tailing sales by 20 percent. At other times, the manager has to search actively for a worthwhile problem or opportunity. For example, a human resources manager sought a way for her firm to celebrate cultural diversity.

A thorough diagnosis of the problem is important because the real problem may be different from the one the first look suggests. To diagnose a problem properly, you must clarify its true nature. For example, what might at first glance seem like a problem of quality is really one of consumer misuse of the product. To resolve the problem, one would need to better inform the consumer, not modify the product. An extreme example is that an owner of a new digital camera complained that the camera only shot partial images, with a horizontal dark spot across the pictures. The true problem was that the camera user held his index finger across the lens while shooting photos.

Establish Decision Criteria

When solving a problem, it pays to know what constitutes a good decision. **Decision criteria** are the standards of judgment used to evaluate alternatives. The more explicit the criteria, the better the decision will be. In seeking to enhance product quality, several of the decision criteria might include the following:

1. The customers should notice the difference in quality.
2. The price of the product should not increase.
3. The demand for the product should increase.
4. Employees should be involved in making the quality improvements.

A second aspect of establishing decision criteria is specifying ground rules for the decision. These include determining who will make the final decision, establishing a deadline for the decision, and determining how many resources will be invested in the decision. With respect to the last point, only so much money can be invested in a given problem.

Develop Creative Alternatives

The third step in decision making is to generate alternative solutions. All kinds of possibilities are explored in this step even if they seem unrealistic. Often the difference between effective and mediocre decision makers is that the former do not accept the first alternative they think of. Instead, they keep digging until they find the best solution. Creativity is such a key part of decision making that it receives separate treatment later in the chapter.

Evaluate the Alternatives

The next step involves comparing the relative value of the alternatives. The problem solver examines the pros and cons of each one and considers its feasibility. Part of evaluating the pros and cons of alternative solutions is to compare each one against the decision criteria established in the second step. Some alternatives would appear attractive, but implementing them would be impossible or counterproductive. For example, one alternative solution a couple chose for increasing their income was to open an entirely new restaurant and bar in a mall. When they discovered that the start-up costs would be approximately $600,000, they decided that the alternative was impossible for the time being.

Choose One Alternative

After investing a reasonable amount of time in evaluating the alternative solutions, it is time to choose one of them—actually making a decision. An important factor influencing this process is the degree of uncertainty associated with it. People who prefer not to take risks choose alternatives that have the most certain outcomes. In contrast, risk takers are willing to choose alternatives with uncertain outcomes if the potential gains appear to be substantial. Despite a careful evaluation of the alternatives, ambiguity remains in most decisions. The decisions faced by managers are often complex, and the factors involved in them are often unclear.

Implement the Decision

Converting the decision into action is the next major step. Until a decision is implemented, it is not really a decision. Many decisions represent wasted effort because nobody is held responsible for implementing them. Much of a manager's job involves helping group members implement decisions. A fruitful way of evaluating a decision is to observe its implementation. A decision is seldom a good one if workers resist its implementation or if it is too cumbersome to implement.

Evaluate and Control

The final step in the decision-making framework is to evaluate how effectively the chosen alternative solved the problem and met the decision criteria. The results of the decision obtained are controlled when they are the ones set forth during the problem-identification stage.

BOUNDED RATIONALITY AND INFLUENCES ON DECISION MAKING

2

Identify and describe factors that influence the effectiveness of decision making.

Decision making is usually not entirely rational, because so many factors influence the decision maker. Awareness of this fact stems from the research of psychologist and economist Herbert A. Simon. He proposed that bounds (or limits) to rationality are present in decision making. These bounds are the limitations of the human organism particularly related to the processing and recall of information.[6] **Bounded rationality** means that people's finite (somewhat limited) mental abilities, combined with external influences over which they have little or no control, prevent them from making entirely rational decisions. Recent research and opinion on bounded rationality emphasizes that humans use problem-solving strategies which are reasonably rapid, reasonably accurate, and that fit the quantity and type of information available.[7] In short, people do the best with what they have while making decisions.

As a result of bounded rationality, most decision makers do not have the time or resources to wait for the best possible solution. Instead, they search for **satisficing decisions,** or those that suffice in providing a minimum standard of satisfaction. Such decisions are adequate, acceptable, or passable. Many decision makers stop their search for alternatives when they find a satisficing one.

Accepting the first reasonable alternative may only postpone the need to implement a decision that truly solves the problem and meets the decision criteria. For example, slashing the price of a pickup truck to match the competition's price can be regarded as the result of a satisficing decision. A superior decision might call for the firm to demonstrate to end users that the difference in quality is worth the higher price, which in the long term will increase sales.

Partly because of bounded rationality, decision makers often use simplified strategies, also known as **heuristics.** A heuristic becomes a rule of thumb in decision making, such as the policy to reject a job applicant who does not smile during the first three minutes of the job interview. A widely used investing heuristic is as follows: The percent of equity in your portfolio should equal 100 minus your age, with the remainder being invested in fixed-income investments including cash. A 25-year-old would therefore have a portfolio consisting of 25 percent interest-bearing securities such as bonds, and 75 percent in stocks. However, his or her 100-year-old grandparent should hold all debt instruments and no stocks! Heuristics help the decision maker cope with masses of information, but their oversimplification can lead to inaccurate or irrational decision making.

A host of influences on the decision-making process contribute to bounded rationality. We describe eight such influences, as outlined in Exhibit 5-2.

Intuition

Intuition is a key personal characteristic that influences decision making. As supported in an interview study of sixty experienced executives, making decisions by intuition is seen as a viable approach in today's business environment.[8] Effective decision makers do not rely on analytical and methodological techniques alone. Instead, they also use hunches and intuition. **Intuition** is an experience-based way of knowing or reasoning in which weighing and balancing evidence are done automatically. When relying on intuition, the decision maker arrives at a conclusion without using a step-by-step logical process. The fact that experience con-

Exhibit 5-2

Influences on Decision Making Contributing to Bounded Rationality

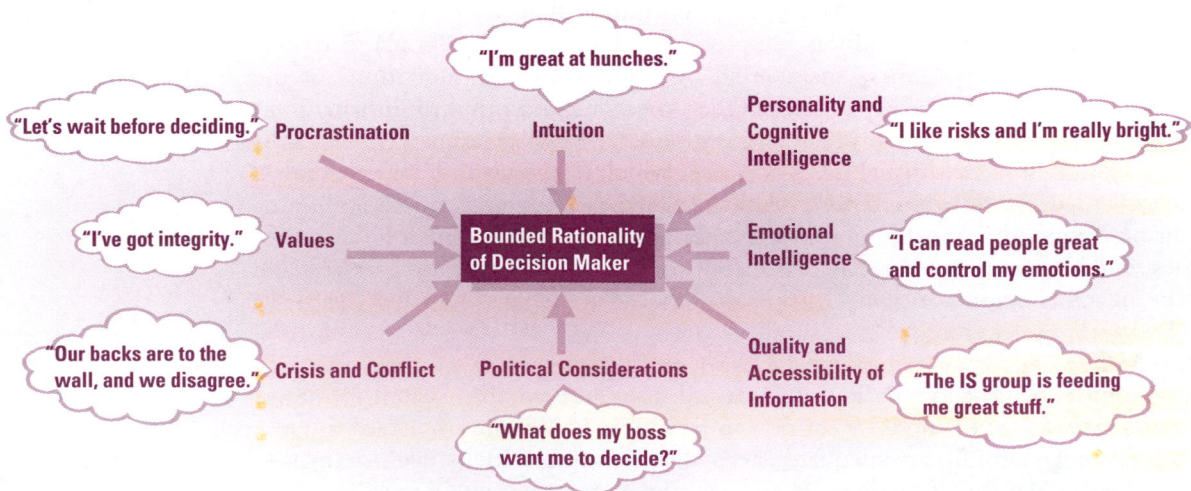

tributes to intuition means that decision makers can become more intuitive by solving many difficult problems. An historically important example follows:

> Ray Kroc has been described as a legend of intuition on the basis of how he started the McDonald's chain. A milkshake-mixer salesman at the time, he came to deliver eight machines to the McDonald brothers' restaurant in 1952. Kroc had a flash that fast-food hamburgers would dominate in the future. So, he made the McDonalds a buyout offer, based on what he later termed his "funny-bone instinct."[9]

The distinction between analytical and intuitive thinking is often traced to which half of the brain is dominant. The left half of the brain controls analytical thinking, whereas the right half controls creative and intuitive thinking. (Note that many researchers have challenged the concept of left- versus right-brain dominance.) Effective problem solvers achieve a balance between analytical (left-brain) and intuitive (right-brain) thinking. Rather than operating independently of each other, the analytical and intuitive approaches should be complementary components of decision making.

Personality and Cognitive Intelligence

The personality and cognitive intelligence of the decision maker influence his or her ability to find effective solutions. One relevant personality dimension is cautiousness and conservatism. A cautious, conservative person typically opts for a low-risk solution. If a person is extremely cautious, he or she may avoid making major decisions for fear of being wrong. Cautiousness and conservatism can be in opposition to self-confidence. Confident people are willing to take reasonable risks because they have faith in the quality of their decisions.

According to behavioral economist Daniel Kahneman, the overconfidence of investors contributed to the stock market plunge that began in the late 1990s and lasted for almost four years. According to prospect theory (mentioned earlier in this chapter) people may suffer from optimistic overconfidence—they believe they can do what they cannot do. Investors believed they were in a new world in which the stock market bubble would be sustained for a long time.[10]

Perfectionism is another personality factor that has a notable impact on decision making. People who seek the perfect solution to a problem are usually indecisive because they are hesitant to accept the fact that a particular alternative is good enough. **Self-efficacy,** the feeling of being an effective and competent person with respect to a task, also has an influence. Researchers note, for example, that having the right amount of "gall" contributes to innovative thinking.[11]

Rigid people have difficulty identifying problems and gathering alternative solutions. People who are mentally flexible perform well in these areas. Optimism versus pessimism is another relevant personality dimension. Optimists are more likely to find solutions than pessimists are. Pessimists are also likely to give up searching because they perceive situations as being hopeless.

Cognitive intelligence has a profound influence on the effectiveness of decision making. In general, intelligent and well-educated people are more likely to identify and diagnose problems and make sound decisions than are those who have less intelligence and education. A notable exception applies, however: Some intelligent, well-educated people have such a fondness for collecting facts and analyzing them that they suffer from analysis paralysis.

Emotional Intelligence

Emotional intelligence is important for decision making because how effectively you manage your feelings and read other people affects the quality of your decisions. For example, if you cannot control your anger, you are likely to make decisions that are motivated by retaliation, hostility, and revenge. You might shout and swear at your team leader because of a work assignment you received.

Your emotional intelligence could also influence career decision making. If you understand your own feelings, you are more likely to enter an occupation or accept a position that matches your true attitudes. A common problem is that many people pursue *hot* and/or well-paying fields even when they are not passionate about the field. As a result they are likely to become discouraged and leave the field—even as early as switching majors. Admitting this lack of passion to oneself might have prevented misdirected time and effort.

Quality and Accessibility of Information

Reaching an effective decision usually requires high-quality, valid information. One of the most important purposes of management information systems is to supply managers and professionals with high-quality information. A vice president of manufacturing might contemplate the establishment of a manufacturing plant in a distant city. She would more likely make an effective decision if the information systems group had accurate information about such factors as the quality of the workforce and environmental regulations.

Accessibility of information may be even more important than quality in determining whether or not information is used. Sometimes it takes so much time and effort to search for quality information that the manager relies on lower-quality information that is close at hand. Think of the decision-making process involved in purchasing a new automobile. Many people are more likely to rely on the opinion of friends than to search through reference sources for more systematic information.

Even when high-quality, accessible information is available, it will not lead to better decision making if the decision maker denies its importance. Sixteen months prior to the explosion of the space shuttle *Columbia* in 2003, the General Accounting Office concluded that the downsizing of NASA's workforce had left it ill equipped to manage its safety upgrade program for the shuttle. Furthermore, a Rand report released in late 2002 said that "Decaying infrastructure and shuttle component obsolescence are significant contributions to a future declining safety posture." Equally significant, NASA later released a batch of e-mails revealing that dozens of NASA workers at the Johnson Space Center were aware that engineers were concerned about a potentially catastrophic re-entry for Columbia. A NASA official later said it would have been impossible for him to be aware of all the conversations among NASA's 18,000 employees.[12]

Political Considerations

Under ideal circumstances, organizational decisions are made on the basis of the objective merits of competing alternatives. In reality, many decisions are based on political considerations, such as favoritism, alliances, or the desire of the decision maker to stay in favor with people who wield power. Political factors sometimes influence which data are given serious consideration in evaluating alternatives. The decision maker may select data that support the position of an influential person whom he or she is trying to please. For instance, a financial analyst was asked to investigate the cost effectiveness of outsourcing the payroll department, so he gave considerable weight to the "facts" supplied by a provider of payroll services. This allowed him to justify having an outside firm assume responsibility for the payroll function. Political factors in decision making therefore present an ethical challenge to the decision maker.

Crisis and Conflict

In a crisis, many decision makers panic. They become less rational and more emotional than they would in a calm environment. Decision makers who are adversely affected by crisis perceive it to be a stressful event. As a consequence, they concentrate poorly, use poor judgment, and think impulsively (see the InfoTrac sidebar). Under crisis, some managers do not bother dealing with differences of opinion because they are under so much pressure. A smaller number of managers perceive a crisis as an exciting challenge that energizes them toward their best level of problem solving and decision making.

Conflict is related to crisis because both can be an emotional experience. One study analyzed strategic decision making by top management teams in both the food-processing and furniture-making industries. The researchers found that the quality of a decision appears to improve with the introduction of conflict. However, the conflict often had the negative side effect of creating antagonistic relationships among some members of the top management team.[13] (More will be said about the positive and negative aspects of conflict in Chapter 8.)

Values of the Decision Maker

Values influence decision making at every step. Ultimately, all decisions are based on values. A manager who places a high value on the personal welfare of employees tries to avoid alternatives that create hardship for workers and therefore implements decisions in ways that lessen turmoil. Another value that significantly influences decision making is the pursuit of excellence. A manager or professional who embraces the pursuit of excellence (and is therefore conscientious) will search for the high-quality alternative solution.

Attempting to preserve the status quo is a value held by many managers, as well as others. Clinging to the status quo is perceived as a hidden trap in decision making that can prevent people from making optimum decisions. People tend to cling to the status quo because they think they can prevent making a bad decision simply by not taking action at all.[14] If you value the status quo too highly, you may fail to make a decision that could bring about major improvements. At one company, the vice president of human resources received numerous inquiries about when the firm would begin offering benefits for domestic partners (of both the opposite or same sex). The vice president reasoned that since the vast majority of employees rated the benefit package highly, a change was not needed. A few employees took their complaints about "biased benefits" to the CEO. The chief executive then chastised the vice president of human resources for not suggesting an initiative that would keep the company in the forefront of human resources management.

The Firestone tire recall of 2000 was one of the biggest public relations nightmares of recent memory for both tire maker Firestone and automobile manufacturer Ford, which had installed the defective tires on its popular Explorer SUV. How well did the companies handle the situation? Log on to InfoTrac at **http://www.infotrac -college.com** and locate a selection of articles that discuss Ford CEO Jacque Nasser's performance under threat. (Nasser has since been ousted as Ford's CEO.) Have Ford and Firestone recovered from the recall?

Procrastination

Many people are poor decision makers because they **procrastinate,** or delay taking action without a valid reason. Procrastination results in indecisiveness and inaction and is a major cause of self-defeating behavior. People can overcome procrastination by learning how to become more self-disciplined. Part of the process involves setting goals for overcoming procrastination and conquering the problem in small steps. For example, a person might first practice making a deadline for a decision over a minor activity such as responding to a group of e-mail inquiries.

THE NATURE OF CREATIVITY

3

Understand the nature of creative decision making in organizations.

Creative thinking is an obvious asset when searching for creative alternatives, yet it also makes a contribution at other decision-making stages. Out-of-the-ordinary thinking, for example, makes a contribution to identifying and diagnosing problems and implementing solutions. Creativity in organizations has surged in importance in recent years for several reasons. First, the high-velocity economy requires that business firms come up with new ideas frequently. Second, a creative business culture attracts, retains, and often motivates knowledge workers. Third, using creative techniques helps generate ideas that the normal mode of brain functioning might miss.[15]

Creativity can be defined simply as the process of developing good ideas that can be put into action. The term *innovation* emphasizes the action part of creativity, such as developing an innovative product. The Crest Spinbrush™, a $6 retail battery-powered toothbrush that helped turn Crest into a billion-dollar brand, is considered to be an innovative product.

We approach the nature of creativity from three perspectives: steps in the creative process, characteristics of creative people, and conditions necessary for creativity.

Steps in the Creative Process

Understanding the steps involved in creativity helps a person become more creative and better manage creativity among others. An old but well-accepted model of creativity can be applied to organizations. The model divides creative thinking into five steps, as shown in Exhibit 5-3.

Exhibit 5-3

Steps in the Creative Process

"I see something of potential value here."

"Time for a warm bath and a long sleep."

"Time to raise some money and get a few early customers."

| Step 1 Opportunity or Problem Recognition | Step 2 Immersion | Step 3 Incubation | Step 4 Insight | Step 5 Verification and Application |

"I'm going to gather all I can find on this subject."

"Wow! I'll sell moon rocks over the Net."

Source: The original source for these stages is Graham Wallace, *The Art of Thought* (New York: Harcourt Brace, 1926.)

Step 1 is *opportunity or problem recognition:* A person discovers that a new opportunity exists or a problem needs resolution. Step 2 is *immersion:* The individual concentrates on the problem and becomes immersed in it. He or she will recall and collect information that seems relevant, dreaming up alternatives without refining or evaluating them. Step 3 is *incubation:* The person keeps the assembled information in mind for a while. He or she does not appear to be working on the problem actively, yet the subconscious mind takes over. While the information simmers, it is arranged into meaningful patterns. One way to capitalize on the incubation phase of creativity is to deliberately take a break from creative thinking. Instead, engage in a routine activity such as updating your electronic address book or sorting through mail. By immersing yourself in an entirely different and less taxing mental activity, a solution to the creative problem may emerge. Step 4 is *insight:* The problem-conquering solution flashes into the person's mind at an unexpected time, such as on the verge of sleep, during a shower, or while running. Insight is also called the Aha! Experience; all of a sudden, something clicks. Step 5 is *verification and application:* The individual sets out to prove that the creative solution has merit. Verification procedures include gathering supporting evidence, logical persuasion, and experimenting with new ideas. Application requires tenacity because most novel ideas are at first rejected as being impractical.

Although creativity usually follows the same steps, it is not a mechanical process that can be turned on and off. Much of creativity is intricately woven into a person's intellect and personality. Furthermore, creativity varies among individuals, and creative people themselves have highs and lows in their creativity.[16]

Characteristics of Creative People

Creative workers are different in many ways from their less creative counterparts. The characteristics of creative people, including creative leaders, can be grouped into three key areas: knowledge, intellectual abilities, and personality. A caution is in order. As explained by Robert J. Sternberg, so many things are true about some creative people, but there are exceptions. For example, most creative people are high in self-esteem, but not all. Yet one consistent attribute of creative people stands out—the decision to be creative. Creative people decide that they will forge their own path and follow it, for better or worse.[17]

Before studying the characteristics of creative people, compare your thinking to theirs by taking the accompanying Self-Assessment, found on page 90.

Knowledge

Creative problem solving requires a broad background of information, including facts and observations. This is particularly true because creativity often takes the form of combining two or more existing things in a new and different way. For example, Internet search engines become more profitable by combining the exquisite technology of the search engines with the concept behind the Yellow Pages. The founders of GoTo.com developed the concept of pop-up ads specifically in response to a search; a person would search for tire stores, then receive ads for tire stores. The simple model of the advertiser paying the search engine company resurrected the Internet advertising business.[18]

Intellectual Abilities

Creative problem solvers tend to be bright rather than brilliant. Intelligence and creativity tend to be moderately correlated up until an IQ of about 120 (the

SELF-ASSESSMENT

The Creative Personality Test

Directions: Describe each of the following statements as "mostly true" or "mostly false."

	Mostly True	Mostly False
1. It is generally a waste of time to read articles, Web sites, and books outside my immediate field of interest.	❏	❏
2. I frequently have the urge to suggest ways of improving products and services I use.	❏	❏
3. Reading fiction and visiting art museums are time wasters.	❏	❏
4. I am a person of very strong convictions. What is right is right; what is wrong is wrong.	❏	❏
5. I enjoy it when my boss hands me vague instructions.	❏	❏
6. Making order out of chaos is actually fun.	❏	❏
7. Only under extraordinary circumstances would I deviate from my To Do list (or other ways in which I plan my day).	❏	❏
8. Taking a different route to work is fun, even if it takes longer.	❏	❏
9. Rules and regulations should not be taken too seriously. Most rules can be broken under unusual circumstances.	❏	❏
10. Playing with a new idea is fun even if it doesn't ultimately benefit me.	❏	❏
11. Some of my best ideas have come from building on the ideas of others.	❏	❏
12. Writing should try to avoid the use of unusual words and word combinations.	❏	❏
13. I frequently jot down improvements in the job I would like to make in the future.	❏	❏
14. I prefer to avoid learning new high-technology devices as much as possible.	❏	❏
15. I prefer writing personal notes or poems to loved ones rather than relying on greeting cards.	❏	❏
16. At one time or another in my life, I have enjoyed doing puzzles.	❏	❏
17. If my thinking is clear, I will find the one best solution to a problem.	❏	❏
18. It is best to interact with coworkers who think much like I do.	❏	❏
19. Detective work would have some appeal to me.	❏	❏
20. Tight controls over people and money are necessary to run a successful organization.	❏	❏

Scoring and Interpretation: Give yourself one point for each answer in the creative direction for each question, indicated as follows:

1) Mostly False	2) Mostly True	3) Mostly False	4) Mostly False
5) Mostly True	6) Mostly True	7) Mostly False	8) Mostly True
9) Mostly True	10) Mostly True	11) Mostly True	12) Mostly False
13) Mostly True	14) Mostly False	15) Mostly True	16) Mostly True
17) Mostly False	18) Mostly False	19) Mostly True	20) Mostly False

Total _____

Extremely high or low scores are the most meaningful. A score of 15 or more suggests that your personality and attitudes are similar to those of creative people, including creative managers. A score of 8 or less suggests that you are more of an intellectual conformist at present. Don't be discouraged. Most people can develop in the direction of becoming more creative. The brainstorming exercise described in the Skill-Development Exercise on page 95 can help you enhance your creative problem solving.

How does your score compare to your self-evaluation of your creativity? We suggest that you also obtain feedback on your creativity from somebody familiar with your thinking and your work.

superior range of intelligence). Beyond that point, the relationship between intelligence and creativity becomes smaller.[19] Applying the triarchic theory of intelligence, the creative type of intelligence would obviously be important for creative problem solving. A good sense of humor and intellectual playfulness are outstanding characteristics of a creative problem solver. Humor helps release creativity, and some creativity is required to be funny.

Creative people maintain a youthful curiosity throughout their lives. The curiosity is not centered just on their own field of expertise; they are enthusiastic about solving puzzling problems. Creative people are also open and responsive to the feelings and emotions of others. They score high on the dimension of Openness. Creative people are able to think divergently. They can expand the number of alternatives to a problem, thus moving away from a single solution. Yet the creative thinker also knows when it is time to think convergently, narrowing the number of useful solutions.

Creativity can stem from both *fluid intelligence* and *crystallized intelligence*. Fluid intelligence depends on raw processing ability, or how quickly and accurately you learn information and solve problems. Like raw athletic ability, fluid intelligence begins to decline by age 30, partly because our nerve conduction slows. Crystallized intelligence is accumulated knowledge that increases with age and experience.[20] The implication for a manager who wants to assemble a creative group is to staff it with workers of varying ages. Generation X members of the group might have the wildest, most unique ideas. However, the baby boomers might have better intuition into what will work.

Personality

Creative people tend to have a positive self-image without being blindly self-confident. Because of this self-confidence, creative people are able to cope with criticism of their ideas. The type of self-confidence particularly helpful for creativity is **creative self-efficacy,** the belief that one can be creative in a work role. The major contributors to creative self-efficacy are self-efficacy about the job in general, experience on the job, and a supervisor who serves as a good model and persuades the worker that he or she is capable of finding imaginative solutions.[21]

Creative people can tolerate the isolation necessary for developing ideas. Talking to others is a good source of ideas, yet at some point the creative problem solver has to work alone and concentrate. Creative people are frequently nonconformists and do not need strong approval from a group. Many creative problem solvers are thrill seekers who find developing imaginative solutions to problems to be a source of excitement. Creative people are also persistent, which is especially important for the verification and application stage of creative thinking. Creative people enjoy dealing with ambiguity and chaos. Less creative people become quickly frustrated when task descriptions are unclear and disorder exists.

The accompanying Skill-Development Exercise gives you a chance to apply your creative personal characteristics to a challenging problem.

Conditions Necessary for Creativity

Certain individual and organizational conditions are necessary for, or at least enhance, the production of creative ideas. The most consistent of these conditions are described here.

SKILL-DEVELOPMENT EXERCISE

COLLABORATE

The Forced Association Technique

The task is for individuals or groups to solve a problem by making associations between the properties of two objects. Working alone or within a group, select a word at random from a textbook or dictionary. If you choose a preposition or adverb instead of a noun, verb, or adjective, try again. Next, list properties and attributes of this word.

Assume that your problem is to improve the job satisfaction of employees. Assume also that the word you chose at random was *jaguar*. Its attributes might include "fast moving," "energetic," "intense," "self-sufficient," and "freedom loving." The forced association is supposed to help solve the problem. Look for a link between the properties of the jaguar and the problem object. To increase job satisfaction, you might give employees more autonomy (freedom loving) and offer them opportunities for job rotation (fast moving).

Expertise, Creative-Thinking Skills, and Internal Motivation

Well-known creativity researcher Teresa M. Amabile has summarized 22 years of research about the conditions necessary for creativity in organizations. Creativity takes place when three components join together: expertise, creative-thinking skills, and the right type of motivation.[22]

Expertise refers to the necessary knowledge to put facts together. The more facts floating around in your head, the more likely you are to combine them in some useful way.

Creative thinking refers to how flexibly and imaginatively individuals approach problems. If you know how to keep digging for alternatives and avoid getting stuck in the status quo, your chances of being creative multiply. Persevering, or sticking with a problem to a conclusion, is essential for finding creative solutions. A few rest breaks to gain a fresh perspective may be helpful, but the creative person keeps coming back until a solution emerges. Quite often an executive will keep sketching different organization charts on paper or with a graphics program before the right one surfaces that will help the firm run smoothly.

The right type of motivation is the third essential ingredient for creative thought. A fascination with or passion for a task is more important than searching for external rewards. (Emotional intelligence also contains this type of motivation.) People will be the most creative when they are motivated primarily by the satisfaction and challenge of the work itself. Although Jeff Bezos ultimately became wealthy from building Amazon.com, he was primarily motivated by the challenge of finding a way to capitalize upon the potential of the Internet as a marketing vehicle.

Passion for the task and high intrinsic motivation contribute to a total absorption in the work and intense concentration, which is known as the **experience of flow.** When an experience is engrossing and enjoyable, the task becomes worth doing for its own sake regardless of the external consequences.[23] Perhaps you have had this experience when completely absorbed in a hobby or being at your best in a sport or dance. (Flow also means being "in the zone.") A highly creative businessperson, such as an entrepreneur developing a plan for worldwide distribution of a product, will often achieve the experience of flow.

Environmental Needs

Three factors outside the person play a key role in fostering creativity. An environmental need must stimulate the setting of a goal. This is another way of saying, "Necessity is the mother of invention." The attacks on the World Trade Center in September 2001 triggered safety fears among many workers in skyscrapers. In response to this need, John Rivers developed the Executive-Chute. The device enables people in high-rises to jump at least ten stories high and land safely on solid ground. Retailing for $995, the Executive-Chute was first advertised through pamphlets distributed in the Empire State Building in New York City.[24] What do you think of the sales potential for the Executive-Chute?

Conflict and Tension

Another condition that fosters creativity is the right amount of conflict and tension to put people on edge. Jerry Hirschberg, founder and president of Nissan Design International, says that people should be asked to hold what appears to be conflicting ideas in the mind simultaneously while encouraging their opposition to do the same. Understanding opposing ideas helps you gain a new perspective. An example Hirschberg offers is that Nissan asked his design team to produce a "world" car. Many staff members were threatened by the idea of a world car because it implied an ordinary vehicle of mass taste. A brave design manager, however, introduced a conflicting opinion. He said, "Whether we like it or not, there are some very successful world cars out there." (See the Video sidebar on this page.)

Once someone in the group said that producing such a car would not mean designing one to appease some low common denominator, the group no longer felt threatened. The group became eager to accept the assignment. By moving past their fears, the group conquered those fears and "embraced the dragon."[25]

Encouragement from Others

Another external factor in creativity is encouragement, including a permissive atmosphere that welcomes new ideas. A manager who encourages imaginative and original thinking, and does not punish people for making honest mistakes, is likely to receive creative ideas from employees. New research suggests that encouragement from family and friends, as well as from a supervisor, enhances creative thinking on the job. The participants in the study were both administrative and production employees in the Bulgarian knitwear industry. Support for creativity was measured by questions such as, "My family and friends outside this organization give me useful feedback about my ideas concerning the workplace." Supervisors rated employee creativity. The researchers concluded that: (a) supervisors and coworkers, and (b) family and friends each made their own contribution to worker creativity.[26]

Mood

A positive mood contributes to creative job performance, even if mood might not be truly classified as a condition necessary for creativity. In the study just mentioned, positive mood made a positive, significant contribution to creativity. A study of 222 employees in seven companies in three high-tech industries indicated that a positive mood leads to creativity.[27]

GMC Terra Cross, Concept Car (02:22)

For comparative look at creativity in the auto industry, go to **http://dubrin .swlearning.com** and view a video segment about the creation of the GMC Terra Cross, a concept car unveiled at the 2002 Detroit Auto Show aimed at a new target market, the Millenials (kids aged 11 to 22). To get to the Auto Show is no small feat, yet true concept cars rarely make it to production without serious modification. *So why commit the resources?* Our discussion of decision making and creativity offers some clues. *How important is it for car companies to explore new design trends?*

Moderate Time Pressures

Some people are at their creative best when facing heavy time pressures. Creativity studies conducted by Amabile, however, suggest that feeling crunched leads to a creativity drop for most people. The greater the time pressure, the less likely workers are to solve a tricky problem, envision a new product, or have the type of "aha!" experiences that lead to innovation. Time pressure is a creativity dampener because it limits people's freedom to reflect on different options and directions. When workers believe they are faced with an urgent mission, the negative effects of time pressures are reduced.[28]

The accompanying Organizational Behavior in Action box insert illustrates two major points about creativity already covered in this chapter.

---

4 ENHANCING AND IMPROVING CREATIVITY

Enhance your creative problem-solving ability.

A unifying theme runs through all forms of creativity training and suggestions for creativity improvement: Creative problem solving requires an ability to overcome traditional thinking. The concept of traditional thinking is relative and hard to pin down, but generally refers to a standard and frequent way of finding a solution to a problem. A non-traditional solution to a problem is thus a modal or recurring solution. For example, traditional thinking suggests that to increase revenue, a retail store should conduct a sale. Creative thinking would point toward other solutions. Bookstore chains such as Barnes & Noble, and Borders increased revenues substantially by also selling CDs and DVDs and opening cafes in their stores.

Organizational Behavior *in Action*
The Benefits of Brainstorming

Robert Barker, a *Business Week* reporter, was told by a well-known business executive Larry Bossidy that "Ideas come at unsuspecting times, at unusual places." Not long after speaking with Bossidy, Barker saw a TV commercial for the Fram SureDRAIN Fast Access Oil Change System. Anyone who has ever changed a car's oil knows that this valve-and-hose gizmo is a great idea. The valve replaces a car's drain plug. The hose directs the old oil into a container. No spills! No mess on your garage floor. Who had this brainstorm?

The reporter found out that Honeywell owns Fram. Jim Brown, director of new product development for Honeywell's Consumer Product Group, gets the credit for the SureDRAIN. "I was on an airport shuttle in Phoenix, going to our sales meeting, and I was talking to our international sales manager," Brown said. "He had just burned his hand while changing his oil, and it got all over his driveway." In a flash of insight, Brown had an idea. He saw a way to sell valve-and-hose oil drain systems that had been available only to owners of heavy-duty trucks up until then.

Why, Barker asked, had inspiration struck in the airport shuttle? "Because it was the beginning of the sales meeting and I was keyed up and enthusiastic," Brown said. "I was receptive."

Questions

1. How does this case incident relate to the stages of creative thought?
2. What might this case incident illustrate about the conditions necessary for creativity?

Source: Based on Robert Barker, "The Art of Bainstorming," *Business Week*, August 26, 2002, p. 169.

The central task in becoming creative is to break down rigid thinking that blocks new ideas. A conventional-thinking manager might accept the long-standing policy that spending more than $5,000 requires three levels of approval. A creative leader might ask, "Why do we need three levels of approval for spending $5,000? If we trust people enough to make them managers, why can't they have budget authorization to spend up to $10,000?"

Overcoming traditional thinking is so important to creative thinking that the process has been characterized in several different ways. A representative concept is that *a creative person thinks outside the box*. A "box" in this sense is a category that confines and restricts thinking. Many executives have saved millions of company dollars by thinking outside the box that says headquarters must be located in a major city or that a firm must do its own manufacturing.

Here we describe several illustrative approaches and techniques for enhancing employee creativity. Recognize also that the conditions for creativity just described can be converted into techniques for creativity enhancement. For example, a manager might be able to enhance creativity by encouraging imaginative thinking.

1. *Brainstorming.* Brainstorming is the best-known technique for developing mental flexibility, which most of you have already done. As a refresher, do the Skill-Development Exercise that follows, which presents rules and guidelines for brainstorming and also gives a challenging Internet business development task. Brainstorming is also accomplished through e-mail, in which participants simultaneously enter their suggestions into a computer. Each participant's input appears simultaneously on the screen of the other participants. In this way, nobody feels intimidated by a dominant member, and participants think more independently. The forced-association technique presented in the earlier Skill-Development Exercise is a variant of brainstorming.

SKILL-DEVELOPMENT EXERCISE

COLLABORATE

Brainstorming

After studying the following rules for brainstorming, organize into groups to play "Get Rich Dot Com":

1. Use groups of five to seven people.
2. Encourage the spontaneous expression of ideas. All suggestions are welcome, even if they seem outlandish or outrageous at first glance. Avoid evaluating suggestions at this point, particularly with respect to making negative statements about suggestions.
3. Quantity and variety are important. The greater the number of ideas, the greater is the likelihood of a breakthrough idea.
4. Encourage combination and improvement of ideas. This process is referred to as piggybacking or hitchhiking.
5. Use a room with natural light if possible. Sunlight, and the cheerfulness of a real window, facilitates creativity for many people.
6. One person serves as the secretary and records ideas, writing them on a sheet of paper, white board, chalkboard, flip chart, or computer.
7. Do not overstructure the session by following any of the rules too rigidly. Brainstorming is a spontaneous process.

Group Activity: Your group assumes the role of a team of people who want to start an Internet company. Your task is to develop a domain name (URL) and a general explanation of your business model. In other words, explain how you intend to generate revenue (or a profit) from your site. Strive to think of a business that would actually stand a chance of making money.

2. *Idea quotas.* A straightforward and effective technique for enhancing worker creativity is to simply demand that workers come up with good ideas. Dana Corporation sets idea quotas—two ideas per employee per month. Everyone in the company, from the CEO to production workers, must generate ideas. The company strives for 80 percent participation and 80 percent implementation. Employees are asked to focus on quality, customer service, production control, office efficiency, and security. At one Dana division, profitability increased 40 percent after idea quotas were imposed.[29]

3. *Heterogeneous groups.* Forming heterogeneous groups can enhance creativity because a diverse group brings various viewpoints to the problem at hand. Key diversity factors include professional discipline, job experiences, and a variety of demographic factors. Diverse groups encourage diverse thinking, which is the essence of creativity.[30] A culturally diverse group can be effective at developing creative marketing ideas to appeal to a particular cultural group. Levi-Strauss has on occasion included an adolescent in a problem-solving group to help understand what type of jeans appeal to members of that age group.

4. *Financial incentives.* A variety of laboratory studies have concluded that working for external rewards, particularly financial rewards, dampens creativity.[31] If you focus on the reward, you may lose out on the joy (internal rewards) of being creative. In work settings, however, financial incentives are likely to spur imaginative thinking. Such incentives might include paying employees for useful suggestions, and paying scientists royalties for patents that become commercially useful. For example, IBM has ranked first for 10 consecutive years (up through 2002) with respect to being awarded patents. IBM employees who are awarded patents are paid cash bonuses.[32]

5. *Architecture and physical layout.* Many companies restructure space to fire up creativity, harness energy, and enhance the flow of knowledge and ideas. Any

IMPLICATIONS FOR MANAGERIAL PRACTICE

1. When making nonprogrammed decisions of importance, follow carefully the decision-making steps. Although going through the steps may appear time consuming, the payout can be decisions of higher quality. Because so many decisions about organizational behavior are nonprogrammed, it is worthwhile to follow the decision-making steps.

2. A key strategy for improving managerial decision making is for the manager to enhance his or her creativity. When faced with a problem, the manager should exercise discipline to search for several alternative solutions, which is the essence of creativity.

3. To unleash creativity, it may be necessary to help group members overcome the feeling that bringing about change is almost impossible. An approach worth a try is to use the simple phrase, "Up until now" in a brainstorming session or staff meeting. Here is how it works: The group says, "Management won't let us try that." You reply, "Up until now, we haven't asked to try that."[33]

4. Learning to be more creative is like learning other skills: Patience and time are required. As a manager, by practicing techniques and attitudes, you will gain the confidence and skill to build a group (or company) where creative thinking is widespread. A desirable goal is to find a way to tap the creativity of everyone for whom you are responsible.[34]

configuration of the physical environment that decreases barriers to divergence, incubation, and convergence is likely to stimulate the flow of creative thinking.[35] The reasoning is that creative thinking is more likely to be enhanced by cubicles rather than corner offices, by elevators rather than escalators, and by atriums rather than hallways. In short, creating the opportunity for physical interaction facilitates the flow of ideas, which in turn facilitates creative thinking.

6. *Inspiration.* A leadership strategy for enhancing creativity and innovation is to inspire workers to think creatively. Inspiring creativity encompasses a wide range of behaviors, including establishing a permissive atmosphere. David Vasella, the chairman and CEO of a pharmaceutical company, offers an illustrative approach to inspiring innovation in product development and operations. Leadership at the company attempts to align business objectives with the company's ideals. Vasella says that people "do a better job when they believe in what they do and in how the company behaves, when they see that their work does more than enrich shareholders."[36]

SUMMARY OF KEY POINTS

1 Work through the classical/behavioral decision-making model when faced with a major decision.

A decision takes place when a person chooses from among two or more alternatives in order to solve a problem. Programmed decisions are made in response to uncomplicated problems, while nonprogrammed decisions are unique responses to complex problems. The degree of risk associated with a decision can be classified into three categories: certainty, risk, and uncertainty. If you frame a decision in terms of winning, you are more likely to take a chance on an outcome of potential value.

A classical/behavioral decision-making model incorporates the ideas that managers make decisions in a generally rational framework, yet intuition and judgment also enter into the model. The seven steps in the model are as follows: (1) identify and diagnose the problem, (2) establish decision criteria, (3) develop creative alternatives, (4) evaluate the alternatives, (5) choose one alternative, (6) implement the decision, and (7) evaluate and control.

2 Identify and describe factors that influence the effectiveness of decision making.

Bounded rationality means that people's limited mental abilities, combined with external influences over which they have little or no control, prevent them from making entirely rational decisions. Satisficing decisions result from bounded rationality. A host of influences contribute to bounded rationality, including the following: intuition, personality and cognitive intelligence, emotional intelligence, quality and accessibility of information, political considerations, crisis and conflict, the values of the decision maker, and procrastination.

3 Understand the nature of creative decision making in organizations.

Understanding the steps involved in creativity can help a person become more creative and better manage creativity among others. The steps are as follows: (1) opportunity or problem recognition, (2) immersion, (3) incubation, (4) insight, and (5) verification and application.

Creative workers are different from others in several key areas. They typically have a broad background of knowledge, tend to be bright rather than brilliant, have a youthful curiosity, and think divergently. Both fluid intelligence and crystallized intelligence contribute to creativity. Creative workers tend to have a positive self-image, including creative self-efficacy, and are often nonconformists who enjoy intellectual thrills, along with ambiguity and chaos.

For creativity to occur, three components must join together: expertise, creative-thinking skills, and internal motivation characterized by a passion for the task. Total absorption in the work, also known as the experience of flow, is also important. An environmental need should be present, along with some conflicting opinions. A positive mood also contributes to creativity, as does moderate time pressures.

4 Enhance your creative problem-solving ability.

A unifying theme runs through all forms of creativity training and suggestions for creativity improvement: Creative problem solving requires an ability to overcome traditional thinking. Techniques for enhancing creativity include brainstorming, imposing idea quotas, forming heterogeneous groups, offering financial incentives for creative problem solving, using a physical layout conducive to creative thinking, and developing inspiration.

KEY TERMS AND PHRASES

Decision, *79*
The act of choosing among two or more alternatives in order to solve a problem.

Problem, *79*
A discrepancy between the ideal and the real.

Programmed (or Routine) Decision, *79*
A standard response to an uncomplicated problem.

Non-programmed (or Non-routine) Decision, *79*
A unique response to a complex problem.

Classical Decision Model, *80*
An approach to decision making that views the manager's environment as certain and stable and the manager as rational.

Behavioral Decision Model, *80*
An approach to decision making that views managers as having cognitive limitations and acting only in terms of what they perceive in a given situation.

Decision Criteria, *82*
The standards of judgment used to evaluate alternatives.

Bounded Rationality, *83*
The idea that people's limited mental abilities, combined with external influences over which they have little or no control, prevent them from making entirely rational decisions.

Satisficing Decision, *83*
A decision that provides a minimum standard of satisfaction.

Heuristics, *84*
Simplified strategies that become rules of thumb in decision making.

Intuition, *84*
An experience-based way of knowing or reasoning in which weighing and balancing evidence are done automatically.

Self-efficacy, *85*
The feeling of being an effective and competent person with respect to a task.

Procrastinate, *88*
Delaying to take action without a valid reason.

Creativity, *88*
The process of developing good ideas that can be put into action.

Creative Self-efficacy, *91*
The belief that one can be creative in a work role.

Experience of Flow, *92*
Being "in the zone"; total absorption in one's work.

DISCUSSION QUESTIONS AND ACTIVITIES

1. What really was the problem that a reverse mortgage was intended to resolve?
2. Can you give an example of a failed decision in business? Explain why you consider the decision to be a failure.
3. Which decision criteria are relevant for you in choosing a career?
4. How would the concept of bounded rationality apply to making decisions about financial investments?
5. A technique for creative problem solving is to remind oneself of a problem just before going to sleep. Upon waking up, a good solution often presents itself. How does this technique relate to the stages of creative thought?
6. How does your mood contribute to your creativity? Describe the evidence supporting your answer.
7. Ask an experienced worker what he or she believes is the most important action a manager can take to enhance creative thinking among group members. Compare the response you get with the information in this chapter.

ORGANIZATIONAL BEHAVIOR ONLINE

TO DO

Creativity Training
Many Web sites offer creativity training. One such site is http://www.before-after.com. Before and After, Inc. mentions many reasons for improving creativity including helping visitors to "Bring greater creativity to your sales process," "Infuse your meeting with creative energy," and "Find creative inspiration." We especially recommend going to the 2-minute Creative IQ test. How does this test compare to the creativity test you took in this chapter? If http://www.before-after.com is no longer in operation, insert "creativity training" in your search engine to find a comparable site.

TO BOOKMARK

Decision Making
http://www.instituteforstrategicclarity.org/dmp.htm

Problem Solving
http://www.gocreate.com/animal

Creativity
http://www.myskillsprofile.com (see the test in the Creativity and Innovation section)

Critical Thinking
http://www.businesspotential.com/critic_think.htm

CASE PROBLEM: Big Electricity Fights Little Squirrel

Robin Folcik was reading the newspaper at breakfast one Sunday when the lights blinked, smoke poured from the sockets, and a charged buzz came over the room. "I thought my house was blowing up," recalls Ms. Folcik, a waitress in Southington, Conn.

Connecticut Light & Power found "remnants of a squirrel" and shards of a ceramic electrical switch at the base of utility pole #85324. The conclusion: A squirrel had electrocuted itself and, in so doing, triggered a massive power surge that blew out appliances all over the neighborhood.

Like many other utilities, Connecticut Power is having trouble these days with squirrel-induced damage. In recent years utilities have stepped up efforts to fight off acrobatic rodents—buying everything from predator urine to baffles that look like pizza pans to fend them off. It's a war that the squirrels are winning, escalating as the electrical grid spreads and more wires are closer to animals whose natural habitat has been destroyed. Longmont Power & Communications, which serves 35,000 customers north of Denver, has reported that more than 90% of its significant outages were caused by squirrels, that cut the power 393 times in 2002, despite measures Longmont had taken to thwart them by banding utility poles with slippery, hard plastic.

What customers don't understand, say exasperated utility workers, is that the cute little forager is an obsessive foe. A squirrel's teeth grows six to ten inches a year, unless the rodent has plenty to gnaw on. Squirrels follow paths that they have taken before, and have an internal navigation system for following a route over and over, using remembered objects to plot a fix with singular determination. "A squirrel thinks, 'This is the way I've gone all my life, and just because you built a substation, don't think for one minute I'm not going to go there,'" says Shelia Frazier, who advises utilities as a senior project manager for Energy Consulting Group LLC of Marietta, GA.

Falling trees and branches obviously cause plenty of outages, too, but dealing with squirrels is a persistent aggravation. Many utilities say trapping squirrels is too expensive. Shooting them is costly and in many places restricted. Thus the development of anti-squirrel gear is surging.

Entrepreneur Douglas Wulff, of Columbia, Mo. hopes for a high sales with his $50 "Critter Pole Guard." Introduced last year, it looks like a string of polypropylene bratwurst that wraps around a utility pole. When a squirrel tries to clamber over it, the bratwurst spins and tosses the animal off. In Chicago, Joe Seid, sales manager at Bird-X, Inc. is pushing products such as the $95 Transonic IXL. Based on, he says, "psycho acoustic jamming" principles, it blasts high intensity sound waves that can't be heard by humans but sound like jackhammers to squirrels.

More than 100 Connecticut Light and Power customers have sought damages for ruined appliances, including Ms. Folcik, who protested that she lost two TV sets, a Sony PlayStation, two video-recorders, an air conditioner, a stereo and speakers, and a treadmill. Customers also want the utility to spend more on maintenance, and have taken their case to the state's Department of Public Utility Control. They don't buy the squirrel story and have suggested that "perhaps C&P maintenance crews were responsible." "I thought, 'A squirrel? Oh yeah? Again?'" says Ms. Flocik. "It has happened before, and they always blame it on a squirrel."

Case Questions

1. What is the real problem facing the utility companies in the conflict with squirrels? Provide a diagnosis.
2. Of the several solutions to the squirrel problem mentioned in the case, which one do you think is the most likely to ward off squirrels?
3. What creative solution can you offer to the squirrel problem facing the utilities?
4. How might the interests of the utility companies, their customers, and animal rights activists be balanced in resolving the dilemma facing the utility companies?

Source: Reprinted with permission of *The Wall Street Journal* from Barbara Carton, "Fried Squirrel Is Not a Favorite Dish with Public Utilities," *The Wall Street Journal*, February 4, 2003, pp. A1, A15. Permission conveyed through Copyright Clearance Center, Inc.

ENDNOTES

1. Paul C. Nutt, *Why Decisions Fail* (San Francisco: Berrett-Koehler, 2002).
2. Research by Daniel Kahneman and Amos Tversky cited in Deborah Smith, "Psychologist Wins Nobel Prize," *Monitor on Psychology,* December 2002, p. 22; "You Can't Beat the Market, Nobel Laureate Advises," Associated Press, January 2, 2003.
3. James L. Bowditch and Anthony F. Buono, *A Primer on Organizational Behavior,* 5th ed. (New York: Wiley, 2001), p. 50.
4. "Solving Problems," in *Business: The Ultimate Resource* (Cambridge, MA: Perseus Books Group, 2002), p. 409.
5. Min Basadur, "Managing Creativity: A Japanese Model," *Academy of Management Executive,* May 1992, p. 30.
6. Herbert A. Simon, "Rational Choice and the Structure of the Environment," *Psychological Review* 63, 1956, pp. 129–138.
7. Gerd Gigerenzer and Reinhard Selten (eds.), *Bounded Rationality: The Adaptive Toolbox* (Cambridge, MA: MIT Press, 2001).
8. Lisa A. Burke and Monica K. Miller, "Taking the Mystery Out of Intuitive Decision Making," *Academy of Management Executive,* November 1999, pp. 91–99.
9. Russell Wild, "Naked Hunch," *Success,* June 1998, p. 55.
10. Interview with Daniel Kahneman in Hope Yen, "Kahneman Says Overconfidence Prefaced Plunge," Associated Press, January 5, 2003.
11. Michael A. West and James L. Farr (eds.), *Innovation and Creativity at Work: Psychological and Organizational Strategies* (New York: John Wiley, 1990).
12. The quote is from "Inquiry Puts Early Focus on Heat Tiles," *New York Times,* February 2, 2003; Larry Wheeler, "NASA Chief Calls on Columbia," *The New York Times,* February 28, 2003.
13. Allen C. Amason, "Distinguishing the Effects of Functional and Dysfunctional Conflict on Strategic Decision-making

Effectiveness," *Academy of Management Journal,* February 1996, pp. 123–148.

14. John S. Hammond, Ralph L. Keeney, and Howard Rafia, "The Hidden Traps in Decision Making," *Harvard Business Review,* September–October 1998, p. 50.

15. Juanita Weaver, "The Missing Think," *Entrepreneur,* January 2003, p. 68.

16. Teresa M. Amabile, "The Social Psychology of Creativity: A Componential Conceptualization," *Journal of Personality and Social Psychology,* August 1983, pp. 357–376.

17. Robert J. Sternberg, "Creativity as a Decision," *American Psychologist,* May 2002, p. 376.

18. Ben Elgin and Timothy J. Mullaney, "Search Engines Are Picking Up Steam," *Business Week,* March 24, 2003, p. 86.

19. Dorothy Leonard and Walter Swap, *When Sparks Fly: Igniting Creativity in Small Groups* (Boston: Harvard Business School Press, 1999).

20. "Why Kids Beat Adults at Video Games: The Two Types of Intelligence," *USA Weekend,* January 1–3, 1999, p. 5.

21. Pamela Tierney and Steven M. Farmer, "Creative Self-Efficacy: Its Potential Antecedents and Relationship to Creative Performance," *Academy of Management Journal,* December 2002, pp. 1137–1148.

22. Teresa M. Amabile, "How to Kill Creativity," *Harvard Business Review,* September–October 1998, pp. 78–79.

23. Mihaly Csikzentmihalyi, "If We Are So Rich, Why Aren't We Happy?" *American Psychologist,* October 1999, p. 824.

24. Janet Morrissey, "Executive-Chute Addresses New Fears," *The Wall Street Journal,* July 17, 2002.

25. "Creativity First," *Leadership* (American Management Association International), May 1998, pp. 5–6.

26. Nora Madjar, Greg R. Oldham, and Michael G. Pratt, "There's No Place Like Home? The Contributions of Work and Nonwork to Creativity Support to Employee's Creative Performance," *Academy of Management Journal,* August 2002, pp. 757–767.

27. Teresa M. Amabile, Sigal G. Barsade, Jennifer S. Mueller, and Barry M. Staw, "Affect and Creativity at Work: A Daily Longitudinal Test," submitted for publication, March 2003.

28. Research cited in Bridget Murray, "A Ticking Clock Means a Creativity Drop," *Monitor on Psychology,* November 2002, p. 24; Teresa M. Amabile, Constance N. Hadley, and Steven J. Kramer, "Creativity Under the Gun," *Harvard Business Review,* August 2002, pp. 52–61.

29. "Generate More Ideas with Quotas," *Managers Edge,* November 1998, p. 5.

30. Leonard and Swap, *When Sparks Fly;* G. Pasacal Zachary, "Mighty Is the Mongrel," *Fast Company,* July 2000, p. 272.

31. Beth' A. Hennessey and Teresa M. Amabile, "Reward, Intrinsic Motivation, and Creativity," *American Psychologist,* June 1998, pp. 674–675.

32. "Xerox Ranks 19th, Kodak 21st for Most '02 Patents," *Bloomberg News,* January 14, 2003.

33. "Three 'Creative' Words," *Managers Edge,* September 1998, p. 1.

34. Juanita Weaver, "Food for Thought," *Entrepreneur,* March 2003, pp. 62, 63.

35. Dorothy Leonard and Walter Swap, "Igniting Creativity," *Workforce,* October 1999, pp. 87–89.

36. Quoted in "Inspiring Innovation," *Harvard Business Review,* August 2002, p. 48.

CHAPTER 6

Foundation Concepts of Motivation

Hank McKinnell is the chairman and CEO of Pfizer in New York. When asked by the editors of *Harvard Business Review,* how you inspire ordinary people to do extraordinary things, he replied, "You motivate people by moving quickly toward a goal, especially if getting to the goal involves pain. Knowing that the organization is committed to quick, decisive action frees people to think creatively and work in concert.

"We saw this in the integration of Pfizer and Warner-Lambert a few years ago. We won our bid for the company, but what we won was a firm thoroughly demoralized by a takeover battle. In my first meetings with the transition teams, I emphasized that we had to build a new company quickly, particularly before our largest competitor settled its own merger issues. The vision was ambitious—integrate Pfizer and Warner-Lambert, seek best practices where appropriate, and be ready to operate as a totally unified organization barely five months after the two companies agreed to the union.

"We gave people permission to move fast and to make mistakes—as long as their actions were in keeping with our values of integrity, performance, and respect for people. The emphasis on speed tamped down resentment, turf issues, and 'paralysis by analysis.' In our U.S. sales force alone, for example, teams from both companies recommended more than 200 changes in operations and policies, and nearly all of them were accepted. Ultimately, hundreds of transition teams, composed of excellent people from both companies, knit together a nearly seamless new Pfizer that was totally operational just a few hours before signing the closing papers."

OBJECTIVES

After reading and studying this chapter and doing the exercises, you should be able to:

1 Describe several need theories of motivation, including the needs hierarchy, the two-factor theory, and the achievement–power–affiliation triad.

2 Summarize the key propositions of goal theory and reinforcement theory.

3 Explain the expectancy theory of motivation.

4 Explain how equity and social comparison contribute to motivation.

5 Use social learning theory to motivate yourself.

6 Recognize the importance of both intrinsic and extrinsic motivators.

7 Explain how personality factors are related to motivation.

NOW ASK YOURSELF: What setting challenging goals has to do with motivating a workforce? Setting challenging goals, even ones generally acknowledged to be painful to implement, is a way to focus attention and energize employees' efforts. Goal setting in the workplace is one of the foundation explanations of motivation presented in this chapter. Another involves reinforcement. In the following chapter, we describe managerial techniques designed to enhance motivation, all based on motivation theory. This chapter also touches on practical approaches to motivation, but it starts with the basics—the basics of motivation. Knowledge and skill in motivating people is a topic of perennial interest to managers and professionals and important contributors to their eventual success.

Motivation (in a work setting) is the process by which behavior is mobilized and sustained in the interest of achieving organizational goals. We know a person is motivated when he or she actually expends effort toward goal attainment. Motivation is complex and encompasses a broad range of behaviors, many of which are described in this and the following chapter. To assess the effectiveness of your present knowledge of motivating others, take the Self-Assessment on page 103.

NEED THEORIES OF MOTIVATION

The simplest explanation of motivation is one of the most powerful: People are willing to expend effort toward achieving a goal because it satisfies one of their important needs. Self-interest is thus a driving force. This principle is referred to as "What's in it for me?" or WIIFM (pronounced "wiff 'em"). Reflect on your own experience. Before working hard to accomplish a task, you probably want to know how you will benefit. If your manager asks you to work extra hours to take care of an emergency, you will most likely oblige. Yet underneath you might be thinking, "If I work these extra hours, my boss will think highly of me. As a result, I will probably receive a good performance evaluation and maybe a better-than-average salary increase."

Here we describe three classic need theories of motivation: the need hierarchy, the two-factor theory, and the achievement–power–affiliation triad.

Maslow's Hierarchy of Needs

Based on his work as a clinical psychologist, Abraham M. Maslow developed a comprehensive view of individual motivation.[1] **Maslow's hierarchy of needs** arranges human needs into a pyramid-shaped model with basic physiological needs at the bottom and self-actualization needs at the top (see Exhibit 6-1). Lower-order needs must be satisfied to ensure a person's existence, security, and requirements for human contact. Higher-order needs are concerned with personal development and reaching one's potential. Before higher-level needs are activated, the lower-order needs must be satisfied. The five levels of needs are described next.

1. *Physiological needs.* At the first level are basic bodily needs such as the need for water, air, food, rest, and sleep. Should these needs be unfulfilled, the individ-

Describe several need theories of motivation, including the needs hierarchy, the two-factor theory, and the achievement–power–affiliation triad.

SELF-ASSESSMENT

Motivating Others

Describe how often you act or think in the way indicated by the statements below when you are attempting to motivate another person. Use the following scale: very infrequently (VI); infrequently (I); sometimes (S); frequently (F); very frequently (VF).

		VI	I	S	F	VF
1.	I ask the other person what he or she is hoping to achieve in the situation.	1	2	3	4	5
2.	I attempt to figure out if the person has the ability to do what I need done.	1	2	3	4	5
3.	When another person is heel-dragging, it usually means he or she is lazy.	5	4	3	2	1
4.	I tell the person I'm trying to motivate exactly what I want.	1	2	3	4	5
5.	I like to give the other person a reward up front so he or she will be motivated.	5	4	3	2	1
6.	I give lots of feedback when another person is performing a task for me.	1	2	3	4	5
7.	I like to belittle the person enough so that he or she will be intimidated into doing what I need done.	5	4	3	2	1
8.	I make sure that the other person feels treated fairly.	1	2	3	4	5
9.	I figure that if I smile nicely enough I can get the other person to work as hard as I need.	5	4	3	2	1
10.	I attempt to get done what I need by instilling fear in the other person.	5	4	3	2	1
11.	I specify exactly what needs to be accomplished.	1	2	3	4	5
12.	I generously praise people who help me get my work accomplished.	1	2	3	4	5
13.	A job well done is its own reward. I therefore keep praise to a minimum.	5	4	3	2	1
14.	I make sure to let people know how well they have done in meeting my expectations on a task.	1	2	3	4	5
15.	To be fair, I attempt to reward people about the same no matter how well they have performed.	5	4	3	2	1
16.	When somebody doing work for me performs well, I recognize his or her accomplishments promptly.	1	2	3	4	5
17.	Before giving somebody a reward, I attempt to find out what would appeal to that person.	1	2	3	4	5
18.	I make it a policy not to thank somebody for doing a job he or she is paid to do.	5	4	3	2	1
19.	If people do not know how to perform a task, their motivation will suffer.	1	2	3	4	5
20.	If properly designed, many jobs can be self-rewarding.	1	2	3	4	5

Total Score _____

Scoring and interpretation: Add the numbers circled to obtain your total score.

90–100   You have advanced knowledge and skill with respect to motivating others in a work environment. Continue to build on the solid base you have established.

50–89   You have average knowledge and skill with respect to motivating others. With additional study and experience, you will probably develop advanced motivational skills.

20–49   To effectively motivate others in a work environment you will need to greatly expand your knowledge of motivation theory and techniques.

Source: The idea for this quiz, and a few of the items, are from David A. Whetton and Kim S. Cameron, *Developing Management Skills*, 5th ed. (New York: HarperCollins, 2002), pp. 302–303.

Exhibit 6-1

Maslow's Hierachy of Needs

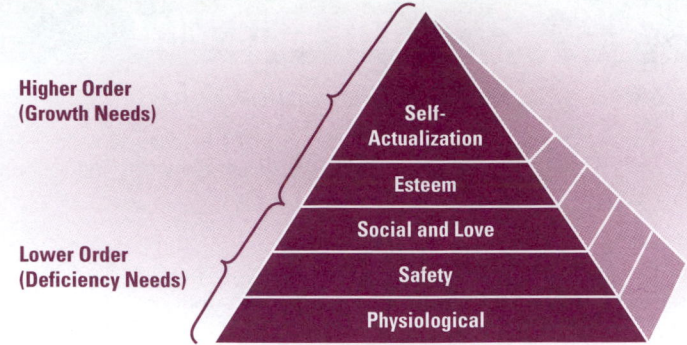

Higher Order (Growth Needs)

Self-Actualization

Esteem

Social and Love

Lower Order (Deficiency Needs)

Safety

Physiological

ual will be preoccupied with satisfying them. Once met, the second level of needs emerges.

2. *Safety needs.* At the second level are needs relating to obtaining a secure environment without threats to well-being. These include needs for security and freedom from environmental threat. Many employees who work at dangerous jobs, such as loggers and miners, would be motivated by the chance to have safer working conditions. Sexual harassment is an example of the safety need for security becoming frustrated, because the harassed person is subjected to an environmental threat. After a person feels safe and secure, a third level of needs emerges.

3. *Social and love needs.* Needs at this level include belonging to a group, affiliating with people, giving and receiving love, and sexual activity. Frustration of needs at this level can lead to serious personal problems. Managers can contribute to the satisfaction of social needs by promoting teamwork and encouraging social interaction in matters concerning work problems. When social and love needs are reasonably met, the person seeks to satisfy esteem needs.

4. *Esteem needs.* Needs at this level include self-respect based on genuine achievement, respect from others, prestige, recognition, and appreciation. Occupations with high status satisfy esteem needs. Managers can satisfy the esteem needs of employees by praising their work and giving them the opportunity for recognition. After reasonable satisfaction of esteem needs, most people will strive to achieve more of their potential through self-actualization.

5. *Self-actualization needs.* At the top of the hierarchy are needs for self-fulfilment and personal development and the need to grow to one's fullest potential. Self-actualized people are those who have become what they are capable of becoming. Managers can help employees move toward self-actualization by giving them challenging assignments, including the chance to do creative work. The U.S. Army ad campaign slogan "Be all that you can be" was pitched at self-actualization needs.

A key principle of the needs hierarchy is that, as needs at a given level are gratified, they lose their potency (strength). The next level of need is then activated. A satisfied need ceases to be a motivator. For instance, once employees can pay for the necessities of life, they ordinarily seek opportunities for satisfying social relationships.

Many people think that, for the vast majority of workers, the only sensible way to motivate them is to satisfy higher-level needs. Many exceptions still exist. A program of providing backup child care helps workers deal with social and love needs.

Another consideration is that, even during prosperous times, there are many corporate downsizings that pose a threat to satisfying basic needs, such as security. The many sweatshops still operating in the garment-manufacturing business pay workers wages that make paying for food and rent a major struggle.[2] The practical implication here is that many workers today can be motivated by offering them an opportunity to satisfy basic needs through such means as job security and a living wage.

Herzberg's Two-Factor Theory

The study of the needs hierarchy led to the **two-factor theory of work motivation.** According to the research of Frederick Herzberg, there are two different sets of job factors.[3] One set, the motivators or satisfiers, can motivate and satisfy workers. The other set, dissatisfiers, or hygiene factors, can only prevent dissatisfaction. Motivators relate to higher-order needs, while hygiene factors relate to lower-order needs.

Key Points in the Theory

The two-factor theory explains how to design jobs to make them motivational. The motivational elements are the intrinsic, or job content, factors that make a job exciting. Motivator factors include achievement, recognition, advancement, responsibility, the work itself, and personal growth possibilities. The extrinsic, or job context, factors are hygienic. Although they are health maintaining and desirable, they are not motivational. Examples of hygiene factors are pay, status, job security, working conditions, and quality of leadership. Herzberg believed that motivation increases when one combines pay with a motivator such as challenging work. (Money is so widely used to enhance motivation that the topic will be treated separately in Chapter 7.) Exhibit 6-2 presents examples of motivator and hygiene factors.

According to the two-factor theory, only the presence of motivator factors leads to more positive energized behavior. For example, challenging work will motivate many people to exert increased effort. If intrinsic factors such as challenging work are not present, the result is neutral rather than negative, and the worker will feel bland rather than angry or unhappy. Although the presence of hygiene (or extrinsic) factors is not motivational, their absence can cause dissatisfaction as in the following illustration. A police captain reported that when officers were assigned old patrol cars, they complained frequently. However, when assigned brand new patrol cars, they did not express much appreciation. Nor did they increase their productivity as measured by the number of citations issued.

Evaluation

The two-factor theory has made two lasting contributions to work motivation. First, it has helped managers realize that money is not always the primary motivator. Second, it has spurred much of the interest in designing jobs to make them more intrinsically satisfying. The enrichment of individual jobs led to the enrichment of work group activities, which in turn spurred the development of self-managing work teams. All these topics are discussed in subsequent chapters.

A major problem with the two-factor theory is that it de-emphasizes individual differences and glosses over the importance of hygiene factors in attracting and retaining workers. Hygiene factors such as good benefits and company management satisfy and motivate many people. Many working parents will work extra

Exhibit 6-2

Examples of Motivator and Hygiene Factors

Motivator Factors (Sources of Job Satisfaction and Motivation)	Hygiene Factors (Sources of Job Dissatisfaction; Neutral to Motivation)
Challenge of the work itself	Physical working conditions
Responsibility	Company policies
Recognition	Quality of supervision
Achievement	Coworker relationships
Job advancement and professional growth	Salary
	Status
	Job security
	Benefits, such as medical insurance

hard to keep their jobs at a company that offers on-site child care or flexible working hours. Another problem with the two-factor theory is that some workers show no particular interest in such motivators as opportunities for growth and advancement. They work primarily so they can pay their bills and enjoy their time with family and friends.

McClelland's Achievement—Power—Affiliation Triad

Many other needs influence job behavior in addition to those mentioned specifically in the need hierarchy. (One example is the need for thrill seeking, as implied from the discussion of the trait for risk taking and thrill seeking described in Chapter 2.) David C. McClelland and his associates have provided a useful explanation of several of these needs.[4] They have proposed a theory of motivation based on the premise that people acquire or learn certain needs from their culture. Among the cultural influences are family, peer groups, television shows, and Web sites. When a need is strong enough, it prompts a person to engage in work activities to satisfy it. Three key acquired needs are achievement, power, and affiliation.

The Need for Achievement

The **need for achievement** is the desire to accomplish something difficult for its own sake. People with a strong need for achievement frequently think of how to do a job better. They are also concerned with how to progress in their careers. Workers with a high need for achievement are interested in monetary rewards primarily as feedback about how well they are achieving. Responsibility seeking is another characteristic of people with a high need for achievement. They also set realistic yet moderately difficult goals, take calculated risks, and desire feedback on performance. (A moderately difficult goal challenges a person but is not so difficult as to most likely lead to failure and frustration.) In general, those who enjoy building business, activities, and programs from scratch have a strong need for achievement.

The Need for Power

The **need for power** is the desire to control other people, to influence their behavior, and to be responsible for them. Managers with a high need for power wish to control resources (such as money and real estate) in addition to people. A person with a strong need for power spends time thinking about influencing and controlling others and about gaining a position of authority and status. Wanting to make a positive impact is also part of the power motive. Executives who have buildings named after themselves or buy professional athletic teams have strong power needs. The need for power is the primary motivator of successful managers.[5]

For managing big companies, a manager's desire to have an impact and be strong and influential is more important than the need to get things done or the desire to be liked. One problem with someone with a strong achievement drive in a large company is that the manager will attempt to accomplish too much personally rather than spread the task among many workers.[6]

The Need for Affiliation

The **need for affiliation** is the desire to establish and maintain friendly and warm relationships with others. People motivated this way care about restoring disrupted relationships and soothing hurt feelings. They want to engage in work that permits close companionship. Successful managers have low affiliation needs, but managers with an extremely low need for affiliation may not show adequate concern for the needs of others.

The needs just described were originally studied through a projective test, called the Thematic Apperception Test. The term *projective* describes when subjects project their needs into a stimulus, such as a photograph or drawing. Visualize a photograph of a young woman carrying a briefcase and entering a large office building. She is standing outside the elevator. A person with a strong need for power might make the interpretation, "The woman is hoping to become an executive some day. I can see how longingly she is looking at the offices above." A person with a strong need for achievement might say, "The woman is on her way to making a big sale. She is determined to do what it takes to close the sale today." A person with a strong need for affiliation might say, "It's lunch time. The woman is on her way to meet her friends and have a great time socializing."

In reality, the projections are much more subtle. Projective tests have elaborate scoring schemes that are interpreted only by psychologists or professionals working under their supervision.

The acquired needs theory has made an important contribution in identifying needs related to managerial performance. For example, many studies have shown that successful executives have a strong need for power. Another consistent finding is that entrepreneurs have a strong need for achievement. However, the achievement–power–affiliation triad is not a complete explanation of work motivation, because it focuses on just several key needs. Similarly, needs theories in general explain only part of motivation. The remaining sections of the chapter describe other approaches to understanding work motivation.

The direct implication of needs theories for managing and leading people is that to get the most from workers' talents, it is necessary to "push their hot buttons." Two examples are as follows:

- Employees with strong security needs are likely to seek assurance, be cautious, and carefully stay within their job description. The manager might encourage risk taking from these workers by telling them about other employees who have tried something new and been successful. It is best to avoid surprises about change and offer frequent feedback.
- Employees with strong achievement needs are likely to display initiative and set personal goals, work well independently, take pride in work well done, and seek recognition for their good work. The manager might include them in the process of establishing work goals, give them ample resources, give

them feedback on their work outcomes, and encourage professional growth opportunities.[7]

The Skill–Development Exercise that follows will help you focus on the importance of identifying psychological needs when attempting to motivate others—and perhaps yourself as well.

2 GOAL THEORY

Summarize the key propositions of goal theory and reinforcement theory.

Goal setting is a basic process that is directly or indirectly part of all major theories of work motivation. Managers widely accept goal setting as a means to improve and sustain performance. Based on several hundred studies, the core finding of goal–setting theory is as follows: Individuals who are provided with specific hard goals perform better than those given easy, nonspecific, or "do your best" goals—or no goals at all. At the same time, however, the individuals must have sufficient ability, accept the goals, and receive feedback related to the task.[8] Our overview of goal–setting theory elaborates on this basic finding.

The premise underlying goal-setting theory is that behavior is regulated by values and goals. A **goal** is what a person is trying to accomplish. Our values create within us a desire to behave consistently with them. For example, if an executive values honesty, she will establish a goal of trying to hire only honest employ-

---

SKILL-DEVELOPMENT EXERCISE

Need Identification among Members of Generations X and Y

Following is a list of work preferences characteristic among members of Generations X and Y. Identify what psychological need or needs might be reflected in each work preference. Jot down the needs right after the work preference on the line indicated. In addition to the information presented in this chapter, the section about personality presented in Chapter 2 will give you some concepts for analysis.

- They like variety, not doing the same thing every workday. _____

- Part of their career goals is to face new challenges and opportunities. It's not all based on money, but on growth and learning. _____

- They want jobs that are cool, fun, and fulfilling. _____

- They believe that if they keep growing and learning then that's all the security they need. Advancing their skill set is their top priority. _____

- They have a tremendous thirst for knowledge. _____

- Unlike baby boomers, who tend to work independently, members of Generations X and Y like to work in a team environment. _____

- They prefer learning by doing and making mistakes as they go along. _____

- They are apt to challenge established ways of doing things, reasoning that there is always a better way. _____

- They want regular, frequent feedback on job performance. _____

- Career improvement is a blend of life and job balance. _____

Source: Reprinted with permission from the TemPositions Group of Companies, 420 Lexington Avenue, Suite 2100, New York, NY, 10170-0002.

ees. The executive would therefore make extensive use of reference checks and honesty testing. Edwin A. Locke and Gary P. Latham have incorporated hundreds of studies about goals into a theory of goal setting and task performance.[9] Exhibit 6-3 summarizes some of the more consistent findings, along with more recent developments. The list that follows describes these findings.

1. *Specific goals lead to higher performance than do generalized goals.* Telling someone to "do your best" is a generalized goal. A specific goal would be, "Decrease the cycle time on customer inquiries via the Internet to an average of three hours." (Here is an example in which common sense can be wrong. Many people believe that telling others to "do your best" is an excellent motivator.)

2. *Performance generally increases in direct proportion to goal difficulty.* The more difficult one's goal, the more one accomplishes. An important exception is that when goals are too difficult, they may lower performance. Difficulty in reaching the goal leads to frustration, which in turn leads to lowered performance. At times when a major goal seems overwhelming, establishing smaller, interim goals is more motivational.

3. *For goals to improve performance, the worker must accept them.* If one rejects a goal, one will not incorporate it into planning. This is why it is often helpful to discuss goals with employees, rather than imposing goals on them. Updated research, however, suggests that the importance of goal commitment may be overrated. Two meta-analyses of studies conducted in laboratories about the effect of goal commitment on performance concluded that commitment has a small impact on performance. Goals appeared to improve performance whether or not people participating in the studies felt committed to their goal.[10] Despite these recent findings, many managers think employee commitment to goals is important. Participating in setting goals has no major effect on the level of job performance except when it improves goal acceptance. Yet participation is valuable because it can lead to higher satisfaction with the goal-setting process.

4. *Goals are more effective when they are used to evaluate performance.* When workers know that their performance will be evaluated in terms of how well they attained their goals, the impact of goals increases.

5. *Goals should be linked to feedback and rewards.* Workers should receive feedback on their progress toward goals and be rewarded for reaching them. **Feedback** is information about how well someone is doing in achieving goals. Rewarding people for reaching goals as a motivational technique is perhaps the most widely accepted principle of management.

6. *A learning goal orientation improves performance more than a performance goal orientation.* A person with a learning goal orientation wants to develop competence

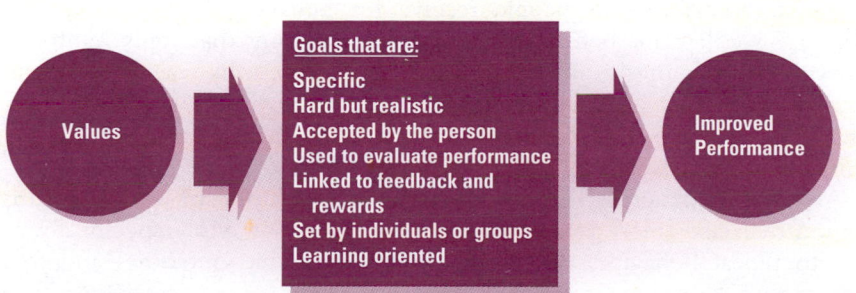

Exhibit 6-3

Goal-Setting Theory

by acquiring new skills and mastering new situations. In contrast, the person with a performance goal orientation wants to demonstrate and validate his or her competence by seeking favorable judgments and avoiding negative judgments. A study with medical supply sales representatives found that a learning-goal orientation had a positive relationship with sales performance. In contrast, a performance-goal orientation was unrelated to sales performance.[11]

7. *Group goal setting is as important as individual goal setting.* Having employees work as teams with a specific team goal, rather than as individuals with only individual goals, increases productivity. Furthermore, the combination of compatible group and individual goals is more effective than either individual or group goals alone. A related consideration is when a team member perceives that team members share his or her personal goals, the individual will be more satisfied and productive. A study of 324 members of 64 short-term project teams found that a perceived fit between individual and group performance goals brought about greater individual satisfaction and contribution to the team. Congruence had less of an impact on mastery goals.[12]

Despite the contribution of goals to performance, technically speaking, they are not motivational by themselves. Rather, the discrepancies created by what individuals do and what they aspire to do creates self-dissatisfaction. The dissatisfaction in turn creates a desire to reduce the discrepancy between the real and the ideal.[13] When a person desires to attain something, the person is in a state of arousal. The tension created by not having already achieved a goal spurs the person to reach the goal. If your goal is to update your company Web site in ten days, your dissatisfaction with not having started would propel you into action.

An effective way to apply goal theory is for the manager to set short-term goals or to encourage others to do the same. The short-term goals should support the organization's long-term goals, but are established in "bites" that are more readily achievable. Assume, for example, that a manufacturing site wants to reduce absenteeism from 20 percent to 5 percent to remain competitive. Going from 20 percent to 5 percent in three months might not be achievable. However, moving down 2 percent per month would be feasible. As each 2-percent reduction in absenteeism is achieved, employees are fed back the results. The feedback serves as a reward for further progress.

The accompanying Organizational Behavior in Action box insert illustrates how challenging and complex goals in business can lead to better-than-anticipated performance (see also the InfoTrac sidebar).

REINFORCEMENT THEORY

A well-established explanation of motivation is **reinforcement theory,** the contention that behavior is determined by its consequences. The consequences are the rewards and punishments people receive for behaving in particular ways. In Chapter 7 we describe behavior modification programs that apply reinforcement theory to enhance motivation. Reinforcement theory, unlike needs-based theories of motivation, de-emphasizes understanding the needs a person attempts to satisfy. Instead, the manager looks for rewards that will encourage certain behaviors, and punishments that discourage other behaviors.

At the foundation of reinforcement theory is **operant conditioning,** or learning that takes place as a consequence of behavior. More specifically, people learn to repeat behaviors that bring them pleasurable outcomes and to avoid

The fortunes of Apple have long been inextricably tied to the actions and desires of one man—Steve Jobs. Jobs is a household name, Palmisano is not. As rumors of a proposed Apple buyout of Universal Music Group started to surface, *Business Week* cast a jaundiced eye at the news, declaring that "the Mac stage has room for only one impresario. . . . Does Jobs really want to share his space with this crowd?" [Salkever, Alex; *Business Week Online* (April 23 2003.]

You can read this short article about Steve Jobs by logging on to InfoTrac College Edition at **http://www.infotrac-college.com,** where you can find this article (key in record number A100486848) and many others that confirm Jobs's partiality for center stage. Then sample some additional articles about Palmisano. *What can you infer about how each of these high-tech CEOs motivates the troops? How might their personalities influence their actions?*

Organizational Behavior *in Action*

Demanding Goals at IBM

Sam Palmisano, now Chairman and CEO of IBM Corporation, was not going to let anything get in the way of his success. It was 1994, and for 21 years Palmisano had proved himself at one IBM division after another. Now he was running Big Blue's outsourcing subsidiary, ISSC, and making a modest profit. Until, that is, he inherited a money-losing business that did consulting and systems integration.

Palmisano instructed his lieutenants to turn the new unit around. Immediately, Gordon Myers, his right-hand man, dug into the project but reported back with bad news: There was no way it was going to happen. The systems integration business, which had lost tens of millions the year before, would just break even. But make much more than

that? Not likely. Palmisano listened—then, with his ever present smile, replied, "Gordon, we set an objective to be profitable this year, and you have to figure out how to get there. I'm not willing to accept than you can't."

And that was that, Myers recalls. "Firm management actually motivates creative thinking," he says wryly. Myers monitored employees to find ways to increase their time spent on projects rather than on the sidelines, forced the disparate groups in ISSC to share resources, and pressed them to cross-sell each other's services. By year-end, the new business was profitable.

Source: Suzanne Koudsi, "Sam's Big Blue Challenge," *Fortune,* August 13, 2001, p. 144.

behaviors that lead to uncomfortable outcomes. After people learn a behavior through operant conditioning, they must be motivated by rewards to repeat that behavior.

According to the famous experimental psychologist B. F. Skinner, to train or condition people, and then later motivate them, the manager does not have to study the inner workings of the mind. Instead, the manager should understand the relationships between behaviors and their consequences. After these relationships are understood, the manager arranges contingencies to reward desirable behaviors and discourage undesirable behaviors.[14] Four basic strategies exist for arranging contingencies, which can modify individual (or group) behavior: positive reinforcement, avoidance motivation, extinction, and punishment.

Positive reinforcement is the application of a pleasurable or valued consequence when a person exhibits the desired response. After positive reinforcement, the probability increases that the behavior will be repeated. The term *reinforcement* means that the behavior (or response) is strengthened or entrenched. A manager who expresses appreciation when a team member works late strengthens the worker's propensity to work late.

Avoidance motivation is rewarding people by taking away an uncomfortable consequence. The process is also referred to as *negative reinforcement* because a negative situation is removed. Negative reinforcement is thus a reward, not a punishment, as commonly thought. Avoidance motivation is a way of strengthening a desired response by making the removal contingent on the right response. Assume that an employee is placed on probation because of poor attendance. After 30 consecutive days of coming to work, the employer rewards the employee by removing the probation.

Extinction is weakening or decreasing the frequency of undesirable behavior by removing the reward for such behavior. It is the absence of reinforcement.

Suppose an employee engages in undesirable behavior such as creating a disturbance just to get a reaction from coworkers. If the teammates ignore the disturbance, the perpetrator no longer receives the reward of getting attention and therefore stops the disturbing behavior. The behavior is said to be extinguished.

Punishment is the presentation of an undesirable consequence for a specific behavior. An indirect form of punishment is to take away a privilege, such as working on an interesting project, because of some undesirable behavior. The most direct managerial application of reinforcement theory is to reward those behaviors that support the goals of the organization.

EXPECTANCY THEORY OF MOTIVATION

3

Explain the expectancy theory of motivation.

According to **expectancy theory,** motivation results from deliberate choices to engage in activities in order to achieve worthwhile outcomes. People will be well motivated if they believe that a strong effort will lead to good performance and good performance will lead to preferred outcomes. The basic version of expectancy theory shown in Exhibit 6-4 is useful to managers and professionals. Components of the model are described next, followed by the guidelines for motivation stemming from expectancy theory.[15]

Expectancy, Instrumentality, and Valence

The key components of expectancy theory are expectancy, instrumentality, and valence. Each one of these components exists in each situation involving motivation. An **expectancy** is a person's subjective estimate of the probability that a given level of performance will occur. The effort-to-performance (E → P) expectancy refers to the individual's subjective hunch about the chances that increased effort will lead to the desired performance. If a person does not believe that he or she has the skill to accomplish a task, that person might not even try to perform.

The importance of having high expectancies for motivation meshes well with a conception of work motivation that emphasizes the contribution of self-efficacy. If you have high self-efficacy about the task, your motivation will be high. Low self-efficacy leads to low motivation. Some people are poorly motivated to skydive because they doubt they will be able to pull the ripcord while free-falling at 120 mph. This definition, which is more complete than the one presented in Chapter 5, will help you appreciate the contribution of self-efficacy to motivation:

> Self-efficacy refers to an individual's convictions (or confidence) about his or her abilities to mobilize the motivation, cognitive resources, and course of action needed to successfully execute a specific task within a given context.[16]

An **instrumentality** is the individual's estimate of the probability that performance will lead to certain outcomes. The (P → O) instrumentality refers to the

Exhibit 6-4

A Basic Version of Expectancy Theory

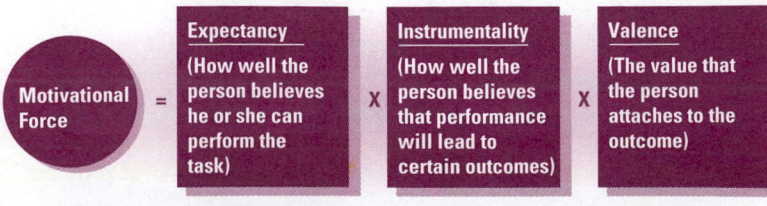

person's subjective evaluation of the chances that good performance will lead to certain outcomes. Among the outcomes might be an increase in status and salary, a promotion, more job security, and appreciation from management. Performance almost always leads to multiple outcomes. In formulating the instrumentality, the employee seeks a subjective answer to the question: "If I do perform well, will the organization really make good on promises to me?" Expectancies and instrumentalities range from 0.00 to 1.00 because both are probabilities.

Valence refers to the value a person places on a particular outcome. People attach positive valences to rewards and negative valences to punishments. An advertising copywriter might place a high positive valence on making a presentation to a client and assign a high negative valence to having his work insulted by the manager or client. The maximum value of a positive valence is +100, while the maximum value of a negative valence is −100. Neutral outcomes (indifference) carry a valence of zero. (Most versions of expectancy theory limit the range of valences from −1.00 to +1.00. However, such a limited range fails to capture the intensity of highly preferred or feared outcomes.) The numerical values of valences are unknown in most situations, yet it is reasonable to assume that people attach values of "good," "bad," and "neutral" to potential outcomes derived from their efforts.

The Calculation of Motivation

In expectancy theory, motivation force $M = (E \rightarrow P) \times (P \rightarrow O) \times V$. The potential of an expected outcome increasing motivation can be high only if the expectancies, instrumentalities, and valences are high. Because anything multiplied by zero is zero, a zero value for $(E \rightarrow P)$, $(P \rightarrow O)$, or V will reduce motivation to zero. Suppose an employee places a maximum value on receiving a raise (V = 100). The employee is confident that she can perform the task required ($E \rightarrow P$ = 0.85). And the employee is even more confident that the firm will come through with the raise if she performs well ($P \rightarrow O$ = 0.90). Note that the values of 0.85 and 0.90 are subjective estimates, not true calculations. The employee's motivation is consequently $(100) \times (0.85) \times (0.90) = 76.5$ (above average on a scale of −100 to +100).

A note of caution: The simple formula just presented does not tell the entire story because each task involves multiple expectancies, instrumentalities, and valences. Desirable and undesirable outcomes may cancel one another out, resulting in zero valence and therefore producing zero motivational force. For example, a person might not strive for a promotion because its positive valences (such as more money and status) are neutralized by its negative valences (such as having to relocate and leave friends behind). To create a situation of high motivation, the manager should take steps to elevate expectancies, instrumentalities, and valences. One approach would be for the manager to make sure the worker had the right training and to boost the worker's self-confidence—thus elevating expectancies. Assuring the worker that good performance would lead to a reward could boost instrumentalities. Choosing meaningful rewards would elevate the valences.

The Influence of Affect on Expectancy Theory

We have already mentioned the influence of affect on attitudes and creativity (Chapters 4 and 5). Positive affect may also exert influence on the components of expectancy theory, as suggested by two laboratory studies with ninety-seven college students. The task was solving anagrams (rearranging letters to make new words such as *item* from *mite*). Affect, or mood, was manipulated by giving students in the experimental group a bag of candy. A key finding was that when the link between performance and outcomes was specified, being in the positive affect group increased expectancies, instrumentalities, and valences.[17]

The implication is that managers might be able to increase the effectiveness of expectancy theory by finding ways to elevate the mood of group members. Dispensing bags of candy would be a short-term expedient, because as Chapter 7 will describe, the same reward repeated too often can become stale. Creating a positive work climate would probably be more effective at sustaining positive affect.

Cross-Cultural Factors and Expectancy Theory

In applying expectancy theory, as well as other explanations of motivation, the manager must be alert to cross-cultural factors. Cross-cultural factors typically factor into which rewards or outcomes are likely to have the highest valence for a particular cultural group. Hispanic people, for example, generally favor outcomes that enable them to maintain cordial relations with other members of the work group. Another example would be that Asians would ordinarily prefer not to receive rewards that singled them out for attention.

As analyzed by Nancy J. Adler, expectancy theory depends on the extent to which workers believe they have control over the outcome of their efforts and how much faith they have in leaders to deliver rewards.[18] The assumption that workers believe they have control over their fate may be culturally dependent. In countries where individualism dominates, such as the United States, employees may believe more strongly that they can influence performance and outcomes. In collectivist societies, such as Taiwan, an individual may feel that group effort has a stronger influence on performance and outcomes. Taiwanese are also more likely to believe that the company has a moral obligation to deliver on outcomes.

EQUITY THEORY AND SOCIAL COMPARISON

4

Explain how equity and social comparison contribute to motivation.

Expectancy theory emphasizes the rational and thinking side of people. Similarly, another theory focuses on how fairly people think they are being treated in comparison to certain reference groups. According to **equity theory,** employee satisfaction and motivation depend on how fairly the employees believe they are treated in comparison to peers. The theory contends that employees hold certain beliefs about the outcomes they receive from their jobs, as well as the inputs they invest to obtain these outcomes.

The outcomes of employment include pay, benefits, status, intrinsic job factors, and anything else stemming from the job that workers perceive as useful. The inputs include all the factors that employees perceive as being their investment in the job or anything of value that they bring to the job. These inputs include job qualifications, skills, education level, effort, and cooperative behavior.

The core of equity theory is that employees compare their inputs and outcomes (making social comparisons) with others in the workplace.[19] When employees believe that they receive equitable outcomes in relation to their inputs, they are generally satisfied. When workers believe that they are being treated equitably, they are more willing to work hard. Conversely, when employees believe that they give too much as compared to what they receive from the organization, a state of tension and dissatisfaction ensues. The people used for reference are those whom the employee perceives as relevant for comparison. For example, an industrial sales representative would make comparisons with other industrial sales reps in the same industry about whom he has information.

There are two kinds of comparisons. People consider their own inputs in relation to outcomes received, and they also evaluate what others receive for the same inputs. Equity is said to exist when an individual concludes that his or her own outcome/input ratio is equal to that of other people. Inequity exists if the person's ratio is not the same as that of other people. All these comparisons are similar to those judgments made by people according to expectancy theory—they are subjective hunches that may or may not be valid. Inequity can be in either direction and of varying magnitude. The equity ratio is often expressed as follows:

$$\frac{\text{Outcomes of Individual}}{\text{Inputs of Individual}} \quad \text{compared to} \quad \frac{\text{Outcomes of Others}}{\text{Inputs of Others}}$$

According to equity theory, the highest level of motivation occurs when a person has ratios equal to those of the comparison person. When people perceive an inequity, they are likely to engage in one of the following actions:

1. *Alter the outcome.* The person who feels mistreated might ask for more salary or a bonus, promotional opportunities, or more vacation time. Some people might even steal from the company to obtain the money they feel they deserve. Others might attempt to convince management to give less to others. One sociology professor donated $2,000 of his $60,000 annual salary to a custodial worker at his university. The professor's intent was to help create equity in the university pay system.

2. *Alter the input.* A person who feels treated inequitably might decrease effort or time devoted to work. The person who feels underpaid might engage in such self-defeating behavior by faking sick days to take care of personal business. Another extreme would be to encourage others to decrease their inputs so they will earn less money.

3. *Distort the perception.* To combat feelings of inequity, people can distort their perceptions of their own (or others') inputs or outcomes. Recognizing that she is overpaid in comparison to coworkers, a financial analyst might say, "Of course, I attended a much tougher program at college, so I deserve more money." Another distortion would be to look for evidence that coworkers are contributing less effort.

4. *Change the reference source.* A convenient way of restoring equity is to change to another reference source whose outcome/input ratio is similar to one's own. A recently graduated MBA accepted a job offer for $20,000 less per year than average compared to other graduates of her program. At first she grumbled about being underpaid but then reanalyzed the situation. Her conclusion was, "The MBAs I was comparing myself with took jobs in New York City or Boston where the cost of living is much higher. If I compare myself to MBAs getting hired outside of New York or Boston, I'm being paid well."

5. *Leave the situation.* As an extreme move, the person who feels treated inequitably might quit a job. He or she would then be free to pursue greater equity in another position.

Equity theory has much face validity and has direct relevance for pay systems. No matter how well designed a program of productivity or cost cutting might be, it must still provide equitable pay. Otherwise, the negative perceptions of workers might lead to less effort to accomplish the goals of management.

SOCIAL LEARNING THEORY

5

Use social learning theory to motivate yourself.

116

As described in Chapter 3, people learn various behaviors by observing and imitating others. At a later point, they are motivated to repeat the learned behaviors. **Social learning** is the process of observing the behavior of others, recognizing its consequences, and altering behavior as a result. According to social learning theory, individual behavior is influenced by a combination of a person's cognitions and social environment. A person has to make some interpretations of the efficacy and suitability of the behavior being observed; otherwise the model will not be imitated.

Social learning does not take place automatically just because environmental models are available. If social learning were that easy, almost every employee would be a model worker. Effective social learning, and therefore motivated behavior, is most likely to take place when several of the following conditions are met:[20]

1. The person should have high expectancies that he or she can learn the observed behavior, and high instrumentalities that the learned behavior will result in valued rewards. The high expectancies center around the person having high self-efficacy. Social learning will be facilitated when the person is confident of performing well in the modeled task.

2. Self-administration of rewards should take place. The person doing the modeling should find the behavior intrinsically satisfying and not have to rely exclusively on extrinsic rewards such as increased earnings and recognition. Modeling the new behavior should result in personal satisfaction and an enhanced self-image. Assume that you learned how to negotiate effectively by observing a mentor negotiate a deal. You would most likely experience increased personal satisfaction from having acquired a valuable new business skill. At a later point, external rewards would be forthcoming if your new skill led to a higher performance evaluation or saving money when purchasing a home.

3. The behavior to be learned should involve mostly tangible mechanical and verbal activities such as physical and interpersonal tasks. It is thus easier to be motivated by watching another person negotiate than engage in internalized strategic planning. We cannot readily imitate the cognitive processes of another person.

4. Social learning can only take place when we possess the physical and mental ability needed to imitate the behavior. A frail person cannot learn to move furniture by simply watching others do it correctly. Also, one cannot imitate effective negotiating practices if he or she is not intelligent enough to figure out what the other side really wants.

Social learning may appear to be more about learning than motivation, but the motivational aspects are still important. Workers typically model the behavior of people from whom they seek approval, such as superiors and high-performing teammates. Part of the motivation for learning and repeating the target behavior is to receive approval from significant people in the work environment. Have you ever noticed how people from the same organization often talk alike?

INTRINSIC VERSUS EXTRINSIC MOTIVATION

6

Recognize the importance of both intrinsic and extrinsic motivators.

Many management experts contend that if you make jobs more interesting, there may be less need for motivating people with external rewards. The two-factor theory of motivation is based on this idea. Also, attempting to motivate people by extrinsic rewards may not be sufficient. Motivating people through interesting work is based on the principle of **intrinsic motivation.** It refers to a person's beliefs about the extent to which an activity can satisfy his or her needs for competence and self-determination. The intrinsically motivated person has energy and passion for the task,[21] as implied in the discussion in Chapter 5 about the experience of flow. Values contribute to intrinsic motivation. People who highly value work tend to be intrinsically motivated, while people who place a low value on work have low intrinsic motivation. You will recall the contribution of intrinsic motivation to creativity in Chapter 4.

Intrinsic motivation is therefore also referred to as **self-determination theory,** the idea that people are motivated when they experience a sense of choice in initiating and regulating their actions. Instead of looking to somebody else for rewards, a person is motivated by the intrinsic or internal aspects of the task. Reinforcement theory, in contrast, emphasizes external rewards associated with the task.

The Rationale behind Intrinsic Motivation Theory

Intrinsic motivation and self-determination theory are closely related. According to self-determination theory, workers are active agents of, rather than passive reactors to, environmental forces. Two factors influence the perception of intrinsic motivation. Certain characteristics of a task, such as challenge and autonomy, promote intrinsic motivation because they allow a person to satisfy the needs for competence and self-determination. Workers' perceptions of why they perform a task can also affect intrinsic motivation. Such motivation is likely to increase when people perceive that they perform tasks for themselves rather than for an external reward. To understand intrinsic motivation, visualize a computer programmer joyously working until midnight to write software that will give her company a competitive edge in satisfying customers. She is so wrapped up in her work that she is unaware of the time. Furthermore, she gives no particular thought to whether she will receive a bonus for her outstanding work.

When an individual performs a task to achieve an external reward such as money or recognition, a shift occurs. The individual believes that the external reward caused the behavior, and money or recognition now controls his or her actions. The worker no longer perceives that he or she is self-determining. As a result, intrinsic motivation may decrease.[22]

Kenneth W. Thomas presents a view, shared by many others, of the importance of intrinsic motivation in today's workplace. He reasons that the world of work has evolved from the command-and-control era to one in which encouraging workers to manage themselves plays a major role in leading workers. Intrinsic motivation is necessary for self-management because self-management implies that you find your work rewarding in itself.[23]

Problems Associated with Extrinsic Rewards

Intrinsic motivation theory is based on the fact that external rewards have disadvantages. Extrinsic rewards can sometimes lower a person's job performance and be demotivating, particularly when a creative task is involved. The appeal of extrinsic rewards can also cause people to:

- Focus narrowly on a task.
- Rush through a job to get a reward.
- Regard the task as a drudgery that must be suffered to receive a reward.
- See themselves as less free and less self-determining.[24]

Despite these problems, a firm should not abandon financial bonuses and other forms of extrinsic motivation. Even the people who enjoy work intensely still expect to be paid well and crave recognition from management. Also, people who love their work, such as top executives, successful novelists, entertainers, and athletes, demand huge fees. The sensible solution is for managers to balance intrinsic and extrinsic rewards. For example, a purchasing agent who saved the company $300,000 by finding a low-price alternative for a component might be rewarded with the opportunity to work on a cross-functional team. He might also be given a hefty year-end bonus.

THE INFLUENCE OF PERSONALITY ON MOTIVATION

7

Explain how personality factors are related to motivation.

For many people, being well motivated comes easily because they have personality traits that predispose them to this. Two key examples are *conscientiousness* and the *achievement need*. (A need usually functions like a personality trait.) The conscientious person will strive to get the job done, and the achievement-driven person welcomes accomplishing tasks. Conversely, it will be more difficult for the manager to motivate people who score low on conscientiousness, and have a weak achievement need.

A study involving 164 telemarketing sales representatives at a large financial services firm provides empirical evidence for the link between personality factors and motivation. As most readers would suspect, high motivation is crucial to perform well as a telemarketer—particularly in light of all the rejection a telemarketer encounters. Motivation was measured in relation to three factors. *Communion striving* represents actions directed toward being accepted in personal relationships and getting along with coworkers. *Status striving* refers to actions directed toward obtaining power and dominance within a status hierarchy, such as a business firm. *Accomplishment striving* reflects an individual's intention to accomplish tasks, as included in most definitions of work motivation. The Five Factor Model was used to study personality.

IMPLICATIONS FOR MANAGERIAL PRACTICE

The explanations of motivation presented in this chapter all have implications for managerial practice. Nevertheless, we emphasize suggestions derived from expectancy theory because its components include ideas from other theories:

1. *Determine what levels and kinds of performance are needed to achieve organizational goals.* Motivating others proceeds best when workers have a clear understanding of what needs to be accomplished. At the same time, the manager should make sure that the desired levels of performance are possible.
2. *Train and encourage people.* Managers should give group members the necessary training and encouragement to be confident that they can perform the required task. Some group members who appear to be poorly motivated simply lack the right skills and self-confidence.
3. *Understand individual differences in valences.* To motivate workers effectively, managers must recognize individual differences in preferences for rewards. An attempt should be made to offer workers rewards to which they attach a high valence. Cross-cultural differences in valences may also occur.
4. *Use positive reinforcement more than punishment.* At times, punishment is necessary. Yet it can produce such negative side effects as anxiety and retaliation against the firm, including employees making costly mistakes intentionally.

The strongest correlations found in the aspect of the study dealing with the personality–motivation relationship are listed here. We also include findings about job performance because motivation is assumed to be a major contributor to job performance:

- Extraversion was correlated with communion striving and status striving.
- Conscientiousness was correlated with accomplishment striving and status striving.
- Extraversion and conscientiousness were correlated with sales performance.
- Status striving and accomplishment striving were correlated with sales performance.[25]

The study therefore demonstrated that personality factors are correlated with motivation, and that both personality factors and motivation are related to job performance. The researchers thus provided one more brick in the wall of evidence that personality and motivation make a difference in job performance.

SUMMARY OF KEY POINTS

1 Describe several need theories of motivation, including the needs hierarchy, the two-factor theory, and the achievement–power–affiliation triad.

Motivation is the process by which behavior is mobilized and sustained in the interest of achieving organizational goals. As reflected in need theories of motivation, self-interest is a driving force.

According to Maslow's needs hierarchy, human needs fall into five groups: physiological, safety, social and love, esteem, and self-actualization. As needs at one level are gratified, they lose their strength and the next level of needs is activated.

Herzberg's two-factor theory of work motivation divides job factors into motivators and satisfiers versus maintenance factors or dissatisfiers. Motivational factors are the intrinsic or job content factors (such as achievement and recognition) that make a job rewarding. Maintenance factors are the extrinsic aspects of the job (such as working conditions and benefits). Dissatisfaction stems from substandard extrinsic factors.

McClelland's acquired needs theory explains that certain needs people strive to satisfy are acquired or learned from the culture. His research centers on three needs of particular significance in understanding entrepreneurs and managers: achievement, power, and affiliation. The need for power is the primary motivator of successful managers.

2 Summarize the key propositions of goal theory and reinforcement theory.

Goal setting is an important part of all major theories of motivation. Specific and difficult goals result in higher performance than generalized goals. Goals must be accepted by workers and goals are more effective when they are used to evaluate performance and linked to feedback and rewards. A learning goal orientation is more effective than a performance goal orientation and group goal setting is as important as individual goal setting.

According to reinforcement theory, behavior is determined by its consequences, or rewards and punishments for behaving in particular ways. At the foundation of reinforcement theory is operant conditioning, or learning that takes place as a consequence of behavior. People learn to repeat behaviors that bring them pleasurable outcomes and to avoid behaviors that lead to uncomfortable outcomes. The four basic strategies for arranging contingencies to modify behavior are positive reinforcement, avoidance motivation, extinction, and punishment.

3 Explain the expectancy theory of motivation.

Expectancy theory is based on the idea that work motivation results from deliberate choices to engage in certain activities in order to achieve worthwhile outcomes. The three components of expectancy theory are effort-to-performance expectancies, instrumentalities, and valence. Positive affect may increase any of these factors. Individual differences and cultural factors influence valence. Most situations have multiple outcomes and valences. Motivational force is the result of the multiplication of expectancies, instrumentalities, and valence.

4 Explain how equity and social comparison contribute to motivation.

Equity theory explains that workers compare their inputs and outcomes with relevant people in the workplace. When employees believe that they are receiving equitable outputs in relation to their inputs, they are generally satisfied and motivated. When workers believe they are giving too much in relation to what they are receiving from the organization, dissatisfaction ensues. People will usually take action to bring their equity ratio into balance. Two such actions would be seeking greater outputs or decreasing input.

Use social learning theory to motivate yourself.
According to social learning theory, individual behavior is influenced by a combination of a person's cognitions and social environment. People learn by imitating a model and becoming motivated to repeat the behavior. Conditions favoring social learning include high expectations, self-administration of rewards, observation of tangible behavior to imitate, and the necessary physical and mental ability.

 Recognize the importance of both intrinsic and extrinsic motivators.
The theory of intrinsic motivation, or self-determination, emphasizes that people are active agents rather than recipients of environmental forces. Passion and energy are part of being intrinsically motivated. Intrinsic motivation is tied in with needs for competence and self-

determination. Extrinsic rewards can sometimes lower a person's job performance and be demotivating, particularly when a creative task is involved. A combination of intrinsic and extrinsic rewards is best for motivation, although intrinsic motivation is essential for self-management.

 Explain how personality factors are related to motivation.
Certain personality traits can predispose a person to being well motivated. A study demonstrated various links between the Five Factor Model of personality and motivation, such as a correlation between extraversion and communion striving and status striving, and a correlation between conscientiousness and accomplishment and status striving. Motivation was also shown to be correlated with sales performance.

KEY TERMS AND PHRASES

Motivation, *102*
In a work setting, the process by which behavior is mobilized and sustained in the interest of achieving organizational goals.

Maslow's Hierarchy of Needs, *102*
A classical theory of motivation that arranges human needs into a pyramid-shaped model, with basic physiological needs at the bottom and self-actualization needs at the top.

Two-factor Theory of Work Motivation, *105*
Herzberg's theory contending that there are two different sets of job factors. One set can satisfy and motivate people (motivators or satisfiers); the other set can only prevent dissatisfaction (dissatisfiers or hygiene factors).

Need for Achievement, *106*
The desire to accomplish something difficult for its own sake.

Need for Power, *106*
The desire to control other people, to influence their behavior, and to be responsible for them.

Need for Affiliation, *107*
The desire to establish and maintain friendly and warm relationships with others.

Goal, *108*
What a person is trying to accomplish.

Feedback, *109*
Information about how well someone is doing in achieving goals. Also, messages sent back from the receiver to the sender of information.

Reinforcement Theory, *110*
The contention that behavior is determined by its consequences.

Operant Conditioning, *110*
Learning that takes place as a consequence of behavior.

Positive Reinforcement, *111*
The application of a pleasurable or valued consequence when a person exhibits the desired response.

Avoidance Motivation, *111*
Rewarding by taking away an uncomfortable consequence.

Extinction, *111*
Weakening or decreasing the frequency of undesirable behavior by removing the reward for such behavior.

Punishment, *112*
The presentation of an undesirable consequence for a specific behavior.

Expectancy Theory, *112*
The theory that motivation results from deliberate choices to engage in activities in order to achieve worthwhile outcomes.

Expectancy, *112*
A person's subjective estimate of the probability that a given level of performance will occur.

Instrumentality, *112*
The individual's subjective estimate of the probability that performance will lead to certain outcomes.

Valence, *113*
The value a person places on a particular outcome.

Equity Theory, *114*
The theory that employee satisfaction and motivation depend on how fairly the employees believe that they are treated in comparison to peers.

Social Learning, *116*
The process of observing the behavior of others, recognizing its consequences, and altering behavior as a result.

Intrinsic Motivation, *117*
A person's beliefs about the extent to which an activity can satisfy his or her needs for competence and self-determination.

Self-determination Theory, *117*
The idea that people are motivated when they experience a sense of choice in initiating and regulating their actions.

DISCUSSION QUESTIONS AND ACTIVITIES

1. How does WIIFM explain the fact that many busy managers and professionals devote considerable amounts of their time to community activities and charities?
2. How would you know if a particular person had strong needs for power, achievement, or affiliation?
3. Why are goals motivational?
4. How can a manager strengthen the expectancies of group members?
5. How does a person formulate an instrumentality for estimating the extent to which hard work will lead to a promotion?

6. Which of your personality traits are likely to enhance your motivation to perform well on the job and at school? What evidence do you have for the strength of these traits?
7. Scan a newspaper, search the Internet, or watch news programs on television to identify an incident of motivated behavior. Analyze whether you think the key person was motivated more by intrinsic or extrinsic rewards. Be prepared to discuss your findings in class.

ORGANIZATIONAL BEHAVIOR ONLINE

TO DO

Risky Investment Strategies

The need for risk taking and thrill seeking will often manifest itself in making investment decisions. Visit http://riskaversion.hypermart.net/fbgn_eng.html and fill out a questionnaire designed to analyze what percent of stocks you should have in your present or future investment portfolio. The questionnaire is based on a data set of more than 8,000 people. After answering the questions you will receive a personal risk profile. How does your risk profile about stock purchases compare to your propensity to take risks in work-related areas such as trying out new ideas and making innovative suggestions?

TO BOOKMARK

Equity
http://www.businessballs.com/adamsequitytheory.htm

Positive Reinforcement
http://www.p-management.com

Intrinsic Motivation
http://fed.org/resrclib/articles/building.html

CASE PROBLEM: Lonely Work at Home

Missed package deliveries and phone calls, and the occasional barking dog, were not exactly what Tom Galloway had in mind when he launched a digital printing business from his home a few years ago. His hopes were to roll out of bed each morning, start the coffeepot and PC, and make a fortune without ever getting out of his pajamas. The reality was that within a few weeks, Galloway was buried under paperwork and was lonely. After six months, he hung up his bathrobe for good.

Although he no longer works at home, Galloway still deals with that type of frustration, but now as a source of revenue. His new venture, a franchised chain of upscale small-business service centers called Your Office USA, targets people facing the same problems he did. "From the Fortune 500 Sales Rep to the part-time home business, you'll look like a million bucks with us and have more time to enjoy the rewards" the Your Office Web site promises.

Your Office is one among many firms serving the almost 40 million people in the United States who operate small businesses from home or are corporate telecommuters. Many of these people seek the professional services and social interaction characteristic of a traditional work environment. Along with executive-suite operators such as HQ and Regus, Your Office positions itself as being a more elegant version of Kinko's. Superstores like Office Depot and Staples are looking to follow the lead of Kinko's by adding more in-house digital offerings.

Your Office is a subsidiary of IB Your Office, a $50 million-a-year company with more than 100 franchises in Europe and Asia. A company executive describes Your Office as a "superstore for the home-based entrepreneur." The 6,000-square foot interiors have the familiar appearance of a corporate office: a receptionist area and long hallways with art on the wall, leading to individual offices and cubicles. Yet few corporate sites house such varied activity. For instance, in one room a customer who is a security expert trains security guards, and in another room a computer specialist is at a workstation.

Randolph Blatt, 41, of Raleigh, North Carolina, is one of those computer specialists. After working from home for four years, Blatt, who recruits computer professionals, became tired of the distractions. "I would get phone calls, and I had screaming babies in the background. I would duck into my laundry room to hide. It never worked. At Your Office, I regularly run into people, and I feel like I'm part of the world."

Your Office also hopes to serve millions of sales representatives who have lost their desks to downsizings and have become corporate nomads, as well as on-the-go entrepreneurs who want satellite offices in several cities. By the hour, the day, or the month, they can rent office space, hire a secretary, check their mailboxes or e-mail, or conduct a videoconference. Whenever New York City bankruptcy attorney Garret Rubin has to meet clients near the Brooklyn courts, he uses a nearby Your Office. "I wish my office was this nice," he says.

At any Kinko's outlet, day or night, graphic artists and bank presidents alike can access a uniform set of PCs, fax machines, and color copiers and printers to update résumés, and can create flyers, trade ideas, and confer with clients. "We're the intellectual meeting place in any community," claims Paul Orfalea, who started Kinko's in an old Santa Barbara, California, hamburger stand in 1970 (the Kinko's name comes from his kinky red hair). Susan Cummins, a Miami public relations expert, calls Kinko's "the only office social experience I connect with. It's like the office, but without the politics." To make things cozier, Kinko's has opened a few Citibank mini-branches in its stores. At Your Office fran-

chisees hold pizza parties and holiday bashes to bring their disparate customers together.

Case Questions

1. What needs are the small business owners and telecommuters described in this case attempting to satisfy by frequenting the small-business service centers?
2. What recommendations would you give to the operators of the service centers to make their services even more attractive to small business owners and telecommuters?
3. What recommendations can you make to the small-business owners and telecommuters for obtaining more intrinsic satisfaction in their work?

Source: Daniel Eisenberg, "Offices by the Hour," *Time,* February 1, 1999, pp. 40–41. Used with permission of the publisher.

ENDNOTES

1. Abraham H. Maslow, "A Theory of Human Motivation," *Psychological Review,* July 1943, pp. 370–396; *Motivation and Personality* (New York: Harper & Row, 1954), Chapter 5.
2. Florence M. Stone, "Motivating Employees: The Danger of Applying '60s Theories to '90s Situations," *HR/OD* (A Member Newsletter of the American Management Association International), June 1998, p. 3.
3. Frederick Herzberg, Bernard Mausner, and Barbara Snyderman, *The Motivation to Work,* 2nd ed. (New York: John Willey & Sons, 1959); Herzberg, *Work and the Nature of Man* (Cleveland: World Publishing, 1966).
4. David C. McClelland, "Business Drive and National Achievement," *Harvard Business Review* July–August 1962, pp. 99–112; McClelland, *The Achieving Society* (New York: Van Nostrand, 1961).
5. Edwin T. Cornelius III and Frank B. Lane, "The Power Motive and Managerial Success in a Professionally Oriented Service Industry Organization," *Journal of Applied Psychology,* February 1984, pp. 32–39.
6. David C. McClelland and David H. Burnam, "Power Is the Great Motivator," *Harvard Business Review,* January 2003, pp. 117–126, 142 (reprint of 1976 article plus *HBR* editor update).
7. Jane Churchouse and Chris Churchouse, *Managing People* (Hamshire, England: Gower Publishing Ltd. 1998); "Recognizing Workers' Needs," *Manager's Edge,* March 1999, p. 1.
8. Book review in *Personnel Psychology,* Winter 1991, p. 872.
9. Edwin A. Locke and Gary P. Latham, *A Theory of Goal Setting and Task Performance* (Upper Saddle River, NJ: Prentice Hall, 1990).
10. John J. Donavan and David J. Radosevich, "The Moderating Role of Goal Commitment on the Goal Difficulty-Performance Relationship: A Meta-Analytic Review and Critical Reanalysis," *Journal of Applied Psychology,* April 1998, pp. 308–315; Howard J. Klein, Michael J. Wesson, John R. Hollenbeck, and Bradley J. Alge, "Goal Commitment and the Goal-Setting Process: Conceptual Clarification and Empirical Synthesis," *Journal of Applied Psychology,* December 1999, pp. 885–896.
11. Don VandeWalle, Steven P. Brown, William L. Cron, and John W. Slocum, Jr., "The Influence of Goal Orientation and Self-Regulation Tactics on Sales Performance: A Longitudinal Field Test," *Journal of Applied Psychology,* April 1999, pp. 249–259.
12. Amy L. Kristof-Brown and Cynthia Kay Stevens, "Goal Congruence in Project Teams: Does the Fit Between Members' Personal Mastery and Performance Goals Matter?" *Journal of Applied Psychology,* December 2001, pp. 1083–1095.
13. P. Christopher Earley and Terri R. Lituchy, "Delineating Goal and Efficacy Effects: A Test of Three Models," *Journal of Applied Psychology,* February 1991, p. 872.
14. B. F. Skinner, *Science and Human Behavior* (New York: Macmillan, 1953).
15. Victor H. Vroom, *Work and Motivation* (New York: John Wiley & Sons, 1964); Lynn E. Miller and Joseph E. Grush, "Improving Predictions in Expectancy Theory Research: Effects of Personality, Expectancies, and Norms," *Academy of Management Journal,* March 1988, pp. 107–122.
16. Alexander D. Stajkovic and Fred Luthans, "Social Cognitive Theory and Self-Efficacy: Going Beyond Traditional Motivational and Behavioral Approaches," *Organizational Dynamics,* Spring 1998, p. 66.
17. Amir Erez and Alice M. Isen, "The Influence of Positive Affect on the Components of Expectancy Motivation," *Journal of Applied Psychology,* December 2002, pp. 1055–1067.
18. Nancy J. Adler, *International Dimensions of Organizational Behavior,* 2nd ed. (Boston: PWS-Kent, 1991), pp. 157–160.
19. J. Stacy Adams, "Toward an Understanding of Inequality," *Journal of Abnormal and Social Psychology,* Vol. 67, 1963, pp. 422–436; M. R. Carrell and J. E. Dettrich, "Equity Theory: The Recent Literature, Methodological Considerations, and New Directions," Academy of Management Review, April 1978, pp. 202–210.
20. Robert Wood and Albert Bandura, "Social Cognitive Theory of Organizational Management," *Academy of Management Review,* July 1989, pp. 361–384.
21. Kenneth W. Thomas, *Intrinsic Motivation at Work: Building Energy and Commitment* (San Francisco: Berrett-Koehler Publishers, 2000).
22. Gregory Moorehead and Ricky W. Griffin, *Organizational Behavior: Managing People and Organizations,* 4th ed. (Boston: Houghton Mifflin, 1995), pp. 147–148; Robert P. Vecchio, *Organizational Behavior,* 2nd ed. (Mason, OH: South-Western/Thomson Learning, 1991), p. 193.
23. Thomas, *Intrinsic Motivation at Work.*
24. Richard M. Ryan and Edward L. Deci, "Self-Determination Theory and the Facilitation of Intrinsic Motivation, Social Development, and Well-Being," *American Psychologist,* January 2000, pp. 68–78; Jeffrey Pfeffer, *Human Equation: Building Profits by Putting People First* (Boston: Harvard Business School Press, 1998), pp. 213–217.
25. Murray R. Barrick, Greg L. Stewart, and Mike Piotrowski, "Personality and Job Performance: Test of Mediating Effects of Motivation among Sales Representatives," *Journal of Applied Psychology,* February 2002, pp. 43–51.

Chapter 7

Motivational Methods and Programs

Rewarding employees for meeting important goals—whether or not the company is raking in lots of money—is the heart of the "goalsharing" program at Corning Inc. Started in the early 1990s, the variable pay plan can give each U.S.–based Corning employee an annual bonus of up to 10 percent of salary. Employees helped develop the system, which is reviewed and adjusted annually at the business unit level by committees that include workers, managers, and union representatives.

One-fourth of the bonus is based on earnings per share of company stock for the preceding year. The rest of the payment depends on how well the worker has met job performance goals established for his or her business unit over the year.

"One of the basic premises of goalsharing is that every employee would have line of sight" to the corporate goal, says Larry Lukefahr, Corning's manager of variable pay programs. Individual performance standards "are set with the idea that each employee can somehow contribute to meeting that goal."

"Everybody must improve from where they ended up last year," say Hank Jonas, the corporation's manager of organizational effectiveness. But in addition, "everybody has an equal chance of success."

It's not always easy to set goals that satisfy the interests of the employee and the company, Lukefahr and Jonas note. A research scientist "might say 10 failures is a success. How do you measure 10 failures and pay someone for 10 failures?" asks Lukefahr. And it's not always easy to explain handing out bonus checks with the company losing money. Corning has a portfolio of businesses, some of which are in the black, which helps support bonuses for all eligible workers.

"I envisioned that there would be good times and bad times," Jonas says. "We want it to fairly reflect how we're doing as a company in good times and bad." Adds Lukefahr: "Our employees are very aware of goalsharing and how goalsharing works. I've never heard anyone question goalsharing."

OBJECTIVES

After reading and studying this chapter and doing the exercises, you should be able to:

1 Explain how to enhance motivation through job enrichment, the job characteristics model, job crafting and work group design.

2 Summarize the basics of a behavior modification program in the workplace.

3 Identify rules and suggestions for motivating group members through behavior modification.

4 Describe why recognition is a good motivator, and the nature of reward and recognition programs in the workplace.

5 Describe how to effectively use financial incentives to motivate others, including the use of stock options and gainsharing.

6 Choose an appropriate motivational model for a given situation.

Source: Steve Bates, "Goalsharing at Corning," *HR Magazine,* January 2003, p. 33. Reprinted with the permission of *HR Magazine* published by the Society for Human Resource Management, Alexandria, VA.

NOW ASK YOURSELF: What does the goalsharing program at Corning tell us about how companies systematically use financial incentives to motivate workers? Rewarding work in a manner that motivates employees to perform at the high levels expected of them is a decisive competency for companies to develop if they are to succeed. The value of actively involving employees in the design of bonus programs is also seen. In this chapter, we describe motivational programs based on financial incentives, but we also examine motivation through job design, behavior modification, and reward and recognition programs. We also describe choosing an appropriate motivational model, a topic that relates to both the present and previous chapter.

Explain how to enhance motivation through job enrichment, the job characteristics model, and work group design.

MOTIVATION THROUGH JOB DESIGN

A major strategy for enhancing motivation is to make the job so challenging and the worker so responsible that he or she is motivated just by performing the job. We will approach motivation through job design by explaining job enrichment, the job characteristics model, job crafting, and self-managed work teams. Research and practice with motivation through job design has its roots in the two-factor theory described in Chapter 6.

Job Enrichment

Job enrichment refers to making a job more motivational and satisfying by adding variety, responsibility, and managerial decision making. At its best, job enrichment gives workers a sense of ownership, responsibility, and accountability for their work. Because job enrichment leads to a more exciting job, it often increases employee job satisfaction and motivation. People are usually willing to work harder at tasks they find enjoyable and rewarding, just as they will put effort into a favorite hobby (see the video sidebar). Managers and professionals in organizations typically have enriched jobs.

Exciting or enriched jobs appeal strongly to new business graduates. A survey of 2,221 MBA students indicated that they wanted to make a quick impact on their jobs. Major employers of MBAs—such as consulting firms, Intel, Disney, Microsoft, and Johnson & Johnson—have responded by promising new MBAs broader exposure than normal and the chance to work with a high-profile task force outside their functional area.[1]

Characteristics of an Enriched Job

According to Frederick Herzberg, the way to design an enriched job is to include as many of the characteristics described next as possible.[2] Exhibit 7-1 summarizes the characteristics and consequences of enriched jobs.

1. *Direct feedback.* Employees should receive immediate evaluation of their work. Feedback can be built into the job (such as the feedback that closing a sale gives a sales representative) or provided by the manager.
2. *Client relationships.* A job is automatically enriched when a worker has a client or customer to serve, whether that client is internal or external. Serving a client is more satisfying to most people than performing work solely for a manager. An information systems specialist at a bank who interacts with loan officers is said to have a client relationship. However, interacting with hostile and verbally abusive customers is demotivational and stressful rather than enriching.

Welcome to the Buffalo Zoo (10:58)

When Donna Fernandez became its zoo director, the Buffalo Zoo was run down, sparsely visited, and in danger of losing its accreditation. Not surprisingly, employees were unenthusiastic and morale was low. They were often reprimanded for minor infractions and managers consistently undermined people's sense of worth. Fernandez knew she had to motivate a broad spectrum of employees, from board members to animal handlers, in order to save the zoo. For a look at the actions she took and the programs she implemented, go to **www.dubrin.swlearning.com** and view the video segment. *What types of job enrichment programs are now in play? How important are direct communication and personal accountability in the "new" zoo?*

3. *New learning.* An enriched job allows its holder to acquire new knowledge. The learning can stem from job experiences themselves or from training programs associated with the job.

4. *Control over scheduling.* The ability to schedule one's work contributes to job enrichment. Scheduling includes the authority to decide when to tackle which assignments and having some say in setting working hours, such as flexible working hours.

5. *Unique experience.* An enriched job has unique qualities or features. A public relations assistant, for example, has the opportunity to interact with visiting celebrities.

6. *Control over resources.* Another contributor to enrichment is the ability to have some control over resources, such as money, material, or people.

7. *Direct communication authority.* An enriched job provides workers the opportunity to communicate directly with other people who use their output. A software engineer with an enriched job, for example, handles complaints about the software she developed. The advantages of this dimension of an enriched job are similar to those derived from maintaining client relationships.

8. *Personal accountability.* In an enriched job, workers are responsible for their results. They accept credit for a job well done and blame for a job done poorly.

A highly enriched job has all eight of the preceding characteristics and gives the job holder an opportunity to satisfy growth needs such as self-fulfilment. A job with some of these characteristics would be moderately enriched. An impoverished job has none.

Before implementing a program of job enrichment, a manager must ask if the workers need or want more responsibility, variety, and growth in the first place. Some employees' jobs are already enriched enough. Other employees do not want an enriched job because they prefer to avoid the challenge and stress of responsibility. A study conducted in a government service organization indicated that employees with a strong need for growth were more likely to respond to an opportunity for performing enriched work. The independent variable studied was the manager offering a case-processing specialist the opportunity to collaborate with him or her on a case.[3]

The Job Characteristics Model

The concept of job enrichment has been expanded to the **job characteristics model,** a method of job design that focuses on the task and interpersonal demands of a job.[4] The model is based on both needs theory and expectancy theory, with its emphasis on workers looking to satisfy needs through the job. To illustrate, a basic proposition of the model is that workers value outcomes to the extent that the outcomes can help satisfy their deficiency and growth needs. As Exhibit 7–2 shows, five measurable characteristics of a job can improve employee motivation, satisfaction, and performance. These characteristics are:

1. *Skill variety,* the degree to which there are many skills to perform.
2. *Task identity,* the degree to which one worker is able to do a complete job, from beginning to end, with a tangible and possible outcome.
3. *Task significance,* the degree to which work has a heavy impact on others in the immediate organization or the external environment.
4. *Autonomy,* the degree to which a job offers freedom, independence, and discretion in scheduling and in determining procedures involved in its implementation.
5. *Feedback,* the degree to which a job provides direct information about performance.

As indicated in Exhibit 7–2, these core job characteristics relate to critical psychological states or key mental attitudes. Skill variety, task identity, and task significance lead to a feeling that the work is meaningful. The task dimension of autonomy leads logically to a feeling that one is responsible for work outcomes. The feedback dimension leads to knowledge of results. According to the model, a redesigned job must lead to these three psychological states for workers to achieve the outcomes of internal motivation, job satisfaction, growth satisfaction, low turnover and absenteeism, and high-quality performance.

The task significance characteristic can be a potent motivator at all job levels. Donald Schneider, the owner and president of a major trucking firm, motivates truckers in this way: "I help them see that everything they do in their jobs contributes to America's economy. I'm always telling then that every idea or action they take to lower our logistics costs lowers the price of products we deliver."[5]

The job characteristics model combines the five characteristics into a single index that reflects the overall potential of a job to trigger high internal work motivation. Called the Motivating Potential Score (MPS), the index is computed as follows:

Exhibit 7-2

The Job Characteristics Model of Job Enrichment

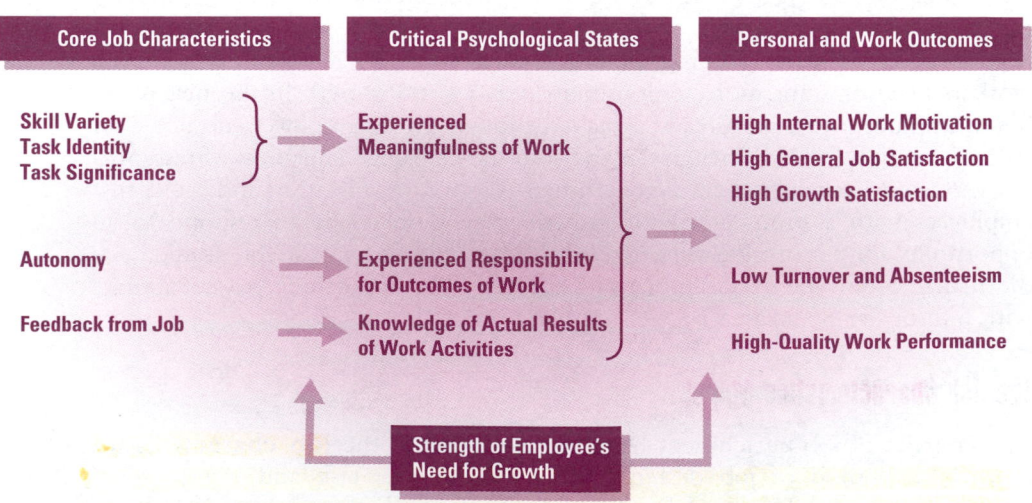

Core Job Characteristics	Critical Psychological States	Personal and Work Outcomes
Skill Variety Task Identity Task Significance	Experienced Meaningfulness of Work	High Internal Work Motivation High General Job Satisfaction High Growth Satisfaction
Autonomy	Experienced Responsibility for Outcomes of Work	Low Turnover and Absenteeism
Feedback from Job	Knowledge of Actual Results of Work Activities	High-Quality Work Performance

Strength of Employee's Need for Growth

Source: J. R. Hackman and G. R. Oldham, *Work Redesign* (Reading, MA: Addison-Wesley, 1980), p. 77.

126

$$MPS = \frac{\overset{\text{Skill}}{\text{Variety}} + \overset{\text{Task}}{\text{Identity}} + \overset{\text{Task}}{\text{Significance}}}{3} \times \text{Autonomy} \times \sigma \text{ Feedback}$$

Numeric values for each of the five job characteristics are obtained by tabulating the job holder's answers to the Job Diagnostic Survey, a written questionnaire. After computing the MPS, a researcher can evaluate whether redesigning a job actually changed employees' perceptions of its motivational value.

A potential problem in implementing the job characteristics model, as well as job enrichment in general, is that supervisors and group members may not agree on what constitutes an enriched job. A study conducted in a university office setting with a variety of jobs found that supervisors and subordinates perceived their job characteristics differently. (The dimensions studied were the same as those contained in the job characteristics model.)

The most notable difference was found for task significance, with the supervisors rating this dimension higher than group members did. A possible interpretation was that the supervisors had a clearer view of the "big picture," and thereby had a better understanding of the potential impact of a task. Another finding was that the group members perceived the enriched quality to have a bigger impact on job outcomes than did the supervisors level. Your perception of task significance has a bigger impact on your satisfaction and motivation than your supervisor's perception of the same factor. An implication of these findings is that employees should play a major role in job redesign, since their perceptions of enrichment differ from their supervisor's perceptions.[6]

Job Crafting

The traditional view of a job is that a competent worker carefully follows a job description, and good performance means that the person accomplishes what is specified in the job description. A contemporary view is that a job description is only a guideline: The competent worker is not confined by the constraints of a job description. He or she takes on many constructive activities not mentioned in the job description.

One way workers frequently deviate from their job descriptions is to modify their job to fit their personal preferences and capabilities. According to the research of Amy Wrzesniewski and Jane E. Dutton, employees craft their jobs by changing the tasks they perform, and their contacts with others, to make their jobs more meaningful.[7] To add variety to her job, for example, a team leader might make nutritional recommendations to team members. The team leader has altered her task of coaching about strictly work-related issues to also coaching about personal health. She has also broadened her role in terms of her impact on the lives of work associates.

Job crafting refers to the physical and mental changes workers make in the task or relationship aspects of their job. Three common types of job crafting involve changing: (1) the number and type of job tasks, (2) the interaction with others on the job, and (3) one's view of the job. The most frequent purpose of crafting is to make the job more meaningful or enriched. A cook, for example, might add flair to a meal just to inject a little personal creativity. Exhibit 7-3 illustrates these three forms of job crafting, including how crafting affects the meaning of work. After studying the exhibit, think through whether you have ever engaged in job crafting.

127

Exhibit 7-3

Forms of Job Crafting

Form	Example	Effect on Meaning of Work
Changing number, scope, and type of job tasks	Design engineers engage in changing the quality or amount of interactions with people, thereby moving a project to completion	Work is completed in a more timely fashion; engineers change the meaning of their jobs to be guardians and movers of projects
Changing quality and/or amount of interaction with others encountered in the job	Hospital cleaners actively care for patients and families, integrating themselves into the workflow of their floor units	Cleaners change the meaning of their jobs to be helpers of the sick; see the work of the floor unit as an integrated whole of which they are a vital part
Changing the view of the job	Nurses take responsibility for all information and "insignificant" tasks that may help them to care more appropriately for a patient	Nurses change the way they see the work to be more about patient advocacy, as well as high-quality technical care

Source: Adapted with permission from the Academy of Management Review from Amy Wresniewski and Jane E. Dutton, "Crafting a Job: Revisioning Employees as Active Crafters of Their Work," *Academy of Management Review,* April 2001, p. 185. Permission conveyed through the Copyright Clearance Center, Inc.

Self-Managed Work Teams

A dominant trend in job design is to organize workers into teams with considerable authority to direct and supervise themselves. A majority of U.S. corporations incorporate team structures, utilizing some form of self-management, in their organizations. Team structures are also prevalent in European and Asian industry particularly in manufacturing. A **self-managed work team** is a formally recognized group of employees who are responsible for an entire work process or segment that delivers a product or service to an internal or external customer.[8] Other terms for self-managed work teams include *self-directed work teams, autonomous group, semi-autonomous team, production work team,* and *work team.* The difference in title sometimes refers to varying amounts of authority held by the group. Self-managed work groups originated as an outgrowth of job enrichment. Working in teams broadens the responsibility of team members.

Implementing self-managed work teams requires that managers focus on empowering and motivating, rather than controlling. A manager who uses a command-and-control style would not be comfortable with self-managed teams.[9]

Small as well as large companies make use of this form of job design. The key purposes for establishing self-managed teams are to increase productivity, enhance quality, reduce cycle time (the amount of time required to complete a transaction), and respond more rapidly to a changing workplace. Next we describe the method of operation of these teams and take a brief look at the results.

Method of Operation

Members of a self-managed work team typically work together on an ongoing, day-by-day basis, thus differentiating it from a task force or committee. The work team is often given total responsibility or "ownership" of a product or service. A work team might be assigned the responsibility for preparing a merchandise catalog. At other times, the team is given responsibility for a major chunk of a job, such as building a truck engine (but not the entire truck). The self-managed work team is taught to think in terms of customer requirements. The team members might ask, "How easy would it be for a left-handed person to use this can opener?"

To promote the sense of ownership, workers are taught to become generalists rather than specialists. Each team member learns a broad range of skills and switches job assignments periodically. Members of the self-directed work team also receive training in team skills. Cross-training in different organizational functions is also important to help members develop an overall perspective of how the firm operates. As compiled by a team of experts,[10] the distinguishing characteristics of a self-directing work team are presented in Exhibit 7-4. Studying these characteristics will provide insight into work teams.

As a result of having so much responsibility for a product or service, team members usually develop pride in their work and team. At best, the team members feel as if they are operating a small business, with the profits (or losses) directly attributable to their efforts. An entry-level worker, such as a data-entry specialist in a market research firm, is less likely to have such feelings.

Self-Managed Work Team Effectiveness

Self-managed work teams demonstrate a reasonably good record of improving productivity, quality, and customer service. Corporate executives and small-business owners have found that self-managed work teams are a highly effective form of work group design. About 50 percent of the time, they result in at least some productivity gains, and effective teams can produce remarkable results. When self-management works, productivity gains of 10 to 20 percent are typical.[11] A representative example of the potential productivity gains from a self-managed work team took place at Monarch Marking Systems, based in Dayton, Ohio. The company manufactures labelling, identification, and tracking equipment. The teams trimmed the square footage needed in the assembly area by 70 percent, reduced past-due shipments by 90 percent, and increased productivity by 100 percent.[12]

A major contributor to work team effectiveness is the suitability of its members to a team operation. The Self-Assessment that follows gives you a chance to think about your mental readiness to work on a team.

Work teams also have some potential disadvantages. Absenteeism is sometimes higher than in traditional work group designs. The reason might be that team members believe that other team members can cover for them because they are multiskilled. (Yet the evidence here is mixed. Sometimes attendance is better in high-morale teams because the members do not want to let each other down.)

Exhibit 7-4

Characteristics of a Self-Managed Work Team

1. Team members are empowered to share many management and leadership functions, such as making job assignments and giving pep talks.
2. Members plan, control, and improve their own work processes.
3. Members set their own goals and inspect their own work.
4. Members create their own schedules and review their group performance.
5. Members often prepare their own budgets and coordinate their work with other departments.
6. Members typically order materials, keep inventories, and deal with suppliers.
7. Members are sometimes responsible for obtaining any new training they might need. (The organization, however, usually mandates the start-up training as described previously.)
8. Members are authorized to hire their own replacements or assume responsibility for disciplining their own members.
9. Members assume responsibility for the quality of their products and services, whether provided to internal or external customers.

SELF-ASSESSMENT

Mental Readiness for Assignment to a Work Team

Directions: Respond to each statement on the following scale: SD, strongly disagree; D, disagree; N, neutral; A, agree; SA. strongly agree.

			Amount of Agreement		
1. Employees should make the majority of decisions related to their work.	SD	D	N	A	SA
2. It is possible for corporate employees to take as much pride in their work as if it were their own business.	SD	D	N	A	SA
3. Workers who lack advanced training and education are capable of making useful work improvements.	SD	D	N	A	SA
4. Groups can work effectively without a clear-cut center of authority.	SD	D	N	A	SA
5. It is worth sacrificing some specialization of labor to give workers a chance to develop multiple skills.	SD	D	N	A	SA
6. Competent workers do not require too much supervision.	SD	D	N	A	SA
7. Having authority over people is not as important as being part of a smoothly working team.	SD	D	N	A	SA
8. Given the opportunity, many workers could manage themselves without much supervision.	SD	D	N	A	SA
9. Cordial relationships are important even in a factory setting.	SD	D	N	A	SA
10. The more power workers are given, the more likely they are to behave responsibly.	SD	D	N	A	SA

Scoring and Interpretation: Score the answers 1 through 5, with SD being 1 and SA being 5. Add the numerical value you assigned to each statement and total your scores. The closer your score is to 50, the higher is your degree of mental readiness to lead or participate on a work team. If your score is 30 or less, attempt to develop a more optimistic view of the capabilities and attitudes of workers. Start by looking for evidence of good accomplishments by skilled and semiskilled workers.

Another potential disadvantage is that a high–quality workforce is needed because team members have to be flexible and intelligent and think broadly. Finally, in a manufacturing setting, establishing work modules for the team can require substantial space, and costs can skyrocket when each group has its own equipment.

2

Summarize the basics of a behavior modification program in the workplace.

ORGANIZATIONAL BEHAVIOR MODIFICATION

One of the more elaborate systems for motivating employees is based upon reinforcement theory. **Organizational behavior modification (OB Mod)** is the application of reinforcement theory for motivating people in work settings. OB Mod programs typically use positive reinforcement rather than punishment to modify behavior. Linking behavior with positive consequences is more effective than using negative motivators, and positive consequences arouse less controversy. Tom Osbourne (R–Neb), former national championship winning football coach at the University of Nebraska—and also an educational psychologist—says that rewards shape behavior better than punishment. He believes that his emphasis on positive motivators contributed to his winning attitude and dedication.[13] Here we present a framework for a formal OB Mod program, followed by suggestions for everyday managerial application of behavior modification.

Steps in a Formal OB Mod Program

As outlined in Exhibit 7-5, the OB Mod program begins with identifying behaviors that require change.[14] For example, the regional manager of a chain of convenience stores might believe strongly that cashiers should always ask "What else can I get for you?" before a customer pays. Market research has shown that this statement enhances sales. The behavior that needs to change is that the cashiers are not asking this question frequently enough (see the InfoTrac sidebar).

The second step is for the manager to measure baseline performance; for example, how frequently cashiers ask the sales-inducing question. The behavior is stated in terms of a percentage frequency for various intervals. Store observers assigned by the regional manager might find, for example, that cashiers ask "What else can I get you?" only about 20 percent of the time.

Step three is to analyze the behavioral antecedents and contingent consequences in the performance-related context (analyzing the functional consequences). This analysis attempts to answer two questions: (1) What are the antecedents of the performance-related behavior measured in the first two steps?, and (2) What are the contingent consequences when workers make the desired response? Antecedents can include many factors such as equipment, technological processes, job design, and/or performance training. However, here we are concerned with antecedents that set the occasion for the behavior to occur—a customer bringing goods to the counter.

The contingent consequences are the outcomes that stem from the behavior. The behavior is what the cashier does (asking the question). Consequences are the outcomes that stem from the behavior, such as the customer saying, "Yes, please get me six Beef Jerkies." A more general consequence would be that sales increase an average of $3.00 per customer when the cashier asks, "What else can I get for you?"

Next the manager decides upon an intervention strategy appropriate to the situation. Environmental variables affecting the linkage between reward and behavior include the nature of the industry, structure, size, processes, and technology. For example, the information technology built into the cash registers will influence how easy it is to record sales above baseline. The manager is now ready to apply an appropriate contingency strategy.

Positive reinforcement is applied to increase functional behaviors and decrease dysfunctional behaviors. Punishment of dysfunctional behaviors might also be used as a last resort. Punishment, however, is followed by positive reinforcement as the worker improves.

After intervening, the manager measures performance again to assess whether the desired effect—asking the sales-inducing question frequently—has been achieved. If the appropriate behavior does not occur frequently, the manager must choose a new intervention strategy or repeat the entire process.

If performance increases as planned, the manager must maintain the desirable behavior through a schedule of reinforcement. Under a continuous schedule, the cashier receives a reward each time a customer responds positively to the question. An intermittent schedule offers rewards from time to time. (A ratio schedule gives the reward on a ratio, such as one reward per six right responses; an interval schedule gives the reward based on the amount of time between the right responses.) The cashier might receive continuous reinforcement in terms of earning a small commission on every sale. The fact that customers will not always respond "Yes" to the key question creates an intermittent schedule.

Customer service is also critical for online retailers, not just at brick-and-mortar convenience stores. Designing sites to give customers the information they need, such as what's new and what's on sale, are typical ways that e-tailers such as Bluefly (**http://www .bluefly.com**) "talk" to their customers. Think about some of your favorite retailers. Then visit their online sites to see if they have successfully recreated online what you like best about a store's atmosphere. *What kinds of positive reinforcement do the sites employ to encourage you to make a purchase or come back?* To help you understand more about how online retailers use positive reinforcement, log on to InfoTrac at **http://www .infotrac-college.com.**

Exhibit 7-5

OB Mod Application Model

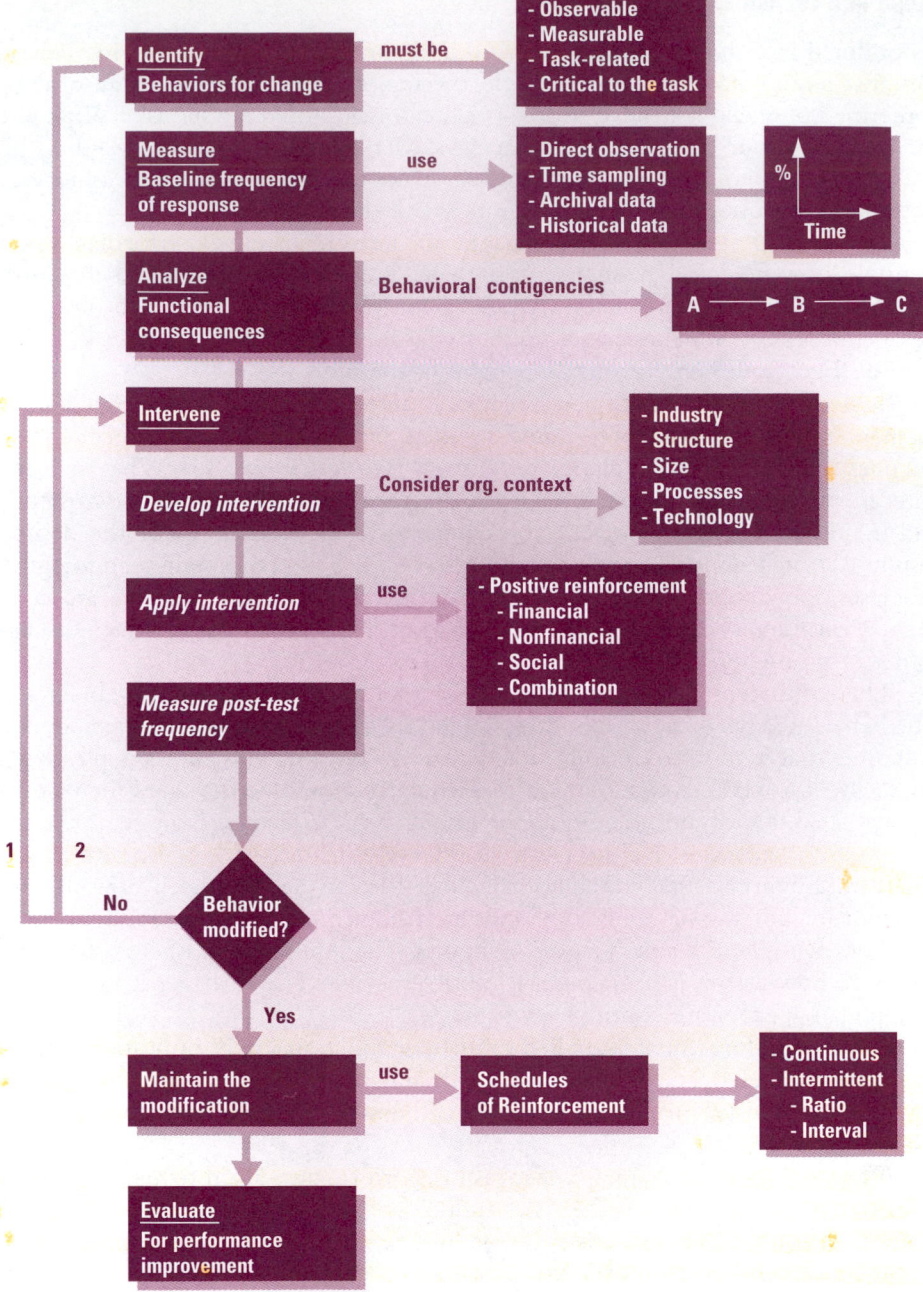

Note: A = antecedent, B = behavior, C = consequences

Source: Reprinted with permission of the Academy of Management Review from Fred Luthans and Alexander D. Stajkovic, "Reinforce for Performance: The Need to Go Beyond Pay and Even Rewards," *Academy Management Executive*, May 1999, p. 53.

The last step answers the question of whether the OB Mod program leads to performance improvement in observable and measurable terms. The manager looks for improvements in the employee's behavior. A store observer might monitor how often the key question is asked; receipts might provide an index of change in sales volume.

Rules for the Application of OB Mod

Principles of behavior modification can also be applied outside of a structured company program. Our focus here is with managers' day-by-day application of OB Mod, with an emphasis on positive reinforcement. An individual contributor attempting to motivate somebody else can also apply these rules. Following these eight rules increases the probability that an OB Mod program will achieve its intended result of increasing the motivation and productivity of individuals and groups. Although the rules have generally been developed with individuals, they also apply to rewarding group performance.

Identify rules and suggestions for motivating group members through behavior modification.

133

Rule 1: Choose an appropriate reward or punishment. An appropriate reward or punishment is effective in motivating a worker or group and is feasible from the company standpoint. Rewards should have a high positive attraction and punishments a negative one. If one reward does not work, another should be tried. Feasible rewards include money, company stock, recognition, challenging new assignments, and status symbols such as a private work area. Often the most basic type of reward, such as an expression of appreciation, has the strongest effect in achieving higher productivity and employee retention.[15] It is generally best to use the mildest form of punishment that will motivate the person, such as verbally expressing disappointment. Although widely used, fear is a generally ineffective form of punishment because it may cause resentment, revenge, and a degree of immobilization.

Rule 2: Reinforce the behaviors you really want to encourage. An axiom of behavior modification is that you get what you reinforce. If you give rewards to customer service representatives based on the number of requests for help they process, you will increase the number of calls. Customer service may not improve, however, because the representatives will feel compelled to quickly process the calls for help. Rewards for resolving customer problems have a greater probability of enhancing customer service. (It takes time and patience to resolve some problems called in to a help desk.)

Rule 3: Supply ample feedback. OB Mod tactics cannot work without frequent feedback to individuals. Feedback can take the form of simply telling people they have done something right or wrong. Brief e-mail messages or handwritten notes are another common form of feedback. Be aware, however, that many employees resent seeing a message with negative feedback on their computer monitor.

Rule 4: Rewards should be commensurate with the good deed. Average performance is encouraged when all forms of accomplishment receive the same reward. Suppose one employee made substantial progress in reducing customer complaints. She should receive more recognition (or a more valuable reward) than a group member who makes only a minor contribution to solving the problem.

Rule 5: Schedule rewards intermittently. Intermittent rewards sustain desired behavior longer and slow the process of desired behavior fading away when it is not rewarded. A reward that is given continuously may lose its impact. A practical value of intermittent reinforcement is that it saves time. Few managers have enough time to dispense rewards for every appropriate response forthcoming from group members.

Rule 6: Rewards and punishments should follow the observed behavior closely in time. For maximum effectiveness, workers should be rewarded shortly after doing something right and punished shortly after doing something wrong. A built-in feedback system, such as software working or not working, capitalizes on this principle. If you administer rewards and punishments, strive to administer them the same day they are earned.

134

Rule 7: Make rewards visible to the recipient and to others. The person who receives the reward should be aware that it has been received. A person might receive a small bonus for good performance with the payment being virtually hidden in the paycheck. Because the reward is not noticed, it has a negligible impact on behavior.[16] Ideally, rewards should also be made visible to other employees besides the recipient. Rewards that are made public increase the status of the recipient and also let other employees know what kinds of behavior get rewarded.

Rule 8: Change the reward periodically. Rewards do not retain their effectiveness indefinitely. A major criticism of positive reinforcement as a motivational technique is that rewards go stale. Employees and customers lose interest in striving for a reward they have received many times previously. This is particularly true with a repetitive statement such as "Nice job" or "Fantastic." It is helpful for the manager to formulate a list of feasible rewards and try different ones from time to time.

Now do the Skill-Development Exercise that follows to practice several of these rules for using behavior modification.

Behavior modification has a long history of improving productivity on the job. Fred Luthans and Alexander D. Sajkovic performed a meta-analysis of all the empirical findings of research conducted with the OB Mod method over a 20-year period. The study indicated a substantial 17 percent average improvement in performance. The overall improvement in manufacturing settings was 33 percent, and was 13 percent in service settings. Another notable finding was that social reinforcers such as recognition and positive feedback were as effective as monetary rewards.[17]

The same researchers conducted an experiment in the operations division of a company that processes and mails credit card bills for several hundred financial institutions, e-commerce customers included. The four reward groups in the study were: (1) routine pay for performance; (2) monetary incentives based on behavior mod; (3) social recognition, such as public compliments; and (4) performance feedback. Monetary rewards based on the principles of behavior modification outperformed routine pay for performance, with a performance increase of 37 percent versus

SKILL-DEVELOPMENT EXERCISE

COLLABORATE

Organizational Behavior Modification

In both of the following scenarios, one student plays the role of the manager attempting to modify the behavior of, or motivate, the other individual. Another student plays the role of the recipient of these attempts at motivation.

Scenario 1: Rewarding a Customer Service Representative. The customer service manager reviews customer service reports and discovers that one service rep has resolved the most complaints for four consecutive weeks. Since this rep has only been on the job for six months, the manager wants to ensure that the rep feels amply rewarded and appreciated. The manager also wants to sustain this high level of performance. The manager calls the rep into the office to discuss this outstanding performance and administer an appropriate reward.

Scenario 2: Punishing a Customer Service Representative. The customer service manager reviews customer service reports and discovers that one service rep has resolved the fewest complaints for four consecutive weeks. Furthermore, three customers have written the company complaining of rude treatment by this representative. Since this rep has only been on the job 6 months, the manager wants to make sure that the rep makes substantial improvements. The manager calls the rep into the office to discuss this poor performance and administer an appropriate punishment.

Others in the class should observe the two scenarios so they can provide feedback on how well OB Mod principles were applied.

11 percent. Behavior mod also had stronger effects on performance than social recognition and performance feedback.[18] Evidence like this reassuring to the leader/manager who intends to apply behavior modification in the workplace.

MOTIVATION THROUGH RECOGNITION

Motivating workers by giving them praise and recognition can be considered a direct application of positive reinforcement. Nevertheless, recognition is such a potentially powerful motivator that it merits separate attention. Also, reward and recognition programs are a standard practice in business and nonprofit firms. An example would be rewarding high performing employees with electronic gift cards or designating them "employees of the month." A reward and recognition program essentially focuses on rewards as a form of recognition. The gift card just mentioned might have a commercial value of $100, but its main value is to recognize a job well done.

Recognition is a strong motivator because it is a normal human need to crave recognition. At the same time, recognition is effective because most workers feel they do not receive enough recognition. Several studies conducted over a 60-year time span indicate that employees welcome praise for a job well done as much as a regular paycheck. This finding should not be interpreted to mean that praise is an adequate substitute for compensation. Employees tend to regard compensation as an entitlement, whereas recognition is perceived as a gift.[19] Workers, including your coworkers, want to know that their output is useful to somebody.

To appeal to the recognition need of others, identify a meritorious behavior and then recognize that behavior with an oral, written, or material reward. The rules for the use of behavior modification are directly applicable. An example of employee recognition is as follows. As the team leader of a production unit, you observe that Janice, one of the manufacturing technicians, has the best safety record in the plant—zero accidents in five years. You send an e-mail message notifying every company employee of Janice's accomplishment.

An outstanding advantage of using recognition, including praise, as a motivator is that a person can give it with little or no cost, yet can still be powerful. Recognition thus has an enormous return on investment in comparison to a cash bonus. The following are several more points to consider to better understand and implement reward and recognition programs:

1. *Feedback is an essential part of recognition.* Specific feedback about what the worker did right makes recognition more meaningful. For example, "The clever cartoon you inserted on our Web site increased sales by 22 percent for replacement keyboards."

2. *Praise is one of the most powerful forms of recognition.* Praise works well because it enhances self-esteem if the praise is genuine. As indicated previously, praise is a supplement to other rewards such as compensation. A challenge in using praise as a form of recognition is that not everybody responds well to the same form of praise. A germane example is that highly technical people tend not to like general praise like "Great job." Instead, they prefer a laid-back yet factual statement about how their output made a contribution. Jim Grenier, a human resources director at Intuit (a developer of financial software) administers an elaborate rewards and recognition program. He notes that public recognition is an important component of any employee award.[20]

3. *Reward and recognition programs should be linked to organizational goals.* Many organizations understand that the biggest return on reward and recognition

Describe why recognition is a good motivator, and the nature of reward and recognition programs in the workplace.

programs takes place when the rewards and recognition are linked to a business strategy.[21] For example, if the company strategy is to develop a more culturally diverse workforce at all levels, an employee should be recognized for recruiting a Latino computer scientist.

4. *Employee input into what type of rewards and recognition are valued is useful.* A company might spend a lot of money giving away grandfather clocks to employees, only to find that they would prefer gift certificates to movies as a form of reward and recognition. Exhibit 7-6 illustrates how a not-for-profit firm solicited employee input to enhance the possibility of having a reward and recognition program meaningful to employees.

5. *It is important to evaluate the effectiveness of the reward and recognition program.* As with all organizational behavior and human resources interventions, it is useful to assess how well the reward and recognition program is working. For example, the company could establish baseline measures of performance, administer the reward and recognition program, and then measure performance again. (Review the section about research methods in Chapter 1.)

MOTIVATION THROUGH FINANCIAL INCENTIVES

Describe how to effectively use financial incentives to motivate others, including the use of stock options and gainsharing.

A natural reinforcer for workers at any level is to offer them financial incentives for good performance. Using financial incentives as a motivator is another application of behavior modification. Financial incentives, however, predate behavior modification in the workplace and are also an application of common sense. The following sections describe four current issues about money as a reinforcer: link–

Exhibit 7-6

Survey to Measure Employee Attitudes toward Rewards and Recognition

1. Do you receive positive feedback from your supervisor on a regular basis? Does your supervisor thank you for the work you do?
   ____ Mostly yes   ____ No or rarely

2. Have you ever wanted to be able to recognize good work done by coworkers?
   ____ Frequently   ____ Seldom

3. Would you prefer to receive recognition initiated by supervisors and managers or by your peers? Or both? (Check all that apply.)
   ____ Managers   ____ Supervisors   ____ Peers
   Keeping in mind that this program is intended to involve "non-cash" tangible rewards that are limited by University and IRS regulations, please respond to the following:

4. What kind of "rewards" would you like to see given?
   ____ Mugs, other items with a special department of University logo
   ____ Flowers   ____ Certificates of appreciation   ____ Catalog of gift certificates
   ____ T-shirts   ____ CDs   ____ Parking passes
   ____ Transit passes   ____ Dinner certificates   ____ Tickets to events
   ____ Other: List suggestions below

5. How could we be sure such a program would work effectively and positively?

6. What drawbacks do you see to such a program?

7. Would you be willing to participate in a work group to implement a program?

   For more information on Berkeley's reward/recognition program, check out the University's Web site for human resources at http://hrweb.berkeley.edu.

Source: University of California, Berkeley, as reprinted in "Employee Input Can Maximize Recognition/Reward Program Success," *HRfocus*, November 1999, p. 15. By permission of the University of California, Berkeley.

ing pay to performance, stock options, gainsharing, and problems associated with financial incentives.

Linking Pay to Performance

Financial incentives are more effective when they are linked to (or contingent upon) good performance. Linking pay to performance generally motivates people to work harder because the link acts as a reinforcer. The recommended approach is to tie employee pay to specific performance criteria and link it directly to value-enhancing business results.[22] The variable pay must be re-earned each year and does not permanently increase base salary.

A representative example of variable pay is the system at MetLife. The company measures performance of employees and managers by comparing each person to others who are on the same level. Performance is measured on a 1-to-5 scale. The company then calculates which employees are categorized as top, middle, or bottom. Employees in the top category receive about 65 percent more in bonuses than those in the middle. Employees in the bottom category might receive no bonus.[23]

Pay for performance is not based on achieving financial goals exclusively. Other performances factors might include providing good customer service, on-time delivery, ratings from client satisfaction surveys, being a good team player, and sharing knowledge with other workers. Merit (or variable) pay for both individuals and the team is based on actual results. Merit pay runs from 5 percent to over 15 percent of total compensation.

Although many employers believe they link pay to performance, research suggests that merit pay may not be so closely linked to performance. A team of researchers meta-analyzed the results of 39 studies about the relationship between pay and performance. A striking conclusion was that pay had little relationship to the quality of work, but did show a moderately positive relationship with the *quantity* of work. However, managers are not completely to blame. It is often easier to measure how much work employees are performing than how well they are performing. The meta-analysis in question also confirms the obvious: People will produce more work when money is at stake.[24] In defense of employers, it is easier to evaluate quantity than quality.

A major concern about pay-for-performance plans is that the ratings assigned to people (such as the high, medium, and low categories at MetLife) are too subjective. Another concern is that individual accomplishment is difficult to measure because most of a worker's contribution in an organization is partially attributed to the work of others, or the organizational system.

The accompanying Organizational Behavior in Action box helps explain why some managers perceive variable pay as a way of boosting productivity and lowering payroll costs.

Stock Options

A widely used method of motivating workers through financial means is to make them part owners of the business through stock purchases. Stock ownership can be motivational because employees participate in the financial success of the firm as measured by its stock price. If employees work hard, the company may become more successful and the value of the stock may increase. Stock options also have other goals related to organizational effectiveness including attracting and retaining

Organizational Behavior *in Action*

Companies Shift to More Variable Pay

When sales at privately held Kaehler Luggage Inc. declined significantly after the terrorist attacks in 2001, President and CEO Wallace W. Kaehler Jr. froze salaries for the 100 employees at 14 stores in Chicago and its surrounding suburbs. With same-store sales showing single-digit increases in 2002, salaries were raised by 3 percent in 2003. But raises are not the only way Kaehler employees are now earning more money. The company's total compensation package was revised, tripling the percentage of potential compensation attributed to bonuses geared to sales. Some of Kaehler's high-end luggage suppliers are even underwriting bonuses based on sales of their products. Under the new plan, employees can earn 5 percent to 15 percent of salary in bonus.

"We've always had incentives for selling," Kaehler said. "By moving more of our payroll dollars to commission-based and bonus-based incentives, it's a way to reward performance and funnel more money to employees, while keeping our payroll in line."

The company has been selling luggage for 74 years. Experts say its recent decision represent two current trends in compensation: Record-low spending on base salaries and record-high spending for bonuses and other forms of compensation.

"We're seeing a fundamental shift in the thinking at companies as to how they're planning to reward employees," says consultant Ken Abosch of Hewitt Associates Inc. His information is based on a survey of compensation trends among 1,000 companies. "Base salaries are a fixed component of costs," he explains. "They're keeping that expense minimal so it won't jeopardize profits and earnings per share. But bonuses are variable costs. They can positively impact sales and job performance. There's tremendous upside for companies to move compensation to the variable cost column." Overall, companies now invest 10.9 percent of compensation expenses on bonuses.

Questions

1. Why might the shift to more compensation in the form of bonuses enhance employee motivation?
2. What problems might retailers like Kaehler Luggage encounter as they place more emphasis on bonuses and less on base salary?

Source: Anne Therese Palmer, "Big Raises Just Not in the Cards: Emphasis Shifts to Bonuses, Other Compensation," *Chicago Tribune*, December 26, 2002 (http://www.chicagotribune.com/business).

---

talent, focusing employee attention on organizational performance, and creating a culture of ownership.[25]

Stock options give employees the right to purchase a certain number of company shares in the future at a specified price, generally the market price on the day the option is granted. If the stock rises in value, you can purchase it at a discount. If the stock sinks below your designated purchase price, your option is worthless (or "under water"). In the late 1990s, thousands of workers in the information technology field became millionaires and multimillionaires (at least on paper) with their stock options. However, within two years most of these gains evaporated as technology stocks plunged. Exhibit 7-7 shows the mathematics behind a stock option.

One of the best publicized uses of stock options is at a low-technology firm, Starbucks Corp. Approximately 40 percent of Starbucks employees participate in the plan. After exercising their options, these employees have made down payments on houses, purchased cars, and paid for their college education. Stock options have also helped reduce turnover to approximately one-third the industry norm.

The true impact of stock options as a motivational device is difficult to evaluate. A major confounding factor is that firms that offer stock options (an extrin-

Exhibit 7-7

How a Stock Option Works

Employee decides to exercise option for 400 shares at $10.57 each when stock reaches $35 per share.

Brokerage sells 400 shares of company stock at $35 each (400 shares × $35)	=	$14,000
Brokerage deducts exercise price (400 shares × $10.57)		– 4,228
		9,772
Taxes withheld (28% for federal income tax + 7.56% for social security tax)		– 3,475
		6,297
Brokerage deducts fees/commissions/interest		– 100
		6197
Brokerage pays profit to employee $ 6,197		$6197

Source: Carrington Nelson, "Exercising Your Stock Options," *Gannett News Service,* 26 July 1998. Copyright 1998, Gannett Co., Inc. Reprinted with permission.

sic motivator) also offer exciting work (an intrinsic motivator). As explained by Mike Butler, a compensation specialist, many of the workers who are attracted to high-tech, entrepreneurial companies find the work stimulating. "Pay isn't the only issue or even the primary issue for some workers. It's the ability to have an impact and do something exciting."[26]

A major potential problem with stock options as a motivational tool is that they become worthless if a stock plunges because the employees left with the option to purchase stock at above the market value! The employee suffers from disappointed expectations, and the company looks foolish. Another particularly acute problem arises with high-tech start-ups that offer relatively low salary combined with generous stock options. If the stock price never rises or plunges, the employee has worked for less than equitable total compensation, creating dissatisfaction.

Gainsharing

Many organizations attempt to increase motivation and productivity through a company-wide plan of linking incentive pay to increases in performance. **Gainsharing** is a formal program of allowing employees to participate financially in the productivity gains they have achieved. Gainsharing Inc. is the institute that helps promote this motivational method (see **http://www.gainsharing .com**). Gainsharing is based on principles of positive reinforcement and the motivational impact of money.

The formulas used in gainsharing vary widely, but there are common elements. Managers begin by comparing what the employees are paid to what they sell or produce. Assume that labor costs make up 50 percent of production costs. Any reduction below 50 percent is placed in a bonus pool. The company's share of productivity savings in the pool can then be distributed to stockholders as increased profits. The savings may allow managers to lower prices, a move that could make the company more competitive.

The second element of gainsharing is employee involvement. Managers establish a mechanism that actively solicits, reviews, and implements employee suggestions about productivity improvement. A committee of managers and employees reviews the ideas and then implements the most promising suggestions.[27]

Gainsharing plans have a 64-year history of turning unproductive companies around and making successful companies even more productive. Gainsharing Inc.

contends that most companies will achieve an increase in their productive output of 10 percent to 30 percent within 30 to 90 days after implementing gainsharing. The reason is that it becomes the employees' self-interest to maximize company output.[28] Gainsharing programs began in manufacturing but are also used widely in service firms such as in financial services.

Lincoln Electric is often cited as an ideal example of gainsharing because its productivity is almost double the industry average. Gainsharing is a key aspect of the company's Incentive Performance System. In addition to exceptional productivity, motivation is high, absenteeism and turnover are exceedingly low, and no layoffs have occurred. Over the life of the system, bonuses have averaged 95.5 percent of base pay. Bonuses are paid at the end of the year in one check, thus magnifying the perception of the importance of the bonus.[29] Although the year-end bonus does not fit the suggestion of giving rewards close in time to the good behavior, it does make the bonus a reward of higher valence.

A research team conducted an experimental evaluation of gainsharing in two hubs of a Fortune 500 company. One hub served as the experimental group where the gainsharing plan was implemented, and the other served as the control group (with no gainsharing). Survey data were collected from several thousand employees participating in the study. The data were analyzed before the beginning of the program and then at 7 and 24 months into the program. Another data analysis took place at 20 months, 3 months after the gainsharing bonus had been eliminated.

The researchers found that even a short-lived gainsharing program can foster and sustain long-term job performance. It was also found that gainsharing contributes to positive employee attitudes, even after the termination of program. The study concluded that the gainsharing program enhanced peer communication. In turn, the improved communication became a source of learning that eventually led to behavioral changes in the workers.[30]

Problems Associated with Financial Incentives

Although financial incentives are widely used as motivators, they can create problems. For example, workers may not agree with managers about the value of their contributions. Financial incentives can also pit individuals and groups against each other. The result may be unhealthy competition rather than cooperation and teamwork. A problem noted with pay for performance is that the method typically rewards immediate, short-term actions. Sales representatives may receive bonuses based on the number of contracts they close, but not bonuses for suggesting new products based on customers' changing needs. Also, if employees focus on immediate results to earn bonuses, they will sometimes not invest effort in working on long-range ideas and exploratory tasks that could lead to innovation.[31]

The most researched argument against financial rewards is that they focus the attention of workers too much on rewards such as money or stocks. (This follows the logic of the opposition to extrinsic motivation in general.) In the process, the workers lose out on intrinsic rewards such as joy in accomplishment. Instead of being passionate about the work they are doing, people become overly concerned with the size of their reward. One argument is that external rewards do not create a lasting commitment. Instead, they create temporary compliance, such as working hard in the short run to earn a bonus. A frequent problem with merit pay systems is that a person who does not receive a merit increase one pay period often feels that he or she has been punished. Another argument against financial incentives is that the rewards manipulate people in the same manner as bribes.

Jeffrey Pfeffer explains that people do work for money, but they work even more for meaning in their lives. Work brings people a meaningful type of fun. Pfeffer believes that people who ignore this truth are essentially bribing their employees and will pay the price in lack of loyalty and commitment. He illustrates his position with the SAS Institute, a successful software company that emphasizes excellent benefits and exciting work rather than financial incentives.[32]

In reality, workers at all levels want a combination of internal rewards and financial rewards, along with other external rewards such as praise. Bob Nelson, the employee rewards specialist who preaches the importance of non-financial rewards, demands $12,500 for a talk about employee motivation.[33] The ideal combination is to offer exciting (internally rewarding) work to people and simultaneously pay them enough money so they are not preoccupied with matters such as salary and bonuses. Money is the strongest motivator when people have financial problems. Another reality is that even if a firm offers exciting work, great benefits, and wonderful coworkers, they usually need to offer financial incentives to attract quality workers.

CHOOSING AN APPROPRIATE MOTIVATIONAL MODEL

In this and the previous chapter, thirteen approaches to understanding and enhancing motivation have been presented. Although these approaches have different labels, most of them have elements in common. In quick review, the thirteen approaches are: (1) the needs hierarchy, (2) the two-factor theory, (3) the achievement–power–affiliation triad, (4) goal theory, (5) reinforcement theory, (6) expectancy theory, (7) equity theory, (8) social learning theory, (9) intrinsic versus extrinsic motivation, (10) job design, (11) organizational behavior modification, (12) recognition, and (13) financial incentives.

A fruitful approach to choosing an effective motivation theory or program for a given situation is for the manager (or other would-be motivator) to carefully diagnose the situation. Choose a motivational approach that best fits the deficiency or neglected opportunity in a given situation. Observe the people that need motivation, and also interview them about their interests and concerns. Then apply a motivational approach that appears to match the interests, concerns, deficits, or missed opportunity. Four examples will help clarify the diagnostic approach:

6

Choose an appropriate motivational model for a given situation.

1. The manager observes that group members perform their jobs well enough to meet standards, but they are not excited about their work. Introducing job enrichment and intrinsic motivation could be just what the organizational behaviorist ordered.
2. The manager observes that group members appear interested in their work and that they like the company and their coworkers. Yet they spend too much time grumbling about personal financial problems. The most direct approach to enhancing motivation in this situation would be to introduce a program of financial incentives. To be effective, the financial payouts should be large enough to make a difference in the financial welfare of the workers.
3. The manager attempts to use recognition to motivate workers at different occupational levels. He or she should choose recognition methods that are likely to have the highest valence for the particular level of worker. Symbolic forms of recognition such as company hats, ties, and desk clocks are likely to have the highest valence for people at lower occupational levels, such as clerical and production workers. Professional-level workers are likely to be more motivated

IMPLICATIONS FOR MANAGERIAL PRACTICE

1. Although motivation through job design is complex, time consuming, and expensive, it must be given careful consideration in any strategic attempt to enhance motivation and productivity. This is especially true because motivation through job design is the conceptual core for a major change to take place in the organization of work—the shift to self-managed work teams.

2. Employees chosen for work teams should be those who show pride in their work and enjoy working cooperatively with others. Self-nomination, or asking for volunteers for the self-directed work team, will decrease selection

errors. After employees are selected, they must be trained thoroughly to become productive members of work teams. Essential training areas include problem-solving techniques, technical skills, and interpersonal and leadership skills.

3. No motivational program is a substitute for adequate compensation, including pay and benefits. One of the many reasons that money remains an all-important reinforcer is that most people have financial worries. One problem is that family income has not kept up with the high cost of housing, creating financial pressures for many wage earners.

by written forms of recognition, including letters to their personal files documenting their contributions.

4. The manager attempts to motivate members of the contingent workforce such as temporary workers and part-time workers. Recognizing these workers' needs for security, company benefits might prove to have high valence, since many contingent workers lack a good benefits package.

SUMMARY OF KEY POINTS

1 Explain how to enhance motivation through job enrichment, the job characteristics model, and work group design.

A major strategy for enhancing motivation is to increase the challenge and responsibility in a job. An enriched, and therefore motivational, job includes some of the following characteristics: direct feedback, client relationships, new learning, control over scheduling, unique experience, control over resources, direct communication authority, and personal accountability. Job enrichment works best when workers want or need more responsibility, variety, and growth, which is not a given.

Job enrichment has been expanded to create the job characteristics model, which focuses on the task and interpersonal dimensions of a job. Five characteristics of a job can improve employee motivation, satisfaction, and performance: skill variety, task identity, task significance, autonomy, and feedback. These characteristics relate to critical psychological states, which in turn lead to outcomes such as internal motivation, satisfaction, low absenteeism, and high quality performance.

Workers often enrich their own jobs by modifying their job descriptions themselves through crafting, or adapting their jobs in terms of: (1) the number and types of tasks, (2) interactions with others, and (3) their view of the job.

A dominant trend in job design is to organize workers into self-managed work teams in order to increase productivity and quality and reduce cycle time. The team is given total responsibility for a product or service in dealing with an external or internal customer. Each team member learns a broad range of skills and switches job assignments periodically. Team members plan, control, and improve their own work processes. They usually order materials, keep inventories, and deal with suppliers.

Self-managed work team members have to be mentally flexible and alert and possess at least average interpersonal skills. They must take pride in their work and enjoy working cooperatively.

2 Summarize the basics of a behavior modification program in the workplace.

Organizational behavior modification (OB Mod), an application of reinforcement theory, is an elaborate motivational system. A formal program includes steps such as: identifying behavior performance problems, developing a contingency intervention strategy, maintaining desirable behavior, and measuring improvement. OB Mod programs are well documented as a method of enhancing productivity in manufacturing and service settings. Social reinforcers work as well as financial ones.

3 **Identify rules and suggestions for motivating group members through behavior modification.**

Behavior modification can also be applied outside of a formal program by the manager following these rules: choosing an appropriate reward or punishment, reinforcing the behaviors you want to encourage, supplying ample feedback, making rewards commensurate with the good deed, scheduling rewards intermittently, giving rewards and punishments promptly, making the rewards visible to the recipient and others, and changing the reward periodically.

4 **Describe why recognition is a good motivator, and the nature of reward and recognition programs in the workplace.**

Recognition is a strong motivator because it is a normal human need to crave recognition; most workers feel they do not receive enough recognition. To appeal to the recognition need of others, identify a meritorious behavior and then recognize that behavior with an oral, written, or material reward. Praise is a powerful form of recognition. Reward and recognition programs should be linked to organizational goals. Employee input into what types of rewards and recognition are valued is useful.

5 **Describe how to effectively use financial incentives to motivate others, including the use of stock options and gainsharing.**

Financial incentives are a widely used motivator at all worker levels. Such incentives are more effective when they are linked to performance. In some firms, members of self-managed work teams receive part of their compensation based on team performance.

A widely used way of motivating workers with financial incentives is to make them part owners of the business through stock purchases. Stock options give employees the right to purchase a certain number of company shares in the future at a specified price. If the stock price drops, the option is worthless.

Gainsharing is a formal program that enables employees to participate financially in the productivity gains they have achieved, thus enhancing motivation. Bonuses are distributed to employees based on how much they decrease the labor cost involved in producing or selling goods. Employee involvement in increasing productivity is an important part of gainsharing.

Financial incentives can create problems such as poor cooperation and focusing too much attention on external rewards such as money or stocks. Instead of being passionate about the work they are doing, people become overly concerned with the size of the reward. In reality, workers at all levels want a combination of internal rewards and financial rewards, along with other external rewards such as praise.

6 **Choose an appropriate motivational model for a given situation.**

A fruitful approach to choose an effective motivation theory or program for a given situation is for the manager to carefully diagnose the situation. A motivational approach is then chosen that best fits the deficiency or neglected opportunity in the situation. An example would be to understand that part-time workers might be strongly motivated by good benefits.

KEY TERMS AND PHRASES

Job Enrichment, *124*
The process of making a job more motivational and satisfying by adding variety, responsibility, and managerial decision making.

Job Characteristics Model, *125*
A method of job design that focuses on the task and interpersonal demands of a job.

Job Crafting, *127*
The physical and mental changes workers make in the task or relationships aspects of their job.

Self-managed Work Team, *128*
A formally recognized group of employees responsible for an entire work process or segment that delivers a product or service to an internal or external customer.

Organizational Behavior Modification (OB Mod), *130*
The application of reinforcement theory for motivating people in work settings.

Stock Option, *138*
A financial incentive that gives employees the right to purchase a certain number of company shares at a specified price, generally the market price of the stock on the day the option is granted.

Gainsharing, *139*
A formal program of allowing employees to participate financially in the productivity gains they have achieved.

DISCUSSION QUESTIONS AND ACTIVITIES

1. How might the job of a telemarketer for debt consolidation services be enriched?
2. Give an example of how a technical support representative for an Internet service provider might *craft* his or her job.
3. Give your own example of how rewarding one type of work behavior might result in behavior that the company really does not want to occur.

4. Critics of behavior modification contend that it is a method of manipulating workers. What is your assessment of this criticism?

5. What forms of recognition would be the most effective in motivating you? How do you know?

6. In what way do stock options interfere with intrinsic motivation?

7. Why does gainsharing enhance cooperation rather than competition?

8. ![COLLABORATE] Ask a classmate whether he or she would prefer to take a new position that offered: (a) below-average pay but some stock options, or (b) above-average pay but no stock options. What might the answer tell you about your friend's personality?

ORGANIZATIONAL BEHAVIOR ONLINE

TO DO

Employee Ownership
Visit the National Center for Employee Ownership, http://www.nceo.org. The site provides useful information about ESOPs, stock options, and ownership culture. Go to the section called *ownership culture*. The developers of the site conclude that an ownership culture combines with employee ownership to improve productivity and satisfaction. What is your opinion of the soundness of their logic? Compare their comments about an employee ownership culture with the same topic in Chapter 14 of this text.

TO BOOKMARK

Recognition Programs
http://www.goalkeeperincentive.com (Go the link, "A Study of the Incentive Merchandise and Travel Marketplace.")

Salary Comparisons
http://www.wageweb.com

Gainsharing
http://www.gainshare.com/profile.html

CASE PROBLEM: A Tale of Two Motivators

At first blush, Mike Weinbach and Justin Sewell seem to have a lot in common. Mike is 27 and Justin is 29. Both run successful dot-coms, and both are in the business of motivation and inspiration. But dig deeper, and oh, what a difference you will find. Weionbach is CEO of U-inspire, Inc., a one-stop source for motivational workplace products and services. Sewell and twin brother Jef co-lead Despair, Inc., which sells parody posters, plaques, mugs, and more. The two companies are on the Web at http://uninspire.com and http://despair.com.

One of the many items sold by U-inspire is a poster titled "Vision." It shows a majestic lighthouse guiding the way through a foggy night. The caption reads, "Vision is not seeing things as they are, but as they will be." Compare this to one of Despair's posters. Called, "Apathy," it is emblazoned with a cobweb-covered phone and the caption, "If we don't take care of the customer, maybe they'll stop bugging us."

How did these two arrive at their world views? Consider Weinbach's story. Early in high school, he was a pretty good wrestler who wanted to win more matches. Nothing seemed to help—until a coach gave him a quote book with these words on the cover:

> In the battle of life it is not the critic who counts. . . .
> The credit belongs to the man who is actually in the arena. . . . Who, at the best, knows in the end the triumph of high achievement; and who, at the worst, if he fails, at least fails while daring greatly, so that his place shall never be with those cold and timid souls who know neither victory nor defeat.

The quotation from Theodore Roosevelt went straight to Weinbach's head and heart. He explains: "I had this watershed realization that the biggest thing holding me back was the fear that if I tried to do better, I might not do as well as I

hoped." Wanting to be anything *but* a "timid soul," Weinbach turned into his own Rocky Balboa. He started waking up earlier to work out. He practiced after regular practice hours. And neighbors got used to seeing him jogging in their streets. Before long, the high schooler was winning tournaments and heading for the state championship. Ever since, through his two years at Harvard Business School and beyond, he has been keeping Roosevelt's wisdom nearby.

Justin Sewell took a different path. At age 19, he left the University of Texas at Austin and went to work as a contract graphic designer and multi-media author. Then in 1994, he became one of five employees at a start-up Internet service provider. Things went pretty informally at the company, so a spoken promise of stock options seemed good enough for the trusting 23-year old. When the company started growing, Sewell asked to have the promise put in writing. Nothing happened, he says. He asked again. Again, nothing. Several other people, including his brother, had received the same promise—and all of them grew deeply discouraged when their equity expectations vaporized before their eyes.

Then an opportunity fell into Sewell's hands—in the form of a catalog from a motivational-products company. He took it to his brother, Jef, and coworker Larry Kersten. They flipped through the pages and had a few painful laughs. "We started talking about success, teamwork, excellence, customer service," Sewell recalls. "We began to joke that there weren't any products in this catalog that addressed companies like the one we worked for or situations that we were in. Someone said, 'There's no failure poster—they need one. There's no mediocrity poster—they need one. There's no apathy poster—they need one. There's no burnout poster—they need one.'"

Now there *are* posters for failure, mediocrity, apathy, burnout, and other grim workplace realities. The brothers Sewell and coworker Kersten saw to it by pooling their severance bucks to launch Despair, Inc. "It sounds hokey, but we really came out of our prior jobs with a newfound appreciation for just how critical it is to keep your word," Sewell said. "Despair would not exist if so many things had not gone so wrong, most of them involving promises being broken."

Sewell concedes there *is* a place for serious products like those sold by U-inspire. He cites Southwest Airlines as one organization where inspirational posters proliferate and make a positive difference. "There's no tension between the messaging that's on the walls and the environment itself, because people there are treated with respect," he explains. "The culture is one that loves the customer, customers love the company, and it all works. Everything is in harmony with itself. But if you put those same motivational posters in an environment where there are massive layoffs, where management seems completely out of touch, where there's lot of politics, it creates enormous tensions."

Weinbach echoes the actions-speak-louder-than-words philosophy. "I stay away from saying 'this is inspirational,' then giving three quotes that I think will inspire everyone. That's now what this is about. It's really about being respectful, getting to know people, communicating, creating a learning environment, and giving people latitude to make decisions."

Case Questions

1. If you were in charge of your company motivational program, would you purchase products from either uinspire.com or despair.com for your workplace? Or both? Or neither? Explain your reasoning.

2. Which theory or explanation of motivation presented in Chapters 6 or 7 would justify motivational workplace products and services?

3. Design an experiment to see if motivational products like those sold by U-inspire and Despair actually enhance employee motivation.

Source: Tom Terez, "What Works: A Tale of Two Motivators," *Workforce,* July 2001, p. 22. Used with permission.

ENDNOTES

1. Shelly Branch, "MBAs: What They Really Want," *Fortune,* March 16, 1998, p. 167.
2. Frederick Herzberg, "The Wise Old Turk," *Harvard Business Review,* September–October 1974, pp. 70–80.
3. George B. Graen, Terri A. Scandura, and Michael R. Graen, "A Field Experimental Test of the Moderating Effects of Growth Need Strength on Productivity," *Journal of Applied Psychology,* August 1986, pp. 484–491.
4. John Richard Hackman and Greg R. Oldham, *Work Redesign* (Reading, MA: Addison-Wesley, 1980).
5. "Driving toward Success," *Executive Leadership,* October 2002, p. 3.
6. Marc C. Marchese and Robert P. Delprino, "Do Supervisors and Subordinates See Eye-to-Eye on Job Enrichment?" *Journal of Business and Psychology,* Winter 1998, pp. 179–191.
7. Amy Wrzesnierski and Jane E. Dutton, "Crafting a Job: Revisioning Employees as Active Crafters of Their Work," *The Academy of Management Review,* April 2001, pp. 179–201.
8. Richard S. Wellings, William C. Byham, and Jeanne M. Wilson, *Empowered Teams: Creating Self-Directed Work Groups that Improve Quality, Productivity, and Participation* (San Francisco: Jossey-Bass, 1991), p. 3.
9. Andrew Leigh and Michael Maynard, "Self-Managed Teams: How They Succeed or Fail," in Perseus Publishing's *Business: The Ultimate Resource Business* (Cambridge, MA: Perseus, 2002), p. 202.
10. This list is paraphrased from Wellings, Byham, and Wilson, *Empowered Teams,* p. 4.
11. The evidence is reviewed in Roy A. Cook and J. Larry Goff, "Coming of Age with Self-Managed Teams: Dealing with a Problem Employee," *Journal of Business and Psychology,* Spring 2002, pp. 487–488; Leigh and Maynard, "Self-Managed Teams," p. 202.
12. Data in this paragraph are from Carla Johnson, "Teams at Work," *HR Magazine,* May 1999, p. 32.
13. Jennifer Daw, "Rep. Osborne is Given Award for Psychology in Management," *Monitor on Psychology,* May 2001, p. 12.
14. Fred Luthans and Alexander D. Stajkovic, "Reinforce for Performance: The Need to Go Beyond Pay and Even Rewards," *Academy of Management Executive,* May 1999, pp. 52–54.
15. Gregory Smith, "Simple Rewards Are Powerful Motivators," *HRfocus,* August 2001, p. 10.
15. Stephen Kerr, "Practical, Cost-Neutral Alternatives that You May Know, but Don't Practice," *Organizational Dynamics,* Summer 1999, p. 65.
17. Luthans and Stajkovic, "Reinforce for Performance," pp. 54–55.
18. Alexander D. Stajkovic and Fred Luthans, "Differential Effects of Incentive Motivators on Work Performance," *Academy of Management Journal,* June 2001, pp. 580–590.
19. Jennifer Laabs, "Satisfy Them With More Than Money," *Workforce,* November 1998, p. 43; Smith, "Simple Rewards," p. 10.
20. Janet Wiscombe, "Rewards Get Results," *Workforce,* April 2002, p. 42.
21. Gillian Flynn, "Is Your Recognition Program Understood?" *Workforce,* July 1998, p. 30.
22. Barbara Davison, "Strategies for Managing Retention," Human Resources Forum (supplement to *Management Review*), November 1997, p. 1.
23. Janet Wiscombe, "Can Pay for Performance Really Work?" *Workforce,* August 2001, p. 29.
24. G. Douglas Jenkins, Jr., "Are Financial Incentives Related to Performance? A Meta-Analytic Review of Empirical Research," *Journal of Applied Psychology,* October 1998, pp. 777–787.
25. "How Stock Options Are Changing," *HRfocus,* October 2002, p. 7.
26. Quoted in Samuel Greengard, "Stock Options Have Their Ups & Downs," *Workforce,* December 1999, p. 46.
27. Larry L. Hatcher and Timothy L. Ross, "Organization Development through Productivity Sharing," *Personnel,* October 1985, p. 44.
28. Cited in "Why Gainsharing Works Even Better Today than in the Past," *HRfocus,* April 2000, p. 3.
29. Richard S. Sabo, "Linking Merit Pay with Performance at Lincoln Electric," in *The Quest for Competitiveness: Lessons from America's Productivity and Quality Leaders,* Y. K. Shetty and Veron M. Buehler (eds.) (Westport, CT: Quorum Books, 1993).
30. Susan C. Hanlon, David C. Meyer, and Robert R. Taylor, "Consequences of Gainsharing: A Field Experiment Revisited," *Group and Organizational Management,* Vol. 19, 1994, pp. 87–111.
31. "Has Usefulness of Pay for Performance Run Its Course?" *Ioma's Report on Salary Surveys®,* January 2003, pp. 1, 14.
32. Jeffrey Pfeffer, "Six Dangerous Myths about Pay," *Harvard Business Review,* May–June 1998, p. 110.
33. Leslie Gross Klaff, "Getting Happy with the Rewards King," *Workforce,* April 2003, p. 48.

Chapter 8

Conflict, Stress, and Well-Being

OBJECTIVES

After reading and studying this chapter and doing the exercises, you should be able to:

1 Understand the nature of conflict in organizations and what its leading causes are.

2 Have the necessary information to resolve many workplace conflicts, including dealing with difficult people.

3 Understand the nature, causes, and consequences of work stress.

4 Explain what organizations can do to manage and reduce stress.

5 Do a more effective job of managing your own stress.

Maggie Wicken, a technology instructor at Boeing Corp., has a high-tech way of monitoring her anxiety. She literally plugs herself into her desktop PC and takes a reading of her own stress level. This is the latest trend in biofeedback, a field that is getting a fresh look in the battle against chronic stress. In the past, biofeedback was mostly done in the doctor's office. But some major corporations—including Boeing, Cisco Systems and Unilever—are trying to put it into practice in real office situations.

Using a finger clip attached to the PC, employees at these companies regularly hook themselves up to a biofeedback software program called Freeze-Framer. By measuring your heart rhythms the same way you take your temperature, it can give people a window on exactly how their body is handling stress throughout the day.

The goal is to learn to read signals from your body and then adjust the way you breathe (the more deeply the better), sit (drop your shoulders) or even what you're thinking about (imagine yourself on the beach). The software even includes video games that you play by manipulating your own heart rate. The ability to bring the body back to a state of calm is what stress-resistant people do naturally.

Skeptics say a lot of this is a placebo effect [similar to the Hawthorne effect described in Chapter 1]. But Ms. Wicken at Boeing, whose anxiety skyrocketed after massive layoffs at her company, says she has learned to bring down her anxiety in under a minute.

Source: Reprinted with permission of *The Wall Street Journal* from Jane Spencer, "Are You Stressed Out Yet?" *The Wall Street Journal*, March 11, 2003, pp. D1, D5. Permission conveyed through Copyright Clearance Center, Inc.

NOW ASK YOURSELF: What does this story about a technology instructor using computerized biofeedback tell us about how workers and organizations invest resources in managing job stress? By using the latest technology tools, in conjunction with techniques and insights from organizational behavior, the potential negative consequences of conflict and stress can be minimized. At the same time, stress and conflict can sometimes be converted into positive forces to enhance productivity. The purpose of this chapter is to present information that will help the reader better understand two closely related processes: conflict and stress.

CONFLICT IN ORGANIZATIONS

Conflict refers to the opposition of persons or forces giving rise to some tension. A conflict occurs when two or more parties perceive mutually exclusive goals, values, or events. Each side believes that what it wants is incompatible with what the other wants. Conflict can also take place at the individual level when a person has to decide between two incompatible choices. For example, a person might have to choose between accepting a job transfer and remaining in town with family and friends. Refusing to transfer could mean a job loss, whereas accepting the transfer would mean less contact with family and friends. Conflict has enough emotional content to lead to stress for the individuals involved. This is why conflict is presented here as the final chapter in the section of the text dealing with individual behavior.

Our study of conflict concentrates on sources of conflict, and various methods, including negotiation, for resolving conflict. We also discuss briefly how and why managers sometimes deliberately stimulate conflict.

Sources and Antecedents of Conflict

Conflict is pervasive in organizations. Managers allegedly spend between 20 and 30 percent of their work activities directly or indirectly resolving conflict. The sources, antecedents, or outright causes of conflict are numerous, and the list is dynamic. At any given time, a new and potent source of conflict might emerge, such as management's current emphasis on hiring temporary workers rather than offering full-time employment. Here we describe five illustrative sources of workplace conflict.

Perceived Adverse Changes

A high-impact source of conflict is a change in work methods, conditions of work, or employment opportunities that the people involved perceive negatively. **Downsizing,** the laying off of workers to reduce costs and increase efficiency, is one such change. The people eliminated from the payroll do not remain in conflict with the organization. Survivors, however, suffer from guilt, anger, and bereavement as they feel sorry for the departed coworkers.[1] Continuous downsizing, even when business conditions improve, can precipitate labor versus management conflict. Management wants to eliminate as many jobs as possible, whereas the labor union values job security for its members.

Despite these conditions, all parties do not perceive downsizing as an adverse change. Company executives may believe that downsizing is rightsizing, leading to an efficient, competitive firm that will attract investors.

147

1

Understand the nature of conflict in organizations and what its leading causes are.

Line versus Staff Differentiation

A major form of conflict takes place between line and staff units. Line units deal with the primary purposes of the firm, such as the sales group in a business firm. Staff units deal with the secondary purposes of the firm, such as the environmental protection unit in a business firm. They also deal with the activities necessary to make the line activities more efficient and effective. Staff units might do the hiring and the labor contract interpretations, and verify that the line group complies with environmental laws. Yet they would not manufacture or sell the product or service.

Staff managers and professionals advise managers but cannot make certain decisions about themselves. A human resources professional, for example, might advise top management about the adverse consequences of downsizing following a merger. Nevertheless, the professional does not have the authority to halt the downsizing. Line and staff workers may conflict when the line manager perceives that the staff professional is attempting to heavily influence his or her decisions. Another source of conflict is that staff professionals are often more loyal to their own discipline than to the organization. An organizational behavior specialist working for a large firm might feel that attending professional meetings is her right. In contrast, her manager feels she should only attend such meetings while on vacation.

Sexual Harassment

Some employees experience conflict because of sexually harassment by a manager, coworker, customer, or vendor. **Sexual harassment** is generally defined as unwanted sexually oriented behavior in the workplace that results in discomfort and/or interference with the job. Sexual harassment is divided into two types. In *quid pro quo* harassment, the employee's submission to or rejection of unwelcome sexual advances is used as the basis for a tangible employment action about the employee. (A tangible employment action is defined by the Supreme Court as "hiring, firing, failing to promote, reassignment with significantly different responsibilities, or a decision causing a significant change in benefits.") The demands of a harasser can be explicit or implied.

Hostile working environment harassment occurs when someone in the workplace creates an intimidating, hostile, or offensive working environment. A tangible employment advantage or adverse economic consequence does not have to exist. The hostile environment type of harassment is subject to considerable variation in perception and interpretation. A company executive might decide to hang a French impressionist painting of a partially nude woman in the lobby. Some people would find this offensive and intimidating, and complain that they were harassed. Others might compliment the executive for being a patron of the arts.

A group of researchers provided useful insights into the role of perception in deciding which behaviors of supervisors and coworkers constituted either type of harassment.[2] Typical harassment behaviors include physical contact, inappropriate remarks, a sexual proposition, a threat or promise associated with a job, comments on the other person's physical appearance, or a glaring stare at the person harassed. The setting for the survey was a manufacturing plant that had a strict policy against sexual harassment. Furthermore, supervisory and professional personnel had training in dealing with sexual harassment. Employee perceptions were compared to U.S. federal guidelines of sexual harassment—the basis for a "correct" response.

Exhibit 8-1

*Accuracy in Identifying
Sexually Harassing Behavior*

149

Supervisory Behaviors	Correspondence with U.S. Federal Guidelines	
If your supervisor did this, would you consider this sexual harassment?	Inaccurate	Accurate
1. Asks you to have sex with the promise that it will help you on the job.	18	96
2. Asks you to have sex with the threat that refusing to have sex will hurt you on the job.	17	97
3. Asks you to go out on a date with the promise that it will help you on the job.	18	96
4. Asks you to go out on a date with the promise that it will hurt you if you do not go.	16	98
5. Touches you on private parts of the body; for example, breasts, buttocks, etc.	22	92
6. Touches you on parts of the body not considered private; for example, shoulder, hand, arm, etc.	77	37
7. Looks at you in a flattering way.	75	39
8. Makes gestures (signs) of a flattering nature.	51	63
9. Makes comments about your dress or appearance that are meant to be complimentary.	96	18
10. Makes comments about your appearance meant to be insulting.	91	23
11. Makes sexually offensive comments.	49	65
12. Tells sexually oriented jokes.	75	39

Source: Marjorie L. Icenogle, Bruce W. Eagle, Sohel Ahman, and Lisa A. Hanks, "Assessing Perceptions of Sexual Harassment Behaviors in a Manufacturing Environment," *Journal of Business and Psychology*, Summer 2002, p. 607. Used with permission.

Exhibit 8-1 presents the responses of the 114 participants in the survey with regard to supervisory behavior. The accuracy versus inaccuracy tabulations for perceptions of coworker behavior were essentially the same as the perceptions of supervisory behavior. The responses indicated that the majority of workers can accurately identify behaviors frequently associated with quid pro quo harassment. However, the same workers had difficulty identifying behaviors used to establish evidence of a hostile work environment. Male workers had a slight edge in the accuracy of their perceptions about what constitutes harassment, and women in white-collar jobs were more accurate than women in blue-collar jobs.

The meanings and interpretations of what constitutes sexual harassment continue to evolve with judicial rulings. Three U.S. Supreme Court decisions in 1998 are now given considerable weight by lower courts and employers:

- In *Oncale vs. Sundowner Offshore Services Inc.,* the Court unanimously declared that sexual harassment is actionable, even when the people involved are of the same sex. What matters is the conduct at issue, not the sex of the people involved, nor the presence or absence of sexual desire. The case involved a roustabout (a waterfront laborer) who was forcibly subjected on numerous occasions to humiliating sex–related actions. His harassers were three crew members, including two supervisors.

- In *Burlington Industries, Inc. vs. Ellerth,* the Court ruled that an employer can be liable for sexual harassment and can be sued regardless of whether a supervisor's threats against an employee are carried out. However, employers can assert an affirmative defense. This means that the employer may be relieved of liability if it genuinely tried to prohibit and remedy sexual harassment, and the employee did not take advantage of corrective opportunities offered by the employer. The case involved a marketing assistant who claimed that her boss made repeated passes at her and advised her to wear short skirts. The assistant never informed management about her supervisor's misconduct.

- In *Faragher vs. City of Boca Raton*, *Florida*, the Court ruled that an employer is liable for a pervasive, hostile atmosphere of harassment and is potentially liable for its supervisors' misconduct whether the company was aware of the harass-ment or not. The case involved an ocean lifeguard who claimed she endured repeated sexual harassment from two male supervisors during five years of employment.[3]

At least 50 percent of women perceive that they have been harassed at some point in their career. Sexual harassment is widely considered an ethical and legal problem, and harassment also has negative effects on the well-being of its victims. The harassed person may experience job stress, lowered morale, severe conflict, and lowered productivity. A study with both business and university workers doc-umented some of the problems associated with sexual harassment. It was found that even at low levels of frequency, harassment exerts a significant impact on women's psychological well–being, job attitudes, and work behaviors. For both business and university workers, women who had experienced high levels of harassment reported the worst job–related and psychological effects. The study also found that women who had experienced only a moderate level of harassment also suffered from negative outcomes.[4]

Exhibit 8-2 presents information employers can use to minimize the fre-quency of harassment in the workplace, as well as defend themselves against charges of harassment.

Exhibit 8-2

Guidelines for Minimizing Sexual Harassment and Protecting the Company Against Harassment Charges

- Develop a zero-tolerance policy on harassment and communicate it to employees. Inform employees that harassment between members of the same sex is also forbidden. Ensure that victims can report abuses without fear of retaliation.
- Deflect the sexual harassment charge with an affirma-tive defense. First, take reasonable care to prevent and correct promptly any sexually harassing behavior. Second, show that an employee failed to use internal procedures for reporting abusive behavior.
- Publicize the antiharassment policies as aggressively and regularly as possible—in handbooks, on posters, in training sessions, in reminders in paychecks, and on the company intranet.
- Ensure that employees will not face reprisals if they report offending behavior. Appoint several managers

to take complaints, and train these managers in sex-ual harassment issues. Have at least two methods of reporting charges available, such as a toll-free number, an open-door policy, or internal review procedures.
- Conduct training for employees and all levels of man-agers on antidiscrimination and antisexual harass-ment policies and practices.
- Punishments against employees found guilty of harassment should be swift and sure.

Source: Susan B. Garland, "Finally, A Corporate Tip Sheet on Sexual Harassment," *Business Week,* July 13, 1998; Jennifer Laabs, "Steps to Protect Your Company Against Sexual Harassment," *Workforce,* October 1998, p. 41.

Competing Work and Family Demands

Balancing the demands of career and family has become a major challenge facing today's workforce. The challenge is particularly intense for employees who are part of a two-wage earning family. **Work–family conflict** occurs when the individual has to perform multiple roles: worker; spouse; and, often, parent.[5] This type of conflict is frequent because the multiple roles are often incompatible. Imagine having planned to attend your child's championship soccer game and then being ordered at the last minute to attend a late-afternoon meeting. A survey revealed the following evidence of work–family conflict and the potential of such conflict:

- About 45 percent of college students say their top consideration in selecting a first employer is the opportunity to achieve a balance between work and life outside of work.
- Approximately 80 percent of workers consider their effort to balance work and personal life as their first priority.
- More than one-third of employed Americans are working ten or more hours a day, and 39 percent work on weekends.
- One-third of employees say they are forced to choose between advancing in their jobs or devoting attention to their family or personal lives.[6]

Work–family conflict is significant for the individual. A meta-analysis of 50 studies with 50 groups found a negative relationship among all forms of work–family conflict and both job and life satisfaction. A tendency was found for women to be more adversely affected by work–family conflict. Family-to-work conflict (family life interfering with work) was less strongly related to dissatisfaction than work-to-family conflict, or conflict that ran in both directions.[7] A more recent survey conducted with 513 employees in a Fortune 500 company also supports the plausible finding that working long hours interferes with family life. The long hours, in turn, leads to depression for some individuals, and stress–related health problems such as ulcers.[8] This study supports the well-accepted proposition that conflict leads to stress.

Work–family conflict is a problem for employers because stressed–out workers are often less productive because of reduced ability to concentrate on work. Furthermore, a study revealed that dual-earner couples who experienced work–family conflict were more likely to engage in family interruptions at work, tardiness, and absenteeism.[9]

Organizational programs to help reduce work–family conflict include flexible working hours, work-at-home programs, dependent care centers, and parental leave programs. Francine M. Deutsch, a specialist in gender equality, advises that parents must also take responsibility for reducing work–life conflicts. She says, "Both parents can have successful work lives and also well-balanced personal lives by fully sharing all responsibilities."[10]

Personal Dispositions, Personality Clashes, and Workplace Bullies

Many instances of workplace conflict stem from individual's dispositions as well as personality clashes. (A *disposition* is a characteristic attitude, similar to a personality trait.) People who are rude, aggressive, inconsiderate, hostile, intensely pessimistic, or bullying readily enter into conflict. Incivility (or rudeness) has gained attention as a cause of workplace conflict. (Think of making a presentation at a meeting while one of the participants chats on a cell phone about personal matters.) The underlying problem is that workplace incivility can spiral downward because the offended party might reciprocate with a counterincivility. More rudeness results, and the interpersonal conflict becomes intense.

On a larger scale, an organizational climate characterized by rudeness can result in aggressive behavior, high turnover, and lost customers.[11] Visualize a person dousing coffee on a person making a telephone call. People with low self-esteem and those with authoritarian (rigid-thinking) attitudes are also conflict prone. They are predisposed to defend themselves against objectively trivial threats.[12]

Many other workplace conflicts arise because of people simply disliking each other. A **personality clash** is an antagonistic relationship between two people based on differences in personal attributes, preferences, interests, values, and styles. People involved in personality clashes often have difficulty in specifying why they dislike each other. Generational differences can result in personality clashes based on differences in values. As described in Chapter 4, members of different generations often have different values, and these differences can lead to workplace conflict.

Bullying behavior contributes to substantial interpersonal conflict in the workplace. An example of such a bully is one who tries to control his or her victim fear and intimidation. According to bullying specialist Gary Namie, "The vast majorities of bullies are bosses because they can make good on their threats."[13] As with sexual harassment, bullying behavior leads to conflict because a worker's demands for tranquility on the job are incompatible with the demands of the harasser or bully.

Functional and Dysfunctional Consequences of Conflict

Although conflict sparks images of negative behavior, it has both positive and negative consequences. Exhibit 8-3 illustrates that conflict in the right amount improves performance, while too little or too much conflict can decrease performance. **Functional conflict** occurs when the interests of the organization are served as a result of a dispute or disagreement. **Dysfunctional conflict** occurs when a dispute or disagreement harms the organization. When destructive conflict erupts, the manager may wish to intervene.

Functional conflict fosters higher levels of performance by arousing motivation, problem-solving ability, creativity, and constructive change. For example, conflicts between various functions in an organization, such as engineering and manufacturing, have led to the establishment of cross-functional teams. Because these teams contain representatives from the different functions, it has been easier to resolve areas of conflict.

Dysfunctional conflict is disruptive in many ways; it wastes people's time and creates a selfish climate that distracts workers from the interests of the firm. For example, a labor union may call a strike or a company may eliminate some jobs primarily to demonstrate power. Conflict can divert time and energy away from reaching important goals. It is not uncommon for two managers in conflict to spend time exchanging e-mail messages proving each other wrong in a particular dispute. Another dysfunctional consequence of conflict is that it may result in one party retaliating for the perceived wrongdoing of another party.

Many of the negative consequences of conflict take place because conflict leads to anger. Angry behavior in the office is often referred to as *desk rage,* incorporating aggression, hostility, and physical violence. According to one report, angry employees have sabotaged employers' equipment and operations in sophisticated

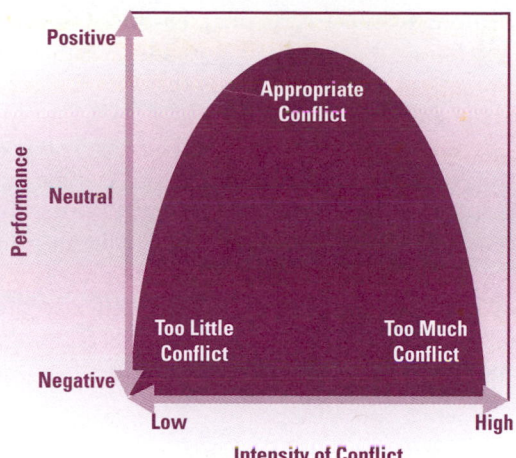

and novel ways. Anger-induced sabotage can be as simple as acts of vandalism or pranks, or as complex as disabling software. Angry employees have put rodents into food products, put needles into baby food, set company property on fire, and wiped out entire company databases.[14]

Workplace violence is a dysfunctional consequence of growing concern, and workplace homicide is a leading cause of workplace death. Workplace violence is estimated to cost U.S. employers between $6.4 billion and $36 billion in lost productivity, tarnished image, insurance payments, and increased security.[15] Most workplace killings result from a robbery or commercial crime. Many of these killings, however, are perpetrated by disgruntled workers or former employees harboring an unresolved conflict. John Byrnes, a workplace violence consultant, advises employers to be aware of behavior that could lead to violence. Extreme acts of violence are preceded by a series of incidents—screaming, verbal threats, or throwing something such as a stapler or floppy disk.[16]

Oganizational forces sometimes trigger unstable employees into dysfunctional behavior. Michael D. Kelleher believes that downsizing or a firing can trigger an angry outburst in an unstable worker. Many instances of violence can be prevented if managers ensure that employees perceive their own value and if managers communicate openly with employees.[17]

An implication of Exhibit 8-3 is that a manager may need to stimulate the right amount of conflict to enhance performance. One method of introducing a moderate degree of conflict would be to assign two groups the same problem and have them compete for the best solution. Another method is for the manager to play the role of the devil's advocate. The manager looks for something to criticize in any proposal made by an individual or a group. Potential flaws in the proposal are therefore uncovered, leading to a superior result.

Stimulating the Right Type of Conflict within Teams

The right amount of conflict can enhance performance. Recent case history analysis in organizations suggests that stimulating the right *type* of conflict is perhaps more important (see the InfoTrac sidebar). Building on earlier knowledge about conflict, a team of researchers classifies the conflict found in teams into two types.[18] **C-type conflict** focuses on substantive, issue-related differences. The C stands for *cognitive,* indicating that the conflict relates to tangible, concrete issues

Most people view conflict negatively, but the right kind of conflict, as we have just learned, can result in much better team functioning and decision making. Delve deeper into the issue of C-type conflict by logging on to InfoTrac College Edition at **http://www.infotrac -college.com.** Search for articles related to the breakup of the Space Shuttle Columbia and the team assembled to investigate the accident. As you scan the headlines and read the coverage, look for examples of C-type conflict. *How do the investigative teams manage conflict?*

that can be dealt with more intellectually than emotionally. **A-type conflict** focuses on personalized, individually oriented issues. The A stands for *affective,* indicating that the conflict relates to subjective issues that are dealt with more emotionally than intellectually.

C-type conflict is functional because it requires teams to engage in activities that foster team effectiveness. Team members engaged in C-type conflict critically examine alternative solutions and incorporate different points of view into their mission statement. Because frank communication and different points of view are encouraged, C-type conflict encourages innovative thinking. In contrast, A-type conflict is dysfunctional because it undermines group effectiveness by blocking constructive activities and processes. By such means as directing anger toward individuals and blaming one another for mistakes, A-type conflict leads to cynicism and distrust.

Conflict Management Styles

2

Have the necessary information to resolve many workplace conflicts, including dealing with difficult people.

Before describing specific methods of resolving conflict, it is useful to understand five styles of handling conflict. As shown in Exhibit 8-4, the five styles are based on a combination of satisfying one's own concerns (assertiveness) and satisfying the concerns of others (cooperativeness).[19]

1. *Competitive.* The competitive style is a desire to win one's own concerns at the expense of the other party, or to dominate. A person with a competitive orientation is likely to engage in win–lose power struggles.
2. *Accommodative.* The accommodative style favors appeasement, or satisfying the other's concerns without taking care of one's own. People with this orientation may be generous or self-sacrificing just to maintain a relationship. A

Exhibit 8-4

Conflict-Handling Styles According to Degree of Cooperation and Assertiveness

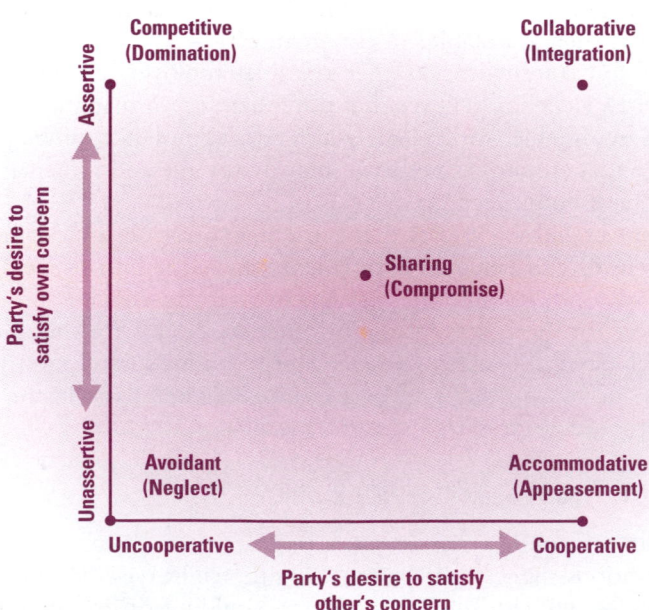

Source: Kenneth W. Thomas, "Organizational Conflict," in Steven Kerr (ed.), *Organizational Behavior* (Columbus, Ohio: Grid Publishing, 1979), p. 156.

154

dissatisfied employee might be accommodated with a larger-than-average pay raise just to calm down the person and obtain his or her loyalty.

3. *Sharing.* The sharing style is halfway between domination and appeasement. Sharers prefer moderate but incomplete satisfaction for both parties, which results in a compromise. The term "splitting the difference" reflects this orientation and is commonly used in such activities as negotiating a budget or purchasing equipment.

4. *Collaborative.* In contrast to the other styles, the collaborative style reflects a desire to fully satisfy the desires of both parties. It is based on an underlying philosophy of **win–win,** the belief that after conflict has been resolved, both sides should gain something of value. A win–win approach is genuinely concerned with arriving at a settlement that meets the needs of both parties, or at least one that does not badly damage the welfare of either side. When a collaborative approach is used, the relationship between the parties improves.

    A win–win approach by Daimler-Chrysler executive Dieter Zetsche took this form: At one time he told Chrysler dealers the company planned to take away subsidies worth $300 to $500 per vehicle. The cutbacks would save the company as much as $1 billion. When dealers balked, Zetche agreed to explore alternatives that would bring about the same savings. Finally, he accepted a proposal that would enable dealers to compensate for the lost money with bonuses for besting new sales targets.[20] So both Daimler-Chrysler and the dealers won.

5. *Avoidant.* The avoider is both uncooperative and unassertive. He or she is indifferent to the concerns of either party. The person may actually withdraw from the conflict or rely on fate. A manager sometime uses the avoidant style to stay out of a conflict between two team members, who are left to resolve their own differences.

Conflict Resolution Methods

Styles of dealing with conflict are closely related to methods of resolving conflict. For example, a collaborative style is a way of managing and resolving conflict. Here we present a sampling of conflict resolution methods by describing confrontation and problem solving, as well as several structural methods.

Confrontation and Problem Solving

A widely applicable approach to resolving conflict is **confrontation and problem solving,** a method of identifying the true source of conflict and resolving it systematically. The confrontation approach is gentle and tactful rather than combative and abusive. Reasonableness is important because the person who takes the initiative in resolving the conflict wants to maintain a harmonious working relationship with the other party. D. H. Stamatis has developed six steps for confrontation and problem solving:

Step 1: Awareness. Party A recognizes that a conflict exists between himself or herself and Party B.
Step 2: The decision to confront. Party A decides the conflict is important enough to warrant a confrontation with Party B and that such a conflict is preferable to avoiding the conflict.
Step 3: The confrontation. Party A decides to work cooperatively and confronts Party B. At this point, Party B may indicate a willingness to accept the

confrontation or may decide to gloss over its seriousness. Often the conflict is resolved at this step, particularly if it is not serious or complicated.

Step 4: Determining the cause of the conflict. The two parties discuss their own opinions, attitudes, and feelings in relation to the conflict, attempting to identify the real issue. For example, the real cause of conflict between a manager and a team member might be that they have a different concept of what constitutes a fair day's work.

Step 5: Determining the solution to the conflict and further steps. In this step, the parties attempt to develop specific means of reducing or eliminating the cause of the conflict. If the cause cannot be changed (such as changing one's opinion of a fair day's work), a way of working around the cause is devised. If both parties agree on a solution, then the confrontation has been successful.

Step 6: Follow-through. After the solution has been implemented, both parties should check periodically to ensure that their agreements are being kept.[21]

The collaborative style of conflict resolution meshes with confrontation and problem solving. A major factor is that trust builds between two parties as they search for the real reason for conflict.

Confront, Contain, and Connect for Anger

A variation of confrontation and problem solving has developed specifically to resolve conflict with angry people, which involves confronting, containing, and connecting. You *confront* by jumping right in and getting agitated workers talking to prevent future blowups. The confrontation, however, is not aimed at arguing with the angry person. If the other person yells, you talk more softly. You *contain* by moving an angry worker out of sight and out of earshot. At the same time, you remain impartial. The supervisor is advised not to choose sides or appear to be a friend. Finally, you *connect* by asking open-ended questions such as "What would you like us to do about your concern?" to get at the real reasons behind an outburst. Using this approach, one worker revealed he was upset because a female coworker got to leave early to pick up her daughter at day care. The man also needed to leave early one day a week for personal reasons but felt awkward making the request. So instead of asserting himself in explicit and direct fashion about his demands, he flared up.

An important feature of the confront, contain, and connect technique is that it provides angry workers a place where they can vent their frustrations and report the outbursts of others. Mediator Nina Meierding says: "Workers need a safe outlet to talk through anger and not feel they will be minimized or put their job in jeopardy."[22]

Structural Methods

A structural method of resolving conflict emphasizes juggling work assignments and reporting relationships so that disputes are minimized. One structural method for resolving conflict is for a manager to have direct control over all the resources he or she needs to get the job done. In this way, the manager is less likely to experience conflict when attempting to get the cooperation of people who do not report directly to him or her.

Conflict can often be reduced or prevented by one or more members from one organizational unit exchanging places with those of another unit; for example, shifting from purchasing to manufacturing. Working in another unit can foster empathy. Reassigning people in this way can also encourage people to develop different viewpoints in the affected groups. As the group members get to know one another better, they tend to reduce some of their distorted perceptions of one another. (As described previously, cross-functional teams accomplish the same purpose.) Exchanging members works best when the personnel exchanged have the technical competence to perform well in the new environment.

A long-standing structural approach to conflict resolution is an appeals procedure. When the person cannot resolve a problem with his or her manager, the person appeals to a higher authority. The higher authority is ordinarily the next level of management or a member of the human resources department. The ability to help two group members in dispute resolve their conflicts is considered a high-level management skill. Exhibit 8-5 presents some of the competencies and strategies required to help subordinates resolve their conflicts. Few managers would have the time to learn all these competencies, but listening to the disputants and helping them to understand the true problem facing them would be an useful start.

Top management in some firms maintains an **open-door policy,** in which any employee can bring a gripe to attention without checking with his or her immediate manager. The open-door policy is a popular grievance procedure because it allows problems to be settled quickly.

Dealing with Difficult People

A challenge all workers face from time to time is dealing constructively with workers who appear intent on creating problems. For a variety of reasons, these difficult or counterproductive people perform poorly themselves or interfere with the job performance of others. A **difficult person** is an individual who creates problems for others, yet has the skill and mental ability to do otherwise. The bully mentioned earlier is an example of a difficult person. Another of many examples is the yes-person who will agree to any commitment and promise any deadline, but will rarely deliver. The techniques described next have wide applicability for helping difficult people change to a more constructive behavior pattern.

1. *Use tact and diplomacy in dealing with annoying behavior.* Coworkers who irritate you rarely do annoying things on purpose. Tactful actions on your part can sometimes take care of these annoyances without having to confront the problem. Close your door, for example, if noisy coworkers are gathered outside. When subtlety does not work, it may be necessary to proceed to the confrontation tactics described earlier. Tact and diplomacy can also be

Exhibit 8-5

Managerial Ways of Intervening in Conflicts between or among Other People

- Clarify the issues and interests at stake.
- Examine the interrelationships between interests and their degree of convergence or divergence.
- Facilitate the choice of the relevant approach for resolving the conflict.
- Identify appropriate conflict-resolution processes.
- Clarify the dynamics of interaction and implications for resolving the conflict.
- Identify assumptions and reframe the understanding of the conflict.
- Identify and re-examine mutual stereotypes and perceptions.
- Facilitate communications.

- Model appropriate communications through restating, reflecting, and summarizing.
- Propose appropriate communication processes and procedures.
- Identify inappropriate behaviors and propose more effective ones.
- Increase awareness of the conflict's real cost and benefits.

Source: Republished with permission of the Academy of Management Executive from Patrick Nugent, "Third-Party Interventions for Managers," *Academy of Management Executive,* February 2002, p. 147. Permission conveyed through Copyright Clearance Center, Inc.

incorporated into confrontation. In addition to confronting a person, you might also point out an individual's good qualities.

2. *Use nonhostile humor.* Nonhostile humor can often be used to help a difficult person understand how his or her behavior has blocked others. Also, the humor will help defuse conflict between you and that person. The humor should point to the person's unacceptable behavior, yet not belittle him or her. Assume that you and a coworker are working jointly on a report. Whenever you turn over a portion of your work for her to review, she finds some fault. You point out lightly that her striving for perfection is admirable but the striving is creating stress for you.

3. *Give recognition and attention.* Counterproductive or difficult people, like misbehaving children, are sometimes crying out for attention. By giving them recognition and attention, their counterproductive behavior will sometimes cease. If their negative behavior is a product of a more deeply rooted problem, recognition and attention alone will not work. Other actions will need to be taken, such as referring the person for counseling.

4. *Help the difficult person feel more confident.* Many counterproductive employees are simply low in self-confidence and self-efficacy. They use stalling and evasive tactics because they are afraid to fail. You might be able to arrange a project or task in which you know the difficult person will succeed. With a small dose of self-confidence and self-efficacy, the person may begin to complain less. With additional successes, the person may soon become less difficult.[23] Self-confidence building takes time. However, self-efficacy can build more quickly as the person learns a new skill.

5. *Reinforce civil behavior and good moods.* In the spirit of positive reinforcement, when a generally difficult person behaves acceptably, recognize the behavior in some way. Reinforcing statements would include, "It's enjoyable working with you today," and "I appreciate your professional attitude."

WORK STRESS

3

Understand the nature, causes, and consequences of work stress.

Stress is closely related to conflict because conflict is a major contributor to stress. As used here, **stress** is the mental and physical condition that results from a perceived threat that cannot be dealt with readily. Stress is therefore an internal response to a state of activation. The stressed person is physically and mentally aroused. Stress will ordinarily occur in a threatening or negative situation, such as worrying about losing one's job or being reprimanded. However, stress can also be caused by a positive situation, such as receiving a large cash bonus.

The topic of work stress is of enormous interest to managers and other professionals because of its impact on productivity and its legal and human consequences. A group of industrial health specialists noted that American workers are working harder and longer than they have in the past two decades simply to maintain their current standard of living. The result is a workforce more at risk than ever for psychological, physical, and behavioral health problems.[24] Among 320,000 employees surveyed by International Survey Research, 38 percent claimed that job stress has seriously reduced their work effectiveness. However, in those companies identified as "high performing," only 31 percent of employees reported reduced work effectiveness. The researchers noted that high-performing companies offer more support to workers.[25]

Our study of work stress centers on its consequences and sources, along with individual and organizational methods for managing stress. Because stress deals heavily with personal perceptions, you will be invited to take two questionnaires, starting with the stress questionnaire on page 160.

A Cybernetic Theory of Stress, Coping, and Well-Being in Organizations

A theory of work stress developed by Jeffrey R. Edwards serves as a useful framework for understanding the symptoms, consequences, and management of stress. The **cybernetic theory of stress, coping, and well-being in organizations** views stress as a discrepancy between an employee's perceived state and desired state.[26] The worker must consider the discrepancy important to experience stress. Consistent with other theories, stress damages psychological and physical well-being. As a result, the person engages in coping—attempts to reduce the negative impacts of stress on well-being. The coping approaches could be any method of stress reduction, such as those described later in the chapter. For example, the worker experiencing stress might take a nap during a rest break.

Coping influences stress by altering the perceptions and desires surrounding the stressful discrepancy as well as by putting the stress in context. If coping is successful, it can also improve well-being directly; for example, by allowing a person to take constructive action about a troublesome experience. The total stress a person experiences is determined by all of his or her discrepancies.

An important implication of the cybernetic theory of stress is that to manage stress properly, a person must seek to narrow the discrepancies between actual conditions and a desired state.

Symptoms and Consequences of Work Stress

A person experiencing stress displays certain symptoms indicating that he or she is trying to cope with a **stressor,** any force creating the stress reaction. These symptoms can include a host of physiological, emotional, and behavioral reactions. A problem with stress symptoms is that they lead to an adverse impact on employee health and well-being.

Physiological symptoms of stress include increased heart rate, blood pressure, breathing rate, pupil size, and perspiration. Men in particular who respond most intensely to mental stress have a higher risk of blocked blood vessels, which increases their risk of heart attack and stroke.[27] If stress symptoms are severe or persist over a prolonged period, the result can also be other stress–related disorders such as hypertension, migraine headache, ulcers, colitis, or allergies. Stress also leads to a chemical imbalance that adversely affects the body's immune system. Thus, the overly stressed person becomes more susceptible to disease and suffers more intensely from existing health problems.

Emotional symptoms of stress include anxiety, tension, depression, discouragement, feeling unable to cope, boredom, prolonged fatigue, feelings of hopelessness, and various kinds of defensive thinking. Behavioral symptoms include nervous habits such as facial twitching, as well as sudden decreases in job performance due to forgetfulness and errors in concentration or judgment. If the stress is particularly uncomfortable or distasteful (large and enduring discrepancies), it will lower job performance. The effect is greater for more complex jobs. An example of a stressor that will lower job performance for all people is a bullying, abrasive boss who wants to see the employee fail. Also, an 8-hour meeting on a Monday is a stressor for most managers and professionals who have other urgent work to perform.

160

SELF ASSESSMENT

The Stress Questionnaire

Directions: Apply each of the following questions to the last 6 months of your life. Check the appropriate column.

	Mostly Yes	Mostly No
1. Have you been feeling uncomfortably tense lately?	☐	☐
2. Are you engaged in frequent arguments with people close to you?	☐	☐
3. Is your social life very unsatisfactory?	☐	☐
4. Do you have trouble sleeping?	☐	☐
5. Do you feel lethargic about life?	☐	☐
6. Do many people annoy or irritate you?	☐	☐
7. Do you have constant cravings for candy and other sweets?	☐	☐
8. Is your cigarette or alcohol consumption dramatically up?	☐	☐
9. Are you habituated to soft drinks or coffee?	☐	☐
10. Do you find it difficult to concentrate on your work?	☐	☐
11. Do you frequently grind your teeth?	☐	☐
12. Are you increasingly forgetful about little things such as mailing a letter?	☐	☐
13. Are you increasingly forgetful about big things such as appointments and major errands?	☐	☐
14. Are you making too many trips to the restroom?	☐	☐
15. Have people commented lately that you do not look well (or "good")?	☐	☐
16. Do you get into verbal fights with people too frequently?	☐	☐
17. Have you been involved in more than one physical fight lately?	☐	☐
18. Do you have a troublesome number of tension headaches?	☐	☐
19. Do you feel nauseated frequently?	☐	☐
20. Do you feel light headed or dizzy almost every day?	☐	☐
21. Do you have churning sensations in your stomach too often?	☐	☐
22. Are you in a big hurry all the time?	☐	☐
23. Are far too many things bothering you?	☐	☐
24. Do you frequently feel tired and exhausted for no particular reason?	☐	☐
25. Do you have difficulty shaking colds or other infections?	☐	☐

Scoring: The following guidelines are only of value if you answered the questions sincerely:

0–7   Mostly Yes answers: You seem to be experiencing a normal amount of stress.

8–17   Mostly Yes answers: Your stress level seems high. Become involved in some kind of stress management activity, such as those described later in this chapter.

18–25   Mostly Yes answers: Your stress level appears much too high. Discuss your stress levels with a mental health professional or visit your family doctor (or both).

Similar to conflict, not all stress is bad. People require the right amount of stress to keep themselves mentally and physically alert. A person's perception of something or somebody usually determines whether it will be a positive or negative stressor. For example, one manager might perceive a quality audit by a corporate executive to be so frightening that he is irritable toward team members. Another manager might welcome the visit as a chance to proudly display her department's high-quality performance.

After prolonged exposure to job stress, a person runs the risk of feeling burned out—a drained, used-up feeling. **Burnout** is a pattern of emotional, physical, and mental exhaustion in response to chronic job stressors. The same syndrome (collection of symptoms) is sometimes regarded as work exhaustion. Cynicism, apathy, and indifference are the major behavior symptoms of the burned-out worker. Personal accomplishment finally diminishes as a result of burnout.[28]

A study of workers and their supervisors in a hospital verified that work exhaustion can have negative consequences for the individual and the organization. Employees completed questionnaires measuring emotional exhaustion, organizational commitment, and turnover intentions. Supervisors rated the same employees on job performance and organizational citizenship behavior. The major findings of the study were that emotional exhaustion led to lower commitment to the organization, and a higher rate of intention to leave the organization. Exhaustion also led to lower job performance and lower organizational citizenship behavior in terms of helping both the supervisor and the organization.[29] An important implication of this study is that burnout can adversely affect behavior and attitudes.

Factors Contributing to Work Stress

A host of internal factors within a person, as well as adverse organizational conditions, can cause or contribute to job stress. As with sources of conflict, the list is dynamic. New sources of stress surface as the work environment changes. For example, today thousands of industrial and retail salespeople feel less job security because so much of the sales function has moved to the Internet.

Factors within the Individual

A general stressor that encompasses both individual and organizational factors is having to cope with significant change. The more significant the change you have to cope with in a short period of time, the greater the probability that you will experience a stress disorder.[30] Exhibit 8-6 presents the impact of various life changes, measured in life-change units. Hostile, aggressive, and impatient people find ways of turning almost any job into a stressful experience. Such individuals are labeled as having Type A personalities, in contrast to their more easygoing Type B personality counterparts. In addition to being angry, the outstanding trait of Type A personality people is their strong sense of time urgency, known as "hurry sickness." This sense of urgency compels them to achieve more and more in less and less time. Type A personality people are prone to cardiovascular disorders, particularly when the individual is hostile. A study of 774 males found that hostility was a good predictor of who would develop heart disease three years later. Hostility was defined as "a stable tendency to interpret the world and other people in a cynical and negative manner."[31]

Recognize, however, that not every hard-driving, impatient person is correctly classified as having a Type A personality. Managers and professionals who love their work and enjoy other people are not particularly prone to heart disease. These people experience more positive emotion than hostility and anger.

Having an external locus of control predisposes people to job stress because they do not believe they can control key stressors in their environment. Managers and professionals with a limited tolerance for ambiguity are prone to frustration and stress because high-level job responsibilities are often ambiguous. **Negative lifestyle factors** also predispose one to job stress. Among them are poor exercise and eating habits and heavy consumption of caffeine, alcohol, tobacco, and other drugs. Another factor predisposing a person to stress is a pessimistic attitude. Being optimistic, in contrast, helps you ward off stress.

The numbers to the right of each life event represent the scale value in life-change units.

1. Death of a spouse (100)
2. Divorce (73)
3. Marital separation (65)
4. Jail term/imprisonment (63)
5. Death of a family member (63)
6. Major personal injury or illness (53)
7. Marriage (50)
8. Fired from the job (47)
9. Marital reconciliation (45)
10. Retirement (45)
11. Major change in health of family member (44)
12. Pregnancy (40)
13. Sexual difficulties (39)
14. Change in financial state (38)

15. Change in number of arguments with spouse (35)
16. Mortgage or loan for major purpose (31)
17. Foreclosure of mortgage or loan (30)
18. Change in responsibilities at work (29)
19. Son or daughter leaving home (29)
20. Trouble with in-laws (29)
21. Outstanding personal achievement (28)
22. Spouse begins or stops work (26)
23. Begin or end school (26)
24. Change in living conditions (20)
25. Revision of personal habits (15)

Source: These stressors have changed over time. This version is from Thomas H. Holmes and Richard H. Rahe, "The Social Adjustment Rating Scale," *Journal of Psychosomatic Research*, 15, 1971, pp. 210–223, with permission of Elsevier; with an interview updating it from Sue MacDonald, "Battling Stress," *Cincinnati Enquirer*, October 23, 1995.

Exhibit 8-6

The Top 25 Stressors as Measured by Life-Change Units

Adverse Organizational Conditions

Under ideal conditions, workers experience just enough stress to prompt them to respond creatively and energetically to their jobs. Unfortunately, high stress levels created by adverse organizational conditions lead to many negative symptoms. According to the **job demands–job control model,** workers experience the most stress when the demands of the job are high yet they have little control over the activity[32] (see Exhibit 8-7). A customer service representative dealing with a major blooper by the firm would fit into this category. In contrast, when job demands are high and the worker has high control, the worker will be energized, motivated, and creative. An information systems specialist who decides which projects to work on might fit here.

A major contributor to work stress is *role overload*. Demands on managers and professionals are at an all-time high, as companies attempt to increase work output and decrease staffing at the same time. A current managerial strategy is to increase layoffs even when sales increase in order to boost worker productivity.[33] Better financial results are achieved by having fewer employees accomplish more work, thereby fostering role-overload stress. Worrying about being next on the "hit list" during downsizing is another major job stressor. In contrast to being overloaded, many other workers suffer from role underload (too little to do) or the job monotony associated with repetitive work. In one situation, a manager left town for three weeks, without giving his newly hired executive assistant an assignment. The assistant suffered anxiety attacks after the fifth day of make-work activities.

A long-recognized contributor to work stress is **role conflict**—having to choose between competing demands or expectations. We have already touched upon role conflict in the study of value conflicts in Chapter 4 and work–family conflicts in the present chapter. If a person complies with one aspect of a role, compliance with the other is difficult. Role conflict has been divided into four types:

1. *Intrasender* conflict occurs when a person is asked to accomplish two objectives that are in apparent conflict. A request by a manager for a group member to increase speed and decrease errors could result in this type of conflict.

Exhibit 8-7

The Job Demands–Job Control Model

163

	Low Job Demands	High Job Demands
Low Control	Passive Job	High-strain Job
High Control	Low-strain Job	Active Job

2. *Intersender* conflict occurs when two or more senders give a person incompatible directions. A worker's manager might request that he begin a project immediately, but upper management insists that new projects should be postponed for the time being.
3. *Interrole* conflict results when two different roles a person occupies are in conflict. Work–family conflict fits the interrole category, as does the situation of a mentor who must give a harsh performance evaluation to the person she is mentoring.
4. *Person–role* conflict occurs when the role(s) an employer expects a worker to perform conflict with the person's basic values. An office assistant in the bursar's office at a vocational technical school in Montreal experienced role conflict because the administration asked her to pressure students to pay their outstanding bills. The woman, herself in poor financial condition, sympathized with the students.[34]

The wider the gap between the two or more roles in role conflict, the more intense the stress. Assume that a sales representative's spouse threatened divorce if the rep's travel exceeded two nights per month. The sales rep would experience intense stress if job demands suddenly required 15 nights away from home per month.

Another role-related stressor is **role ambiguity,** a condition in which the jobholder receives confusing or poorly defined expectations. Role ambiguity involves several factors. First, there is insufficient information about the worker's expected performance. Second, there is unclear or confusing information about expected job behaviors. Third, there is uncertainty about the outcome (such as promotion or dismissal) of certain on-the-job behaviors.[35] The person facing extreme role ambiguity proclaims, "I don't know what I'm supposed to be doing or what will happen to me if I do it."

Another contributor to stress and burnout is emotional labor, the burden of having to modify or fake emotions, or at least facial expressions, when dealing with customers (as described in our discussion of emotions in Chapter 4). Alicia Grandey contends that sales workers and customer service representatives carry the biggest emotional labor of any occupational group.[36] Similar to other stressors, faking emotion can overwork the cardiovascular and nervous systems and weaken the immune system.

Repetitive strain injuries (RSI), including carpal tunnel syndrome, account for two-thirds of all work-related injuries. Computer workers, meat cutters, as well as interpreters for the deaf who use sign language, are among the workers at high risk for repetitive strain injuries. Repetitive strain injury victims often suffer severe mental stress as well as physical pain. One of the many stressors is worrying about not being able to work again in one's chosen field because of the physical disability. Although physical pain is at the root of the problem, emotional stress can lead to more muscle tension and intensify the physical pain.[37] Although RSI can be caused by organizational factors, a disability management specialist reports that more than half of carpal tunnel syndrome cases stem from off-the-job factors. Individuals who spend a lot of time at the keyboard off hours, are obese or diabetic or both, and who have poor circulation, predispose themselves to this problem.[38]

A final organizational stressor mentioned here is being part of a culturally diverse workforce. Although cultural diversity brings many advantages to organizations (as will be described in Chapter 16), it may lead to interpersonal stress. As analyzed by Richard S. DeFrank and John M. Ivancevich, these stressors include competition among groups for attention and resources, and decreased interaction because of the perceived need for political correctness in dealing with demographic groups other than one's own. Not knowing how to respond well in a diverse setting is also a stressor; for example, a 55-year-old white man feeling awkward because his manager is a 25-year-old African-American woman. Furthermore, it is stressful for a person to feel that he or she is not a good cultural fit with most members of the organization.[39] The accompanying Organizational Behavior in Action box illustrates how specialists can help employees deal better with cultural diversity.

4

Explain what organizations can do to manage and reduce stress.

Organizational Approaches to Stress Management

Negative stress is disruptive to both productivity and employee well-being. As a consequence, organizations are actively involved in stress management. Several illustrative approaches to stress management include providing emotional support to employees, sponsoring a wellness and fitness program, giving on-site massages, and providing the opportunity to take nap breaks on the job. Creating a high-

---

Organizational Behavior *in Action*
Employee Assistance Programs and Cultural Diversity

Mary Ellen Rogers, CEO of Family Care and Workforce Diversity Consultants, says that employee-assistance programs today offer a wealth of work/life and diversity services such as helping to find child and elder care, or providing tips on working with foreign customers. Twenty years ago, EAPs provided only services for personal crises such as substance abuse or marriage counseling. Rogers notes that management is beginning to realize that diversity issues, such as discrimination and cultural alienation, affect productivity. "Diversity is not just about race and religion. It's about global etiquette, understanding other cultures, and helping people feel comfortable in foreign surroundings."

At the law firm of Halloran & Sage, in Hartford, Connecticut, services to help employees recover from alcohol and drug abuse aren't commonly needed. The highly paid, busy professionals on the staff are more interested in support services from an employee assistance program (EAP), such as finding elder or child care. To meet their needs, the firm developed a Generations Program. It is a hotline referral service through Family Care and Workforce Diversity Consultants that helps employees find care, schools, community centers, housing, and scholarship programs for members of their families.

The company's diversity reps help employees research cultural or work/life questions that come up, such as finding a school or community center with a diverse ethnic makeup. Many employees use the program to find concierge services and to handle travel and cultural questions related to business, such as how to address colleagues from another culture, or where to get basic foreign-language training.

Source: Sarah Fister Gale, "Companies Find EAPs Can Foster Diversity," *Workforce*, February 2002, pp. 66–67. Used with permission.

job-demand, high-control job, as described previously, is also an approach to stress prevention.

Emotional support from an immediate superior can help group members cope better with job stress. One study compared the illness rate between two groups of employees who faced comparable heavy stressors. Those employees who felt they had their manager's support suffered only half as much illness in 12 months as those who felt they lacked such support. The most helpful managers ask themselves the question, "How can I make my subordinates feel as effective as I do?" Supportive behaviors that help employees feel more effective include the following:

1. Keep communication channels open.
2. Provide the right kind of help (such as verbal encouragement or time off from work to recover from a heavy stressor).
3. Act as a catalyst (such as helping an employee look at a troublesome problem in a new perspective).
4. Hold back on disseminating stressful information (such as passing along rumors about downsizing).[40]

To help combat negative stress, as well as to promote wellness, many employers offer programs that encourage employees to stay in good physical and mental shape. A **wellness program** is thus a formal organization-sponsored activity to help employees stay well and avoid illness. Workshops, seminars, activities, and medical procedures offered in a wellness program include the following: medical examinations, stress management techniques, smoking cessation programs, and preventive health care. Biofeedback, as described in the chapter opener, is often included in wellness programs. A study conducted by the Nevada Stress Center demonstrated that employees who participated in a stress management program had fewer sick days than those who did not participate. Furthermore, the stress center participants visited physicians 34 percent less than did their non-participating counterparts.[41] At the same time, one could ask the question: Are employees who are healthier to begin with more likely to participate in stress-management programs in the first place?

An emerging approach to help employees combat stress is to give them the opportunity to nap on company premises. Napping is one of the most effective methods of treating and preventing stress. Everyday job stress can often be alleviated by taking a 15- to 20-minute nap to restore alertness and memory and to decrease the effects of fatigue. Naps beyond 30 minutes place people in their normal sleep cycle, with people often waking up feeling groggy and disoriented. 42 IS, a California information systems firm, is an example of a company that commits resources to facilitate employee napping. 42 IS created a sleeping loft complete with queen-size bed, pillows and blankets.[42] For career-minded people, the slogan "You snooze, you win" replaces "You snooze, you lose."

Individual Approaches to Stress Management

5

Do a more effective job of managing your own stress.

Techniques individuals can use to manage stress can be divided into three categories: control, symptom management, and escape.[43]

Control

Methods of controlling and reducing stress include getting the right emotional support. Receiving social support—encouragement, understanding, and friendship—from other people is a key strategy for coping with work and personal stress.

An equally important control technique is to practice good work habits and time management. By establishing priorities and minimizing procrastination, people can gain better control of their lives. Gaining control is especially important because feeling out of control is a major stressor. The lowly To Do list could thus save you an ulcer or heart attack! Demanding less than perfection from oneself can also help prevent stress. Not measuring up to one's own unrealistically high standards is a substantial stressor.

Symptom Management

Dozens of symptom management techniques have been developed, and no stress management program is complete without using at least one. Getting appropriate physical exercise is an excellent starting point in symptom management. Physical exercise helps dissipate some of the tension created by work stress and also helps the body ward off future stress-related disorders. One way in which exercise helps combat stress is by releasing endorphins. These are morphine-like chemicals produced in the brain that act as painkillers and antidepressants.

Another widely, applicable symptom management technique is the **relaxation response,** a general-purpose method of learning to relax by yourself. The key ingredient of this technique is to make yourself quiet and comfortable. At the same time, think of the word "one" (or any simple chant or prayer) with every breath for about ten minutes. The technique slows you down both physiologically and emotionally and at the same time reduces the adverse effects of stress. Much of the benefit of the relaxation response can also be achieved by napping or visualizing a pleasant fantasy for about ten minutes. Yoga offers many of the benefits of the relaxation response; however pushing yoga too far can be dangerous for people with high blood pressure or disorders of the joint. The relaxation response is physically harmless. The stress busters listed in Exhibit 8-8 are mostly aimed at symptom management.

Escape

Escape methods of stress management are actions and reappraisals of situations that provide the stressed individual some escape from the stressor. Eliminating the stres-

Exhibit 8-8

Stress Busters

- Take a nap when facing heavy pressures. Napping is one of the most effective techniques for reducing and preventing stress.
- Give in to your emotions. If you are angry, disgusted, or confused, admit your feelings. Suppressing your emotions adds to stress. Talk to a friend or counsellor about your problems.
- Take a brief break from the stressful situation and do something small and constructive such as washing your car, emptying a wastebasket, or cleaning out a drawer.
- Get a massage because it can loosen tight muscles, improve your blood circulation, and calm you down.
- Get help with your stressful task from a coworker, manager, or friend.
- Concentrate intensely on reading, a sport, a hobby, or surfing the Internet. Contrary to common sense, concentration is at the heart of stress reduction.

- Have a quiet place at home and enjoy a brief idle period there every day.
- Take a leisurely day off from your routine, or at least take a brief walk during a particularly stressful day.
- Finish something you have started, however small. Accomplishing almost anything reduces some stress.
- Stop to smell the flowers, make friends with a young child or elderly person, or play with a kitten or puppy.
- Strive to do a good job, but not a perfect job.
- Work with your hands, doing a pleasant task.
- Find somebody or something that makes you laugh, and have a good laugh.
- Minimize drinking caffeinated or alcoholic beverages, and drink fruit juice or water instead. Eat fruits or vegetables for snacks rather than junk food.

IMPLICATIONS FOR MANAGERIAL PRACTICE

1. A manager's goal should be to maintain optimal levels of conflict in his or her unit. Sometimes this will involve the reduction of conflict; at other times, conflict stimulation may be necessary.

2. Approximately 20 to 30 percent of a manager's time involves resolving conflict. It is therefore important for a manager to develop effective conflict resolution skills. A good starting point is to use confrontation and problem solving.

3. A manager should encourage C-type conflict within the organizational unit and at the same time discourage A-type conflict. A mechanism for doing this would be for the manager to take the steps necessary within the group to encourage focused activity, creative problem solving, open communication, and integration.

4. Given that an optimal amount of stress facilitates performance, a manager should strive to design the appropriate amount and kinds of stressors for both individuals and groups. Manipulating stressors is much like manipulating the challenge level of a job. Stress can be increased or decreased by manipulating the amount of job responsibility, goal difficulty, tightness of deadlines, amount of supervision, and critical feedback.

5. Managers should encourage team members to embark upon a systematic program of stress management, considering today's turbulent work environment. Workers who are already managing stress well should be encouraged in their efforts.

sor is the most effective escape technique. For example, if a manager experiences stress because of serious understaffing in his department, he should negotiate to receive authorization to hire additional staff. Mentally blocking out a stressful thought is another escape technique, but it may not work in the long run. Without constructive action about the problem, a stressor will usually return.

SUMMARY OF KEY POINTS

1 **Understand the nature of conflict in organizations and what its leading causes are.**

Workplace conflict has many sources, including the following: perceived adverse changes, line versus staff differentiation, sexual harassment, competing work and family demands, and personal dispositions and personality clashes.

Functional conflict occurs when the interests of the organization are served as a result of a dispute or disagreement. Dysfunctional conflict occurs when a dispute or disagreement harms the organization, calling for managerial intervention. At times, the manager may want to stimulate conflict to enhance performance. Team performance is enhanced by stimulating C-type conflict, which deals with substantive, work-related issues. A-type conflict, which deals with personal issues and emotions, generally lowers team performance.

2 **Have the necessary information to resolve many workplace conflicts, including dealing with difficult people.**

Five styles of handling conflict based on a combination of assertiveness (looking out for oneself) and cooperativeness have been identified: competitive, accomodative, sharing, collaborative (win–win), and avoidant. A widely applicable approach to resolving conflict is confrontation and problem solving, in which the true source of the conflict is identified and then resolved systematically. The recommended confrontation approach is a gentle and tactful one. To resolve conflict with an angry person, you might confront him or her, contain the angry situation, and connect with the person. A structural method of resolving conflict emphasizes juggling work assignments and reporting relationships so that disputes are minimized. An appeals procedure is a structural approach.

Techniques for dealing with difficult people include: using tact and diplomacy, using nonhostile humor; giving recognition and attention; helping the difficult person feel more confident, and reinforcing civil behavior and good moods.

3 **Understand the nature, causes, and consequences of work stress.**

Stress is an internal response to a state of activation, ordinarily occuring in a threatening or negative situation. The cybernetic theory of stress views stress as an important discrepancy between an employee's perceived state and a desired state. To manage stress properly, the person attempts to narrow the discrepancy.

Stress symptoms include a host of physiological, emotional, and behavioral reactions. Many of these symptoms can adversely affect job performance. After prolonged job stress, a person may experience burnout. A general stressor that encompasses both individual and organizational factors is having to cope with significant change. Factors within a person contributing to work stress include a Type A personality, an external locus of control, negative lifestyle factors, and a pessimistic attitude.

Adverse organization conditions are another set of stressors. According to the job demands–job control model, workers experience the most stress when the demands of the job are high yet they have little control over the activity. Other stressors include role overload and worry about potential job loss. Role conflict in its various forms and role ambiguity are other stressors of significance. Emotional labor is a recently recognized stressor. Repetitive strain injuries contribute to work

stress, and so might being part of a culturally diverse group.

 Explain what organizations can do to manage and reduce stress.
Organizational approaches to stress management include providing emotional support to employees, the establishment of a wellness program, and allowing for napping on the job.

5 **Do a more effective job of managing your own stress.**
Individual methods of preventing and controlling stress can be divided into three categories: attempts to control stressful situations, symptom management, and escape from the stressful situation. Specific tactics include eliminating stressors, getting sufficient physical exercise, using relaxation techniques, getting emotional support from others, and improving work habits. Also see the stress buster list in Exhibit 8-8.

KEY TERMS AND PHRASES

Conflict, *147*
The opposition of persons or forces giving rise to some tension.

Downsizing, *147*
The laying off of workers to reduce costs and increase efficiency.

Sexual Harassment, *148*
Unwanted sexually oriented behavior in the workplace that results in discomfort and/or interference with the job.

Work–Family Conflict, *151*
Conflict that ensues when the individual has to perform multiple roles: worker; spouse; and, often, parent.

Personality Clash, *152*
An antagonistic relationship between two people based on differences in personal attributes, preferences, interests, values, and styles.

Functional Conflict, *152*
A situation that occurs when the interests of the organization are served as a result of a dispute or disagreement.

Dysfunctional Conflict, *152*
A situation that occurs when a dispute or disagreement harms the organization.

C-Type Conflict, *153*
Conflict that focuses on substantive, issue-related differences.

A-Type Conflict, *154*
Conflict that focuses on personalized, individually oriented issues.

Win–Win, *155*
The belief that, after conflict has been resolved, both sides should gain something of value.

Confrontation and Problem Solving, *155*
A method of identifying the true source of conflict and resolving it systematically.

Open-Door Policy, *157*
An understanding in which any employee can bring a gripe to the attention of upper-level management without checking with his or her immediate manager.

Difficult Person, *157*
An individual who creates problems for others, yet has the skill and mental ability to do otherwise.

Stress, *158*
The mental and physical condition that results from a perceived threat that cannot be dealt with readily.

Cybernetic Theory of Stress, Coping, and Well-Being in Organizations, *159*
The view that stress is a discrepancy between an employee's perceived state and desired state.

Stressor, *159*
Any force creating the stress reaction.

Burnout, *160*
A pattern of emotional, physical, and mental exhaustion in response to chronic job stressors.

Negative Lifestyle Factors, *161*
Behavior patterns predisposing a person to job stress, including poor exercise and eating habits and heavy consumption of caffeine, alcohol, tobacco, and other drugs.

Job Demands–Job Control Model, *162*
An explanation of job stress contending that workers experience the most stress when the demands of the job are high yet they have little control over the activity.

Role Conflict, *162*
Having to choose between competing demands or expectations.

Role Ambiguity, *163*
A condition in which the job holder receives confused or poorly defined role expectations.

Wellness Program, *165*
A formal organization-sponsored activity to help employees stay well and avoid illness.

Relaxation Response, *166*
A general-purpose method of learning to relax by oneself, which includes making oneself quiet and comfortable.

DISCUSSION QUESTIONS AND ACTIVITIES

1. In what way does the presence of *spam* advertising on e-mail represent conflict? Who are the parties in conflict?
2. Conflict is said to have some functional consequences. Describe an example of how conflict has ever improved your work or personal life.
3. Several analyses have concluded that sexual harassment is costly to the organization. What do you think are the costs associated with sexual harassment?
4. Why are entrepreneurs and other business owners more likely to experience work–family conflict than corporate employees?
5. Identify at least three ways in which customers are rude to employees. What suggestions might you have for overcoming this type of rudeness problem?
6. Give an example from your own life of how the cybernetic model of stress might be valid.
7. Identify an information technology job that you think creates negative stress for most incumbents, and pinpoint the stressors.

ORGANIZATIONAL BEHAVIOR ONLINE

TO DO

Anger Toolkit
A current thrust in both resolving conflict and managing stress is learning how to manage anger—one of the strongest emotions. Visit http://www.angermgmt.com to learn more about this important development in work and personal life. You will find useful information on the site about managing anger. In addition, go to "Measure Your Anger Right Now." Compare the results of this test with your own evaluation of how angry you are. Also, reflect on any feedback you may have received recently about your anger.

TO BOOKMARK

American Institute of Stress
http://www.stress.org

Evaluation of Resistance to Stress
http://www.pressanykey.com/stresstest.html

Employee Assistance Programs
http://www.eapintl.com

CASE PROBLEM: Burning Out at SalaryPro

Pete Ambrose started his employment with SalaryPro, Inc. in its Client Service Center 18 months ago. SalaryPro administers the payroll function for small- and medium-size companies as well as several other human resource activities including training and recruitment. The service center is composed of five teams, with each one consisting of approximately eight specialists. Each of the teams specialized in a different knowledge base to direct incoming calls efficiently. Pete's team answered inbound calls from participants in 401(k) retirement plans or Section 125 flexible spending account plans with their employer, although Pete had limited knowledge about how these plans were administered. The first two weeks of his employment at SalaryPro were spent in intensive training to learn about the products. By week three of his employment, Pete was answering client questions on his own.

Pete's training focused on knowledge about retirement and flexible plans, and he was also given guidance on what would be expected of him as a specialist. Because the center serviced clients across the United States, assistance was available from 8 AM to 8 PM Eastern Standard Time. Pete expressed a preference to his manager for working days; nevertheless, he was informed that he would work a rotating shift in which his hours would be either 8–5, 9–6, or 11–8, depending on the telephone coverage needed on any given day.

A shift consisted of eight hours of phone work, one hour of lunch, and two highly encouraged fifteen-minute breaks. The breaks were designed to refresh the call specialist both physically and mentally. The remaining seven-and-one-half hours were to be spent taking calls, submitting research requests, completing follow-ups for client inquiries, and attending any necessary meetings or training. To ensure that everyone had a similar workload, the supervisors decided that it was fair to expect that a specialist should either be available to take calls or actually be taking calls for a total of six hours each day. The total amount of uncommitted time available to complete other work was approximately one-and-one-half hours per day.

Call specialists were given worksheets every day on which to indicate the times they were not available to take calls and the reasons for not being available. When a specialist did not meet the six-hour expectation on any given day, regardless of the amount of calls taken, his or her day was evaluated as *unfavorable*. While specialists were evaluated on their entire daily performance, they were also evaluated on the individual calls they took. A monitoring system recorded five random conversations each week, enabling the supervisors to see and hear what a specialist was saying and doing while servicing any given client. The calls were then reviewed by a monitoring committee and graded on five dimensions:

1. Completing the required greeting and closing with the client.
2. Using the client's name at least twice.
3. Completing the necessary security checks before releasing any sensitive information to the client.
4. Relaying accurate information to the client.
5. Diagnosing any future calls or problems for the client.

The five areas totalled 100 points. A specialist was expected to obtain at least 90 percent of the points on every call; anything less than 90 percent was considered to be *unfavorable*. An award called "Stars" was given to specialists who provided exceptional service. The Stars could come from receiving compliments in spoken or written form from clients, or from nominations from other specialists or supervisors. The Stars were hand delivered to the specialist from the department manager to be displayed in his or her cubicle for other specialists to see.

By the start of week three, Pete was up and running on his own. He still had the occasional question about the different products and expectations, but he completed the work the best he could. Pete found that he could talk to the participants on the phone with ease and even calm down clients when they were upset. Between his first and sixth months at SalaryPro, Pete received five Stars derived from client compliments.

Pete believed he was communicating with clients efficiently, yet his monitoring scores indicated otherwise. Pete scored consistently low on "diagnosing future calls or problems." He made a conscious effort to improve his calls but each monitor reflected a below average, or *unfavorable* score, primarily because he was unable to recognize the potential for future problems. Not only were Pete's monitoring scores continuously decreasing, but his daily statistics were almost always under the six-hour expectation. He tried to

decide which was more important—servicing the client efficiently or being available to spend time with the client. Although Pete knew it was important to do both, he struggled with being able to receive a favorable rating on both dimensions. Pete's direct supervisor encouraged Pete to take home his training material to review it in the evenings.

Pete began leaving work each day feeling exhausted. The rotating schedule meant Pete was getting home at a different time each week, shortening the time available to be with his family. When at home, he felt he should be studying his training materials. Furthermore, Pete always went to bed feeling overwhelmed with exhaustion. Yet he often could not fall asleep because he worried about how his job performance might affect his review. Pete noticed that many of the muscles in his neck and shoulder were so tense that it made it difficult to get in a comfortable position when he was trying to fall asleep.

The call volume began to increase as the end of the year approached. Pete worried about how his supervisors would view his service with the clients. Pete knew that this would be the review period in which he would be eligible for his 10 percent raise. On December 28, Pete met with his supervisor to discuss his performance during the past six months. The meeting did not go as well as Pete hoped. His supervisor completed the performance review and indicated that she did not feel that Pete's performance entitled him to the full 10 percent raise. After discussing Pete's performance with her manager, the supervisor decided to give him a 5 percent salary increase.

For Pete, the smaller-than-anticipated raised was the last straw, and he decided to quit SalaryPro that day. He sent his supervisor an e-mail saying that he quit, picked up his belongings, and left the building.

Case Questions

1. What were some of the conditions that contributed to Pete's work exhaustion?
2. What initiatives could Pete have taken to prevent his stress problems from escalating?
3. What steps could management at SalaryPro have taken to prevent the type of turnover that Pete's situation represented?

Source: Case researched by Katie Kovar, Rochester Institute of Technology, 2003.

ENDNOTES

1. David M. Noer, *Healing the Wounds: Overcoming the Trauma of Layoffs and Revitalizing Downsized Organizations* (San Francisco: Jossey-Bass, 1993).
2. Marjorie L. Icenogle, Bruce W. Eagle, Sohel Ahman, and Lisa A. Hanks, "Assessing Perceptions of Sexual Harassment Behaviors in a Manufacturing Environment," *Journal of Business and Psychology,* Summer 2002, pp. 601–616.
3. These rulings are summarized in Jennifer Laabs, "What You're Liable for Now," *Workforce,* October 1998, pp. 34–42.
4. Kimberly T. Schneider, Suzanne Swan, and Louise F. Fitzgerald, "Job-Related and Psychological Effects of Sexual Harassment in

the Workplace: Empirical Evidence from Two Organizations," *Journal of Applied Psychology,* June 1997, p. 406.
5. Linda Elizabeth Duxbury and Christopher Alan Higgins, "Gender Differences in Work-Family Conflict," *Journal of Applied Psychology,* February 1991, p. 64.
6. "When Work and Private Lives Collide," *Workforce,* February 1999, p. 27.
7. Ellen Ernst Kossek and Cynthia Ozeki, "Work-Family Conflict, Policies, and the Job-Life Satisfaction Relationship: A Review and Directions for Organizational Behavior—Human Resources

Research," *Journal of Applied Psychology,* April 1998, pp. 139–149.

8. Virginia Smith Major, Katherine J. Klein, and Mark G. Ehrhart, "Work Time, Work Interference With Family, and Psychological Distress," *Journal of Applied Psychology,* June 2002, pp. 427–436.

9. Leslie B. Hammer, Talya N. Bauer, and Alicia A. Grandey, "Work-Family Conflict and Work-Related Withdrawal Behaviors," *Journal of Business and Psychology,* Spring 2003, pp. 419–436.

10. Quoted in Carol Kleiman, "Finding Balance with Work, Family," *Chicago Tribune* syndicated story, November 23, 1998. See also Francine M. Deutsch, *Having It All: How Equally Shared Parenting Works* (Boston: Harvard University Press, 1998).

11. Lynne M. Andersson and Christine M. Pearson, "Tit for Tat? The Spiraling Effect of Incivility in the Workplace," *Academy of Management Review,* July 1999, pp. 452–471.

12. J. M. Rabbie and F. K. Bekkers, "Threatened Leadership and Intergroup Competition, " *European Journal of Social Psychology,* Vol. 8, 1978, pp. 19–20. (As cited in Robert P. Vecchio, *Organizational Behavior,* 2nd ed. (Mason, OH: South Western/Thomson Learning, 1991), p. 415.)

13. Julie Ellis, "Knock Down Workplace Bullying; Improve Office Morale," *Managing Workplace Conflict,* Sample Issue, The Dartnell Corporation, 2002.

14. Jennifer Laabs, "Employee Sabotage: Don't Be a Victim," *Workforce,* July 1999, p. 33.

15. Jennifer Daw, "Road Rage, Air Rage, and Now 'Desk Rage,'" *Monitor on Psychology,* July/August 2001, p. 52.

16. Cited in Susan Strother, "He's Defusing the Workplace," *Rochester Democrat and Chronicle,* December 27, 1999, p. 3F.

17. Michael D. Kelleher, *Profiling the Lethal Employee: Case Studies of Violence in the Workplace* (Westport, CT: Praeger, 1997), p. 12. Understanding how the environment contributes to violence is also an underlying theme in Ricky W. Griffin, Ann O'Leary-Kelly, and Judith M. Collins (eds.), *Dysfunctional Behavior in Organizations, Part A: Violent and Deviant Behavior, Part B: Non-Violent Dysfunctional Behavior in Organizations,* Volume 23 (Stamford, CT: JAI Press, 1998).

18. Allen C. Amson, Wayne A. Hockwarter, Kenneth R. Thompson, and Allison W. Harrison, "Conflict: An Important Dimension in Successful Management Teams," *Organizational Dynamics* (Autumn 1995), pp. 20–33.

19. Kenneth Thomas, "Conflict and Conflict Management," in Marvin D. Dunnette (ed.), *Handbook of Industrial and Organizational Psychology* (Chicago: Rand McNally College Publishing, 1976), pp. 900–902.

20. Joann Muller and Christine Tierney, "Can This Man Save Chrysler?" *Business Week,* September 17, 2001.

21. D. H. Stamatis, "Conflict: You've Got to Accentuate the Positive," *Personnel,* December 1987, pp. 48–49.

22. The quote and technique are both from Kathleen Doheny, "It's a Mad, Mad Corporate World," *Working Woman,* April 2000, pp. 71–72.

23. "How to Deal with 'Problem' Workers," *Positive Leadership,* sample issue distributed 2001.

24. Patrick A. McGuire, "Worker Stress, Health, Reaching Critical Point," *Monitor On Psychology,* May 1999, p. 1.

25. Survey cited in "Stop Burnout—Before It Stops Your Employees," *HRfocus,* February 2002, p. 3.

26. Jeffery R. Edwards, "A Cybernetic Theory of Stress, Coping, and Well-Being in Organizations," *Academy of Management Review,* April 1992, pp. 256–257.

27. Research reviewed in "Mental Stress Is Linked to Blocked Blood Vessels," *Monitor on Psychology,* February 1998, p. 7.

28. Cynthia L. Cordes and Thomas W. Dougherty, "A Review and Integration of Research on Job Burnout," *Academy of Management Review,* October 1993, p. 622.

29. Russell Cropanzano, Deborah E. Rupp, and Zinta S. Byrne, "The Relationships of Emotional Exhaustion to Work Attitudes, Job Performance, and Organizational Citizenship Behavior," *Journal of Applied Psychology,* February 2003, pp. 160–169.

30. Rabi S. Bhagat, "Effects of Stressful Life Events on Individual Performance and Work Adjustment Processes within Organizational Settings: A Research Model," *Academy of Management Review,* October 1983, pp. 660–671.

31. Research reported in Etienne Benton, "Hostility Is Among Best Predictors of Heart Disease in Men," *Monitor on Psychology,* January 2003, p. 15.

32. Marilyn L. Fox, Deborah J. Dwyer, and Daniel C. Ganster, "Effects of Stressful Job Demands and Control on Physiological and Attitudinal Outcomes in a Hospital Setting," *Academy of Management Journal,* April 1993, pp. 290–292.

33. Lisa Takeuchi Cullen, "Where Did Everyone Go?", *Time,* November 18, 2002, p. 66.

34. Daniel Katz and Robert L. Kahn, *The Social Psychology of Organizations* (New York: Wiley, 1966); updated in "Working Smart," *Personal Report for the Executive,* May 15, 1988, p. 3.

35. J. B. Teboul, "Facing and Coping with Uncertainty during Organizational Encounter," *Communication Quarterly,* Vol. 8, 1994, pp. 190–224.

36. Alicia A. Grandey, "Emotion Regulation in the Workplace: A New Way to Conceptualize Emotional Labor," *Journal of Occupational Health Psychology* 5, no. 1, 2000, pp. 95–110; Grandey, "When the 'Show Must Go On': Surface Acting and Deep Acting as Determinants of Emotional Exhaustion and Peer-Related Service Delivery," *Academy of Management Journal,* February 2003, pp. 86–96.

37. Haeyoun Park, "Emotional Impact on RSI Sufferers Is Often Overlooked," Knight Ridder, August 2, 1999.

38. Cited in William Atkinson, "The Carpal Tunnel Conundrum," *Workforce,* September 2002, p. 17.

39. Richard S. DeFrank and John M. Ivancevich, "Stress on the Job: An Executive Update," *Academy of Management Executive,* August 1998, p. 56.

40. Sandra L. Kirmeyer and Thomas W. Dougherty, "Work Load, Tension, and Coping: Moderating Effects of Supervisor Support," *Personnel Psychology,* Spring 1988, pp. 125–139.

41. Kathryn Tyler, "Cut the Stress," *HR Magazine,* May 2003, p. 101.

42. M. Waters, "Naps Could Replace Coffee as Workers' Favorite Break," *Monitor On Psychology,* July 1998, p. 6.

43. The framework for this section is from Janina C. Latack, "Coping with Job Stress: Measures and Future Directions for Scale Development," *Journal of Applied Psychology,* August 1986, pp. 522–526.

Chapter 9

Interpersonal Communication

OBJECTIVES

After reading and studying this chapter and doing the exercises, you should be able to:

1 Describe the communication process.

2 Describe the impact of information technology on interpersonal communication in organizations.

3 Explain how nonverbal communication can be used to enhance communication.

4 Present details about the various channels of communication in organizations.

5 Summarize barriers to effective communication and how to overcome them.

6 Explain how to overcome potential cross-gender and cross-cultural communication problems.

7 Recognize the basics for becoming a more power-oriented communicator.

When Shaw's Supermarkets acquired another company, rumors ran rampant. How many stores would be closed? How many people would be laid off? Controlling the rumor mill is never easy, especially for a company with 32,000 employees in seven New England states. The solution: introduction of *The Rumor Buster,* a newsletter published on an as-needed—but at least weekly—basis during the merger, says Ruth Bramson, senior vice president of human resources in East Bridgewater, Mass. "Communication is the major stumbling block to a successful merger," says Bramson. *The Rumor Buster* "addressed whatever horrendous rumors were going around at the moment. We found it to be an incredibly successful tool."

HR (human resources) discovered just how useful the newsletter was when employees of the newly acquired company were polled; they indicated that the newsletter had been an important and positive part of the integration. "They told us that they looked forward to getting *The Rumor Buster* because it focused on the things that they were worried about," Bramson says.

Source: Len Grensing-Pophal, "Got the Message," *HR Magazine,* April 2001, pp. 75–76. Reprinted with the permission of *HR Magazine* published by the Society for Human Resource Management, Alexandria, VA.

NOW ASK YOURSELF: Why do the leaders of many successful organizations make a conscious and deliberate effort to address potential communication issues before they fester into major problems such as damaging a merger? Communication is the basic process by which managers and professionals accomplish their tasks, and people in positions of authority consistently rank communication skills as vital for success. At times, a newsletter distributed in hard copy or electronically can be the communication medium of choice. Yet such communication is enhanced by interacting with employees at all levels about issues large and small. The Nierenberg Group's survey on the top job skills for the 21st century identified interpersonal communication skills as the number one workplace skill. Communication was also rated as a top 5 skill by 95 percent of Nierenberg survey respondents.[1]

The purpose of this chapter is to explain key aspects of interpersonal communication in organizations and make suggestions for improved communication. To achieve this purpose, we include information about the communication process, the impact of information technology on communication, overcoming various barriers to communication, and how to develop a more power-oriented communication style.

THE COMMUNICATION PROCESS

1

Describe the communication process.

Interpersonal communication takes place through a series of steps, as illustrated in Exhibit 9-1. For effective communication to take place, six components must be present: a communication source or sender, a message, a channel, a receiver, feedback, and the environment. "Noise" can also have an impact on communication. As you study this model, you will observe that perception and communication are closely linked. To help explain the communication process, assume that a production manager wants to inform a team leader that productivity in his department slipped last month.

1. *Source (the sender).* The source of a communication event is usually a person attempting to send a spoken, written, sign language, or nonverbal message to another person or persons. The perceived authority and experience of the sender are important factors in influencing how much attention the message will receive.

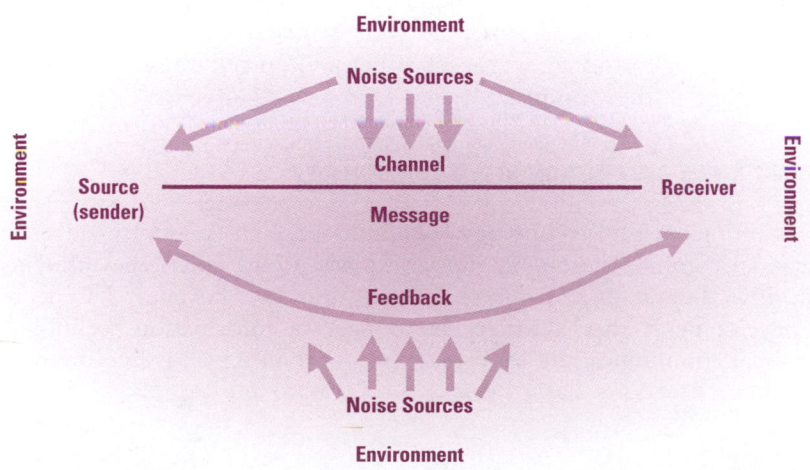

Exhibit 9-1

The Communication Process

Various sources of interference can prevent a message getting from sender to receiver as intended.

2. *Message.* The heart of a communication event is the **message,** which is a purpose or an idea to be conveyed. Many factors influence how a message is received. Among them are clarity, the alertness of the receiver, the complexity and length of the message, and how the information is organized. The production manager's message will most likely get across if she says directly, "I need to talk to you about last month's below-average productivity figures."

3. *Channel (medium).* Several communication channels, or media, are usually available for sending messages in organizations. Typically, messages are written, spoken, or a combination of written and spoken. Some kind of nonverbal cue, such as a smile or hand gesture, accompanies most spoken messages. Heavy reliance is now placed on electronic transmission of messages. In the production manager's case, she has chosen to drop by the team leader's office and deliver her message in a serious tone.

4. *Receiver.* A communication event can only be complete when another party receives the message and understands it properly. In the example under examination, the team leader is the receiver. Perceptual distortions of various types (as described in Chapter 3) act as filters that can prevent a message from being received as intended by the sender. If the team leader is worried that his job is at stake, he might get defensive when he hears the production manager's message.

5. *Feedback.* Without feedback, it is difficult to know whether a message has been received and understood. The feedback step also includes the reactions of the receiver. If the receiver takes action as intended by the sender, the message has been received satisfactorily. The production manager will know her message got across if the team leader says, "OK, when would you like to review last month's production figures?" Effective interpersonal communication therefore involves an exchange of messages between two people. The two communicators take turns being receivers and senders.

6. *Environment.* A full understanding of communication requires knowledge of the environment in which messages are transmitted and received. The organizational culture is a key environmental factor that influences communication. It is easier to transmit controversial messages when trust and respect are high than when they are low.

7. *Noise.* Distractions such as noise have a pervasive influence on the components of the communication process. In this context, **noise** is anything that disrupts communication, including the attitudes and emotions of the receiver. Noise includes work stress, fear, ambivalence, and strong advocacy for an opposing position. In a more literal sense, the whir of machinery, piped-in music, and the chatting of coworkers with each other and on cell phones are also examples of noise in the workplace.

COMMUNICATION AND INFORMATION TECHNOLOGY

2

Describe the impact of information technology on interpersonal communication in organizations.

Advances in information technology have influenced the quantity and quality of interpersonal communications in the workplace. Quite often the influence has been positive, but at other times communication effectiveness has decreased. Three developments that illustrate the impact of information technology on interpersonal communication are e-mail, telecommuting, and slide presentations by computer.

E-mail

E-mail has had two major impacts on interpersonal communication. First, written messages have replaced many telephone and in-person interchanges, with the majority of office workers being connected by e-mail networks. Group members often keep in regular contact with one another without having lengthy meetings or telephone conversations. Second, people receive many more messages than they did by paper and telephone. Many managers and professionals process over 100 e-mail messages per day.

E-mail facilitates communication in many ways, including people in various parts of the world exchanging information without worrying about trying to connect through different time zones. A more subtle consequence of e-mail is that it enhances industrial democracy. Ray Maghroori notes: "Ten or 20 years ago, there was no way for average workers to communicate with leaders."[2] Today messages are no longer filtered through layers of management.

A widespread problem with e-mail is that it encourages the indiscriminate sending of messages including trivial information, mass distribution of information of interest to a limited number of people, the exchange of jokes and sports news, and requests for seemingly unimportant information. The blitz of messages requires many people to work extra hours just to sort through their mail on matters that do not add value to the organization. Although processing e-mail overwhelms many people, as the technology has matured the situation has been more manageable for many workers.

According to a survey of 2,447 workers conducted by Pew Internet and the American Life Project, the majority of e-mail users find that it is a manageable part of their job. The typical work e-mailer spends approximately 30 minutes during his or her workday processing e-mail, receives about 10 incoming messages, and sends five messages. A subgroup of these e-mailers—labeled power e-mailers—spend two hours or more daily on e-mail. They handle between 30 and 50 messages per day, yet only 11 percent say they feel overwhelmed by processing e-mail. Furthermore, company e-mail systems receive less spam than home systems partially because the company is more likely to use spam filters.

The most impersonal use of e-mail is for firing people, either for poor performance or as part of a downsizing. A consultant notes, "Most people consider firing by e-mail one of the most heartless things you can do. E-mail is a faceless, cowardly way to fire someone."[3]

The distractions associated with e-mail are widely recognized, leading various specialists to suggest ways for more productive use of this mode of communication. The accompanying Organizational Behavior in Action box presents representative ideas for the productive use of e-mail.

Telecommuting

A major deviation from the traditional work schedule is having a full-time or part-time schedule working away from company premises. An estimated 30 million to 40 million people in the United States work at home as either corporate employees or for self-employment.[4] The majority of people who work at home do so only a day or two per week at their residence. Concerns about terrorist threats and contagious diseases have made working at home appear even more desirable for many workers in recent years.

Organizational Behavior *in Action*
Ten E-Mail Time Management Tips

A recent study estimated that managers spend about an hour every day processing e-mail. Here are ten tips for making better use of this time.

1. *Check e-mail less often.* Check e-mail only during natural breaks in your workday, such as between tasks. Turn off all automatic notifications regarding incoming messages.
2. *Clear out your inbox.* A cluttered e-mail inbox results in a lot of rereading and worrying about work piling up.
3. *Cancel unnecessary mail.* Unsubscribe to listserves of questionable value.
4. *Filter incoming mail.* Use software to move mail to appropriate folders, such as "Urgent" and "Trash."
5. *Set aside reading time.* Set aside "for information only" e-mail to read later.

6. *Delete spam.* The simplest way to deal with unsolicited e-mail is to delete it.
7. *Send to less people.* Watch your list of recipients. Your colleagues are already sagging under a mountain of information. They will thank you for not contributing to it.
8. *Use mailing lists.* Mailing to an address list saves time.
9. *Quote messages.* Include the fragment of the sender's original message for clarification.
10. *Use the telephone!* The telephone is preferable to e-mail, when dealing with complex issues, emotional discussions, sensitive material, and reprimands.

Source: Gihan Perera, "Ten E-Mail Time Management Tips," http://www.firststep.com.au/articles/email-tm.html. Accessed 6 November 2003.

Telecommuting is an arrangement in which employees use computers to perform their regular work responsibilities at home or in a satellite office. Employees who telecommute usually use computers tied to the company's main office. People who work at home are referred to as telecommuters or teleworkers. The vast majority of people who work at home are either assigned a computer by the company or possess their own computer and related equipment. Yet a person might do piecework at home, such as making garments or furniture, without using a computer. In addition to using computers to communicate with their employer's office, telecommuters may attend meetings on company premises and stay in contact by telephone and teleconferences.

A major communication challenge to telecommuters is that they rely so heavily on e-mail, and therefore lose out on the social interaction of work, which is so important to many people. You will recall the case at the end of Chapter 6 about telecommuters and small business people spending time congregating in office centers that cater to people who work independently. Teleworkers are also encouraged to spend some time in the traditional office in face-to-face communication with other workers. Avoiding such contact can lead to feelings of isolation, that one isn't a part of the office communication network. People who are successful at telecommuting are usually those with relatively low affiliation needs. A study of employees and managers showed that teleworkers have worse relationships with their managers and coworkers than people who work in a traditional office.[5]

Presentation Technology

Virtually every reader of this text has witnessed or given a talk using presentation technology. Computer-generated slide software, such as PowerPoint, is currently in vogue, yet overhead projectors are also part of presentation technology. Speakers in all types of organizations supplement their talk with computer slides and often organize their presentation around them. Some speakers sit slumped in a chair, narrating the slides. Many people want presentations reduced to bulleted items and eye-catching graphics. (Have you noticed this tendency among students?) The ability to prepare a slide presentation has become an dispensable corporate survival skill. Audiences have become accustomed to watching an array of impressive graphics during oral presentations.

The communication challenge here is that during an oral presentation, the predominant means of connection between sender and receiver is eye contact. When an audience is constantly distracted from the presenter by movement on the screen, sounds from the computer, or lavish colors, eye contact suffers and so does the message. Another problem is that the speaker who relies on multimedia to the exclusion of person-to-person contact may be communicating the subtle message, "I am not really necessary."[6] The implication for presenters is to find a way to integrate speaking skills with the new technology. One of the biggest challenges is to learn how to handle equipment and maintain frequent eye and voice contact at all times. Jean Mausehund and R. Neil Dortch offer these sensible suggestions:

- *Reveal points only as needed.* Project the overhead transparencies or computer slides only when needed and use a cursor, laser pointer, or metal pointer for emphasis.
- *Talk to the audience and not the screen.* A major problem with computer slides is that the presenter as well as the audience is likely to focus continually on the slide. If the presenter minimizes looking at the slide, and spends considerable time looking at the audience, it will be easier to maintain contact with the audience.
- *Keep the slide in view until the audience gets the point.* A presenter will often flash a slide or transparency without giving the audience enough time to comprehend the meaning of the slide. It is also important for presenters to synchronize the slides with their comments.[7]

The Impact of Computer-Mediated Communication on Behavior

As alluded to previously, computerized communication has had a major impact, both positive and negative, on behavior in organizations. On the positive side, communication can be more widespread and immediate than in making telephone calls, holding meetings, or sending hard-copy memos. With computer-mediated communication, information be exchanged at a torrid pace, keeping large numbers of people informed and alert. More people have a voice because e-mail, and sometimes instant messaging, is possible with senior managers. For example, it is much easier for an entry-level worker to send an e-mail to the division president than to telephone, send a letter to, or have a meeting with the executive.

Computerized information has also had substantial negative impacts on behavior in organizations. Above all, many workers suffer from the lack of a human touch—they want to relate to a person rather than engage in so many electronic exchanges. It is more difficult to motivate, listen to, or encourage a worker electronically than in person. Many workers suffer from substantial productivity losses as they become enticed into excessive Internet surfing during company time. As a result these workers may suffer from lowered performance evaluations and even job loss. Similarly, reading e-mail messages and searching the Internet becomes so time consuming that the worker neglects the human interaction aspects of the job, such as dealing with coworker and customer problems.

Excessive use of computers often leads to repetitive motion disorder, leaving the worker discouraged and pained. Customer service often deteriorates as a result of information technology. Many banks, for example, force customers with a service problem to call a toll-free number rather than allowing them to deal with a branch representative. A voice-response system instructs the customer to punch in a lengthy account number and make choices from a complicated menu. The process is time consuming and difficult for customers not familiar with information technology. The result can be resentment, frustration, and the loss of a customer.

Computer-mediated communication often results in *wired managerial workers.* Being electronically connected to the office at all times leads many managers and professionals to complain that their employers expect them to be always available for consultation. The more recent Wi-Fi–enabled laptops systems enable workers to stay connected to company data even more readily than with the traditional systems.[8]

Finally, computerized communication encourages multitasking to the point that many workers feel they are wasting time unless they are attempting two tasks at once, such as talking on a cell telephone and accessing e-mail at the same time. The problem is that diminished concentration often leads to poorer quality work, and almost precludes the flow experience so necessary for creativity. Also, multitasking is inherently rude when dealing with another person. Many complaints have been made about customer-contact workers who deal with one customer while talking to another on a cell phone.

To capitalize on the benefits of computer-mediated communication devices, it is important to keep in mind that the human touch is still important. The capability to sending and receiving messages electronically should not mean that human contact has become undesirable or unnecessary.

NONVERBAL COMMUNICATION

3

Explain how nonverbal communication can be used to enhance communication.

The most obvious modes of communication are speaking, writing, and sign language. (Many large business meetings today include an interpreter who signs for deaf members of the audience.) A substantial amount of interpersonal communication also occurs through **nonverbal communication,** the transmission of messages by means other than words. Body language refers to those aspects of nonverbal communication directly related to movements of the body, such as gestures and posture. Nonverbal communication usually supplements rather than substitutes writing, speaking, and sign language.

The general purpose of nonverbal communication is to express the feeling behind a message. Suppose that a sales representative stands tall when saying, "Our payroll processing service is devoid of bugs and glitches." The representative's posture reveals confidence in making this pitch. The same message delivered in a slouched position with one hand over the mouth would communicate a feeling of limited confidence.

Nonverbal communication incorporates a wide range of behavior. Nevertheless, it can be divided into the following eight categories.[9]

1. *Environment.* The physical setting in which the message takes place communicates meaning. This would include office décor, a type of automobile, and the type of restaurant or hotel chosen for a business meeting. Bigger deals are typically negotiated and consummated in more luxurious restaurants, whereas discussions about work assignments might be held in a family-style restaurant.

2. *Body placement.* The placement of one's body in relation to someone else is widely used to transmit messages. Facing a person in a casual, relaxed style indicates acceptance. Moving close to another person is also a general indicator of acceptance. However, moving too close may be perceived as a violation of personal space, and the message sender will be rejected.

3. *Posture.* Another widely used clue to a person's attitude is his or her posture. Leaning toward another person suggests a favorable attitude toward the message one is trying to communicate. Leaning backward communicates the opposite. Standing up straight is generally interpreted as an indicator of self-confidence, while slouching is usually a sign of low self-confidence.

4. *Hand gestures.* Gestures of the hand, such as frequent movements to express approval and palms spread outward to indicate perplexity, provide meaningful hints in communication.

5. *Facial expressions and movement.* The particular look on a person's face and movements of the person's head provide reliable cues as to approval, disapproval, or disbelief.

6. *Voice tone.* Aspects of the voice such as pitch, volume, quality, and speech rate may communicate confidence, nervousness, or enthusiasm. Intelligence is often judged by how people sound. Research suggests that the most annoying voice quality is a whining, complaining, or nagging tone.[10]

7. *Clothing, dress, and appearance.* The image a person conveys communicates such messages as "I feel powerful" and "I think this meeting is important." For example, wearing one's best business attire to a performance appraisal interview would communicate the idea that "I think this meeting is very important."

8. *Mirroring.* To mirror is to build rapport with another person by imitating his or her voice tone, breathing rate, body movement, and language. Mirroring relies 10 percent on verbal means, 60 percent on voice tone, and 30 percent on body physiology. A specific application of mirroring is to conform to the other person's posture, eye movements, and hand movements. The person feels more relaxed with you as a result of your imitation.

One of many practical applications of nonverbal communication is to project enthusiasm and confidence with body language. Ron Huff recommends the following:

- *Loosen your facial expression.* A tight, grim look gives the appearance of being unapproachable. Relax your muscles, and look for opportunities to smile and offer encouraging nods.
- *Move closer to message senders.* Work associates feel you are listening intently when you lean slightly toward them when they speak. It is a subtle way of showing that you want to hear every word.
- *Gesture to reinforce a point.* If you are excited or pleased with an idea, do not rely exclusively on words to communicate these feelings. Pump a fist, clap your hands, or point approvingly at the speaker. Use the gesture that feels the most natural to you.[11]

Another workplace application of nonverbal communication is to help combat drug trafficking and terrorism. The art of spotting nervous or threatening

180

behavior has gained respect among airport security officials. Since the terror attacks on September 11, 2001, the Federal Bureau of Investigation started teaching nonverbal behavior analysis to all new recruits. Instead of selecting people to be interrogated on what they look like, custom agents have been trained to observe what people do and to ask pointed questions when suspicious nonverbal behavior surfaces. Among the indicators of suspicious behavior are darting eyes, hand tremors, a fleeting smile, and an enlarged carotid artery (indicating the rapid blood flow associated with anxiety). Failure to make eye contact with the custom official is a strong red flag.[12]

Despite the recommendations and implications of the information about nonverbal communication, keep in mind that many nonverbal signals are ambiguous. For example, a smile usually indicates agreement and warmth, but can also indicate nervousness.

4 ORGANIZATIONAL CHANNELS OF COMMUNICATION

Present details about the various channels of communication in organizations.

Messages in organizations travel over many different channels, or paths. Communication channels can be formal or informal and can be categorized by the direction they follow.

Formal Communication Channels

Formal communication channels are the official pathways for sending information inside and outside an organization. The primary source of information about formal channels is the organization chart. It indicates the channels the messages are supposed to follow. By carefully following an organization chart, an entry-level worker would know how to transmit a message to the CEO. Formal communication channels are often bypassed through information technology. Using e-mail, anybody can send a message to anybody else in the organization. During an emergency, workers are also likely to bypass formal channels, such as a technician telephoning the plant manager directly about a chemical spill.

In recent years, companies have developed formal communication channels for managing crises such as fires and explosions, massive product recalls, financial scandals, and terrorist attacks. One of the most crucial parts of a disaster plan is how to communicate with the company's work force during a crisis. A key part of the challenge is to locate and re-establish contact with employees who may be scattered in the streets or stranded in airports around the world. Aon Corporation, an international insurance, risk-management, and consulting company, improvised to use its Web site as an official communication channel during the crisis of September 11. A company official said, "With everything else down, we decided to use the company Web site. That seemed like the only option we had."[13] Web sites have now become the premier formal crisis communication channel. Formal channels during a crisis are necessary for informing employees about a disaster, work assignments, health services and grief counselling, and assistance in returning to work.

Other formal communication channels during a crisis include the television or radio. Oppenheimer Funds, which occupied five floors at the World Trade Center, wanted to transmit a message to both employees and customers that it would be operating again as soon as the markets opened. The solution was for the CEO to appear on CNBC's *Squawk Box* to deliver that message. Messages sent through the media also offer the advantage of appearing more credible than messages directly from management, particularly when management is distrusted. American Airlines has a long-standing relationship of distrust with its unions, so during a crisis, company officials prefer to communicate to employees through the media.[14]

The formal communication channels are precisely specified in a traditional bureaucratic organization with its many layers. Communication channels are more difficult to follow in the modern **network organization**, a spherical structure that can rotate self-managing teams and other resources around a common knowledge base. The key purpose of the network organization is to enter into temporary alliances with other firms in order to capitalize on the combined talents. A strategic alliance is the term often used to describe these temporary, multifirm ventures.

IBM and Apple Computer have entered into strategic alliances for certain products and services, such as microprocessor chips. Later on, they terminated some of their strategic alliances, pointing to the fluid nature of network organizations. Digital cameras are usually the product of strategic alliances among several electronic and photo companies, and so are hybrid cars (using engines powered by gasoline and hydrogen).

Exhibit 9-2 shows the contrast between a bureaucracy (pyramid shape) and a network organization (spherical shape). The connecting lines can be considered formal communication channels.

Informal Communication Channels

An **informal communication channel** is the unofficial network of channels that supplements the formal channels. Most of these informal channels arise out of necessity. For example, people will sometimes depart from the official communication channels to consult with a person with specialized knowledge. Suppose an administrative professional in the inventory control department spoke and wrote fluent German. Employees from other department would regularly consult her when they were dealing with a customer from Germany.

Information communication channels help explain why changes in organizational structure (one which specifies the formal communication channels) sometimes do not change the quantity and quality of work that gets accomplished. The same pattern of networks that workers use to accomplish their tasks may not change despite the changes on the organization chart.[15]

The **grapevine** is the major informal communication channel in organizations. The grapevine refers to the tangled pathways that can distort information.

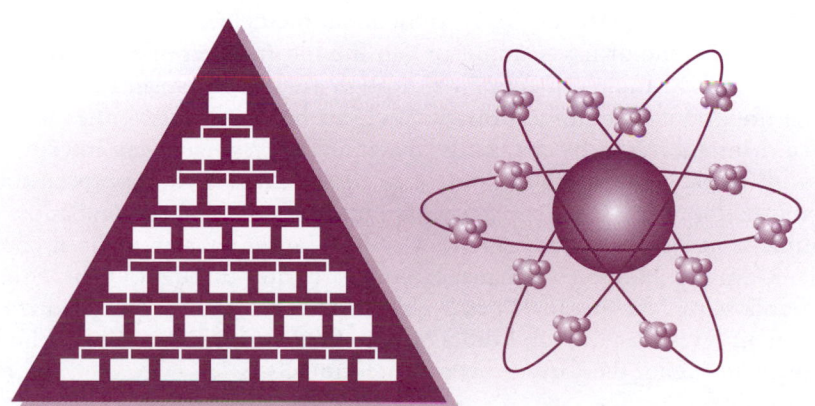

Exhibit 9-2

Communication Pathways in a Hierarchical Organization and a Spherical Organization

Communication pathways are more complex in a spherical organization than in a hierarchical organization.

181

The term referred originally to the snarled telegraph lines on the battlefield during the U.S. Civil War. The grapevine is often thought to be used primarily for passing along negative rumors and negative gossip. Gossips sometimes use the Internet and e-mail as channels for transmitting negative gossip. When left to fester, gossip can cause individuals chagrin, and also lead to turnover, conflict, and lawsuits. Gossip often increases when workers are bored or lack ample information about company events. Managers can often stop negative gossip by confronting the source of the gossip, demanding that he or she stop. Positive gossip, however, makes a contribution to the organization because trading information strengthens ties among workers and humanizes the workplace.[16]

The grapevine is sometimes used purposely to disseminate information along informal lines. For example, top management might want to hint to employees that certain work will be outsourced unless the employees become more productive. Although the plans are still tentative, feeding them into the grapevine may result in improved motivation and productivity.

Rumors are an important communication force within organizations, and they tend to thrive in organizations with poor corporate communication, such as a penitentiary. Furthermore, an active grapevine is correlated with higher levels of stress, threat, and insecurity. Respondents to a worldwide survey agreed that rumors are an important early source of information. Executives from the United Kingdom and the United States agreed most strongly, whereas those from Switzerland and Japan agreed the least. To ensure that rumors are more helpful than harmful, management might do the following:

- Be wary of vague communication, which fosters misinterpretation and anxiety.
- Promote healthy, accurate communication.
- Avoid concealing bad news.
- Correct erroneous communications that relate to organizational policies, practices, and strategic plans.[17]

A problem with inaccurate rumors is that they can distract workers, create anxiety, and decrease productivity. A frequent by-product of false rumors about company relocation or a pending merger is that some of the more talented workers leave in the hopes of more stable employment.

Another informal channel of significance is *chance encounters.* Unscheduled informal contact between managers and employees can be an efficient and effective communication channel. John P. Kotter found that effective managers do not confine their communication to formal meetings.[18] Instead, they collect valuable information during chance encounters. Spontaneous communication events may occur in the cafeteria, near the water fountain, in the halls, and on the elevator. In just two minutes, the manager might obtain the information that would typically be solicited in a 30-minute meeting or through a series of e-mail exchanges.

One important communication channel can be classified as either formal or informal. **Management by walking around** involves managers intermingling freely with workers on the shop floor or in the office, as well as with customers. By spending time in personal contact with employees, the manager enhances open communication. Because management by walking around is systematic, it could be considered formal. However, a manager who circulates throughout the company is not following the formal paths prescribed by the organization chart. Management by walking around differs from chance encounters in that the latter are unplanned events; the former occurs intentionally.

Communication Directions

Messages in organizations travel in five directions: downward, upward, horizontally, diagonally, and spherically. *Downward communication* is the flow of messages from one level to a lower level. It is typified by a middle manager giving orders to a lower-level supervisor or by top management sending announcements to employees. Information is sometimes transmitted from a higher level to a lower one without the sender inviting a response. When this occurs, the feedback built into two-way communication is lost.

Upward communication is the transmission of messages from lower to higher levels in an organization. It is the most important channel for keeping management informed about problems within the organization. Management by walking around, chance encounters, and simply talking regularly to employees are factors that improve upward communication. An **open-door policy** is a more formal upward communication channel that allows employees to bring a gripe to top management's attention without first checking with their manager. Upward communication is more widely used in less bureaucratic firms than in highly bureaucratic firms. Almost all executives contend that they value upward communication, whether or not the majority of employees agree.

Horizontal communication is sending messages among people at the same organization level. It often takes the form of coworkers from the same department talking to one another. Horizontal communication is the basis for cooperation. When coworkers are not sharing information with and responding to one another, they are likely to fall behind schedule. Also, efforts are duplicated and quality suffers. Another type of horizontal communication takes place when managers communicate with other managers at the same level.

Diagonal communication is the transmission of messages to higher or lower organizational levels in different departments. A typical diagonal communication event occurs when a manager from one department contacts a lower-ranking person from a department outside of his or her chain of command.

Spherical communication is communication among members from different teams in the network organization. The communication events take place with team members from the same or different organizations. Visualize a team member from Nike Corporation communicating directly with a team member from Nokia Corporation. He wants to talk about a strategic alliance to develop a basketball shoe with a built-in cell phone!

BARRIERS TO INTERPERSONAL COMMUNICATION

5

Summarize barriers to effective communication and how to overcome them.

The information presented so far has been helpful in understanding how communication takes place in organizations. Let us now explore further why messages sent from one person to another are often not received exactly as intended. As was shown in Exhibit 9–1, barriers (or noises) exist at every step in the communication process. Interference is the most likely to occur when a message is complex, arouses emotion, or clashes with a receiver's mental set. An emotionally arousing message may deal with such topics as money or personal inconvenience. A message that clashes with a mental set challenges the receiver to make a radical shift in thinking. For example, a human resources manager had difficulty getting across the message that managers could no longer make a specific request for a woman to fill an administrative assistant position.

183

Seven communication barriers are described here. The first four relate primarily to the sending of messages; the last three relate more to receiving them. Exhibit 9-3 lists barriers to communication, as well as the means for overcoming them, which will be described in the next section of the chapter.

1. *Semantics.* Many communication problems are created by **semantics,** the varying meanings people attach to words. The symbols (both words and nonverbal behavior) used in communication can take on different means for different people. Consequently, it is possible for a person to misinterpret the intended meaning of the sender. One phrase fraught with varying interpretations is "essential personnel." When a CEO announces before a downsizing that only essential personnel will be retained, many people are left wondering about their status. Few people can accept the message that they are "nonessential."

2. *Filtering of negative information.* A formidable upward communication barrier is **filtering,** the coloring and altering of information to make it more acceptable to the receiver. Many managers and individual workers filter information to avoid displeasing their superiors, such as when describing a revenue shortfall. Filtering is most likely to take place when top-level management has a history of punishing the bearer of bad news.

3. *Lack of credibility of the sender.* The more trustworthy the source or sender of a message, the greater the probability that the message will get through clearly. In contrast, when the sender of the message has low credibility, many times it will be ignored. Credibility in sending messages is so important that it is a major contributor to effective leadership.

4. *Mixed signals.* Communications can break down with a subtle variation of low credibility. The disconnect occurs from **mixed signals**—sending different messages about the same topic to different audiences. For example, a company might brag about the high quality of its products in public statements. Yet on the shop floor and in the office, the company tells its employees to cut corners whenever possible to lower costs. Another type of mixed signal occurs when you send one message to a person about desired behavior, yet behave in another way yourself. A mixed signal of this type would occur when an executive preaches the importance of social responsibility, yet practices blatant job discrimination.

5. *Different frames of reference.* People perceive words and concepts differently depending on their **frame of reference,** a perspective and vantage point based on past experience. (A frame of reference means about the same thing as a *paradigm*.) A typical example of the frame of reference problem took place

Exhibit 9-3

Barriers to Communication and Means for Overcoming Them

Understanding barriers to communication should be followed up with effective tactics for overcoming them.

Barriers	Overcoming Barriers
Semantics	Clarify ideas before sending.
Filtering of negative information	Motivate the receiver.
Lack of credibility of the sender	Discuss differences in paradigms.
Mixed signals	Foster informal communication.
Different frames of reference	Communicate feelings behind the facts.
Value judgments	Be aware of nonverbal behavior.
Communication overload	Obtain feedback.
	Adapt to the other person's communication style.
	Engage in meta-communication.

in a financial service company that was instituting work-streamlining teams to improve productivity. The vice president of operations announced the program with great enthusiasm, only to find that the message was received in a distorted, negative fashion. The problem was that the vice president perceived productivity improvement as a vehicle for ensuring increased profits and survival. Lower-ranking employees, however, perceived productivity improvement as a way for the company to maintain output while laying off workers.

6. *Value judgments.* Making value judgments prior to receiving an entire message interferes with the communication of its intended meaning. A **value judgment** is an overall opinion of something based on a quick perception of its merit. When value judgments are made too hastily, the receiver hears only the part of the message that he or she wishes to hear. A manager might begin to read an announcement about a dependent-care center to be sponsored by the company. The manager might make a quick value judgment that this program is "just another human resources initiative to keep people happy." By so doing, the manager will block out the information that dependent-care facilities often increase productivity by reducing absenteeism and turnover. It is also possible that a hasty value judgment will prompt a person to discount a message despite listening to it fully.

7. *Communication overload.* Electronic communication has contributed to the problem of too much information being disseminated throughout most private and public firms. **Communication (or information) overload** occurs when people are so overloaded with information that they cannot respond effectively to messages. As a result, they experience work stress. Managers and staff professionals alike are exposed to so much printed, electronic, and spoken information that their capacity to absorb it all is taxed. The human mind is capable of processing only a limited quantity of information at a time.

The receiver and sender both contribute to communication overload. The receiver's "circuits are jammed," yet many senders contribute to the problem by disseminating too much information to the same person.

Overcoming Communication Barriers

An effective strategy for improving communication in organizations is to overcome communication barriers. Improving communication is important because successful firms are characterized by an abundance of straightforward communication.[19] The following sections provide an overview of tactics and techniques for improving the sending and receiving of messages. In addition, they describe methods of overcoming problems in communicating with people of the opposite sex and from different cultures.

Improving the Sending of Messages

Improving the way messages are sent will help overcome communication barriers. Implementing the following suggestions will improve the chances that messages are received as intended.

1. *Clarify ideas before communicating.* Many communications fail because of inadequate planning and lack of understanding of the true nature of the message to be communicated. To plan effectively, managers and professionals must consider the goals and attitudes of those who will receive the message and those who will be affected by it. Part of clarifying ideas is to present them in a clear, exciting manner, at a level appropriate for the audience.

2. *Motivate the receiver.* The recipient of the message has to be motivated to attend to the message. This is best accomplished by appealing to the receiver's interests or needs. In sending a message to higher-level management, it is important to frame it in terms of how it contributes to earning money, saving money, or productivity.

3. *Discuss differences in paradigms.* A method for understanding and dealing with differences in frames of reference is to recognize that people have different paradigms that influence how they interpret events. A **paradigm** is a model, framework, viewpoint, perspective, or frame of reference. When two people look at a situation with different paradigms, a communication problem may occur. For instance, a business owner might say, "We should be able to get this order ready for shipment by Monday morning if we work all day Saturday and Sunday." The employee may respond "How horrible. Nobody works on Saturday and Sunday; those are family days." From the paradigm of the business owner, you work as much as necessary to meet a business goal. But from the standpoint of this worker in particular, a person works a limited number of hours, and reserves other times for personal activities.

   The solution to this communication clash is to discuss the paradigms. Both people live by different rules or guidelines (a major contributor to a paradigm). If the two people can recognize that they are operating with different paradigms, the chances for agreement are improved. People can change their paradigms when the reasons are convincing.[20] For example, the worker in the preceding situation may never have thought about investing time on weekends to help the employer succeed.

4. *Foster informal communication.* An abundance of informal, open communication enhances trust within an organization. Negative rumors are less likely to appear on the grapevine when talking about sensitive topics comes naturally. Ample casual meeting areas such as lounges and conference rooms also contribute to informal communication. Management by walking around and chance encounters are other contributors to the flow of informal communication. Informal communication also fosters gossip, yet when the trust level is high, the gossip is more likely to be positive, such as buzzing about who is going to receive a major promotion. The accompanying Organizational Behavior in Action box illustrates the importance of getting to know workers better by visiting them at their workplace.

5. *Communicate feelings behind the facts.* The facts in a message should be accompanied by the appropriate feelings. Feelings add power and conviction to the message. The sender of the message should explain his or her personal feelings and encourage the receiver to do the same. For example, a manager who is disappointed with the quality of a finished product might say, "The product has a cheap look. I'm disappointed with the attention you paid to product design. How do you feel about my criticism?" A less-effective approach would be to simply criticize the poor design without mentioning feelings. Expressing feelings is part of *speaking directly*. As noted business executive Larry Bossidy states, "A lot of people tend to soften their message instead of simply saying what they want or what they believe. All this does is prevent you from being understood."[21]

6. *Be aware of nonverbal behavior.* A speaker's tone of voice, expression, and apparent receptiveness to the responses of others have an impact on the receiver. These subtle nonverbal aspects of communication often affect the listener's reaction to a message even more than the content of the communication.

Organizational Behavior *in Action*
Retirement Home Chief Practices Empathy

Michael Daly's staff told him he needed to hire another dining room helper to pour coffee at breakfast. But Daly, 38, the chief executive officer of a small chain of upscale retirement rental residences, wasn't buying it. Why hire someone else when the nursing aides could pitch in and serve? "I'm the CEO. I've got a big ego. I didn't believe it," he said. That is until Daly ditched his suit and cell phone for a day on the job, following a work schedule set by the staff.

So far, Daly has done his "Walking in Your Shoes Program" at three of the company's nine facilities. "They want me to have the most difficult day they can," he said. Typically he works in the kitchen, handles a stint on the reception desks, empties trash, makes repairs, and cleans apartments. "They give me the dirtiest room, and I don't know how to clean a room," he said.

Daly agrees that the work gives him a grass-roots knowledge of a facility, particularly when he manages to penetrate layers of middle management. His favorite spot for picking up knowledge is folding laundry with the housekeeping staff, though it takes the crew about half an hour to loosen up enough to give him the lowdown. He also learns who the good workers are. For example, a longtime waitress at another facility taught him how to serve a meal and carry a tray properly. "I felt very comfortable with her teaching me," he said. Daly said he learned that she was a great mentor. "Now, I'm working on the budget, and I can see why we are paying her more. You look at her job description, and say: 'Why is this woman paid so much?' Now I know. She's just a statistic in a budget until you work side by side with her and learn her value."

At Chancellor Park retirement home, Daly's day started in the dining room. He saw how frantic it was. "I realized the aides were barely able to keep up with the shower schedule. They couldn't pour coffee," he said. "We'll have to do something." After breakfast, William Brown, executive director of Chancellor Park, assigned Daly to complete four repair jobs in one hour and twenty minutes. It took Daly an hour longer, and he still did not get everything done. At one point Daly had to stop to help a resident go the bathroom—a 15-minute interruption. He said the interruption made him wonder whether all the maintenance staff had been trained to help out. Daly gained a new understanding of why work orders would accumulate.

Then Daly visited Edith Creskoff, 94, who wanted a television moved in her apartment. "You're pretty efficient for a president," she said. Then it was on to Ron Polenz, a man in his 60s, who needed the hinges on his refrigerator door switched so he could open it from his wheelchair. "I had no idea they were reversible," Daly said. "I have to order 166 refrigerators, and now that I know, I'll make sure I order reversible ones." Polenz watched Daly struggle to turn the refrigerator on its side as Daly muttered under his breath about not having the right tools for the job. "You're seeing my first bead of sweat of the day," Daly said.

"I thought you were hot stuff already with that tool kit," Polenz joked before delivering his opinion of Daly's "Walking in Your Shoes" Program. "The man's the CEO, and he comes down and sees for himself rather than wait for somebody to report to somebody else," said Polenz. "The more I think about it, the more I like the idea."

Questions

1. In what way does this case anecdote illustrate empathy on the job?
2. What changes in Daly's behavior and management practices are likely to result from the Walking in Your Shoes program?

Source: "CEO Demotes Himself for a Day," Knight Ridder story, September 23, 2002.

When sending messages to others, it is important to keep in mind all the aspects of nonverbal behavior previously described.

7. *Obtain feedback.* The best efforts at communication may be wasted if feedback on how well the message came across is not received. Asking questions, encouraging the receiver to express reactions, following up on contacts,

188

and subsequently reviewing performance are ways of obtaining feedback. A powerful method of obtaining feedback is to request, "Could you please summarize what you heard me say?"

8. *Adapt to the other person's communication style.* People communicate more freely with those who match their communication style. If you want to assume the burden for decreasing communication barriers with another person, then make some adaptations to his or her style. If your communication target prefers e-mail messages to telephone calls, use e-mail rather than phone calls, except for highly sensitive matters. If your manager prefers brief, bulleted summaries rather than well-developed narrative reports, prepare such brief reports for him or her. If your target responds best to anecdotes, develop anecdotes to support your major points. In contrast, if the receiver prefers statistics to anecdotes, prepare statistics to support major points. It is usually possible to learn the other person's style by careful observation, and by posing a question such as, "How do you like your information presented?"

9. *Engage in meta-communication.* When having a difficult time getting through to another person, it helps to talk about your communication difficulty. To **meta-communicate** is to communicate about your communication to help overcome barriers or to resolve a problem. If, as a manager, you are trying to get through to a group member with an angry facial expression, you might say, "You look upset about our conversation. Is this a bad time to talk with you about something important?" The group member might counter, "I think I'm carrying too big a workload, so I'm not very happy." With the air cleared, communication might now flow more smoothly.

Improving the Receiving of Messages

Listening is a basic part of communication, and many communication problems stem from the intended receiver not listening carefully. Reducing communication barriers requires a special type of listening. **Active listening** means listening for full meaning without making premature judgments or interpretations (see the InfoTrac sidebar). The active listener listens intently, with the goal of empathizing with the speaker. As a result of listening actively, the listener can feed back to the speaker what he or she thinks the speaker meant. Observing nonverbal cues is another facet of active listening. For example, if an employee laughs slightly whenever he mentions a deadline, dig for more information. The laughter may signal that he thinks the deadline is unrealistic.[22]

An active listener also avoids traps such as reacting too quickly to a word or phrase that stirs emotion. Instead he or she carefully interprets the word and analyzes what the word or phrase might mean to the sender. The active listener might hear a speaker say, "People with a weak work ethic have no place in this company." Before getting angry or accepting the entire message, the active listener would wait to find out what the sender really means by a "weak work ethic."

A foundational skill for the active listener is to ask open-ended questions because these questions invite an explanation rather than a one-word response. Open-ended questions begin with words such as: "Tell me about," "Explain to me," "How are you doing with our project?", and "Where are you headed?" Two examples of closed-end questions are, "Will you make your deadline?" and "Do you like your job?"

Listening can be an important factor in business success. Many companies invest considerable time and energy to better understanding the thinking, values, and behavior patterns of their customers. Quite often the same processes the com-

Active listening is an important skill in many kinds of business situations. From salary negotiations to upselling customers, communication and active listening are key components of many different types of exchanges. Delve deeper into the issue of active listening by logging on to InfoTrac College Edition at **http://www.infotrac -college.com.** Use "active listening" in a keyword search to see how many different tips and techniques you can find for improving your active listening skills. If you get stuck, call up "Active Listening Is More Than Just Hearing," an article from *Supervision* magazine [record no.A65077526]. *What advice do these articles provide to help you become a better listener?*

panies use to gain insights into their external customers can be used to learn more about their own employees. One executive who emphasized the importance of listening to employees was Sam Walton, founder of Wal-Mart. Walton was fanatical about visiting his stores, learning through listening and watching.[23] More recent Wal-Mart executives have followed in his tradition.

The suggestions for effective listening presented in Exhibit 9-4 support active listening. In addition, do the Skill-Development Exercise to build your ability to listen actively.

Dealing with Gender Differences in Communication Style

Despite the trend toward equality in organizations, substantial interest has arisen in identifying differences in communication styles between men and women. People who are aware of these differences will face fewer communication barriers between themselves and members of the opposite sex. As we describe these differences, recognize them as group stereotypes, reflecting how the average man or woman is likely to behave. Individual differences in communication style are usually more important than group (men versus women) differences. Key differences in sex-related communication styles are as follows:

- Women prefer to use communication for rapport building and building social connections.
- Men prefer to use talk primarily as a means of preserving independence and status by displaying knowledge and skill, and women tend to downplay their status.

6

Explain how to overcome potential cross-gender and cross-cultural communication problems.

Exhibit 9-4

Twelve Keys to Effective Listening

These keys are a positive guideline to better listening. In fact, they're at the heart of developing better listening habits that could last a lifetime.

Twelve Keys to Effective Listening	The Bad Listener	The Good Listener
1. Find areas of interest	Tunes out dry subjects	Seeks opportunities; asks "What's in it for me?"
2. Judge content, not delivery	Tunes out if delivery is poor	Judges content, skips over delivery errors
3. Hold your fire	Tends to enter into argument	Doesn't judge until comprehension is complete
4. Listen for ideas	Listens for facts	Listens for central themes
5. Be flexible	Takes intensive notes using only one system	Takes fewer notes; uses four or five different systems, depending on speaker
6. Work at listening	Shows no energy output; fakes attention	Works hard; exhibits active body state
7. Resist distractions	Is distracted easily	Fights or avoids distractions, tolerates bad habits, knows how to concentrate
8. Exercise your mind	Resists difficult expository material; seeks light, recreational material	Uses heavier material as exercise for the mind
9. Keep your mind open	Reacts to emotional words	Interprets color words; does not get hung up on them
10. Capitalize on the fact that *thought* is faster than speech	Tends to daydream with slow speakers	Challenges, anticipates, mentally summarizes, weighs the evidence, listens between the lines to tone of voice
11. Restate what you hear	Reacts to what he or she hears	Clarifies what he or she hears until other person says, "Yes, this is what I'm saying."
12. Notices eye color	Does not observe speaker's eyes	Observes eye color at start of conversation

Sources: John W. Richter, "Listening: An Art Essential to Success," *Success,* (September 1980): p. 26; Lyman K. Steil, "How Well Do You Listen?" *Executive Female,* Special Issue No. 2 (1986): p. 37; "Train Yourself in the Art of Listening," *Positive Leadership* (Ragan Communications, Inc.), Sample issue distributed 2003.

COLLABORATE

SKILL-DEVELOPMENT EXERCISE

Actively Listening to a Coworker

Before conducting the following role plays, review the keys to effective listening presented in Exhibit 9-4. Suggestion 11 about summarization is particularly important when listening to a person who is talking about an emotional topic.

One student plays the role of a coworker who has just been offered the position of manager of another department. He or she will be receiving 10 percent higher pay and be able to travel overseas twice a year for the company. He or she is eager to describe full details of this good fortune to a coworker. At the same time, the person has some concerns about the promotion. The person is concerned that his or her spouse might not appreciate the idea of overseas travel.

Another student plays the role of the coworker to whom the first worker wants to describe his or her good fortune. The second worker wants to listen intently to the first worker. At the same time, the listener is facing some urgent work problems and therefore may have to fight being distracted.

Other class members will rate the second person on his or her listening ability.

- Men prefer to work out their problems by themselves, whereas women prefer to talk out solutions with another person.
- Women want empathy, not solutions. When women share feelings of being stressed out, they seek empathy and understanding.
- Women are more likely to compliment the work of a coworker, while men are more likely to be critical.
- Men tend to be more directive in their conversation, while women emphasize politeness.
- Women tend to be more conciliatory when facing differences, while men become more intimidating.
- Men are more interested than women in calling attention to their accomplishments or hogging recognition.
- Men tend to dominate discussions during meetings.
- Women tend to downplay their certainty about a subject, while men are more likely to minimize their doubts. As a result, women tend to appear less confident than men, even when their confidence levels are equal.
- Women are more likely to use a gentle expletive, whereas men tend to be harsher. (Do you think this difference really exists?)[24]

Understanding these differences can help you interpret the behavior of people, thus avoiding a communication block. For example, if a male team member is not as effusive with praise as you would like, remember that he is simply engaging in gender-typical behavior. (Again, this is a gender stereotype that is not universally applicable.) Factor in this gender difference before taking the shortfall personally.

Overcoming Cross-Cultural Communication Barriers

The modern workforce has become more culturally diverse in two major ways. Many subgroups within our own culture have been assimilated into the workforce, and there is increasing interaction with people from other countries. Cultural differences within a diverse country, such as the United States or Canada, can be as pronounced as differences between two countries. Managers therefore face the challenge of preventing and overcoming communication barriers created by differences in language and customs. Sensitivity to cultural differences goes a long way toward overcoming these potential communication barriers. In addition, communicators should keep in mind several suggestions:

1. *Be sensitive to the fact that cross-cultural communication barriers exist.* If you are aware of these potential barriers, you will be ready to deal with them. When you are dealing with a work associate with a different cultural background than yours, solicit feedback in order to minimize cross-cultural barriers to communication.

2. *Show respect for all workers.* The same behavior that promotes good cross-cultural relations in general helps overcome communication barriers. A widely used comment that implies disrespect is to say to a person from another culture, "You have an accent." If you were in that person's culture, you, too, might have an accent.

3. *Use straightforward language and speak slowly and clearly.* When working with people who do not speak your language fluently, speak in an easy-to-understand manner. Minimize the use of idioms and analogies specific to your language. Particularly difficult for foreigners to interpret are sports analogies such as "This should be a slam dunk." Also perplexing are general idioms such as "My manager passed the buck," or "Our competitor is over the hill."

4. *Be alert to cultural differences in customs and behavior.* To minimize cross-cultural communication barriers, recognize that many subtle job-related differences in customs and behavior may exist. For example, Asians may feel uncomfortable when asked to brag about themselves in the presence of others. From their perspective, calling attention to oneself at the expense of another person is rude and unprofessional. Exhibit 9-5 presents a sampling of cross-cultural differences in customs and behavior that relate to communications.

Exhibit 9-5

Cross-Cultural Differences in Communication

- Members of Asian and some Middle-Eastern cultures consider direct eye contact rude.
- Japanese people rarely use the word "no." When they say "yes" ("hai"), it only acknowledges they have heard what was said.
- When Japanese people say "We'll consider it," they probably mean "No."
- Korean people are hesitant to say "no," even when they have rejected a proposal. Koreans feel it is important to have visitors leave with good feelings.
- British people understate their feelings. If a British person says "Your report does raise a few questions," the real meaning is probably "Your report is atrocious."
- People from Latin America are very conscious of rank, and they expect the manager to be the voice of authority. Consequently, Latin Americans may be hesitant to make suggestions to a superior.
- Americans are eager to get down to business quickly and will therefore spend less time than people from other cultures in building a relationship.
- Americans value time much more than do people from other cultures. They are therefore more likely than people from other cultures to appear perturbed when a person shows up late for a meeting.
- French-speaking people tend to use polite forms of greeting, particularly in business settings, while Americans are less formal. When greeting a business contact in a French-speaking country, it is therefore important to include prefixes such as *sir, monsieur, madame, ms., mademoiselle,* or *miss.*

Skill Development: The above information will lead to cross-cultural skill development if practiced in the right setting. During the next 30 days, look for an opportunity to relate to a person from a given culture in the way described above. Observe the reaction of the other person to provide feedback on your cross-cultural effectiveness.

5. *Be sensitive to differences in nonverbal communication.* All cultures use nonverbal communication, but the specific cues differ across cultures. To receive messages accurately when working with people from diverse cultures, one must be sensitive to these differences. When visiting another country, Americans must be careful not to use the OK signal of a circle formed by the thumb and forefinger. Such a signal is considered an extreme vulgarity in several other cultures, including Germany. (It could be argued that the OK signal is really verbal communication because it is a symbol.)

6. *Do not be diverted by style, accent, grammar, or personal appearance.* Although these superficial factors all relate to business success, they are difficult to interpret when judging a person from another culture. It is therefore better to judge the merits of the behavior.[25] (This is also good advice in dealing with people from your own culture.) A brilliant individual from another culture may be still learning your language and thus make basic mistakes when speaking in your tongue. He or she might also not have yet developed a sensitivity to dress style in your culture.

7. *Listen for understanding, not agreement.* When working with diverse teammates, the differences in viewpoints can lead to conflict. If you listen for understanding, you prepare yourself to consider the viewpoints of others as a first resort. If everyone listens to understand, they can begin to appreciate one another's paradigms and accept differences of opinion.[26]

THE POWER-ORIENTED LINGUISTIC STYLE

7

Recognize the basics for becoming a more power-oriented communicator.

A major part of being persuasive involves choosing the right **linguistic style,** which is a person's characteristic speaking pattern. According to Deborah Tannen, linguistic style involves such behaviors as the amount of directness used, pacing and pausing, word choice, and the use of such communication devices as jokes, figures of speech, anecdotes, questions, and apologies.[27] A linguistic style is complex because it includes the culturally learned signals by which people communicate what they mean, along with how they interpret what others say and how they evaluate others. The complexity of linguistic style makes it difficult to offer specific prescriptions for using a power-oriented style. Nevertheless, here are many components of a linguistic style that would give power and authority to the message sender:[28]

- Choose words that show conviction, such as "I'm convinced," or "I'm confident that. . . ." Similarly, avoid expressions that convey doubt or hesitancy, such as "I think," or "I hope." Be bold in expressing ideas, yet do not attack people.
- Use the pronoun "I" to receive more credit for your ideas. (Of course, this could backfire in a team-based organization.)
- Emphasize direct rather than indirect talk, such as saying, "I need your report by 3 tomorrow afternoon," rather than, "I'm wondering if your report will be available by noon tomorrow."
- Frame your comments in a way that increases your listener's receptivity. The frame is built around the best context for responding to the needs of others. An example would be to use the frame "Let's dig a little deeper" when the other people in the room know something is wrong, but find pinpointing the problem to be elusive. Your purpose is to enlist the help of others in finding the underlying nature of the problem.

- Speak at length, set the agenda for a conversation, make jokes, and laugh. Be ready to offer solutions to problems, as well as suggest a program or plan. All of these points are more likely to create a sense of confidence in listeners.

- Minimize the number of questions you ask that imply you lack information on a topic, such as, "What do mean that most dot-com companies are burning cash?"

- Apologize infrequently and particularly minimize saying, "I'm sorry."

- Take deep breaths to project a firm voice. People associate a firm voice with power and conviction.

- Occupy as much space as possible when speaking before a group. Stand with your feet approximately 18 inches apart, and place your hands on the top of your hips occasionally. The triangles you create with arms occupy space, and the hand-on-hip gesture symbolizes power to most people.

- Let others know of your expertise because people tend to defer to experts. Mention how much experience you have had in a particular phase of the business to get people to take your message more seriously. An executive might say, "I've brought two companies out of crises before, and I can do it for us right now."[28]

Despite these suggestions for developing a power-oriented linguistic style, Tannen cautions that here is no one best way to communicate. How to project your power and authority is often dependent upon the people involved, the organizational culture, the relative rank of the speakers, and other situational factors. The power-oriented linguistic style should be interpreted as a general guideline. Another consideration is that you may not want to project a powerful, imposing image. Some managers and professionals prefer to play a more, laid back, behind-the-scenes role.

IMPLICATIONS FOR MANAGERIAL PRACTICE

1. Interpersonal communication is the basic process by which managers and professionals carry out their functions. It is therefore critical to work toward unclogging communication channels in all directions. Part of unclogging these channels is to overcome communication barriers following some of the guidelines presented in this chapter. It is particularly important to be aware of communication barriers and to recognize the receiver's frame of reference.

2. Two-way communication is usually superior to one-way communication. Interact with the receiver to foster understanding. While delivering your message, ask for verbal feedback and be sensitive to nonverbal signals about how your message is getting across. By so doing,

many communication barriers (such as value judgments) will be overcome.

3. Managers and professionals are well advised to pay attention to the nonverbal messages they send and receive. A starting point is to become more conscious of one's facial expression and those of other people. Managerial workers can also listen more carefully to vocal inflections, look closer to see what other people's eyes show about their true feelings, and pay attention to what they wear to transmit the desired messages about themselves. By paying close attention to nonverbal communication, managerial workers can improve communication and consequently improve productivity.

SUMMARY OF KEY POINTS

1 **Describe the communication process.**

Interpersonal communication takes place through the following steps: source (the sender), message, channel (medium), receiver, and feedback. The environment in which the message is sent and noise are also part of the communication process.

2 **Describe the impact of information technology on interpersonal communication in organizations.**

Advances in information technology have influenced the quantity and quality of interpersonal communications in the workplace. Three such advances are e-mail, telecommuting, and presentation technology. E-mail facilitates communication but contributes to information overload. Telecommuters can lose out on face-to-face human interaction. People who make extensive use of presentation technology sometimes neglect to connect with the audience. Computer-mediated communication can enhance communication by being more widespread and rapid. Yet many negative impacts are possible, including communication without the human touch, stress from repetitive motion disorder, the existence of wired managerial workers, and the encouragement of multitasking that leads to errors.

3 **Explain how nonverbal communication can be used to enhance communication.**

Nonverbal communication helps express the feeling behind a message and includes the following forms: environment (physical setting), body placement, posture, hand gestures, facial expressions and movements, voice tone, dress and appearance, and mirroring (to establish rapport). One of the many practical applications of nonverbal communication is to project enthusiasm and confidence with body language, such as when a person loosens his or her facial expression.

4 **Present details about the various channels of communication in organizations.**

Formal communication channels are specified precisely in bureaucratic organizations. These channels are more difficult to follow in a network organization because of its spherical structure of self-directed teams. Informal communication channels supplement the formal channels, with the grapevine being the major informal communication channel. Rumors are an important communication force within organizations and provide information early. Management by walking around can be classified as both a formal and an informal channel.

Messages in organization travel in five directions: downward, upward, horizontally, diagonally, and spherically (in the network organization). An open-door policy is an example of a formal upward communication channel.

5 **Summarize barriers to effective communication and how to overcome them.**

Key barriers to communication include: semantics, filtering of negative information, lack of credibility of the sender, mixed signals, different frames of reference, value judgments, and communication overload. Overcoming these barriers can involve such activities as clarifying ideas before sending, motivating the receiver, discussing differences in paradigms, fostering informal communication, communicating feelings behind the facts, being aware of nonverbal behavior, obtaining feedback, adapting to the other person's communication style, and engaging in meta-communications. Active listening facilitates receiving messages more accurately.

6 **Explain how to overcome potential cross-gender and cross-cultural communication problems.**

Sensitivity to gender differences in style is important for overcoming communication barriers. For example, men tend to be more directive in their conversation, whereas women emphasize politeness. Cross-cultural communication barriers can be overcome in general by sensitivity to cultural differences. Two specific tactics are to show respect for all workers and to use straightforward language and speak slowly and clearly.

7 **Recognize the basics for becoming a more power-oriented communicator.**

To become a more power-oriented communicator, it is important to choose the right linguistic style. Among the features of a power-oriented linguistic style are choosing words that show conviction, emphasizing direct talk, and apologizing infrequently.

KEY TERMS AND PHRASES

Message, *174*
A purpose or an idea to be conveyed in a communication event.

Noise, *174*
Anything that disrupts communication, including the attitude and emotions of the receiver.

Telecommuting, *176*
Working at home and sending output electronically to the office.

Nonverbal Communication, *178*
The transmission of messages by means other than words.

Formal Communication Channels, *180*
The official pathways for sending information inside and outside an organization.

Network Organization, *181*
A spherical structure that can rotate self-managing teams and other resources around a common knowledge base.

Informal Communication Channels, *181*
The unofficial network of channels that supplements the formal channels.

Grapevine, *181*
The major informal communication channel in organizations.

Management by Walking Around, *182*
The process of managers intermingling freely with workers on the shop floor, in the office, and with customers.

Open-Door Policy, *183*
An understanding in which any employee can bring a gripe to the attention of upper-level management without checking with his or her immediate manager.

Semantics, *183*
The varying meanings people attach to words.

Filtering, *184*
The coloring and altering of information to make it more acceptable to the receiver.

Mixed Signals, *184*
Communication breakdown resulting from the sending of different messages about the same topic to different audiences.

Frame of Reference, *184*
A perspective and vantage point based on past experience.

Value Judgment, *185*
An overall opinion of something based on a quick perception of its merit.

Communication (or Information) Overload, *185*
A situation that occurs when people are so overloaded with information that they cannot respond effectively to messages, resulting in stress.

Paradigm, *186*
A model, framework, viewpoint, perspective, or frame of reference.

Meta-communicate, *188*
To communicate about your communication to help overcome barriers or resolve a problem.

Active Listening, *188*
Listening for full meaning without making premature judgments or interpretations.

Linguistic Style, *192*
A person's characteristic speaking pattern, involving the amount of directness used, pacing and pausing, word choice, and the use of jokes, figures of speech, questions, and apologies.

DISCUSSION QUESTIONS AND ACTIVITIES

1. When a large number of job applicants are available to fill technical positions, hiring managers and human resource professionals are even more insistent about finding technical workers who have good communication skills. What might be the reasoning of these people hiring the technical workers?

2. A manager said, "By the time I answer all my e-mail and voice mail, it's time to go home." What advice can you offer this manager?

3. Watch a business executive on television and evaluate how effectively the person uses nonverbal communication. Be ready to report your findings back to class.

4. In what ways do cell phones: (a) contribute to enhanced communication in organizations, and (b) create communication barriers?

5. How can an organization benefit from good upward communication?

6. A business analyst from the Dominican Republic, working in the United States, said to her manager, "I am having a problem in meetings. When my coworkers are laughing, I do not know what they are laughing about. They all speak English too fast for me." What should the manager do in this situation?

7. Ask a successful person his or her impression of the importance of being a power-oriented communicator. Be prepared to share your observations with classmates.

ORGANIZATIONAL BEHAVIOR ONLINE

TO DO

Practicing Listening Skills
Your tax dollars are at work to help you listen. The U.S. Government Department of Veterans Affairs has prepared a Web site to help people develop their listening skills. Go to http://www.va.gov/adr/listen.html. The VA advises you that "Hearing becomes listening only when you pay attention to what is said and follow it very closely." After studying the site, identify two responding skills and two nonverbal techniques you think will be particularly valuable for you.

TO BOOKMARK

Presentation Tips
http://www.fastcompany.com/online/07/124present.html

Telecommuting
http://www.rileyguide.com/telecomm.html

Cross-Cultural Communication and Miscommunication
http://business-english-training.com/integr.htm

Nonverbal Communication
http://www.casualpower.com/intro.htm

C A S E   P R O B L E M : The Scrutinized Team Member Candidate

HRmanagerPLUS.com is a human resources management firm that provides human resource services such as payroll, benefits administration, affirmative action programs, and technical training to other firms. During its seven years of operation, HRmanagerPLUS.com has grown from 3 to 50 employees, and last year had total revenues of $21 million.

Most of the work of the firm is performed by teams, led by a rotating team leader. Each team member takes an 18-month turn at being a team leader. The four-person new ventures team is regarded by CEO and founder, Jerry Clune, as vital for the future of the company. In addition to developing ideas for new services, team members are responsible, initially, for obtaining clients for any new service they propose.

As with other teams at HRmanagerPLUS.com, the new ventures team has a voice in hiring. In conjunction with Clune, the team decided it should expand to five members. The team posted a job opening for a new member on an Internet recruiting service, ran classified ads in the local newspaper, and also asked present employees for referrals. One of the finalists for the position was Gina Cleveland, a 27-year-old business school graduate. In addition to interviewing with Clune and two company vice presidents, Cleveland spent one-half day with the new ventures team, breakfast and lunch included.

The team agreed that Cleveland appeared to be a strong candidate on paper. Her education and experience were satisfactory, her résumé was impressive, and she presented herself well during a telephone screening interview. Team leader, Lauren Nielsen, suggested that the group hold a debriefing session. The purpose of the session would be to share ideas about Cleveland's suitability for joining the team. Nielsen commented, "It seems like we think that Gina is a strong candidate based on her credentials and what she said. But I'm a big believer in nonverbal communication. Let's each share our observations about what Gina's body language tells us she is really like. I'll go first."

Lauren: I liked the way Gina looks so cool and polished when she joined us for breakfast. She's got all the superficial movements right to project self-confidence. But did anybody else notice how she looked concerned when she had to make a choice from the menu? She finally did choose a ham-and-cheese omelet, but she raised her voice at the end of the sentence when she ordered it. I got the hint that Gina is not very confident. I also noticed Gina biting her lips a little when we asked her how creative she thought she was. I know that Gina said she was creative and gave us an example of a creative project she completed. Yet nibbling at her lips like that suggests she's not filled with fire power.

Michael: I didn't make any direct observations about Gina's being self-confident or not, but I did notice something that could be related. I think Gina is on a power trip, and this could indicate high or low self-confidence. Did anybody notice how Gina put her hands on her hips when she was

standing up? That's a pure and clear signal of somebody who wants to be in control. Her haircut is almost the same length and style like most women who've made it to the top in Fortune 500 companies. I think she cloned her hairstyle from Carly Fiorina, the HP honcho. Another hint I get of Gina's power trip is the way she eyed the check in the restaurant at lunch. I could see it in her eyes that she really wanted to pay for the entire team. That could mean a desire to control and show us that she is very important. Do we want someone on the team with such a strong desire to control?

Brenda: I observed a different picture of Gina based on her nonverbal communication. She dressed just right for the occasion—not too conservatively, not too far business casual. This tells me she can fit into our environment. Did you notice how well groomed her shoes were? This tells you she is well organized and good at details. Her attaché case was a soft, inviting leather. If she were really into power and control, she would carry a hard vinyl or aluminium attaché case. I see Gina as a confident and assertive person who could blend right into our team.

Larry: I hope that because I'm last, I'm not too influenced by the observations that you three have shared so far. My take is that Gina looks great on paper, but she may have a problem in being a good team player. She's too laid back and distant. Did you notice her handshake? She gave me the impression of wanting to have the least possible physical contact with me. Her handshake was so insincere. I could feel her hand and arm withdrawing from me as she shook my hand. I also couldn't help noticing that Gina did not lean much toward us during the round table discussion. Do you remember how she would pull her chair back ever so slightly when we got into a heavy discussion? I interpreted that as a sign that Gina does not want to be part of a close-knit group.

Lauren: As you have probably noticed, I've been typing as fast as I can with my laptop, taking notes on what you have said. We have some mixed observations here, and I want to summarize and integrate them before we make a decision. I'll send you an e-mail message with an attached file of my summary observations by tomorrow morning. Make any changes you see fit and get back to me. After we have finished evaluating Gina carefully, we will be able to make our recommendations to Jerry (Clune).

Case Questions

1. To what extent are new ventures team members making an appropriate use of nonverbal communication to size up Gina Cleveland?

2. Which team member do you think made the most realistic interpretation of nonverbal behavior? Why?

3. Should Lauren, the team leader, have told Gina in advance that the team would be scrutinizing her nonverbal behavior? Justify your answer.

ENDNOTES

1. Cited in "The Top Job Skills for the 21st Century," *People@work,* May 1999, Professional Training Associates Inc.
2. Quoted in "Like It or Not, You've Got Mail," *Business Week,* October 4, 1999, p. 178.
3. Quoted in Todd Raphael, "E-mailing Your Way to Disaster," *Workforce,* July 2002, p. 88.
4. Mahlon Apgar, IV, "The Alternative Workplace: Changing Where and How People Work," *Harvard Business Review,* May–June 1998, p. 121; "Time to Take Another Look at Telecommuting," *HRfocus,* May 2002, p. 6.
5. Susan J. Wells, "Two Sides to the Story," *HR Magazine,* October 2001, p. 41.
6. Jean Mausehund and R. Neil Dortch, "Presentation Skills in the Digital Age," *Business Education Forum,* April 1999, pp. 30–32.
7. Mausehund and Dortch, "Presentation Skills," pp. 31–32.
8. Jim Kerstetter and Peter Burrows, "Why the Tech Turnaround Looks Real," *Business Week,* May 5, 2003, p. 30.
9. Michael Argyle, *Bodily Communication,* 2nd ed. (Madison, CT: International Universities Press, 1990).
10. Jeffrey Jacobi, *The Vocal Advantage* (Upper Saddle River, NJ: Prentice Hall, 1996).
11. Research cited in "Use Body Language to Gain Their Trust," *Managers Edge,* April 2000, p. 5.
12. Ann Davis, Joseph Pereira, and William M. Bulkeley, "Silent Signals: Security Concerns Bring New Focus on Body Language," *The Wall Street Journal,* August 15, 2002, pp. A1, A6.
13. Patrick Kiger, "Lessons from a Crisis: How Communication Kept a Company Together," *Workforce,* November 2001, p. 28.
14. Paul Argenti, "Crisis Communication Lessons from 9/11," *Harvard Business Review,* December 2002, p. 106.
15. Interview by Bob Rosner, "Studying the World beneath the Org Chart," *Workforce,* September 2001, p. 65.
16. Samuel Greengard, "Gossip Poisons Business: HR Can Stop It," *Workforce,* July 2001, pp. 26–27.
17. Cited in Mildred L. Culp, "Rumor Important, Say Managers Worldwide," WorkWise® syndicated column, March 28, 1999.
18. John P. Kotter, *The General Managers* (New York: Free Press, 1991).
19. Robert A. Dilenschneider, *A Briefing for Leaders: Communication as the Ultimate Exercise of Power* (New York: Harper/Business 1991).
20. Suzette Haden Elgin, *Genderspeak* (New York: Wiley, 1993).
21. Quoted in "For Honeywell Exec, BS Doesn't Pay," *Executive Leadership,* September 2002, p. 3.
22. The comment about nonverbal cues is from "See How Much You're Missing? How to Listen When You'd Rather Talk," *Working Smart,* April 2000, p. 7.
23. "Listen and Respond: The Communication Two-Step," *Leadership* (American Association International), June 1998, p. 4.
24. Deborah Tannen, *Talking from 9 to 5* (New York: William Morrow, 1994); Tannen, "The Power of Talk: Who Gets Heard and Why?" *Harvard Business Review,* September–October 1995, pp. 138–148; Daniel J. Canary and Kathryn Dindia, *Sex Differences and Similarities in Communication* (Mahwah, NJ: Erlbaum, 1998), p. 318; John Gray, *Men Are from Mars, Women Are from Venus* (New York: HarperCollins, 1992).
25. Roger E. Axtell, *Gestures: The Do's and Taboos of Body Language Around the World* (New York: Wiley, 1990).
26. "Use Team's Diversity to Best Advantage," *ExecutiveSTRATEGIES,* April 2000, p. 2.
27. Deborah Tannen, "The Power of Talk: Who Gets Heard and Why?", *Harvard Business Review,* September–October 1995, pp. 138–148.
28. Tannen, "The Power of Talk," pp. 138–158; "How You Speak Shows Where You Rank," *Fortune,* February 2, 1998, p. 156; "Proven Strategies for Gaining Cooperation," *Manager's Edge,* April 2000, p. 4; Robert B. Ciadini, "Harnessing the Science of Persuasion," *Harvard Business Review,* October 2001, p. 77.

Chapter 10

Group Dynamics and Teamwork

Ray Olgelthorpe, president of AOL Technologies, America Online Inc., was asked "What's the secret to a great team?" "Think small," he replied. "Ideally your team should have 7 to 9 people. If you have more than 15 or 20, you're dead. The connections between team members are hard to make.

"Two and one-half years ago, AOL was feeling hamstrung at the technologies level. There was a bottleneck at the top. We decided to make that division team-based, and created core teams that were empowered to make decision about products.

"It was the best thing we could have done. The core teams spun off satellite teams (also made up of small groups of people) that focused on specific projects, with specific goals and expectations.

"The management challenge is to understand that the people who report to you may get most of their direction from another person or from several other people: their team leaders. And people can be on more than one team, of course. It's the manager's job to think about whether *this* person is being stretched too thin, or whether *that* person needs some special training.

"Size is the key. Have the smallest number of people possible on each team."

Source: Regina Fazio Maruca, "Unit of One: What Makes Teams Work?" *Fast Company,* November 2000, p. 110. Permission conveyed through Copyright Clearance Center, Inc.

NOW ASK YOURSELF: What does this story about teams of AOL tell us about how group size can contribute to group effectiveness? Understanding the characteristics of an effective work group, including size, is one of the major topics about group and teams discussed in this chapter. Corporate America has made its position on teamwork known in countless above-the-fold stories in the business press that emphasize the important correlations between people and profits. The heavy emphasis on teams and group decision making in today's organizations only increases the importance of understanding teams and groups for tomorrow's managers. In modern organizations, standard practice is to organize all sorts of work around groups and teams. Groups are vital to the understanding of organizational behavior because they are the building blocks of the larger organization.

TYPES OF GROUPS AND TEAMS

A **group** is a collection of people who interact with one another, work toward some common purpose, and perceive themselves as a group. The head of a customer service team and her staff would be a group. In contrast, twelve people in an office elevator would not be a group because they are not engaged in collective effort. According to Jon R. Katzenbach and Douglas K. Smith, groups and teams function differently.[1] A **team** is a special type of group. Team members have complementary skills and are committed to a common purpose, a set of performance goals, and an approach to the task. An important part of team functioning is **teamwork**—an understanding and commitment to group goals on the part of all team members.

1

Describes the various types of groups in organizations.

Groups and teams can also be differentiated in other ways. A working group has a strong, clearly focused leader, while a team leader shares leadership roles. A group is characterized by individual accountability, while a team has individual and mutual accountability. Another distinction is that the team delivers actual joint work products. Also, a group strives to run efficient meetings, while a team encourages open-ended discussion and full participation in problem solving.

Groups and teams have been classified in many different ways. Here we describe the distinctions between formal versus informal groups and among three different types of work teams.

Formal versus Informal Groups

Some groups are formally sanctioned by management and the organization itself, while others are not. A **formal group** is one deliberately formed by the organization to accomplish specific tasks and achieve goals. Examples of formal or work groups include departments, projects, task forces, committees, and search teams to find a new executive. In contrast, **informal groups** emerge over time through the interaction of workers. Although the goals of these groups are not explicitly stated, informal groups typically satisfy a social or recreational purpose. Members of a department who dine together occasionally would constitute an informal group. Yet the same group might also meet an important work purpose of discussing technical problems of mutual interest.

Types of Work Teams

All workplace teams have the common elements of people working together cooperatively who possess a mix of skills. We have already described self-managed work teams in Chapter 7. Three other representative work teams are cross-functional teams, top-management teams, and virtual teams. Projects, task forces, and committees are quite similar in design to cross-functional teams, so they do not receive separate mention here. No matter what label the team carries, its broad purpose is to contribute to a collaborative workplace in which people help one another achieve constructive goals. The idea is for workers to collaborate (a high level of cooperation) rather than compete with or prevent others from getting their work done.

As teams have become more common in the workplace, much effort has been directed toward specifying the skills and knowledge needed to function effectively on a team, particularly a self-directed work team. The Self-Assessment that follows presents a representative listing of team skills perceived as necessary by employers. How many team skills do you possess?

SELF-ASSESSMENT

Team Skills

A variety of skills are required to be an effective member of various types of teams. Several different business firms use this skill inventory to help guide team members toward the competencies they need to become high-performing team members. Review each team skill listed and rate your skill level for each one, using the following classification:

S = strong (capable and comfortable with effectively implementing the skill)
M = moderate (demonstrated skill in the past)
B = basic (minimum ability in this area)
N = not applicable (not relevant to the type of work I do)

	Skill Level (S, M, B, or N)		Skill Level (S, M, B, or N)
Communication Skills		**Organizational Skills**	
Speak effectively	_____	Know the business	_____
Foster open communications	_____	Use technical/functional expertise	_____
Listen to others	_____	Use financial/quantitative data	_____
Deliver presentations	_____	**Strategic Skills**	
Prepare written communication (both e-mail and hardcopy)	_____	Recognize big picture impact	_____
Self-Management Skills		Promote corporate citizenship	_____
Act with integrity	_____	Focus on customer needs	_____
Demonstrate adaptability	_____	Commit to quality	_____
Engage in personal development	_____	Manage profitability	_____
Strive for results	_____		
Show commitment to work	_____		
Thought Process Skills			
Innovate solutions to problems	_____		
Use sound judgment	_____		
Analyze issues	_____		
Think "outside the box"	_____		

Cross-Functional Teams

It is common practice for teams to be composed of workers from different specialties. A **cross-functional team** is a work group composed of workers from different specialties but about the same organizational level, coming together to accomplish a task. The purpose of the cross-functional team is to get workers from different specialties to blend their talents toward a task that requires such a mix. Product development is the most frequent purpose of a cross-functional team. In addition, cross-functional teams are used for such purposes as improving quality, reducing costs, and engaging in systems development. In the life and health insurance field, many companies have reorganized the field sales support or policy-holder services into cross-functional teams. In practice, this means going from a customer service approach in which one person handles one function, such as new applications for insurance, to a team approach where each team member can handle any request.

A key success factor for cross-functional teams is that the team leader has both technical and process skills. The leader needs the technical background to understand the group task and to recognize the potential contribution of members from diverse specialities. At the same time the leader must have the interpersonal skills to facilitate a diverse group of people with limited, zero, or even negative experiences in working collectively.[2]

A major advantage of cross-functional teams is that they enhance communication across groups, thereby saving time. The cross-functional team also offers the advantage of a strong customer focus because the team orients itself toward satisfying a specific internal or external customer or group of customers. A challenge with these teams, however, is that they often breed conflict because of the different points of view. Also, the members may lack the teamwork skills to bring about a strong collaboration.[3]

To perform well on a cross-functional team, a person has to think in terms of the good of the larger organization, rather than in terms of his or her own specialty. For example, a manufacturing technician might say, "If I propose using expensive components for the Net-access pager, would the product cost too much for its intended market?"

Virtual Team

Some teams conduct most of their work by sending electronic messages to one another rather than conducting face-to-face meetings. A **virtual team** is a small group of people who conduct almost all of their collaborative work by electronic communication rather than face-to-face meetings. The team members are typically dispersed physically, but could also work in the same organization and contribute input at different times. Teleworkers are often part of a virtual team. E-mail is the usual medium for sharing information and conducting meetings. Groupware is another widely used approach to conducting a virtual meeting. Using groupware, several people can edit a document at the same time or in sequence. Desktop videoconferencing is another technological advance that facilitates the workings of virtual team.[4] Electronic brainstorming, as described in Chapter 5, is also well-suited for a virtual team.

Most high-tech companies make some use of virtual teams. Strategic alliances, in which geographically dispersed companies work with one another, are a natural fit for virtual teams. It's less expensive for the field technician in Iceland to hold a virtual meeting with her counterparts in South Africa, Mexico, and California than to bring them all together in one physical location. IBM makes some use of virtual teams in selling information technology systems, partially because so many IBM field personnel work from their homes and vehicles. Virtual teams are also an effective way of responding to new workforce demographics where the most talented employees may be located anywhere in the world, and may demand personal flexibility in terms of when and where to perform work.[5]

Mutual trust is a major factor for the success of most teams, and even more critical for a virtual team. Wayne F. Cascio and Stan Shurygailo observe that in a virtual team trust is established by repeatedly setting expectations and then delivering results that meet or surpass those expectations. An analysis of the development of trust in 29 global virtual teams that communicated exclusively by e-mail over a six-week period found that three characteristics were associated with the highest level of trust. First, the interactions began with warm-up introductions about members, including the exchange of personal information. Second, clear roles were established for each member. Third, all team members demonstrated positive attitudes such as by showing enthusiasm and giving quick responses to all e-mail messages. The researchers also noted that the presence of just one pessimist in the group might undermine trust in the entire virtual team. Lack of trust, in turn, often lowers overall group productivity.[6]

Although members of a virtual team have limited or minimum face-to-face contact with each other, they still need guidance and direction. In many firms, members of the virtual team participate in face-to-face team training before beginning the formal work of the team. Exhibit 10-1 provides a variety of useful suggestions for managing a virtual team and enhancing teamwork.

Despite the efficiency of virtual teams, there are times when face-to-face interaction is necessary to deal with complex and emotional issues. Negotiating a new contract between management and a labor union, for example, is not well-suited to a virtual meeting.

Exhibit 10-1

How to Achieve Virtual Teamwork

Establishing trust and commitment, encouraging communication, and assessing team members poses tremendous challenges for virtual team managers. Here are a few tips to make the process easier:

- Establish regular times for group interaction.
- Set up rules for communication.
- Use visual forms of communication where possible.
- Emulate the attributes of co-located teams. For example, allow time for informal chit-chat and socializing, and celebrate achievements.
- Give and receive feedback and offer assistance on a regular basis. Be persistent with people who aren't communicating with you or each other.
- Agree on standard technology so all team members can work together.
- Consider using 360-degree feedback (feedback from several different raters) to better understand and evaluate team members.

- Provide a virtual meeting room via intranet, Web site, or bulleting board.
- Note which employees effectively use e-mail to build team rapport.
- Smooth the way for an employee's next assignment if membership on the team, or the team itself, is not permanent.
- Be available to employees, but don't wait for them to seek you out.
- Encourage informal, off-line conversation among team members.

Source: Carla Johnson, "Virtual Teamwork," *HR Magazine,* June 2002, p. 71. Reprinted with the permission of HR Magazine published by the Society for Human Resource Management, Alexandria, VA.

Top Management Team

The group of managers at the top of most organizations is referred to as a team, the management team, or the top management team. Yet as team expert Jon R. Katzenbach observes, few groups of top managers function as a team in the sense of the definition presented earlier in this chapter.[7] The CEO gets most of the publicity, along with credit and blame for what goes wrong. Nevertheless, groups of top managers are teams in the sense that most major decisions are made collaboratively with all members of the top-management group included. Reuben Marks (Colgate-Palmolive) and Michael Dell (Dell Computers) are examples of highly visible and brilliant CEOs who regularly consult with their trusted advisors before making major decisions.

The term top management team has another less frequent meaning. A handful of companies are actually run by a committee of two or more top executives who claim to share power equally. The executives agree between themselves as to which type of decisions each one makes independently, and which decisions they make collaboratively. In this way, they are like a husband-and-wife team running a household. An example of a two-person team sharing power at the top comes from the merger of Exxon and Mobil. Some observers, however, are skeptical that a company can really be run well without one key executive having the final decision. Can you imagine your favorite athletic team having two head coaches?

STAGES OF GROUP DEVELOPMENT

2

Summarize the stages of group development and key roles members occupy within a work group.

Key to understanding the nature of work groups is knowing what the group does (the content) and how it proceeds (the process). A key group process is the group's development over time. To make this information more meaningful, relate it to any group to which you have belonged for at least one month. Understanding the stages of group development can lead to more effective group leadership or membership. The five group stages are shown in Exhibit 10-2 and described next.[8]

Stage 1: Forming. At the outset, members are eager to learn what tasks they will be performing, how they can benefit from group membership, and what constitutes acceptable behavior. Members often inquire about rules they must follow. Confusion, caution, and communality are typical during the initial phase of group development.

Stage 2: Storming. During this "shakedown" period, individual styles often come into conflict. Hostility, infighting, tension, and confrontation are typical. Members may argue to clarify expectations of their contributions. Coalitions and cliques may form within the group, and one or two members may be targeted for exclusion. Subgroups may form to push for an agenda of interest to them. (Despite the frequency of storming, many workplace groups work willingly with one another from the outset, thus skipping stage 2.)

Stage 3: Norming. After storming comes the quieter stage of overcoming resistance and establishing group standards of conduct (norms). Cohesiveness and commitment begin to develop. The group starts to come together as a coordinated unit, and harmony prevails. Norms stem from three sources. The group itself quickly establishes limits for members, often by effective use of glares and nods. For example, the team member who swears at the leader might receive angry glances from other members. Norms may also be

Exhibit 10-2

The Stages of Group Development

Most groups follow a predictable sequence of stages.

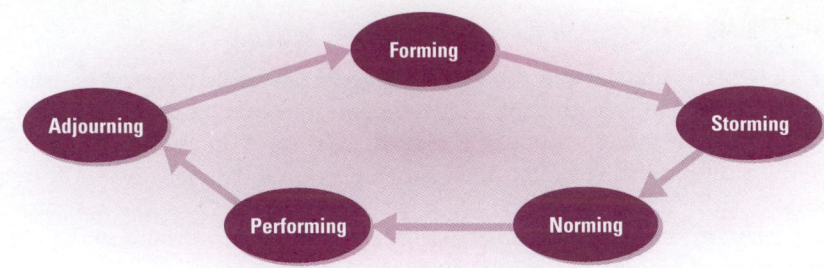

imposed that are derived from the larger organization and from professional codes of conduct. A third source of norms might be an influential team member who inspires the group to elevate its performance or behavior. A member of a sales team at Western New York Computing (systems and software) said to the other team members, "Why stop at being the best in this city? Let's develop a regional reputation."

Stage 4: Performing. When the group reaches the performing stage, it is ready to focus on accomplishing its key tasks. Issues concerning interpersonal relations and task assignment are put aside as the group becomes a well-functioning unit. Intrinsic motivation and creativity are likely to emerge as the group performs. At their best, members feel they are working "for the cause," much like a political campaign team or a team bringing a breakthrough product to market.

Stage 5: Adjourning. Temporary work groups are abandoned after their task has been accomplished, much like a project team to erect an office tower. The same group members, however, have developed important relationships and understandings they can bring with them should they be part of the same team in the future. The link between adjourning and forming shown in Exhibit 10-2 is that many groups do reassemble after one project is completed. The link between Stages 1 and 5 would not apply for a group that disbanded and never worked together again.

A key managerial challenge is to help the group move past the first three stages into performing. At times, group members may have to be confronted that they are spending too much time on process issues and not enough on the task at hand.

Roles within Groups

Another perspective on group process is to identify team members' roles (see the video sidebar).[9] Positive roles are described here to help you identify areas of possible contribution in group efforts:

1. *Knowledge contributor.* Being technically proficient, the knowledge contributor provides the group with useful and valid information. He or she is intent upon helping with task accomplishment and also values sharing technical expertise with team members.

2. *Process observer.* A person occupying this role forces the group to look at how it functions with statements such as: "We've been at it for two and a half hours, and we have only taken care of one agenda item. Shouldn't we be doing better?" The process observer might also point to excellent team progress.

Cannondale Teams (13:02)

Cannondale Corporation, based in Bethel, Connecticut, specializes in high-performance bicycle design and production, a never-ending race that pits strength against weight. Continually boosting performance is no easy feat, and Cannondale has turned to teams to fuel product design innovations. But with all its emphasis on engineering, high technology, and materials science, you might think the human touch never enters into Cannondale's calculations. For a look at a Cannondale team in action, go to **http:// dubrin.swlearning.com** and view the video segment. *Watch for examples of the various roles played by members of the team. How well do members understand the roles that others play? In what ways do members show support for each other?*

3. *People supporter.* A person occupying this role assumes some of the leader's responsibility for providing emotional support to teammates and resolving conflict. He or she serves as a model of active listening while others make presentations. The people supporter helps others relax by smiling, making humorous comments, and appearing relaxed. He or she supports and encourages team members even when disagreeing with them.

4. *Challenger.* To prevent complacency and non-critical thinking, a team needs one or more members who confront and challenge bad ideas. A challenger will criticize any decision or preliminary thinking that is deficient in any way, including being ethically unsound. Effective interpersonal skills are required to be a challenger. Antagonistic, attack-oriented people who attempt the challenger role lose their credibility quickly because they appear more interested in attacking than solving problems.

5. *Listener.* Listening contributes so substantially to team success that it comprises a separate role, even though other roles involve listening. If other people are not heard, the full contribution of team effort cannot be realized. As a result of being a listener, a team member or team leader is able to summarize discussion and progress for the team.

6. *Mediator.* Disputes within the group may become so intense and prolonged that two people no longer listen or respond to each other. The two antagonists develop such polarized viewpoints that they are unwilling to move toward each other's point of view. Furthermore, they have moved beyond the point that conciliation is possible. At this point, the team leader or a team member must mediate the dispute.

7. *Gatekeeper.* A recurring problem in group effort is that some members may fail to contribute because other team members dominate the discussion. Even when the viewpoints of the timid team members have been expressed, they may not be remembered because one or two other members contribute so frequently to discussion. When the opportunity gate is closed to several members, the gatekeeper pries it open. He or she requests that a specific team member be allowed to contribute or that the member's past contribution be recognized.

8. *Take-charge leader.* Some teams cry out for direction because either a formal leader has not been appointed or the appointed leader is unusually laid back. In such situations, a team member can assume the role of the take-charge leader. The problem could be that team members are hesitant to make even simple decisions or take a stand on controversial matters. A starting point for the take-charge leader is to encourage the team to define its mission and list its three main objectives.

According to the team-role theory developed by R. Meredith Belbin, it is important for group members to understand the roles that others play, when and how to let another group member take over, and how to compensate for the shortcomings of others in the group. Roles tend to be based on the psychological makeup of individuals, who adopt them naturally.[10] For example, a person who has developed good listening skills will gravitate toward the listener role, and a knowledgeable, bright person will naturally assume the knowledge-contributor role.

The Skill-Development Exercise on page 206 gives you an opportunity to identify and observe the roles just described. Recognize, however, that these roles may overlap; they are not entirely independent of each other.

SKILL-DEVELOPMENT EXERCISE

COLLABORATE

Team Member Roles

Form small teams to conduct a 20-minute meeting on a significant topic. Possibilities include: (1) a management team deciding on whether to lay off one-third of the workforce in order to increase profits, or (2) a group of fans who have volunteered to find a new team mascot name to replace "Redskins." While team members conduct their heated discussions, other class members should make notes of which team members carry out which roles. Watching for the eight different roles can perhaps be divided among class members, such as people in the first row looking for examples of a knowledge contributor. Use the following role worksheet to help you make your observations. Summarize the comments indicative of the role.

Knowledge contributor: _____
_____
_____

Process observer: _____
_____
_____

People supporter: _____
_____
_____

Challenger: _____
_____
_____

Listener: _____
_____
_____

Mediator: _____
_____
_____

Gatekeeper: _____
_____
_____

Take-charge leader: _____
_____
_____

3

Identify characteristics of an effective work group.

CHARACTERISTICS OF EFFECTIVE WORK GROUPS

Groups, like individuals, have characteristics that contribute to their uniqueness and effectiveness. As shown in Exhibit 10-3, these characteristics can be grouped into ten categories. Our description of work group effectiveness follows this framework.[11]

Job Design

Effective work groups follow the principles of job design embodied in job enrichment and the job characteristics model described in Chapter 7. For example, both task significance and task identity should be strong. Group members therefore perceive their work as having high intrinsic motivation.

A Feeling of Empowerment

An effective group or team believes that it has the authority to solve a variety of problems without first obtaining approval from management. Empowered teams share four experiences: potency, meaningfulness, autonomy, and impact. *Potency* refers to team members believing in themselves and exhibiting a confident can-do attitude. Teams with a sense of *meaningfulness* have a strong collective commit-

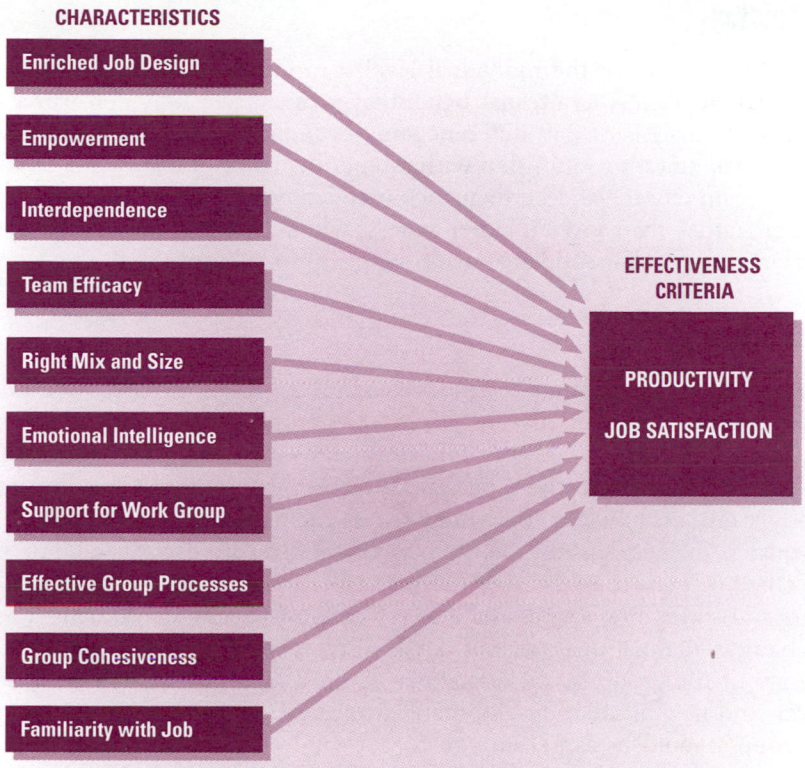

Exhibit 10-3

Work Group Characteristics Related to Effectiveness

CHARACTERISTICS

- Enriched Job Design
- Empowerment
- Interdependence
- Team Efficacy
- Right Mix and Size
- Emotional Intelligence
- Support for Work Group
- Effective Group Processes
- Group Cohesiveness
- Familiarity with Job

EFFECTIVENESS CRITERIA

PRODUCTIVITY

JOB SATISFACTION

Sources: Michael A. Campion, Ellen M. Papper, and Gina Medsker, "Relations between Work Team Characteristics and Effectiveness: A Replication and Extension," *Personnel Psychology*, Summer 1996, p. 431; Bradley L. Kirkman and Benson Rosen, "Powering Up Teams," *Organizational Dynamics*, Winter 2000, pp. 48–52; Stanley M. Gulley, Kara A. Incalcaterra, Aparna Joshi, and J. Matthew Beaubien, "A Meta-Analysis of Team Efficacy, Potency, and Performance: Interdependence and Level of Analysis as Moderators of Observed Relationships," *Journal of Applied Psychology*, October 2002, pp. 819–832; Scott W. Lester, Bruce M. Meglino, and M. Audrey Korsgaard, "The Antecedents and Consequences of Group Potency: Longitudinal Investigation of Newly Formed Work Groups," *The Academy of Management Journal,* April 2002, pp. 352–368; Vanessa Urch Druskat and Steven B. Wolff, "Building the Emotional Intelligence of Groups," *Harvard Business Review*, March 2001, pp. 80–90.

ment to their mission and see their goals as valuable and worthwhile. *Autonomy* refers to the freedom, discretion, and control the teams experience (the same as in job enrichment). A team experiences impact when members see the effect of their work on other interested parties such as customers and coworkers.[12]

Interdependence

Several types of interdependence characterize effective work groups. Such groups show task interdependence in the sense that members interact and depend on one another to accomplish work. *Task interdependence* is valuable because it increases motivation and enhances the sense of responsibility for the work of other group members. *Goal interdependence* refers to the linking of individual goals to the group's goals. For example, a member of a sales team might establish a compensation goal for herself, but she can realize this goal only if the other team members achieve similar success. Aside from the reality of interdependence, clearly defined goals are a major requirement for group effectiveness. Interdependent feedback and rewards also contribute to group effectiveness. Individual feedback and rewards should be linked to group performance to encourage good team play.

Team Efficacy

As with self-efficacy at the individual level, a productive group believes in itself. **Team efficacy** refers to a team's belief that it can successfully perform a specific task. A meta-analysis of 259 different samples indicated that team efficacy had a statistically significant relationship with job performance of teams. The relationship between team efficacy and performance was stronger when task interdependence was high rather than low. In other words, when group cohesiveness was more important, group self-confidence made a bigger contribution.[13]

Right Mix and Size

A variety of factors relating to the mix of group members are associated with effective work groups. A diverse group of members—in terms of experience, knowledge, and education—generally improves problem solving. Cultural diversity tends to enhance creativity because various viewpoints are brought into play. A study cautions, however, that only when each member of the group enjoys high-quality interactions can the full benefits of diversity be realized. The interactions relate to both the task itself (such as talking about improving a motorcycle starter) and social interactions (such as chatting about children during a break).[14] A problem with functional (technical speciality) diversity is that it can decrease the tendency of the group to stick together, as illustrated in a study of ninety-three research and new product development groups.[15]

Groups should be large enough to accomplish the work, but when groups become too large, confusion and poor coordination may result. Also, larger groups tend to be less cohesive. Cross-functional teams, work teams, committees, and task forces tend to be most productive with seven to ten members. Another important composition factor is the quality of the group or team members. Bright people with constructive personality characteristics contribute the most to team effectiveness. A study involving 652 employees composing 51 work teams found that teams with members higher in mental ability, conscientiousness, extraversion, and emotional stability received higher supervisor ratings for team performance.[16] (In other words, put winners on your team, and you are more likely to have a winning team.)

Emotional Intelligence

As described in Chapter 2, emotional intelligence makes a major contribution to individual effectiveness. Teams also benefit from having members with high emotional intelligence in such ways as building relationships both inside and outside the team, and understanding the subtle human aspects of their environment. An emotionally intelligent group, for example, would not propose a costly, elaborate program during a period of corporate downsizing. For a group to be emotionally intelligent, it must do more than assemble a handful of emotionally intelligent members. High group emotional intelligence requires creating norms that establish mutual trust among members, a sense of group identity, and team efficacy. The emotionally intelligent group deals constructively with emotion within the group, such as recognizing that the group is sad because a likeable member has been downsized, or that the group is ecstatic because it has surpassed its annual productivity goal.[17]

Support for the Work Group

The resources available to support the group and the context (environment) influence effectiveness. Key support factors include giving the group the information it needs, coaching group members, providing the right technology, and receiving recognition and other rewards. Training quite often facilitates work group effectiveness. The training content typically includes group decision making, interpersonal skills, technical knowledge, and the team philosophy. Managerial support in the form of investing resources and believing in group effort fosters effectiveness. Communication and cooperation between groups improves group effectiveness, although management must help create the right environment for it to occur.

A representative example of how company-sponsored training improves group effectiveness took place at Centria, a manufacturer of wall and roof systems. One aspect of the training was to teach supervisors the STAR (Specific Task Action Result) system, a tool for positive feedback, as explained by the HR director:

> When you give somebody positive feedback, you say, "Today when you were running the line and set the new record, I was really impressed with the way you worked with all the team members and kept them focused on what they needed to do. By doing that, you were able to set a record that was 10% higher than any time before." That would be a positive STAR. The theory is if you give enough feedback and reward and recognize people for when they do it right, they're going to it right all the time.[18]

Effective Processes within the Group

Many processes (activities) that influence effectiveness take place within the group. One is the belief that the group can do the job (team efficacy), reflecting high team spirit. Effectiveness is also enhanced when workers provide *social support* to one another through such means as helping one another have positive interactions. *Workload sharing* is another process characteristic related to effectiveness. *Communication and cooperation* within the work group also contribute to effectiveness.

Interpersonal processes are important, and so are work processes. Teams that can be trusted to follow work processes and procedures tend to perform better. Adhering to such processes and procedures is also associated with high-quality output. Although following processes and procedures might appear to be a routine expectation, many problems are created by workers who fail to do so. For example, a group might show a productivity dip if workers on a project fail to back up computer files and a computer virus attacks.

Group Cohesiveness

A group in which members work closely with each other, in a unified, cooperative manner, is likely to be effective. *Group cohesiveness* is closely linked to several other dimensions of an effective work group. Collectively, the process characteristics described previously contribute to a group that pulls together. Without cohesiveness, a group will fail to achieve synergy. The right size and mix within a group will also foster group cohesiveness.

Familiarity with Jobs, Coworkers, and the Environment

Another important set of factors related to work-group effectiveness is familiarity. It refers to the specific knowledge group members have of their jobs, coworkers, and the environment. Familiarity, as it ties into experience, is an asset for many types of jobs—at least if one has a certain level of proficiency. The contribution of familiarity is evident also when new members join an athletic team. Quite often the team loses momentum during the adjustment period.

The characteristics of an effective work group or team should be supplemented by effective leadership. Team leaders must emphasize coaching more than controlling. Instead of being a supervisor, the leader should become a team developer.

GROUP PROBLEM SOLVING AND DECISION MAKING

4

Implement two different methods of group problem solving and decision making.

The majority of U.S. business firms, as well as other organizations, use some types of teams. A major activity of many of these teams is to make decisions. Furthermore, teams and other groups make most major decisions in organizations. In general, decision making by groups has proven superior to individual decision making. An exception is that people working alone generate a larger number of creative alternative solutions to a problem than they do during group brainstorming.[19] One reason might be that if you spend your time thinking of solutions rather than listening to other group members, you produce more ideas.

One method of group problem solving, brainstorming, was described in Chapter 5. Here we describe group decision-making styles, along with two other methods of group decision making and problem solving—the nominal group and delphi techniques.

Group Decision-Making Styles

The term *group decision making* refers to a group playing a role in making a decision. Group decision making takes place in different degrees. One extreme is *consultative* decision making in which the group leader consults with members before making a decision. The other extreme is *democratic* decision making in which the problem at hand is turned over to the group, and they are empowered to make the decision themselves.

Midway between the two is *consensus* decision making, in which the manager shares the problem with group members. Together they generate and evaluate alternatives and attempt to reach agreement on a solution. Consensus is achieved when every member can say, "I have had an opportunity to express my views fully, and they have been thoughtfully considered by the group. Even though this solution is not the one I believe is optimal, it is acceptable and I will support it. I endorse the validity of the process we have undertaken."[20]

The Nominal Group Technique

The opposite of an interacting group is a nominal group whose distinguishing characteristic is silent effort during part of group problem solving. Brainstorming by computer allows for the same non-interactive input by group members. The steps in the **nominal group technique (NGT)** proceed as follows:

1. Members of the target group are chosen and brought together.
2. If the group is too large, it is divided into subgroups of eight or fewer.

3. The group leader presents a specific question.
4. Individual members silently and independently record their ideas in writing.
5. Each group member (one at a time, in turn, around the table) presents one idea to the group without discussion. The ideas are summarized and recorded on a chalkboard, flipchart, or sheet of paper on the wall. If computers are used, the output can be displayed on a large monitor.
6. After all members have presented their ideas, a discussion takes place to clarify and evaluate the ideas.
7. The meeting terminates with silent, and independent, voting by individuals through a rank ordering system (such as using a 1-to-10 scale). The nominal group decision is the pooled outcome of the individual rankings.[21]

The NGT has met with acceptance because it results in a disciplined decision. An advantage of this technique is that it combines the merits of individual reflection with the scrutiny of collective thought. One study demonstrated that the NGT overwhelmingly outperformed a standard brainstorming group.[22] Also, the NGT helps introverted people become actively involved in group activity.

The Delphi Technique

In some decision-making situations, group input is needed, yet it is difficult to bring people together because of the cost or time away from the office. Another problem is that some groups conflict so much in face-to-face meetings that it is difficult to solve problems and reach decisions. Managers might also believe that teleconferencing is not appropriate for decision making. The **Delphi technique** is well suited for these purposes. It is a group decision-making technique designed to provide group members with one another's ideas and feedback, while avoiding some of the problems associated with interacting groups.[23]

The Delphi technique incorporates a carefully structured sequence of questionnaires distributed to each group member, usually by e-mail. Each person answers the questionnaire about the problem at hand and transmits his or her responses and thoughts to the coordinator on an attached file or directly on the e-mail message. The leader aggregates the responses, and then sends them back to the team, and asks for feedback. Group members must trust the leader to aggregate and integrate the responses honestly.

Problem solving ordinarily improves with each successive input. In the last round of the questionnaire, group members are asked to vote for their choice of solutions. The coordinator edits the final version containing successive input from all the participants. The Delphi technique becomes a type of chain letter, and might be classified as a virtual group. Responses are sometimes averaged if the questionnaire calls for quantitative data. At other times, some people's choices and decisions are given more weight than those of other group members.

One problem with the Delphi technique is that it is more time consuming than group brainstorming or the nominal group technique. Delphi-technique sessions can last several days or even weeks.

POTENTIAL PROBLEMS WITHIN GROUPS

Chapter 7 included mention of the potential productivity advantages of self-directed work teams. However, group activity, including group decision making, does not always lead to superior results. Failure to attain outstanding results typically stems from lacking the characteristics of effective work groups, as summarized in

Pinpoint several potential problems with group effort and know how to prevent them.

Exhibit 10-3. For example, a work group might fail if it was not empowered, the group was low on emotional intelligence, and the members were poorly trained. Furthermore, similar results would occur if the group lacked the support of management, members did not support one another, and members were quite unfamiliar with the task and one another. For these and perhaps other reasons, informal studies, formal studies, and anecdotal evidence from consultants estimate a failure rate of at least 50 percent for self-directed teams.[24]

Work group failures also stem from dysfunctional processes. Here we look at three major processes within groups that can hamper their effectiveness: group polarization, social loafing, and groupthink.

Group Polarization

During group problem solving, or group discussion in general, members often shift their attitudes. Sometimes, the group moves toward taking greater risks; this is called the *risky shift*. At other times, the group moves toward a more conservative position. The general term for moving in either direction is **group polarization,** a situation in which post-discussion attitudes tend to be more extreme than pre-discussion attitudes.[25] For example, as a result of group discussion, members of an executive team become more cautious about entering a new market.

Group discussion facilitates polarization for several reasons. Discovering that others share our opinions may reinforce and strengthen our position. Listening to persuasive arguments may also strengthen our convictions. The "it's not my fault" attitude is another contributor to polarization. If responsibility is diffused, a person will feel less responsible—and guilty—about taking an extreme position.

Group polarization has a practical implication for managers who rely on group decision making. Workers who enter into group decision making with a stand on an issue may develop more extreme post-decision positions. For example, a group of employees who were seeking more generous benefits may decide as a group that the company should become an industry leader in employee benefits.

Social Loafing

An unfortunate by-product of group effort is that an undermotivated person can often squeeze by without contributing a fair share. **Social loafing** is freeloading, or shirking individual responsibility, when a person is placed in a group setting and removed from individual accountability. If you have worked on group projects for courses, you may have encountered this widely observed dysfunction of collective effort.

Two motivational explanations of social loafing have been offered. First, some people believe that because they are part of a team, they can "hide in the crowd." Second, group members typically believe that others are likely to withhold effort when working in a group. As a consequence, they withhold effort themselves to avoid being played for a sucker.

An experiment by Tina L. Robbins demonstrated that social loafing can occur even when a task is thought provoking and personally involving, and allows for unique contribution. She concludes that "the performance of self-directed work teams or groups which are formed for the purpose of brainstorming, product idea generation, or for making proposal implementation decisions may suffer the consequences of social loafing."[26] Even some workers involved in exciting tasks look for a free ride.

Groupthink

A potential disadvantage of group decision making is **groupthink, a deterioration of mental efficiency, reality testing, and moral judgment in the interest of group cohesiveness.** Simply put, groupthink is an extreme form of consensus. Those in this group atmosphere value getting along more than getting things done.[27] The group thinks as a unit, believes it is impervious to outside criticism, and begins to have illusions about its own invincibility. As a consequence, the group loses its powers of critical analysis. Groupthink is most likely to take place under certain conditions. A highly cohesive group favors groupthink because members identify strongly with the group. Other contributing factors include directive leadership, high stress, group insulation and a lack of built-in mechanisms for evaluating decisions. Having to choose between two unfavorable alternatives can lead to groupthink. An example would be an executive group deciding whether to recall a potentially unsafe product (and taking a huge loss) or leaving the product in distribution (and risking human suffering and negative publicity). Having limited time to make a major decision is another contributor to groupthink because the contributors may rush through the process.

Groupthink appears to have taken place at the many long-distance service providers who engage in slamming, or illegally switching people to its long-distance service without permission. The management group in the companies involved in this practice assumed that the customers who were involuntarily switched to their service either wouldn't notice or complain about the problem. However, many customers do complain, such as the 1,400 complaints against the group of long-distance companies known as The Fletcher Companies. The owner of the companies was ultimately fined $5 million for violating federal rules against slamming.[28]

A negative implication of groupthink is that it interferes with effective decision making. The emotional factors of wanting to achieve consensus and not wanting to be perceived as an irritant by other group members interferes with that person making an optimum decision. You might think that the alternative chosen by the group is terrible, yet you suppress your dissent to avoid being perceived as a dissident.

Groupthink can often be prevented if the team leader or member encourages all group members to express doubts and criticism of proposed solutions to the problem. It is also helpful to periodically invite qualified outsiders to meet with the group and provide suggestions. A specific technique proposed for combating groupthink is for the group leader in advance of the meeting to ask group members to write down their views anonymously on the decision in question. The leader then aggregates the individual statements into one list and distributes it to the group before the meeting. This kind of pre-commitment decreases group member's tendency to conform, even though the views remain anonymous.[29]

BUILDING TEAMWORK

6

Explain how to foster teamwork.

The team player roles described previously point to actions the individual can take to become a team player. The Self-Assessment on page 214 gives you the opportunity to gauge your current mental readiness to be a contributing team member. Here we highlight managerial actions and organizational practices that facilitate teamwork.[30] Good teamwork enhances, but does not guarantee, a successful team. Most executives, including CEO Jeffrey R. Immelt of GE, believe that teamwork is fundamental to the success of their organizations. Immelt often plays on the guilt of poor performers by telling them they are letting the team down.[31]

The manager can begin by helping team members believe that they have an *urgent constructive purpose.* A demanding performance challenge helps create and sustain the team. Early in the history of the group, the manager should establish trust by *empowering the group to determine how to meet the objectives.* Teamwork is fostered when the team leader establishes the direction, then steps aside to allow the group to work out the details of getting the job done. A major strategy for teamwork is to promote the attitude that *working together effectively is the established norm.* Developing such a culture of teamwork will be difficult when a strong culture of individualism exists within the firm. The team leader can communicate the norm of teamwork by *making frequent use of words and phrases that support teamwork.* Emphasizing the words team *members* or *teammates,* and de-emphasizing the words *subordinates* and *employees* helps communicate the teamwork norm.

Using the *consensus decision-making style* is another way to reinforce teamwork. A sophisticated approach to enhancing teamwork is to *feed team members valid facts and information that motivate them to work together.* New information prompts the team to redefine and enrich its understanding of the challenge it is facing, thereby allowing them to focus on a common purpose. A subtle yet potent method of building teamwork is for the team to *use language that fosters cohesion and commitment.* In-group jargon bonds a team and sets the group apart from others. An example is a team of information technology specialists saying "Send me a deck" to mean "Send me a PowerPoint presentation."

SELF-ASSESSMENT

Team Player Attitudes

Directions: Describe how well you agree with each of the following statements, using this scale: Disagree Strongly (DS); Disagree (D); Neutral (N); Agree (A); Agree Strongly (AS).

	DS	D	N	A	AS
1. I am at my best working alone.	5	4	3	2	1
2. I have belonged to clubs and teams ever since I was a child.	1	2	3	4	5
3. It takes far too long to get work accomplished with a group.	5	4	3	2	1
4. I like the friendship of working in a group.	1	2	3	4	5
5. I would prefer to run a one-person business than to be a member of a large firm.	5	4	3	2	1
6. It's difficult to trust others in the group on key assignments.	5	4	3	2	1
7. Encouraging others comes naturally to me.	1	2	3	4	5
8. I like the give and take of ideas that is possible in a group.	1	2	3	4	5
9. It is fun for me to share responsibility with other group members.	1	2	3	4	5
10. Much more can be accomplished by a team than by the same number of people working alone.	1	2	3	4	5

Total Score_____

Scoring and interpretation: Add the numbers you have circled to obtain your total score.

41–50   You have strong positive attitudes toward being a team member and working cooperatively with other members.

30–40   You have moderately favorable attitudes toward being a team member and working cooperatively with other members.

10–29   You much prefer working by yourself than being a team member. To work effectively in a company that emphasizes teamwork, you may need to develop more positive attitudes toward working jointly with others.

Organizational Behavior *in Action*

Give Others Credit

In her 25 years at U.S. Bank of Washington, Phyllis Campbell has climbed the ladder to become president and chair of the bank's advisory board. She attributes her success in large part to her ability to give others credit. She compares her leadership philosophy to an old, majestic tree. Just as the roots and branches must be strong for the tree to survive, your employees must provide reliable support to advance your goals.

Step Back to Get Ahead

For Campbell, shoving aside her ego to let her coworkers and employees strut their stuff has enhanced her stature. She rarely brags about her accomplishments and looks for ways to let staffers take center stage. "Early in my career, colleagues began to recognize my willingness to step aside so they could get acclaim," Campbell says. "I'd get promotions because I had all these people saying, 'She's a great boss. She gave me credit. She develops people well.' I gained a reputation as a someone who focused on the work, not myself."

Campbell often passed along smart ideas to coworkers, who in turn would act on her suggestion to achieve their own triumphs. When that happened, no one would be happier than Campbell.

Earn Lasting Trust

Some would-be leaders try to hog all the praise. Campbell insists that, "people damage themselves over time by over-worrying about getting credit, because they forget the organization's needs."

As a midlevel manager years ago, Campbell was assigned to chair a task force to propose a new service-delivery program. When her group was ready to make its recommendations, senior management asked Campbell to give the presentation alone. She refused.

"I wanted all six people in my group to take part," she recalls. "Senior management reluctantly agreed. At first they said, 'Oh geez, that's too many people.' But I assured them it would still take the same 20 minutes they'd allotted for it. As a result, these six people gained exposure to top executives."

Questions

1. What lesson about teamwork does Campbell provide?
2. How does Campbell risk losing power by her method of leadership?

Source: "Spotlight Your Team," *Executive Leadership,* July 2001, p. 3. Used with permission.

To foster teamwork, the manager should avoid **micromanagement,** or supervising group members too closely and second-guessing their decisions. Micromanagement can hamper a spirit of teamwork because team members do not feel in control of their own work. A practical initiative that gets at the heart of teamwork is for team members to *learn what other members of the team are working on.* In this way, team members can fill in for each other, thereby fostering a spirit of teamwork.

Creating physical structures suited for teams is an effective organizational intervention to support teamwork. Group cohesiveness, and therefore teamwork, is enhanced when teammates are located close together and can interact frequently and easily. Frequent interaction often leads to camaraderie and a feeling of belonging. A useful method for getting people to exchange ideas is to establish a shared physical facility, such as a conference room, research library, or break lounge. Recognize, however, that workers still need private space so they can concentrate on work without interruption. A key strategy for encouraging teamwork is to *reward the team as well as individuals.* The most convincing team incentive is to calculate compensation partially on the basis of team results. Team-based pay is useful for motivating employees to work more cooperatively, providing the corporate culture emphasizes collaboration rather than individualism.

IMPLICATIONS FOR MANAGERIAL PRACTICE

1. Be aware of group norms and the extent to which they facilitate or inhibit reaching organizational objectives. Reward systems must be developed that encourage high group performance. For example, if a group performs well on a given task and management then elevates performance standards, a norm toward lowered productivity may result.

2. When forming a new work group or team, recognize that time is needed before the group will be able to achieve maximum performance. Be alert to somewhat predictable stages of group formation and development: forming, storming, norming, and performing.

3. Be aware that group effectiveness is not a random occurrence. Strive to incorporate into the group many of the characteristics associated with work group effectiveness, such as proper job design, the right composition, and workload sharing. At the same time, if the task to be performed does not really require interdependent work, a group is not likely to make a better contribution than individuals working independently.

4. Managers can remove themselves as impediments to self-management of teams, while retaining the role of adviser and resource person, by asking these questions of team members: (a) What is the cause of the problem?, (b) What are you doing to fix it?, (c) How will you know when it is accomplished?, and (d) How can I help?[32]

High-excitement team-building courses, like the kayak-racing course developed at Charles Schwab, can get pretty strange. Rattlesnake hunts, paintball wars, fire-walking, and rescuing Barbie dolls from tanks of "deadly" plastic sharks have all had their corporate adherents. Log on to InfoTrac College Edition at **http://www .infotrac-college.com** to see how many outlandish exercises, all in the name of building camaraderie and risk taking, you can find. Then ask yourself whether you believe these sorts of team-building efforts really transfer into results back at the office.

Another option available to organizations for enhancing teamwork is to *send members to outdoor (or off-site) training,* a form of experiential learning. Participants acquire leadership and teamwork skills by confronting physical challenges and exceeding their self-imposed limitations. Rope activities are typical of outdoor training. Participants attached to a secure pulley with ropes will climb up a ladder and jump off to another spot. Walking over white-hot coals to promote bonding is another team-building activity. (Yes, some participants have been hospitalized.) All of these challenges are faced in teams rather than individually, which fosters the development of teamwork. Outdoor training is likely to have the most favorable outcomes when the trainer helps the team members comprehend the link between such training and on-the-job behavior.

Many companies invest in off-site training. A case in point is Daniel Hubbard, director of corporate communications at Charles Schwab, the large brokerage firm. He created an adventure kayak racing club for employees at the company's San Francisco headquarters (see the InfoTrac sidebar). Hubbard believes that adventure racing develops personal and team skills. He also thinks that kayak racing together will help Schwab employees get to know one another better or meet for the first time, and will promote loyalty to the company. Hubbard chose an activity that he thought would fit employee demographics and personal characteristics. The average Schwab employee is around 30 years old, educated, affluent, competitive, and team oriented.[33]

SUMMARY OF KEY POINTS

1 **Describe the various types of groups in organizations.**
Groups and teams can be classified in various ways. Formal groups are deliberately formed by the organization, whereas informal groups emerge over time through worker interaction. Three types of work teams described here are cross-functional teams, virtual teams (ones that meet electronically), and top management teams.

2 **Summarize the stages of group development and key roles members occupy within a work group.**

Groups are thought to go through five predictable stages of development: forming, storming, norming, performing, and adjourning. Group member roles include: knowledge contributor, process observer, people supporter, challenger, listener, mediator, gatekeeper (letting others into the discussion), and take-charge leader.

3 **Identify the characteristics of an effective work group.**

Effective work group characteristics are well documented. The jobs should be enriched, and the members should have a feeling of empowerment. Group members should be interdependent in terms of tasks, goals, and feedback and rewards. Team efficacy, the feeling of being able to accomplish the task, is important. The group should be composed of heterogeneous members who are flexible and have a preference for group work. Group emotional intelligence—especially in terms of developing trust—is useful. The group should have support including giving the group the information it needs, coaching group members, providing the right technology, and receiving recognition and other rewards. The group process should include team spirit, social support, and workload sharing, and following work processes and procedures enhances performance. Group cohesiveness contributes to performance and satisfaction, and members should be familiar with the jobs, coworkers, and the work environment.

4 **Implement two different methods of group problem solving and decision making.**

Group decision-making styles follow a continuum from being consultative, through based on consensus, to being democratic. When consensus is reached, all group members are at least willing to support the decision. The nominal group and Delphi techniques capitalize on the value of collective thought, yet minimize some of the problems that occur in interacting groups. Using the NGT, each person writes down ideas separately and later shares ideas with the group before all the ideas are ranked by group members. With the Delphi technique, each member responds to a questionnaire about the problem, passing along his or her input to the team leader who aggregates the information and redistributes it as often as necessary. Finally, group members vote on the best solution.

5 **Pinpoint several potential problems with group effort and know how to prevent them.**

Group effectiveness can be hampered in several ways. Polarization, or taking extreme positions, can result. Members may engage in social loafing, or freeloading. Groupthink, an extreme form of consensus and lack of critical reasoning, may occur as members strive for solidarity.

6 **Explain how to foster teamwork.**

Managers and leaders can enhance teamwork through many behaviors, attitudes, and organizational actions including the following: give the team an urgent, constructive purpose; develop a norm for teamwork; refrain from micromanagement; create physical structures suited for teams; and support outdoor (or off-site) training.

KEY TERMS AND PHRASES

Group, *199*
A collection of people who interact with one another, work toward some common purpose, and perceive themselves as a group.

Team, *199*
A special type of group in which the members have complementary skills and are committed to a common purpose, a set of performance goals, and an approach to the task.

Teamwork, *199*
A situation in which there is understanding and commitment to group goals on the part of all team members.

Formal Group, *199*
A group deliberately formed by the organization to accomplish specific tasks and achieve goals.

Informal Group, *199*
A group that emerges over time through the interaction of workers, typically to satisfy a social or recreational purpose.

Cross-Functional Team, *201*
A work group, composed of workers with different specialties but from about the same organizational level, who come together to accomplish a task.

Virtual Team, *201*
A group that conducts almost all of its collaborative work via electronic communication rather than face-to-face meetings.

Team Efficacy, *208*
A team's belief that it can successfully perform a specific task.

Nominal Group Technique (NGT), *210*
An approach to developing creative alternatives that requires group members to generate alternative solutions independently.

Delphi Technique, *211*
A group decision-making technique designed to provide group members with one another's ideas and feedback,

while avoiding some of the problems associated with inter-acting groups.

Group Polarization, *212*
A situation in which post-discussion attitudes tend to be more extreme than pre-discussion attitudes.

Social Loafing, *212*
Freeloading, or shirking individual responsibility when placed in a group setting and removed from individual accountability.

Groupthink, *213*
A deterioration of mental efficiency, reality testing, and moral judgment in the interest of group cohesiveness.

Micromanagement, *215*
Supervising group members too closely and second guessing their decisions.

DISCUSSION QUESTIONS AND ACTIVITIES

1. Explain the meaning of this sentence: "All teams are groups, but not all groups are teams."
2. How will your study of individual behavior help you better understand how groups operate?
3. Why is membership on a cross-functional team such good experience for becoming an executive?
4. Critics of the group and team movement in organizations often make a quip like "Have you ever seen a statue of a committee in a park?" What is their point?
5. How might you use the Delphi technique to help you prepare a more effective job résumé?
6. Identify an example of groupthink in a work or social setting that you have observed or read about.
7. Outdoor (or off-site) training has achieved enormous popularity as a method for developing teamwork (even without research substantiation). What factors do you think account for its popularity?
8. Form a small group with three or four of your classmates. See if you can make a checklist of ten or more items for assessing the effectiveness of a team.

ORGANIZATIONAL BEHAVIOR ONLINE

TO DO

Hundreds of consulting firms and training organizations offer team-building exercises, including Dale Carnegie Training®, the organization that became famous by offering training in public speaking, the development of self-confidence, and sales skills. Visit http://www.dalecarnegie.com to investigate what type of group and teamwork training Dale Carnegie offers. Compare the ideas of Dale Carnegie with those presented in the chapter. What similarities and differences do you see? What is your impression of the Dale Carnegie approach to building group effectiveness and teamwork?

TO BOOKMARK

Teamwork Development
http://www.creativecookingschool.com/corporate.asp

Teamwork Suitability Self-Quiz
http://content.monster.com/tools/quizzes/teamplayer

Cross-Functional Teams
http://www.glennparker.com/Freebees/teaming-with-strangers.html

Cross-Cultural Virtual Teams
http://www.grovewell-global.com/virtual-teams.html

CASE PROBLEM: The Speed Team at IBM

Steve Ward, the vice president of business transformation and chief information officer at IBM, was having dinner with a few members of his approximately 200-member leadership council. During dinner he decided that saving time, through making decisions faster, writing software faster, and completing projects faster, needed higher priority at IBM. If smaller telecommunications companies could continue to work faster than IBM, they would keep nibbling away at Big Blue's market share.

The morning after the leadership council dinner, the Speed Team was born. Ward contacted 21 IBMers and give them an assignment: Get the 100,000-person information technology group moving faster than ever, with a focus on the rapid development Web-oriented applications. At IBM, the IT group has high status and reports to the senior vice president of strategy.

The Speed Team's co-leaders—Jane Harper, director of technology operations, and Ray Blair, director of e-procurement—had strong reputations for pushing projects forward at a blazing pace. The two leaders decided that the team should have a life span of approximately six months. "I think that we will have failed if the Speed Team is still together three years from now," explains Harper. "Our plan, when we started this, was to come together, look at what works, look at why projects get bogged down, create some great recommendations about how to achieve speed, get executive buy-in, and try to make those recommendations part of the fabric of the business."

Steve Ward built the Speed Team with IBM employees who had led breakthrough projects that were completed in an unusually short period of time. One example is Gina Poole, founder of developerWorks, a Web site to help IBM forge stronger relationships with software companies. She was drafted based on how quickly she was able to get the site up and running. Members of the Speed Team shared success stories about how rapidly they accomplished projects in the past. They also shared information about how they were able to overcome barriers to speed.

The Speed Team then picked up some ideas about quick turnaround times by studying the IBM WebAhead lab, which develops prototypes for new technologies. WebAhead employees work in a single shared-office setup—long tables of several employees arranged in rows. The overall atmosphere is casual. A sign on the door reads, "This is not your father's IBM." The lab's purpose is simple and liberating: "Our team is funded to do cool stuff for IBM," says Bill Sweeney, a WebAhead manager. "We don't have to think about increasing sales of a product line. We just have to think about the next important thing that might hit us." One of the secrets that the WebAhead team unlocked is that speed is its own reward. Employees were encouraged and energized when they saw their pet projects being deployed in weeks rather than months or quarters.

After examining many fast-moving projects, including e-procurement, the Speed Team began outlining what those projects had in common. It then created the "Success Factors for Speed," six attributes that all successful projects had in common: strong leaders, team members who were speed demons, clear objectives, a strong communication system, and a process carefully tailored to the requirements of the group. The general principle discovered by the Speed Team is that going faster is all about how you relate to time. If your treat time as a tangible (like money), you wind up moving faster.

The Speed Team decided that it needed a medium for gathering fast feedback, so the team held a weeklong online "town hall" meeting. The goal was to encourage other employees to contribute ideas about getting projects accomplished quickly. Some of the suggestions confirmed what the Speed Team had learned. Many projects wind up in the breakdown lane because of overly rigorous measurement. The coordinator of the online meeting said, "People complained about breaking down 13-week projects into 13 phases and having to produce measurement reports at the end of each week." The Speed Team also picked up some information about speed they did not discover on their own. Information overload at IBM was slowing people down. Newsletters, e-mail, and the intranet can create duplication and mixed messages.

Soon the Speed Team began implementing both its "quick hit" ideas and its long-term initiatives. Quick hits included things like creating a speed rating for employee-performance reviews and getting all leads to specify more clearly their time-oriented priorities. Long-term initiatives involved addressing the occasional disconnect between finance-department employees who supervise the funding of company projects and those employees who actually run the projects. Sometimes by the time a project is ready for implementation, its funding has been cut.

Although the Speed Team has a specified termination date, its members and its leaders believe its influence will not end. "These people will work together for years, whether you call them the Speed Team or not," says Ward. "People have begun to think about the need for speed in their work. We're no longer necessary. Our job was to be catalysts, and catalysts can't linger around."

Case Questions

1. What characteristics of an effective work group does the Speed Team appear to have?
2. To what extent was a team structure really necessary to carry out the mission of the Speed Team?
3. Should the Speed Team really adjourn at this point?

Source: Based on information in Scott Kirsner, "Faster Company," *Fast Company,* May 2000, pp. 162–172. Permission conveyed through Copyright Clearance Center, Inc.

ENDNOTES

1. Jon R. Katzenbach and Douglas K. Smith, "The Discipline of Teams," *Harvard Business Review,* March–April 1993, p. 113.
2. Glenn Parker, "Team with Strangers: Success Strategies for Cross-Functional Teams," http://www.glennparker.com/Freebees/teaming-with-strangers.html. Material copyright © 1998 Glen Parker.
3. Avan R. Jassawalla and Hemant C. Sashittal, "Building Collaborative Cross-Functional New Product Teams," *Academy of Management Executive,* August 1999, pp. 50–63.
4. James L. Creighton and James W. R. Adams, "The Cybermeeting's About to Begin," *Management Review,* January 1998, pp. 29–31.
5. Anthony M. Townsend, Samuel M. DeMarie, and Anthony R. Hendrickson, "Virtual Teams: Technology and the Workplace of the Future," *Academy of Management Executive,* August 1998, p. 17.
6. Wayne F. Cascio and Stan Shurgailo, "E-Leadership and Virtual Teams," *Organizational Dynamics,* Number 4, 2003, pp. 362–376.
7. Jon R. Katzenbach, "The Myth of the Top Management Team," *Harvard Business Review,* November–December 1997, pp. 82–99.
8. J. Steven Heinen and Eugene Jacobsen, "A Model of Task Group Development in Complex Organizations and a Strategy of Implementation," *Academy of Management Review,* October 1976, pp. 98–111; Bruce W. Tuckman and Mary Ann C. Jensen, "Stages of Small Group Development Revisited," *Group & Organization Studies,* Vol. 2, 1977, pp. 419–427.
9. Glen M. Parker, *Team Players and Teamwork: The New Competitive Business Strategy* (San Francisco: Jossey-Bass, 1990); Thomas L. Quick, *Successful Team Building* (New York: AMACOM, 1992), pp. 40–52; "Lead or Lay Back? How to Play the Right Role on a Team," *Executive Strategies,* November 1999, p. 2.
10. R. Meredith Belbin, "Team Builder," in *Business: The Ultimate Resource Business* (Cambridge, MA: Perseus Books Group, 2002), p. 966.
11. Based on literature reviews and original material in Michael A. Campion, Ellen M. Papper, and Gina Medsker, "Relations between Work Team Characteristics and Effectiveness: A Replication and Extension," *Personnel Psychology,* Summer 1996, p. 431; Bradley

L. Kirkman and Benson Rosen, "Powering Up Teams," *Organizational Dynamics,* Winter 2000, pp. 48–52; Stanley M. Gulley, Kara A. Incalcaterra, Aparna Joshi, and J. Matthew Beaubien, "A Meta-Analysis of Team Efficacy, Potency, and Performance: Interdependence and Level of Analysis as Moderators of Observed Relationships," *Journal of Applied Psychology,* October 2002, pp. 819–832; Scott W. Lester, Bruce M. Meglino, and M. Audrey Korsgaard, "The Antecedents and Consequences of Group Potency: A Longitudinal Investigation of Newly Formed Work Groups," *The Academy of Management Journal,* April 2002, pp. 352–368; Vanessa Urch Druskat and Steven B. Wolff, "Building the Emotional Intelligence of Groups," *Harvard Business Review,* March 2001, pp. 80–90.

12. Bradley L. Kirkman and Benson Rosen, "Powering Up Teams," *Organizational Dynamics,* Winter 2000, pp. 48–52.

13. Stanley M. Gulley, Kara A. Incalcaterra, Aparna Joshi, and J. Matthew Beaubien, "A Meta-Analysis of Team Efficacy, Potency, and Performance: Interdependence and Level of Analysis as Moderators of Observed Relationships," *Journal of Applied Psychology,* October 2002, pp. 819–832.

14. Priscilla M. Elsass and Laura M. Graves, "Demographic Diversity in Decision-Making Groups: The Experiences of Women and People of Color," *Academy of Management Review,* October 1997, p. 968.

15. Robert T. Keller, "Cross-Functional Project Groups in Research and New Product Development: Diversity, Communications, Job Stress, and Outcomes," *Academy of Management Journal,* June 2001, pp. 547–555.

16. Murray R. Barrick, Greg L. Stewart, Mitchell J. Neubert, and Michael K. Mount, "Relating Member Ability and Personality to Work-Team Processes and Team Effectiveness," *Journal of Applied Psychology,* June 1998, pp. 377–391.

17. Vanessa Urch Druskat and Steven B. Wolff, "Building the Emotional Intelligence of Groups," *Harvard Business Review,* March 2001, pp. 80–90.

18. "Centria's Hybrid Approach Trains Promoted-from-Within Plant Supervisors," *IOMA Report on Training Programs,* January 2003, p. 11.

19. Larry K. Michaelsen, Warren E. Watson, and Robert H. Black, "A Realistic Test of Individual versus Group Decision Making," *Journal of Applied Psychology,* October 1989, pp. 834–839; Leigh Thompson, "Improving the Creativity of Organizational Work Groups," *The Academy of Management Executive,* February 2003, p. 99.

20. William B. Eddy, *The Manager and the Working Group* (New York: Praeger, 1985), pp. 150–151.

21. Andrew J. Van de Ven and André L. Delberq, "The Effectiveness of Nominal, Delphi, and Interacting Group Decision-Making Processes," *Academy of Management Journal,* December 1974, p. 606.

22. The evidence is reviewed in Thompson, "Improving the Creativity of Organizational Work Groups," p. 104.

23. Normal Dalkey, *The Delphi Method: An Experimental Study of Group Opinions* (Santa Monica, CA: Rand Corporation, 1969); Thomson, "Improving the Creativity of Organizational Work Groups," p. 104.

24. Carla Joinson, "Teams at Work," *HR Magazine,* May 1999, p. 32; Jac Fitz-Enz, "Measuring Team Effectiveness," *HRfocus,* August 1997, p. 3.

25. Our discussion is based on Gregory Moorhead and Ricky W. Griffin, *Organizational Behavior: Managing People and Organizations,* 4th ed. (Boston: Houghton Mifflin, 1995), pp. 278–279.

26. Tina L. Robbins, "Social Loafing on Cognitive Tasks: An Examination of the 'Sucker Effect'," *Journal of Business and Psychology,* Spring 1995, pp. 278–279.

27. Irving L. Janis, *Victims of Groupthink: A Study of Foreign Policy Decisions and Fiascoes* (Boston: Houghton Mifflin, 1972), pp. 39–40; Glenn Whyte, "Groupthink Reconsidered," *Academy of Management Review,* January 1989, pp. 40–56.

28. "FCC Pulls the Plug on Phone Slammer," Associated Press syndicated story, April 22, 1998.

29. Research reported in "Avoid 'Groupthink,'" *Manager's Edge,* March 2003, p. 2.

30. Many of the ideas in this section come from Ruth Wagemen, "Critical Success Factors for Creating Superb Self-Managing Teams," *Organizational Dynamics,* Summer 1997, p. 57; "What Makes Teams Work?" *HRfocus* (Special Report on Teams), April 2002, S1, S3–S4; Katzenbach and Smith, "The Discipline of Teams," pp. 118–119; Rebecca Winters, "Extreme Offsites," *Time,* August 9, 1999, pp. 75A–76A; Charlotte Garvey, "Steer Teams with the Right Pay," *HR Magazine,* May 2002, pp. 70–78.

31. Matt Murray, "GE's Immelt Starts Renovations on the House that Jack Built," *The Wall Street Journal,* February 6, 2003, p. A6.

32. Milan Moravec, Odd Jan Johannessen, and Thor A. Hjelmas, "The Well-Managed SMT," *Management Review,* June 1998, p. 58.

33. Valerie Marchant, "Am I Up to This?" *Time,* August 9, 1999, p. 79A.

Chapter 11

Leadership in Organizations

Several years ago Finbar O'Neill, the chief counsel for Hyundai Motor America, was serving as acting chief operating officer while the parent company searched for someone—*anyone*—to lead the struggling brand. A Hyundai dealer recalls that during a dealer's conference in Monterey, California, "Fin got up and asked what direction we thought the company should be going in. We started throwing out suggestions, yelling out advice. Fin called time-out, left the room, came back with an easel with lots of paper on it, and started writing a bunch of things down."

By the meeting's end, O'Neill had recorded 100 suggestions—and was facing a decidedly less angry mob of dealers. "Fin said, 'I can't work on all of these at once, so let's pick the top 10, and that's where I'll start,'" Reilly remembers. "That was Hyundai's defining moment. It was the day that somebody took charge. It's when we got leadership."

A few months after that meeting, Hyundai handed over the reins of its American unit to O'Neill. Using his most lawyerly attributes—disciplined thinking, attention to detail, patience for steady progress—O'Neill began attacking the brand's problems one by one. During the next four years, the CEO led Hyundai through the industry's most unlikely transformation. Hyundai Motor America achieved record sales for an 18-month stretch, and sales in the United States quadrupled. Bright prospects for the future? Hyundai says yes.

OBJECTIVES

After reading and studying this chapter and doing the exercises, you should be able to:

1 Differentiate between leadership and management.

2 Describe key leadership traits, styles, and behaviors.

3 Explain the basics of four different contingency theories of leadership.

4 Present an overview of transformational and charismatic leadership.

5 Explain how 360-degree feedback is used to improve leadership effectiveness.

6 Identify forces that can sometimes decrease the importance of leadership.

Source: Fara Warner, "Finbar O'Neill Is Not a Car Guy," *Fast Company,* November 2002, pp. 84, 86. Permission conveyed through Copyright Clearance Center, Inc.

NOW ASK YOURSELF: In what ways does this inspiring story about "Fin" and Hyundai illustrate a fundamental activity of successful leaders?" Granting group members the opportunity to contribute input to major decisions doesn't seem like too far a stretch from common sense, but many managers squander such occasions. In this chapter we describe a variety of leadership theories and practices. Many of them involve some type of participative decision making. Leadership has always been a topic of major importance to scholars and practitioners, and current interest is intense as organizations struggle to survive in a hyper-competitive world. We turn to a *Fortune* magazine analysis of the 10 most admired companies in the world to sum up our argument: "The truth is that no one factor makes a company admirable, but if you were forced to pick the one that makes the most difference, you'd pick leadership."[1] Executives themselves think that knowledge of leadership is important for organizational success. Samuel J. Palmisano, the CEO of IBM, invested $100 million of company funds into teaching 30,000 employees to lead, rather than control, their staffs so that employees would not feel like cogs in a machine.[2]

Leadership is not just the domain of a few members of top management. Take-charge ability is important at all levels of management. Employees who are in direct contact with customers and clients often require stronger leadership than do higher-level workers. Entry-level workers often lack experience, direction, and a strong work ethic. Furthermore, the current emphasis on teams means that effective team leaders are needed throughout the organization.

The discussion of leadership in this chapter centers on several topics of interest to managers and professionals: leadership traits, styles, and behaviors; contingency theories of leadership; transformational and charismatic leadership; 360-degree feedback for improving leadership effectiveness; and substitutes for leadership. The following chapter deals with other topics closely associated with leaders, such as power and influence. First, however, let us look at the nature of leadership.

THE NATURE OF LEADERSHIP

1

Differentiate between leadership and management.

Leadership involves influencing others to achieve objectives important to them and the organization. With effective leadership, people want to contribute to the organization's success. A representative definition is that **leadership** is the ability to inspire confidence and support among the people on whose competence and commitment performance depends.[3] Although leadership is a major function of management, it is not the same thing *as* management. In the view of John Kotter, management copes with complexity, which requires preserving order and consistency. Leadership, in comparison, copes with change in a competitive, rapidly evolving world. Effective leaders deal with change by formulating a vision of the future and setting a direction for that vision.[4] Leaders are also heavily involved in persuading, inspiring, and motivating others and spearheading useful changes.

Exhibit 11-1 presents a broad view of the difference between leadership and management. The same information provides more insight into the nature of leadership. Effective leadership and management are both required in the modern workplace. Managers must be leaders, but leaders must also be good managers. Workers need to be inspired and persuaded, but they also need assistance in developing and maintaining a smoothly functioning workplace. Another important perspective on leadership is that it contributes to organizational effectiveness. The

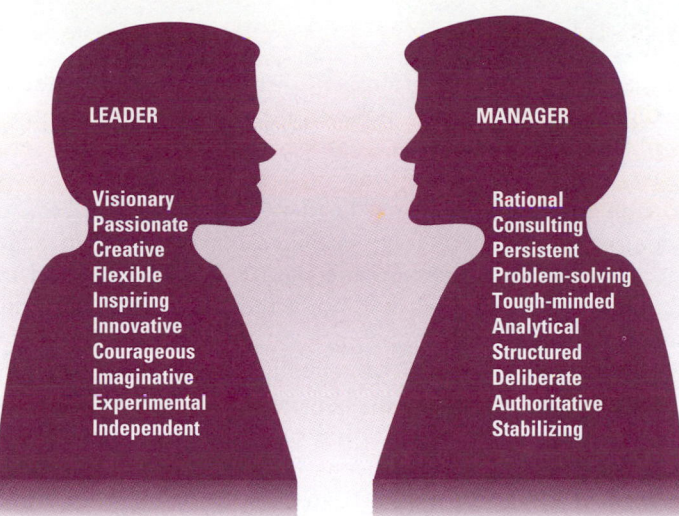

Exhibit 11-1

Leaders versus Managers

223

Source: Genevieve Capowski, "Anatomy of a Leader: Where Are the Leaders of Tomorrow?" *Management Review* (March 1994): 12. Copyright © 1994 American Management Association International. Reprinted by permission of American Management Association International, New York, NY. All rights reserved. http://www. amanet.org.

leaders featured in this chapter are people whose personal attributes help them achieve good results for the organization.

A growing body of evidence supports the common-sense belief that leadership matters. For example, a comprehensive study of many organizations concluded that incompetent managers are responsible for billions of dollars of lost productivity each year.[5] A later study with forty-eight Fortune 500 firms found that the presence of a charismatic leader contributed to a firm's net profit margin, particularly in an uncertain environment.[6] (One explanation for this is that a leader with a strong personality helps people focus on their work.) The argument that leaders do not contribute to organizational effectiveness is presented later.

LEADERSHIP TRAITS AND CHARACTERISTICS

A logical approach to understanding leadership is to study the traits and characteristics of effective leaders. For many years, scholars downplayed the study of leadership characteristics, but an interest in the inner qualities of leaders has reawakened, particularly with respect to ethical qualities and charisma. The traits of leaders relate closely to the degree to which others perceive these people to be leaders. For example, a person who exudes self-confidence would generally be perceived as having leadership qualities (see the video sidebar). Research evidence confirms that effective leaders are different from other people—they have the "right stuff." The differences relate to the traits and characteristics described in this section.[7] The current interest in leadership traits is also reflected in a demand for leaders with vision and charisma.

Hundreds of traits and personal characteristics of leaders have been researched over the years, dating back to the early 1900s. Here we discuss illustrative leadership qualities, under the categories of cognitive skills and personality traits and motives, that research and careful observation support.

2

Describe key leadership traits, styles, and behaviors.

224

Cognitive Skills

An effective leader must have appropriate **cognitive skills,** or mental ability and knowledge. Organizational leaders possess effective problem-solving ability. They anticipate problems before they occur, and persevere until the problems are solved. In the process, they demonstrate imagination, creativity, and a willingness to experiment with unproven methods. Leadership positions place a continuously increasing demand on problem-solving ability. For example, managers are pressured to perform tasks in a shorter time with a smaller staff, and contribute to developing a business strategy that will point the firm in the right direction.

Technical and professional competence, or knowledge of a particular business, is another cognitive requirement for effective leadership. When outsiders are brought into a company to fill senior management positions, they usually need a specialty to complement their leadership and administrative skills. One reason Carly Fiorina was recruited from Lucent Technologies to become the CEO of Hewlett Packard was because of her extensive knowledge of how to provide Internet equipment and services to other businesses. Several years ago GM hired the legendary car developer Bob Lutz to help them design cars with more flair and consumer appeal. Based heavily on his design talent, the expectations were that Lutz would spur the company to take risks to create exciting, popular products that would enhance revenues.[8] In lesser leadership positions, technical competence is important because it is difficult to establish rapport with group members when the leader does not understand the technical details of the work.

Personality Traits

Personality traits and characteristics have an important influence on leadership effectiveness. Which traits and characteristics are the most relevant varies with the situation. For example, enthusiasm may be more important for a sales manager for term life insurance than for an inventory control manager. The sales manager's enthusiasm may be needed to help sales representatives cope with rejection by customers.

A foundation trait for leadership effectiveness is **self-awareness,** insightfully processing feedback about oneself to improve personal effectiveness. Other aspects of self-awareness can be categorized as emotional intelligence, as described in Chapter 2. The leader must be able to benefit from feedback that is sometimes obvious and at other times subtle. For example, a leader might notice a blank stare (a form of nonverbal feedback) while explaining a new initiative to group members. The leader could profitably use this feedback to use another approach to describe the initiative.

A realistic degree of *self-confidence* is frequently associated with leadership effectiveness. A leader who is self-confident without being overbearing instills confidence among group members. The concept of self-confidence is useful in studying leadership because it illustrates the relationship between traits and behavior. A manager who is inwardly self-confident will behave confidently and will be perceived as acting cool under pressure. Projecting self-confidence is especially important when leading an organization or a group out of a crisis, because most people need to rely on a strong person when faced with turmoil. A financial executive observed that a confident boss finds the right balance between micromanaging (looking over every possible detail) versus delegating so much that his or her authority is diluted.[9] The point is that an insecure boss will obsessively check on every detail to avoid mistakes that reflect poorly on his or her leadership. At the other extreme, a leader who lacks confidence in his or her own abilities will overly rely on others to accomplish tasks.

Trustworthiness contributes to leadership effectiveness in most situations. Being perceived as trustworthy involves many different behaviors. At the top of the list, however, are behavioral consistency and integrity. Consistency refers to reliability and predictability, such as when a manager conducts performance evaluations and reimburses for expenses as agreed. Integrity centers around telling the truth and keeping promises.[10] Judy George, the founder of the home furnishings retail chain Domain, makes this comment about trustworthiness: "Running a successful business has a lot to do with integrity, work ethic, treating people fairly and kindly, and being honest in all your dealings."[11] The accompanying Self-Assessment exercise pinpoints the type of behaviors that prompt people to trust a leader.

SELF-ASSESSMENT

Behaviors and Attitudes of a Trustworthy Leader

Listed here are behaviors and attitudes of leaders who are generally trusted by their group members and other constituents. After you read each characteristic, check to the right whether this is a behavior or attitude that you appear to have developed already, or does not fit you at present.

	Fits Me	Does Not Fit Me
1. Tells people he or she is going to do something, and then always follows through and gets it done	❑	❑
2. Described by others as being reliable	❑	❑
3. Good at keeping secrets and confidences	❑	❑
4. Tells the truth consistently	❑	❑
5. Minimizes telling people what they want to hear	❑	❑
6. Described by others as "walking the talk"	❑	❑
7. Delivers consistent messages to others in terms of matching words and deeds	❑	❑
8. Does what he or she expects others to do	❑	❑
9. Minimizes hypocrisy by not engaging in activities he or she tells others are wrong	❑	❑
10. Readily accepts feedback on behavior from others	❑	❑
11. Maintains eye contact with people when talking to them	❑	❑
12. Appears relaxed and confident when explaining his or her side of a story	❑	❑
13. Individualizes compliments to others rather than saying something like "You look great" to a large number of people	❑	❑
14. Doesn't expect lavish perks for himself or herself while expecting others to go on an austerity diet	❑	❑
15. Does not tell others a crisis is pending when it isn't just to gain their cooperation	❑	❑
16. Collaborates with others to make creative decisions	❑	❑
17. Communicates information to people at all organizational levels	❑	❑
18. Readily shares financial information with others	❑	❑
19. Listens to people and then acts on many of their suggestions	❑	❑
20. Generally engages in predictable behavior	❑	❑

Scoring and Interpretation: These statements are mostly for self-reflection, so no specific scoring key exists. However, the more the statements that fit you, the more trustworthy you are—assuming you are answering truthfully. The usefulness of this self-quiz increases if somebody who knows you well answers it for you to supplement your self-perceptions. Your ability and willingness to carry out some of the behaviors specified in this quiz could have an enormous impact on your career because so many business leaders in recent years have not been perceived as trustworthy. Being trustworthy is therefore a career asset.

Emotional intelligence is a major contributor to leadership effectiveness. As described in Chapter 2, the concept refers to managing ourselves and our relationships effectively. A newer conception of emotional intelligence is so broad that it encompasses many traits and behaviors related to leadership effectiveness, including self-confidence, empathy, and visionary leadership.[12] Passion for the work and the people is a particularly important aspect of emotional intelligence for leadership effectiveness. It is difficult to inspire others if you are not passionate about your major work activities.

Continuing research into emotional intelligence suggests another reason for its contribution to effective leadership. When a company faces a sudden crisis, how leaders handle their emotions can determine whether the company survives. The emotionally intelligent leader is able to articulate a group's shared yet unexpressed feelings, and develop a mission that inspires others. An example of a sudden crisis facing a company would be if it did not win a major government contract that could ensure its short-term survival.[13] A leader would talk about the grief the group was feeling and then point toward other areas of profitable activity for the group.

Many leaders have failed because of glaring deficits in emotional intelligence. When Frank Lorenzo took over Eastern Air Lines (which he later led into bankruptcy), the animosity that developed between him and union bosses grew so great that it hastened the airline's demise. Leona Helmsley played evil stepmother to all the employees of her real estate mogul husband. She fired employees at whim (one for taking an apple while she worked through lunch). Eventually Helmsley was convicted of tax evasion and sent to prison.[14]

More evidence for the contribution of personality to leadership effectiveness stems from research with the Five Factor Model of personality, combining the results of seventy-three samples. The four factors with the highest correlations with leadership effectiveness were neuroticism (lower was better), extraversion, openness, and conscientiousness. Extraversion was related to leadership effectiveness most consistently across different studies and different criteria of leadership effectiveness. When the five factors were combined, the relationship with leadership effectiveness was quite high (a correlation coefficient of .48).[15] Therefore, personality does matter for leadership, at least to some degree.

Motives

The power and achievement motives, described in Chapter 6, are closely associated with leadership effectiveness. A strong power motive propels the leader to be interested in influencing others. When a power motive is too intense, it can manifest itself in ruthless leadership behavior. The two leaders just cited for having low emotional intelligence fit here.

A need for achievement often facilitates leadership effectiveness. As a leader, a person with a strong need for achievement will typically have a strong sense of time urgency, which can be a positive force for innovation.[16] For example, a leader desiring to be the first mover on a product exhibits this sense of urgency.

Even if one understands the dispositions of the leader, however, the situation in which the leader functions is also enormously important. Consultant Larraine Segil explains: "My research revealed that you can be a wonderful manager or leader, but if you have an organization that doesn't support or enable you, you're either going to leave the company or put on the cloaks and clothes of a non-dynamic leader to protect your position."[17]

LEADERSHIP BEHAVIORS AND STYLES

After the trait approach comes a focus on the activities carried out by leaders to enhance productivity and morale. The **behavioral approach to leadership** attempts to specify how the behavior of effective leaders differs from their less effective counterparts. The behavioral approach assumes that leaders are relatively consistent in how they attempt to influence group members in different situations. A key concept here is **leadership style,** which is the relatively consistent pattern of behavior that characterizes a leader. Much of this consistency occurs because a leadership style is based somewhat on an individual's personality. Despite this consistency, some managers can modify their style as the situation requires.

Our presentation of leadership styles and behaviors consists of three parts: the pioneering Ohio State University and University of Michigan studies, the Leadership Grid, and the leader–member exchange model. Before reading ahead, assess your leadership style in the Self-Assessment that follows.

SELF-ASSESSMENT

What Style of Leader Are You or Would You Be?

Directions: Answer the following questions, keeping in mind what you have done, or think you would do, in the scenarios and attitudes described.

	Mostly Ture	Mostly False
1. I am more likely to take care of a high-impact assignment myself than turn it over to a group member.	❏	❏
2. I would prefer the analytical aspects of a manager's job rather than working directly with group members.	❏	❏
3. An important part of my approach to managing a group is to keep the members informed almost daily of any information that could affect their work.	❏	❏
4. It's a good idea to give two people in the group the same problem, and then choose what appears to be the best solution.	❏	❏
5. It makes good sense for a leader or manager to stay somewhat aloof from a group, so her or she can make a tough decision when necessary.	❏	❏
6. I look for opportunities to obtain group input before making a decision, even on straightforward issues.	❏	❏
7. I would reverse a decision if several of the group members presented evidence that I was wrong.	❏	❏
8. Differences of opinion in the work group are healthy.	❏	❏
9. I think that activities to build team spirit, like a team fixing up a poor family's house on a Saturday, are an excellent investment of time.	❏	❏
10. If my group were hiring a new member, I would like the person to be interviewed by the entire group.	❏	❏
11. An effective team leader today uses e-mail for about 98 percent of communication with team members.	❏	❏
12. Some of the best ideas are likely to come from the group members rather than the manager.	❏	❏
13. If our group were going to have a banquet, I would get input from each member on what type of food should be served.	❏	❏

(continued)

SELF-ASSESSMENT

(continued)

14. I have never seen a statue of a committee in a museum or park, so why bother making decisions by a committee if you want to be recognized?   ❑   ❑
15. I dislike it intensely when a group member challenges my position on an issue.   ❑   ❑
16. I typically explain to group members how (which method) they should accomplish an assigned task.   ❑   ❑
17. If I were out of the office for a week, most of the important work in the department would get accomplished anyway.   ❑   ❑
18. Delegation of important tasks is something that would be (or is) very difficult for me.   ❑   ❑
19. When a group member comes to me with a problem, I tend to jump right in with a proposed solution.   ❑   ❑
20. When a group member comes to me with a problem, I typically ask that person something like, "What alternative solutions have you thought of so far?"   ❑   ❑

Scoring and Interpretation: The answers in the participative/team-style leader direction are as follows:

1.	Mostly False	8.	Mostly True	15.	Mostly False
2.	Mostly False	9.	Mostly True	16.	Mostly False
3.	Mostly True	10.	Mostly True	17.	Mostly True
4.	Mostly False	11.	Mostly False	18.	Mostly False
5.	Mostly False	12.	Mostly True	19.	Mostly False
6.	Mostly True	13.	Mostly True	20.	Mostly True
7.	Mostly True	14.	Mostly False		

If your score is 15 or higher, you are most likely (or would be) a participative leader. If your score is 5 or lower, you are most likely (or would be) an authoritarian leader.

Skill Development: The quiz you just completed is also an opportunity for skill development. Review the twenty questions and look for implied suggestions for engaging in participative leadership. For example, question 20 suggests that you encourage group members to work through their own solutions to problems. If your goal is to become an authoritarian leader, the questions can also serve as useful guidelines. For example, question 19 suggests that an authoritarian leader looks first to solve problems for group members.

Pioneering Studies on Leadership Dimensions

Much of the theory underlying leadership styles can be traced back to studies conducted at Ohio State University and the University of Michigan beginning in the late 1940s. A major output of the Ohio State studies was the emphasis placed on two leadership dimensions, initiating structure and consideration.

Initiating structure describes the degree to which the leader establishes structure for group members. Structure is initiated by activities such as assigning specific tasks, specifying procedures to be followed, scheduling work, and clarifying expectations. **Consideration** describes the degree to which the leader creates an environment of emotional support, warmth, friendliness, and trust. He or she does so by engaging in such behaviors as being friendly and approachable, looking out for the personal welfare of the group, keeping the group informed of new developments, and doing small favors for group members.[18] Exhibit 11-2 shows how leadership style can be based on a combination of these two key dimensions.

Exhibit 11-2

Leadership Styles Based on a Combination of Initiating Structure and Consideration

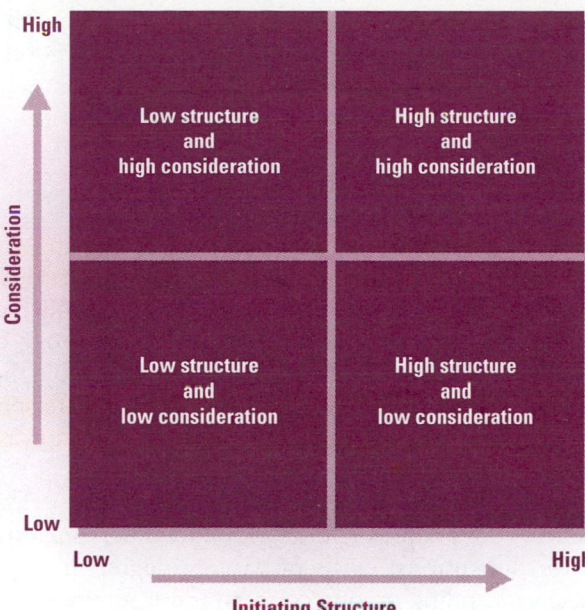

Many of the Ohio State studies were conducted with first-level supervisors and therefore may not apply well to executive leadership. It was discovered that employee turnover was lowest and job satisfaction highest under leaders who were rated highest in consideration. Research also indicated that leaders high on initiating structure were generally rated highly by superiors and had higher producing work groups.

Researchers at the University of Michigan also investigated the differences in results obtained by production-centered and employee-centered managers (about the same idea as initiating structure versus consideration). Production-centered managers set tight work standards, organized tasks carefully, prescribed the work methods to be followed, and supervised closely. Employee-centered managers encouraged group members to participate in goal setting and other work decisions, and helped to ensure high performance by engendering trust and mutual respect.

A dominant finding of the Michigan studies was that the most productive work groups tended to have leaders who were employee centered rather than production centered. Also, the most effective leaders were those who had supportive relationships with group members. They also tended to use group rather than individual decision making and encouraged subordinates to set and achieve high performance goals. Despite this dominant finding, exceptions were found. A study conducted with 20,000 employees at a heavy-equipment manufacturer indicated that supervisors with the best production records were both production and employee centered.[19]

In practice, effective leaders exhibit a wide range of behaviors in addition to the key behaviors mentioned here. The behaviors associated with trustworthiness are relevant here. Another example is the leader's ability to manage polarities, or extremes of positions and interests. Philosopher Peter Koestenbaum believes that the central leadership attribute is the ability to manage polarity. In every aspect of life, these polarities are inevitable. Questions regarding on-the-job polarities include: "How can I invest myself heavily in both family and career?" "Am I a boss or a friend?" "How do I reconcile my own needs for glory with those of the team?", and "How do I cut costs drastically yet not lay off good employees?" Koestenbaum believes that how a leader manages polarity separates greatness from mediocrity.[20]

The Leadership Grid®

The **Leadership Grid®** is a framework for classifying leadership styles that simultaneously examines a leader's concerns for task accomplishment and people. With roots in the Ohio State leadership dimensions, the Grid is the nucleus of a system of leadership training and organization development. No history of the formal study of leadership is complete without some mention of the Grid. The Leadership Grid describes leadership style in terms of concerns for production and people. The concerns reflect attitudes rather than actual behavior. However, attitudes *often* translate into behavior.

Concern for production includes results, the bottom line, performance, profits, and mission. Concern for people includes group members and coworkers. Each of these concerns (or dimensions) exists in varying degrees along a continuum from 1 to 9. A manager's standing on one concern is not supposed to influence his or her standing on the other.

According to the Grid, a 9,9 style (team management) is the best because it leads to such positive consequences as high productivity, satisfaction, and creativity. The 9,9 style has built-in flexibility, rather than a "one size fits all" philosophy. With it, the manager can evaluate a situation and then use principles of human behavior to handle problems.[21]

The Leader–Member Exchange Model

The behavioral models presented so far assume that the leader relates in approximately the same manner toward all group members. George Graen and his associates have developed a leadership model that challenges the reality of such consistency in behavior. The **leader–member exchange model (LMX)** recognizes that leaders develop unique working relationships with each group member.[22] A leader might be considerate and compassionate toward one team member yet rigid and unfeeling toward another.

Each relationship between the leader/manager differs in quality. One subset of employees, the in-group, is given additional rewards, responsibility, and trust in exchange for their loyalty and performance. In contrast, another subset of employees (the out-group) is treated in accordance with a more formal understanding of the supervisor–subordinate relations. The leader's first impression of a group member's competency heavily influences where he or she becomes a member of the in-group or out-group.

In-group members have attitudes and values similar to the leader and interact frequently with the leader. Out-group members have less in common with the leader and operate somewhat detached from the leader. The one-to-one relationships have a major influence on the subordinate's behavior in the group. Members of the in-group become part of a smoothly functioning team headed by the formal leader. Out-group members are less likely to experience good teamwork.

Interest in the leader–member exchange model has intensified in recent years, with many field studies conducted. A contributing factor the stream of research about LMX is that it is sensible: The quality of your relationship with your manager has a big impact on your job behavior and performance. Here we highlight research findings with the most direct implications for organizational behavior:

1. Being a member of the in-group facilitates achieving high productivity and satisfaction. Out-group members receive less challenging assignments and are more likely to quit because of job dissatisfaction.[23]

2. High-quality leader–member exchanges lead to more effective delegation, in addition to higher productivity and satisfaction. The study in question showed that the quality of exchanges from the standpoints of both supervisors and group members were associated with improved delegation, which in turn enhanced performance and satisfaction.[24]

3. Despite the many consequences of positive leader–member exchanges, most supervisors are not overly influenced by them in making performance appraisals. Supervisors may have their "pets," but research has shown that supervisors can overcome these biases to make objective performance appraisals.[25]

4. The disability status of group members can have an effect on leader–member exchange relationships, according to an organizational simulation and a field study with 41 supervisors and 220 subordinates. Ingratiation (using techniques to make somebody like you) was more effective in developing a positive leader–member exchange for persons with a physical disability. The study also demonstrated that when subordinates with disabilities did not make much use of ingratiation, they received lower LMX ratings, suggesting negative bias against disabilities.[26]

5. A study conducted with 146 supervisor–subordinate pairs in a hospital laboratory suggested that the link between LMX and performance, as measured by supervisory ratings, is strongest when job conflict is low, task ambiguity is high, and intrinsic job satisfaction is high.[27]

An important implication of the leader–member exchange is that the quality of the relationship between the leader/manager and each group member has important job consequences. Favorable exchanges can lead to such important effects as higher productivity and satisfaction, improved motivation, and smoother delegation.

Before focusing our attention on several precise theories of leadership, the Organizational Behavior in Action box offers some wisdom from experienced leaders about effective behavior in dealing with group members.

CONTINGENCY THEORIES OF LEADERSHIP

The behavioral theories of leadership provide general guidelines for leadership effectiveness, emphasizing both production and people. After development of behavioral theories came an attempt to specify the conditions under which various leadership styles would lead to the best results. The intent was to make explanations of leadership precise and scientific. According to **contingency theory of leadership,** the best style of leadership depends on factors relating to group members and the work setting. A major contingency factor, for example, involves the needs of the group.[28] For example, a leader might want to push ahead immediately with the implementation of a new technology, but if the group needs more training before implementation, the leader must first help the group develop the necessary skills. Here we present four contingency theories, or explanations, of leadership: Fiedler's contingency theory, the path-goal theory, the situational leadership model, and the normative decision model.

3

Explain the basics of four different contingency theories of leadership.

Organizational Behavior *in Action*

Practical Advice from Acknowledged Leaders

The editors of *Success* magazine asked a group of acknowledged leaders what they advise others. A few words of their wisdom from members of the group interviewed or researched follows:

Scott McNealy, CEO of Sun Microsystems. Rise and shine. "I leave the vision thing to the gurus and scientists. Fundamentally, the CEO's job is to figure out what the vision is, not necessarily to create it."

Oprah Winfrey, CEO of Harpo Media. Be O-Positive. "The power to maintain a positive attitude is the key to success."

Lee Iacocca, formerly of Chrysler Corp., now head of E-Bike. Be a big-time wheeler-dealer. "Surround yourself with good people, especially if you're the leader of a small company. Never go it alone."

Andrea Jung, CEO and president of Avon. Get the best advice. "Seek advice from the best leaders available to you. When in doubt, ask for some advice from your key team members. You never know. It may just lead you to greatness."

Bob McDonald, founder of the training and development company The Highlands Program. Know thyself—and your people. "Great leaders find out what their own natural talents are and use them. They stop worrying about what they are not naturally gifted at doing and focus their energy where they will have the greatest impact."

Source: "How You Can Be a Great Leader," *Success,* April 2001, pp. 28–35.

Fiedler's Contingency Theory of Leadership

Fred E. Fiedler developed an elaborate contingency model, which holds that the best style of leadership is determined by the leader's work situation. Although historically important, research and managerial training related to Fiedler's contingency theory have diminished substantially in recent years. Fiedler's model specifies the conditions under which leaders should use task- and relationship-motivated styles.[29] (Observe again the two key leadership dimensions of initiating structure and consideration.) To implement Fiedler's theory, leadership style and the situation are measured through questionnaires.

Fiedler measures the leader's style by means of the least-preferred coworker scale (LPC). Whether the leader is primarily task or relationship motivated is measured by how favorably the leader describes his or her least-preferred coworker. The LPC is defined as the past coworker with whom he or she would least like to work. Ratings of coworkers are made on a scale of polar-opposite adjectives such as pleasant versus "unpleasant." The logic is that people who describe their least-preferred coworker in relatively positive terms are relationship oriented. In contrast, people who describe their least-preferred coworker in very negative terms are task oriented.

Situational control is the degree to which the leader can control and influence the outcomes of group effort. Measurements of situational control (or favorableness to the leader) are based on three factors, listed in order of importance:

1. *Leader–member relations.* The extent to which group members accept and support their leader.
2. *Task structure.* The extent to which the leader knows exactly what to do, and how well and in what detail the tasks to be completed are defined.
3. *Position power.* The extent to which the organization provides the leader with: (a) the means of rewarding and punishing group members, and (b) appropriate formal authority to get the job done.

Numerous studies have investigated the relationship among leadership-style situational control by the leader and leadership effectiveness. Exhibit 11-3 summarizes the major findings of these studies with over 800 groups in various settings. The task-motivated style generally produces the best results when the leader has very high or very low control of the situation. The relationship-motivated style is best when the situation is under moderate or intermediate control.

A practical implication of Fielder's theory would be for the leader to understand how to make the situation more favorable by: (a) improving relationships with group members, (b) enhancing task structure by providing more guidelines and instructions, and (c) requesting more position power from the organization.

The Path–Goal Theory of Leadership

The path–goal theory of leadership specifies what the leader must do to achieve high morale and productivity in a given situation.[30] Path–goal refers to a focus on helping employees find the correct path to goal attainment. Exhibit 11-4 presents a model of the theory. It indicates that the leader should choose the right leadership style to match the contingency factors in order to achieve results.

An important contribution of the path–goal theory is that it both specifies what leaders need to do in different situations and explains the reasoning behind such behavior. The key propositions relate to motivation, satisfaction, and performance. (Path–goal theory is based on the expectancy theory of motivation.)

1. Leaders perform a motivational function by increasing personal payoffs (rewards) to group members for achieving work objectives and making the path to payoffs smoother. Clarifying the path, reducing roadblocks and pitfalls, and increasing opportunities for satisfaction on the way to the goal are behaviors that make the path smoother.
2. When group members perceive that clear paths to work goals exist, they will be motivated because they will be more certain of how to reach the goals.
3. Attempts by the leader to clarify path–goal relationships will be seen as redundant by group members if the work system already carefully defines the path to the goal. Under these conditions, control may increase performance, but it will also decrease satisfaction.

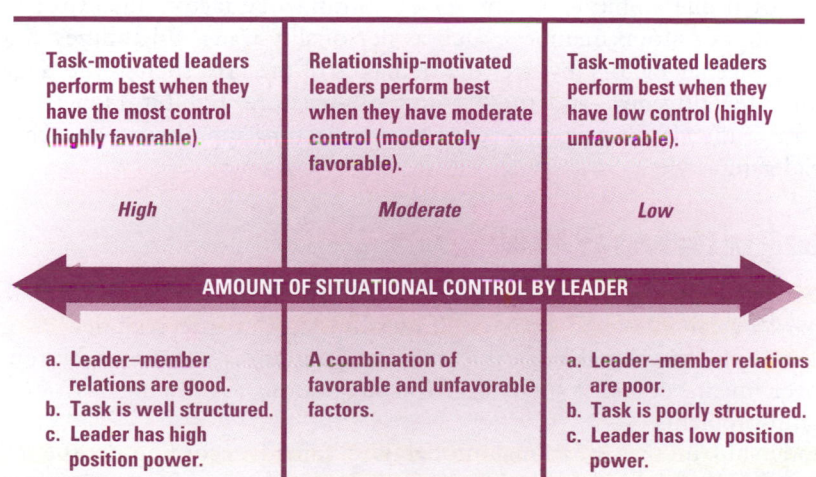

Exhibit 11-3

Summary of Findings from Fiedler's Contingency Theory

233

Exhibit 11-4

The Path–Goal Theory of Leadership

The leader chooses the right leadership style to match the contingency factors in order to achieve outcomes.

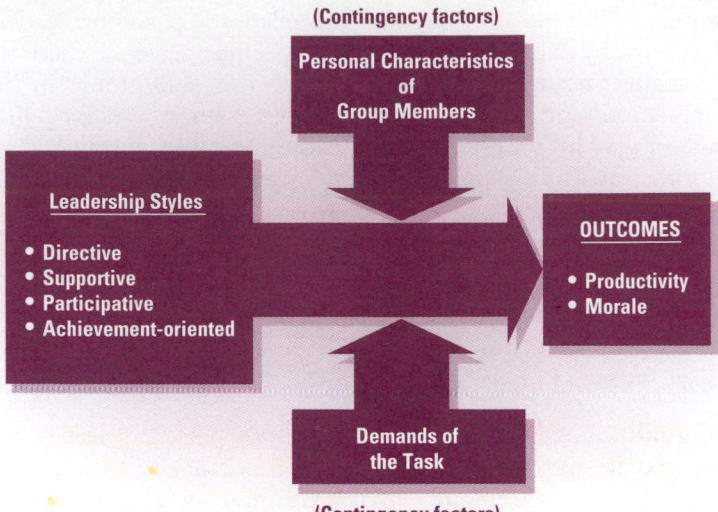

According to path–goal theory, the leader needs to consider choosing among four different leadership styles to handle the contingency demands of a given situation. *Directive leadership* involves initiating structure, setting guidelines on standards, and conveying expectations. *Supportive leadership* emphasizes showing concern for the well-being of group members and developing mutually satisfying relationships.

Participative leadership involves consulting with group members to solicit their suggestions and then using this input for decision making. As mentioned at the outset of the chapter participative leadership fits the modern organization with its emphasis on teamwork. Michael Useem formulates participative leadership as *trickle-up leadership* because the process emphasizes group members advising the leaders. As technology continues to change and organizations decentralize, workers on the front line have more independence and responsibility. Consequently, these workers have valuable inputs for leaders.[31] In *achievement-oriented leadership,* the leader sets challenging goals, promotes work improvement, sets high expectations, and expects group members to assume responsibility.

Each of these leadership styles works well in some situations but not in others. As shown in Exhibit 11-4, one set of contingency factors involves personal characteristics of group members, such as personality traits and abilities. Another set of contingency factors involves the demands of the task, such as the degree of ambiguity, repetitiveness, and the amount of structure. Exhibit 11-5 presents a statement of the circumstances, or contingency factors, appropriate to each of the four leadership styles.

The Situational Leadership® Model

The **Situational Leadership®** **model** of Paul Hersey and Kenneth H. Blanchard explains how to match a leadership style to the readiness of group members.[32] The situational leadership training program is widely used in business and government because it offers practical suggestions for dealing with everyday leadership problems.

Leadership in the situational model is classified according to the relative amount of task and relationship behavior the leader engages in (quite similar to

Leadership Style	Situation in which Appropriate
Directive	Positively affects satisfaction and expectancies of subordinates working on ambiguous tasks.
	Negatively affects satisfaction and expectancies of subordinates working on clearly defined tasks.
Supportive	Positively affects satisfaction of subordinates working on dissatisfying, stressful, or frustrating tasks.
Participative	Positively affects satisfaction of subordinates who are ego-involved with nonrepetitive tasks.
Achievement-oriented	Positively affects confidence that effort will lead to effective performance of subordinates working on ambiguous and nonrepetitive tasks.

Exhibit 11-5

Contingency Relationships in Path–Goal Leadership

235

initiating structure and consideration). Task behavior is the extent to which the leader spells out the duties and responsibilities of the individual or group. Relationship behavior is the extent to which the leader engages in two–way or multi–way communication. It includes such activities as listening, providing encouragement, and coaching. As Exhibit 11-6 shows, the situational model places combinations of task and relationship behaviors into four quadrants. Each quadrant calls for a different leadership style.

The Situational Leadership model states that there is no one best way to influence group members. The most effective leadership style depends on the readiness level of group members. **Readiness** in situational leadership is defined as the extent to which a group member has the ability and willingness or confidence to accomplish a specific task. The concept of readiness is therefore not a characteristic, trait, or motive; it relates to a specific task.

Readiness has two components—ability and willingness. Ability is the knowledge, experience, and skill an individual or a group brings to a particular task or activity. Willingness is the extent to which an individual or group has the confidence, commitment, and motivation to accomplish a specific task.

The key point of the Situational Leadership model is that as a group member's readiness increases, a leader should rely more on relationship behavior and less on task behavior. As a person becomes more skilled, he or she needs less direction about the job, but motivation and encouragement might still be important. When a group member becomes very ready (or self-sufficient), a minimum of task or relationship behavior is required by the leader. Notice that at the readiness condition R4 (as shown in Exhibit 11-6), the group member is able and willing or confident. The manager therefore uses a delegating leadership style (quadrant 4). He or she turns over responsibility for decisions and implementation.

The situational model represents a consensus about leadership behavior in relation to group members: Competent people require fewer specific directives than less competent people. The situational model is also appealing because it supports common sense. You can benefit from the model by attempting to diagnose the readiness of group members before choosing the right leadership style.

Nevertheless, the model presents categories and guidelines so precisely that it gives the impression of infallibility. In reality, leadership situations are less clear-cut than the four quadrants suggest. Also, the prescriptions for leadership will work only some of the time. For example, many supervisors use a telling style with unable and unwilling or insecure team members (R1) and still achieve poor results.

Exhibit 11-6

The Situational Leadership Model

The Situational Leadership Model offers precise guidelines for supervising group members, depending on their readiness.

236

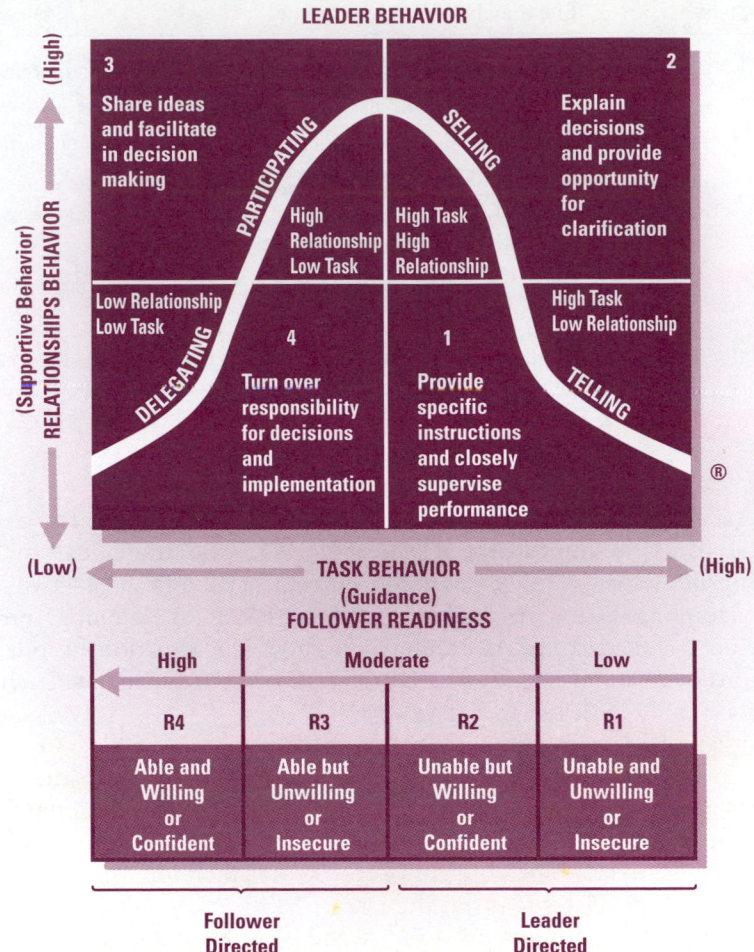

P. Hersey, K. Blanchard, and D. E. Johnson, *Management and Organizational Behavior: Leading Human Resources*, 8th ed. (Upper Saddle River, NJ: Prentice Hall, 2001), 182. Situational Leadership® is a registered trademark of the Center for Leadership Studies. Reprinted with the permission of the Center for Leadership Studies, Escondido, CA 92025. All rights reserved.

The Normative Decision Model

Another contingency viewpoint is that leaders must choose a style that elicits the correct degree of group participation when making decisions. Given that much of a leader's interactions with group members involves decision making, this perspective is sensible. The **normative decision model** views leadership as a decision-making process in which the leader examines certain factors within the situation to determine which decision-making style will be the most effective. Here we present the latest version of the model that Victor Vroom and his associates have been building upon for 30 years, based on research with over 100,000 managers.[33]

The normative model (formerly known as the leader-participation model) identifies five decision-making styles, each reflecting a different degree of participation by group members:

Decide. The leader makes the decision alone and either announces or sells it to the group. The leader might use expertise in collecting information from the group or others who appear to have information relevant to the problem.

Consult (Individually). The leader presents the problem to group members individually, gathers their suggestions, and then makes the decision.

Consult (Group). The leader presents the problem to group members in a meeting, gathers their suggestions, and then makes the decision.

Facilitate. The leader presents the problem, then acts as a facilitator, defining the problem to be solved and the boundaries in which the decision must be made. The leader wants concurrence and avoids having his or her ideas receive more weight based on position power.

Delegate. The leader permits the group to make the decision within prescribed limits. Although the leader does not directly intervene in the group's deliberations unless explicitly asked, he or she works behind the scenes, providing resources and encouragement.

The leader diagnoses the situation in terms of seven variables. Based on answers to those variables, the leader/manager follows the path through decision matrices to choose one of the five decision-making styles. The model includes two versions: one when time is critical and one when a more important consideration is the development of the decision-making capabilities of group members. Exhibit 11-7 depicts the matrix for time-driven group problems, a situation in which a decision must be reached rapidly. The situational factors, or problem attributes, are listed at the top of the matrix. Specifying the situational factors makes the model a contingency approach. The decision-making style chosen depends on these factors:

Decision Significance. The significance of the decision to the success of the project or the organization.

Importance of Commitment. The importance of team members' commitment to the decision.

Leader's Expertise. Your knowledge or expertise in relation to the problem.

Likelihood of Commitment. The likelihood that the team would commit itself to a decision that you might make on your own.

Group Support for Objectives. The degree to which the team supports the organization's objectives at stake in the problem.

Group Expertise. Team members' knowledge or expertise in relation to the problem.

Team Competence: The ability of the team members to work together in solving problems.

Accurate answers to these seven situational factors are not always easy to obtain. The leader may have to rely heavily on intuition and minimize distorted thinking; for example, in believing he or she has expertise when it might be lacking.

To use the model, the decision maker begins at the left side of the matrix, at "Problem Statement." At the top of the matrix are seven situational factors, each of which may be present (H for high) or absent (L for low) for that problem. You begin by ascertaining if the decision is significant. If so, you select H and answer the second question, concerning the importance of gaining group commitment. If you continue the process without crossing any horizontal line on the matrix, you will arrive at one of the five recommended decision styles. Sometimes a conclusive determination can be made based on two factors, such as L, L. Others require three (L, H, H), four (H, H, H, H), or as many as seven factors (such as H, H, L, L, H, H, H). Different people giving different answers to the situational factors will arrive at different conclusions about the recommended decision style in the situation.

Exhibit 11-7

The Time-Driven Model

Source: Victor H. Vroom's Time-Driven Model reproduced from *A Model of Leadership Style*, copyright 1998.

Instructions: The matrix operates like a funnel. You start at the left with a specific decision problem in mind. The column headings denote situational factors that may or may not be present in the problem. You progress by selecting High or Low (H or L) for each relevant situational factor. Proceed down from the funnel, judging only those situational factors for which a judgment is called for, until you reach the recommended process.

Problem Statement	Decision Significance	Importance of Commitment	Leader Expertise	Likelihood of Commitment	Group Support	Group Expertise	Team Competence	
	H	H	H	H	–	–	–	Decide
				L	H	H	H	Delegate
							L	Consult (Group)
						L	–	Consult (Group)
					L	–	–	Consult (Group)
			L	H	H	H	H	Facilitate
							L	Consult (Individually)
						L	–	Consult (Individually)
					L	–	–	Consult (Individually)
				L	H	H	H	Facilitate
							L	Consult (Group)
						L	–	Consult (Group)
					L	–	–	Consult (Group)
		L	H	–	–	–	–	Decide
			L	–	H	H	H	Facilitate
							L	Consult (Individually)
						L	–	Consult (Individually)
					L	–	–	Consult (Individually)
	L	H	–	H	–	–	–	Decide
				L	–	–	H	Delegate
							L	Facilitate
		L	–	–	–	–	–	Decide

To help you apply the model, the following Skill–Development Exercise presents a scenario developed by Vroom, along with the suggested answer or path.

The normative model provides a valuable service to practicing managers and leaders. It prompts them to ask questions about important contingency variables in decision-making situations. For previous versions of the model, managers who follow its procedures are likely to increase their decision-making effectiveness. Furthermore, managers who make decisions consistent with the model (again, based on previous versions) are more likely to be perceived as effective managers.[34] These same good results are probable for Vroom's new model.

When the leader concludes that group decision making is appropriate, morale will often be elevated. Lois Juliber, a Colgate-Palmolive executive, implemented a program of encouraging people throughout the organization to make decisions. She noted:

SKILL-DEVELOPMENT EXERCISE

Applying the Time-Driven Model

Setting: Auto Parts Manufacturer
Your Position: County Manager

Your firm has just acquired a small manufacturer of spare auto parts in Southeast Asia. A recent collapse of the economies in the region made values very attractive. Your senior management decided to acquire a foothold in this region. It was less interested in the particular acquired firm, which produces parts for the local market, than it was in using it as a base from which to produce parts at reduced cost for the worldwide market.

When you arrived at your new assignment two weeks ago, you were somewhat surprised by the less than enthusiastic reception that you received from the current management. You attribute the obvious strain in working relations not only to linguistic and cultural differences but also to a deep-seated resentment to their new foreign owners. Your top management team

members seem to get along very well with one another, but the atmosphere changes when you step into the room.

Nonetheless, you will need their help in navigating your way through this unfamiliar environment. Your immediate need is to develop a plan for land acquisition on which to construct new manufacturing and warehouse facilities. You and your administrative assistant, who accompanied you from your previous assignment, should be able to carry out the plan, but its development would be hazardous without local knowledge.

How much should you involve the team in developing the plan about constructing new manufacturing and warehouse facilities?

Source: Victor H. Vroom, "Leadership and the Decision-Making Process," *Organizational Dynamics*, Spring 2000, p. 90. (Question added.)

All of a sudden, people got the sense that they could really make a decision, and no one was going to second-guess them. And for morale, that was just fantastic. Second-guessing is the absolute paralyzer of an organization, and not what you do in a turnaround, when you need speed.[35]

TRANSFORMATIONAL AND CHARISMATIC LEADERSHIP

4

Present an overview of transformational and charismatic leadership.

In recent years, considerable attention has been paid to the type of leader who goes beyond merely conducting transactions with people, such as rewarding and disciplining them. The **transformational leader** is one who helps organizations and people make positive changes in the way they conduct their activities. Transformational leadership is closely linked to strategic leadership, which provides direction and inspiration to an organization (see the InfoTrac sidebar). However, the emphasis in transformational leadership is on sweeping, positive changes. A major contributing factor to transformational leadership is **charisma,** the ability to lead others based on personal charm, magnetism, inspiration, and emotion. The study of transformational leadership and charismatic leadership is based on trait theory, because the focus of analysis is the leader's personal characteristics.

Transformational Leadership

James McGregor Burns originated the idea of transformational leadership, stating that it occurs when one or more persons engage with others in such a way that leaders and followers raise one another to higher levels of motivation and morality. The purposes of leaders and followers become fused, and the power bases are linked as mutual support for a common purpose.[36] In its pure form, transformational leadership is moral and uplifting, and is concerned with engaging the hearts

Log on to InfoTrac College Edition at **http://www .infotrac-college.com**; using the PowerTrac search tool, enter the journal name "Vital Speeches." (**Vital Speeches** provides a record of the important addresses of recognized leaders of public opinion.) Choose one or two speeches to sample. Select a speech given by a favorite public figure or peruse speeches recently given on a topic of concern to you. Look for particular ways in which the speakers attempt to transform their audiences. For example, if the speaker asks an audience to transcend self-interest, for what purpose is the appeal made? Make a list of salient examples.

and minds of many people. The responsibility for leadership is thereby shared with many people. A recent study supports the idea that a leader with good moral reasoning is more likely to be perceived as transformational by group members. Managers with the highest moral reasoning scores on a questionnaire exhibited more transformational leadership behaviors than leaders with lower scores, as rated by subordinates on a questionnaire about transformational leadership.[37]

The transformational leader exerts a higher level of influence than does a transactional (routine) leader, and thereby motivates people to do more than expected. Transformational leadership is key to revitalizing large organizations of many types. A transformational leader can develop new visions for a firm and mobilize employees to accept and work toward attaining these visions. Transformations take place in one or more of the following ways:

1. By raising people's level of consciousness about the importance and value of designated rewards and ways to achieve them.
2. By getting people to transcend their self-interests for the sake of the work group and the firm.
3. By raising people's focus on minor satisfactions to a quest for self-fulfillment. At the same time, group members are encouraged to seek satisfaction of higher-level needs.
4. By helping workers to adopt a long-range, broad perspective and focus less on day-by-day concerns.
5. By helping people understand the need for change. The transformational leader must help group members understand the need for change both emotionally and intellectually. A transformational leader recognizes this emotional component to resisting change and deals with it openly.
6. By investing managers with a sense of urgency. If managers throughout the organization do not perceive a vital need for change, the leader's vision will not be realized.
7. By committing to greatness. Greatness encompasses striving for business effectiveness such as profits and high stock value, as well as impeccable ethics.[38]

Several different concepts of the characteristics and qualities of transformational leaders have been developed. An analysis of the components of transformational leaders was based on 1,440 subordinates who assessed the leadership behavior of 695 branch managers in a large Australian financial institution.[39] As summarized in Exhibit 11-8, the results are useful because they reinforce other understandings of transformational leadership. The statements accompanying each leadership dimension are essentially behavioral descriptions as expressed in survey statements about transformational leadership. For example, empowerment is operationally defined as "My manager fosters trust, involvement, and cooperation among team members."

Few leaders can qualify as meeting all the behavioral and moral criteria of transformational leadership, yet if we focus on achieving a business turnaround while still treating workers humanely, many executives qualify. One example is Mike S. Zafirovski, the chief operating officer of Motorola Inc. who revitalized their cell phone unit. Under his direction, Motorola's flagship cellular-telephone business was uplifted from losing money in 2001 to a nearly seven percent margin within eight months. The Motorola CEO said, "Mike Z's leadership style is the best I've seen at energizing a broad-based organization while driving it to make the tough but right decisions."[40]

1. **Vision**
   Communicates a clear and positive vision of the future
2. **Staff Development**
   Treats staff as individuals; supports and encourages their development
3. **Supportive leadership**
   Gives encouragement and recognition to staff
4. **Empowerment**
   Fosters trust, involvement, and cooperation among team members
5. **Innovative Thinking**
   Encourages thinking about problems in new ways and questions assumptions

6. **Lead by Example**
   Is clear about his or her values, and practices what he or she preaches
7. **Charisma**
   Instills pride and respect in others and inspires me by being highly competent

Source: Sally A. Carless, Alexander J. Wearing, and Leon Mann, "A Short Measure of Transformational Leadership," *Journal of Business and Psychology,* Spring 2000, p. 396.

Exhibit 11-8

Dimensions and Corresponding Behaviors of Transformational Leadership

Turnarounds of the type engineered by "Mike Z" reflect the actions of a transformational leader. Some turnaround leaders, however, use brutal tactics to restore profitability to a firm, including slashing the payroll by as much as 50 percent, selling off assets, and delaying payments to suppliers. The positive turnaround artist works closely with people to restore a healthy psychological climate. According to Rosabeth Moss Kanter, these leaders replace secrecy and denial of problems with dialogue, and blame and scorn with respect. The transformational leader also rewards initiative, and encourages people to stop protecting their turf and begin collaborating.[41]

Charismatic Leadership

Charisma in a leader generally inspires group members and facilitates transformations. A recent perspective on charisma is that it reflects executive presence, or simply "it," as in "This person has *it*."[42] Charisma, to a large extent, lies in the eye of the beholder and involves a relationship between the leader and the follower. A good example is Steve Jobs, considered by many to be the number-one visionary of Silicon Valley. One of his latest visions has been to make his Pixar Animation Studios as successful as Disney studios. His earlier visions for Apple Computer may have changed personal computing. Despite Jobs's wide popularity, for many people he is too arrogant, sarcastic, and impatient to be charismatic and inspirational. When a charismatic leader has good ethics, the transformations will be beneficial to society. An immoral charismatic leader, in contrast, can lead people toward evil ends. Who in your mind is an *evil charismatic?*

A key characteristic of charismatic leaders is their *vision*. They offer a vision (or lofty goal) of where the organization is headed and how it can get there (a plan). A vision is multifaceted, extending beyond organizational goals. It also involves a way of identifying with the organization, aligning with the organization's actions and strategies, and even building a collective identity for the firm.[43] A sense of vision inspires employees to perform well. Charismatic leaders often use input from workers to craft their visions so that the vision will appear more realistic. Jürgen Schrempp, the CEO of Daimler-Chrysler, puts it this way: "You have to know what you are talking about. I go to the factories, and we have debates on how cars should look five years from now."[44]

Charismatic leaders are *masterful communicators.* They formulate believable dreams and portray their vision of the future as the only path to follow. Charismatics also use metaphors to inspire people. An example is a favorite aphorism of Richard Marcus, the president of Neiman-Marcus stores, is: "If you follow in someone else's footsteps, you never get ahead."

Charismatic leaders at their best *inspire trust.* Quite often their followers are willing to gamble with their careers to follow their chief's vision, such as accepting a low starting salary with stock options based on the start-up's vision of great success. Charismatic leaders are *energetic* and use an *action-oriented leadership style.* They exude energy, serving as a model for getting things done well and on time.

Charismatic leaders are adept at *managing their impression well,* which helps them be perceived as charismatic.[45] Impression management can take place at the physical level, such as an appealing appearance, yet can also take place at an intellectual level. An intellectual example would be if the person indicates he or she has powerful contacts, such as by saying, "Bill Gates and I were discussing the future of the PC just last week."

Charisma is not necessarily a mystical, in-born set of characteristics and behaviors. As the Skill-Development Exercise that follows shows, charisma is an

---

SKILL-DEVELOPMENT EXERCISE

Developing Charisma

Establishing the goal of becoming more charismatic is the starting point for developing charisma. In addition, you can then discipline yourself to develop some of the traits and characteristics described in the text. Here are eleven specific suggestions for skill development:

1. *Use visioning.* If you are the leader of an organizational unit, develop a dream about its future. Discuss your vision with others in the unit and your immediate superior.
2. *Make frequent use of metaphors.* Develop metaphors to inspire people around you. A commonly used one after a group has suffered a substantial setback is, "Like the phoenix, we will rise from the ashes of defeat."
3. *Inspire trust and confidence.* Make your deeds consistent with your promises. Get people to believe in your competence by making your accomplishments known in a polite, tactful way.
4. *Make others feel capable.* Give out assignments on which others can succeed, and lavishly praise their success.
5. *Be highly energetic and goal oriented.* Impress others with your energy and resourcefulness. To increase your energy level, exercise frequently, eat well, and get ample rest.

6. *Express your emotions frequently.* Freely express warmth, joy, happiness, and enthusiasm.
7. *Develop and display a sense of humor.* Appropriate use of humor helps build workplace relationships because people feel more comfortable with people who make them feel good, and humor often puts people in a good mood. Self-effacing humor is often effective, whereas humor that pokes fun at others is usually highly ineffective.
8. *Smile frequently, even if you are not in a happy mood.* A warm smile seems to indicate a confident, caring person, which contributes to a perception of charisma.
9. *Make everybody you meet feel that he or she is quite important.* For example, at a company meeting, shake the hand of every person you meet.
10. *Focus on the positive.* Charismatic people are optimists who minimize complaints and emphasize what positive steps can be taken to overcome a problem.
11. *Maintain positive body language.* To radiate authenticity and confidence, stand and sit up straight. When standing, keep your feet about 12 inches apart. When sitting, do not tap your feet nervously.[46]

attainable skill if you have the discipline to practice the techniques the exercise outlines. Observe that several of the suggestions are geared toward impression management.

A major concern about the heavy emphasis on charisma for leadership is that too many CEOs are evil charismatics who win the support of thousands, and then plunder the organization for personal gain.[47] Former key executives at Enron Corporation and Global Crossing serve as prominent examples. As a backlash to relying so heavily on charismatic executives, major corporations in recent years have sought hard-working, ethical individuals as CEOs, even if they are less flamboyant. The ideal executive leader would be an ethical, hard-working, and charismatic person. One of many possible examples is CEO Andrea Jung of Avon Corporation.

360-DEGREE FEEDBACK FOR IMPROVING LEADERSHIP EFFECTIVENESS

5

A widely used method for improving leadership effectiveness is for the manager/leader to receive feedback on his or her traits, attitudes, and behaviors from multiple raters. A **360-degree survey** is a formal evaluation of superiors based on input from people who work for and with them, sometimes including customers and suppliers in the evaluation process. The 360-degrees refers to the fact that people all around the leader are making the ratings and evaluations. Such evaluations can also be used as part of the performance appraisal. Particularly when used for learning about leadership effectiveness, the individual completes the same form that all others used to describe his or her behavior. The feedback is communicated to the leader and interpreted with the assistance of a psychologist or organizational behavior specialist.

Explain how 360-degree feedback is used to improve leadership effectiveness.

The data from the survey can be used to help leaders fine-tune their attitudes and behaviors. For example, if all the raters gave the leader low ratings on "sensitivity to the needs of others," the leader might be prompted to improve this trait. Action plans for improving sensitivity would include reading about understanding others, attending a seminar, taking a suitable online course, and making a deliberate attempt to understand the feelings and needs of others.

A standard approach to a 360-degree survey is for a sampling of work associates to complete a lengthy questionnaire about dozens of specific behaviors.[48] Self-ratings are then compared to ratings by others. Assume that a leader rates himself in the 90th percentile on "displays warmth and a good sense of humor." If others rated him at the 15th percentile on this dimension, the leader might be counseled about how to put others at ease. The example just cited hints at the importance of professionally trained counselors being involved in 360-degree surveys. Some people feel emotionally crushed when they find a wide discrepancy between their self-perception on an interpersonal skill and the perception of others.

A challenge facing the effective use of 360-degree feedback is the problem of defensiveness. Many people reject negative feedback, perceiving that the raters are wrong. A study was conducted with MBA students who had full-time jobs, with the students obtaining 360-degree feedback from at least six raters at their employers. The study showed that less favorable ratings were associated with the negative reaction that the feedback was inaccurate and not useful.[49]

6

Identify forces that can sometimes decrease the importance of leadership.

SUBSTITUTES FOR LEADERSHIP

An implicit theme of this chapter has been that leadership is important because it affects such outcomes as productivity and satisfaction. At times, however, competent leadership is not necessary, and incompetent leadership can be counterbalanced by certain factors in the work situation. Under these circumstances, leadership is of little consequence to the performance and satisfaction of team members. According to this viewpoint, many organizations have **substitutes for leadership.** Such substitutes are factors in the work environment that provide guidance and incentives to perform well, making the leader's role almost superfluous.[50] Leadership substitutes, in effect, neutralize the effects of leadership.

Group member characteristics that can substitute for leadership include ability, experience, training, and professional orientation. For example, a highly capable employee with strong professional values will accomplish the job with *any* plausible person acting as the formal leader. Task characteristics that can substitute for leadership include standardized methods, jobs with built-in feedback, and intrinsically satisfying work. Information technology can also substitute for leadership (or at least supervision) when instructions for tasks are entered into the computer. Organizational factors that can substitute for leadership include explicit plans and goals and cohesive work groups. The cohesive work group, for example, will exert its own influence over group members.

CHOOSING AN APPROPRIATE LEADERSHIP MODEL

Twelve different leadership theories, models, and explanations have been presented. Although these approaches have different labels, there are many common elements. Furthermore, all the different theories, models, and explanations are useful for guiding and influencing group members. In quick review, the twelve approaches are: (1) developing the right traits, (2) the initiating structure and consideration dimensions of leadership, (3) the Leadership Grid, (4) the leader–member exchange model, (5) Fiedler's contingency theory of leadership, (6) the path–goal theory of leadership, (7) the situational leadership model, (8) the normative decision model, (9) transformational leadership, (10) charismatic leadership, (11) 360-degree feedback, and (12) substitutes for leadership.

A fruitful approach to choosing an effective leadership theory, model, or explanation is for the manager to carefully diagnose the situation. Choose a leadership approach that best fits the deficiency or neglected opportunity in a given situation. Observe the people to be led, and also interview them about their interests, goals, and concerns. Then apply a leadership approach that appears to match the interests, concerns, deficits, or missed opportunities. The following two examples will help clarify this diagnostic approach:

1. A manager observes that many important decisions are being made and that group members are eager to get involved. Nevertheless, the group members are overworked and pressed for time. The leader would be advised to use the normative decision model to help decide how important it is to involve the group in a particular decision. (The leader wants to involve group members, but needless involvement will intensify the overwork problem.)
2. A manager observes that the group is accomplishing its job, and morale is satisfactory. Yet something is missing; a sense of urgency and excitement does not pervade the atmosphere. In this situation, the leader is advised to take the steps in his or her power to behave like a transformational and charismatic leader.

IMPLICATIONS FOR MANAGERIAL PRACTICE

1. Technically competent and well-motivated employees require less guidance and control than do their less competent and poorly motivated counterparts.

2. When group members face ambiguity, heavy work demands, and heavy job stress, a relationship-oriented leadership style may increase morale and productivity.

3. Exhibiting charisma can benefit the vast majority of leaders. Although charisma is somewhat dependent on longstanding personality characteristics, it can be enhanced through such means as suggested in the Skill-Development Exercise on page 242.

4. Although the modern organization emphasizes team-oriented, collaborative leadership, organizations still need decisive, creative, and independent-thinking leaders.

5. Transformational leadership is sometimes not necessary. The transformational leader might attempt to make sweeping changes in a system that only needs modification. In many situations, practicing small acts of leadership, such as listening to workers, is all that is needed. Michael E. McGill and John W. Slocum, Jr. observe, "A little leadership is what followers want and what leaders can do. Moreover, it can be learned. No less important, it is exactly the amount and kind of leadership that most organizations need."[51] (An example of a little act of leadership would be to set a realistic weekly goal, or given encouragement and support to a group member.)

SUMMARY OF KEY POINTS

1 **Differentiate between leadership and management.**
Leadership involves influencing others to achieve important objectives. Leaders are heavily involved in persuading, inspiring, and motivating others and spearheading change. Managers are more involved with stability and control.

2 **Describe key leadership traits, styles, and behaviors.**
Certain traits and characteristics contribute to leadership effectiveness in many situations. These personal attributes fall into the general categories of cognitive skills and personality characteristics, including emotional intelligence. Self-confidence, trustworthiness, and good problem-solving ability are three examples of key traits.

A foundation concept of the behavioral approach to leadership includes the two dimensions of initiating structure and consideration; and similarly, production-centered and employee-centered leadership. The Leadership Grid® describes a manager's leadership style along the dimensions of concern for production and concern for people. Each of these concerns exists in varying degrees. The leader-member exchange model emphasizes that leaders have unique relationships with group members. In-group members have good relationships with the leader, whereas out-group members have poor relationships. Being part of the in-group enhances productivity and satisfaction.

3 **Explain the basics of four different contingency theories of leadership.**
Fiedler's contingency theory specifies the conditions under which leaders need to use task-motivated and relationship-motivated styles. In situations of high control and low control, the task-motivated style is better. Relationship-motivated leaders have the highest producing groups under situations of moderate control.

According to the path-goal theory, leaders can enhance motivation by increasing personal payoffs to group members for achieving work objectives and by making the paths to payoffs smoother. The effective leader will choose among leadership styles according to two sets of contingency factors: characteristics of subordinates and task demands.

The situational leadership model explains how to match leadership style to the readiness of group members. Leadership is classified according to the amount of task and relationship behavior. Readiness is the extent to which a group member has the ability and willingness or confidence to accomplish a specific task. As a group member's readiness increases, a leader should rely more on relationship behavior and less on task behavior. When a group member becomes very ready, a minimum of task or relationship behavior is required by the leader.

The normative decision model explains that leadership is a decision-making process. A leader examines certain contingency factors in the situation to determine which decision-making style will be the most effective, in either a time-driven or a developmental situation. The model identifies five decision-making styles: two based on individuals and three on groups. By answering a series of seven diagnostic questions in a matrix, the manager follows the path to a recommended decision style.

4 **Present an overview of transformational and charismatic leadership.**

The transformational leader is a charismatic person who helps bring about profound changes in people and the organization, often transforming the culture. Charismatic leaders are known to have vision, be masterful communicators, and inspire trust. They are also adept at managing their impression well. Charisma can be developed to some extent.

5 **Explain how 360-degree feedback is used to improve leadership effectiveness.**

Using 360-degree feedback, a person receives feedback on his or her traits, attitudes, and behaviors from multiple raters. Self-evaluation is often included. The data from the 360-degree survey can be used to help the leaders fine-tune their attitudes and behaviors.

6 **Identify forces that can sometimes decrease the importance of leadership.**

Although leadership is important, in certain situations, other factors may function as substitutes for leadership. These factors can be found within group members, the task, or the organization. Effective followers also decrease the need for leadership.

KEY TERMS AND PHRASES

Leadership, *222*
The ability to inspire confidence and support among the people on whose competence and commitment performance depends.

Cognitive Skills, *224*
Mental ability and knowledge.

Self-Awareness, *224*
Insightfully processing feedback about oneself to improve personal effectiveness.

Behavioral Approach to Leadership, *227*
An attempt to specify how the behavior of effective leaders differs from their less effective counterparts.

Leadership Style, *227*
The relatively consistent pattern of behavior that characterizes a leader.

Initiating Structure, *228*
The degree to which a leader establishes structure for group members.

Consideration, *228*
The degree to which the leader creates an environment of emotional support, warmth, friendliness, and trust.

Leadership Grid®, *230*
A framework for classifying leadership styles that simultaneously examines a leader's concerns for task accomplishment and people.

Leader–Member Exchange Model, *230*
The model that recognizes that leaders develop unique working relationships with each group member.

Contingency Theory of Leadership, *231*
The position that the best style of leadership depends on factors relating to group members and the work setting.

Situational Control, *232*
The degree to which the leader can control and influence the outcomes of group effort.

Path–goal Theory of Leadership, *233*
An explanation of leadership that specifies what the leader must do to achieve high morale and productivity in a given situation.

Situational Leadership Model, *234*
The model that matches leadership style to the readiness of group members.

Readiness, *235*
The extent to which a group member has the ability and willingness or confidence to accomplish a specific task.

Normative Decision Model, *236*
A contingency viewpoint of leadership that views leadership as a decision-making process in which the leader examines certain situational factors to determine which decision-making style will be most effective.

Transformational Leader, *239*
One who helps organizations and people make positive changes in the way they conduct their activities.

Charisma, *239*
The ability to lead others based on personal charm, magnetism, inspiration, and emotion.

360-Degree Survey, *243*
A formal evaluation of superiors based on input from people who work for and with them, sometimes including customers and suppliers.

Substitutes for Leadership, *244*
Factors in the work environment that provide guidance and incentives to perform, making the leader's role almost superfluous.

DISCUSSION QUESTIONS AND ACTIVITIES

1. Describe how a person might be a good leader but a poor manager.
2. Describe how a person might be a good manager but a poor leader.
3. What factors or forces would prompt a leader to be highly ethical and trustworthy working for one company, yet highly unethical and untrustworthy working for another company?
4. Assuming you believe that the leader–member exchange theory is valid, how would you go about becoming part of a leader's in-group?

5. How would the situational theory help you do a better job of managing or leading poorly motivated workers?
6. What do you perceive to be a major difference between a contingency leader and a charismatic leader?
7. Which of the theories or explanations of leadership presented in this chapter do you think would be the most useful for a team leader? For a CEO? Explain your reasoning.

ORGANIZATIONAL BEHAVIOR ONLINE

TO DO

Developing Your Self-Confidence Online

As described in this chapter, self-confidence is a major contributor to leadership effectiveness in a variety of situations. http://www.self-confidence.co.uk offers a free self-confidence course online. After you sign up for the course, you will receive your first installment immediately. After that you will receive one tutorial a week for six weeks. The lessons include self-confidence–boosting stories, information and quotes, and skill-development exercises. Sponsors of the site will invite you to take related courses for a fee.

TO BOOKMARK

Center for Creative Leadership
http://www.ccl.org

Developing as a Leader by Understanding Human Nature
http://www.levinsoninst.com/Lship-G.htm

Servant-Leadership
http://www.greenleaf.org

CASE PROBLEM: The Unflappable John Chambers of Cisco

A few years ago at a technology conference, John T. Chambers, the CEO of networking giant Cisco Systems Inc., was talking with Carl Russo, the CEO of the telecom-equipment start-up Cerent Corp. After a few pleasantries, Chambers got right to the point. "How much would it cost me to buy you?" Cisco later agreed to pay a staggering $6.9 billion in stock for Cerent, even though the two-year start-up had sold only $10 million worth of equipment. Convinced that Cerent's technology was critical for linking the Internet and telephone-system worlds, Chambers would not back down.

Much of Cisco's growth has come through acquisitions, having bought over 70 companies in an eight-year span. During the period of intensive acquisitioning, the company invested heavily in internal R&D (research and development). The strategy has led to tremendous growth in sales and stock price, in the first ten years since it went public. During the 2000–2002 period, Cisco stock declined substantially along with the rest of the Internet and telecommunications industries.

When Chambers became CEO in 1995, Cisco had a market cap of $9 billion. Five years later, the cap was $486 billion, but then slipped down to $154 billion by January 2002. By 2003 the stock was climbing back up again rapidly, as the company returned to profitability after a two-year slump.

Salesman and Visionary

Chambers is considered the leading salesperson in the Internet world. He persistently hawks the Internet. One day he is preaching Net religion to Chinese President Jiang Zemin, and the next he's meeting with six technology enthusiasts in a garage who are sketching a new networking technology. Chambers approaches managing his company with the same zeal. He has helped Cisco become the ultimate model of an efficient Net company. The company sells about 80 percent of its products over the Internet, speeding up the process of and eliminating costly and needless steps between order-taking and delivery. Chambers evangelizes about how he can do the same for every other industrial company.

Chambers spins a far-reaching vision of an Internet future. He declares that there will be a day when a New World Network will seamlessly blend the technology of the Internet with high-speed optical fibers, cable, and wireless systems to carry voice and data everywhere. Chambers thinks that his company can become the top supplier for the New World Network. "If we do it right, we have the chance to become one of the most influential companies in history," he says. Chambers frequently makes statements such as, "We want to change the world."

Many industry analysts agree that Chambers has built one of the deepest management teams in Silicon Valley. Managers are empowered more at Cisco than at other well-known high-tech firms. One Cisco executive says, "One thing John does well is stretch people's responsibilities and change the boxes they are in. It makes our jobs new all the time."

Much of Chambers' reputation stems from his engaging and unassuming personality. Armed with a soft West Virginian accent and the ability to come across as a regular guy rather than a high-powered, well-paid, well-connected executive, Chambers oozes charm. Despite the warmth Chambers projects when he assumes a sales role, some competitors perceive him as a bully. "Cisco's competitors hate the company—I mean really hate it," says Shannon Pleasant, a networking analyst.

Chambers has adopted the role of industry statesman. He has frequent meetings at the White House and spends face time with Washington insiders during their pilgrimages to Silicon Valley. In a one-year period, he met with more than 30 heads of state and George W. Bush before the latter became U.S. President. Chambers heavily emphasizes customer relations in his approach to leading Cisco. When Chambers joined the company, it was engineering oriented. Today the emphasis is strongly marketing oriented despite being so high tech. All company executives have their bonuses tied to customer-satisfaction ratings. Cisco managers and professionals emphasize listening to their customers and often buy whatever technology they think their customers want. Chambers invests considerable time building customer relationships, making good use of his folksy charm.

Chambers works relentlessly, although he takes off Sunday to spend time with his family. He spends 30 hours per week meeting with customers, and his work ethic helps set the tone for Cisco employees. A former Cisco employee says, "It's a very demanding place. The peer pressure is intense. For Type A personalities only. To be successful, you have to commit to it. It's not an eight-hour day."

Dealing with the Downturn

By the end of 2001, Cisco Systems encountered some of the problems facing the rest of the manufacturers of Internet and telecommunications equipment. Cisco was losing money in early 2002, but was then profitable again during the first quarter of 2003. At one point, Cisco laid off 8,500 employees. With the decrease stock value, it became more difficult to purchase other companies. A business analyst commented "Cisco was at the right place at the right time and exploited it very well. Chances are they won't be able to do it again." Other observers accused Cisco of using aggressive accounting practices to make the company look more profitable than reality. Two of these practices would be a massive write-down of assets and understating the true costs of certain acquisitions.

A concern about the future growth of Cisco is that it will not be able to find another bonanza, like network switching, to help fuel continued rapid growth. However, one of several promising products is the voice-over-Internet system. Using Internet phones, a company would no longer have to invest in building and serving a traditional telephone system.

In the face of critics, Chambers stays optimistic. During a meeting with financial analysts he contended that the company's customer focus, culture of empowerment, skills in acquiring other companies, and dominant market share will allow it to overcome adversity. "Let's not kid ourselves," he says. "This market is coming to us. It is going to consolidate. Who in this industry is better at consolidation than Cisco? And who, by the way, has the assets that Cisco does?"

A former colleague of Chambers, John Thibault, questions his ability to deal well with business downturns. "He's almost too nice to kick the asses that need to be kicked." During the layoff of 8,500 workers, Chambers cut his own salary down to $1, and visited the company outplacement center in order to boost morale. Cisco management developed a program for laid-off employees in which it agreed to pay employees one-third of their salary and continue their health benefits and stock-option grants if they worked for a local charity or community organization.

New Emphasis on Employee Development

Under the leadership of John Chambers, Cisco had relied heavily on acquiring technical talent from the outside—particularly through purchasing companies staffed with the talent Cisco needed. Today when Cisco must fill a key position, the talent often comes from the inside. Pathfinder, a software system, enables Cisco employees to search for internal jobs that interest them, and to contact the hiring manager for an interview. Approximately 20 percent of Cisco engineers have used the system to find an internal transfer. A key purpose of Pathfinder is to enable employees to move within the company and develop skills that feed Cisco's goal of relying more on internally grown talent.

Chambers has a tremendous thirst for knowledge related to his business, but dyslexia has made reading a struggle for him. Nevertheless, he attended Duke University and West Virginia University as an undergraduate, earned a law degree at W.V.U., and an MBA from Indiana University. Chambers uses a sharp memory to compensate for his mediocre reading skills.

Case Questions

1. How would you describe John Chambers's approach to leadership, including his style?
2. What suggestions for improvement as a leader might you offer Chambers?
3. What is your evaluation of the effectiveness of shifting from acquiring talent from the outside to developing talent from within Cisco?
4. What are Chambers's major leadership challenges for the future?

Sources: Andy Reinhardt, "Meet Mr. Internet: Cisco Systems CEO John Chambers Has a Vision of a New World Order—with Cisco as Its No. 1 Supplier," *Business Week*, September 13, 1999, pp. 128–140; Andy Serwer, "There's Something About Cisco," *Fortune*, May 15, 2000, pp. 114–138; Patrick J. Kiger, "Cisco's Homegrown Gamble," *Workforce*, March 2003, pp. 28–34; John A. Byrne and Ben Elgin, "Cisco Behind the Hype," *Business Week*, January 21, 2002, pp. 54–61; Mark Evans, "The Charming John Chambers: Few CEOs Garner—or Earn—This Kind of Respect," *National Post* (http://www.cisco.com/ca/newsroom/np_johnchambers.shtml; John Chambers, "CEO Visions: Networks Have to Think Smarter," *InformationWeek.com* (http://www.informationweek.com /shared/printableArticle.jhtml?articleID=6512258).

ENDNOTES

1. Thomas A. Stewart, "America's Most Admired Companies," *Fortune,* March 2, 1998, p. 72.
2. Spencer E. Ante, "The New Blue," *Business Week,* March 17, 3003, p. 83.
3. W. Chan Kim and Renee A. Mauborgne, "Parables of Leadership," *Harvard Business Review,* July–August 1992, p. 123.
4. John P. Kotter, "What Leaders Really Do," *Harvard Business Review,* May–June 1990, pp. 103–111.
5. Robert Hogan, Gordon J. Curphy, and Joyce Hogan, "What We Know about Leadership Effectiveness and Personality," *American Psychologist,* June 1994, p. 494.
6. David A. Waldman, Gabriel G. Ramírez, Robert J. House, and Phanish Puranam, "Does Leadership Matter? CEO Leadership Attributes and Profitability under Conditions of Perceived Environmental Uncertainty," *Academy of Management Journal,* February 2001, pp. 134–143.
7. Shelly A. Kirkpatrick and Edwin A. Locke, "Leadership: Do Traits Matter?" *Academy of Management Executive,* May 1991, pp. 48–60; Edwin A. Locke and Associates, *The Essence of Leadership: The Four Keys to Leading Successfully* (New York: Lexington/Macmillan, 1991), pp. 13–34.
8. Frank Gibney Jr., "Vrroooom At The Top," *Time,* January 14, 2002, pp. 42–43.
9. Carol Hymowitz, "The Confident Boss Doesn't Micromanage or Delegate Too Much," *The Wall Street Journal,* March 11, 2003, p. B1.
10. Ellen M. Whitener, Susan E. Brodt, M. Audrey Korsgaard, and Jon M. Werner, "Managers as Initiators of Trust: An Exchange Relationship Framework for Understanding Managerial Trustworthy Behavior," *Academy of Management Review,* July 1998, p. 516.
11. Quoted in "The Top 500 Women-Owned Businesses," *Working Woman,* June 1999, p. 44.
12. Daniel Goleman, "Leadership that Gets Results," *Harvard Business Review,* March–April 2000, p. 80.
13. Loren Gray, "Becoming a Resonant Leader," *Harvard Management Update,* July 2002, pp. 4–5; Daniel Goleman, Richard Boyatzis, and Annie McKee, *Primal Leadership: Realizing the Power of Emotional Intelligence* (Boston: Harvard Business School Publishing, 2002).
14. Joel Stein, "Bosses from Hell," *Time,* December 7, 1998, p. 181.
15. Timothy A. Judge, Joyce E. Bono, Remus Ilies, and Megan W. Gerhardt, "Personality and Leadership: A Qualitative and Quantitative Review," *Journal of Applied Psychology,* August 2002, pp. 765–780.
16. Martin L. Maher and Douglas A. Klieber, "The Greying of Achievement Motivation," *American Psychologist,* July 1981, pp. 787–793.
17. Quoted in Shari Caudron, "Where Have All The Leaders Gone?" *Workforce,* December 2002, p. 31.
18. Ralph M. Stogdill and Alvin E. Coons (eds.), *Leader Behavior: Its Description and Measurement* (Columbus: Ohio State University Bureau of Business Research, 1957); Carroll L. Shartle, *Executive Performance and Leadership* (Upper Saddle River, NJ: Prentice Hall, 1956).
19. Arnold S. Tannenbaum, *Social Psychology of the Work Organization* (Monterey, CA: Wadsworth, 166), p. 74; Robert Dubin, "Supervision and Productivity: Empirical Findings and Theoretical Considerations," in Walter Nord (ed.), *Concepts and Controversies in Organizational Behavior* (Glenview, IL: Scott, Foresman and Company, 1972), pp. 524–525.
20. Polly Labarre, "Do You Have the Will to Lead?" *Fortune,* March 2000, pp. 227–228.
21. Robert R. Blake and Anne Adams McCanse, *Leadership Dilemmas—Grid Solutions* (Houston: Gulf Publishing Company, 1991).

22. George Graen and J. F. Cashman, "A Role-Making Model of Leadership in Formal Organizations: A Developmental Approach," in J. G. Hunt and L. I. Larson (eds.), *Leadership Frontiers* (Kent, OH: Kent State University Press, 1975), pp. 143–165; Robert P. Vecchio, "Leader-Member Exchange, Objective Performance, Employment Duration, and Supervisor Ratings: Testing for Moderation and Mediation," *Journal of Business and Psychology,* Spring 1998, pp. 327–341.
23. Robert P. Vecchio, "Are You In or OUT with Your Boss?" *Business Horizons,* vol. 29, 1987, pp. 76–78.
24. Chester A. Schriesheim, Linda L. Neider, and Terri A. Scandura, "Delegation and Leader-Member Exchange: Main Effects, Moderators, and Measurement Issues," *Academy of Management Journal,* June 1998, pp. 298–318.
25. Vecchio, "Leader-Member Exchange," p. 340.
26. Adrienne Colella and Arup Varma, "The Impact of Subordinate Disability on Leader-Member Exchange Relationships," *Academy of Management Journal,* August 2001, pp. 304–315.
27. Kenneth J. Dunnegan, Mary Uhl-Bien, and Dennis Duchon, "LMX and Subordinate Performance: The Moderating Effects of Task Characteristics," *Journal of Business and Psychology,* Winter 2002, pp. 275–285.
28. Michael Useem, "The Leadership Lessons of Mount Everest," *Harvard Business Review,* October 2001, p. 53.
29. Fred E. Fiedler, Martin M. Chemers, and Linda Mahar, *Improving Leadership Effectiveness: The Leader-Match Concept,* 2nd ed. (New York: John Wiley & Sons, 1984); Martin M. Chemers, *An Integrative Theory of Leadership* (Mahwah, NJ: Lawrence Erlbaum Associates, 1997), pp. 28–38.
30. Robert J. House and Terence R. Mitchell, "Path-Goal Theory of Leadership," *Journal of Contemporary Business* (Fall 1974), p. 83.
31. Bill Breen, "Trickle-Up Leadership," *Fast Company,* November 2001, p. 70; Michael Useem, *Leading Up: How to Lead Your Boss So You Both Win* (New York: Crown, 2001).
32. Paul Hersey, Kenneth H. Blanchard, and Dewey E. Johnson, *Management of Organizational Behavior: Utilizing Human Resources,* 7th ed. (Upper Saddle River, NJ: Prentice Hall, 1996), pp. 188–227.
33. Victor H. Vroom, "Leadership and the Decision-Making Process," *Organizational Dynamics,* Spring 2000, pp. 82–93.
34. Richard H. G. Field and Robert J. House, "A Test of the Vroom-Yetton Model Using Manager and Subordinate Reports," *Journal of Applied Psychology,* June 1990, pp. 362–366.
35. Susan Caminiti, "Turnaround Titan," *Working Woman,* December/January 1999, p. 57.
36. Quoted in "Leadership," in *Business: The Ultimate Resource Business* (Cambridge, MA: Perseus Books Group, 2002), p. 916; James McGregor Burns, *Leadership* (New York: Harper & Row, 1978).
37. Nick Turner, et al., "Transformational Leadership and Moral Reasoning," *Journal of Applied Psychology,* April 2002, pp. 304–311.
38. John J. Hater and Bernard M. Bass, "Supervisors' Evaluations and Subordinates' Perceptions of Transformational and Transactional Leadership," *Journal of Applied Psychology,* November 1988, p. 695; Noel M. Tichy and May Anne Devanna, *The Transformational Leader* (New York: Wiley, 1990).
39. Sally A. Carless, Alexander J. Wearing, and Leon Mann, "A Short Measure of Transformational Leadership," *Journal of Business and Psychology,* Spring 2000, pp. 389–405.
40. Roger O. Crockett, "Can Mike Z Work More Magic at Motorola?" *Business Week,* April 14, 2003, p. 58.
41. Rosabeth Moss Kanter, "Leadership and the Psychology of Turnarounds," *Harvard Business Review,* June 2003, pp. 58–67.

42. Michelle Conlin, "She's Gotta Have 'It,'" *Business Week,* July 22, 2002, p. 88.

43. Jay A. Conger and Rabindra N. Kanungo, *Charismatic Leadership in Organizations* (Thousand Oaks, CA: Sage, 1998).

44. Alex Taylor III, "Schrempp Shifts Gears," *Fortune,* March 18, 2002, p. 98.

45. William L. Gardner and Bruce J. Avolio, "The Charismatic Relationship: A Dramaturgical Perspective," *Academy of Management Review,* January 1998, p. 33.

46. Several of the suggestions are from Roger Dawson, Secrets of Power Persuasion: Everything You'll Need to Get Anything You'll Ever Want (Upper Saddle River, NJ: Prentice Hall, 1992), pp. 179–194: "Secrets of Charismatic Leadership," *WorkingSMART,* February 1998, p. 1.

47. Rakesh Khurana, *Searching for a Corporate Savior* (Princeton, NJ: Princeton University Press, 2002).

48. Craig T. Chappelow, "360-Degree Feedback," in Cynthia D. McCauley, Russ S. Moxley, and Ellen Van Velsor, *The Center for Creative Leadership Handbook of Leadership Development* (San Francisco: Jossey-Bass, 1998), pp. 29–65; Angelo S. DeNisi and Avraham N. Kluger, "Feedback Effectiveness: Can 360-Degree Appraisals Be Improved?" *Academy of Management Executive,* February 2000, pp. 129–139.

49. Joan F. Brett and Leanne E. Atwater, "360° Feedback: Accuracy, Reactions, and Perceptions of Usefulness," *Journal of Applied Psychology,* October 2001, pp. 930–942.

50. Jon P. Howell, David E. Bowen, Peter W. Dorfman, Steven Kerr, and Philip Podsakoff, "Substitutes for Leadership: Effective Alternatives to Ineffective Leadership," *Organizational Dynamics,* Summer 1990, p. 23.

51. Michael E. McGill and John W. Slocum Jr., "A Little Leadership, Please?" *Organizational Dynamics,* Winter 1998, p. 48.

Chapter 12

Power, Politics, and Influence

After reading and studying this chapter and doing the exercises, you should be able to:

1 Identify sources of power for individuals and sub-units within organizations.

2 Describe the essence of empowerment.

3 Pinpoint factors contributing to, and examples of, organizational politics.

4 Identify and describe a variety of influence tactics.

5 Explain how managers can control dysfunctional politics.

6 Differentiate between the ethical and unethical use of power, politics, and influence.

Vincent Lai landed a job as a business analyst with a big telecommunications company several years ago, but as soon as he started work, he realized that the hiring manager had been more interested in replacing his predecessor than bringing him on board. The manager ignored him, and he had little to do. Within weeks, he felt his career coming to a halt.

Office politics never came up in the interview, says Mr. Lai, who is 36 years old. But looking back, there were several clues to his boss's indifference that he wished he had heeded. For instance, when he asked why his predecessor was leaving, the manager vaguely cited "creative differences." When Mr. Lai tried to meet with that person, the manager said the person was "too busy."

"When she was interviewing me, she was thinking more about pushing this other guy out," says Lai, an East Hanover, NJ resident who has been looking for work for 17 months since he left another post that turned out to be a "poor fit." He's wary about making another poor choice.

John Murphy, co-founder of the Interview Club, a job-hunting and interview-skills practice group in New York, says companies will always "tell you the good parts and leave out the bad parts" about a position. Many job seekers he works with say they feel shut down after they ask hiring managers tough questions during interviews. But doing research before you even get to the interview stage can help you ask more focused questions and even read an interviewer's evasion more clearly, he says.

The three major areas to focus on are a company's financial health, the responsibilities of the position, and the office environment.

Source: Republished with permission of *The Wall Street Journal* from Kris Maher, "The Jungle: Focus on Recruitment, Pay and Getting Ahead," *The Wall Street Journal,* March 25, 2003, p. B8. See also http://www.CareerJournal.com for extensive advice about many phases of career management.

NOW ASK YOURSELF: What advice about career management can we glean from the incident about job hunter Vincent Lai? For starters, an awareness of organizational politics can help prevent major career mistakes, such as a failed job experience. Power, politics, and influence are such major parts of the workplace that they have become standard topics of organizational behavior. How they are invoked—whether with aggression in a spirit of cooperation—presents interesting dilemmas suitable for our analysis.

In this chapter, we approach power, politics, and influence from multiple perspectives. We describe the meaning of these concepts, how power is obtained, and how it is shared (empowerment). We examine why organizational politics is so prevalent, and then describe the tactics of politics and influence. In addition, we describe the control of dysfunctional politics, and ethical considerations about the use of power, politics, and influence. As you read the chapter, you will learn that some tactics of power, politics, and influence violate ethical codes and therefore should be avoided.

THE MEANING OF POWER, POLITICS, AND INFLUENCE

A challenge in understanding power, politics, and influence in organizations is that the terms appear close in meaning. Here we present meanings of these terms aimed at providing useful distinctions. **Power** is the potential or ability to influence decisions and control resources. The predominant view of power is that it is the influence over other's actions, thoughts, and outcomes.[1] Many definitions of power center on the ability of a person to overcome resistance in achieving a result. Some researchers suggest that power lies in the potential, while others focus on use.[2] As a hedge, our definition includes both potential and use. If you have a powerful battery in your car, isn't it still powerful whether or not it is in use?

Politics is a way of achieving power. As defined by Jeffrey Pfeffer, "Organizational politics involves those activities taken in organizations to acquire, develop, and use power and other resources to obtain one's preferred outcomes in a situation in which there is uncertainty or dissensus about choices."[3] As used here, **organizational politics** refers to informal approaches to gaining power through means other than merit or luck.

Influence is close in meaning to power. Influence is also the ability to change behavior, but it tends to be more subtle and indirect than power. Power indicates the ability to affect outcomes with greater facility and ease than influence.[4]

Managers and professionals often need to use political tactics to achieve the power and influence they need to accomplish their work. An example would be a human resources manager cultivating the support of a top executive so she can proceed with a program of employee wellness. Without the ethical and effective use of politics, the company would not be able to work toward total customer satisfaction.

SOURCES OF INDIVIDUAL AND SUBUNIT POWER

1

Identify sources of power for individuals and subunits within organizations.

The sources or bases of power in organizations can be classified in different ways. A useful starting point is to recognize that power can be used to forward either the interests of the organization or personal interests. **Socialized power** is the use of power to achieve constructive ends. An example would be the manager who attempted to gain power to spearhead a program of employee wellness. **Personalized power** is the use of power primarily for the sake of personal aggrandizement and gain.[5] An example would be a new CEO using his power to insist that company headquarters be moved to a location near his home.

Here we classify the sources (and also the bases and origins) of power, which stem from the organization, from the individual, and from providing resources.[6]

Power Granted by the Organization (Position Power)

Managers and professionals often have power because of the authority, or right, granted by their positions. The power of a manager's position stems from three sources: legitimate power, coercive power, and reward power. **Legitimate power** is based on the manager's formal position within the hierarchy. A government agency head, for example, has much more position power than a unit supervisor in the same agency. Managers can enhance their position power by formulating policies and procedures. For example, a manager might establish a requirement that she must approve all new hires, thus exercising authority over hiring.

Coercive power comes from controlling others through fear or threat of punishment. Typical organizational punishments include bypassing an employee for promotion and terminating employment, giving damaging performance appraisals to people who do not support your initiatives, even if the initiatives are unethical or illegal. The threat of a lawsuit by an employee who is treated unjustly serves as a constraint on legitimate power, and is referred to as *subordinate power*. **Reward power** involves controlling others through rewards or the promise of rewards. Examples of this include promotions, challenging assignments, and recognition given to employees.

The effectiveness of coercive power and reward power depends on the perceptions and needs of group members. For coercive power to be effective, the employee must fear punishment and care about being a member of the firm. Conversely, an employee who did not care much for recognition or power would not be strongly influenced by the prospects of a promotion.

Executives who abuse power by voting themselves extraordinary compensation during a business downturn have been under attack from many observers of business. At American Airlines, the labor union was able to constrain executive abuse of legitimate power as follows:

> In 2003, after sharp criticism from angry employees, the head of American Airlines apologized as the company dropped a plan to give bonuses to six top executives if they stayed with the airline for two more years. The bonuses were equal to twice the executives' salaries. The employees learned of the perks after agreeing to cut their own benefits by $10 billion over six years, to help save the company. American Airlines did not tell the workers about the executive perks until workers agreed to pay cuts of 15.6 percent to 23 percent.
>
> Chairman and CEO Donald J. Carty, who would have received a $1.6 million bonus, said, "I have apologized to our union leaders for this and for the concern it has caused our employees."[7]

Power Stemming from the Individual (Personal Power)

Managers and professionals also derive power from two separate personal characteristics: knowledge and personality. **Expert power** is the ability to influence others because of one's specialized knowledge, skills, or abilities. For expertise to be an effective source of power, group members must respect that expertise.

254

Exercising expert power is the logical starting point for building one's power base. Powerful people in business, government, and education almost invariably launched their career by developing expertise in a specialty of value to their employers. Furthermore, expert power also keeps a person in demand for executive positions. A case in point is Paul Pressler, the former chairman of Global Theme Parks at Walt Disney Co. who was recruited for the chief executive position at Gap, Inc. a few years ago. Pressler's expertise was in running giant retail locations, albeit in the form of theme parks. Pressler also had developed retail expertise with Disney Stores earlier. The Gap chairman said that Pressler was not an extraordinary merchant but he complemented the kinds of expertise Gap needed: information technology, a strong marketing background, and an understanding of consumer segmentation.[8]

Referent power is the ability to influence others that stems from one's desirable traits and characteristics. It is based on the desire of others to be led by or identify with an inspiring person. Having referent power contributes to a perception of being charismatic, but expert power also makes a contribution.[9]

Power from Providing Resources

Another way of understanding the sources of power is through the **resource dependence perspective.** According to this perspective, the organization requires a continuing flow of human resources, money, customers, technological inputs, and material to continue to function. Subunits or individuals within the organization who can provide these resources derive power from this ability.[10]

A variation on power from providing resources is the derivation of power from gossip, which is an important resource in many organizations. Most people know that an influential member of the grapevine can accrue a small degree of power, and a recent scientific analysis supports this idea. The authors of the analysis define gossip as "informal and evaluative talk in an organization, usually among no more than a few individuals, about another member of that organization who is not present."[11] According to the model developed, a supplier of gossip will develop the sources of power already described, such as reward, expert, and coercive power. However, if the person provides mostly negative gossip, his or her referent power will decrease. Another problem is that negative gossip can be perceived as a form of harassment that creates an unsafe workplace for employees.[12]

EMPOWERMENT OF GROUP MEMBERS

2

Describe the essence of empowerment.

Distributing power throughout the organization has become a major strategy for improving productivity, quality, and satisfaction. Employees experience a greater sense of self-efficacy (self-confidence for a particular task) and ownership in their jobs when they share power. **Empowerment** is the process of sharing power with group members, thereby enhancing their feelings of self-efficacy.[13] You can begin to personalize the meaning of empowerment by doing the Skill-Development Exercise that follows.

Exhibit 12-1 shows a model of the empowerment process. According to this model, managers must act in specific ways to empower employees, such as those mentioned in stage 2. Participative management is the general strategy for empowering workers. The techniques of participative management listed in stage 2, such as goal setting, modeling, and job enrichment, have been described in previous chapters. The information about empowering teams presented in Chapter 10 is also relevant here.

SKILL-DEVELOPMENT EXERCISE

Becoming an Empowering Leader

To empower employees, leaders and managers must convey appropriate attitudes and develop the right inter-personal skills. The following list of attitudes and skills will help you become an empowering manager and leader. To the best of your self-evaluation, indicate which skills and attitudes you have and which ones require development.

Empowering Attitude or Behavior	Can Do Now	Would Need to Develop
1. Believe in the ability of team members to be successful.	_____	_____
2. Be patient with people and give them time to learn.	_____	_____
3. Provide group members with direction and structure.	_____	_____
4. Teach group members new skills in small, incremental steps so they can easily learn those skills.	_____	_____
5. Ask group members questions that challenge them to think in new ways.	_____	_____
6. Share information with team members, sometimes just to build rapport.	_____	_____
7. Give group members timely feedback and encourage them throughout the learning process.	_____	_____
8. Offer group members alternative ways of doing things.	_____	_____
9. Exhibit a sense of humor and demonstrate caring for workers as people.	_____	_____
10. Focus on group members' results and acknowledge their personal improvement.	_____	_____

Source: Republished with permission of Supervisory Management from Richard Hamlin, "A Practical Guide to Empowering Your Employees," *Supervisory Management* (April 1991), p. 8. Permission conveyed through Copyright Clearance Center, Inc.

To bring about empowerment, managers must remove conditions that keep employees powerless, such as authoritarian supervision or a job over which they have little control. An example of a person in a low-control job would be a manager who cannot shut off interruptions even to prepare budgets or to plan. Employees must also receive information that increases their feelings of self-efficacy. As shown in Exhibit 12–1, when employees are empowered, they will take the initiative to solve problems and strive hard to reach objectives.

Empowerment may not proceed smoothly unless certain conditions are met. A major consideration is that the potentially empowered workers must be competent and interested in assuming more responsibility. Otherwise the work will not get accomplished. W. Alan Randolph observed ten companies that made the transition to empowerment.[14] The first key to effective empowerment is *information sharing*. Lacking information, it is difficult for workers to act with responsibility.

Another critical factor for successful empowerment is for management to *provide more structure* as teams move into self-management. To initiate empowerment, managers must teach people new skills and make the parameters clear. Workers need to know, for example, "What are the limits to my empowerment?" The third critical factor Randolph observed was that *teams must gradually replace the traditional organizational hierarchy.* Empowered teams do not only make recommendations, they make and implement decisions and are held accountable. A major contributor to successful empowerment at a large food company studied was that

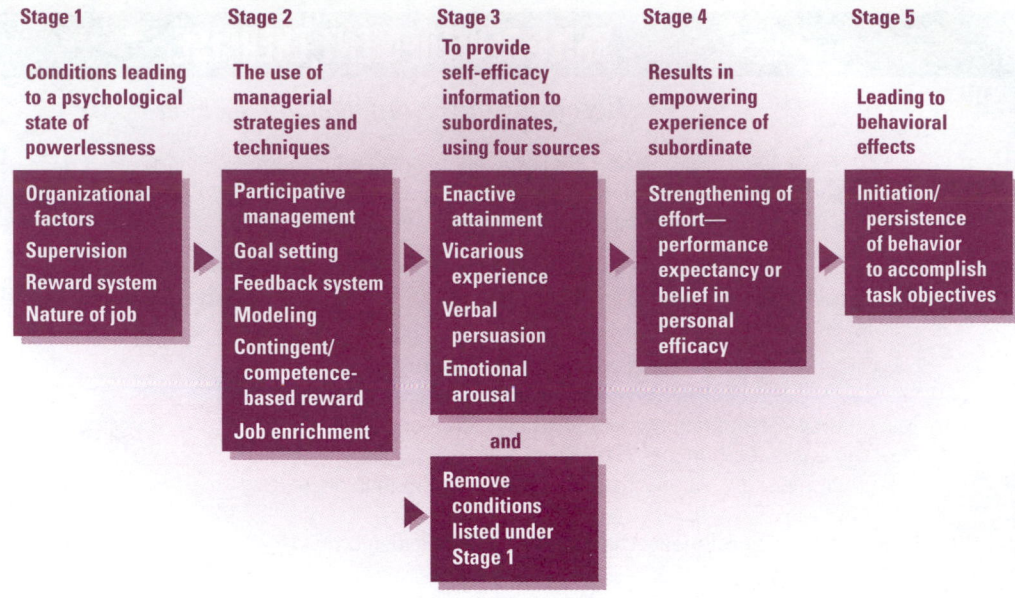

Stage 1	Stage 2	Stage 3	Stage 4	Stage 5
Conditions leading to a psychological state of powerlessness	**The use of managerial strategies and techniques**	**To provide self-efficacy information to subordinates, using four sources**	**Results in empowering experience of subordinate**	**Leading to behavioral effects**
Organizational factors Supervision Reward system Nature of job	Participative management Goal setting Feedback system Modeling Contingent/competence-based reward Job enrichment	Enactive attainment Vicarious experience Verbal persuasion Emotional arousal	Strengthening of effort—performance expectancy or belief in personal efficacy	Initiation/persistence of behavior to accomplish task objectives

and

Remove conditions listed under Stage 1

Source: Republished with permission of the Academy of Management Review from Jay A. Conger and Rabindra N. Kanungo, "The Empowerment Process: Integrating Theory and Practice," *Academy of Management Review* (July 1988): p. 475. Permission conveyed through Copyright Clearance Center, Inc.

Exhibit 12-1

Five Stages in the Process of Empowerment

teams acted as managers. They hired and fired people, appraised performance, scheduled work, and managed a budget.

Empowerment is also more effective when the empowered individuals and teams are told what needs to be done but are *free to determine how to achieve the objectives.* Consultant Norman Bodek says, "Allowing people to determine the most efficient work techniques is the essence of empowerment."[15]

A final consideration for successful empowerment is implied in the other conditions. *Unless managers trust employees,* empowerment will not be effective or even take place. For example, when employees are trusted, they are more likely to be given the information they need and be granted the freedom to choose an appropriate method. Without trusting employees, according to Oren Harari, companies cannot capitalize on intellectual assets to the optimal extent in achieving competitive advantage.[16]

Exhibit 12-2 provides additional insight into empowerment by listing indicators of whether group members show signs of empowerment or disempowerment.

Now that we have described the sources of power and empowerment, we shift focus to more details about political behavior and influence tactics.

FACTORS CONTRIBUTING TO, AND EXAMPLES OF, POLITICAL BEHAVIOR

3

Pinpoint factors contributing to, and examples of, organizational politics.

The most fundamental reason for organizational politics is the political nature of organizations. Coalitions of interests and demands arise both within and outside organizations. Similarly, organizations can be viewed as loose structures of interests and demands in competition with one another for attention and resources. The interaction among different coalitions results in an undercurrent of political tactics, such as when one group tries to promote itself and discredit another.

Another contributor to political activity is the pyramid structure of organizations. The people at the top of the organization hold most of the power, while people at each successive level down the hierarchy hold less power. The amount

One valuable way to track progress in empowerment is to look for the behaviors exhibited by employees who are moving toward effective empowerment. Compare those behaviors with the behaviors you might see from disempowered employees:

Empowered Employees	**Disempowered Employees**
Take initiative in ambiguous situations and define problems in a way that enables further analysis of decisions	Wait for a designated authority to define the problem and assign responsibilities
Identify opportunities in ambiguous situations, such as when customers complain or competitive threats arise	Address a problem effectively but fail to notice the possible opportunity
Apply critical thinking skills, such as surfacing and testing assumptions or evaluating arguments	Accept information, reasoning, or conclusions without testing (especially when presented by an authority)
Offer judgments about how and why specific decisions or actions support the shared purpose	Discuss but may not be able to apply the available information about shared purpose
Build consensus for decisions and actions both within and across functional groups	Expect to attempt consensus building, but appeal to hierarchical authority if the attempt fails
Identify and act on opportunities to systematize activities, document and communicate system information, identify and resolve systemic problems, and adapt or dismantle systems that no longer add value	Focus on improving individual or team effectiveness, yet fail to notice problems that extend beyond the group, create good one-time solutions yet fail to systematize them, rely on existing systems even if they are less valuable
Optimize resources by reducing expenses and finding opportunities to invest new resources (process improvements, technology upgrades, etc.)	Focus on the resources question only when and as directed by a designated authority

Source: Republished with permission of Management Review from Kyle Dover, "Avoiding Empowerment Traps," *Management Review* (January 1999): 53. Copyright © 1999 American Management Association International. Reprinted by permission of Association International, New York, NY. All rights reserved. http://www.amanet.org.

Exhibit 12-2

Signs of Empowerment and Disempowerment

of power that can be distributed in a hierarchy is limited. Power-oriented managers sometimes cope with the limited amount of power available by expanding their sphere of influence sideways. For example, the director of the food stamp program in a government agency might attempt to gain control over the housing assistance program, which is at the same level.

Downsizing and team structures create even less opportunity for climbing the hierarchy, thus intensifying political behavior for the few remaining powerful positions. Worried about layoffs themselves, many workers attempt to discredit others so that the latter would be the first to go. Internal politics generally increase as good jobs, promotions, and bonuses become scarcer. As a business column noted recently, "The art of fawning over a boss may be more important now because of the stagnant economy and shortage of well-paying, full-time jobs."[17]

Organizational politics is also fostered by the need for power. Executives have much stronger needs than others, and thus propel themselves toward frequent episodes of political behavior. Because executives are responsible for controlling resources, their inner desire to do so helps them in their jobs. A personalized power need is more likely to trigger political behavior than a socialized power need.

Finally, a devious reason for the existence of politicking is **Machiavellianism,** a tendency to manipulate others for personal gain. (Niccolo Machiavelli was a fifteenth century political philosopher whose book, *The Prince,* describes how leaders may acquire and maintain power by placing expediency above morality.) One study found that people who scored very high on an organizational politics questionnaire also scored high on a test of Machiavellianism.[18] A more recent analysis suggests that many ambitious and successful corporate executives have strong Machiavellian tendencies, such as acquiring other companies just to give the appearance of true corporate growth.[19]

To make effective use of organizational politics, managerial workers must be aware of specific political strategies and tactics. To identify and explain the majority of political behaviors would require years of study and observation. Managers so frequently need support for their programs that they search for innovative political maneuvers. Furthermore, new tactics continue to emerge as the workplace becomes increasingly competitive. Here we show twelve political tactics, with the first eight being mostly ethical and the last five mostly unethical.

1. *Develop power contacts through networking.* A fundamental principle of success is to identify powerful people and then establish alliances with them. Cultivating friendly, cooperative relationships with powerful organizational members and outsiders can make the managerial worker's cause much easier to advance. These contacts can support a person's ideas and recommend him or her for promotions and visible temporary assignments. A challenge in the era of electronic communications is that face time, or in-person contact, is helpful for building contacts. It is important to converse with powerful people in person in addition to sending them electronic messages. Although still electronic, an occasional telephone call is a useful supplement to e-mail for purposes of building a network. The accompanying Organizational Behavior in Action box describes an executive who has relied heavily on networking to advance her career.

2. *Manage your impression.* You will recall that charismatic leaders rely heavily on impression management, and the same technique is important for other success-oriented people. An example of an ethical impression-management tactic would be to contribute outstanding performance and then make sure key people know of your accomplishments. Making others aware of what you accomplish is often referred to as *achieving visibility.* When tactics of impression management appear insincere, they are likely to create a negative impression and thus be self-defeating (see the InfoTrac sidebar). A key person to impress is your immediate superior. Many firms send professionals to etiquette training, because displaying proper etiquette makes a positive impression on customers and clients.[20] The accompanying Self-Assessment on page 260 will help you think through how sensitive you are to effectively managing your impression.

3. *Control vital information.* Power accrues to those who control vital information, such as knowing how to maneuver contracts through private and governmental bureaucracies. Here, control generally refers to keeping the information covert until it serves one's purpose. If the information is made public, the person loses control.

4. *Keep informed.* In addition to controlling vital information, it is politically important to keep informed. Successful managers and professionals develop a pipeline to help them keep abreast, or even ahead, of developments within the firm. For example, a politically astute individual might befriend a major executive's assistant.

5. *Be courteous, pleasant, and positive.* According to employment consultant Robert Half, courteous, pleasant, and positive people are the first to be hired and the last to be fired (assuming they are also technically qualified).[21]

6. *Ask satisfied customers to contact your manager.* A favorable comment by a customer receives considerable weight because customer satisfaction is a top corporate priority. If a customer says something nice, the comment will carry more weight than one from a coworker or subordinate. The reason is that

Organizational Behavior *in Action*

Ryder System Executive Challis M. Lowe Networks Her Way to the Top

Challis M. Rowe earned more than $740,000 last year as an executive vice president at Ryder System, a logistics and commercial truck-leasing company headquartered in Miami. Women outnumber men at the top at Ryder. In 1977, Lowe was making just over $25,000 as a Continental Bank middle manager. As the Chicago bank's first black female officer, she suffered from sexism on the job and working-mother guilt at home.

Her subsequent career trajectory shows how minority women might reach the summit of major corporations. One lesson is clear: Take risks. "I've never let being scared stop me from doing something," explains Ms. Lowe, a thin woman who talks fast and gestures often. "Just because you haven't done it before doesn't mean you shouldn't try."

That attitude helped her gain admission to Northwestern University's executive MBA program while she toiled 12 hours a day for Continental. The 1978 graduate degree "was probably one of the defining experiences in my life," says Ms. Lowe. "It put me in a position to later look for a different job." Lowe made her first risky career shift several years later: staying with the company after a foreign takeover. In late 1984, Sanwa Bank of Japan bought the Continental equipment-leasing subsidiary in Chicago, where she had risen to vice president. "I was scared," she admits. She thought it would be even tougher for a black woman to be a manager in a Japanese business.

As the Sanwa unit's senior vice president for administrative services, Lowe oversaw everything from advertising to human resources and purchasing. Yet she says her Japanese boss ignored her when they first met with her all-male lieutenants. Lowe persisted, and soon got the unit to attract and retain quality American employees by instituting American-style pay incentives.

Laid off during a 1993 downturn, Lowe heard that Heller Financial needed a human-resources chief who could eliminate duplicative operations at the Chicago commercial-finance company. But its recruiter refused to recommend her. He said,

"You're not an HR person." Undaunted, Lowe called a Heller executive she had met through a local women's networking group. The woman gave her résumé to the chief executive. Heller, majority owned by Fuji Bank, hired Lowe partly because of her experience working with a Japanese parent company.

In 1997, Lowe left Heller to become executive vice president for human resources and administration services at Beneficial, a consumer-financial concern. "Oh, man, a chance to shape a U.S. public company," she recalls thinking, rubbing her palms with glee. She wrangled the same hefty compensation paid to business-unit chiefs, arguing she needed the parity to give her the clout to revamp the corporate structure.

Lowe stuck with Beneficial until the company was sold, leaving her jobless again in 1999. When she began job-hunting six months later, she resisted Ryder's feelers for weeks. The concern served a largely male industry that she knew nothing about. "The question," she recollects, "was could I fit?" Since her May 2000 arrival, the retired Ryder CEO reports, "she has met our high expectations."

Lowe, who yearns to run a midsize business someday, understands why many minority female managers still feel blocked by a "concrete ceiling." The solution? Networking with white women "has been an important part of my success," she says. "You have to get out of your comfort zone if you are going to progress."

Questions

1. In addition to networking, what other political tactics has Lowe used to advance her career?
2. Which sources of power has Lowe accumulated?
3. To what extent do you think that Lowe's frequent job changes will hurt her career?

Source: Adapted with permission of the Wall Street Journal from Joann S. Lublin, "How One Black Woman Lands Her Top Jobs: Risks and Networking," *The Wall Street Journal,* March 4, 2003, p. B1. Permission conveyed through Copyright Clearance Center, Inc.

insiders might praise you for political reasons, whereas a customer's motivation is thought to be pure.

7. *Avoid political blunders.* A strategy for retaining power is to refrain from making power-eroding blunders. Committing these politically insensitive acts can also

SELF-ASSESSMENT

The Manager Impression Survey

Respond to each of the following statements on a 1 to 5 scale: very infrequently (VI), infrequently (I), sometimes (S), frequently (F), or very frequently (VF). If you do not have a manager currently, think of a previous relationship with a manager or how you would behave if you were placed in the situation being described.

To what extent do you:	Frequency				
	1	2	3	4	5
1. Do personal favors for your manager (such as getting him or her coffee or a soft drink)	VI	I	S	F	VF
2. Offer to do something for your manager that you are not required to do, as a personal favor	VI	I	S	F	VF
3. Compliment your immediate manager on his or her dress or appearance	VI	I	S	F	VF
4. Praise your immediate manager on his or her accomplishments	VI	I	S	F	VF
5. Take an interest in your manager's personal life	VI	I	S	F	VF
6. Try to be polite when interacting with your manager	VI	I	S	F	VF
7. Try to be a friendly person when interacting with your manager	VI	I	S	F	VF
8. Try to act as a "model" employee such as never taking longer than the established time for lunch	VI	I	S	F	VF
9. Work hard when you know the results will be seen by your manager	VI	I	S	F	VF
10. Let your manager know that you try to do a good job in your work	VI	I	S	F	VF

Total Score _____

Scoring and Interpretation: Score each circled response 1, 2, 3, 4, or 5, according to the scale indicated previously. Use the following interpretive guide:

45–50 You are working diligently at creating a good impression with your manager. You show good political savvy. Be aware, however, that insincere attempts at impressing management will backfire because they will appear unethical.

30–44 You show moderate concern for creating a good impression with your manager. Become more sensitive to the impression you make on your manager.

10–29 You are not making enough effort to create a good impression with your manager. If you want to be recognized, do a more effective job of managing your impression.

Source: Sandy J. Wayne and Robert C. Liden, "Effects of Impression Management on Performance Ratings: A Longitudinal Study," *Academy of Management Journal* (February 1995), p. 246.

prevent you from attaining power. Leading blunders include strong criticism of a superior in a public forum and going around your manager with a complaint. Another blunder is burning your bridges by creating ill will with former employees.

8. *Sincere flattery.* A powerful tactic for ingratiating yourself to others is to flatter them honestly and sincerely. Although one meaning of the term flattery is insincere praise, another meaning refers to a legitimate compliment. Charismatic people use flattery regularly. The Skill-Development Exercise on page 261 will help you develop flattery skills. Such development should come easy to you because Organizational Behavior students typically have great potential interpersonal skills, along with high cognitive and emotional intelligence.

9. *Backstabbing.* The ubiquitous backstab requires that you pretend to be nice but all the while plan someone's demise. A frequent form of backstabbing is to inform your rival's immediate superior that he or she is faltering under the pressure of job responsibilities. The recommended approach to dealing with a

SKILL-DEVELOPMENT EXERCISE

A Short Course in Effective Flattery

Flattering others is an effective way of building personal relationships (or engaging in organizational politics) if done properly. Suggestions for effective flattery are presented here. *Flattery* here refers to pleasing others by complimentary remarks or attention. We are not referring to flattery in the sense of giving insincere or excessive compliments. To build your skills in flattering others, practice these suggestions as the opportunity presents itself. Rehearse your flattery approaches until they feel natural. If your first attempt at flattery does not work well, analyze what went wrong the best you can.

- *Use sensible flattery.* Effective flattery has at least a spoonful of credibility, implying that you say something positive about the target person that is quite plausible. Credibility is also increased when you point to a person's tangible accomplishment. Technical people in particular expect flattery to be specific and aimed at genuine accomplishment.

- *Compliment what is of major importance to the flattery target.* You might find out what is important to the person by observing what he or she talks about with the most enthusiasm.

- *Flatter others by listening intently.* Listening intently to another person is a powerful form of flattery. Use active listening (see Chapter 9) for best results.

- *Flatter by referring to or quoting the other person.* By referring to or quoting (including para-

phrasing) another person, you are paying that person a substantial compliment.

- *Use confirmation behaviors.* Use behaviors that have a positive or therapeutic effect on other people, such as praise and courtesy. Because confirmation behaviors have such a positive effect on others, they are likely to be perceived as a form of flattery.

- *Give positive feedback.* A mild form of flattering others is to give them positive feedback about their statements, actions, and results. The type of feedback referred to here is a straightforward and specific declaration of what the person did right.

- *Remember names.* Remembering the names of people with whom you have infrequent contact makes them feel important. To help remember the person's name, study the name carefully when you first hear it and repeat it immediately.

- *Avoid flattery that has a built-in insult or barb.* The positive effect of flattery is eradicated when it is accompanied by a hurtful comment, such as "You have good people skills for an engineer" or "You look good. I bet you were really beautiful when you were younger."

Source: Andrew J. DuBrin, *Personal Magnetism: Discover Your Own Charisma and Learn to Charm, Inspire, and Influence Others* (New York: AMACOM, 1997), pp. 75–92; Karen Judson, "The Fine Art of Flattery," *Kiwanis*, March 1998, pp. 34–36, 43.

---

backstabber is to confront the person directly, ask for an explanation of his or her behavior, and demand that he or she stop. Threaten to complain to the person's superior.[22]

10. *Embrace-or-demolish.* The ancient strategy of embrace-or-demolish suggests that you remove from the premises rivals who suffered past hurts through your efforts. (The same tactic is called "take no prisoners.") Otherwise the wounded rivals might retaliate at a vulnerable moment. An illustration of embrace-or-demolish is when, after a hostile takeover, many executives lose their jobs because they opposed the takeover.

11. *Stealing credit.* For many workers, the most detestable form of office politics is for their boss, or other worker, to take credit for their ideas without acknowledging the source of the idea. Paul Lapides estimates that up to 80 percent of workers suffer this indignity at some time in their careers. The credit stealing breeds distrust, damages motivation, and is sometimes misperceived as a perk of power.[23] A good starting point in stopping idea thieves is to hold a one-on-one

session with the thief, and confront the issue. If the issue is not resolved, tell key decision makers about the idea theft.[24]

12. *Territorial games.* Also referred to as *turf wars,* **territorial games** involve protecting and hoarding resources that give a person power, such as information, relationships, and decision-making authority. The purpose of territorial games is to compete for three kinds of territory in the modern corporate survival game: information, relationships, and authority. A relationship is "hoarded" in such ways as not encouraging others to visit a key customer, or blocking a higher performer from getting a promotion or transfer by informing other managers that he or she is mediocre.[25] Other examples of territorial games include monopolizing time with clients, scheduling meetings so someone cannot attend, and shutting out coworkers on an important assignment.

E-mail, including Instant Messaging, has become a major vehicle for conducting both ethical and unethical organizational politics. To help manage their impressions, many people send e-mails with distribution to many key people regarding their positive contribution to a project. E-networking is a convenient way to maintain minimum contact with many people, until the in-person meeting can be arranged. People flatter their target person via e-mail, and send copies to key people. On the downside, some people reprimand others by e-mail, and let others know of the target's mistakes. Sometimes managers who are haggling with each other will send a copy to a common boss, hoping that the boss will intervene in the dispute.[26] A productivity problem with so many people being copied for political purposes is that in-boxes can become overloaded.

ORGANIZATIONAL INFLUENCE TACTICS

4

Identify and describe a variety of influence tactics.

In addition to using power and political tactics to get people to their way of thinking, managerial workers also use a variety of influence tactics. Extensive research has been conducted on social influence tactics aimed at upward, horizontal, and downward relations.[27] The person doing the influencing chooses which tactic seems most appropriate for a given situation. Seven of the most frequently used influence tactics are described here.

1. *Leading by example* means that the manager influences group members by serving as a positive model of desirable behavior. A manager who leads by example shows consistency between actions and words. For example, suppose a firm has a strict policy on punctuality. The manager explains the policy and is always punctual. The manager's words and actions provide a consistent model.

2. *Assertiveness* refers to being forthright in your demands. It involves a person expressing what he or she wants done and how he or she feels about it. A manager might say, for example, "Your report is late, and that makes me angry. I want you to get it done by noon tomorrow." Assertiveness, as this example shows, also refers to making orders clear.

3. *Rationality* means appealing to reason and logic. Strong managers and leaders frequently use this influence tactic. Pointing out the facts of a situation to group members to get them to do something exemplifies rationality. Intelligent people respond the best to rational appeals.

4. *Ingratiation* refers to getting someone else to like you, often through the use of political skill. A typical ingratiating tactic would be to act in a friendly manner just before making a demand. Effective managerial workers treat people well consistently to get cooperation when it is needed.

5. *Exchange* is a method of influencing others by offering to reciprocate if they meet your demands. When asking favors in a busy workplace, it is best to specify the amount of time the task will take, such as by saying "I will need ten minutes of your time sometime between now and next Wednesday." Be aware of what skills or capabilities you have that you can barter with others. Perhaps you are good at retrieving crashed computer files or explaining the tax code. You can then offer to perform these tasks in exchange for favors granted to you.[28]

   An example of exchange among two of the mostly highly compensated people in business was alleged to have taken place at Citigroup several years ago. Sanford Weill, at the time co-CEO of Citigroup, asked star analyst Jack Grubman to "take a fresh look" at his rating for AT&T. Grubman informed Weill of "his progress with AT&T" and asked his boss (Weill) for help in getting his twin daughters accepted at an elite nursery school in New York City. Grubman upgraded AT&T to "buy" from neutral, and Grubman's unit of Citigroup later received $45 million in fees from AT&T for underwriting new stock. Citigroup began donating $1 million a year for five years to the nursery school (the 92nd Street Y). A reporter uncovered a Grubman e-mail that read, "I used Sandy to get my kids in 92nd St. Y preschool (which is harder than Harvard) and Sandy needed Armstrong's vote on our board to nuke Reed [the co-CEO at Citigroup] in showdown." Grubman says his e-mail was baseless and simply a lie to inflate his importance.[29]

6. *Inspirational appeal and emotional display* is an influence method centering on the affective (as opposed to the cognitive) domain. Given that leaders are supposed to inspire others, such an influence tactic is important. As Jeffrey Pfeffer observes, "Executives and others seeking to exercise influence in organizations often develop skill in displaying, or not displaying, their feelings in a strategic fashion."[30] An inspirational appeal usually involves an emotional display by the person seeking to influence. It also involves appealing to group members' emotions.

7. *Joking and kidding,* according to one survey, are widely used to influence others on the job.[31] Good-natured ribbing is especially effective when a straightforward statement might be interpreted as harsh criticism. A manager concerned about the number of errors in a group member's report might say, "Now I know what you are up to. You planted all those errors just to see if I really read your reports."

Which influence tactic to choose? Managers are unlikely to use all the influence tactics in a given situation. Instead, they tend to choose an influence tactic that fits the demands of the circumstance. Researchers found support for this conclusion in a study with 120 managers, along with about 1,200 subordinates, peers, and superiors. (The tactics studied were similar to many of those mentioned in this chapter.) An effective tactic was one that led to task commitment, used by managers who were perceived to be effective by the various raters.

The results suggested that the most effective tactics were rational persuasion, inspirational appeal, and consultation. In contrast, the least effective influence tactics were pressure, coalition formation, and appealing to legitimate authority. The researchers cautioned that the outcome of a specific influence attempt is also determined by such factors as the target's motivation and organizational culture.[32] Also, any influence tactic can trigger target resistance if it is inappropriate for the situation or is applied unskillfully. Tact, diplomacy, and insight are required for effective application of influence (and political) tactics.

5

Explain how managers can control dysfunctional politics.

The Control of Dysfunctional Politics and Ethical Considerations

Carried to excess, organizational politics and influence tactics can hurt an organization and its members. One consequence is that when political factors far outweigh merit, competent employees may become unhappy and quit. Another problem is that politicking takes time away from tasks that could contribute directly to achieving the firm's goals. Many managers spend more time developing political allies (including "kissing up") than coaching group members or doing analytical work.

The most comprehensive antidote to improper, excessive, and unethical organizational politics is to rely on objective measures of performance. This is true because people have less need to behave politically when their contributions can be measured directly. With a formal system of goal setting and review, the results a person attains should be much more important than the impression the person creates. However, even a goal-setting program is not immune from politics. Sometimes the goals are designed to impress key people in the organization. As such, they may not be the most important goals for getting work accomplished. Another political problem with goal setting is that some people will set relatively easy goals so they can look good by attaining all their goals.

Meshing individual and organizational objectives would be the ideal method of controlling excessive, negative political behavior. If their objectives, needs, and interests can be met through their jobs, employees will tend to engage in behavior that fosters the growth, longevity, and productivity of the firm. L. A. Witt investigated how goal congruence between the individual and the organization affected political behavior. When employees perceived considerable politics in the workplace, their commitment to the organization and job performance both suffered. However, when employees and their superiors shared the same goals, commitment and performance were less negatively affected by politics. Witt concluded that one way to reduce the negative impact of organizational politics is for the manager to ensure that his or her subordinates hold the appropriate goal priorities. In this way, group members will have a greater sense of controversy over, and understanding of, the workplace and thus be less affected by the presence of organizational politics.[33]

Finally, open communications can also constrain the impact of political behavior. For instance, open communication can let everyone know the basis for allocating resources, thus reducing the amount of politicking. Organizational politics can also be curtailed by threatening to discuss questionable information in a public forum. If one employee engages in backstabbing of another, the manager might ask her or him to repeat the anecdote in a staff meeting. It has been said that sunlight is the best disinfectant to deviousness.

6

Differentiate between the ethical and unethical use of power, politics, and influence.

Our discussion of sources of power, political tactics, and influence tactics should not imply an endorsement of all of these methods to gain an advantage in the workplace. Each strategy and tactic must be evaluated on its merit by an ethical test, such as those described in Chapter 4. One guiding principle is to turn the strategy or tactic inward. Assume that you believe that a particular tactic (for example, ingratiation) would be ethical in working against you. It would then be fair and ethical for you to use this tactic in attempting to influence others.

Another guiding principle is that it is generally ethical to use power and influence to help attain organizational goals. In contrast, it is generally unethical to use the same tactics to achieve a personal agenda and goals not sanctioned by the organization. Yet even this guideline involves enough "grayness" to be open for interpretation. The following Skill-Development Exercise provides an opportunity to evaluate the ethics of behavior.

Another perspective on organizational politics is to recognize that both the means and the ends of political behavior must be considered. A study of the subject cautioned, "Instead of determining whether human rights or standards of justice are violated, we are often content to judge political behavior according to its outcomes."[34] The authors of the study suggest that when it comes to the ethics of organizational politics, respect for justice and human rights should prevail for its own sake.

SKILL-DEVELOPMENT EXERCISE

The Ethics of Influence Tactics

You decide if the following manager made ethical use of influence tactics.

Sara Nelson is a marketing manager for a finance company that lends money to companies as well as individuals. She comes up with the idea of forming a division in the company that would collect delinquent student loans, strictly on commission. Her company would retain about one-third of the money collected. The clients would be banks having difficulty collecting loans after students graduate. Nelson brings her idea to the CEO, and he grants her the opportunity to make a presentation about the new idea to top management within one month. The CEO states that he sees some merit in the idea, but that the opinion of the rest of the committee will be given considerable weight.

With 29 days to go before the meeting, Sara invites all five members of the executive committee to join her for lunch or breakfast individually. All five finally agree on a date for the lunch or breakfast meeting. During the meals, Sara makes a strong pitch for her idea, and explains that she will need the person's support to sell the idea to the rest of the committee. She also promises, "If you can help me get this collection division launched, you will have one big IOU to cash." Sara stays in touch with the CEO about the upcoming meeting, but does not mention her "pre-selling" lunches.

During the new-initiative review meeting, the five members of the committee support Sara's idea, and the CEO says that he is encouraged, and will now warmly consider the idea of a student loan collection division.

1. Was Sara Nelson behaving ethically?
2. Which influence tactic did she use in attempting to achieve her goals?

IMPLICATIONS FOR MANAGERIAL PRACTICE

1. Recognize that a significant portion of the efforts of organizational members will be directed toward gaining power for themselves or their group. At times, some of this behavior will be directed more toward self-interest than organizational interest. It is therefore often necessary to ask, "Is this action being taken to help this person or is it being done to help the organization?" Your answer to this question should influence your willingness to submit to that person's demands.
2. If you want to establish a power base for yourself, a good starting point is to develop expert power. Most powerful people began their climb to power by demonstrating their expertise in a particular area. (This tactic is referred to as becoming a subject matter expert.)
3. In determining if a particular behavior is motivated by political or merit considerations, evaluate the intent of the actor. The same action might be based on self-interest or concern for others. For instance, a team member might praise you because he believed that you accomplished something of merit. On the other hand, that same individual might praise you to attain a favorable work assignment or salary increase.

SUMMARY OF KEY POINTS

1 **Identify sources of power for individuals and sub-units within organizations.**

Power, politics, and influence are needed by managers to accomplish their work. In the model presented here, managers and professionals use organizational politics to achieve power and influence, thus attaining desired outcomes.

Socialized power is used to forward organizational interests, whereas personalized power is used to forward personal interests. Power granted by the organization consists of legitimate power, coercive power, and reward power. Power stemming from the individual consists of expert power and referent power (the basis for charisma). According to the resource dependence perspective, subunits or individuals who can provide key resources to the organization accrue power. At times, gossip can be a power-giving source.

2 **Describe the essence of empowerment.**

Managers must act in specific ways to empower employees, including removing conditions that keep employees powerless and giving information that enhances employee feelings of self-efficacy. Five critical conditions for empowerment are for an organization to share information with employees, provide them structure, use teams to replace the traditional hierarchy, grant employees the freedom to determine how to achieve objectives, and trust employees.

3 **Pinpoint factors contributing to, and examples of, organizational politics.**

Contributors to organizational politics include: the political nature of organizations, the pyramid structure of organizations, decision making in the absence of formal policy, the need for power, and Machiavellianism. Among the ethical tactics of organizational politics are: developing power contacts; managing your impression; controlling vital information; keeping informed; being courteous, pleasant, and positive; asking satisfied customers to contact your manager; avoiding political blunders; and using sincere flattery. Among the unethical tactics are backstabbing, embrace-or-demolish, stealing credit, and playing territorial games.

4 **Identify and describe a variety of influence tactics.**

Influence tactics frequently used by managerial workers include leading by example, assertiveness, rationality, ingratiation, exchange, inspirational appeal and emotional display, and joking and kidding.

5 **Explain how managers can control dysfunctional politics.**

Approaches to controlling dysfunctional politics include: relying on objective performance measures, meshing individual and organizational objectives, minimizing political behavior by top management, and open communications, including threatening to discuss politicking publicly.

6 **Differentiate between the ethical and unethical use of power, politics, and influence.**

Political behaviors chosen by an individual or organizational unit must rest on ethical considerations. A guiding principle is to use only those tactics you would consider fair and ethical if used against you. Also recognize that both the means and the ends of political behavior must be considered.

KEY TERMS AND PHRASES

Power, *252*
The potential or ability to influence decisions and control resources.

Organizational Politics, *252*
Informal approaches to gaining power through means other than merit or luck.

Socialized Power, *252*
The use of power to achieve constructive ends.

Personalized Power, *252*
The use of power primarily for the sake of personal aggrandizement and gain.

Legitimate Power, *253*
Power based on one's formal position within the hierarchy of the organization.

Coercive Power, *253*
Controlling others through fear or threat of punishment.

Reward Power, *253*
Controlling others through rewards or the promise of rewards.

Expert Power, *253*
The ability to influence others because of one's specialized knowledge, skills, or abilities.

Referent Power, *254*
The ability to influence others that stems from one's desirable traits and characteristics; it is the basis for charisma.

Resource Dependence Perspective, *254*
The need of the organization for a continuing flow of human resources, money, customers, technological inputs, and material to continue to function.

Empowerment, *254*
The process of sharing power with group members, thereby enhancing their feelings of self-efficacy.

Machiavellianism, *257*
A tendency to manipulate others for personal gain.

Territorial Games, *262*
Also known as turf wars, territorial games refer to behaviors involving the hoarding of information and other resources.

DISCUSSION QUESTIONS AND ACTIVITIES

1. What might be the negative consequences to a manager if he or she ignored power, politics, and influence tactics?
2. How might having a lot of power help a person achieve ethical ends within an organization?
3. Describe how the exercise of personal power can lead to position power for an individual.
4. Using concepts from the theory presented about power, explain why people who are skilled at wireless communication (Wi-Fi) have so much power today.
5. Why does the replacement of hierarchy with teams assist the empowerment process?
6. Job hunters are advised to "size up the political climate" before accepting a job at a company. How might the candidate go about sizing up the political climate?
7. What can you do today to start increasing your power? Compare your observations with classmates.

ORGANIZATIONAL BEHAVIOR ONLINE

TO DO

Knowledge of Influence Tactics

Now that you have studied a little bit about influence tactics, here is an opportunity to take an online quiz measuring your mastery of the topic. To measure your iNfluence Quotient, go to http://:www.influenceatwork.com/nq_test.html. A scoring key is provided, and the Web site advises you not to be too hard on yourself if you do not achieve a high score. The authors of the site explain, "It's taken thousands of psychological researchers many decades to discover answers to questions like those above."

TO BOOKMARK

Employee Empowerment
http://www.isixsigma.com/library/content/c000527.asp

Office Politics
http://www.officepolitics.com/home.php

Organizational Politics
http://www.andersonconsulting.com/org/doopsup.htm

CASE PROBLEM: High-Tech Hooky in the Office

David Wiskus gives new meaning to the term "working lunch." The Denver tech-support worker installed a program in his Handspring Visor hand-held that allowed him to manipulate the screen in his office computer from a booth at a local diner. As he lingered over burgers and fries, he could actually open windows and move documents around on his screen via the hand-held—creating the impression to anyone who walked by that the diligent Mr. Wiskus had just stepped away from his desk.

It has never been easier to be a white-collar slacker. While the uninitiated are still grousing about how mobile technology has created a 24/7 work culture and sabotaged their private time, a savvier crowd has moved on to a more rewarding pursuit: using technology to make it look like you're working when you're not.

The Technology for Slackers

An office assistant from New York explains four of her methods for faking work: With her printer she can dial in and print documents on the office printers so people will think she is in. She has her telephone calls forwarded so they follow her from place to place throughout the day. She can go to bed early and use the timer feature in Microsoft Outlook to send e-mails to her boss at 4 A.M. The same assistant also uses remote-control technology to open documents on her office computer screen.

The Wall Street Journal reporter Jane Spencer notes that the shirking tactic is not new, but the tools have become a lot more powerful. Executives have long discreetly asked their secretaries to flip on the office light to make Friday absences

less glaring; leaving a jacket on the back of your chair is also an old trick. But the latest generation of office accessories, from cell phones to the RIM Blackberry, have brought a new level of sophistication—and a host of new strategies for manipulating perceptions of your diligence.

The new options allow people to do far more than send e-mails from the beach. Services like GoToMyPC.com—similar to the one Wiskus used on his hand-held—let you operate your office computer by remote control. You can even move the cursor on your screen, opening documents and printing them on the shared office printer. Other strategies involve using existing technology in new ways. E-mail timers, a standard feature in Microsoft Outlook, let you send e-mails hours after you've gone to bed—a painless way to suggest to the boss that you're burning the midnight oil. (In Outlook, open up a message, [go] to "options," and fill in the "do not deliver before" option.)

Stuart Gilman, director of the Ethics Resource Center in Washington, DC is concerned about this new application of office technology. He says, "If you're out playing golf, and you look like you've spent four hours in the office . . . If everybody does that, the company goes bankrupt."

Even some lower-tech tools, such as call forwarding, have grown more sophisticated, making it a snap to answer your desk phone from your daughter's soccer game or the pedicure chair. Services like Yahoo By Phone also let you pick up your e-mail from afar, even without a hand-held gadget. For about $5.00 per month, a computerized voice named Jenni will read your messages over the phone.

Stretching the Truth

Some business executives say these new tools are dangerous because they play into employees' increasing willingness to fudge the truth about their work life. A recent ethics survey by the Society for Human Resource Management found that 59% of human-resource professionals said they personally observed employees lying about the number of hours they worked; some 53% reported that they saw employees lying to a supervisor, an eight-percentage-point jump in six years.

Some employers not only tolerate the technology, but use it themselves. Skip Coghill, who runs a trucking company, does a lot more than send e-mails in the middle of the night. When he recently took a cruise off the coast of Acapulco, many of his clients never knew he'd left the office. Between casino visits and midnight-buffet runs, Mr. Coghill used the GoToMyPC.com software to operate his office computer by remote control. He could even spy on his employees from the deck of the ship: He brought up Global Positioning Systems maps that showed him the precise location of each of his trucks, down to the intersection. If an employee was off-track, he could fire off a text message to the truck. "I was drinking a piña colada, sitting in my swimsuit, having a total ball," says Mr. Coghill.

David Wiskus Moves On

David Wiskus, the Denver tech worker who manipulated his computer from a nearby diner so he could take three-hour lunches, is no longer with the company. He says he was eventually fired for habitual lateness.

Case Questions

1. In what way is this case, and report, about impression management?

2. What is your evaluation of the ethics of employees who use information technology to distort the truth about whether they are working, or at what time they are working?

3. What is your evaluation of the ethics of the trucking executive who tracked his workers while he was on vacation in Acapulco?

4. Which technique of combating organizational politics might managers use to decrease or eliminate high-tech hooky?

Source: Adapted with permission of the Wall Street Journal from Jane Spencer, "Shirk Ethic: How to Fake a Hard Day at the Office," *The Wall Street Journal,* May 15, 2003, pp. D1, D3. Permission conveyed through the Copyright Clearance Center, Inc.

ENDNOTES

1. Book review in *Personnel Psychology,* Summer 2002, p. 502.
2. Daniel J. Brass and Marlene E. Burkhardt, "Potential Power and Power Use: An Integration of Structure and Behavior," *Academy of Management Journal,* June 1993, pp. 441–442.
3. Jeffrey Pfeffer, *Power in Organizations* (Marshfield, MA: Putman, 1981), p. 7.
4. Robert P. Vecchio, *Organizational Behavior: Core Concepts,* 4th ed. (Mason, OH: South-Western/Thomson Learning, 2000), p. 126.
5. Leonard H. Chusmir, "Personalized vs. Socialized Power Needs among Working Men and Women," *Human Relations,* February 1986, p. 149.
6. John R. P. French and Bertram Raven, "The Basis of Social Power," in Dorwin Cartwright and Alvin Zander, eds., *Group Dynamics: Research and Theory* (Evanston, IL: Row, Peterson and Company, 1962), pp. 607–623.
7. David Koenig, "American Airlines Dumps Executive Bonuses after Criticism from Unions," Associated Press, April 19, 2003. Reprinted with permission of the Associated Press.
8. Amy Merrick and Bruce Orwall, "Leaving Disney, Pressler Will Fill Top Job at Gap," *The Wall Street Journal,* September 27, 2002, pp. B1, B4.
9. Jeffrey D. Kudisch, Mark L. Poteet, Gregory H. Dobbins, Michael C. Rush, and Joyce E. A. Russell, "Expert Power, Referent Power, and Charisma: Toward the Resolution of a Theoretical Debate," *Journal of Business and Psychology,* Winter 1995, p. 189.
10. Jeffrey Pfeffer, *Managing with Power* (Boston: Harvard Business Review Publications, 1990), pp. 100–101.
11. Nancy B. Kurland and Lisa Hope Pelled, "Passing the Word: Toward a Model of Gossip and Power in the Workplace," *Academy of Management Review,* April 2000, p. 429.
12. Anita Bruzzese, "Office Gossip Really Harassment," Gannett News Service, June 2, 2003.
13. Jay A. Conger and Rabindra N. Kanungo, "The Empowerment Process: Integrating Theory and Practice," *Academy of Management Review,* July 1988, pp. 473–474.
14. W. Alan Randolph, "Navigating the Journey to Empowerment," *Organizational Dynamics,* Spring 1995, pp. 19–31.
15. Phillip M. Perry, "Seven Errors to Avoid When Empowering Your Staff," *Success Workshop,* A supplement *to Manager's Edge,* 1999, p. 4.
16. Oren Harari, "The Trust Factor," *Management Review,* January 1999, p. 28.
17. Chad Graham and Dawn Sagario, "'Good Fawning' Over Boss Can Help in Tough Times," *The Des Moines Register* syndicated story, April 20, 2003.
18. Gerald Biberman, "Personality and Characteristic Work Attitudes of Persons with High, Moderate, and Low Political Tendencies," *Psychological Reports,* 1985, pp. 1303–1310.
19. Stanley Bing, *What Would Machiavelli Do?* (New York: HarperCollins, 2000).
20. "Etiquette for the Young—with Bite," The Associated Press, June 8, 2002.
21. "'Career Insurance' Protects DP Professionals from Setbacks, Encourages Growth," *Data Management,* June 1986, p. 33. The same principle is equally valid today.
22. "Face Cowardly Backstabbers in the Workplace," Knight Ridder story, February 13, 2000.
23. Jared Sandberg, "Some Bosses Never Meet a Success That Isn't Theirs," *The Wall Street Journal,* April 23, 2003, p. B1.
24. "Stopping Idea Thieves: Strike Back When Rivals Steal Credit," *Executive Leadership Extra!* April 2003, p. 3.
25. Annette Simmons, *Territorial Games: Understanding & Ending Turf Wars at Work* (New York: AMACOM, 1998).
26. Jeffrey Zaslow, "The Politics of the 'CC' Line," *The Wall Street Journal,* May 28, 2003, p. D2.
27. Several of the tactics are from Gary Yukl and Cecilia M. Falbe, "Influence Tactics and Objectives in Upward, Downward, and Lateral Influence Attempts," *Journal of Applied Psychology,* April 1990, pp. 132–140.
28. "Aloofness Doesn't Pay," *Executive Strategies,* April 2000, p. 1.

29. Daniel Kadlec, "Did Sandy Play Dirty?" *Time,* November 25, 2002, pp. 21–22.

30. Pfeffer, *Managing with Power,* p. 224.

31. Andrew J. DuBrin, "Sex Differences in the Use and Effectiveness of Tactics of Impression Management," *Psychological Reports,* Vol. 74, 1994, pp. 531–544.

32. Gary Yukl and J. Bruce Tracey, "Consequences of Influence Tactics Used with Subordinates, Peers, and the Boss," *Journal of Applied Psychology,* August 1992, pp. 525–535.

33. L. A. Witt, "Enhancing Organizational Goal Congruence: A Solution to Organizational Politics," *Journal of Applied Psychology,* August 1998, pp. 666–674.

34. Gerald F. Cavanagh, Dennis J. Moberg, and Manuel Velasquez, "The Ethics of Organizational Politics," *Academy of Management Review,* July 1981, p. 372.

Chapter 13

Organization
Structure and Design

When describing why it had been difficult to get the giant chipmaker into the Internet age, Intel Chief Executive Craig R. Barrett used the metaphor of Intel's microprocessor business being a creosote bush, a tall desert plant that drips poisonous oil, killing off all vegetation that attempts to grow within anywhere near itself. Microprocessors so dominated the company's strategy, Barrett explains, that other businesses could not sprout around it. Chips, he says, "are a dream business with wonderful margins and a wonderful market position. How could anything else compete here for resources and profitability?"

Barrett works to reshape Intel into a supplier of a full range of semiconductors for networking gear, information appliances, and PCs. His efforts move Intel toward radically different areas such as e-commerce, consumer electronics, Internet servers, and wireless telephones. "We're putting a new image on top of the big powerful chip monster that eats the world," Barrett says.

The old Intel was dedicated to a single product (Intel inside). The core of the changes at Intel will divide the company into five groups so as to better pursue new products and acquisitions. The groups are Computer Processors, Information Appliances, Intel Online Service, New Business Group, and Web-hosting Business. The Computer Processors group is still the heart of Intel's business. Processors and companion chips still contribute the vast majority of Intel's sales and profits, but the new divisions are poised to help the company grow.

Source: Andy Reinhardt, "The New Intel: Craig Barrett Is Leading the Chip Giant into Riskier Terrain," *Business Week*, March 13, 2000, pp. 110–124.

NOW ASK YOURSELF: What is the point of this Intel story? It illustrates how organization structure influences organization behavior. A company's success sometimes depends on the organization structure it creates to meet the demands of the future. Intel has moved away from essentially a one-product company to a multidivision firm organized according to products and services. As a consequence, work is now organized differently at Intel. In this chapter, we describe organization structure because understanding structure is part of organizational behavior. Structure and behavior influence each other. For example, a loose organization structure, such as a collection of teams, requires employees to work productively without the benefit of close supervision. In contrast, some employees need careful guidelines for conducting their work, and therefore need a tighter structure, such as a bureaucracy.

The purpose of this chapter is to understand the various types of organization structures and factors that influence the structure for a given purpose. Three terms need to be clarified first. An **organization** is a collection of people working together to achieve a common purpose (or simply a big group). **Organization structure** is the arrangement of people and tasks to accomplish organizational goals. The structure is usually indicated on the organization chart, along with specifying who reports to whom. **Organizational design** is the process of creating a structure that best fits a purpose, strategy, and environment. For example, a giant motor company like Ford Motors emphasizes organization by product, such as having a separate division for Jaguar Motors. The organization design is a guided process for integrating the workers, information, and technology of a firm.[1]

FOUNDATION CONCEPTS OF ORGANIZATIONAL STRUCTURE

Organizations are so complex that many different variables are required to describe them, similar to describing people or machines. To get started understanding how organizations are structured, we look at five key concepts: mechanistic versus organic, formal versus informal, degree of formalization, degree of centralization, and complexity. You will observe that several concepts about organization structure overlap, thereby simplifying the understanding of organizations (see the video sidebar).

Identify and define the foundation concepts of organization structure, including the informal organization.

Mechanistic versus Organic

A major variable for understanding organization structure is whether it is mechanistic or organic. A **mechanistic organization** is primarily hierarchical with an emphasis on specialization and control and vertical communication; with heavy reliance on rules, policies, and procedures. An old-fashioned manufacturing organization such as the General Motors of yesteryear is an example of a mechanistic organization. The term has become synonymous with the term bureaucracy.

An **organic structure** is laid out like a network and emphasizes horizontal specialization, extensive use of personal coordination, and extensive communication among members; with loose rules, policies, and procedures. Knowledge resides wherever it is most useful to the organization. Organic structures are known for their responsiveness to a changing environment. A small high-tech start-up would be an example of an organic structure. Also, a shop that makes custom racing cars would have an organic form.

Machado & Silvetti Associates, Inc. (12:24)

As you begin your exploration of organization structure and organizational design, take an inside look at Boston-based architectural firm Machado and Silvetti by viewing a video segment about the firm at **http://dubrin.swlearning .com.** Pay particular attention to how roles overlap and how project manager Mike Yusem describes his own role and responsibilities. Then after you have read the chapter, think about the firm's structure. Try to explain the horizontal and vertical associations that exist at Machado and Silvetti. *Where would you place the firm on a continuum from mechanistic to organic? From formal to informal? Why does Mike Yusem seem to have difficulty in delegating? Does the firm's structure contribute to his difficulties?*

272

Formal versus Informal Structure

Understanding the difference between the formal and informal structure is akin to understanding the difference between formal and informal groups, as described in Chapter 10. The **formal organization structure** is an official statement of reporting relationships, rules, and regulations. The rules and regulations are designed to cover all the events and transactions that are likely to take place in conducting the business of the organization. For example, the formal organization structure tells managers how to respond to employee requests for an education leave of absence or what to do with damaged parts from vendors.

The **informal organization structure** is a set of unofficial working relationships that emerges to take care of the events and transactions not covered by the formal structure. The informal structure supplements the formal structure by adding a degree of flexibility and speed. A widespread application of the informal structure is the presence of "tech fixers" in most firms who supplement the technical support center. For example, marketing assistant Rick might be skilled at resolving Internet-related problems. As a consequence, many people call on Rick for some quick assistance even though the formal organization indicates that they should use the tech support center for help with Internet problems.

Another perspective on the informal organization structure is that all companies have hidden shadow organizations where much of the real work gets accomplished. The shadow organization is revealed by social network analysis, which traces who talks to whom, who listens, and how most of the information and influence really flows. Consultants Ernst & Ernst LLP reported finding opportunities to save a large auto industry supplier more than $14 million by using social network analysis to uncover inefficient communication that was deterring innovation.[2]

Social network analysis reveals the informal social relationships and the unofficial communication channels, so it also helps to understand informal groups and informal communication channels. Tracking the informal relationships within an organization can help explain how and why new hires either succeed or fail to assimilate into the corporate culture. Workers who connect to the right information flow will perform better because of the connections they make.

Network mappers begin by surveying company employees to find answers to several key questions. The basic one is "To whom do you go for information about what's going on?" Other questions are asked about the frequency of interaction or are used to differentiate between requests for information and requests for influence. Based on the answers, the mappers draw diagrams that graphically show who is connected to whom.[3] (In the past, such diagrams were referred to as sociograms.)

Social network analysis can benefit managers by revealing if people are getting the information they need to perform their jobs well. The same analysis can point to which employees are in the best position to disseminate useful information to other workers.

Degree of Formalization

The dimension of **formalization** is the degree to which expectations regarding the methods of work are specified, committed to writing, and enforced. The more policies, rules, and procedures there are specifying how people should behave, the more formalized the organization. An organization with a high degree of formalization is likely to have a high degree of specialization of labor and high delegation of authority. A more formal organization is more mechanistic and bureaucratic. A motor vehicle bureau usually has a high degree of formalization, especially in dealing with the public. (People cannot order vanity license plates without paying a fee, no matter how sweetly they ask!)

Degree of Centralization

Centralization refers to the extent to which executives delegate authority to lower organizational units. The smaller the amount of delegation, the more centralized the organization. In a decentralized firm, however, some decisions are more centralized than others. Strategic decisions—those involving the overall functioning of the firm—are more likely to be centralized than operational decisions. An organization that relies heavily on functional (specialized) units will be more centralized because top management needs to coordinate the functions of the various units.

Domino's Pizza is a highly centralized firm. Company headquarters makes all the major decisions about matters such as the menu and décor of their establishments, the quality of their products, and the speed of their deliveries. An example of a highly decentralized firm is Tyco, a worldwide collection of loosely associated business firms (a conglomerate) engaged in both manufacturing and services. CEOs of the affiliated companies have considerable latitude in running their businesses yet must meet financial targets set by headquarters.

Complexity

Complexity refers to the number of different job titles and organizational units. Large organizations often have hundreds of departments and thousands of job titles. In a complex organization, many of the job titles are esoteric, such as "risk analyst," "contract administrator," and "fleet manager." The more complex the organization, the more difficult it is to manage. Complexity typically increases in direct proportion to size. Small organizations have fewer job titles and departments.

The concept of *differentiation* is closely linked to complexity. A horizontally differentiated organization has many different job titles, and many different departments doing separate work, whereas a vertically differentiated organization has many levels. A giant bureaucracy such as Citigroup has considerable horizontal and vertical differentiation.

THE BUREAUCRATIC FORM OF ORGANIZATION

As already implied, a **bureaucracy** is a rational, systematic, and precise form of organization in which rules, regulations, and techniques of control are precisely defined. *Bureau* is the French word for office, indicating that a bureaucracy is a form of organization with many different offices. Exhibit 13-1 depicts the basic concept of the bureaucratic form of organization. A bureaucracy was conceived of by Max Weber to be the ideal organization, having the following characteristics:

2

Specify the basic features of the bureaucratic form of organization structure, including how it is divided into departments.

- Rules and procedures controlling organizational activities
- A high degree of differentiation among organizational functions
- A high degree of job specialization
- An organization of offices determined by hierarchy, with each unit reporting to a higher unit and no unit free-floating
- A heavy emphasis on rules and norms to regulate behavior

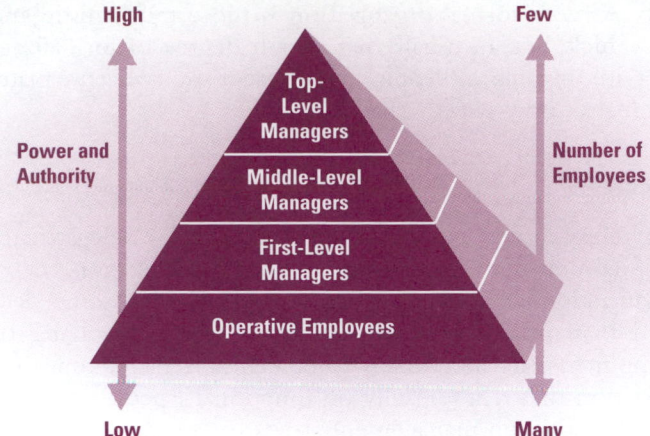

Exhibit 13-1

The Bureaucratic Form of Organization

In a bureaucracy, power is concentrated at the top. Note that team leaders are typically found at the first level or middle level of management.

- Interpersonal relations characterized by impersonality in place of favoritism
- Selection and promotion based on merit
- All administrative actions recorded in writing[4]

The ideal organization just described is called a **machine bureaucracy** because it standardizes work processes and is efficient. It is best suited to large organizations whose work is largely performed by production, technical, and support workers. In contrast, a **professional bureaucracy,** composed of a core of highly trained professionals, standardizes skills for coordination. Professional bureaucracies include organizations such as accounting firms, consulting firms, hospitals, and universities. Because it is difficult to regulate the work of professionals performing complex work, the professional bureaucracy decentralizes decision making and is less formal than a machine bureaucracy. The professional bureaucracy is relatively flat, with considerable differentiation across units.[5]

In visualizing a typical bureaucracy, it appears that one person is in charge of every function, including running the enterprise. In reality, authority is shared to some extent in top-level positions. You will recall the existence of top management teams as described in Chapter 10, in which major executives share responsibility for directing an enterprise. A dual-executive team is becoming more frequent in major corporations. A company founder will often divest day-to-day responsibilities to another executive, so the former can concentrate more on strategy and building relationships with the outside world. Starbucks, Charles Schwab, and Amazon.com had major changes in leadership to create two-person executive teams who share a company vision. Bill Gates of Microsoft transferred his role as chief executive to company CEO Steve Ballmer. Gates assumed the job of chief software architect. Despite this power sharing, one person still stands out as the symbolic leader of each firm. The arrangement is a softening of having one person in charge, but not an abandonment of the principle.

Before reading about the good and bad side of bureaucracy, do the accompanying Self-Assessment, which follows on page 276. It will help you assess how well you might fit into a bureaucracy.

The Contribution of Bureaucracy

Bureaucratic forms of organization have persisted because, used properly, they make possible large-scale accomplishments that cannot be achieved by small groups of people working independently. The Social Security Administration is an example of a large bureaucracy that accomplishes an astonishing amount of work each month in paying benefits to approximately 50 million Americans. Elliot Jacques has aptly expressed the contribution of bureaucracy:

> Thirty-five years of research has convinced me that managerial hierarchy (or bureaucracy) is the most efficient, hardiest, and in fact the most natural structure ever devised for large corporations. Properly structured, hierarchy can release energy and creativity, rational productivity, and actually improve morale.[6]

An analysis by Paul S. Adler also points to the important contributions of bureaucracy. One of his major arguments is that slashing bureaucracy can backfire. Many firms have discovered that the layers of managers eliminated to reduce bureaucracy are often the repository of precious skills and expertise.[7] After many middle manager positions have been eliminated, their loss is recognized and regretted.

A similar argument is that dumping the policies and procedures characteristic of a bureaucracy can weaken an organization. In many cases, these procedures embody a vast organizational memory of best practices. Having tossed out the manuals, many organizations discover that their employees are frustrated because they have to improvise with little guidance. A lot of time is wasted in reinventing and redeveloping useful procedures that have been discarded. For example, a newly appointed credit manager might not have a policy for dealing with a long-term, reliable customer who suddenly becomes delinquent with payments.

The hierarchical form of organization called bureaucracy emerged from necessity. It is the only form of organization that enables a firm to employ large numbers of people and still hold them clearly accountable for their results. Bureaucracy is also important for the emotional reason that they fulfill our deep need for order and security.[8] As an employee, it is comforting to know that there is an efficient system in place to deposit your pay directly into your bank twice per month, and that if the fluorescent bulb in your office burns out, you know which office (bureau!) to call.

Potential Dysfunctions of a Bureaucracy

Not all bureaucracies work like Max Weber intended. The major problem is that members of the bureaucracy often carry out its characteristics to the extreme. Organizations that rely heavily on formal controls to direct people sometimes suppress initiative and decision making at lower levels of management. Too many controls and too much review of decisions can also lower productivity. A bureaucracy is subject to rigidity in handling people and problems. Although a bureaucratic design is supposed to hold people accountable for results, some people in large bureaucracies tend to *pass the buck,* or claim that a particular problem is the responsibility of another department or person. A bureaucracy's well-intended rules and regulations sometimes create inconvenience and inefficiency. Some experts blame the demise of the Pontiac Fiero, five years after it was introduced, on a bureaucracy that was rigid and inefficient. For example, the car died after the company decided not to spend enough money to make changes as basic as power steering.

A major problem within large bureaucracies is that they are clumsy and slow, often prompting companies to go outside when they need something done in a hurry, such as developing a prototype of a new product. (As described later, almost all bureaucracies have built-in structures to overcome the slowness problem.) Business writer Keith H. Hammonds has expressed the extreme negative view of

SELF-ASSESSMENT

The Bureaucratic Orientation Scale

Directions: Answer each question "mostly agree" (MA) or "mostly disagree" (MD). Assume the mindset of attempting to learn something about yourself rather than attempting to impress a prospective employer.

	MA	MD
1. I value stability in my job.	❏	❏
2. I like a predictable organization.	❏	❏
3. I enjoy working without the benefit of a carefully specified job description.	❏	❏
4. I would enjoy working for an organization in which promotions are generally determined by seniority.	❏	❏
5. Rules, policies, and procedures tend to frustrate me.	❏	❏
6. I would enjoy working for a company that employed 95,000 people worldwide.	❏	❏
7. Being self-employed would involve more risk than I'm willing to take.	❏	❏
8. Before accepting a job, I would like to see an exact job description.	❏	❏
9. I would prefer a job as a freelance Web designer to one as a supervisor for the Department of Motor Vehicles.	❏	❏
10. Seniority should be as important as performance in determining pay increases and promotion.	❏	❏
11. It would give me a feeling of pride to work for the largest and most successful company in its field.	❏	❏
12. Given a choice, I would prefer to make $125,000 per year as a vice president in a small company than $150,000 per year as middle manager in a large company.	❏	❏
13. I would feel uncomfortable if I was to wear an employee badge with a number on it.	❏	❏
14. Parking spaces in a company lot should be assigned according to job level.	❏	❏
15. I would generally prefer working as a specialist instead of performing many different tasks.	❏	❏
16. Before accepting a job, I would want to make sure that the company has a good program of employee benefits.	❏	❏
17. A company will not be successful unless it establishes a clear set of rules and regulations.	❏	❏
18. Regular working hours and vacation are more important to me than finding thrills on the job.	❏	❏
19. You should respect people according to their rank.	❏	❏
20. Rules are meant to be broken.	❏	❏

Scoring and Interpretation: Give yourself one point for each question that you answered in the bureaucratic direction:

1. Mostly agree	8. Mostly agree	15. Mostly disagree
2. Mostly agree	9. Mostly disagree	16. Mostly agree
3. Mostly disagree	10. Mostly agree	17. Mostly agree
4. Mostly agree	11. Mostly agree	18. Mostly agree
5. Mostly disagree	12. Mostly disagree	19. Mostly agree
6. Mostly agree	13. Mostly disagree	20. Mostly disagree
7. Mostly agree	14. Mostly agree	

15–20   You would enjoy working in a bureaucracy.

8–14   You would experience a mixture of satisfaction and dissatisfaction if working in a bureaucracy.

0–7   You would most likely be frustrated by working in a bureaucracy, especially a large one.

Source: Updated from *Human Relations: A Job Oriented Approach,* 5th ed., by Andrew J. DuBrin © 1988. Reprinted by permission of Pearson Education, Inc., Upper Saddle River, NJ.

large bureaucracies as inefficient and monolithic entities: "Big companies are broken. Nearly a century old, the modern business organization is nearing the end of its useful life. The old model is dying."[9] (Has Hammonds visited a Wal-Mart lately?)

Another frequent problem in a bureaucracy is high frustration accompanied by low satisfaction. The sources of these negative feelings include red tape, slow decision making, and an individual's limited influence on how well the organization performs.

The accompanying Organizational Behavior in Action box illustrates how an extremely successful organization can be heavily bureaucratic in key respects, yet still retain a climate of democracy, and quickly respond to problems.

Departmentalization

In bureaucratic and other forms of organization, the work is subdivided into departments or other units. The departmentalization capitalizes upon the classic bureaucratic principle of specialization and also helps avoid confusion. Can you imagine the chaos if all the workers in an organization of more than fifty people worked in one large department? The process of subdividing work into departments is called **departmentalization.**

Here we will use charts to illustrate four frequently used forms of departmentalization: functional, territorial, product service, and customer. Most organization charts show a combination of these various types. The majority of business firms use a combination of the first four structures, leading to the creation of a fifth type of departmentalization—a hybrid.

Functional Departmentalization

Functional departmentalization involves grouping people according to their expertise. Bureaucracies are almost always organized into functional departments. Within a given department, the work may be further subdivided. For instance, finance may include subunits for accounts receivable, accounts payable, and payroll. The names of functional departments vary widely with the nature of the business or enterprise. Exhibit 13-2 illustrates a representative type of functional structure. The advantages and disadvantages of functional departmentalization follow those of a bureaucracy.

Territorial Departmentalization

Grouping subunits according to the geographic area served is **territorial departmentalization.** In this structure, those responsible for all the activities of a firm

Exhibit 13-2

Functional Departmentalization within the Davenport Machine Company

Observe that each box below the level of chief executive officer (CEO) indicates an executive in charge of a specific function or activity, such as having responsibility for sales and marketing.

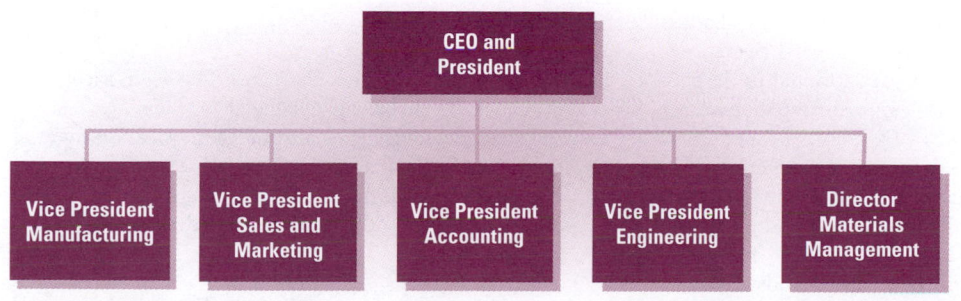

Organizational Behavior *in Action*

Park Memorial Hospital Skillfully Blends Hierarchy with Democracy

Parkland Memorial Hospital in Dallas, Texas is the busiest maternity hospital in America. In a recent year, Parkland delivered 16,597 babies. Not only is that more babies than any other maternity ward in America, it's also more babies born in one Dallas hospital than were born in 10 of America's states, as well as the District of Columbia. Indeed, it's *4 out of every 1,000 babies born in the United States.*

But what's most impressive about all of those babies is how good Parkland is at getting them born safely. On neonatal death rates—how many babies die within the first month—Parkland beats the national average. For African-American babies, Parkland's rate of stillbirths is lower than the national average; its rate of very-low-birth-weight babies is lower than the national average, and its C-section rate is 21%, compared with a national average of 24.4%. (All figures refer to stillbirths.)

That impressive performance becomes astonishing when you consider the population that Parkland serves: 95% of the women who deliver at the hospital are indigent. Because Parkland is the county hospital in Dallas, its maternity service takes all comers, from private patients to illegal immigrants. Parkland spends less money per baby than the national average.

Parkland has a strategy for performance, innovation, and customer care that embraces a set of contradictory—even counterintuitive—ideas. The L&D (labor and delivery) areas, for instance, operate within rigidly, carefully codified rules about medical practice, a method that is unusual even for an academic medical center. But those rules play out in a workplace culture of notable informality and flexibility. Parkland's L&D staff constantly manages to turn adversity into advantage.

Practically overwhelmed by the increasing number of babies, critically short of nurses, and operating in a building designed for 3,000 fewer births a year, Parkland's L&D department has had to reengineer how it delivers babies several times over the past 20 years. Some measures adopted in desperate efforts to keep pace have improved patient care.

The professional staff in Parkland's L&D areas is divided into an elaborate hierarchy. At any given moment, there are 14 distinct levels of medical staff, from nurse's aides ("OB* techs") to attending physicians with years of experience. The hierarchy involves a precise definition of duties and authority at every level: There are three different kinds of nurses, for instance, each allowed to do different

*Obstetrics, not organizational behavior.

things. And yet in practice, the L&D floors could not be less hierarchical. L&D has an egalitarian, all-hands-on-deck spirit.

At 7 AM each day, clerks, nurses, and doctors all change hands. Everyone needs to brief everyone else. The new charge nurse takes command of the board and a walkie-talkie that links her to the other charge nurses and physicians. New nurses coming on duty stand by for assignments and to learn details about each patient. The senior resident takes command of a half-dozen more-junior doctors.

People call one another by their first—or last—names, without resorting to titles. Everyone wears the same blue scrubs, and doctors and support staff share locker rooms without regard to rank. "It's important that there be roles," says Dr. George Wendel. "It's not important there be boundaries."

There is a careful system behind the success of L&D, one that's been honed for over 50 years. Parkland's L&D areas rely on a set of protocols that define every step of the medical experiences for women. The protocols—actual rules that are written down and taught—specify which questions a woman should be asked in a satellite clinic during her first prenatal visit. Another example is [that] the protocols specify that at Parkland, RNs do not do pelvic exams—those are for doctors, midwives, or nurse practitioners.

Miriam Sibley, the senior VP of Parkland's Women and Children's Services Divisions, says the rules "give us a way to organize a tremendous amount of work." Says Dr. Steve Bloom, associate medical director of L&D: "Without the protocols, well, you've got 50 faculty members, 40 midwives, and 100 nurses, all practicing medicine. It would be chaos. The protocols reduce variability, error, and cost, and they increase care. It seems Parkland's is a better way of doing things."

Questions

1. In what ways is the Parkland L&D division bureaucratic or hierarchical?
2. In what way is the Parkland L&D division democratic or non-hierarchical?
3. In what way might organization structure be contributing to the success of deliveries at Parkland?

Source: Reprinted with permission of Fast Company from Charles Fishman, "Miracle of Birth," *Fast Company,* October 2002, pp. 106–116. Permission conveyed through Copyright Clearance Center, Inc.

in a given geographic area report to one manager. The internationalization of business has increased the relevance of organizing by territory. Service organizations make extensive use of territorial departmentalization. For example, large insurance and financial services firms organize territorially. Territorial departmentalization is used frequently to supplement functional groupings. In a frequently used structure, a corporate headquarters might departmentalize by function while the field forces would organize by territory.

Product/Service Departmentalization

Product/service departmentalization is the arrangement of departments according to the products or services they provide. When specific products or services are so important they almost become independent companies, product departmentalization makes sense. Exhibit 13-3 presents a version of product service departmentalization at the capital (financial-services) unit of General Electric Company. Notice that the four finance divisions offer product or services with unique demands of their own. For example, the sale of insurance and investment products is a different business than lending money to business firms. Notice also that the same customer might purchase services from one or more subdivisions, such as a small business purchasing life insurance from one unit, and borrowing money to finance a new machine from another. As a consequence, the structure is not customer departmentalization.

Customer Departmentalization

Customer departmentalization creates a structure based on customer needs. When the demands of one group of customers are quite different from the demands of another, customer departmentalization often results. Many manufacturing companies organize their efforts according to business and retail departments, such as the marketing of Hewlett-Packard personal computers. Many manufacturers and retailers now have an e-commerce or e-tailing division or department. Such units represent customer departmentalization because the divisions or departments cater to the customer group that chooses to trade over the Internet. Sometimes the e-groups have their own physical facilities, such as a distribution center and dedicated servers.

The overriding advantage of organizing by territory, product service, or customer is that it gives major attention to enhancing that product's growth or providing good service to customers. Such units also foster employee pride. The same types of departmentalization present problems identical to any other form of decentralization. It can be expensive because of duplication of effort and the difficulty of controlling the organization units.

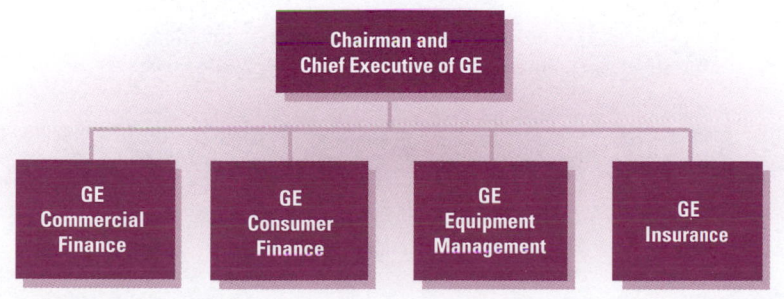

Exhibit 13-3

Product/Service Departmentalization at GE Capital

Notice that the four divisions of GE Capital could be considered separate business firms.

Hybrid Organization Structure

Almost all complex organizations contain several forms of departmentalization, either in the overall organization chart or in various divisions. Referring back to Exhibit 13-3, imagine that the Consumer Finance Division departmentalized into subdivisions for car loans, credit cards, and boats/recreational vehicles. You would then have an organization that featured product-service departmentalization yet also contained a division with customer departmentalization. A **hybrid (or mixed) organization structure** combines the advantages of two or more types of organization forms into one structure. Some functions may be highly specialized and located at corporate headquarters, whereas other units (such as product or territorial units) may be self-contained and located elsewhere. Exhibit 13-4 illustrates a hybrid organization structure. It is doubtful any large, complex organization could function effectively or efficiently without using a hybrid design.

Line versus Staff Units

In Chapter 8, line and staff groups were mentioned in relation to conflict. Line and staff groups are present in most forms of departmentalization, yet the organization chart rarely makes such designations. In Exhibit 13-2, the manufacturing, sales and marketing, and materials management units would all be considered staff units. The accounting and engineering groups would *sometimes* be considered staff groups. If a sixth box were added, human resources, we would definitely have a staff group.

The distinction between line and staff is often blurred. (Line groups are responsible for the primary purposes of the firm, whereas staff groups are responsible for the secondary purposes.) Members of some departments are not sure if they are perceived as line or staff by top management, leading to role ambiguity. A marketing executive said, "The key purpose of our firm is to provide goods to customers. Yet when cutbacks take place, marketing people get chopped first. It makes no sense to me."

Exhibit 13-4

Hybrid Organization Structure

Most organizations use different organization structures at each organizational level or at various places throughout the organization.

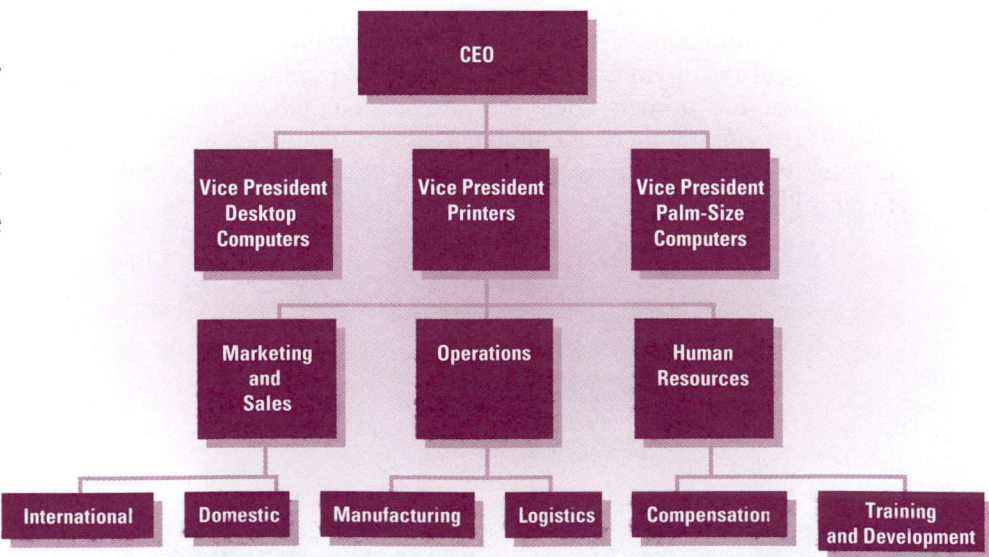

KEY MODIFICATIONS OF THE BUREAUCRATIC STRUCTURE

To overcome several of the disadvantages of the bureaucratic and functional forms of organization, several other structures have developed. Typically these less bureaucratic structures are used to supplement or modify the bureaucratic structure. Teams, as described in Chapter 7 in the context of job design, have emerged as the most widely used supplement to the bureaucratic structure. Task forces and projects follow a similar departure from bureaucracy as do teams. Here we describe the matrix organization structure, the flat structure, and outsourcing as an organization arrangement.

Matrix Organization Structure

Traditional organizations can be slow to respond to change. A frequently used antidote to this problem is the **matrix organization structure,** which consists of a project structure superimposed on a functional structure. A **project** is a temporary group of specialists working together under one manager to accomplish a fixed objective, such as launching a major new product. The word *matrix* refers to the feature of something contained in something else, similar to a grid with numbers in the cells (see Exhibit 13-5). The distinguishing feature of the matrix organization is the responsibility of the project or program manager to achieve results through employees who also report directly to another manager or have dual reporting responsibilities. For example, a person assigned to a project in a matrix organization might report to both the project manager and the manager in his or her regular department.

3

Describe three key modifications of a bureaucratic structure: matrix, flat, and outsourcing.

281

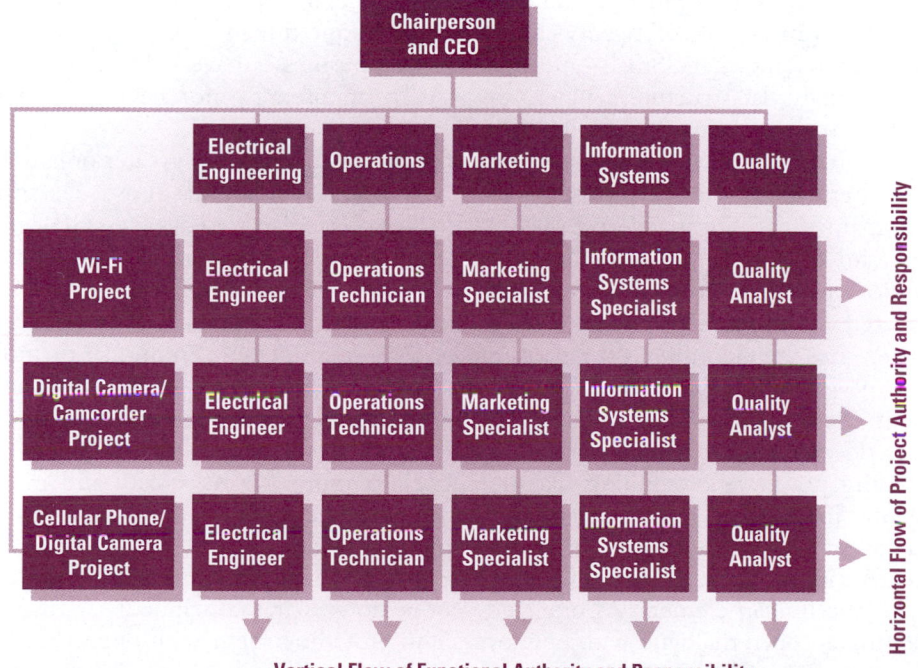

Exhibit 13-5

Matrix Organization in an Electronics Company

In a matrix organization, a project structure is superimposed on a functional structure.

A major purpose of the matrix organization is to allow the firm to take advantage of new opportunities and solve special problems. Instead of developing a new organization containing functional departments, the firm leaves the original organization intact. The project or program managers within the matrix structure have access to the resources of the functional departments. A key advantage of the matrix organization is its ability to implement important projects that demand intense, sustained attention for a limited time. It has been used, for example, to build a prototype for an e-commerce system. On the negative side, the matrix structure often creates problems because people assigned to projects within the matrix have a dual reporting relationship. One study concluded that matrix organizations have proved unworkable, particularly in international settings. Separated by the barriers of distance, language, culture, and different time zones, international managers could not overcome the confusion created by matrix structures.[10]

Despite this potential disadvantage, a project manager in a matrix organization is not doomed to failure. The challenge for the manager is to use a high level of interpersonal skill (such as the ability to resolve conflict) as well as technical skill to achieve goals.

Flat Organization Structures and Downsizing

A **flat organization structure** is one that has relatively few layers. A flat structure is less bureaucratic for two reasons. First, few managers in this form of organization are available to review the decisions of other people. As a by-product, customer service is often improved because many customer problems can be resolved without waiting for layers of approval. Second, because the chain of command is shorter, there is less concern about authority differences among people. Most large organizations have moved toward flatter structures, continuing a trend that began over 25 years ago. General Motors, for example, has moved from a peak of twenty-nine layers to about fifteen today (the number fluctuates somewhat). Small- and medium-size businesses have held on to their traditionally flat structures, which are usually imposed by not having enough money to build management depth.

Flatter organization structures created by downsizing lead to greater organizational efficiency about one-half the time. GE, one of the world's most successful companies, has downsized over 100,000 workers in the last two decades. Hewlett-Packard laid off over 15,000 employees after its merger with Compaq, and became a more profitable company because of it. A controversial aspect of flat structures created by downsizing is that they result in substantial human suffering. Even when jobs are plentiful, losing a job can result in considerable emotional turmoil for the individual. Survivors of the downsizing also experience problems, such as guilt. On a larger scale, when large numbers of companies and government agencies downsize, a recession is perpetuated because fewer people have strong purchasing power. A continuing recession leads to more job insecurity and more layoffs, intensifying human suffering. More will be said about the problems associated with downsizing as a change strategy in Chapter 14.

An important implication for managers when creating flat structures is to deal with the human element. As one study about downsizing concluded: ". . . maintaining an open dialogue with employees and providing them with opportunities to affirm themselves in a positive manner will help to eliminate some of the negative outcomes which accompany layoffs."[11]

Outsourcing as an Organizational Arrangement

An increasingly common practice among organizations of all types and sizes is to **outsource,** or have work performed for them by other organizations. Outsourcing is linked to organization structure because it is a method of dividing work: Certain activities are assigned to groups outside the organization. Another way of framing outsourcing is that it is a vast network of interconnected enterprises that depend on one another for services.[12] By outsourcing, a company can reduce its need for employees and physical assets and reduce payroll costs. Many firms outsource the development and start-up phases of their e-commerce units to outside information technology consultants. Much to the chagrin of labor unions and local workers, many companies outsource work to geographic areas where workers are paid lower wages.

Among the many examples of outsourcing would be for a small company to hire another company to manage its payroll and employee benefits and for a large manufacturing firm to have certain components made by another firm. Even IBM is a contractor for other employers; for example, in making the hard drives for other computer manufacturers or managing their computer systems. A new thrust in outsourcing is for U.S. firms to send white-collar professional jobs overseas, including software development and financial services. A 2003 study revealed that U.S. financial services firms planned to transfer 500,000 jobs, or 8 percent, of total industry employment during the following five years.[13] By mid-2003, however, the U.S. Congress and several states were looking for ways to reduce the outflow of American white-collar jobs overseas (see the InfoTrac sidebar). Overall, the outsourcing movement has been a boon for small- and medium-size firms who perform stable work for larger organizations.

A key implication of outsourcing as an organization design strategy is that people over whom you have no direct control perform work for your company. Other managers are responsible for leading and managing employees who perform important functions for the organization. A frequent concern in the clothing, toy, and consumer electronics industries is that subcontractors sometimes engage in unsavory practices, such as violating wage and child-labor laws. Outsourcing has led to sweatshops as smaller firms compete to offer the lowest possible price for manufacturing goods. Outsourcing can therefore create ethical dilemmas.

Another key human aspect of outsourcing is that it breeds conflict over which functions should be outsourced. Labor unions vehemently oppose a company sending jobs to lower wage countries in order to save money, thereby resulting in job loss for union members. Department heads within a company fight to defend themselves against being outsourced, such as outsourcing the training function of the human resources department. Another example would be the head of a software development unit in a U.S. company struggling against a plan to outsource software development to an Indian company.

Are steep increases in the outsourcing of white-collar jobs the dark side of globalization? Log on to InfoTrac College Edition at **http://www.infotrac -college.com,** and use the Advanced Search tool to locate recent articles on the outsourcing of white-collar work from issues of *Fortune, BusinessWeek, Forbes,* or other similar publications. Find examples of different kinds of jobs that have relocated offshore. Where are the majority of jobs going? What are some of the reasons that jobs are moving to the Far East versus other locations? Also, consider what kind of legislation is being proposed to prevent further shifts of American jobs overseas. Is outsourcing a trend American legislators can reverse?

LEADING-EDGE ORGANIZATION STRUCTURES

4

Spin-offs from traditional organization structures continue to emerge as organizations strive to improve their efficiency and effectiveness. A major reason for these changes is that a traditional mechanistic organization can be too cumbersome to respond to changes in the environment. Two leading-edge forms are the horizontal structure and the network organization.

Describe the two contemporary organizational designs referred to as horizontal structures and network structures.

The Horizontal Structure

A major current development in organizational design is to work horizontally rather than vertically. A **horizontal structure** is the arrangement of work by teams that are responsible for accomplishing a process. The virtual organization is thereby similar to the establishment of work teams. A major difference, however, is that team members are responsible for a process rather than a product or service. The difference is subtle; the team aims at delivering a product or service to a customer rather than focusing on the product or service itself. Instead of focusing on a specialized task, all team members focus on achieving the purpose of all the activity, such as getting a product in the hands of a customer. In a horizontal structure or process organization, employees take collective responsibility for customers.[14]

One approach to switching from a task emphasis to the process emphasis in a horizontal structure is through **reengineering,** the radical redesign of work to achieve substantial improvements in performance. Reengineering searches for the most efficient way to perform a large task. The emphasis is on uncovering wasted steps, such as people handing off documents to one another to obtain approval. Eliminating workers who perform nonessential tasks is another goal of reengineering. E-commerce can be considered a way of reengineering the work of sales representatives. If goods are exchanged over the Internet, the need for industrial sales representatives shrinks considerably. Fewer purchasing agents are needed also because buying over the Internet is more efficient than speaking directly to sales representatives.

As a result of reengineering, work is usually organized horizontally rather than vertically. The people in charge of the process act as team leaders who guide the team toward the completion of an important core process, such as new product development or filling a complicated order. Key performance objectives for the team would include "reduce cycle time," "reduce costs," and "reduce throughput time." Exhibit 13–6 illustrates the horizontal structure, as do the projects embedded in the matrix organization shown in Exhibit 13–5.

A caution to managers and prospective managers is to recognize that the push toward the horizontal structures and reengineering should not be embraced without qualification. Having a "task mentality" is still important because expertise is still crucial in many endeavors. A surgical team, for example, still relies on highly proficient specialists such as a brain surgeon and an anesthetist. Also, wouldn't you prefer that a specialist had designed the operating system on your cellular telephone when you need to call somebody to rescue you from a life-threatening situation?

Exhibit 13-6

A Horizontal Structure

In a horizontal structure, even though specialists are assigned to the team, they are expected to understand one another's tasks and perform some of those tasks as needed.

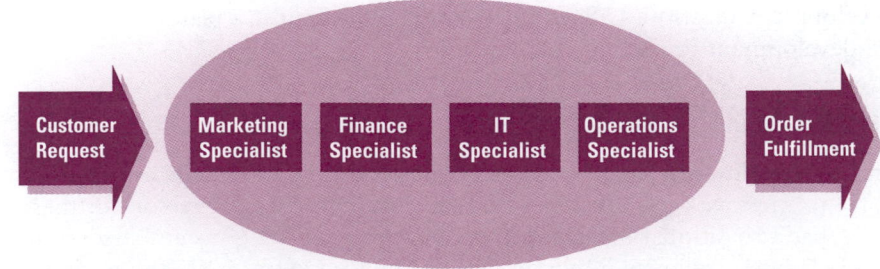

Customer Request → Marketing Specialist | Finance Specialist | IT Specialist | Operations Specialist → Order Fulfillment

The Network Structure

Another fast-growing development in organization structure is for organizations to affiliate with one another based on their need to share resources. Few companies have all the assets and resources in their firm to accomplish new endeavors. The key in many modern firms is not to own the resources, but to have access to them.[15] The best resources and talents are borrowed as needed. A **network structure (or virtual organization)** is a temporary association of otherwise independent firms that are linked by technology to share expenses, employee talents, and access to one another's markets.[16] Outsourcing is somewhat like forming a network structure, except that the relationship is more limited and contractual.

A pure network structure would have neither corporate headquarters nor an organization chart. Hierarchy would be sacrificed to speed of decision making, and vertical integration would be supplanted by horizontal integration across company boundaries. Each contributor to the network would stick to its core competency—what it does best such as manufacturing a particular component, marketing the finished product, or new product development.

For most organizations, the network structure supplements the regular structure, much like a large project. Many large organizations have small units that use the network structure for forming strategic alliances with other companies. Digital cameras, for example, are typically the product of a strategic alliance among several companies. Strategic alliances are also formed to market products. For example, Xerox formed a strategic alliance with several office products stores to provide new channels for customers to obtain many Xerox products. Also, many companies form partnerships with Internet portals to one another's advantage. A portal such as Yahoo! benefits because a link on the Web site of the partner drives traffic to the portal.

Proponents of the network structure see it as a fluid and flexible entity taking the form of a group of collaborators who link together to capitalize on a specific opportunity. After the opportunity has been met, the venture will typically disband. However, some alliances and partnerships are relatively permanent. An essential requirement is that members of the alliance must trust one another. One incompetent or dishonest member of the network can ruin or severely damage the multiple venture. It is not uncommon for an overseas member of a strategic alliance to steal the other's technology and become a direct competitor.

The horizontal and virtual structures place additional demands on the interpersonal skills of the workers involved. Relationships tend to be more stable in a functional structure, whereas horizontal and virtual structures involve more temporary relationships. A person has to get up to speed quickly in establishing working relationships. Furthermore, the authority structure is less clear, so the individual may have to rely more on informal influence tactics. Personal power becomes more important than positional power.

THE CRITERIA FOR AN EFFECTIVE ORGANIZATION DESIGN

One way to integrate information about organization design is to specify what makes for an effective design. Based on their consulting and first-hand research, Michael Goold and Andrew Campbell conclude that most organization structures evolve in fits and starts, shaped more by organizational politics than policies. An example of designing an organization on the basis of politics would be to have a

5

Specify the criteria for an effective organization design.

minor functionary report directly to the CEO because the division head in question was a good friend of the CEO. Goold and Campbell present nine tests that can be used to evaluate an existing design or create a new one.[17]

Four *fit* tests are followed by five *good design* tests, as outlined in Exhibit 13-7. Starting at the left, the company begins with the *market advantage test:* "Does your design direct sufficient management attention to your sources of competitive advantage in each market?" A firm that could adapt well to geographic preferences might use a territorial structure. The *parenting advantage test* asks, "Does your design help the corporate parent add value to the organization?" For example, if one of the key roles of the parent company is to encourage knowledge sharing (see Chapter 15) among units, it is important to create a position on the chart specifying such responsibility. The *people test* asks: "Does your design reflect the strengths, weaknesses, and motivations of your people?" Suppose, for example, the organization has a highly competent chief financial officer in headquarters. It could be helpful to have division-based financial officers to report to that CFO. The *feasibility test* asks, "Have you taken into account all of the constraints that may impede the implementation of your design?" An example would be a foreign government restraint that prohibits a subsidiary of a foreign company to operate independently. Instead, it must establish a strategic alliance with a local partner.

Proceeding to the "Good Design Test" in Exhibit 13-7, first comes the *specialist cultures test* which asks, "Does your design protect units that need distinct cultures?" For example, the company might have a new-product development group that requires a highly organic design, as opposed to a more mechanistic design for the rest of the company. Next is the *difficult-links test* that asks, "Does your design provide coordination solutions for the unit-to-unit links that are likely to be problematic?" Typically the majority of these links are best handled through self-managed networking among the units. When the units do not link well together, it might be necessary to have a clearly defined arbitration process for resolving disputes.

The *redundant hierarchy test* asks, "Does your design have too many parent levels and units?" An upper-level unit must add value to lower-level units (at least by 10 percent) to justify having that layer of management. The *accountability test* asks, "Does your design support effective controls?" (A control is a way of measuring performance against a standard.) Ensure that each unit is accountable for its own results, and cannot blame poor performance on problems created by other units. Finally comes the *flexibility test* that asks, "Does your design facilitate the development of new strategies and provide flexibility required to adapt to change?" See if your design would support the pursuit of future opportunities, such as having a business development unit that has the resources to research the future.

Exhibit 13-7

Nine Criteria for an Effective Organization Design

Source: Diagram developed from text information presented in Michael Goold and Andrew Campbell, "Do You Have a Well-Designed Organization?" *Harvard Business Review,* March 2002, pp. 117–124.

A management team would need to invest considerable time in investigating the nine criteria for an effective organization design. Yet the result could be a superior design that would take into account both organization structure and human capabilities.

ORGANIGRAPHS: DRAWING HOW COMPANIES REALLY WORK

The typical approach to providing an overview of reporting relationships in an organization is to draw an organization chart. Simplified versions of these charts have been presented throughout this chapter. Henry Mintzberg and Ludo Van der Heyden have developed what they believe is a more revealing way to depict the people and operations within an organization. The **organigraph** is a map that provides an overview of the company's functions and the way people organize themselves at work. An organigraph is potentially useful because it depicts the many relationships among people in an organization.[18] Network analysis, as described earlier, provides a similar type of analysis within a small work unit. An organigraph helps you understand several important aspects of organizational functioning:

- What parts connect to one another?
- How should processes and people be linked to one another?
- Whose ideas have to flow to which other people?

According to Mintzberg and Van der Heyden, an organigraph can help a company see untapped competitive opportunities. To illustrate, one such map drawn for Electrocomponents, a British distributor of electrical and mechanical products, led managers to see clearly the company's true expertise—business-to-business relationships. Based on this insight, the company decided to expand in Asia and to increase its Internet business.

Exhibit 13-8 presents three organigraphs for a Canadian Bank, illustrating how understanding work relationships can enhance customer service. A traditional organizational chart would not include information about customer interactions.

6

287

Understand why a new type of organization chart called an *organigraph* can contribute to understanding organization structure.

IMPLICATIONS FOR MANAGERIAL PRACTICE

1. An overriding decision in organizational design is the choice between a mechanistic or an organic structure. Mechanistic structures are better suited to repetitive tasks in a stable environment, in which centralized control is desirable.

2. A design decision for a large organization is usually not an issue of mechanistic versus organic but instead choosing which units should be mechanistic and which ones should be organic.

3. Organization structure influences behavior in many ways. A key factor is that specialization can lead to job dissatisfaction and boredom for many workers. An exception is that some

   highly trained workers prefer to be superspecialists, such as a package designer.

4. Workers with a strong bureaucratic orientation thrive best in a controlled environment with tight job descriptions and predictability in their jobs. Workers with a low bureaucratic orientation prefer a looser and less predictable work environment.

5. Leading-edge organizational designs are becoming increasingly popular. Managers and non-managers alike need high-level interpersonal skills to function effectively in such structures because they must often rely more on informal than formal authority.

Exhibit 13-8

Organigraphs of a Canadian Bank

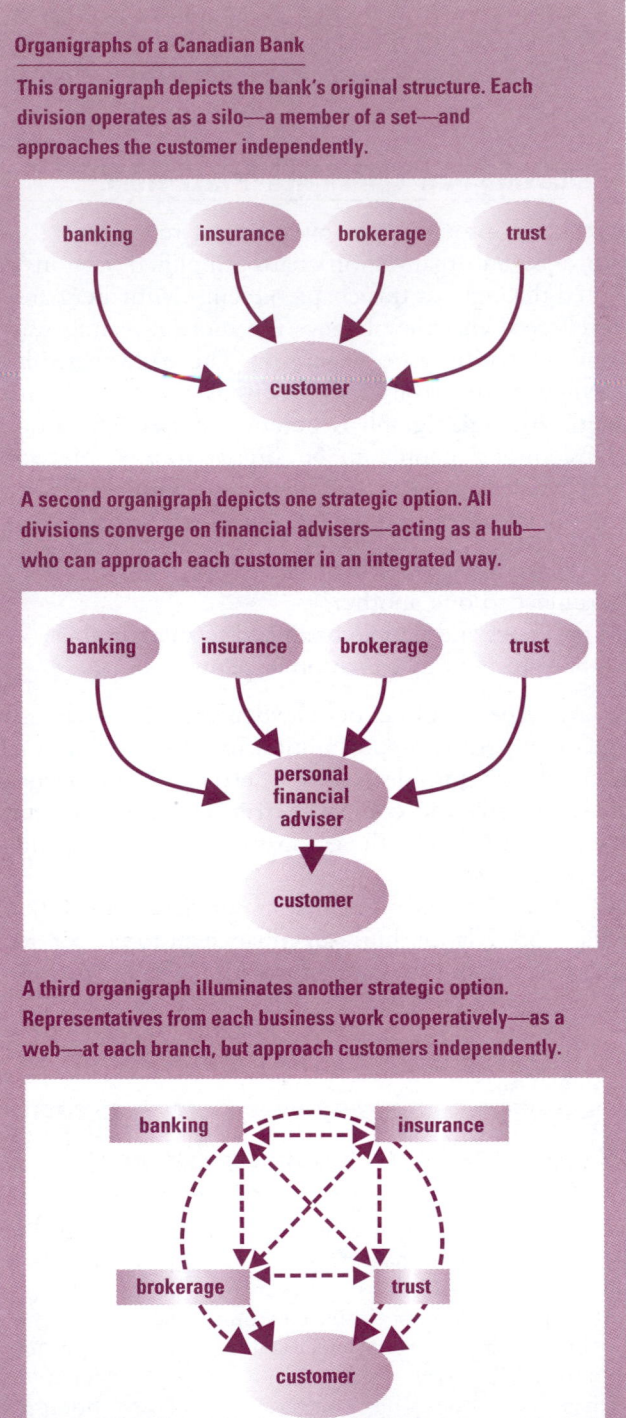

Organigraphs of a Canadian Bank

This organigraph depicts the bank's original structure. Each division operates as a silo—a member of a set—and approaches the customer independently.

A second organigraph depicts one strategic option. All divisions converge on financial advisers—acting as a hub—who can approach each customer in an integrated way.

A third organigraph illuminates another strategic option. Representatives from each business work cooperatively—as a web—at each branch, but approach customers independently.

Source: Adapted and reprinted by permission of *Harvard Business Review*. From "Organigraphs: Drawing How Companies Really Work" by Henry Mintzberg and Ludo Van der Heyden, September–October 1999, p. 90. Copyright © 1999 by the President and Fellows of Harvard College, all rights reserved.

SUMMARY OF KEY POINTS

1 **Identify and describe the foundation concepts of organization structure, including the informal organization.**

Organization structure is the arrangement of people and tasks to accomplish organizational goals, whereas organizational design is the process of creating an appropriate structure. Mechanistic organizations are hierarchical, with an emphasis on specialization and control, as well as rules and regulations. In contrast, an organic structure is laid out like a network and is much looser. An informal organization emerges to take care of the events and transactions not covered by the formal structure. Social network analysis is useful in depicting the informal structure. The more formalized an organization, the more it is mechanistic and bureaucratic. The more centralized an organization, the more extensively top managers delegate responsibility. Organizations vary in their complexity, or differentiation among subunits.

2 **Specify the basic features of the bureaucratic form of organization structure, including how it is divided into departments.**

A bureaucracy is a rational, systematic, and precise form of organization. In it, rules, regulations, and techniques of control are defined precisely. Properly used, bureaucracy allows for large-scale accomplishments. Problems associated with bureaucracy include suppression of initiative through overcontrol, high job frustration, and low job satisfaction. A bureaucracy can also be clumsy and slow.

Departmentalization is the grouping of work into manageable units. The basic forms of departmentalization are functional, territorial, product-service, and customer. Most firms use a hybrid structure composed of several types of departmentalization. The functional organization has both the advantages and disadvantages of a bureaucracy. The other forms give major attention to a customer or market, but can be expensive because of duplication of effort and are also difficult to control. Line and staff units are frequently built into a departmentalized structure.

3 **Describe three key modifications of a bureaucratic structure: matrix, flat, and outsourcing.**

Bureaucratic structures are commonly supplemented by organic, or highly adaptable, organizational units. A matrix structure consists of a project structure imposed on a functional structure. The matrix manager must achieve results through employees who are also responsible to another manager. A flat structure has relatively few layers, which speeds up decision making. Outsourcing is an arrangement whereby one organization has work performed by another. A growing trend is to outsource professional work. Outsourcing is linked to structure because it is a method of dividing work.

4 **Describe the two contemporary organizational designs referred to as horizontal structures and network structures.**

Two leading-edge organization structures are the horizontal structure and the network structure. A horizontal structure arranges work by teams that are responsible for accomplishing a process. A network structure, or virtual corporation, is a temporary association of otherwise independent firms that join forces to exploit an opportunity. Each network member contributes its core competency.

5 **Specify the criteria for an effective organization design.**

To produce a well-designed organization, managers are advised to answer four "fit" tests and five "good design" tests. The fit tests deal with market advantage, corporate parenting advantage, people, and feasibility. The good design tests deal with specialist cultures, difficult links among the units, redundant hierarchy, accountability, and flexibility.

6 **Understand why a new type of organization chart called an organigraph can contribute to understanding organization structure.**

The organigraph is a map that provides an overview of the company's functions and the way people organize themselves at work. Aside from depicting interpersonal relationships in the organization, an organigraph can help a company see untapped competitive opportunities.

KEY TERMS AND PHRASES

Organization, *271*
A collection of people working together to achieve a common purpose (or simply a big group).

Organization Structure, *271*
The arrangement of people and tasks to accomplish organizational goals.

290

Organizational Design, *271*
The process of creating a structure that best fits a purpose, strategy, and environment.

Mechanistic Organization, *271*
A primarily hierarchical organization with an emphasis on specialization and control, vertical communication, and heavy reliance on rules, policies, and procedures.

Organic Structure, *271*
An organization laid out like a network, emphasizing horizontal specialization, extensive use of personal coordination, extensive communication among members, and loose rules, policies, and procedures.

Formal Organization Structure, *272*
An official statement of reporting relationships, rules, and regulations.

Informal Organization Structure, *272*
A set of unofficial working relationships that emerges to take care of the events and transactions not covered by the formal structure.

Formalization, *272*
The degree to which expectations regarding the methods of work are specified, committed to writing, and enforced.

Centralization, *273*
The extent to which executives delegate authority to lower organizational units.

Complexity, *273*
The number of different job titles and units within an organization.

Bureaucracy, *274*
A rational, systematic, and precise form of organization in which rules, regulations, and techniques of control are precisely defined.

Machine Bureaucracy, *274*
An ideal organization that standardizes work processes and is efficient.

Professional Bureaucracy, *274*
An organization composed of a core of highly trained professionals that standardizes skills for coordination.

Departmentalization, *277*
The process of subdividing work into departments.

Functional Departmentalization, *277*
The grouping of people according to their expertise.

Territorial Departmentalization, *277*
An organizational structure in which those responsible for all the activities of a firm in a given geographic area report to one manager.

Product/Service Departmentalization, *277*
The arrangement of departments according to the products or services they provide.

Customer Departmentalization, *279*
An organizational structure based on customer needs.

Hybrid (or Mixed) Organization Structure, *279*
An organization structure that combines two or more types of organization forms into one structure.

Matrix Organization Structure, *280*
An organization consisting of a project structure superimposed on a functional structure.

Project, *280*
A temporary group of specialists working together under one manager to accomplish a fixed objective.

Flat Organization Structure, *281*
An organization structure with relatively few layers.

Outsource, *282*
The practice of having work performed by groups outside the organization.

Horizontal Structure, *283*
The arrangement of work by teams that are responsible for accomplishing a process.

Reengineering, *284*
The radical redesign of work to achieve substantial improvements in performance.

Network Structure (or Virtual Organization), *284*
A temporary association of otherwise independent firms linked by technology to share expenses, employee talents, and access to one another's markets.

Organigraph, *287*
A map that provides an overview of a company's functions and the way people organize themselves.

DISCUSSION QUESTIONS AND ACTIVITIES

1. Many readers of this text are not already in a position to lay out an organization structure. How might they make use of information about organization structure and design?
2. Explain whether Starbucks (or choose Pizza Hut or McDonald's) is a mechanistic or an organic organization. Compare your answer with that of another student who has analyzed the same business.
3. What hints would you look for to analyze the degree of formalization in the company for which you were being interviewed?

4. What evidence could you present that having a *functional mindset* is natural for most people? (*Hint:* For example, when people visit a hospital or grocery store, in what way do they think in terms of departmentalization?)
5. Why is it that so many business owners who say they do not like bureaucracy nevertheless welcome large bureaucratic organizations, like Daimler-Chrysler, as customers?

6. Why is the network organization so well suited to a highly competitive, rapidly changing work environment?
7. Why might an organigraph provide more useful information for organizational behavior than would the standard organization chart?

ORGANIZATIONAL BEHAVIOR ONLINE

TO DO

The Contribution of Organization Charts
Visit http://www.humanconcepts.com/tour_orgcharting/tour_01.htm (Organization Charts: Why They Are Critical to Your Organization). The Web site presents graphic information about organization charts, backed up by narrative descriptions of the potential contribution of the charts. The three main purposes presented are communication, empowerment, and understanding. Study http://www.humanconcepts .com and explain in your own words how the type of organization charts they present achieve these three purposes. Would you recommend such charts to a company in which you have invested money? Explain your reasoning.

TO BOOKMARK

Organization Charts
http://www.rff.com

An Example of a Machine Bureaucracy
http://www.gm.com

Virtual Organizations
http://www.virtual-organization.net

Project Management
http://www.pmi.org

CASE PROBLEM: The J&J Organization Design Team

You and several classmates are seated in a large conference room at the worldwide headquarters of Johnson & Johnson, the medical products giant. Chairman and CEO William C. Weldon addresses the group in a serious yet excited tone: "We are privileged to be here today at an historic moment in the history of J&J, the company we all love and admire. I say with confidence that there is not a person in this room, nor his or her loved ones, who have not used J&J products at some point in their life, perhaps even this week. Can anybody present today say he or she has never used a Band-Aid, or Johnson & Johnson Baby Powder? Is there anybody here who has never used Tylenol or Motrin?

"But I am not here to be sentimental. Rather, I am here to take action. We have a great company with one of the best brands in the world. Johnson & Johnson has been around a long time, and we have taken good care of our customers, employees, and stockholders. Our products have reduced human suffering and saved hundreds of thousands of lives. But I think we can do better.

"Please study our organization chart carefully. (Larsen begins a PowerPoint presentation of the organization structure, as shown in Exhibit 13-9 on page 292.) As you students of organization structure and design can easily recognize, we emphasize a product structure because our products are so vital, and so distinguishable. We know, for example, that personal care products are a different animal than professional pharmaceuticals. Yet what I am asking this design team to do

is give me a new organization structure. That's right—redesign the Johnson & Johnson worldwide organization structure. Give me a design by territory, give me a design by function. Or whatever else you can dream up. Do what you want.

"I and the other members of the executive team may not accept your first attempt at redesign, but at least we will be getting started in the direction of organization redesign. A great organization explores the possibility of change regularly. The breakout rooms are equipped with paper, pencils, transparency masters, laptop computers, and chalkboards. However, the message is more important than the medium. Bring me back your first efforts in thirty minutes."

Your Task
Draw a new organization structure for Johnson & Johnson (http://www.jnj.com) by working in a small group to discuss your redesign. Drawing your final design on a transparency for an overhead projector is often the easiest and quickest method. Sketching directly on a chalkboard or flip chart also works well. After the design teams have completed their tasks, a team leader presents the findings to the entire class. In this way, the various designs can be compared. Speculate about the potential advantage of your design over the existing design.

Exhibit 13-9

*The Johnson & Johnson
Management Structure*

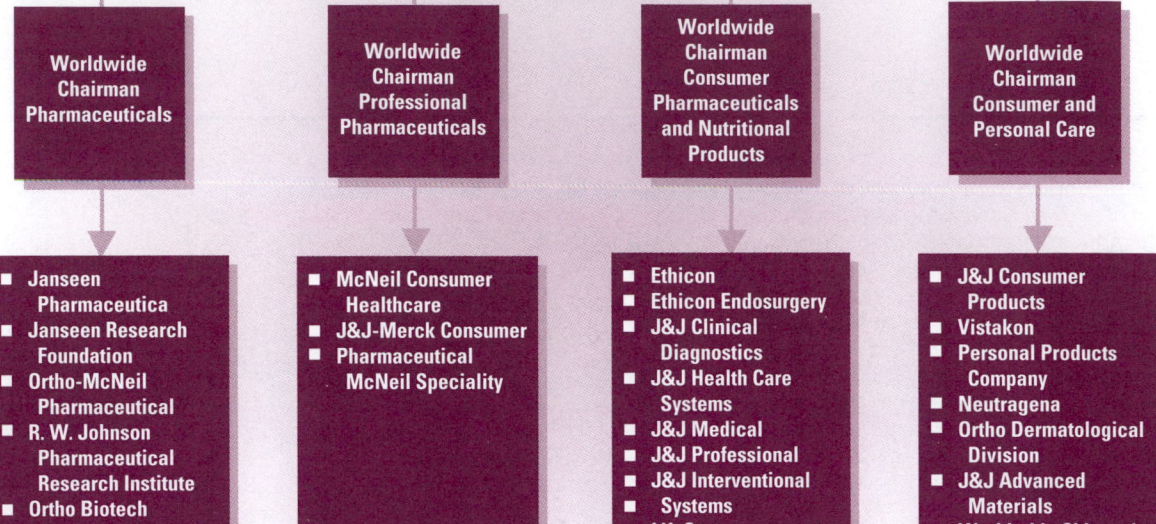

ENDNOTES

1. "What Is Organization Design?" http://www.inovus.com/organiza .htm.
2. Mark Henricks, "The Shadow Knows," *Entrepreneur,* January 2000, p. 110.
3. Ibid., p. 112.
4. Max Weber, *The Theory of Social and Economic Organization* (New York: Free Press, 1947).
5. Henry Mintzberg, *Structure in Fives: Designing Effective Organizations* (Upper Saddle River, NJ: Prentice-Hall, 1983), pp. 189–214.
6. Elliot Jacques, "In Praise of Hierarchy," *Harvard Business Review,* January–February 1990, p. 127.
7. Paul S. Adler, "Building Better Bureaucracies," *Academy of Management Executive,* November 1999, p. 36.
8. Harold J. Leavitt, "Why Hierarchies Thrive," *Harvard Business Review,* March 2003, p. 98.
9. Keith H. Hammonds, "Size Is Not a Strategy," *Fast Company,* September 2002, p. 80.
10. Christopher A. Bartlett and Sumantra Ghosal, "Matrix Management: Not a Structure, a Frame of Mind," *Harvard Business Review,* July–August 1990, p. 145.
11. Barbara J. Petzall, Gerald E. Parker, and Philipp A. Stoeberl, "Another Side to Downsizing: Survivors' Behavior and Self-Affirmation," *Journal of Business and Psychology,* Summer 2000, p. 601.
12. "Outsourcing Proves Value for Doing Business Cheaper," Knight Ridder, May 21, 2000.
13. Michael Schroeder, "More Financial Jobs Go Offshore," *The Wall Street Journal,* May 1, 2003, p. A2.
14. Ann Majchrzak and Qianwei Wang, "Breaking the Functional Mind-Set in Process Organizations," *Harvard Business Review,* September–October 1996, p. 93.
15. Oren Harari, "Transform Your Organization into a Web of Resources," *Management Review,* January 1998, p. 21.
16. William H. Davidow and Michael S. Malone, *The Virtual Corporation: Structuring and Revitalizing the Corporation for the 21st Century* (Edward Burlingame Books/Harper Business, 1992).
17. Michael Goold and Andrew Campbell, "Do You Have a Well-Designed Organization?" *Harvard Business Review,* March 2002, pp. 117–124.
18. Henry Mintzberg and Ludo Van der Heyden, "Organigraphs: Drawing How Companies Really Work," *Harvard Business Review,* September–October 1999, pp. 87–94.

Chapter 14

Organizational Culture and Change

A group of Hewlett-Packard Co. and former Compaq Computer Corp. employees gathered together for an intensive two-day get-to-know-you session. Among the two weighty questions pondered: Did the Compaq group resemble a pack of downhill ski racers? Or were they more akin to an ice hockey team? The sports chatter was all part and parcel of a new employee workshop dubbed, "Fast Start," that HP implemented for its 150,000 staffers worldwide.

At the introductory dinner of one Fast Start session, each attendee received a card with three personal characteristics written on it referring to someone else in the room. The traits on the card included personal achievements such as "went white-water kayaking" and "had a cameo on a TV sitcom." Each attendee was then asked to deduce who the person on their card was by the end of the meal. The exercise set off a furious whirl of hobnobbing as the group of 20 people swapped food and notes. "It really forced people to talk to each other," said an H-P services division manager.

Hewlett-Packard had many major hurdles to overcome in bringing about the merger with Compaq. The giant printer and computer manufacturer had to fight a nasty proxy battle with a company co-founder's son to get the Compaq deal done, and the purchase squeaked by with just the slimmest of shareholder margins. In the process, H-P alienated employees that once rallied around the folksy values of co-founders David Packard and Will Hewlett's storied "H-P Way." H-P began working on cultural issues by creating a strategic-change office and by hiring consultants to study the cultures.

One finding was that H-P was more of a voicemail culture, while Compaq was an e-mail culture. Another finding was that H-P people saw their Compaq counterparts as "shoot from the hip" and "cowboys," whereas Compaq people saw H-P folks as "bureaucrats."

To induce managers to implement Fast Start, the pay of H-P executives—including Chief Executive Carly Fiorina—is tied partly to employees completing the workshop. As some final insurance, H-P has also appointed half a dozen "work-force development coordinators" to police which groups complete the workshop.

OBJECTIVES

After reading and studying this chapter and doing the exercises, you should be able to:

1 Present an analysis of the importance of organizational culture.

2 Present two models of the change process in organizations.

3 Describe why people resist change and how to manage such resistance.

4 Describe three major factors that create organizational change.

5 Explain the nature of organization development.

6 Develop useful insights into managing change in your job and career.

Source: Adapted from Pui-Wing Tam, "H-P Designs Workshops to Break Post-Merger Ice," *The Wall Street Journal,* July 11, 2002, p. B6; Tam, "H-P Is Leaving Nothing to Chance in Compaq Union," *The Wall Street Journal,* April 28, 2003, p. A10. Permission conveyed through Copyright Clearance Center, Inc. A10.

NOW ASK YOURSELF: What does the story about the Fast Start workshops at H-P tell us about the importance of blending organizational cultures? Corporate mergers have to be managed on a number of levels in order for the merger to succeed. By first examining organizational culture, which is much like the personality of an organization, we can dig deeper into three key aspects of organizational change: strategies for bringing about change, the role of organization development in making organizations more adaptive, and dealing with change on a personal level.

ORGANIZATIONAL CULTURE

1

Present an analysis of the importance of organizational culture.

As implied in previous mentions of the term, **organizational culture** is a system of shared values and beliefs that influence worker behavior. Edgar Schein was the first management theorist to define the corporate culture and to explain how the culture is such a dominant force in organizations. Much of his original thinking has influence these more recent ideas about organizational culture.[1] Our study of organizational culture focuses on its determinants, its dimensions, how it is learned, and its consequences.

Determinants of Organizational Culture

Many forces shape a firm's culture. Often its origin lies in the values, administrative practices, and personality of the founder or founders. Also, the leader's vision can have a heavy impact on culture, such as John Chambers's dream of Cisco Systems becoming one of the world's greatest companies in history. A much-publicized example of the impact of a leader on culture is Herb Kelleher, the founder of Southwest Airlines, who is considered pivotal in shaping one of the most distinctive organizational cultures. Up until Kelleher's retirement several years ago, Southwest was considered very dependent on his personality and character. After his retirement for health reasons, his personality could still be felt. At the core of Southwest are the values of humor and altruism. For example, Southwest employees have established a catastrophe fund to help workers who need more assistance than usual employee benefits cover.[2]

Organizational culture responds to and mirrors the conscious and unconscious choices, behavior patterns, and prejudices of top-level managers. As the founders leave or become less active, other top-level managers help define the culture. One of the ways in which Lou Gerstner, the former CEO and chair of IBM, changed the IBM culture was to relax its dress standards. His intent was to create a more relaxed (and less rigid) atmosphere at IBM.

The culture in which a society operates also helps determine the culture of the firm. Sooner or later, society's norms, beliefs, and values find their way into the firm. Societal values are communicated through such means as the media, conversations, and education. The emphasis on sexual and racial equality in U.S. society has become incorporated into the value culture of many employers. The culture at the Finnish electronics company Nokia emphasizes collegiality, reflecting the Finnish character. CEO Jorma Ollila says, "We don't snap our suspenders."[3] The same emphasis on collegiality translates into harmony and cooperation in the workplace at many Scandinavian companies. Another perspective on national culture is that the introduction of values from another society into a retail business can be a competitive advantage. For example, the Japanese values of high quality and reliability, and spotless factories, have helped fuel the success of the Lexus and Infiniti car brands in the United States.

The industry to which a firm belongs helps shape its culture; for example, the culture of a high-tech information technology firm is quite different from that of a meat-packing facility. A public utility will have a culture different from a food manufacturer of comparable size. Heavy competition and low profit margins may force the food manufacturer to operate at a faster pace than the utility, which has more limited competition.

Dimensions of Organizational Culture

The dimensions, or elements, of culture help explain the nature of the subtle forces that influence employee actions. For example, a culture that values risk taking encourages employees to try new ways of doing things. The employees will do so without concern that they will be punished for failed ideas. The following list describes nine influential dimensions of culture:

1. *Values.* The foundation of any organizational culture is values. A firm's philosophy is expressed through values, and values guide behavior on a daily basis. A study demonstrated, for example, that when top management has a lax attitude toward honesty, employee theft increases above the norm of 30 percent. (Two previous studies have shown that about 30 percent of respondents admitted to having stolen from their employers.)[4]

2. *Organizational stories with underlying meanings.* Stories are circulated in many organizations to reinforce principles that top management thinks are important. For example a story circulated at Steelcase about how two night-shift workers shipped prototype models to waiting customers, thus illustrating how much the firm values good customer service. (Prototype models are ordinarily not sold, but are for internal purposes only.)

3. *Myths.* Myths are dramatic narratives or imagined events about the firm's history. They contribute to corporate legends, help unify groups, and can build competitive advantage. At United Parcel Service (UPS), for example, stories are repeated about drivers overcoming severe obstacles or reaching inaccessible locations to deliver packages.

4. *Degree of stability.* A fast-paced, dynamic firm has a different culture from that of a slow-paced, stable one. Top-level managers send out signals by their own energetic or lethargic stance regarding how much they welcome innovation. The degree of stability also influences the strength of a culture and whether or not a culture can take root.

5. *Resource allocations and rewards.* The ways in which money and other resources are allocated have a critical influence on culture. The investment of resources sends a message about what the firm values.

6. *Rites and rituals.* Part of a firm's culture is made up of its traditions, or its rites and rituals. Few companies think they have rites and rituals, yet an astute observer can identify them. Examples include regular staff meetings, retirement banquets (even for fired executives), and receptions for visiting dignitaries.

7. *A sense of ownership.* The movement toward stock ownership for an increasing number of employees has created an ownership culture in many firms where workers are inspired to think and act like owners. An ownership culture includes increased loyalty, improved work effort, and the alignment of worker interests with those of the company. An ownership culture can be reflected in

such everyday actions as conserving electricity, making gradual improvements, and not tolerating sloppy work by coworkers. An ownership culture can backfire, however, if employee wealth stays flat or decreases as a result of stock ownership.[5]

8. *Corporate spiritualism and organizational spirituality.* Organizations differ substantially in two closely related concepts that influence culture. Corporate spiritualism takes place when management is just as concerned about nurturing employee well-being as they are about profits. Many practices, such as work/life programs, contribute to this style of spiritualism.[6] Organizational spirituality refers to workers at all levels believing in something bigger than themselves in addition to traditional religion. This type of spirituality is also seen as an invisible means of support and an ever-reliable resource that keeps you and your career on track when the going gets rough.[7] Workers in a pharmaceutical firm, for example, might believe that the grand purpose of the company is to alleviate and prevent human suffering. In firms with either corporate spiritualism or organizational spirituality (or both), people go about their work with a true sense of purpose. Both of these cultural dimensions contribute to a firm having a soul. (You will recall that the purpose of work/life programs is to help workers balance the demands of career and personal life.)

9. *Innovativeness.* A cultural dimension of significance in most fields is the innovative spirit of the workforce. As described in our study of creativity, an environment that encourages innovation contributes to individual creativity. A striking example is that Nokia conducts an internal competition that rewards creativity, such as giving prizes for the best photos taken by employees using a company-made camera phone. Many creative ideas, such as the user-changeable handset cover, come from workers outside the research and development group.[8]

In addition to the dominant culture of a firm, the subculture also influences behavior. A **subculture** is a pocket in which the organizational culture differs from the dominant culture, as well as other pockets of subculture. In a bank, the consumer loan division may have a culture different from that of the mortgage group, because the consumer group has to work with much shorter time frames in processing loans.

Exhibit 14-1 presents key aspects of the organizational culture of business firms most likely to be familiar to you. Scanning the exhibit, combined with other references to culture in this chapter and elsewhere in the text, will add to your understanding of organizational culture.

How Workers Learn the Culture

Employees learn the organizational culture primarily through **socialization,** the process of coming to understand the values, norms, and customs essential for adapting to the organization. Socialization is therefore a method of indoctrinating employees into the organization in such a way that they perpetuate the culture. The socialization process takes place mostly by learning through imitation and observation.

Another important way in which workers learn the culture is through the teachings of leaders, as implied in the cultural dimension of resource allocations and rewards. Organizational members learn the culture to some extent by

IKEA	Very informal culture with roots in Swedish culture. Emphasis on informality, cost consciousness, and a humble, down-to-earth approach. Workers are allowed considerable responsibility.
Nike	Go-it alone, insular culture characterized by a desire for growth within, rather than taking on the hassles of integrating a merger with another company.
Home Depot	Rowdy corporate culture, with the idea of growing big and fast. Workers used to drive forklift trucks through aisles with customers around. Before former GE exec Bob Nardelli took over in 2001, the culture permitted casual attitudes towards costs.
Coca-Cola	Bureaucratic, slow moving, with major changes taking a long time to implement. Up through end of 2001 it had bloated a corporate staff. Gradually shifting to a faster-moving culture.
Southwest Airlines	Strong, trusting partnerships between managers and workers and unions, that allow all-concerned to execute the intricacies of an airline running smoothly. Strong emphasis on valuing human resources and intrinsic job satisfaction. Positive job attitude a key hiring factor.
United Airlines	Ailing culture, long plagued by tension between management and unions. Employees are hired for functional skills rather than relational skills. Performance is measured in a functionally specific, divisive way rather than allowing cross-functional responsibility for performance.

Exhibit 14-1

A Sampleing of Organizational Cultures of Well-Known Companies

Sources: Katarina Kling and Ingela Goteman, "IKEA CEO Anders Dahlvig on International Growth and IKEA's Unique Corporate Culture and Brand Identity," *Academy of Management Executive*, February 2003, pp. 31–37; Douglas Robson, "Just Do . . . Something," *Business Week*, July 2, 2001, pp. 70–71; Aixa M. Pascual, "Tidying Up at Home Depot," *Business Week*, November 26, 2001, pp. 102–104; Dean Foust, "Shaking Up the Coke Bottle," *Business Week*, December 3, 2001, pp. 74–75; Patrick J. Kiger, "Unite or Die," *Workforce*, February 2003, pp. 26–29.

observing what leaders pay attention to, measure, and control.[9] Suppose a coworker of yours is praised publicly for doing community service. You are likely to conclude that an important part of the culture is to help people outside the company. Senior executives will sometimes publicly express expectations that help shape the culture of the firm. At Paychex Inc., the top executive and founder, Tom Golisano, sets the tone for a practical-minded, action-oriented culture, with dedicated managers. He reflects:

> We expect our senior management to be hands on. And I think when you talk to a lot of people who come from larger organizations, a lot of times they come from a difficult culture and it's hard for them to adapt. They expect in most cases a much healthier benefits and wage package, okay? They expect larger support staffs. They expect a little more freedom in their time and movement than we're willing to give them.[10]

The Consequences and Implications of Organizational Culture

Depending on its strength, a firm's organizational culture can have a pervasive impact on organizational effectiveness. Employees of a firm with a strong culture will follow its values with little questioning. A weaker culture provides only broad guidelines to members. Six major consequences and implications of organizational culture are outlined in Exhibit 14-2 and summarized next.

1. *Competitive advantage and financial success.* The right organizational culture contributes to gaining competitive advantage and therefore achieving financial

Exhibit 14-2

Consequences and Implications of Organizational Culture

Although organizational culture is a soft concept, it has many hard consequences.

- Competitive Advantage and Financial Success
- Productivity, Quality, and Morale
- Innovation
- Compatibility of Mergers and Acquisitions
- Person–Organization Fit
- Direction of Leadership Activity

Organizational Culture

From the moment that America Online and Time Warner announced that they were merging three years ago, analysts warned that the biggest difficulty facing the newly merged company would be an inevitable "clash of cultures." AOL was billed as the quintessential fast and nimble New Economy pioneer. Time Warner was cast as the tradition-bound old-media behemoth. So when the merger failed to deliver on its promise, the press began to wonder if cultural differences were at fault. Other mergers of recent memory—Chrysler and Daimler-Benz, HP and Compaq, ABC and Disney— were also widely heralded as culturally incompatible. Log on to InfoTrac College Edition at **http://www .infotrac-college.com** and do some background reading on any one of these mergers/acquisitions or on another of your choice. Pay particular attention to criticisms of the deal. How often is culture blamed for apparent failures to achieve promised synergies?

success. A study of thirty-four firms investigated the relationship between a high-involvement/participative culture and financial performance. Firms perceived by employees to link individual efforts to company goals showed higher returns on investments and sales than firms without such linkages.[11] An indirect support of the link between corporate culture and organizational success comes from an analysis of Wal-Mart executives who left to manage other larger retailers, such as Kmart and Fleming Cos. Inc., the grocery distributor. Although the executives in question performed well at Wal-Mart, they flopped at the other companies. Many Wal-Mart employees interviewed claimed that the unique culture of the company is more important than an individual executive in creating the company's success.[12] (Do you remember the leadership substitutes position presented in Chapter 11?)

2. *Productivity, Quality, and Morale.* A culture that emphasizes productivity, including high quality, encourages workers to be productive. Productivity and competitive advantage are closely linked because high level productivity contributes heavily to gaining on the competition. A culture that values the dignity of human beings fosters high morale and job satisfaction. The consistently strong performance of Southwest Airlines is partially attributed to its humane and fun-loving culture that leads to high job satisfaction and motivation, often resulting in high productivity.

3. *Innovation.* A major contributor to innovation is a corporate culture that encourages creative behavior. Gary Hamel has identified specific features of a culture that inspire innovation, including the setting of very high expectations, creating a cause that workers can be passionate about, encouraging radical ideas, and allowing talented people in the company to easily transfer to different business areas within the firm. Also, innovators must be paid exceptionally well. As Hamel states, "Entrepreneurs won't work for peanuts, but they'll work for a share of the equity, a piece of the action."[13]

4. *Compatibility of mergers and acquisitions.* A reliable predictor of success in merging two or more firms is the compatibility of their respective cultures. When the cultures clash, such as a mechanistic firm merging with an organic one, the result can be negative synergy (see the InfoTrac sidebar). A consultant who contributed to a major study on mergers and acquisitions said, "Many deals fail to capture the expected synergies due to incompatible cultures, the loss of key talent or clashes of management style." He recommends, therefore, that human resource professionals become an integral part of the merger and acquisition team.[14]

5. *Person–organization fit.* An important success factor for the individual is finding an organization that fits his or her personality. Similarly, an organization will be more successful when the personality of most members fits its culture.

In one study, organizations were measured on such dimensions as stability, experimenting, risk taking, and an orientation towards rules. The preferences of professional employees regarding culture were measured and compared to the culture of their firms. Good person–organization fits result in more commitment and higher job satisfaction.[15]

6. *Direction of leadership activity.* Much of a top-level manager's time is spent working with the forces that shape the attitudes and values of employees at all levels. A key leadership role is to establish what type of culture is needed for the firm and then shaping the existing culture to match that ideal. Charles D. Moran, the top executive at Acxiom Corp., sums up the link between culture and company leadership in these words: "Your culture should be everything you do as a business. It should be how you solve problems, build products and work in teams. For the CEO and other leaders, it's about how you lead."[16]

TWO MODELS OF THE CHANGE PROCESS IN ORGANIZATIONS

2

Present two models of the change process in organizations.

"The only constant is change" is a frequently repeated cliché in the workplace. To meet their objectives, managers and professionals must manage change effectively almost daily. Even companies that appear from the outside to work in a stable environment are faced with change. A surprising example is Hershey Foods Corporation, which has been making chocolate products since 1905—including the remarkably stable brands, Hershey's milk chocolate and Reese's Peanut Butter Cups. However, the technology for distributing chocolate products, including Internet sales, has created enormous challenges for the chocolate maker. A company executive said, "Keeping up with the technology is probably the greatest challenge. Imagine how different it is to make chocolate now than when Milton Hershey was making his first caramel. From the time chocolate is made to the time it reaches the consumer, it's dealing with new technology the whole way."[17]

Competitive threats are a primary mover for changes within an organization, even for market leaders. In 2003, Microsoft CEO Steve Ballmer issued an internal memo outlining the significant challenges the company was facing. He called for employees to "change old habits and seriously re-think business-as-usual." In addition to competition from the free Linux operating system, Ballmer reasoned that the company was facing the problem of slow customer spending because of economic pressures and skepticism that new software would boost productivity. Ballmer believed that the biggest challenge facing Microsoft was its own maturity. As a 30-year old, 50,000-employee successful company, Microsoft was struggling to create breakthrough products and quickly respond to customer needs.[18]

The many types of change in organizations include changes in technology, organizational structure, and the people with whom one works, such as customers and company insiders. Organizational change has been studied from different perspectives. Collectively, the two models described next help explain change from the organizational and individual perspectives.

The Growth Curve Model of Change in Organizations

The **growth curve model** traces the inevitability of change through a firm's life cycle, as shown in Exhibit 14–3. According to this model, businesses pass through three phases in sequence.[19] First is the *formative phase,* characterized by a lack of structure, trial and error, and the presence of entrepreneurial risk taking. Mistakes are seen as learning opportunities, and innovation is extremely important. The firm focuses on its market, with the goal of becoming predictable, stable, and successful.

Exhibit 14-3

*The Growth Curve Model
of Organizational Change*

*Organizations go through
predictable life stages.*

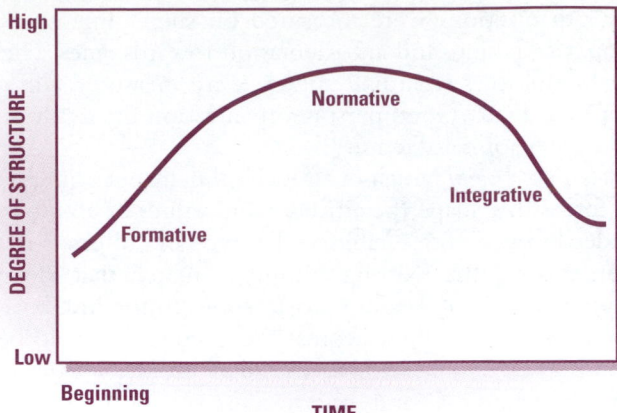

Second is the *normative phase,* in which stability occurs. An emphasis is placed on maintaining the existing structure and developing predictability. Mistakes are frowned upon and perhaps punished, which leads to less risk taking. The firm becomes more bureaucratic, and innovation is mostly given lip service or relegated to the research and development unit. The goal is survival, and the focus is less on the market and more on maintaining the status quo. However, changes continue to occur in the environment, which forces this phase to end.

Third is the *integrative phase,* in which the firm redefines itself and finds a new direction. During this phase, top-level managers attempt many changes, such as introducing a new vision and policies. At the same time, the most resistance to change occurs at this stage, as many members of the firm attempt to resist the discomfort change brings. The integrative phase is associated with ambiguity and uncertainty. In addition, the firm experiences an "organ rejection" of the new systems. During this phase, leadership, inspiration, and interpersonal skills become more important than routine management and technical skills.

During the integrative phase, there is a pulling and tugging between forces for and against change. According to the **force-field theory,** an organization simultaneously faces forces for change (the driving forces) and forces for maintaining the status quo (the restraining forces). Forces for change include new technology, competition from other groups, and managerial pressures. Forces for the status quo include group performance norms, fear of change, employee complacency, and well-learned skills. Considerable managerial skill is required in order for driving forces to outweigh restraining forces. As managers push for change, there is an equal push in the opposite direction from those who want to maintain the status quo.[20]

Another observation about change is that the ability to change is somewhat related to size: Large organizations are more resistant to change than small- or medium-size organizations. In the Microsoft example just cited, the inference could be made that CEO thought the bigness of the company was making it less nimble.

The Unfreezing–Changing–Refreezing Model

Psychologist Kurt Lewin presented a three-step analysis of the change process.[21] His unfreezing–changing–refreezing model is widely used by managers to help bring about constructive change. Many other approaches to initiating change stem from this simple model, illustrated in Exhibit 14-4. Unfreezing involves reducing or eliminating resistance to change. As long as employees oppose a change, it will not be implemented effectively.

Exhibit 14-4

The Change Process

Change is a three-step process.

301

Changing, or moving on to a new level, usually involves considerable two-way communication, including group discussion. According to Lewin, "Rather than a one-way flow of commands or recommendations, the person implementing the change should make suggestions. The changees should be encouraged to contribute and participate." *Refreezing* includes pointing out the success of the change and looking for ways to reward people involved in implementing the change. For the change process to be complete, refreezing must take place.

WHY PEOPLE RESIST CHANGE

Before a company's managers can gain support for change, they need to understand why people resist change. People resist change for reasons they think are important, the most common being the fear of an unfavorable outcome. This outcome could be less money, personal inconvenience, more work, and so forth. People also resist change for such varied reasons as not wanting to disrupt social relationships and not wanting to break well-established habits.

A deep-level reason many employees resist change is that they face competing commitments. Even if the worker wants to go along with a workplace change, he or she might direct productive energy toward a hidden competing commitment. Organizational psychologists Robert Kegan and Lisa Laskow Lahey explain that an employee who moves slowly on a project may have an unrecognized competing commitment to avoid an even tougher assignment that might follow. If he performs well on the present project he might be given an even greater challenge that he fears might be beyond his potential.[22] The competing commitment functions as an immunity to change. Another example of a competing commitment is that a worker might resist performing well in a new supervisory position; if she performs well as a supervisor, she might be perceived as being disloyal to members of the work group of which she was a well-accepted member.

Even when people do not view a change as potentially damaging, they may sometimes resist it because they fear the unknown. People will sometimes cling to a system they dislike rather than change. According to folk wisdom, "People would rather deal with the devil they know." Workers may also resist change because they are aware of weaknesses in the proposed changes that may have been overlooked or disregarded by management.[23]

A sales manager resisted her company's proposal to shift a key product to dealer distribution. She explained that dealers would give so little attention to the product that sales would plunge. Despite her protests, the firm shifted to dealer distribution. Sales of the product did plunge, and the company returned to direct selling.

Gaining Support for Change

Gaining support for change, and therefore overcoming resistance, is an important managerial responsibility. Here we look at nine of these techniques for gaining support for change. Exhibit 14-5 provides an overview of several of these methods plus a few others, as described in a classic article.

3

Describe why people resist change and how to manage such resistance.

Approach	Commonly Used	Advantages	Drawbacks
Education and communication	Where there is a lack of information or inaccurate information and analysis.	Once persuaded, people will often help with the implementation of the change.	Can be very time-consuming if lots of people are involved.
Participation and involvement	Where the initiators do not have all the information they need to design the change, and where others have considerable power to resist.	People who participate will be committed to implementing change, and any relevant information they have will be integrated into the change plan.	Can be very time-consuming if participants design an inappropriate change.
Facilitation and support	Where people are resisting because of adjustment problems.	No other approach works as well with adjustment problems.	Can be time-consuming, expensive, and still fail.
Negotiation and agreement	Where someone or some group will clearly lose out in a change, and where that group has considerable power to resist.	Sometimes it is a relatively easy way to avoid major resistance.	Can be too expensive in many cases if it alerts others to negotiate for compliance.
Manipulation and co-optation	Where other tactics will not work or are too expensive.	It can be a relatively quick and inexpensive solution to resistance problems.	Can lead to future problems if people feel manipulated.
Explicit and implicit coercion	Where speed is essential, and the change initiators possess considerable power.	It is speedy and can overcome any kind of resistance.	Can be risky if it leaves people mad at the initiators.

Source: Adapted and reprinted by permission of *Harvard Business Review*. From "Choosing Strategies for Change" by John P. Kotter and Leonard A. Schlesinger, March–April 1979, p. 111. Copyright © 1979 by the President and Fellows of Harvard College, all rights reserved.

Exhibit 14-5

Methods for Dealing with Resistance to Change

1. *Allow for discussion and negotiation.* Support for change can be increased by discussing and negotiating the more sensitive aspects of the change. The two-way communication incorporated into the discussion helps reduce some employee concerns. Discussion often leads to negotiation, which further involves employees in the change process. When Larry Johnson, the CEO of Albertson's, led a major restructuring of the large food and drug retailer, he emphasized good communication. "You have to give out your e-mail and your phone number, and hold town meetings, to let people ask tough questions," he said.[24]

2. *Allow for participation.* The best documented way of overcoming resistance to change is to allow people to participate in the changes that will affect them. A powerful participation technique is to encourage people who already favor the change to help in planning and implementation. These active supporters of the change will be even more strongly motivated to enlist the support of others.

3. *Point out the financial benefits.* Because so many employees are concerned about the financial effects of work changes, it is helpful to discuss these effects openly. If employees will earn more money as a result of the change, this fact can be used as a selling point. For example, the CEO of a small company told his

employees, "I know you are inconvenienced and ticked off because we have cut way back on office support. But some of the savings will be invested in bigger bonuses for you." Much of the grumbling subsided.

4. *Avoid change overload.* Too much change in too short a time leads to negative stress. So it is helpful to avoid overloading employees with too many sweeping changes in a brief time period. Too much simultaneous change also causes confusion, leading to foot-dragging about the workplace innovation. The more far-reaching the innovation is, such as restructuring a firm, the greater is the reason for not attempting other innovations simultaneously.

5. *Gain political support for change.* Few changes get through organizations without the change agent's forming alliances with people who will support his or her proposals. Often this means selling the proposed changes to members of top-level management before proceeding down the hierarchy. It is much more difficult to create change from the bottom up.

6. *Provide education.* A standard method of reducing resistance to change is through education and communication of relevant information. The method is likely to be the most effective when people resist change because they lack sufficient information. For example, workers may resist making the necessary preparations for outsourcing part of their work until they are informed about the scale of the outsourcing program and how it will affect their jobs.

7. *Avoid citing poor performance as the reason for change.* Instead of criticizing, the change agent should accurately describe market challenges or budget restraints and show employees why change is necessary for survival. For example, do not say to employees, "If things hadn't become so sloppy around here, we wouldn't need to change." Instead, tell them, "Our competitors can deliver finished product in half the time because of this new technology. If we don't make the change, too, we'll lose all our key accounts."[25]

8. *Incorporate the human touch.* Some changes are resisted because they are perceived to diminish valued human contact. Many workers and customers may be impressed with an information technology device that eliminates having to deal with a human to complete a transaction. The same workers, however, may resist the change because they enjoy human contact. Perhaps employees might be able to receive counselling about their benefits through an interactive computer program, or a voice recognition system, yet they would *prefer* to interact face-to-face with a benefits counselor. B2B (business-to-business selling over the Internet) has not grown as fast as predicted a few years ago. A contributing factor to the modest growth has been small-business owners' reluctance. Even business people who are computer savvy will sometimes shy away from B2B because they are uncomfortable with the impersonal nature of the transaction. Instead of being able to sell on the basis of service, they fear they will be compared to competitors strictly on the basis of price. A financial analyst notes, "There's something to be said for some of those good old-fashioned relationships you get from a good supplier."[26]

9. *Pay attention to the emotional aspects of change.* Another aspect of behavior that must be dealt with in overcoming resistance to major change is emotion. Too often the manager attempting to sell the change focuses on cognitive aspects alone, such as making a rational presentation of the merits of the change. One example of paying attention to emotion would be to enable workers to express tension and anxiety they have about the change, such as worrying about whether a merger with another company will make them second-class citizens. Another way of paying attention to emotion is to formulate a

metaphor that evokes positive feelings.[27] In the merger situation, the manager might talk about the group becoming part of a bigger family with room for everyone.

To practice the concepts of managing change, do the Skill-Development Exercise that follows.

4

Describe three major factors that create or force organizational change.

THREE MAJOR FACTORS THAT CREATE ORGANIZATIONAL CHANGE

Organizational change is often created or forced because of initiatives taken by management, changes in technology, or new ways of performing work. Many forces would fit into these categories. Here we pinpoint three representative forces: downsizing, information technology, and a shift in work roles.

Downsizing and Restructuring as a Change Strategy

Downsizing has already been mentioned as a significant stressor and as a method of achieving a flat structure. Downsizing is also the most often used deliberate organization change in recent years. More than 85 percent of the *Fortune* 100 firms initiated major restructuring in the early 1990s. The pace of downsizing diminished only slightly at the end of the decade. Downsizing intensified again in the 2000–2003 period, with major contributors being company mergers and acquisitions, as well as a slower economy. Cost reductions are often necessary because the survival of the firm is at stake. Laying off workers can sometimes make a firm more competitive by lowering costs, but at the same time this causes enormous confusion and resentment. Downsizing can also leave a firm so understaffed that it cannot capitalize on new opportunities. Another concern is that downsizing depletes human assets and interferes with organizational learning (see Chapter 15) because so much information stored in people's memories leaves the firm.[28]

An important perspective on downsizing as a change strategy is to specify the conditions under which it has the best chance of contributing to organizational effectiveness.[29] To begin with, top management should ponder whether downsizing can be avoided. Instead of laying off employees, a way should be sought to better utilize their expertise. Some cost cutting can be achieved by involving employees in improving work methods and processes. Under ideal circumstances, key people can look to penetrate new markets. As a last-ditch maneuver to avoid

SKILL-DEVELOPMENT EXERCISE

COLLABORATE

Overcoming Resistance to Change

One student plays the role of a team leader who is to meet today with team members to sell them on the idea that the company plans to shift from a standard workweek to a 4/40 workweek (work 10 hours per day, four days per week). About six other students play the role of the team members, several of whom have mixed reactions to the proposed change. The team leader should use the techniques for overcoming resistance to change described in this section. Team members who do not like the contemplated change should express what they consider valid reasons for resisting the change. Other class members should observe and then provide feedback.

downsizing, a company might reduce the salaries of all workers, or place workers on a four-day workweek, thereby having enough money to pay a full workforce. Exhibit 14–6 summarizes a few advantages of avoiding downsizing, and also presents several of its potential negative effects.

The first key to a successful restructuring is to integrate downsizing with the company's long-term strategies. The firm must determine where the business is headed and which employees are needed to ensure that future. The company must identify and protect high-potential individuals who are needed to carry the firm forward. After delayering, firms must decentralize and empower key individuals to conduct their jobs. The downsizing survivors must be revitalized by redefining their positions. (A problem is that survivors often have to assume the workload of several people.) It is therefore essential to eliminate low-value and non-value activities such as multiple reviews of other people's work and meetings without meaningful agendas.

After restructuring, teamwork must be emphasized more than previously because much cooperation is required to accomplish the same amount of work with fewer personnel. The downsized organization may require a new structure. It should be redesigned to reflect the changed jobs, processes, and responsibilities. Horizontal as well as vertical relationships must be specified. Considerable attention must be paid to the human element before and after downsizing. A carefully implemented system of performance appraisal increases the chances that good work performance and the possession of vital skills should receive more weight than favoritism in retaining employees.

A progressive approach is to offer training to employees designated for downsizing so they might qualify for any vacant positions in the company. Downsizing survivors in all companies need an outlet to talk about their grief and guilt in relation to laid-off coworkers. As is often done, laid-off workers should be given assistance in finding new employment and redirecting their careers.

Information Technology and Organizational Change

Advances in information technology have facilitated a variety of profound changes in organizations. Your knowledge of information systems and information technology will help you visualize many organizational changes created by digitalizing information. A major change is that electronic access to information has made much of the delayering of organizations possible. Many middle management and coordinator positions have been eliminated because there is less need for people to act as conduits of information. Instead, information seekers obtain information via computers.

Exhibit 14-6

The Costs of Downsizing versus The No-Layoff Payoff

Massive layoffs can backfire after taking into account:	*Companies that avoid downsizing say they get:*
• Severance and rehiring costs	• A fiercely loyal, more productive workforce
• Potential lawsuits from aggrieved workers	• Higher customer satisfaction
• Loss of institutional memory and trust in management	• Readiness to snap back with the economy
• Lacks of staffers when the economy rebounds	• A recruiting edge
• Survivors who are risk averse, paranoid, and political	• Workers who aren't afraid to innovate, knowing that their jobs are safe

Source: Michelle Conlin, "Where Layoffs Are a Last Resort," *Business Week*, October 8, 2001, p. 42.

Information technology has played a key role in making organizations more democratic. Democracy is enhanced because more people have access to information. John Gage of Sun Microsystems said, "Sun's organization structure is who sends e-mail to whom."[30] As implied by this quote, e-mail makes it easier for lower-ranking members to communicate directly with higher-ranking members. Before the surge in information technology, such direct interaction was rare in large firms.

Although information technology has made organizations more democratic, many communications are also more impersonal. (Refer back to Chapter 9.) E-mail messages have replaced many conversations that might have profited from face-to-face interaction. Self-service systems for key functions, such as filing travel and expense reports and obtaining information about benefits, make it difficult to chat with someone about a problem. (At the same time, these impersonal systems save the organization time and money, such as through hiring fewer people to work on expense accounts.)

The Internet is changing the nature of many businesses, such as companies interacting more directly with customers and suppliers. Many retail sales positions and industrial sales positions have been eliminated by e-commerce. The Internet has transformed some industries. A good example is the newspaper industry whose changes mirror what is happening in other industries. To survive, the industry has had to rely on its traditional strength of offering detail and depth. Services must now also be offered in both hard copy and online. Newspapers were among the first commercial entities on the Internet. Information on the Net is now offered free, pay-per-view, and by subscription. *The Wall Street Journal* actually makes money with its online subscription service.[31]

Enterprise software that links together the various functions of the enterprise to one another and to customers affects job behavior. A smaller number of managers are needed because fewer employees are needed when enterprise software is fully implemented. The remaining key workers must be skilled in information technology, problem solving, and interpersonal skills.

Information technology has created substantial changes in how long and where people work. Accessing and responding to e-mail has added hours to the workweek of many employees. Another change is that managers and professionals feel obliged to stay in frequent contact with the office, even during nights, weekends, and vacations. A report on technology in the 21st century put it this way:

> The problem today is that we haven't yet learned to manage technology. All too often our cellular telephones and notebook computers control us. Increasingly, we work all the time, everywhere. We use every available second to handle and prioritize voice mail, e-mail, and paperwork. In the Information Age, it's becoming impossible to know when work is completed. And unless something changes, all this ultimately affects everything from customer service to burnout.[32]

The Transition from Carrying Out a Job to Performing Work

A subtle change in the workplace of concern to organizations and individuals is that traditional job descriptions are becoming too rigid to fit the flexible work roles carried out by many workers. An emerging trend is for companies to hire people to "work" rather than to fill a specific job slot. At both Amazon.com and Koch Industries, job descriptions are rarely used. At Amazon, a person might still hold the same essential job but three months later perform entirely different work.

The "Amazonian" might be working out a software glitch one day and helping lay out a new wing of a distribution center the next.

This sea of change in work design can be overwhelming for people whose paradigm is to think of work as occupying a particular job. A starting point in the shift is to think about how to accomplish work rather than fill a job. Both Koch and Amazon have developed a model to make this shift from filling a job to carrying out a work role. These companies look more for a good person–organization fit than for candidates to fill a particular job. At Amazon, this means hiring people with entrepreneurial drive who are customer focused. The director of strategic growth (human resources) says, "We try not to be too rigid about qualifications, but on the kind of people we hire and how they can apply what they know."[33]

To make this approach to work roles function well, the organization structure has to be flexible and employees have to have access to different opportunities. Also, managers have to be willing to let employees experiment and work in different positions. A cornerstone idea is that workers' skills have to be matched to the project. For example, a creative person from anywhere in the firm might be assigned to a cross-functional product development team.

The implication for managers is that shifting away from relatively fixed job descriptions to emphasizing work roles is part of dealing with change in organizations. For many managers, this shift is difficult because job descriptions are the essence of bureaucracy.

ORGANIZATION DEVELOPMENT AS A CHANGE STRATEGY

5

Explain the nature of organization development.

When it is necessary to bring about long-term, significant changes in a firm, a formal method of organizational change is sometimes used. **Organization development (OD)** is any strategy, method, or technique for making organizations more effective by bringing about constructive, planned change. You might think of a clinical psychologist or executive coach working with the individual to bring about change, whereas an organization development professional focuses on improving the entire organization. OD applies principles of human behavior to promote healing, growth, and constructive change in organizations.[34] In its ideal form, organization development attempts to change the culture toward a more democratic and humanistic model. At other times, organization development aims to help change the technology or structure of the firm.[35]

An appreciation of the number of OD techniques available can be gained from studying Exhibit 14-7. Various techniques are grouped according to whether they deal primarily with individuals, small groups, or the total organization. Several of the techniques, such as team development, conflict resolution, and stress management, have been described in previous chapters. Labeling all of these interventions organization development is somewhat arbitrary because they are practiced in organizations not even aware of the existence of such a label. Here we describe a process model of organization development, followed by more information about two other OD approaches.

A Process Model of Organization Development

To be effective, OD methods must be made to fit a particular firm. Nevertheless, a process model has been developed that incorporates the important features of many different OD change efforts.[36] The model builds on earlier strategies for organization development. A key feature is that the OD specialist and staff members

A wide range of organizational behavior and psychological techniques can be considered techniques of organization development.

Individual Level	Small-Group Level	Organization Level
Executive (or business) coaching	Team development	Six Sigma
Employee assistance programs (EAPs)	Cultural diversity training	Gainsharing
Career development programs	Modified work schedules	Survey feedback (attitude surveys)
Organizational behavior modification (OB Mod)	Creativity training	Action research (employees participate in implementing changes identified as needed by a consultant)
Job enrichment	Intergroup conflict resolution	
Wellness programs, including stress reduction	Quality improvement teams	Implementing organization learning
	Self-managing teams	Knowledge management
Soxual harassment avoidance training		

Exhibit 14-7

A Sampling of Organization Development Interventions

are both involved in bringing about constructive change. The model, which is summarized here, is outlined in Exhibit 14-8.

Step 1: Preliminary Problem Identification
The manager recognizes that a problem exists that interferes with work effectiveness. The problem could include the manager's behavior, such as the manager not making effective use of input by group members in his or her planning.

Step 2: Managerial Commitment to Change
The manager must commit to taking the necessary steps to implement the change program. The manager is warned that the change program could involve negative feedback about his or her behavior.

Step 3: Data Collection and Analysis
Before organization development can proceed, the climate must be assessed through interviews, observations, and a written survey. Information is obtained about such topics as the manager's alertness and open-mindedness, cooperation with other departments, problem-solving ability, and trust. This information is used to develop objectives for constructive changes.

Step 4: Data Feedback
Data collected in Step 3 are shared with the manager and staff members. In this way, staff members can compare their perceptions with those of others, and the manager shows ownership of the problem.

Step 5: Identification of Specific Problem Areas
The OD specialist helps staff members give the manager feedback regarding strengths and weaknesses. Although the manager may not agree with the feedback, he or she must accept the perceptions. Problem areas among the staff members can also be identified in this step.

Step 6: Development of Change Strategies
The emphasis is on identifying root problems and developing action steps. A spirit of teamwork often develops as problems are identified that can be attributed to both the manager and staff members.

Step 7: Initiation of Behavior
An action step(s) is selected and implemented that seems to be the best solution to the problem. The behavioral change strategy considers who, what, when, and where. For example, the manager (who) will make sure that the planning and priority setting (what) are accomplished during staff meetings (when) in the conference room (where).

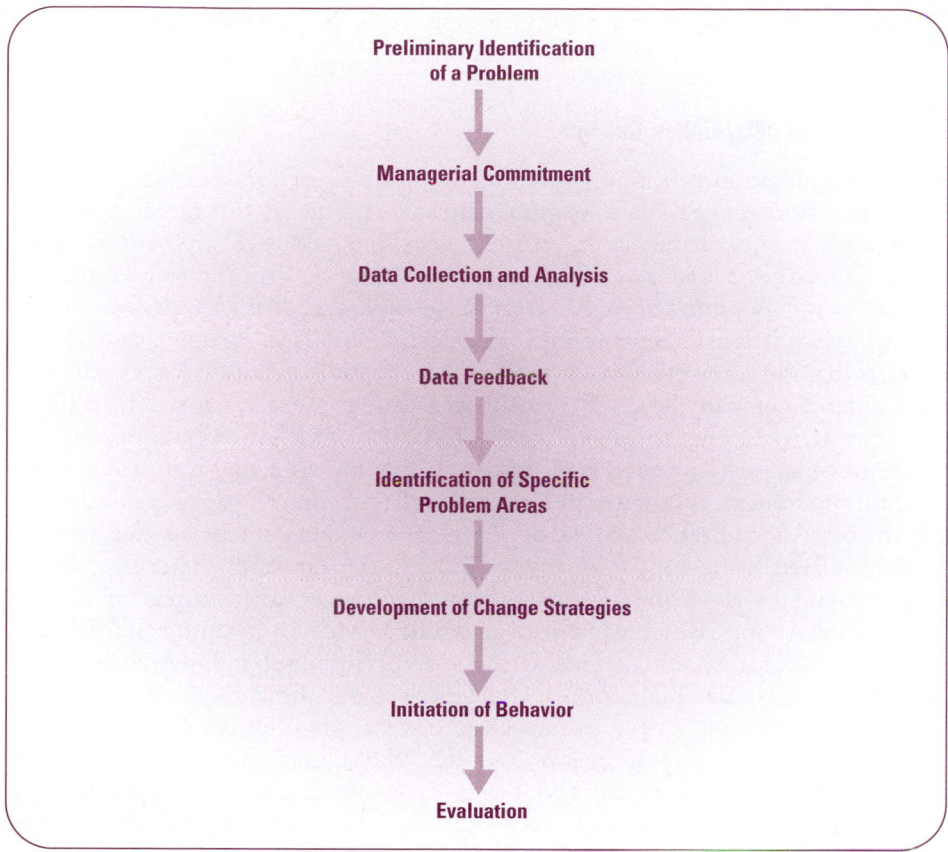

Exhibit 14-8

*A Process Model of
Organization Development*

*A formal program of organi-
zation development follows
certain steps.*

309

Source: Joseph A. Young and Barbara Smith, "Organizational Change and the HR Professional," *Personnel*, October 1988:
p. 48. Reprinted with the permission of *Personnel* published by the Society for Human Resource Management, Alexandria, VA.

Step 8: Evaluation

An attempt is made to evaluate whether the behavior changes made in Step 7 by
both the manager and staff members have improved behavior and work results.
Evaluation data may be collected through more interviews and observations,
including speaking to the manager's superior.

Process Consultation

A widely used OD intervention at the small-group level is called **process consultation.** Using this technique, the OD specialist (process consultant) examines
the pattern of a work unit's communications. A team leader typically asks for
process consultation because team meetings have not been highly productive. The
process consultant directly observes team meetings. At opportune times, the consultant will raise questions or make observations about what has been happening.
The role of the process consultant is to challenge the status quo by asking such
questions as:

- "Why doesn't anybody ever respond to Larry's questions?"
- "How come nobody challenges Jennifer's remarks when she is way off base?"
- "Why does everybody nod their heads in agreement when the CEO speaks?
  Are you all yes–people around here?"

Why process consultation makes a contribution has been explained in these
terms: "It points out the true quality of the emperor's new clothes even when

everyone is pretending they are quite elegant." Also, the process consultant can be helpful in changing a closed communication style.[37]

Large-Scale Organizational Change

At best, organization development is a method of change aimed at breathing new life into a firm. **Large-scale organizational change** is the method used to accomplish a major change in the firm's strategy and culture. The process is sometimes referred to as *bending the frame,* to indicate that the firm is changed in a significant way.[38] A company needs large-scale organizational change, or a turnaround, when it faces major internal or external problems. A high turnover rate suggests that the company is not a good place to work for a variety of possible reasons. When a company develops a reputation for high turnover, it will be difficult to attract talented, motivated replacements. Loss of established business and the failure to obtain new business is virtual proof that the company is in trouble.

Shifting from an authoritarian (or command and control) style organization to a team-based organization would be a typical example of a large-scale change. Closely related is the shift from a slow-moving bureaucracy to a more nimble, entrepreneurial-style firm. One of the most stunning turnarounds of all was Continental Airlines, which went from an airline headed for its third bankruptcy—with low morale and poor customer service—to becoming an industry leader. A key part of the large-scale organizational change was to establish a results-oriented culture. Two components of the culture change were to: (a) let people do their job without interference, and (b) treat one another with dignity and respect.[39]

A starting point in bringing about large-scale organizational change is to place a transformational leader in charge. Another important consideration, as advanced by the research and analysis of Larry Hirschorn, is to organize the transformational effort into three campaigns: political, marketing, and military. Following these procedures will help bring order to the chaos often associated with a large-scale change initiative.[40] The *political campaign* creates a coalition strong enough to support the initiative, and also to receive guidance from the people involved in the change. The change initiator may have to inspire others at first, and then build consensus at a later point. At other times, a change in organizational structure might be necessary to help build the coalition. For example, a layer of management might be eliminated so division heads can interact directly with the CEO who spearheads the large-scale organizational change.

The *marketing campaign* is designed to publicize and sell the benefits of the initiative. The campaign concentrates on listening to ideas that surface from the field as well as on working with lead customers to design the initiative. (A lead customer makes an advanced use of a product or service, or uses it in an imaginative way—such as closing wounds with duct tape!) Another approach to receiving input is to directly observe what is happening in the field. For example, top management at a large insurance company wanted to enhance productivity throughout the organization. During field visits, organizational behavior specialists discovered that in the most successful offices, managers held huddles rather than formal meetings at the beginning of each day, covering the same topics as would the meetings. The huddles were then recommended to all branch offices. The marketing campaign also includes giving a theme to the change initiative, such the classic "Work-Out" theme at GE, meaning that executives would help lower-ranking managers resolve problems and eliminate unnecessary work.

The *military campaign* is aimed at deliberately engaging with others to overcome resistance, using many of the ideas just described for winning support for change. It is essential for the change initiator to stay closely involved with the change effort because many large-scale initiatives fail simply because they are neglected shortly after the kickoff.

A final consideration here about large-scale organization change is to involve as many people as feasible. Richard H. Axelrod explains that efficient and effective implementation of change requires a critical mass of people through the organization who are committed to the outcomes; not just consultants and leaders, but everyone.[41] (A knowledge of individual differences suggests that such total commitment to improving the organization is highly unlikely, even though it's an ideal worth striving for.)

As with most forms of organization development, an external or internal consultant is usually required to bring about large-scale change. Line managers may be responsible for implementing the change, but advisors trained in organizational behavior help in the process.

The accompanying Organizational Behavior in Action tells the story of large-scale organization change in response to a troubled firm.

Six Sigma as Organization Development

The shift to a more quality-conscious firm can be classified as a total systems approach to organization development. Six Sigma stems from **total quality management (TQM)**, a management system for improving performance throughout a firm by maximizing customer satisfaction, making continuous improvements, and relying heavily on employee involvement. Although the term TQM has fallen into almost total disuse, and many people consider the quality movement to have passed, the quest for high quality remains an important thrust. Having high-quality goods and services is considered a necessary minimum to compete effectively.

To qualify as vendors to well-established customers, it is necessary to maintain high-quality standards. One such standard is six sigma, or 3.4 errors in one million opportunities. (The figure is derived from the area under the normal curve from −6 to +6 standard deviations from the mean.) This quality standard has taken the form of company-wide programs for attaining high quality. With capital first letters, Six Sigma® also refers to a philosophy of driving out waste, and improving quality and the cost and time performance of a company. (Six Sigma is a registered trademark of Motorola Inc., based on the statistical techniques developed by Joseph Juran.) Examples of companies with Six Sigma programs besides Motorola are GE and AlliedSignal.

Six Sigma is regarded as a data-driven method for achieving near-perfect quality with an emphasis on preventing problems. The approach emphasizes statistical analysis and measurement in design, manufacturing, and the entire area of customer-oriented activities. Six Sigma also has a strong behavioral aspect, with an emphasis on motivating people to work together to achieve higher levels of productivity. As with all programs of organizational improvement, top-management commitment is critical. Six Sigma is seen as a fusion of technical and social systems because of the emphasis on both technical programs and creating a culture of quality. Without a shift to a culture that believes in and practices quality, it is difficult to sustain the shift to high quality. Six Sigma teams are formed to carry out most of the quality improvement.

Organizational Behavior *in Action*

On the Road Again at Yellow Freight Systems

Several years ago a headhunter called Bill Zollars, a senior vice president of Ryder, a big transportation company. The recruiter urged Zollars to consider the top job at Yellow Freight Systems. Yellow was trying to set out on the road to recovery, after experiencing a $30 million loss, layoffs, and a Teamster strike.

The CEO of Yellow Corp., the parent of Yellow Express, explained to Zollars that the survival strategy was to transform the company from a long-haul carrier into something completely different: a carrier that offered multiple services and that was built around unprecedented customer service. Excited about the prospects, Zollars signed on with Yellow to help a troubled company start over.

The Change Methods

Zollars began changing the company by regularly visiting terminals around the country, and conducting town hall meetings. His journey lasted one-and-one half years. "There were days when I gave the same speech 10 times in ten different locations," he says. "I'd start at 6:30 AM with the drivers, then I'd talk to the dock workers, the people in the office, and the sales staff. At night I'd meet with customers. I wanted as many employees and customers as possible to hear it from me face-to-face."

Again and again he reminded employees of the company's new focus: customers. He knew this represented a new way of thinking about the business. In the past, Yellow reps would tell customers when a package could be delivered rather than asking when the package needed to be delivered.

Another change effort was to hear from customers. With the help of an outside firm, Yellow surveyed 10,000 randomly selected customers using 15-minute conversations. Since then, the company has been surveying 600 different customers a month.

"We had the attitude that speed and price were the most important things," says Greg Ried, chief communications officer. "But according to our research, what matters most is that you pick up when you say you are going to, deliver when you say you're going to, and don't damage the freight." The new Yellow Exact Express, time-definite, guaranteed service has helped achieve a delivery rate promptness of 98 percent. Because of Exact Express, Yellow is moving the sort of "hot" freight that it didn't get before. For example, Yellow was hired to make an overnight shipment of 40,000 flashlights from Los Angeles to Washington, DC for an outdoor event that took place during the 2001 inaugural.

One of the main reasons that Yellow has been able to expand and improve service is its state-of-the-art technology. Since 1994, the company has spent about $80 million a year on its highly integrated information systems. One application of the advanced technology is that each dockworker is equipped with a wireless mobile data terminal, or MDT, designed to speed up the loading and unloading process. Before a tractor trailer arrives, the worker can see what's on board, as well as which doors on the dock correspond to those destinations.

After going through a serious metamorphosis, the new Yellow began hosting an annual conference in Las Vegas called, "Transformation." Each year, 1,000 employees and 500 customers attend workshops on change. The underlying message is that the changes at Yellow are far from over. "Now that people have gotten used to how we do things, I'll tell them, 'Well, it will be different from years from now,'" says Zollars. "And some of them will say, 'I thought we were done.' But I don't think that you're ever done. You have to keep reinventing the company, because the market keeps changing. If you don't, you end up coasting."

Results of the Transformation

Yellow is a different company today. It still hauls primarily big heavy, freight. Gone, however, is the one-dimensional long-haul approach and the complacency ingrained from years of regulation. No more telling customers, "Sorry we can't do that." The new mantra is "Yes we can." In an attempt to offer one-stop shopping, Yellow has added a variety of services, including regional and expedited shipping, to satisfy a broader range of transportation needs.

The new Yellow is faster, more precise, and more profitable. New services continue to grow. The new company is considered to be a technology leader in its industry. Yellow's systems monitor 13,000 trucks nationwide and around 70,000 national and international shipping orders each day. The once rigid delivery schedule is now flexible.

"We've gone from being a company that thought it was in the trucking business to being one that realizes it's in the service business," says Zollars matter-of-factly.

Six Sigma, as with other quality programs, can help an organization achieve reliable products and services. Changes are more likely to take place when Six Sigma is linked to the organization infrastructure, including pay and rewards, and departmental budgets.[42] However, good quality alone does not attract large numbers of customers and job candidates. Products that offer passion, fun, and excitement (such as the Ford Motor Company's Jaguar) are bigger draws than flawless construction.

MANAGING CHANGE YOURSELF

Develop useful insights into managing change in your job and career.

A major factor in managing change is coping well with change yourself. All the approaches to organizational and small-group change described in this chapter work more effectively with individuals predisposed to managing change well. Our approach to providing insight into self-managing change is divided into relevant research and personal suggestions. To help you think through your flexibility about dealing with change, do the Self-Assessment that follows.

Empirical Research about Coping with Organizational Change

A study involving over 500 employees in six organizations and five countries supported the well-accepted belief by practicing managers that some employees adapt better to organizational change than others. The ability to cope with change was measured both by self-reports and managerial assessments of how the workers coped with change. Seven personality factors presumed to be related to change were measured: locus of control, generalized self-efficacy, self-esteem, positive affectivity (similar to optimism), openness to experience, tolerance for ambiguity, and risk aversion. The seven traits were reduced to two factors: positive self-concept and risk tolerance.

A key result was that having a positive self-concept and a tolerance for risk were positively related to both measures of coping with change. The strongest and most consistent dispositional, or personality, variables among the seven traits in terms of their relationship to coping with change were tolerance for ambiguity and positive affectivity.[43] The implication supports what you probably suspected: People who can tolerate a lack of clarity and structure, and who are optimistic cope well with change.

Suggestions for Coping with Change

The research just reported has a few implications for your ability to manage change well: Practice dealing with ambiguous tasks (such as unclear assignments) and work on having a positive general disposition. Consider also the following

SELF-ASSESSMENT

How Flexible Are You?

To succeed as a managerial worker, a person needs a flexible attitude, an ability to be open to others, and a willingness to listen. Where do you stand on being flexible? Test yourself by answering Often, Sometimes, or Rarely to the following questions.

	Frequency		
	Often	**Sometimes**	**Rarely**
1. Do you tend to seek out only those people who agree with your analysis on issues?	❏	❏	❏
2. Do you ignore most of the advice from coworkers or other students about doing your work more efficiently?	❏	❏	❏
3. Do your team members go along with what you say just to avoid an argument?	❏	❏	❏
4. Have people referred to you as "rigid" or "close-minded" on several occasions?	❏	❏	❏
5. When presented with a new method, do you immediately look for a flaw?	❏	❏	❏
6. Do you make up your mind early with respect to an issue and then hold firmly to your opinion?	❏	❏	❏
7. When people disagree with you, do you tend to belittle them or become argumentative?	❏	❏	❏
8. Do you often feel you are the only person in the group who really understands the problem?	❏	❏	❏
9. Do you prefer to hang on to old software even though more than one new update has been published?	❏	❏	❏
10. Do you resist trying new foods?	❏	❏	❏

Check Your Score: If you answered "Rarely" to eight questions, you are unusually adaptable and therefore probably cope well with change. If you answered "Sometimes" to at least six questions, you are on the right track, but more flexibility would benefit your ability to deal with change. If you answered "Often" to five or more questions, you have a long way to go to improve your flexibility and adaptability to change. You are also brutally honest about your faults, which could be an asset.

practical suggestions: *Look for the personal value that could be embedded in a forced change.*[44] If you are downsized, take the opportunity to assume responsibility for your own career rather than being dependent on the organization. Many downsizing victims find a new career for themselves that better fits their interests, or try self-employment in search of more job security.

When faced with a significant change, *ask "What if?" questions* such as "What if my company is sold tomorrow?", "What if I went back to school for more education?", and "What if I did accept that one-year assignment in China?" When confronting major change, *force yourself to enjoy at least some small aspect of the change.* Suppose the edict comes through the organization that purchases can now only be made over the Internet. This means you will no longer be able to interact with a few of the sales reps you considered to be buddies. With the time you save, however, you will have spare hours each week for leisure activities.

You are less likely to resist change if you *recognize that change is inevitable.* Dealing with change is an integral part of life, so why fight it? Keep in mind also to *change before you have to, which can lead to a better deal.* If your manager announces

IMPLICATIONS FOR MANAGERIAL PRACTICE

1. To manage organizational culture, one must first understand the culture of the firm and then use that knowledge to guide one's own behavior and that of group members. For example, an executive might resist downsizing as a way to reduce costs because laying off productive and loyal employees conflicts with the firm's values.

2. The biggest challenge in implementing workplace innovations is to bring about cultural change. Workers' attitudes and values have to change if the spirit of innovation is to keep smoldering. An effective vehicle for bringing about such change is for top-level managers and others to exchange ideas. Formal arrangements, such as regularly scheduled staff meetings, facilitate exchanging ideas, reflecting on values, and learning what behavior is in vogue. Encouraging informal meetings can often achieve the same purpose with a higher degree of effectiveness.

3. Learning how to cope well with change yourself is a key part of managing change.

a new plan, get on board as a volunteer before you are forced to accept a lesser role. If your company has made the decision to start a Six Sigma program, study the subject early and ask for a role as a facilitator or team leader. Stop trying to be in control all the time because you cannot control everything. Many changes will occur that you cannot control, so relax and enjoy the ride. Finally, recognize that change has an emotional impact, which will most likely cause some inner turmoil and discomfort. Even if the change is for the better, you might remain emotionally attached to your old system—or neighborhood, car, or PC.

SUMMARY OF KEY POINTS

1 Present an analysis of the importance of organizational culture.

The origins of organizational culture often lie in the values, administrative practices, and personality of its founders. Other key influences are the societal culture, the industry, and the organization's code of conduct. Organizational culture has various dimensions, such as the values, stories, and myths maintained by the organization; the sense of ownership within the firm; corporate spiritualism; and innovativeness.

The culture is taught primarily through socialization and the teaching of leaders. The consequences of organizational culture include: competitive advantage, productivity and morale, innovation, compatibility of mergers and acquisitions, the person–organization fit, and the direction of leadership activity.

2 Present two models of the change process in organizations.

The growth curve model of change in organizations traces the inevitability of change through a firm's life cycle. During the integrative phase, there is a pulling and tugging between forces for change and against change. Another model of change views it as a three-step process: the unfreezing, changing, and refreezing of behavior.

3 Describe why people resist change and how to manage such resistance.

People resist change for a variety of reasons they think are important, the most common being the fear of an unfavorable outcome. Also, facing competing commitments may create immunity to change. Techniques for overcoming resistance include: (1) allowing for discussion and negotiation, (2) allowing for participation, (3) pointing out financial benefits of a change, (4) avoiding change overload, (5) gaining political support for change, (6) providing education, (7) avoiding citing poor performance as the reason for change, (8) incorporating the human touch, and (9) paying attention to the emotional aspects of change.

4 Describe three major factors that create organizational change.

Downsizing as a change strategy is most likely to be effective when it is integrated into the company's long-term strategies. Low-value work must be eliminated, teamwork must be emphasized, and considerable attention must be paid to the human element. Information technology has facilitated change in organizations, including making them more democratic because of the increased accessibility of information. The Internet is changing the nature of many businesses, such as allowing companies to interact more directly with customers and suppliers. Information technology has created substantial changes in how long and where people work. Another force for change in organizations is the transition from a jobholder meeting the demands of a job description to a person carrying out a variety of work roles, or different kinds of work.

5 **Explain the nature of organization development.**
Organization development brings about constructive, planned change, including modifying the culture. Using the process model of organization development, both the OD consultant and staff members are involved in bringing about constructive change. Process consultation is used to examine the pattern of a work unit's communications. Large-scale organization development is used to accomplish a major change in the firm's strategy and culture. The large-scale change effort should be organized into three campaigns: political, marketing,

and military. As many people as feasible should be involved in the change effort.

Six Sigma programs stem from total quality management, and are an important organization development strategy. Six Sigma is also a philosophy of driving out waste, improving quality and the cost and time performance of a company.

6 **Develop useful insights into managing change in your job and career.**
People who score high on the personality factors of positive self-concept and risk tolerance adapt better to change. Two specific traits related to dealing well with change are tolerance for ambiguity and positive affectivity. Among the suggestions for managing change well are: searching for the personal value that could be embedded in forced change, asking "What if," forcing yourself to enjoy at least some small aspect of the change, recognizing that change is inevitable, and understanding that change has an emotional impact.

KEY TERMS AND PHRASES

Organizational Culture, *294*
A system of shared values and beliefs that influence worker behavior.

Subculture, *296*
A pocket in which the organizational culture differs from the dominant culture, as well as other pockets of subculture.

Socialization, *296*
The process of coming to understand the values, norms, and customs essential for adapting to an organization.

Growth Curve Model, *299*
A model that traces the inevitability of change through a firm's life cycle.

Force-Field Theory, *300*
The theory contending that an organization simultaneously faces forces for change (the driving forces) and forces for maintaining the status quo (the restraining forces).

Organization Development (OD), *307*
Any strategy, method, or technique for making organizations more effective by bringing about constructive, planned change.

Process Consultation, *309*
An intervention in which the organization development specialist examines the pattern of a work unit's communications.

Large-Scale Organizational Change, *310*
The method used to accomplish a major change in the firm's strategy and culture.

Total Quality Management (TQM), *311*
A management system for improving performance throughout an organization by maximizing customer satisfaction, making continual improvements, and relying heavily on employee involvement.

Six Sigma, *311*
A data-driven method for achieving near-perfect quality with an emphasis on preventing problems.

DISCUSSION QUESTIONS AND ACTIVITIES

1. As described in the opening case to this chapter, employees from the two companies involved in a merger indicated which sport team the other side resembled. How would this activity contribute to a smooth corporate merger?
2. How would you describe the organizational culture of Wal-Mart (or any other retailer) based on whatever evidence you have? If necessary, visit your local Wal-Mart (or other retailer) for firsthand observations.
3. Why do so many CEOs believe that their primary responsibility is managing organizational culture? What happened to making a profit?

4. How can a manager tell if an employee is resisting change?
5. Why might the transition from "jobs to work" lead to resistance to change for many people?
6. How does organization development at the individual level contribute to organizational change?
7. Identify a major change you will have to cope with in the next several years and describe your plan of action for coping with it.

ORGANIZATIONAL BEHAVIOR ONLINE

TO DO

Understanding a Company Culture
Visit www.delphi.com/careers/culture, the Web site of the automotive supplier, Delphi. Observe the dimensions that Delphi uses to describe its corporate culture. Delphi is proud of its "Principles" and "Absolutes of Excellence." Yet after reading the information in these two categories, would you classify the information as being dimensions of corporate culture? Why or why not?

TO BOOKMARK

Organizational Culture (Knowledge Maps)
http://www.appliedlearninglabs.com

Managing Change, as Proposed by the Center for Quality of Management
http://www.cqm.org

The American Productivity & Quality Center
http://www.apqc.org

Process Consultation
http://www.cape.org/2003/schein.html

CASE PROBLEM: Patching up the Darwinian Culture at Computer Associates

Sanjay Kumar was on his best behavior. Through winter and spring of 2002, as corporate scandals erupted across America, the Chairman of Computer Associates International Inc. appeared determined to cast the embattled software powerhouse as a model of corporate virtue. It was no easy sell. After a decade of white-hot growth, CA had become legendary for its convoluted accounting, outsized executive handouts, and a take-no-prisoners approach to customers.

Company Problems

The 40-year-old Kumar toiled to turn overcome problems at CA. He coddled customers and worked to clear up accounting questions. He overhauled the board of directors, long considered a rubber stamp. Despite the changes, on July 24, 2002, Kumar stupefied investors and corporate-governance experts alike. After a week of negotiations that ended after midnight, he coughed up $10 million to end a proxy challenge from Texas entrepreneur Sam Wyly. CA justified the deal as a legitimate means to end a management distraction that drained valuable time for Kumar's turnaround effort. But the company is having a difficult time washing off the odor of a scandal.

Although no one at CA has been indicted, the Long Island based company is under investigation by the SEC and the U.S. Justice Department for alleged accounting irregularities. Investors, outraged by accounting shifts and a plunging stock price, have filed nearly a dozen suits.

CA has many frayed relations left to repair. The layoffs from 50-plus acquisitions left hundreds of former employees angry from coast to coast. CA used the fact that products were vital to customers to get them to agree to massive new contracts, critics say, and paid little attention to customer service. That left customers feeling roughed up and angry. "CA bullied and cajoled. They screwed the customers for every cent they could get out of them," says a former CA sales manager.

Now, Kumar is a CEO on the spot. He runs a widely distrusted company in an era where trust is suddenly worth more than growth. He also has to deal with disgruntled buyers who are all too happy to postpone software updates. Kumar says he is out to change the very nature of the software giant, from the way it adds up its numbers to the way it deals with people.

For 15 years, Kumar stood shoulder-to-shoulder with founder and current Chairman Charles B. Wang as the two forged a hard-edged corporate culture focused on creating growth at all costs. For a time, Wang and Kumar succeeded beyond their wildest dreams. In the go-go market of the 1990s, CA emerged as a global tech titan—the world's third largest software company. In the business of managing mainframes and computer networks, CA was king.

Wang and Kumar fashioned together CA's bare-knuckle culture in the 1990s. They encouraged sharp disagreements. Favored employees were encouraged to come up with new ideas and run with them. "It's a thunderously great place to work if you like extreme challenges and opportunities," says Mark Stabler, a former CA senior vice president.

At lower levels, CA was not a happy place. Every year, managers shook up the sales force, reassigning as much as 60 percent of them to new accounts. That meant starting from scratch with customers, year after year. Some employees lived in fear of being punished for making mistakes. A former CA executive who was part of the company's in-crowd says "If you made a mistake, you'd be fired or demoted. We called it spending time in purgatory."

Change Efforts

Kumar wants to recapture CA's glory days. He believes he is striving to create a gentler giant. The path to growth, Kumar says, is to cozy up with customers and develop products they want to buy. It used to be all about landing the big deal. Now, "It's about the customer," he says.

Kumar patches up relations personally with customers that were frustrated with CA, such as KeyCorp Lit. "They were treating us like a captive customer," recalls a KeyCorp executive. "The only time we saw the account team was when we had a contract to be renewed."

Kumar has established a 650-person customer-care organization and launched annual customer-satisfaction surveys, linking pay of 500 senior executives to the results. And he has visited dozens of customers to get back in their good graces. He's humbler now, offering apologies for past mistakes and new flexibility in the way customers buy software. For growth, Kumar is banking on those same customers. Once they're feeling friendlier, and a bit richer, he plans to sell them loads of new software. Monster acquisitions are out. In 12 to 18 months, he plans to deliver a new generation of software to handle wireless communication and Web services that automate communications between Web sites.

To smooth out CA's earnings, Kumar revamped the company's accounting. In the past, CA recognized software-license revenues immediately after a deal was concluded. The new model recognizes software-license revenues over the life of a contract.

Kumar has also launched a major overhaul of the board of directors. He expanded the board from eight to eleven, retiring several veteran members and adding seven new outsiders, including a Harvard Business School corporate-governance expert, Jay W. Lorsch.

But all the while, dual federal probes hang over his head. As president for eight years and CEO for two, Kumar is responsible for the way the company kept its books. He went along with CA's long-standing revenue-accounting policies, including double-counting certain revenues when the company renegotiated long-term contracts. Using the new system, CA retroactively reclassified revenues for the previous five years, slicing $2.5 billion off the total.

Outside director Lewis S. Ranieri says Kumar is the man for the top CA job because he's making progress in customer relations and corporate governance under difficult conditions. "I don't know who did what to whom before I came, but for the two years I've seen, he's the antithesis of the old CA," says Ranieri.

When confronted by critics recently, Kumar vigorously defended himself. "I have nothing to hide. I'm not in the bunker," he said. He denies that he did anything illegal and stresses the progress he is making. "I have a five-year plan, and we're two years into it," he says.

Kumar acknowledges that CA behaved poorly in the past, but he blames the problems on underlings. "Our sales force was very successful, and it gave rise to bad behavior," he says, adding: "Much of what went on, the top of the company had no idea."

At the same time, he's unapologetic about the controversial $1.1 billion in stock grants made to the company's three top officers in 1998—with 30 percent going to him—even though investor outrage forced the trio to give back half the stock.

Kumar defends CA's Darwinian culture. "The company demanded performance," he says. Yet he is remodeling the old CA into a place where employees have more say and less turmoil. During one of the recent annual reorientation of the sales force, only two percent to three percent of the staff switched customers.

While Kumar blames much of CA's customer woes on an overaggressive sales force, interviews with former employees show that Kumar himself was sometimes in the thick of things. At one time, Kumar was accused of threatening to shut down the computers of a grocery chain if they did not sign a new contract with considerable new software. Kumar regards this accusation as unfounded.

As Kumar looks toward the future, he keeps focused on improved relations with CA's customers, investors, and employees.

Diverse Culture

According to interviews conducted by *Vault.com* employees say that Computer Associates is very open to women and minorities, and the Chairman and COO are both minorities. *Fortune* listed CA as one of America's Best 50 Companies for minorities in the July 2001 issue. One employee notes, "The overall attitude is positive towards the advancement of anyone who can generate revenue." Furthermore, employees who cannot meet revenue quotas are out.

Case Questions

1. Analyze the culture at Computer Associates, using a few of the standard dimensions of organizational culture.
2. How feasible is it for Sanjay Kumar to bring about cultural change at CA when he is part of the old culture?
3. In today's business environment, would CA still be able to bully its customers?
4. What suggestions can you offer CA management for revamping its culture in a positive direction?

Source: Steve Hamm, "CEO on the Spot," *Business Week,* September 30, 2002, pp. 88–94; "Computer Associates," http://www.vault.com.

ENDNOTES

1. "Edgar Schein: Careers, Culture, and Organizational Learning," in *Business: The Ultimate Resource* (Cambridge, MA: Perseus Books Group, 2002), p. 1044.
2. Katrina Brooker, "Can Anyone Replace Herb?", *Fortune,* April 17, 2000, pp. 186–192; James Campbell Quick, "Crafting an Organization Culture: Herb's Hand at Southwest Airline," *Organizational Dynamics,* Autumn 1992, pp. 50–53.
3. "Can CEO Ollila Keep the Cellular Superstar Flying High?" *Business Week,* August 10, 1998, p. 54.
4. John Kamp and Paul Brooks, "Perceived Organizational Climate and Employee Counterproductivity," *Journal of Business and Psychology,* Summer 1991, p. 455.
5. Scott Hays, "'Ownership Cultures' Create Unity," *Workforce,* February 1999, pp. 60–64.
6. Joanne Cole, "Building Heart and Soul," *HRfocus,* October 1998, pp. 9–10.
7. Mildred L. Culp, "Spirituality Brings Connectedness, Profit in Today's Fragmented Workplace," WorkWise® syndicated column, September 5, 1999.
8. Christopher Meyer, "The Biology of Business," *Fast Company,* May 2003, p. 46.
9. Literature reviewed in Gerard George, Randall G. Sleeth, and Mark A. Siders, "Organizing Culture: Leader Roles, Behaviors, and Reinforcement Mechanisms," *Journal of Business and Psychology,* Summer 1999, p. 548.
10. Quoted in Andy Meisler, "Spare Him the Gurus," *Workforce,* June 2003, p. 36.
11. Daniel R. Denison, *Corporate Culture and Organizational Effectiveness* (New York: Wiley, 1990).
12. Anna Driver, "Wal-Mart Alumni Don't Always Find Success," Reuters, April 19, 2003.
13. Gary Hamel, "Reinvent Your Company," *Fortune,* June 12, 2000, pp. 97–118. The quote is from page 118.

14. Quoted in Jeffrey A. Schmidt, ed., *Making Mergers Work* (Alexandria, VA: Towers/Perrin/SHRM, 2002).

15. Charles A. O'Reilly III, Jennifer A. Chatman, and David F. Caldwell, "People and Organizational Culture: A Profile Comparison Approach to Assessing Person-Organization Fit," *Academy of Management Journal,* September 1991, pp. 487–516.

16. Charles D. Morgan, "Culture Change/Culture Shock," *Management Review,* November 1998, p. 13.

17. "Hershey Thinks Its Delivery Problems Are Now Over," Associated Press, April 20, 2000.

18. Robert A. Guth, 'Microsoft's CEO Sends Out New Battle Cry," *The Wall Street Journal,* June 5, 2003, p. B4.

19. Harry Woodward and Steve Bucholtz, *Aftershock: Helping People through Corporate Change* (New York: Wiley, 1987).

20. Kurt Lewin, *Field Theory in Social Science: Selected Theoretical Papers* (New York: Harper & Brothers, 1951).

21. Kurt Lewin, *Field Theory and Social Science* (New York: Harper & Row, 1951), Chapters 9 and 10.

22. Robert Kegan and Lisa Laskow Lahey, "The Real Reason People Won't Change," *Harvard Business Review,* November 2001, pp. 84–92.

23. James A. F. Stoner and R. Edward Freeman, *Management,* 4th ed. (Upper Saddle River, NJ: Prentice Hall, 1989), p. 369.

24. Quoted in Carol Hymowitz, "To Maintain Success, Managers Must Learn How to Direct Change," *The Wall Street Journal,* August 13, 2002, p. B1.

25. "When Employees Resist Change," *Success Workshop, A* supplement to *Manager's Edge,* January 2000, p. 1.

26. "Internet B2B Still Isn't Up to Speed," The Associated Press, April 15, 2002.

27. Shaul Fox and Yair Amichai-Hamburger, "The Power of Emotional Appeals in Promoting Organizational Change Programs," *Academy of Management Executive,* November 2001, pp. 84–93.

28. Susan Reynolds Fisher and Margaret A. White, "Downsizing in a Learning Organization: Are There Hidden Costs?" *Academy of Management Review,* January 2000, pp. 244–251.

29. Sherry Kuczynski, "Help! I Shrunk the Company," *HRMagazine,* June 1999, pp. 40–45; Dean Elmuti and Yunus Kathawaia, "Rightsizing for Individual Competitiveness: Important Thoughts to Consider," *Business Forum,* Fall 1993, pp. 8–11; "Layoffs Are Not Inevitable," The Associated Press, November 19, 2001.

30. Quoted in "At Crossroads of Change: An Interview with Tom Peters," *Leadership* (A Member Newsletter of the American Management Association International), May 1998, p. 3.

31. Eric Shoeniger, "Turning a Page on the Internet Economy," Unisys Exec, May–June 2000, pp. 8–10.

32. Samuel Greengard, "How Technology Will Change the Workplace," *Workforce,* January 1998, p. 78. Used with permission.

33. Shari Caudron, "Jobs Disappear: When Work Becomes More Important," *Workforce,* January 2000, pp. 30–32.

34. Book review by Rick Tallarigo, Sr., in *Personnel Psychology,* Winter 2002, p. 1033.

35. Robert T. Golembiewski, *Organization Development: Ideas and Issues* (New Brunswick, NJ: Transaction Books, Rutgers University, 1989).

36. Joseph A. Young and Barbara Smith, "Organizational Change and the HR Professional," *Personnel,* October 1988, p. 46; Wendell L. French, "Organization Development, Objectives, Assumptions, and Strategy," *California Management Review,* Vol. 2, 1969, p. 26.

37. Leonard D. Goodstein and W. Warner Burke, "Creating Successful Organizational Change," *Organizational Dynamics,* Spring 1991, p. 14.

38. Goodstein and Burke, "Creating Successful Organizational Change," p. 4.

39. Greg Brenneman, "Right Away and All at Once: How We Saved Continental," *Harvard Business Review,* September–October 1998, pp. 162–179.

40. Larry Hirschorn, "Campaigning for Change," *Harvard Business Review,* July 2002, pp. 98–104.

41. Richard H. Axelrod, *Terms of Engagement: Changing the Way We Change Organizations* (Williston, VT: BK Publishers, 2000).

42. Joseph A. Defeo, "Six Sigma: Road Map for Survival," *HRfocus,* July 1999, pp. 11–12; "Six Sigma," in *Business: The Ultimate Resource,* pp. 572–573

43. Timothy A. Judge, Carl J. Thoresen, Victor Pucik, and Theresa M. Welbourne, "Managerial Coping with Organizational Change: A Dispositional Perspective," *Journal of Applied Psychology,* February 1999, pp. 107–122.

44. The first two items on the list are from Fred Pryor, "What Have You Learned from Change?" *Managers Edge,* September 1998, p. 2.

The Learning Organization and Knowledge Management

Several years ago, Siemens Medical Solutions decided to change its "knowledge is power" culture into one in which "knowledge sharing" was the norm. The company wanted employees to have easy access to information and expertise across business units so they could do their jobs better and faster without reinventing the wheel, says Richard Wetherell, corporate director for quality, knowledge management, and process improvement.

The problem was that many employees associated sharing knowledge with losing power. For example, says Wetherell, if a software engineer is the only one in a department who can perform a certain skill, he sees that as job security, and doesn't want to give that knowledge away. There was also a scheduling issue. Taking the time to share information or to coach someone in a new skill can be burdensome to busy employees, he says. Employees saw no value in this sort of communication. Wetherell reasoned, "If we reward and recognize people for sharing, then it doesn't feel like losing power."

To support the new environment, the company built three Web-based knowledge-sharing tools, through which employees can collect and disseminate useful information to the rest of the company. "People of Med" is an online database of employee profiles that includes each member's contact information, experience, areas of expertise, and photograph. "Communities of Practice" is an online meeting place where employees volunteer to host forums on specific topics, such as ISO 9000 certification challenges. The "Knowledge Square" is an online database filled with presentations, Web sites, technical papers, specs, and any other materials that might be of value to the company.

"The technology is great, but they only work if people use it," Wetherbell says. To encourage employees to take advantage of the knowledge-sharing opportunities, they receive bonus points every time they use one of the three tools. These can be used to purchase items from a gift catalogue that includes everything from T-shirts to vacations. Whether they store their profiles in People of Med, participate in a community, or download information from the Knowledge Square, they get rewarded.

Siemens Medical Solutions employees naturally turn to the knowledge-sharing tools to gather information and connect with other employees. Wetherell still offers the bonus points, but says the incentive program was intended primarily to lure employees online and get them using the tools. "They see the intrinsic value of knowledge-sharing now," he says. "It make their lives easier and helps them be more productive."

Source: Sarah Fister Gale, "Incentives and the Art of Changing Behavior," *Workforce*, November 2002, p. 82. Used with permission.

NOW ASK YOURSELF: What does the emphasis on knowledge sharing at Siemens Medical tells us about the relevance of helping organizations learn, managing knowledge, and sharing knowledge? (The Siemens anecdote also illustrates the relevance of behavior modification for enhancing organizational effectiveness.) The concept of managing knowledge and sharing information—a major new thrust in organizational behavior—stems from the idea of learning organizations, so in this chapter we look at both. We first examine the nature of learning organizations, then follow that discussion with a description of knowledge management, including knowledge sharing. Becoming a learning organization sets the stage for managing knowledge well and making optimum use of human capital.

THE LEARNING ORGANIZATION

Closely related to organization development is the idea that an effective organization engages in continuous learning by proactively adapting to the external environment. Scholars and managers agree that organizational learning is desirable, yet not all agree on the nature of a learning organization. A **learning organization** is one that is skilled at creating, acquiring, and transferring knowledge; and at modifying behavior to reflect new knowledge and insights.[1] Or as Peter Senge puts it, a learning organization is simply a group of people working together to enhance their capacities to create results they value.[2] Although we speak of organizational learning, it is still individual people who create the conditions for such learning. Chris Argyris notes that organizational learning is done by individuals acting as agents for organizations.[3] An organization may have a collective mind, but it does not have a brain.

Our approach to understanding the learning organization will be to first describe a recent model framework of a learning organization, followed by a list of its building blocks or components. The field of organizational learning and knowledge management has many abstract and nebulous concepts. Our approach is to translate many of these concepts into specific behaviors that practitioners can take to improve the management of knowledge. Before proceeding, however, the Self-Assessment that follows will give you a sense of the day-by-day characteristics of a learning organization.

The 4I Framework of a Learning Organization

As interest in learning organizations has increased, attempts have been made to develop an overall understanding, or framework, for them. The 4I framework is instructive because it describes the processes involved in a firm making systematic use of information. A portion of the model that appears most useful to practitioners is presented here and shown in Exhibit 15-1 on page 324. A premise behind this framework is that organizational learning that results in organizational renewal encompasses the entire enterprise, not simply the individual or group. Another premise is that the organization operates in an open system, rather than having solely an individual focus. As is well known, an organization must satisfy the demands of the external world or it will perish.

As explained by Mary M. Crossan, Henry W. Lane, and Roderick E. White, organizational learning is composed of four processes: intuiting, interpreting, integrating, and institutionalization.[4] The four processes work together to link the individual, group, and organizational levels. The four processes are the glue that

1

Describe the 4I framework of a learning organization.

SELF-ASSESSMENT

Do You Work for a Learning Organization?

Directions: Indicate for each of the following statements whether it is mostly true or mostly false in relation to your current or most recent place of work. Indicate a question mark when the statement is either not applicable or you are not in a position to judge.

	Mostly True	?	Mostly False
1. Company employees often visit other locations or departments to share new information or skills they have learned.	❏	❏	❏
2. Our company frequently repeats mistakes.	❏	❏	❏
3. We get most of our market share by competing on price.	❏	❏	❏
4. Many people in our organization are aware of and believe in our vision.	❏	❏	❏
5. Top management assumes that the vast majority of employees are experts at what they do.	❏	❏	❏
6. Almost all of our learning takes place individually rather than in groups or teams.	❏	❏	❏
7. In our company, after you have mastered your job you do not have to bother with additional learning such as training programs or self-study.	❏	❏	❏
8. Our firm shies away from inviting outsiders into our company to discuss our business because few outsiders could understand our uniqueness.	❏	❏	❏
9. If it weren't for a few key individuals in our company, we would be in big trouble.	❏	❏	❏
10. Our new product launches go smoothly and quickly.	❏	❏	❏
11. Our company creates a lot of opportunities for employees to get together and share information, such as conferences and meetings.	❏	❏	❏
12. We are effective at pricing the service we provide to customers.	❏	❏	❏
13. Very few of our employees have any idea about company sales and profits.	❏	❏	❏
14. I often hear employees asking questions about why the company has taken certain major actions.	❏	❏	❏
15. The company maintains a current database about the knowledge and skills of almost all our employees.	❏	❏	❏
16. Having specialized knowledge brings you some status in our company.	❏	❏	❏
17. It would be stretching the truth to say that many of our employees are passionate about what our organization is attempting to accomplish.	❏	❏	❏
18. Our performance appraisal system makes a big contribution to helping employees learn and improve.	❏	❏	❏
19. Following established rules and procedures is important in our company, so creativity and imagination are not encouraged.	❏	❏	❏
20. Most of our employees believe that if you do your own job well, you don't have to worry about what goes on in the rest of the organization.	❏	❏	❏
21. We get loads of useful new ideas from our customers.	❏	❏	❏
22. I have frequently heard our managers talk about how what goes on in the outside world has an impact on our company.	❏	❏	❏
23. We treat customer suggestions with a good deal of skepticism.	❏	❏	❏
24. During breaks, you sometimes hear employees discussing the meaning and implication of the work they are doing.	❏	❏	❏
25. Employees at every level tend to rely on facts when making important decisions.	❏	❏	❏
26. If a process or procedure works well in our company, we are hesitant to experiment with other approaches to a problem.	❏	❏	❏

(continued)

	Mostly True	?	Mostly False
27. Our company treats mistakes as valuable learning experiences about what not to do in the future.	❑	❑	❑
28. Our company rarely copies ideas from the successful practices of other companies.	❑	❑	❑
29. Each time we face a significant problem, our company seems to start all over to find a solution.	❑	❑	❑
30. It's a waste of time to be reading about a learning organization, when my real interest is in learning how to prevent problems.	❑	❑	❑

Total score: _____

Scoring and Interpretation:

A. Record the number of Mostly True answers you gave to the following questions: 1, 4, 5, 10, 11, 12, 14, 15, 16, 18, 21, 22, 24, 25, 27.

B. Record the number of Mostly False answers you gave to the following questions: 2, 3, 6, 7, 8, 9, 13, 17, 19, 20, 23, 26, 28, 29, 30.

C. Add the numbers for A and B.

D. Add half of your "?" responses to A, and half to B.

25 or higher	You are most likely a member of a learning organization. This tendency is so pronounced that it should contribute heavily to your company's success.
13–24	Your company has an average tendency toward being a learning organization, suggesting an average degree of success in profiting from mistakes and changing in response to a changing environment.
0–12	Your firm is definitely not a learning organization.

Source: Andrew J. DuBrin, *Looking Around Corners: The Art of Problem Prevention* (Madison, WI: CWL Publishing Enterprises, 1999), 181–183. Used with permission of the publisher.

binds the structure together. The three learning levels define the structure through which organizational learning takes place (as does all of organizational behavior).

Individual Level: Intuiting and interpreting take place at the individual level. *Intuiting* is the preconscious (not quite explicit or conscious) recognition of the pattern and/or possibilities inherent in a personal stream of experience. *Intuiting* is essentially intuition and relies on hunches about events taking place in the organization. *Interpreting* is explaining through words and/or actions an insight or idea to oneself and to others. A manager might develop the intuition that the company is not getting its fair share of repeat business. He might then say to coworkers, "Could we be facing some problem with our products that prompts many customers to forget about us after one try?"

Group Level: Integration takes place at the group level. This is the process of developing shared understanding among individuals and of taking coordinated action. Dialogue about the problem and joint action are critical to the development of shared understanding. The group might bat around the problem by asking "What is it about us that prompts so many customers to try us once and not come back?"

Organization Level: Institutionalization takes place at the organization level. This is the process of ensuring that routinized actions occur. At first, the integrating taking place at the group level will be ad hoc and informal. However, if the coordinated action is recurring and substantial, it will become institutionalized. Tasks

Exhibit 15-1

The 4I Framework of Organizational Learning

Organizational learning takes place at three levels and involves four processes.

Individual Level (Intuiting and Interpreting)

Group Level (Integrating)

Organizational Level (Institutionalizing)

Organizational Learning

Source: Mary M. Crossan, Henry W. Lane, and Roderick E. White, "An Organizational Learning Framework: From Institution to Institution," *Academy of Management Review*, July, 1999, p. 525.

become defined, actions specified, and organizational mechanisms put in place to ensure that certain actions occur. Institutionalizing can also be regarded as the process of embedded learning achieved by individuals and groups into the organization. In the example at hand, an institutionalized process might be to follow up with first-time customers regarding the reasons they intend to return or not return.

An implication of the 4I framework for managers is that for organizational learning to take place, individuals should be encouraged to share their intuition and insights with other individuals and the group. In this way, the best insights will eventually become institutionalized.

2 Building Blocks of a Learning Organization

Identify the building blocks, or key characteristics, of a learning organization

To become and remain a learning organization, certain characteristics and behaviors are required of organizational members, as described next.[5] Although organizational theorists speak of a learning organization, the workers do the learning. The collective wisdom of the workers might then translate into a learning organization.

Double-Loop Learning

An in-depth, nondefensive type of learning takes place in a learning organization. **Double-loop learning** occurs when people use feedback to confront the validity of the goal or the values implicit in the situation. When you engage in double-loop learning, you change the governing values or assumptions themselves. As a result, you change your actions. A conventional-thinking manager (one who engages in single-loop learning) at a tire distributor observes that sales have been declining (feedback from the environment). The manager then asks, "How can we more effectively market retread tires for automobiles?" As a double-loop learner, the same manager might ask, "Why are we even selling retreads for the automotive market? The demand is declining and they are not very safe." Note that the sales manager is being open and non-defensive about his or her product line, and is changing the assumption that retreaded tires even make a contribution to society.

Action Learning

Learning while working on real problems, or **action learning,** is a fundamental part of a learning organization. Action learning requires an environment that supports workers developing new skills and reflecting on what they have learned, and is based on the concept of:

$$L = P + Q$$

The equation means that learning (L) is comprised of programmed knowledge (P) plus questioning skills (Q). Programmed knowledge refers to ideas that people have been taught or that they learned through experience. Questioning skills refer to the ability and willingness to challenge programmed knowledge using the stimulus of a real-life problem.[6] A manager might have programmed knowledge that the way to increase productivity is to threaten people with job loss. Working on a live problem about a low-productivity office, the manager might begin to question whether his or her view is oversimplified.

Participants in action learning are asked to work in teams to attack a significant organizational problem, such as decreasing the cycle time on a project. In the process of resolving an actual work problem, the participants acquire and use new skills, tools, or concepts. As the project progresses, new skills are applied later in the process of working with the problem. For example, if the team learned how to eliminate duplication of effort in one aspect of the work process, they would look to eliminate duplication at other points in the cycle. Motorola is one company that uses action learning systematically. Teams of 20 to 25 senior managers from various parts of the company work on significant problems as defined by executives to whom the managers report. Quite often a starting point in problem solving is to enhance product quality.

Systems Thinking

In the learning organization, members regard the organization as a system in which everybody's work affects the activities of everybody else. Systems thinking also means keeping the big picture foremost in everybody's mind and being keenly aware of the external environment. This is true because the organization is part of a system that includes the outside world. A systems thinker at Brooks Brothers said a few years ago, "The trend even among affluent businesspeople is away from our ultraconservative image. Our customer base is declining. If we don't want Brooks Brothers to be perceived as a museum of fashions past, we had better modify our product line." Brooks Brothers was able to modify its product image just enough to satisfy the modern conservative dresser without alienating its remaining die-hard ultraconservatives. Each store has elegant products to satisfy the conservative and ultraconservative dresser.

Shared Vision

Organization members must develop a common purpose and commitment for the organization to keep learning. If the vision inspires enough people, they will keep learning to make the vision come true. A designer at Waterman, for example, might ask, "What can I learn this month that will help us realize our dream of remaining the premier supplier of a full range of high-quality, high-fashion writing instruments?" Developing a shared vision is contingent upon effective leadership. If workers at all levels believe that the company is headed toward greatness, they will be motivated to learn to help deliver greatness.

The Challenging of Mental Models

Organization members must unearth the powerful assumptions that prevent people from working together. For example, higher-level managers might have the assumption that entry-level workers are not capable or interested in strategic thinking. The managers therefore never engage entry-level workers in dialogue about the purpose of the firm and its long-range vitality. As a result, managers miss out on valuable input. To help you challenge mental models, practice asking

"Why?" and "Why not?" Challenging mental models and questioning assumptions can open up a world of opportunities.

Team Learning

A learning organization emphasizes collective problem solving. Members freely share information and opinions with one another to facilitate problem solving. The team learning can take place in several ways. The basic approach is to use group problem solving throughout the firm. However, a large firm might bring people together at a retreat where they work in teams to reflect on ways of improving the organization. At one manufacturing company, a team-based revelation was that too many employee suggestions were too superficial, resulting in minor modifications of procedures or products. Supervisors were encouraged to encourage workers to make suggestions that made dramatic improvements in how a product was manufactured, such as skipping a step or even questioning whether a part was needed at all.

Personal Mastery of the Job

Continuous learning usually is required to master a job in the modern organization. For continuous learning to take place, each member must develop expertise. Quite often this detail is overlooked because of the emphasis on learning in groups. Collective learning is much more productive when every member of the group brings something valuable to the table. As mentioned previously, in a learning organization it is still people who do the learning. To say an organization adapts to its environment really means that a handful of perceptive workers spot environmental trends and figure out how the organization can capitalize on them.

Translation of New Knowledge into New Ways of Behaving

Given that learning involves a change in behavior, a true learning organization translates knowledge into action. Learning at a superficial level would occur if managers attended a seminar on expectancy theory and simply retained key principles. Members of a learning organization would *apply* expectancy theory. Similarly, if you are a learning person, you would incorporate organizational behavior knowledge into your repertoire of skills.

The challenge of translating new knowledge into new ways of behavior became evident during the beginnings of the e-commerce revolution. Companies who learned about e-commerce, then simply used the Internet as an electronic sales catalogue, did not profit much from e-commerce. The true winners were firms that made more far-sweeping changes related to e-commerce, such as transforming the ways they dealt with suppliers, dealers, and distributors.

Systematic Investigation and Problem Solving

A key building block of a learning organization is the widespread use of systematic investigation and problem solving based on the scientific method. A systematic approach can prevent overlooking important facts and not gathering enough information to make an informed decision. As important as problem-solving tools may be, even more important is the disciplined mindset necessary for creating a learning organization. Employees must think with greater discipline and pay more attention to details.

As David A. Garvin notes, workers must continuously ask, "How do we know that's true?" They must "push beyond obvious symptoms to assess underlying causes, often collecting evidence when conventional wisdom says it is unnecessary."[7] A corporate travel coordinator might say to her boss, "Why is it true that at the vice-president level and above, managers must fly first-class and stay at premier hotels? Have we recently collected data on their travel preferences? Suppose we showed how the company could save $150,000 per year by less luxurious flight and hotel accommodations? Isn't it worth investigating?"

Experimentation

One approach to seeking out new opportunities and learning is through experimentation. Most successful companies continuously experiment with new ways of improving their manufacturing or services. The efforts of the United States Postal Service to retain market share by offering new services, and even forming an alliance with FedEx, is a good example of organizational learning. Experimentation can be done on a large scale by conducting demonstration projects or pilot programs. For example, McDonald's Corporation will often try out a new restaurant theme, such as 1950s-style diners in a test market. If the project is profitable, the concept will be expanded. Experimentation requires a risk-taking attitude, characteristic of the entrepreneurial mindset.

Learning from Other Organizations

Some of the best insights an organization can acquire stem from studying competitors and other firms. Borrowing ideas from the competition, also known as *benchmarking,* took place long before the concept of a learning organization arose. A learning organization systematizes the process, while at the same time attempting to be ethical. "Learning from others" is most ethical when the learning does not directly capitalize on an idea a competitor spent considerable time and money developing.

Substantial learning can take place in copying the practices of firms not directly in your line of business. Suppose you would like to establish a worldwide method of distributing hard-to-get automobile parts, like a carburetor for a 1956 Edsel. You carefully study the marketing techniques of Amazon.com and BarnesandNoble.com, distributors of books, music, and other products. You set up an elaborate system, copy the order and shipping process of these firms, and call yourself Oldautoparts.com. Since you don't distribute books, music, and videos and your benchmarking targets don't distribute hard-to-find auto parts, nobody gets hurt. You are a learning organization without directly copying another company's ideas.

Healthy Disrespect for the Status Quo

A general characteristic of a learning organization is to challenge whatever exists and see if anything can be improved in any way. The status quo to be challenged can refer to work processes, products, services, policies, organization structure, organizational culture, or physical location of offices and plants. Managers and other employees should challenge whatever can be changed to prevent the problem of being a less effective organization. When an organization is successful, the desire to change can be weak because success is self-rewarding. Yet highly effective leaders should see the need to change to prevent problems in the long run. A telling example is Amazon.com. Although it sold more books and records at a pace beyond the most optimistic forecasts in its early days, founder Jeff Bezos and his team were not content. The company continually attempted new ways of increasing revenues, including partnerships with hundreds of companies, creating their own mammoth distribution centers, and selling a wide spectrum of merchandise. Challenging the status quo has become standard operating procedure at Amazon.com.

High-Impact Learning

Another perspective on a learning organization is that the significance of the learning must be taken into account. The more significant the learning, the more likely it will move the firm forward and prevent substantial problems. According to one team of researchers, learning capability is demonstrated only if the ideas have impact or add value for the firm's stakeholders for a long time. Three steps facilitate high-impact learning.[8]

The *first step* to facilitate high-impact learning is to build a commitment to learning capability. The challenge in this step is getting managers intellectually and emotionally committed to learning. One way of getting managers and other workers excited about learning is to incorporate ideas about learning into business strategy and mission statements.

The *second step* is to generate ideas with impact. Companies that are successful at high-impact learning have deliberate approaches for acquiring knowledge. Many companies choose continuous improvement as a method for generating new ideas. Two other useful methods for generating ideas are suggestions systems and process-improvement task forces.

The *third step* is to work to disseminate ideas with impact. One way to share ideas is the widespread use of cross-functional teams. Individuals from different functions share some of the best ideas while carrying out group tasks. More ideas about information sharing are presented later in this chapter.

KNOWLEDGE MANAGEMENT

A major consequence of a learning organization is that knowledge is managed more effectively. **Knowledge management (KM)** is a systematic approach to documenting, applying, and transferring the know-how and experience of employees.[9] A major objective of knowledge management is to make effective use of the vast store of useful information experience possessed by employees (see the InfoTrac sidebar). Managing knowledge well achieves such goals as innovation, non-duplication of effort, and competitive advantage. When knowledge is managed effectively, information is shared as needed whether it is printed or stored electronically or in the brains of workers.

The justification for knowledge management is that intellectual capital is a resource that allows for survival and competitive advantage. **Intellectual capital** is knowledge that transforms raw materials and makes them more valuable. It is also a capital asset consisting of intellectual material.[10] The intellectual capital of many firms, consisting of the know-how and intelligence of the workers, is far more valuable than their physical assets, consisting mostly of a handful of machines and furniture. Firms high in intellectual capital and low in physical capital include software development companies, consulting firms, and advertising agencies. Knowledge management also helps deal with the problem of knowledge loss when competent employees leave the firm. If the employee's useful knowledge, including creative ideas, are documented by the firm, a knowledgeable employee's departure is a less serious problem. KM would therefore also be helpful in counteracting the knowledge loss associated with large-scale downsizing.

Although a learning organization leads to knowledge management, it is also true that managing knowledge well helps an organization learn. Our study of knowledge management encompasses the conditions favoring knowledge management, strategies and techniques of knowledge management, and methods for sharing knowledge.

Knowledge work and *knowledge workers* are terms coined by Peter Drucker more than 40 years ago, but it has been only fairly recently that businesses have started to recognize knowledge as a key organizational assest that should be managed right along with cash flows and supply chains. Log on to InfoTrac College Edition at **http:// www.infotrac-college.com** to find examples of ways companies have attempted to use knowledge management to capture the unstructured knowledge that resides in people's heads. One useful search tip might be to combine "KM" and "war stories."

Organizational Conditions Favoring Knowledge Management

3

Certain organizational conditions favor the effective management of knowledge. As already mentioned, being a learning organization facilitates knowledge management because the learning organization creates the conditions for making good use of information. Such an organization is prepared to make good use of knowledge. A closely related condition is an *organizational culture that emphasizes sharing information*. A knowledge management system is unlikely to work without an organization undergoing a significant cultural change. Incentives must exist for knowledge sharing. Those who contribute to the knowledge base and generate the most useful or frequently used information might receive a cash bonus, stock, a plaque, or a company-paid luxury vacation. More important than the incentives themselves is for workers to develop a social obligation to share.[11]

Another organizational condition for making knowledge management a reality is to *provide leadership for the effort*. Senior management should understand the value of knowledge management and support the development of programs and policies to make it a reality. The right kind of leadership usually means more than financial support for a KM initiative. Senior executives must understand the potential contribution of knowledge management and play an active role in making decisions about knowledge management activities. For example, a senior executive might make a decision about new initiatives to retain creative people within the firm.

Another key organizational condition is to *demonstrate the value of knowledge management to encourage commitment*. Workers must understand why the organization has formalized knowledge management and how it will benefit the organization. Thomas Koulopoulos, president of a consulting firm specializing in knowledge management, notes, "Most of us were raised in a culture that doesn't believe in sharing. We've built our careers around proprietary ideas, information, and knowledge."[12] Explaining the benefits of KM can only go so far in creating favorable attitudes. Workers should be shown how the sharing knowledge makes their job easier or better. A high-impact approach is to explain how knowledge management leads to new products, increased sales, cost savings, and more money available for salaries.

Recognize organization conditions favoring knowledge management (KM).

Knowledge Management Strategies and Techniques

4

Given that knowledge management has become one of the fastest growing trends in management of the decade, various strategies and techniques have been developed to foster the process. We make no rigid distinction between strategies and techniques for KM versus conditions favoring knowledge management. The building blocks of a learning organization are also closely tied in with the knowledge-management strategies and techniques to be described next.

Pinpoint strategies and techniques for knowledge management.

Hire the Right Persons

If you want to achieve an important organizational goal, hire the right people. Hiring people who are good at learning and teaching makes a substantial difference in the effectiveness of knowledge management. Tom O. Davenport explains: "Not enough companies have built into their competency models how well people learn and pass on their knowledge informally on the job. If you've got people who are hungry to learn and people who are good at transferring knowledge, the organization will be much more alive."[13]

People with the right stuff for KM are most likely to be those who have demonstrated intelligence, accumulated knowledge, and displayed intellectual curiosity in the past. Interview probing and reference checks would be helpful. Two relevant interview questions would be, "Describe to me how you have shared knowledge with others so far in your career or at school," and "What new development in your field have you learned in the past month or so?" Psychological testing about cognitive ability and openness (intellectual curiosity) would also be appropriate.

Create Knowledge

Creating knowledge is an important first step for managing knowledge. The strategy is easily stated but not so easy to implement. First you need intelligence to create the knowledge, and you also need the conditions favoring creativity and innovation described in Chapter 5. Knowledge is the raw material that allows people to innovate new products, services, processes, and management methods. The 4I model of organizational learning provides a partial explanation of how knowledge is created. To understand the need for creating new knowledge, it is useful to perceive every product, service, and work process as a bundle of knowledge. For example, the Chrysler PT Cruiser is the intelligence bundled in the ability to transform a 67-year-old design to fit modern tastes for the retro look, do the appropriate engineering and manufacturing, and market and distribute the product to customers. The idea of creating knowledge is not new; it has been the foundation of successful organizations for a long time. KM, however, underscores the value of large numbers of people creating knowledge.[14]

Competitive Knowledge Management

An aggressive approach to knowledge management is to develop mechanisms for enabling workers to track knowledge and expertise outside the company. This approach has traditionally been referred to as *competitive intelligence*. With the Internet and company-developed databases now available to the public, company employees might be able to find out useful information about the competition that is public knowledge. If this approach is carried too far, it could move into the area of stealing trade secrets. Michael Dell of Dell Computer makes an Internet search of industry trends part of his work routine. He believes that considerable useful information about industry trends is available on various Web sites. A person needs high-level Internet search skills—knowing where to look—to derive useful information.

Codification versus Personalizing Knowledge

To better understand different approaches to knowledge management, a team of researchers studied KM practices at management consulting firms, health-care providers, and computer manufacturers.[15] The researchers classified the various knowledge management activities into two different strategies. A major finding was that companies dealing with standardized products and services have a different approach to knowledge management than companies that provide highly customized solutions to problems.

For companies that manufacture and sell relatively standardized products that fit the needs of many customers, knowledge is carefully codified and stored in databases. In this way, the information can be readily accessed and used repeatedly by anyone in the firm. The authors of the study call this the *codification strategy*. In companies that provide highly customized solutions to unique customer or client problems, knowledge is shared primarily through interpersonal contacts. (The same strategy could be described as informal learning.) The chief purpose of computers, including e-mail, is to help people communicate. The approach just described is labeled the *personalization strategy*. The researchers noted that a company's choice of knowledge management strategy is not arbitrary; it should be driven by the company's competitive strategy of standardization versus customization. Emphasizing the wrong approach or attempting to do both simultaneously can interfere with productivity and profitability. To help identify whether codification or personalization is the best approach to KM, top management should find accurate answers to the following questions:

- Do you offer standardized or customized products? (If your products are standardized, it is best to codify knowledge. For customized products, use the personalization model because codified knowledge will generally be of little value.)
- Do you have a mature or an innovative product? (Use codified knowledge for mature products and personalized knowledge for innovative products.)
- Do your people rely on explicit or tacit knowledge to solve problems? (Explicit knowledge fits better for a codified strategy of knowledge management. For tacit knowledge, a person-to-person approach works best.)

These guidelines are probably less precise than the authors of the study think. One problem is that products are sometimes a combination of standardization and customization, such as shoes made to fit unusual sizes. Also, knowledge is not always readily classifiable as explicit (well structured) versus tacit (intuitive).

Appointing a Chief Information (or Knowledge) Officer

To help foster knowledge management, about 100 large firms have created a position labeled chief information officer or chief knowledge officer. Contrary to popular expectation, this person is not in charge of training and development. A chief information officer is in charge of systematically collecting information and connecting people who need information with others who might have the information they need. Specific parts of the job description or role include:

- Arranging conferences where workers share information
- Assimilating databases and information systems of company knowledge
- Teaching people how to learn at a deeper level
- Getting people to reflect on their experiences and profit from their mistakes
- Selling people on the idea that brainpower (intellectual capital) is the company's true source of competitive advantage

Because knowledge is the primary output of professional service firms, they were the first to create the position of chief knowledge officer. John Peetz, CKO of Ernst & Young, describes his role: "For us, knowledge management is critical. It's one of our four core processes—sell work, do work, manage people, and manage knowledge."[16]

Deliver Knowledge Just in Time

A technologically advanced method of managing knowledge is to provide workers with information that enhances the effectiveness of their work, just at the point at which they could use the information. Visualize a loan officer at a bank typing in your name and social security number as you apply for a yacht loan. Five seconds after typing in your name, your credit history and driving record appear on screen, giving her the knowledge she needs to process your loan. This type of just-in-time knowledge management system is already gaining hold in medicine. For example software exists that enables a physician to know which drugs a patient is taking, or is allergic to, as the physician types a prescription into a laptop computer.

The central idea of just-in-time delivery of information is to embed specialized knowledge into the jobs of specialized workers. PartnersHealthCare has a system for embedding knowledge into the technology that physicians use in their jobs so that searching for information is no longer a separate activity. When a doctor orders medicine or a lab test, the order-entry system automatically checks the decision against an enormous clinical database, along with the patient's own record. Medical informatics is the name given to this endeavor. Some companies such as Dell have systems for customer-service representatives that rapidly supply knowledge to help them resolve customer problems.[17] For example, Dell might have information of the three most likely things a person who has difficulty getting started with the Dell photo management system is doing wrong.

Closing the Gap between Knowing and Doing

Jeffrey Pfeffer and Robert I. Sutton have investigated why companies don't accomplish more if they have so much knowledge and expertise. (This is a Stanford University Business School twist on the age-old question, "If you're so smart, why aren't you rich?") Pfeffer and Sutton believe that companies have fallen into the knowing–doing gap because doing something requires the hard work of making something happen. Managing knowledge is not enough; it must be converted into action. It is easier and safer to have intellectual discussions, to gather large databases, and to invest in technical infrastructure, than it is to actually execute. The challenge for companies and the people in them is to build a culture of action.[18] Often this means taking decisive action that results in repeat business, such as an airline having a high percent of on-time flights, or a retailer offering commissions to sales representatives in the stores.

An important general point about knowledge management strategies and techniques is that employee behavior is more important than specific techniques in achieving a true knowledge enterprise. A study of ten technology firms identified four behaviors that made the biggest contribution toward effective knowledge management:

- Focusing on system performance rather than on narrow technical outcomes (such as wondering how the technical task you are performing will really increase profits)
- Following systematic work and decision processes (such as following an established process for getting bids from suppliers rather than developing a new process)
- Sharing knowledge (such as letting others know about your really cool ideas)
- Trying new approaches (such as trying a new idea for decreasing the use of energy or water, and testing if it really results in a savings)[19]

5

Specify methods for sharing information within an organization.

METHODS FOR SHARING INFORMATION

A major goal of the learning organization and knowledge management is for organizational members to share relevant information. Many of the strategies and techniques already described in this chapter contribute directly or indirectly to information sharing. Here we describe briefly five focused methods for sharing information.

1. *In-House Yellow Pages.* The basic idea of company Yellow Pages is to compile a directory of the skills, talents, and special knowledge of employees throughout the firm. To be useful, the Yellow Pages have to go far beyond basic information and job experience. The directory should indicate the specialized knowledge of the people listed and their level of expertise. When faced with a problem requiring specialized talent, employees can consult the Yellow Pages for a person to help.

2. *Intranet communication systems.* A growing number of firms use intranets and online forums to spread and share knowledge. Buckman Laboratories has a knowledge sharing system known as K'Netix, used by 1,200 employees in 80 countries including CEO Bob Buckman. Employees working from home or a customer's office can receive information instantaneously on everything from HR practices to perfecting a new chemical process.[20] The accompanying Organizational Behavior in Action box describes the effective use of an intranet system by a company whose services many readers use regularly.

Organizational Behavior *in Action*

Searching for Good Ideas at Google

Most Fridays at Google, the search-engine company, Marissa Mayer and about 50 engineers and other employees sit down to do a search of their own. Mayer, an intense, fast-talking product manager, scribbles rapidly as the engineers race to explain and defend the new ideas that they've posted to an internal Web site. By the end of the hour-long meeting, six, seven, or sometimes even eight new ideas are fleshed out enough to take to the next level of development.

Some of those ideas might become new features on Google, new code or search algorithms, or a new way to juice up the Google home page. "We really jam in there," Mayer says.

To stay on top of competitor search engines, Google needed a stream of new ideas. "We always had great ideas, but we didn't have a good way of expressing them or capturing them," says Craig Silverstein, Google's director of technology. Mayer's proposal: Search for ideas in the same way that the Google search engine combs the Web.

Google's idea search starts with an internal Web page that take minutes to set up. Using a program called Sparrow, even Google employees without Internet savvy (there are a few) can create a page of ideas. That enables the company to cast its net across its 300-plus employees. "We never say, 'This group should innovate, and the rest should do their jobs,'" says Jonathan Rosenberg, vice president of product management. "Everyone spends a fraction of their day on R&D."

Mayer combs the site daily, searching for relevant ideas. She digs out the ones that generate the most comments and that seem the most doable. Relevance isn't necessarily measured by how much money an idea makes; it's more about making Google searches *better*.

In the Friday meetings, Mayer insists on speed. The sessions are kept to one hour, and individual presenters never get more than 10 minutes. But everyone knows that the conversation won't end when the meeting does. Promising ideas are quickly outlined on the intranet site. Usually, the person who came up with the idea is put in charge of turning it into a feature.

Two current ideas include a news-search feature that debuted in 2002 and a pilot project that keeps track of persistent searches on the Web. "You can take Google's temperature just by going to the intranet site," Rosenberg says. "It's a window to everyone's soul."

Questions

1. In what way does Google intranet site qualify as a technique of knowledge management?
2. What possible advantage might the Google intranet have over brainstorming, as a method of collecting useful ideas from company employees?

Source: Fara Warner, "How Google Searches Itself," *Fast Company*, July 2002, pp. 50–52.

3. *Personal explanations of success factors.* An advanced method of information sharing is for key organizational members to teach others what they know through explanations of success factors. Noel Tichy refers to these stories as the *teachable point of view* because they help leaders become teachers. The teachable point of view is a written explanation of what a person knows and believes about what it takes to succeed in his or her own business, as well as in business in general. About two pages in length, the document focuses on critical success factors such as "What would it take to knock out the competition?" Tichy claims that this hard–hitting method of information sharing is used in hundreds of companies.[21]

4. *Foster dialogue among organization members.* To promote the importance of information sharing, company leaders should converse about the importance of intellectual capital and the development of core competencies.[22] At the same time, workers throughout the firm should be encouraged to share useful suggestions, tidbits of knowledge, and success stories about problem solving. This type of information sharing can take place face-to-face, yet e-mail exchanges also play a vital role.

5. *Shared physical facilities and informal learning.* An important method of fostering dialogue is to develop shared physical facilities as described in Chapter 10 regarding teamwork development. Considerable information sharing is likely to take place in a snack lounge or company information resource center. At the same time, informal learning takes place, which is almost synonymous with information sharing.

IMPLICATIONS FOR MANAGERIAL PRACTICE

1. The most important and the most practical aspect of the learning organization and knowledge management is for workers to share useful information with one another. In your role as a manager, you should therefore make a systematic effort to ensure that information is shared in the total organization or your organizational unit. Establish both formal steps (for example, an intranet) and informal methods (such as simply encouraging people to exchange good ideas) to accomplish information sharing.

2. Several theorists have mentioned that a company's true competitive advantage derives from intellectual capital. If this observation is valid, then one of the highest organizational priorities is to recruit and retain knowledgeable and intelligent workers. Even during a downsizing, maximum effort should be invested in retaining the best thinkers and most knowledgeable people in the company.

SUMMARY OF KEY POINTS

1 **Describe the 4I framework of a learning organization.**
According to the 4I framework, organizational learning that results in organizational renewal encompasses the entire enterprise. Organizational learning is composed of four processes: intuiting, interpreting, integrating, and institutionalization. The four processes work together to link the individual, group, and organizational levels. Intuiting and interpreting take place at the individual level; integrating takes place at the group level; and institutionalizing takes place at the organizational level.

2 **Identify the building blocks, or key characteristics, of a learning organization.**
Components of the learning organization include: (a) double-loop learning, (b) action learning (learning while doing), (c) systems thinking, (d) shared vision, (e) the challenging of mental models, (f) team learning, (g) personal mastery of the job, (h) translation of new knowledge into new ways of behaving, (i) systematic investigation and problem solving, (j) experimentation, (k) learning from other organizations, (l) healthy disrespect for the status quo, and (m) high-impact learning.

3 **Recognize organizational conditions favoring knowledge management (KM).**
The importance of intellectual capital justifies knowledge management. Among the conditions favoring KM involve being a learning organization: having an organizational culture that emphasizes information sharing, leadership for knowledge management, and demonstrating the value of knowledge management.

4 **Pinpoint strategies and techniques for knowledge management.**
Strategies and techniques for knowledge management include: (a) hiring the right people, (b) creating knowledge, (c) competitive knowledge management, (d) codifying versus personalizing knowledge, (e) appointing a chief information (or knowledge) officer, (f) delivering knowledge just in time, and (g) closing the gap between knowing and doing. Employee behavior is more important than specific techniques in achieving a true knowledge enterprise.

5 **Specify methods for sharing information within an organization.**
Information sharing is at the heart of a learning organization and knowledge management. Five specific methods are: (a) in-house Yellow Pages, (b) intranet communication systems, (c) personal explanations of success factors, (d) the fostering of dialogue among organizational members, and (e) shared physical facilities and organizational learning.

KEY TERMS AND PHRASES

Learning Organization, *321*
An organization that is skilled at creating, acquiring, and transferring knowledge and at modifying behavior to reflect new knowledge and insights.

Double-Loop Learning, *324*
A change in behavior that occurs when people use feedback to confront the validity of the goal or the values implicit in the situation.

Action Learning, *324*
Learning that occurs while working on real problems, involving the acquisition of new skills, tools, and concepts.

Knowledge Management (KM), *328*
The systematic sharing of information to achieve advances in innovation, efficiency, and competitive advantage.

Intellectual Capital, *328*
Knowledge that transforms raw materials and makes them more valuable; it is also a capital asset consisting of intellectual material.

DISCUSSION QUESTIONS AND ACTIVITIES

1. How might you be able to use a few concepts from the learning organization and knowledge management to manage your career more effectively?
2. How might the behavior modification system for improving knowledge sharing described in the chapter opening case have an unintended negative consequence?
3. What is the difference between a learning organization and an organization that simply offers its employees considerable training and development?
4. Why do mental models sometimes interfere with the goals of diversity?
5. What is your evaluation of McDonald's as a learning organization? Support your conclusion with a few observations.
6. Give an example of how your instructor for this course would be able to be a systems thinker in his or her role as a teacher.
7. **COLLABORATE** Ask an experienced manager what type of information should be included in the in-house Yellow Pages. Be prepared to share your findings with classmates.

ORGANIZATIONAL BEHAVIOR ONLINE

TO DO

Building a Learning Organization

See and hear some interesting tidbits of information about building a learning organization by visiting http://www.leadertalk.com/Pages/LearnOrg.html. The Web site explores many of the key issues covered in this chapter, as described by featured experts. An interesting feature is that each of these experts mentions some key points on a video clip of about one minute. You will probably not have to download software just to watch and see the video clips. Write a bulleted list of the major points you learned about (a) what companies are trying to learn, and (b) how they manage intellectual capital.

TO BOOKMARK

Intranets

http://compnetworking.about.com/library/weekly/aa052799.htm

The Learning Organization—An International Journal

http://www.mcb.co.uk/tlo.htm

Resources for Learning Organizations

http://www.brint.com/km/

Knowledge Management

http://www.amsinc.com/KnowledgeMgmt

Knowledge Organization

http://knowledgepassion.com

Knowledge Sharing

http://www.work.com/sharing.html

CASE PROBLEM: The Reluctant Information Shares

The Flagstaff Marketing Group specializes in offering marketing assistance to business firms. Most of their accounts are small- and medium-size firms without large marketing staffs of their own. The Flagstaff Group often helps a client market a product by assisting in such matters as finding prospective customers and developing marketing slogans. One client, a manufacturer of foot-powered scooters, sought advice on opening a new market. Flagstaff helped them market their product to city dwellers as a vehicle for going to work. The marketing theme was "Scoot Your Way to Success." Sales quadrupled for the scooter manufacturer.

For large client firms, Flagstaff offers specialized expertise that the client firm may lack. For example, Flagstaff develops company logos and names that help give a firm a distinctive identity, such as finding a new name for a company after a merger or spin-off. Although not developed by Flagstaff, an example is the name "Lucent Technologies" for the former equipment-manufacturing division of AT&T.

Peter Flagstaff, the founder of the firm, has been concerned lately that his firm develops ideas inefficiently. He said to Lindsay Gibson, the executive vice president at Flagstaff, "I keep hearing the same discussions over and over about solving a particular client problem. The account executives keep sifting through the alternatives that others have done before. People don't capitalize on all the good problem solving that has taken place in the past. We go through the same agonizing process of dealing with similar problems."

Gibson replied, "Are you suggesting, Peter, that we should offer canned solutions to clients so we could save lots of time?"

"Not at all," responded Peter. "We could at least save some time and offer similar types of assistance to clients that we offered to other clients in the past. I'll give you a good example. Reggie Whitson recently had a pet-clothing manufacturer for a client. The client wanted to expand the market for items like dog raincoats, dog shoes for cold weather, and

a luxury line of dog sweaters for special occasions. So Reggie spent a week researching dog clothing before coming up with some recommendations for his client.

"If Reggie could have picked up some ideas in-house, he could have found some good ideas a lot more quickly. Also, if he had spent less time, the client would not have been so taken back by the large fee."

Looking perplexed, Lindsay said, "But how would Reggie have known about who had tackled a similar client problem in the past?"

Peter jumped in, "Lindsay, you have pinpointed the problem. We have done a poor job of systematically pooling all that great information in our heads. Not only do we reinvent the wheel, we reinvent the idea that a wheel would be useful.

"I'm proposing that we find a way of sharing knowledge that will pay big dividends for the firm. The major consulting firms have developed pretty effective systems of knowledge management and knowledge sharing in recent years.

"I'm not implying that we hire somebody to be our chief information officer or that we invest $500,000 in sophisticated software. I just want us to do a better job of sharing ideas with one another." "I've got an idea," said Lindsay, "let's schedule a combination dinner and focus group for the professional staff. The subject will be why we aren't doing a better job of information sharing." Among the comments that emerged from the dinner/focus group were the following:

GARY: I would like to share more of my experiences with the other account executives. I'm concerned, though, about the good of the firm. Suppose I give some of my best ideas to another account exec, and then he or she leaves the firm. My good ideas are fed right to the competition.

BRENDA: Unlike Gary, I have no hesitancy in sharing ideas. The problem is the time involved. We were encouraged at one time to do a write-up of how we solved unusual client problems. The task proved to be busywork. We had to follow a complicated format. Maybe we should use a briefer method of recording good ideas.

SHARON: I'm not opposed to sharing ideas, but it makes me a little self-conscious. To ask someone else for ideas suggests that I'm not so creative myself. Take that dog-clothing account. If I asked others for ideas, it would have been like I can't think of any good ideas for promoting dog clothing myself. (Laughter from the group.)

JASON: So long as we are all being brutally honest here, let me get to the heart of the problem. We're creative types. Our careers are dependent on having good ideas. After you share an idea with another exec, the idea becomes public knowledge. It loses its originality. So if you use that idea again, you are no longer creative because other account execs are using it.

ANNE: Jason has a point. Teamwork is nice, but you still have to look out for numero uno. Sure I have warm, fuzzy feel-

ings toward top management and the other account executives. Yet I'm still evaluated by Flagstaff in terms of my originality.

Peter Flagstaff said to the group, "Lindsay and I both thank you for being so candid. I see a few glimmers of hope in terms of knowledge sharing in our firm. But this is just the start of a continuing dialogue. We have a long way to go to manage knowledge well at Flagstaff marketing."

Lindsay nodded in agreement.

Case Questions

1. What suggestions can you offer Peter Flagstaff and Lindsay Gibson to improve knowledge sharing at the Flagstaff Marketing Group?
2. How valid are the points made by the account executives for not doing a better job of sharing information?
3. What cultural changes might be needed at Flagstaff to improve knowledge sharing?

ENDNOTES

1. David A. Garvin, "Building a Learning Organization," *Harvard Business Review,* July–August 1993, p. 80.
2. Quoted in Robert M. Fulmer and J. Bernard Keys, "A Conversation with Peter Senge: New Developments in Organizational Learning," *Organizational Dynamics,* Autumn 1998, p. 35.
3. Mary Crossan, "Altering Theories of Learning and Action: An Interview with Chris Argyris," *Academy of Management Executive,* May 2003, p. 40.
4. Mary M. Crossan, Henry W. Lane, and Roderick E. White, "An Organizational Learning Framework: From Intuition to Institution," *Academy of Management Review,* July 1999, pp. 522–537.
5. Robert M. Fulmer and Philip Gibbs, "The Second Generation Learning Organizations: New Tools for Sustaining Competitive Advantage," *Organizational Dynamics,* Autumn 1998, pp. 7–20; Senge, *The Fifth Discipline;* Daniel R. Tobin, *The Knowledge-Enabled Organization* (New York: AMACOM, 1998). William E. Brenneman, Robert M. Fulmer, and J. Bernard Keys, "Learning across a Living Company: The Shell Companies' Experiences," *Organizational Dynamics,* Autumn 1998, pp. 61–70; Chris Argyris, "Double-Loop Learning, Teaching and Research," *Academy of Management Learning & Education,* December 2002, pp. 206–218.
6. George Boulden, "Action Learning," in *Business: The Ultimate Resource* (Cambridge, MA: Perseus Books Group, 2002), p. 12.
7. David A. Garvin, "Building a Learning Organization," *Harvard Business Review,* July–August 1993, pp. 81–82.
8. Dave Ulrich, Todd Jick, and Mary Ann Von Glinow, "High-Impact Learning: Building and Diffusing Capability," *Organizational Dynamics,* Autumn 1993, p. 60.
9. Book review in *Academy of Management Executive,* February 2002, p. 161.
10. Thomas A. Stewart, "Intellectual Capital," in *Business: The Ultimate Resource,* p. 159.
11. Samuel Greengard, "How to Make KM a Reality," *Workforce,* October 1998, p. 91.
12. Greengard, "How to Make KM a Reality," p. 91.
13. Quoted in Louisa Wah, "Making Knowledge Stick," *Management Review,* May 1999, p. 27.
14. William Miller, "Building the Ultimate Resource," *Management Review,* January 1999, p. 43.
15. Morten T. Hansen, Nitin Nohria, and Thomas Tierney, "What's Your Strategy for Managing Knowledge?" *Harvard Business Review,* March–April 1999, pp. 106–116.
16. Thomas A. Stewart, "Is This Job Really Necessary?" *Fortune,* January 12, 1998, p. 154.
17. Thomas H. Davenport and John Glaser, "Just-In-Time Deliver Comes to Knowledge Management," *Harvard Business Review,* July 2002, pp. 107–111.
18. Cited in Alan Webber, "Why Can't We Get Anything Done?" *Fast Company,* June 2000, pp. 168–180.
19. Susan A. Mohrman, David Finegold, and Janice A. Klein, "Designing the Knowledge Enterprise: Beyond Programs and Tools," *Organizational Dynamics,* Autumn 2002, pp. 134–149.
20. Greengard, "Storing, Shaping, and Sharing Collective Wisdom," *Workforce,* October 1998, p. 84.
21. Noel Tichy, "The Teachable Point of View," *Harvard Business Review,* March–April 1999, p. 82.
22. Miller, "Building the Ultimate Resource," p. 45.

Chapter 16

Cultural Diversity and International Organizational Behavior

OBJECTIVES

After reading and studying this chapter and doing the exercises, you should be able to:

1 Understand the scope, competitive advantages, and success factors associated with cultural diversity.

2 Identify and explain key dimensions of cultural differences.

3 Describe what is required for managers and organizations to become multicultural.

4 Be more aware of barriers to good cross-cultural relations.

5 Explain how motivation, ethics, appropriate negotiation skills, conflict resolution, and empowerment practices can vary across cultures.

6 Appreciate the nature of diversity training and cultural training.

The emergence of Hispanics as a force in online shopping has triggered a scramble among retailers to launch Spanish-language Web sites. Nissan North America, Office Depot, and Honda Motors are among dozens of companies that have constructed Spanish-language sites in recent months. More, including JetBlue Airways, are in the process.

"It's a formidable market, and companies finally are starting to take advantage of it," says Richard Israel of researcher comScore Networks. A surge in Spanish-language Web sites should lead to better service for Hispanics. It could also mean more revenue for e-tailers. In April 2003, 12.7 million Hispanics were online, up 7 percent from six months earlier. Overall U.S. Internet growth, by comparison, was 2 percent, according to comScore. Hispanics spend more time online than non-Hispanics and are among the biggest online spenders on travel, consumer electronics and baby supplies. As a result, several industries are wooing Hispanics including the following:

- *Office supplies.* Because Hispanics are one of the fastest-growing segments in small business, "It got our attention," says Monica Luechtefeld, executive vice president of global e-commerce at Office Depot. The Spanish-language Web site, launched in January 2003 was influenced by the company's employees, 15 percent of whom are Hispanic, and by its *Fortune* 500 customers, who have requested a site in Spanish from which to order supplies.
- *Automotive.* Bilingual customers are more likely to research and purchase an expensive product in their native language, says Sam Lopez, a marketing executive at Nissan North America. It launched a Spanish-language version of its Web site last month. Hispanics tend to spend a greater percentage of their income on cars and clothes, online studies show. Autobytel, a leading auto Web site, saw its Hispanic audience nearly triple to 1.1 million since unveiling a Spanish site in December.
- *Portals.* American Online recently began it first nationwide advertising in Spanish. Yahoo! has parlayed high-profile promotions and marketing deals to reach more Hispanics.

Despite the new online emphasis on Hispanics, only 3 percent of all Web content is in Spanish. Part of the reason might be because the percentage of Hispanic households with Internet access is 40 percent, versus a 70 percent rate for non-Hispanic homes, according to Nielsen/NetRatings.

"In this economy, the growing influence of Hispanics online can't be overlooked," says Ingrid Otero-Smart, former president of the Association of Hispanic Advertising Agencies. "And more retailers will take advantage."

Source: John Swartz, "Retailers Constructing Web Sites in Spanish," *USA Today* syndicated story, June 8, 2003.

NOW ASK YOURSELF: What do the Spanish-language marketing initiatives just described tell us about the importance of understanding and appreciating cultural diversity among customers as well as listening to the suggestions of culturally diverse employees? We have already mentioned demographic and cultural diversity at several places in this text. Chapter 2 included a description of demographic factors as a source of individual differences, Chapter 9 described cross-cultural communication barriers, Chapter 14 described how cross-cultural differences can hamper a merger, and cross-cultural issues were raised in relation to many other concepts throughout the text. One purpose of this chapter is to provide additional insights managers and professionals can use to capitalize upon diversity within and across countries.

The fact that business has become increasingly international has elevated the importance of understanding cross-cultural and international organizational behavior. Furthermore, members of minority groups[1] will comprise 40 percent of new entrants to the workforce by 2008. At present, 30 million immigrants work in the United States, with most from Spanish-speaking countries in Central America and South America.[2] Small- and medium-size firms, as well as corporate giants, are increasingly dependent on trade with other countries. An estimated 10 to 15 percent of jobs in the United States depend on imports or exports. Furthermore, most manufactured goods contain components from more than one country. For example, the Jeep Liberty manufactured by the Chrysler division of DaimlerChrysler is made in Toledo, Ohio, but the motor is made in Japan.

Our description of cultural diversity and cross-cultural organizational behavior will include a presentation of key concepts, as well as ideas for developing diversity and cross-cultural skills. Before reading on, do the Self-Assessment on skills and attitudes that follows. It will help you think through how multicultural you are now.

CULTURAL DIVERSITY: SCOPE, COMPETITIVE ADVANTAGES, AND SUCCESS FACTORS

1

Understand the scope, competitive advantages, and success factors associated with cultural diversity.

Cultural diversity can be approached from many different perspectives relating both to its interpersonal and business aspects. In this section, we describe the scope of cultural diversity, and how it affects business results, as well as factors associated with successful cultural diversity initiatives. Diversity training is given separate attention later.

The Scope of Cultural Diversity

Improving cross-cultural relations includes understanding the true meaning of appreciating demographic and cultural diversity. To appreciate diversity, a person must go beyond tolerating and treating people from different racial and ethnic groups fairly. Recognize, however, that some people criticize the diversity movement for being over-inclusive instead of assisting people who have been held back or discriminated against because of demographic factors such as race or age. The true meaning of valuing diversity is to respect and enjoy a wide range of cultural and individual differences, thereby including everybody. Some diversity specialists now prefer the term *inclusion* to diversity.

To be diverse is to be different in some measurable way. Although the diversity factor is measurable in a scientific sense, it may not be visible on the surface.

SELF-ASSESSMENT

Cross-Cultural Attitudes and Skills

Listed here are various skills and attitudes that employers and cross-cultural specialists think are important for relating effectively to coworkers in a culturally diverse environment. Check the appropriate column.

	Applies to Me Now	Not There Yet
1. I have spent some time in another country.	❑	❑
2. At least one of my friends is deaf, blind, or uses a wheelchair.	❑	❑
3. Currency from other countries is as real as the currency from my own country.	❑	❑
4. I can read in a language other than my own.	❑	❑
5. I can speak in a language other than my own.	❑	❑
6. I can write in a language other than my own.	❑	❑
7. I can understand people speaking in a language other than my own.	❑	❑
8. I use my second language regularly.	❑	❑
9. My friends include people of races different from my own.	❑	❑
10. My friends include people of different generations.	❑	❑
11. I feel (or would feel) comfortable having a friend with a sexual orientation different from mine.	❑	❑
12. My attitude is that although another culture may be very different from mine, that culture is equally good.	❑	❑
13. I would be willing to (or already do) hang art from different countries in my home.	❑	❑
14. I would accept (or have already accepted) a work assignment of more than several months in another country.	❑	❑
15. I have a passport.	❑	❑

Scoring and Interpretation: If you answered "Applies to Me Now" to 10 or more of these statements, you most likely function well in a multicultural work environment. If you answered "Not There Yet" to 10 or more of these statements, you need to develop more cross-cultural awareness and skills to work effectively in a multicultural work environment. You will notice that being bilingual gives you at least five points on this quiz.

Source: Some of the statements are derived from Ruthann Dirks and Janet Buzzard, "What CEOs Expect of Employees Hired for International Work," *Business Education Forum,* April 1997, pp. 3–7; Gunnar Beeth, "Multicultural Managers Wanted," *Management Review,* May 1997, pp. 17–21.

Upon meeting a team member, it may not be apparent that the person is diverse from the standpoint of being dyslexic, color-blind, gay, lesbian, or vegetarian. However, all of these factors are measurable.

As just implied, some people are more visibly diverse than others because of physical features or disabilities. Yet the diversity umbrella is supposed to include everybody in an organization. The goal of a diverse organization is for persons of all cultural backgrounds to achieve their full potential, not restrained by group identities such as sex, nationality, or race.[3] Exhibit 16–1 presents a broad sampling of the ways in which work associates can differ from one another. Studying this list can help you anticipate the types of differences in cultural as well as individual factors. Individual factors are also important because people can be discriminated against for personal characteristics as well as group factors. Many people, for example, believe they are held back from promotion because of their weight-to-height ratio.

Diversity has evolved into a wide range of group and individual characteristics.

- Race
- Sex or gender
- Religion
- Age (young, middle aged, and old)
- Generation differences including attitudes (for example, Baby Boomers versus Generation X and
- Generation Y)
- Ethnicity (country of origin)
- Education
- Abilities
- Mental disabilities (including attention deficit disorder)
- Physical disabilities (including hearing status, visual status, able bodied, wheelchair user)
- Values and motivation
- Sexual orientation (heterosexual, homosexual, bisexual, transgender or transsexual)
- Marital status (married, single, divorced, cohabitating, widow, widower)

- Family status (children, no children, two-parent family, single parent, grandparent, opposite-sex parents, same-sex parents)
- Personality traits
- Functional background (area of specialization, such as marketing or HR)
- Technology interest (high tech, low tech, technophobe)
- Weight status (average, obese, underweight, anorexic)
- Hair status (full head of hair, bald, wild hair, tame hair, long hair, short hair)
- Style of clothing and appearance (dress up; dress down; professional appearance; casual appearance; tattoos; body piercing, including multiple ear rings, nose rings, lip rings)
- Tobacco status (smoker versus non-smoker, chewer versus non-chewer)
- Your addition(s) to the list _____

_____

_____

Exhibit 16-1

The Diversity Umbrella

The Competitive Advantage of Diversity

Encouraging cultural and demographic diversity within an organization helps an organization achieve social responsibility goals. Also, diversity sometimes brings a competitive advantage to a firm. Before diversity can offer a competitive advantage to a firm, it must be woven into the fabric of the organization. This stands in contrast to simply having a "diversity program" offered periodically by the human resources department. Instead, the human resource efforts toward accomplishing diversity should be managed as part of organizational strategy. Thomas A. Kochan conducted a 5-year study of the impact of diversity on business results. The study examined large firms with positive reputations for their long-standing commitment to building a culturally diverse workforce and managing diversity effectively. Kochan concluded that diversity can enhance business performance only with proper training and an organizational culture to support it.[4]

The potential competitive (or bottom-line) benefits of cultural diversity, as revealed by research and observations, are described next:[5]

1. *Managing diversity well offers a marketing advantage, including increased sales and profits.* Allstate Insurance Company invests considerable effort into being a culturally diverse business firm. More than coincidentally, Allstate is now recognized as the nation's leading insurer of African Americans and Hispanics. Appeals to specific cultural groups, including Web sites written in the language of the target group, as illustrated in the chapter opener, enhance sales substantially. A study of racial diversity and business strategy in banking indicated that cultural diversity adds value, and within the proper context, contributes to a competitive advantage for the firm. The proper context, however, was that the banks had to have a growth strategy. Racial diversity did not increase profits for firms with a downsizing strategy.[6]

2. *Effective management of diversity can reduce costs.* More effective management of diversity may increase job satisfaction of diverse groups, thus decreasing turnover and absenteeism and their associated costs. A diverse organization that welcomes and fosters the growth of a wide variety of employees will retain more of its minority and multicultural employees. Also, effective management of diversity helps avoid costly lawsuits over being charged with discrimination based on age, race, or sex.

3. *Companies with a favorable record in managing diversity are at a distinct advantage in recruiting talented people.* Those companies with a favorable reputation for welcoming diversity attract the strongest job candidates among women and minorities. A shortage of workers gives extra impetus to cultural diversity. In recent years, there has been a tendency for large firms *not* to decrease diversity and inclusion efforts during a recession. During a tight labor market, companies cannot afford to be seen as racist, sexist, ageist, or even antiunion.

4. *Workforce diversity can provide a company with useful ideas for favorable publicity and advertising.* A culturally diverse workforce or its advertising agency can help a firm place itself in a favorable light to targeted cultural groups. During Kwanzaa, the late December holiday celebrated by many African Americans, McDonald's Corp. has run ads aimed at showing its understanding of and respect for African Americans' sense of family and community. For such ads to be effective, however, the company must also have a customer-contact workforce that is culturally diverse. Otherwise, the ads would lack credibility.

5. *Workforce heterogeneity may also offer a company a creativity advantage.* As mentioned in relation to effective groups (Chapter 10), creative solutions to problems are more likely when a diverse group attacks a problem. A pioneering study of organizational innovation found that innovative companies had above-average records on reducing racism, sexism, and classism.[7]

The Diversity Development department of the United States Postal Service conducted a study to determine whether employing a diverse workforce has an impact on the organization's return on investment (ROI). The goal of the Postal Service diversity development program is to build an inclusive workforce to serve its diverse customer base. To assess the impact of a diverse workforce, the Postal Service evaluated multiple indicators of corporate performance against a measure of workforce inclusiveness. The measure sums the aggregate percentage of under-representation among various ethnic and racial groups within each of the 85 postal districts compared to the local civilian workforce. Each ethnic or racial group was counted separately for males and females. An example of under-representation would be if Hispanic males constituted 2 percent of a given district's workforce, in comparison to 8 percent Hispanic males constituting the local civilian workforce. Greater levels of workforce inclusiveness were positively associated with the following performance measures:

- Customer ratings of overall satisfaction
- Customer ratings of courteous and friendly service from clerks
- Customer ratings of the ability of clerks to explain products and services
- Employee ratings regarding not feeling excluded from the work unit
- Employee ratings regarding concern over being a victim of workplace violence
- Employee ratings regarding freedom from sexual harassment[8]

In short, the United States Postal Service has been able to quantify some of the benefits associated with being a culturally inclusive organization.

Factors Associated with Diversity Success

Business firms, as well as public organizations, achieve varied success with cultural diversity initiatives. Jacqueline A. Gilbert and John M. Ivancevich studied two comparable-size companies that achieved different levels of success with cultural diversity. Both firms were established units of *Fortune* 500 conglomerates. Employee surveys, managerial interviews, and company records were used to provide a detailed account of diversity efforts over time.[9] One firm, designated the Multicultural Organization, has made substantial progress toward becoming more diverse. Evidence for the success included regional and local diversity awards and mention in prominent business publications. The firm designated the Plural Organization was less successful with inclusion of diverse employees and wanted to improve its efforts. Five factors highlight the differences between the Multicultural Organization's fundamental cultural change and the Plural Organization's superficial diversity commitment:

1. *CEO Initiation and Support.* The CEO of the Multicultural Organization played a more active and assertive role in bringing about cultural diversity. For example, he established a clear vision of how a more diverse workforce contributes to the bottom line. Also, he helped established values that defined its culture as one embracing diversity. (The cultural change factor has already been mentioned twice in regard to its favorable impact on the positive consequences of cultural diversity.)

2. *Human Resource Initiatives.* The Multicultural Organization had more human resource programs aimed at achieving diversity. Among these many initiatives include a vice president of diversity position, an annual diversity conference that features best practices from plants throughout the corporation, and an active women and minority recruitment program. The Plural Organization had fewer human resource initiatives for promoting diversity.

3. *Organizational Communication.* At the Multicultural Organization, a wide range of employees were involved in shaping human resource policies. A representative example is the Equality Council, a cross section of employees who meet once a month on issues related to a diverse workforce. Among its many suggestions was an anonymous suggestion box named "Dr. Equality." Employees also designed material to promote diversity such as posters, calendars, and coffee mugs. Efforts to involve employees at the Plural Organization were much less systematic.

4. *Corporate Philosophy.* A corporate-wide philosophy governed diversity policies in the Multicultural Organization, whereas in the Plural Organization each plant had the freedom to develop its own philosophy. Lack of accountability made it easier for plants of the Plural Organization to discontinue diversity initiatives found to be too costly and time consuming.

5. *Measures of Company Success.* At the Multicultural Organization, human capital objectives—including diversity—are presented as essential components of achieving profit and customer satisfaction. Also, many considered the efforts of the human resources department as adding value to the corporation. At the Plural Organization, cultural diversity was seen as a public relations tool and not as a vehicle for creating competitive advantage.

All five success factors can be interpreted as suggestions to management for gaining true advantage from cultural diversity. For example, include achieving cultural diversity as a measure of company success along with financial measures.

2

Identify and explain key dimensions of cultural differences.

Log on to InfoTrac College Edition at **http://www .infotrac-college.com** and use the Advanced Search tool to locate recent articles about key differences among national cultures. Do you find evidence that that cultural values are changing in any particular part of the world? For example, consider the influence the fall of communism has had on the national cultures of Eastern European countries. What about the economic reforms in China? How might the Chinese cultural values change as China gradually moves closer to a market economy?

CROSS-CULTURAL VALUES

Useful background information for understanding how to work well with people from different cultures is to examine their values. We approach this task by first looking at how cultures differ with respect to certain values; and second, how cultural values shape management style. As described in Chapter 4, values are a major force underlying behavior on and off the job.

Key Dimensions of Differences in Cultural Values

One way to understand how national cultures differ is to examine their values (see the InfoTrac sidebar). Here we examine eight values and how selected nationalities relate to them, based on the work of several researchers.[10] Geert Hofstede identified the first five value dimensions in research spanning 18 years, involving over 160,000 people from over 60 countries. The next four on the list have been observed by several researchers, and the last value is based on new international developments. Differences in cultural values are stereotypes, reflecting how an average person from a particular culture might behave. People within a culture are likely to vary considerably among themselves; for example, many Latin Americans have casual attitudes toward time, with others placing a high value on being punctual and making effective use of time. A summary of these cultural values is presented next.

1. *Individualism versus collectivism.* At one end of the continuum is **individualism,** a mental set in which people see themselves first as individuals and believe that their own interests take priority. **Collectivism,** at the other end of the continuum, is a feeling that the group and society receive top priority. Members of a society that values individualism are more concerned with their careers than with the good of the firm. Members of a society that values collectivism, in contrast, are typically more concerned with the organization than with themselves. Highly individualistic cultures include the United States, Canada, Great Britain, Australia, and the Netherlands. Japan, Taiwan, Mexico, Greece, and Hong Kong are among the countries that strongly value collectivism. The current emphasis on teamwork, however, is softening individualism in individualistic cultures.

2. *Power distance.* The extent to which employees accept the idea that members of an organization have different levels of power is referred to as **power distance.** In a high-power-distance culture, the boss makes many decisions simply because she or he is the boss. Group members readily comply because they have a positive orientation toward authority. In a low-power-distance culture, employees do not readily recognize a power hierarchy. They accept directions only when they think the boss is right or when they feel threatened. High-power-distance cultures include India, France, Spain, Japan, Mexico, and Brazil. Low-power-distance cultures include the United States, Israel, Germany, and Ireland.

3. *Uncertainty avoidance.* People who accept the unknown and tolerate risk and unconventional behavior are said to have low **uncertainty avoidance.** In other words, these people are not afraid to face the unknown. A society ranked high in uncertainty avoidance contains a majority of people who want predictable and certain futures. Low uncertainty-avoidance cultures include the United States, Canada, Australia, and Singapore. Workers in Israel, Japan, Italy, and Argentina are more motivated to avoid uncertainty in their careers.

4. *Materialism versus concern for others.* In this context, **materialism** refers to an emphasis on assertiveness and the acquisition of money or material objects. It also means a de-emphasis on caring for others. At the other end of the continuum is **concern for others,** an emphasis on personal relations and a concern for the welfare of others. Materialistic countries include Japan, Austria, and Italy. The United States is considered to be moderately materialistic (according to Hofstede's research). Scandinavian nations all emphasize caring as a national value. Many American CEOs in recent years have been accused of being materialistic to the point of greed and gluttony.

5. *Long-term orientation versus short-term orientation.* Workers from a culture with a **long-term orientation** maintain a long-range perspective, and thus are thrifty and do not demand quick returns on their investments. A **short-term orientation** is characterized by a demand for immediate results and a propensity not to save. Pacific Rim countries are noted for their long-term orientation. In contrast, the cultures of the United States and Canada are characterized by a more short-term orientation.

6. *Formality versus informality.* A country that values **formality** attaches considerable importance to tradition, ceremony, social rules, and rank. At the other extreme, **informality** refers to a casual attitude toward tradition, ceremony, social rules, and rank. Workers in Latin American countries highly value formality, such as lavish public receptions and processions. Americans, Canadians, and Scandinavians are much more informal. Karolina Basic, a Croatian woman studying and working in the United States, provides a practical suggestion for dealing with the formality versus informality dimension: "When I deal with American people, I usually call them by their first names, but when I deal with Croatian people, I still address them by their last names."

7. *Urgent time orientation versus casual time orientation.* Individuals and nations attach different importance to time. People with an **urgent time orientation** perceive time as a scarce resource and tend to be impatient. People with a **casual time orientation** view time as an unlimited and unending resource and tend to be patient. Americans are noted for their urgent time orientation. They frequently impose deadlines and are eager to get started doing business. Asians and Middle Easterners, in contrast, are patient negotiators.

   A paradox about the time orientation dimension is that Chinese get major projects completed quickly despite a casual time orientation. A key part of the ability of Chinese to move projects along so quickly is the value they place on personal relationships. To Chinese managers, a handshake is more important than extensive documentation that has been reviewed and signed off by lawyers.

8. *High-context versus low-context cultures.* Cultures differ in how much importance they attach to the surrounding circumstances, or context, of an event. **High-context cultures** make more extensive use of body language. Some cultures, such as the Asian, Hispanic, and African-American cultures, are high context. In contrast, northern European cultures are **low context** and make less use of body language. The American culture is considered to be medium-low context. People in low-context cultures seldom take time in business dealings to build relationships and establish trust.

9. *Work orientation/leisure orientation.* A major cultural value difference is the number of hours per week people expect to invest in work instead of leisure or other nonwork activities. American corporate professionals typically work about 55 hours per week, take 45-minute lunch breaks, and 2 weeks of

vacation. Japanese workers share similar values with respect to amount of work per week. European professionals, in contrast, are more likely to work 40 hours per week, take 2-hour lunch breaks, and 6 weeks of vacation. European countries have steadily reduced the work week in recent years, while lengthening vacations. The average German worker invests about 1,400 hours a year in work, a 17% decrease from 1980. IG Metall, a German trade-workers union, went on strike recently demanding a 35-hour work week. Europeans, particulary Swedes, also are likely to take much more sick leave than workers from other countries. To compensate for the lesiure orientation of European workers, many European companies are outsourcing jobs outside of Europe. French car manufacturer PSA Peugeot Citroen, for example, more than doubled the size of its workforce ourside France to 68,000 during the last decade. Countries with stronger work orientations, such as Slovakia, Brazil, and South Africa, are absorbing Western European manufacturing jobs.[11]

Although the dimensions of cultural values just described are broad national stereotypes, they still relate to meaningful aspects of organizational behavior. A study related the extent of role conflict, role ambiguity, and role overload—reported by middle managers from 21 nations—to national scores on power distance, individualism, uncertainty avoidance, and materialism. Middle managers from cultures with high power distance and collective attitudes experience less role ambiguity. However, high power distance and collectivism were positively related to role overload. The researchers also found that role stress varies substantially more by country than by demographic or organizational factors.[12]

A more recent study on the impact of cultural values investigated how similarity to peers and supervisors influences career advance in an individualistic versus collectivistic society. The study participants were bank tellers working for the same multinational bank in Hong Kong and the United States. Both personality and individualism versus collectivism were measured by questionnaires. The researchers did not assume that work units in Hong Kong banks were collectivistic, nor that work units in the United States were individualistic. One major finding was that having a personality similar to peers was positively associated with promotion in units with high individualism. In units with high collectivism, having a personality similar to the boss was instead positively associated with advancement.[13] (The lesson here is that if you find yourself in an individualistic work group, emphasize your personality traits that match your coworkers. In a collectivistic work group, do what you can to emphasize personality traits similar to your supervisor.)

How might a person use information about cultural differences to enhance interpersonal effectiveness? A starting point would be to recognize that a person's national values might influence his or her behavior. Assume that the managerial worker wanted to establish a good working relationship with a person from a high-context culture. To begin, he or she might emphasize body language when communicating with the individual.

Culturally Based Differences in Management Style

The impact of culture on management and leadership style is another important influence of culture on organizational behavior. Although personality factors are a major contributor to management style, culture is also important because it serves as a guide to acceptable behavior. Culture provides the values that guide behavior. For example, a person raised in a collectivist culture would find it natural to be a consensus style manager/leader. Because management deals so heavily with people, it is part of the society in which it takes place. To be effective, a manager transplanted to a different culture may have to make some concessions to the national stereotype of an effective leader. National stereotypes of management styles, according to the research of Geert Hofstede and his collaborators, are as follows:[14]

1. *Germany:* German managers are expected to be primarily technical experts, or meisters, who assign tasks and help solve difficult problems. More recent data stemming from the GLOBE (Global Leadership and Organizational Behavior Effectiveness) indicates that a strong performance orientation is the most pronounced German value, with German managers not being overly considerate of others.[15]

2. *Japan:* Japanese managers rely on group consensus before making a decision, and the group controls individual behavior to a large extent. Japanese managers are perceived as more formal and businesslike, and less talkative and emotional, than their American counterparts. Japanese managers in large, successful firms are more likely to fit the consensus stereotype. Many Japanese managers in family-owned businesses have imperial attitudes and behaviors, and have strong sexist attitudes toward women.

3. *France:* French managers, particularly in major corporations, are part of an elite class (having attended select business schools called *Les Grandes Écoles*). As a consequence, they behave in a superior, authoritarian manner. The rigid class distinctions of French society also help shape the managers' attitudes and behaviors. Higher-level managers perceive themselves to be superior to managers at lower levels.

4. *The Netherlands:* Dutch managers emphasize quality and consensus, and do not expect to impress group members with their status. Dutch managers give group members ample opportunity to participate in problem solving. Following the tradition of consensus, most problems are resolved through lengthy discussion.

5. *China:* Many managers from China work in Pacific Rim countries such as Taiwan, Hong Kong, Singapore, Malaysia, and the Philippines. In companies managed by Chinese, major decisions are made by one dominant person, quite often people over 65. The Chinese manager maintains a low profile.

MULTICULTURAL MANAGERS AND ORGANIZATIONS

A major message from the study of international and cross-cultural organizational behavior is that managers and their organizations need to respond positively to cultural diversity. Here we look separately at the multicultural manager and the multicultural organization.

3

Describe what is required for managers and organizations to become multicultural.

The Multicultural Manager

The **multicultural manager** has the skills and attitudes to relate effectively to and motivate people with little regard to race, gender, age, social attitudes, and lifestyles. A multicultural manager has the ability to conduct business in a diverse, international environment. Achieving such competence is a combination of many factors, including some of the traits associated with effective leadership described in Chapter 11. A few skills and attitudes are especially relevant for achieving the status of a multicultural manager.

A good starting point is to make strides toward becoming bilingual. International business people respect the fact that a managerial worker is bilingual even if the second language is not their primary language. For example, if an American speaks French, the American can relate well to Italians and Spanish people. The tortuous reasoning is that many Italians and Spanish speak French as a third language, and respect the American who speaks a little French.

A major requirement for becoming a multicultural manager is to develop **cultural sensitivity,** an awareness of and a willingness to investigate the reasons why people of another culture act as they do.[16] A person with cultural sensitivity will recognize certain nuances in customs that will help build better relationships with people from different cultural backgrounds than his or her own. An example of cultural insensitivity follows:

> A manager in a telecommunications in firm in Washington DC wanted to recognize the outstanding accomplishments of a worker, who was born and raised in India, on a major project. The manager offered the worker guest coupons to a steakhouse, not stopping to think that an Indian raised in India probably does not eat steak. The worker appreciated the recognition but laughed to his coworkers in describing the incident.

Exhibit 16-2 provides specific examples of nuances to consider. In addition, the information in Chapter 9 about overcoming cross-cultural communication barriers is directly relevant. Being able to deal effectively with cultural differences can be a make-or-break factor (or mediating variable) in the success of overseas ventures. Applying the information in Exhibit 16-3 will be the most effective when you understand the cultural values driving the behavior. For example, the information about the importance of business cards in Japan is generated in part

Exhibit 16-2

Protocol Dos and Don'ts in Several Countries

Dorothy Manning of International Business Protocol suggests adhering to the following dos and don'ts in the countries indicated. Remember, however, that these suggestions are not absolute rules.

Great Britain
DO say please and thank you often.
DO arrive promptly for dinner.
DON'T ask personal questions because the British protect their privacy.
DON'T gossip about British royalty. Allow the British to take the initiative with respect to gossiping about royalty, such as mentioning juicy stories in the tabloids.

France
DO shake hands when greeting. Only close friends give light, brushing kisses on cheeks.
DO dress more formally than in the United States. Elegant dress is highly valued.
DON'T expect to complete any work during the French two-hour lunch.
DON'T chew gum in a work setting.

Italy
DO write business correspondence in Italian for priority attention.

DO make appointments between 10:00 A.M. and 11:00 A.M. or after 3:00 P.M.
DON'T eat too much pasta, as it is not the main course.
DON'T hand out business cards freely. Italians use them infrequently.

Greece
DO distribute business cards freely so people will know how to spell your name.
DO be prompt even if your hosts are not.
DON'T expect to meet deadlines. A project takes as long as the Greeks think is necessary.
DON'T address people by formal or professional titles. The Greeks want more informality.

Japan
DO present your business cards with both hands and a slight bow as a gesture of respect.
DO present gifts, American made and wrapped.
DON'T knock competitors.
DON'T present the same gift to everyone, unless all members are the same organizational rank.

Source: *TWA Ambassador* October 1990, p. 69; *Inc. Magazine's Going Global: Japan Inc.*, January 1994; plus updates from direct observation in the present.

because Japanese people value power distance, and the company a person works for helps determine his or her status. The value of collectivism also fosters the exchange of cards.[17]

An effective strategy for becoming a multicultural manager is to simply respect others in the workplace. To respect another culture is to recognize that although the other culture is different, it is equally good. A person from one culture might therefore say, "Eating rattlesnakes for dinner is certainly different from my culture, yet I can see that eating rattlesnakes is as good as eating cows." (Which living organisms constitute palatable food is a major day-by-day cultural difference.) Respect comes from valuing differences. Respecting other people's customs can translate into specific attitudes such as respecting one group member for wearing a yarmulke on Friday or another for wearing an African costume to celebrate Kwanzaa.

A final point for becoming a multicultural manager is to avoid a set of twin dangers. One is **parochialism,** the assumption that the ways of one's culture are the only ways of doing things. (An American might say, "Of course, we give merit pay to workers. There is no other way of motivating them.") The other danger is **ethnocentrism,** the assumption that the ways of one's culture are the best ways of doing things. ("Merit pay is the most effective method of motivating workers.")[18]

The Multicultural Organization

As more workers in a firm develop multicultural skills, the organization itself can achieve the same skill level. A **multicultural organization** values cultural diversity and is willing to encourage and even capitalize on such diversity. Developing a multicultural organization helps achieve the potential benefits that come with valuing diversity. In addition, the multicultural organization helps avoid problems that crop up when managing for diversity such as increased turnover, interpersonal conflict, and communication breakdowns.

An organization passes through developmental stages as it moves from a monocultural organization to a multicultural one, as shown in Exhibit 16-3. At the *monocultural level,* there is implicit or explicit exclusion of racial minorities, women, and other groups underrepresented in powerful positions in society.

The *non-discriminatory* level is characterized by a sincere desire to eliminate the majority group's unfair advantage. Yet the organization does not significantly change its culture. The organization may strive to ensure that the racial and ethnic mix matches the racial and ethnic mix of society in general or its customer base. The organization may also attempt to influence its climate so it is not a hostile environment for the new members of the workforce. Full compliance with a government-mandated affirmative action program helps an organization reach the non-discriminatory level.

At the *multicultural level,* the organization is becoming or has become profoundly diverse. The organization reflects the contributions and interests of the diverse cultural and social groups in the organization's mission, operations, products, and services. A pluralism exists when both minority and majority group members are influential in creating behavioral norms, values, and policies. Another characteristic is full structural integration. The term means that that no one is assigned a specific job just because of his or her ethnicity or gender.[19] The multi-cultural organization strives to be bias free, because bias and prejudice create discrimination.

To move toward being a multicultural organization, business firms take a variety of diversity initiatives. Later, in this chapter we describe diversity and cultural training. Also of importance are a variety of initiatives related to various demographic groups, as listed in Exhibit 16-4. An age initiative, for example, would be to ensure that in downsizing, senior employees are not over-represented. At the same time, junior candidates should not be over-represented in hiring.

4

Be more aware of barriers to good cross-cultural relations.

BARRIERS TO GOOD CROSS-CULTURAL RELATIONS

An important part of achieving a multicultural organization and good cross-cultural relations in general is to understand barriers to such harmony. Major barriers of this type are described as follows:[20]

1. *Perceptual expectations.* Achieving good cross-cultural relations is hampered by people's predisposition to discriminate. They do so as a perceptual shortcut, much like stereotyping. Psychologist Diane Halpern explains how the process works: "Even if you have absolutely no prejudice, you are influenced by your expectations. A small woman of color doesn't look like a corporate executive. If you look at heads of corporations, they are tall, slender, white males. They are not fat. They are not in a wheelchair. They are not too old. Anything that doesn't conform to the expectations is a misfit."[21] Halpern's perception about all corporate executives being slim and not too old may be a misperception (check out a few annual reports), yet the message is important. Because people are not naturally non-discriminatory, a firm has to put considerable effort into becoming multicultural.

Exhibit 16-4

Diversity Initiatives at Major Business Firms

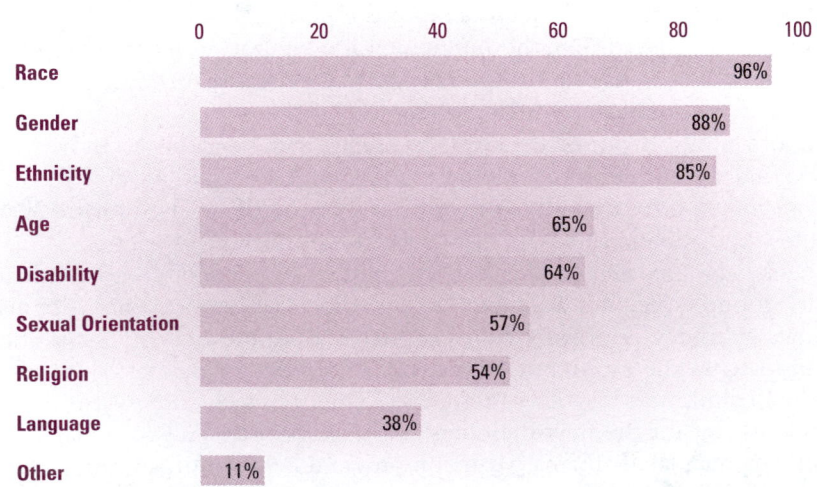

Note: Figures indicate percentage of companies responding that they address certain issues through diversity initiatives.

Source: "Impact of Diversity on the Bottom Line," an SHRM/Fortune survey reflecting the responses of 121 HR professionals from 1,000 companies on *Fortune* magazine's list of the "100 Top Companies to Work For." Presented in Lin Grensing-Pophal, "Reaching for Diversity," *HR Magazine*, May 2002, p. 56. Reprinted with the permission of HR Magazine published by Society for Human Resource Management, Alexandria, VA.

2. *Ethnocentrism.* As stated previously, the multicultural manager avoids ethnocentrism, which impairs intercultural relations in general. Most cultures consider themselves to be the center of the world. One consequence of this attitude is that people from one culture prefer people from other cultures more similar to themselves. English people would therefore have more positive attitudes toward the Scottish than they would toward Brazilians. Despite this generalization, some countries that appear to have similar cultures are intense rivals. Many Japanese disliked Korean people, and vice versa as do French and Belgians.

3. *Intergroup rather than interpersonal relations.* In intergroup relations, we pay attention only to the group membership of the person. In interpersonal relations, we pay attention to a person's characteristics. An interpersonal relationship requires more effort because we have to attend to details about the other person. Automobile manufacturers have in recent years developed extensive training programs to help sales representatives develop interpersonal rather than intergroup relations with women buyers. In the past, many sales reps would lose valuable sales prospects because they assumed that women were not the decision makers about an automobile purchase.

4. *Stereotypes in intergroup relations.* As a result of stereotypes, people overestimate the probability that a given member of a group will have an attribute of his or her category. People tend to select information that fits the stereotype and reject inconsistent information. As a consequence, we readily draw conclusions about people from other cultural groups without carefully listening and observing. As a Chinese-American woman reports, "I'm tired of people assuming that I like math and science and that I'm good with details. I'm a people person with a creative bent. I actually hate math." (A problem here is that the woman may be excluded from job assignments that fit her true capabilities.)

5. *Language differences.* A major barrier to good cross-cultural relations is language differences. When people do not understand each other's languages, the possibility for misunderstanding multiplies. A team member who was a native of France on assignment in the United States, said the boss was *retarded,* so the meeting would have to wait. The other team members thought this was an insult, but *en retard* in French refers to being late. On a more somber note, language barriers cause many industrial accidents in the United States. A researcher notes that Latinos in the U.S. are frequently employed in dangerous industries, particularly construction. Language barriers between workers and supervisors make safety training exceptionally difficult.[22]

CROSS-CULTURAL PROCESSES

Another approach to understanding international and cross-cultural organizational behavior is to examine similarities and differences in important processes. Five such areas in which cross-cultural differences may surface are motivation, ethics, negotiations, conflict resolution methods, and empowerment practices.

Explain how motivation, ethics, appropriate negotiation skills, conflict resolution, and empowerment practices can vary across cultures.

Cross-Cultural Motivation

For managers to effectively lead and influence workers from another culture, they must use a motivational approach that fits the culture in question. Motivational concepts apply across cultures providing that the manager has relevant information about two key factors. The manager must know which needs the people are attempting to satisfy and which rewards will satisfy those needs. A case in point is reinforcement theory. All human beings are motivated by rewards, yet which rewards have high valence varies across cultures. An American worker might respond well to individual recognition, while a South Korean worker might respond better to sharing a reward with the group.

In support of the idea that people in different cultures have similar needs, a study of global leadership by Manfred R. R. Kets De Vries and Elizabeth Florent-Treacy indicates that workers have basic motivational needs. One such need is the *attachment/affiliation need,* which is expressed as a drive for connecting with other people, such as identifying with a group or feeling a sense of community. Another universal need, according to these researchers, is exploratory/assertive and is closely associated with cognition and learning. These needs constitute the foundation for play, creativity, and innovation, thereby being a new label for intrinsic motivation and openness.[23] The similarity of needs across cultures is not surprising when you consider that the Five Factor model can describe the personality structure of people in different continents (as described in Chapter 2).

A study conducted in Russia illustrates how motivation theory can apply across cultures, if modifications are made for cultural differences. Dianne H. B. Welsh, Fred Luthans, and Steven M. Sommer selected three motivational theories and accompanying techniques to test in a Russian factory. Extrinsic rewards, behavioral management, and participation were studied because all three approaches have historical roots in Russian human resource management. The study took place in a cotton mill, using 99 male weavers from three different shifts. All the weavers also assisted other weavers but did not occupy formal supervisory roles.

The extrinsic rewards were American goods that the weavers received contingent upon increasing the amount of top-grade fabric they produced. The behavioral management intervention consisted of the weavers' supervisors administering recognition and praise for functional behaviors. The participative intervention asked for the workers' input and involved elements of job enrichment.

The extrinsic rewards and behavioral management interventions had a positive impact on the job performance of Russian workers. The participation intervention not only failed to improve performance, it actually contributed to a performance decline. The researchers concluded that American-based motivation theories do apply in Russia, but that participative management is a poor cultural fit.[24]

A more recent study also found that cultural factors influence the effectiveness of participative management as a motivational technique. The participants in the study were junior workers in the Hong Kong and U.S. branches of a large multinational bank. Four variables were studied in addition to participative decision making and performance: (1) self-efficacy about participative decision making, (2) group efficacy about participation (believing that the group is competent), (3) *ideocentrism* (viewing the self as separate from others, with an orientation toward personal accomplishment), and (4) *allocentrism* (viewing the self as inseparable from others in the in-group). A major finding of this complex study was that for employees with allocentric beliefs, a strong positive relationship was found between an opportunity to participate and group performance—assuming the participants had high participation efficacy. Also, in groups scoring low on allocentrism, there was no relationship between participative decision-making opportunity and group performance.[25] In short, when people believe in collective effort, it helps them benefit from participative decision making.

Cross-Cultural Ethics

Coping with cross-cultural ethical codes challenges many international managers. When faced with an ethical dilemma, should managers abide by ethical codes of their own country or those of the country they are visiting? A recurring ethical dilemma is that in many countries, including Pakistan and Mexico, government officials demand payments to expedite certain transactions. In the United States, direct payments to government officials to win contracts are illegal and unethical. The Foreign Corrupt Practices Act does not outlaw payment to foreign government officials, providing such payoffs are part of the country's business practices. To get around the direct payment prohibitions, some countries demand that large American companies donate technology to the foreign country, with China being a leading example. Money is not exchanged but the foreign country receives side benefits from dealing with a U.S. company.

Another cross-cultural difference in ethics is that in the United States, ethical values and behavior are the responsibility of the individual. In Europe and Japan, managers typically make ethical decisions based on the shared values and responsibilities of the organization. Another point of differentiation is that American companies are more likely to have a written code of ethics.[26]

One questionable way in which managers cope with cross-cultural differences in ethics is to outsource to another country work that would be unethical, or illegal, in their own countries. A lethal example is the recycling of automobile and truck batteries. During recycling, acid leaks from these batteries and the fumes are extraordinarily toxic. Several countries, including Australia, contract with small firms in India to recycle these batteries. The small Indian firms take virtually no safety precautions for the workers.

Another cross-cultural ethical issue involves pay practices. Many American firms justify high compensation to executives as an issue of supply and demand, with exceptional leadership talent being in short supply. Yet many other countries question the ethics of paying an executive as much as $100 million per year when many employee in the same company work for minimum wage.

Cross-Cultural Negotiations

As world trade increases, so does the need for negotiating with people from different cultures. Negotiation is one of the single most important skills for the international manager or specialist. A major challenge in skill development is that negotiation styles vary from one culture to another. Managers should negotiate when the value of the exchange and the relationship is important.

Managerial negotiation requires significant adaptation when conducted in a foreign culture. A do-or-die attitude is often self-defeating. A list of suggestions for negotiation abroad follows. Each of the first five points includes the American attitude that could be self-defeating and explains how it can be improved.[27]

1. *Use a team approach.* Most American managers are convinced they can handle any negotiation by themselves, while other countries rely on negotiation teams. Bringing several Americans to the negotiating table may convey a seriousness of purpose and commitment.
2. *Be patient.* A striking difference between American negotiations and those in many foreign cultures concerns time. Japanese, Chinese, and Arab negotiators, for example, are willing to spend many days negotiating a deal. Much of their negotiating activity seems to be ceremonial (including elaborate dining) and unrelated to the task. This often frustrates the "strictly business" American.
3. *Learn to tolerate less than full disclosure of information.* Many Americans believe that "laying one's cards on the table" is a valuable negotiating tactic. As a consequence, they expect honest information and are frustrated when it is not forthcoming. Because many foreign negotiators routinely practice small deceptions at the negotiating table, less than full disclosure must be tolerated.

4. *Accept silence as part of negotiating.* Unlike Asian negotiators, Americans often become uncomfortable when more than 10 seconds elapses without somebody making a task-related comment. It is sometimes fruitful to remain silent and wait for the other side to make an offer or reveal the nature of its thinking.

5. *Take no for an answer sometimes.* American are highly competitive in a negotiating session and take each loss personally. Foreign customers and suppliers, in contrast, are often willing to lose one negotiating session to build a solid long-term relationship among people and firms.

6. *Learn about the other culture's negotiating style in advance.* Part of doing your homework for negotiating in another culture involves have an awareness of negotiating stereotypes for the other culture. A few possibilities: Japanese prefer an exchange of information to confrontation; Russians love combat; Spanish negotiators are individualistic; Koreans are team players; Asians are high in context so you have to watch the body language, and what is *not* said.[28]

A useful perspective on these suggestions is that a person is rarely on a level playing field when negotiating in another country. Adapting to the other side's negotiating tactics may help to place negotiations on an equal footing. However, Americans should not necessarily be the only group adapting their negotiating tactics to fit different cultures. Business people from around the world may have to develop a cross-cultural negotiating style.

Conflict Resolution Models across Cultures

Research provides some quantitative evidence that national culture influences which method of conflict resolution a manager chooses. Catherine Tinsley sorted conflict-resolution models into three types; resolving conflict by: (a) deferring to status power, (b) applying regulations, and (c) integrating interests. According to her observations, preference for a model, or method, is influenced by culture that filters information and guides members toward a particular model.

The 396 participants in the study were managers from Japanese, German, and American cultures. All participants had been educated by business programs in their culture and were currently working for a company in their culture. Participants completed surveys about resolving conflict over different approaches to solving a business problem.

A major finding was that Japanese, German, and American managers tended to use different models when resolving workplace conflict. Half the variance (reasons for something taking place) in choosing a conflict model could be accounted for by a manager's cultural group membership. Japanese preferred a status power model (using their authority). Germans preferred a regulations model (appealing to rules and regulations), and Americans preferred an interests (win–win) model. Tinsley cautions that these cross-cultural differences may complicate the work life for expatriate managers who find themselves trying to manage conflict in a foreign cultural system. A particular concern is that American managers may be surprised to learn that colleagues from Japanese and German cultures do not favor the interests model.[29]

Empowerment and Continuous Improvement across Cultures

A team of researchers investigated how well the management practices of empowerment and continuous improvement fit different cultures. Data were collected from employees from a United States–based multinational corporation with operations in the United States, Mexico, Poland, and India. The major findings were as follows:

- Continuous improvement was related to high levels of satisfaction with coworkers and the work itself in all four countries. No negative findings were associated with continuous improvement in any country, suggesting that continuous improvement and self-development are a good fit in all the cultures studied.
- The outcomes associated with empowerment varied with the country and culture. Workers in the United States, Mexico, and Poland had favorable views of their supervisors when they used a high degree of empowerment. Indian employees, however, rated their supervisors low when empowerment was high. (Indians value high-power distance, and therefore expect the supervisor to retain most of the power.)
- In the U.S. and Mexico, empowerment was unrelated to coworker satisfaction, yet in Poland, empowerment was positively related to coworker satisfaction. In India, empowerment was shown to have a negative impact on coworker satisfaction.[30]

In general, the results of the study suggest that multinational managers should consider the cultural context of the management practices they implement. In particular, empowerment may backfire when used in a high-power distance culture. The study might also be interpreted as more evidence of the universal need for personal growth.

DIVERSITY TRAINING AND CULTURAL TRAINING

Many training programs have been developed to help employees value diversity and improve cross-cultural relations, especially overseas relations. The type of information presented so far in this chapter is likely to be included in such programs. In this section, we describe a diversity training program and one for improving cross-cultural relations.

6

Appreciate the nature of diversity training and cultural training.

Diversity Training

Cultural training aims to help workers understand people from other cultures. Understanding can lead to dealing more effectively with them as work associates or customers. **Diversity training** has a slightly different purpose. It attempts to bring about workplace harmony by teaching people how to get along better with diverse work associates. Quite often the program is aimed at minimizing open expressions of racism and sexism. All forms of diversity training center on increasing people's awareness of and empathy for people who are different from themselves.

Diversity training sessions focus on the ways that men and women or people of different races reflect different values, attitudes, and cultural backgrounds. Some diversity programs deal specifically with generational differences, so people with different values based on age can work harmoniously. Diversity training sessions can vary from several hours to several days. Sometimes the program is confrontational, sometimes not. As described by diversity consultant H. Roosevelt Thomas, Jr., the objectives of diversity training include one or more of the following:

- Fostering awareness and acceptance of individual differences
- Helping participants understand their own feelings and attitudes about people who are "different"

- Exploring how differences might be tapped as assets in the workplace
- Enhancing work relations between people who are different from each other[31]

An essential part of relating more effectively to diverse groups is to empathize with their point of view. To help training participants develop empathy, representatives of various groups explain their feelings related to workplace issues. The Skill-Development Exercise provides an opportunity to simulate a diversity training program. The Organizational Behavior in Action box illustrates the type of interpersonal insights gained in some diversity training programs.

COLLABORATE

SKILL-DEVELOPMENT EXERCISE

Developing Empathy for Differences

Class members come up to the front of the room one by one and give a brief presentation (perhaps two or three minutes) about any way in which they have been perceived as different and how they felt about this perception. The difference can be of any kind, relating to characteristics such as ethnicity, race, choice of major, physical appearance, height, weight, hair color, or body piercing. After each member of the class has presented (perhaps also the instructor), class members discuss what they learned from the exercise. It is also important to discuss how this exercise can improve workplace relationships.

Organizational Behavior *in Action*

Dos and Don'ts in Interacting with Blind People

Human behavior specialists at the American Blind Children's Council, have developed guidelines to help sighted people interact more comfortably with blind people. The guidelines are prepared from the perspective of the blind person, and apply equally well to blind children and adults on and off the job.

Don't grab us to lead us. Allow us to take your arm when we are walking together.
Do touch us on the arm or use our names when addressing us. This lets us know you are speaking to us and not someone else in the room.
Don't shout when you speak to us. We cannot see but our hearing is fine.
Do give specific directions like "The telephone is three feet to the right," as opposed to "The telephone is over there."
Don't pet or distract our leader dogs. They are not pets; they are working companions on whom we depend.

Do treat us as individuals. Blind children (and adults) come in all shapes, sizes, and colors.
Don't be afraid to use words like "blind" or "see." Our eyes may not work, but it's still nice to see you.
Do direct your questions directly to us. We do not need to have someone tell you what we need in terms of office supplies, etc.

Questions

1. How might this information help you become a more complete multicultural worker?
2. What did you read that was new information for you?
3. Would you classify blindness as a form of cultural diversity? Demographic diversity? A combination of the two?

Source: Adapted slightly from "Helping Today's Blind Children become the Winners of Tomorrow," brochure for the American Blind Children's Council, undated.

Cultural diversity programs have several potential problems. The diversity trainers and participants are sometimes too confrontational and express too much hostility. Companies have found that when employees are too blunt during these sessions, it may be difficult to patch up interpersonal relations in the work group later on. Another concern about diversity training is that it exaggerates stereotypes in order to promote understanding, such as propagating that Latinos do not start meetings on time.[32]

Mentoring of minority group members has been effective in fostering some of the goals of diversity training. Many companies rely on both informal mentoring and formal mentoring (assigning a mentor to a person) as ways to help minorities and women advance in their careers. A survey of successful minority executives indicated that 48 percent of the respondents said they had a role model who guided them toward early career goals. The role model/mentors were primarily of the same ethnic, racial, or cultural origin. A specific finding was that successful minorities with supportive managers and coworkers have faster compensation growth and progress more rapidly in their firms. A sponsor of the survey said, "Minority executives believe that mentors are very helpful in advocating for upward mobility and teaching them how to navigate through the corporation."[33]

Training in Cross-Cultural Relations

For many years, companies and government agencies have prepared their workers for overseas assignments. The method most frequently chosen is **cultural training,** a set of learning experiences designed to help employees understand the customs, traditions, and beliefs of another culture. In today's diverse business environment, training employees in cross-cultural relations has increased in importance.

A major goal of cultural training, especially for workers on overseas assignments, is to help them avoid **culture shock.** The condition refers to a group of physical and psychological symptoms that can develop when a person is abruptly placed in a foreign culture. Among the symptoms are excessive hand washing and concern for sanitation, fear of physical contact with others, fear of being mugged, and strong feelings of homesickness.[34] A partial explanation for culture shock is that when placed in an unfamiliar environment, and when people behave in ways we do not understand, we feel out of control. Culture shock is a major contributor to the high failure rate of overseas assignments. Recent attention has been paid to the culture shock problems of employees from other countries transferring to the United States. Such employees are referred to as *inpatriates.* One problem is that inpatriates may find no fellow members of their country in the United States, whereas Americans can always find Americans in other countries. Another problem is that many people fear their children will be shot at on the way to or from school.[35] (Again, perceptions have a major influence on attitudes and actions, whether or not they are correct.)

Learning a foreign language is often part of cultural training, yet it can also be a separate activity. Knowledge of a second language is important because it builds better connections with people from other cultures than does having a reliance on a translator. Many workers besides international business specialists also choose to develop skills in a target language. Speaking another language can help build rapport with customers and employees who speak that language.

Cultural training can be used to improve effectiveness in one's own country as well as overseas. For example, the home-building and real estate industries use cultural training. Selected workers in these industries are learning the Asian culture.

Such training does not necessarily involve taking a crash course in Chinese or Japanese. Instead, it means the workers have been learning about subtle cultural differences between Eastern and Western people.

Builders and real estate agents hire cultural diversity specialists to help them learn how to communicate and accommodate their customers from China, Japan, Taiwan, Korea, Vietnam, and the Philippines. Home builders and real estate agents receive cultural training in such issues as:

- Negotiating styles
- Money matters in terms of who is the decision maker in the Asian family
- Use of body language, such as eye contact
- Business etiquette[36]
- Design preferences in a home, such as feng shui. (The term refers to the ancient Chinese philosophy of creating a harmonious home and work environment, leading to good fortune and prosperity for the inhabitants. Other Asian cultures and many Westerners now embrace feng shui principles.)

IMPLICATIONS FOR MANAGERIAL PRACTICE

1. As a manager or cultural diversity specialist, it is important to keep selling the idea that diversity initiatives do not regard white males as the enemy. In contrast, diversity is meant to be inclusive. Many white males are concerned that diversity initiatives are a form of reverse discrimination and that they will be accused of being "advantaged" because of their skin color.[37]

2. A managerial success factor is to become multicultural in terms of conducting business effectively with people from different cultures. The demand for multicultural managers continues to increase despite some disenchantment with the success of overseas business in recent years.

3. To perform well in many positions in the modern world, it may be necessary for you to develop a global mind-set, a feeling of comfort and confidence in dealing with workers from diverse countries. Develop a global mind-set requires perspective, a sincere interest in another country, and a sense of humor to recover from obvious slips.[38] Similarly, second-language proficiency is becoming a key success factor in the global workplace.

SUMMARY OF KEY POINTS

1 **Understand the scope, competitive advantages, and success factors associated with cultural diversity.**

The true meaning of valuing diversity is to respect a wide range of cultural and individual differences. To be diverse is to be different in some measurable, though not necessarily visible, way. Encouraging cultural diversity within an organization is socially responsible and also offers these potential advantages: increased sales and profits, cost reduction associated with turnover and lawsuits, better employee recruitment, better ideas for publicity and advertising, and creativity. The United States Postal Service has been able to quantify some of the benefits associated with being a culturally inclusive organization.

Five factors associated with successful diversity initiatives are: CEO initiation and support, a variety of human resource initiatives, widespread communication about diversity programs; a corporate philosophy favoring diversity, and including diversity in measures of company success.

2 **Identify and explain key dimensions of cultural differences.**

Nine values particularly helpful in understanding how national cultures differ are as follows:

individualism versus collectivism, power distance (respect for hierarchy), uncertainty avoidance, materialism versus concern for others, long-term versus short-term orientation, formality versus informality, urgent time orientation versus casual time orientation, and high-context versus low-context cultures, and work orientation/leisure orientation.

The impact of culture on management and leadership style is another important influence of culture on organizational behavior. Culture serves as a guide to acceptable behavior. For example, a person raised in a collectivist culture would find it natural to be a consensus-style manager/leader. Also, French managers tend to be highly authoritarian.

3 Describe what is required for managers and organizations to become multicultural.

Multicultural managers have the skills and attitudes to relate effectively to and motivate people across race, gender, social attitudes, and lifestyles. Multiculturalism is enhanced by bilingualism, cultural sensitivity, and an absence of parochialism and ethnocentrism.

A multicultural organization values cultural diversity and is willing to encourage and even capitalize upon such diversity. The developmental stages of such an organization are monocultural, nondiscriminatory, and multicultural. To move toward becoming multicultural, business firms can take a variety of initiatives, including not targeting senior employees for downsizing.

4 Be more aware of barriers to good cross-cultural relations.

Barriers to the good cross-cultural relations required of a multicultural organization include perceptual expectations that lead to discriminatory stereotypes and ethnocentrism, intergroup (based on group differences) versus interpersonal (based on individual differences) relations, and language differences.

5 Explain how motivation, ethics, appropriate negotiation skills, conflict resolution, and empowerment practices can vary across cultures.

Certain motivational approaches can apply cross-culturally. Some psychological needs, like attachment/affilia-tion, apply across cultures. Also, extrinsic rewards and behavior management techniques were found to be effective with Russian factory workers. A cultural belief in collective effort enhances the effectiveness of participative decision making. Coping with cross-cultural ethical codes challenges many international managers. A major issue is whether to abide by the home ethical codes or those of the foreign company and country.

Managers need good negotiating skills to achieve their objectives in international business. Americans must adapt their traditional negotiating tactics to fit other cultures. For example, people from other cultures may want to work more slowly than Americans on reaching agreement. When working in other countries, managers must be sensitive to differences in the preferred model of resolving conflict. One study showed that Japanese managers prefer a status power model of conflict resolution, Germans preferred to appeal to rules and regulations, and Americans preferred an interests model. Empowerment is likely to work poorly in a high power-distance culture such as India. However, continuous improvement works across cultures.

6 Appreciate the nature of diversity training and cultural training.

Diversity training attempts to bring about workplace harmony by teaching people how to get along better with diverse work associates. Cultural training is helpful in overcoming culture shock and contributing to better relations with various groups at home. Learning a foreign language is often part of cultural training, yet it can also be a separate activity.

KEY TERMS AND PHRASES

Individualism, *344*
A mental set in which people see themselves first as individuals and believe that their own interests take priority.

Collectivism, *344*
A value emphasizing that the group and society receive top priority.

Power Distance, *344*
The extent to which employees accept the idea that members of an organization have different levels of power.

Uncertainty Avoidance, *344*
The extent to which people accept the unknown and tolerate risk and unconventional behavior.

Materialism, *345*
An emphasis on assertiveness and the acquisition of money and material objects. Usually measured along a continuum, with concern for others at the opposite end.

Concern for Others, *345*
An emphasis on personal relations and a concern for the welfare of others. Usually measured along a continuum, with materialism at the opposite end.

Long-term Orientation, *345*
In describing national culture, taking a long-range perspective.

Short-term Orientation, *345*
In describing a national culture, a demand for immediate results.

Formality, *345*
Attaching considerable importance to tradition, ceremony, social rules, and rank.

Informality, *345*
A casual attitude toward tradition, ceremony, social rules, and rank.

Urgent Time Orientation, *345*
The perception of time as a scarce resource, therefore leading to impatience.

Casual Time Orientation, *345*
The perception of time as an unlimited and unending resource, leading to patience.

High-context Culture, *345*
A culture that makes more extensive use of body language.

Low-context Culture, *345*
A culture that makes less use of body language.

Multicultural Manager, *347*
A manager with the skills and attitudes to relate effectively to and motivate people across race, gender, age, social attitudes, and lifestyles, and to conduct business in a diverse, international environment.

Cultural Sensitivity, *348*
An awareness of and a willingness to investigate the reasons why people of another culture act as they do.

Parochialism, *349*
The assumption that the ways of one's culture are the only way of doing things.

Ethnocentrism, *349*
The assumption that the ways of one's culture are the best ways of doing things.

Multicultural Organization, *349*
An organization that values cultural diversity and is willing to encourage and even capitalize on such diversity.

Diversity Training, *355*
Training that attempts to bring about workplace harmony by teaching people how to get along better with diverse work associates.

Cultural Training, *357*
Training that attempts to help workers understand people from other cultures.

Culture Shock, *357*
A group of physical and psychological symptoms that can develop when a person is abruptly placed in a foreign culture.

DISCUSSION QUESTIONS AND ACTIVITIES

1. What steps can you take to better prepare yourself to become a multicultural manager?
2. What hints can you find in an organization's annual report about whether the organization is culturally diverse?
3. Diversity specialists argue that a firm's employee mix (or base) should match its customer mix. Assume you are the general manager of a nursing home or a retirement village. Explain whether your employee base (or mix) should match your client base.
4. If you knew that group members all had "a strong leisure orientation," how would this information help you do a better job as a manager?
5. Working alone or in a group, develop a policy for a large company to deal with the rights of employees to be exempt from working certain hours, days, and holidays based on their religion.
6. Software is available to translate documents from one language into another, and devices are for sale that will give you a voice translation from one language to another. With this technology available, why should the multicultural worker bother learning another language?
7. A criticism made of cultural training and diversity training is that they usually emphasize Americans adjusting to other cultures rather than the reverse. Where do you stand on this issue?

ORGANIZATIONAL BEHAVIOR ONLINE

TO DO
Developing Your Multicultural Skills through the Internet
A useful way of developing skills in a second language and learning more about another culture is to create a bookmark, or favorite, written in your target language. In this way, each time you go the Internet on your own computer, your cover page will contain fresh information in the language you want to develop.

To get started, use a search engine like that offers choices in several languages. Enter a key word like "newspaper" or "current events" in the search probe. Once you find a suitable choice, enter the edit function for "Favorites" or "Bookmarks" and insert that newspaper as your cover page. For example, imagine that French were your choice; your search might have brought you to http://www.france2.fr, or http://www.cyberpresse.ca. These Web sites keep you abreast of French (or Canadian) international news, sports, and cultural events—written in French. Another example is to find a Spanish-language version of a U.S. newspaper such as found on http://www.elpasotimes.com. Now every time you access the Internet, you can spend 5 minutes becoming multicultural. You can save a lot of travel costs and time using the Internet to help you become multicultural.

CASE PROBLEM: Prudential Managing Director Mark Becomes Margaret

People in the Quantitative Management Department at Prudential Financial Inc. were trading whispers across the rows of cubicles. What's wrong with Mark Stumpp? Why has he dropped so much weight so quickly? Was he sick? Nobody knew.

A Changed Person

One day after lunch, Stumpp, age 51, handed a small, framed snapshot to Jim Scott, his friend and co-manager for 14 years. "Do you know who that is?" Stumpp asked. Scott glanced at the picture of a tall woman with blonde bangs and shook his head. He'd never seen her. "That's the person you're going to be working with a year from now," Stumpp said. "The lady in the photograph, Stumpp, is going to be me."

Prudential's QM department manages billions of dollars of other people's money. It's a business that relies on a nurtured image of solidity, on the value implicit in longtime relationships. Word of Stumpp's intensely private decision spread through Prudential's Newark headquarters. People realized this wasn't going to be about just him. It was going to be about them, too.

Stumpp was uncomfortable in Mark's body as far back as his memories reach. Deep inside something felt terribly wrong. It is called gender dysphoria, a condition characterized by intense feelings of being the wrong gender.

Ron Andrews, a vice president of human resources, said that he had never encountered a more difficult issue. "What was difficult about this," he said, "is I didn't know anything."

Stumpp had a reputation as an office clown. He dropped jokes in the middle of meetings, walked around the office without shoes, and wore jeans when everyone else wore a suit. But he was an acknowledged expert in the serious business of making money grow. His department manages $32 billion on behalf of client pension funds and other institutional investors. Prudential's own $8 billion in pension funds is managed here.

"My business is about trust," Stumpp says, and he knew trust would not be enhanced if people saw him "turn into a girl [woman]." It was two years before his coworkers began to notice he was changing—and to worry. The hormones were reshaping his body. Enlarged breasts could be hidden in loose-fitting shirts, but there was no way to disguise the disappearance of muscle.

Informing the People Who Need to Know

In the summer of 2001, the few executives at Prudential who knew what was going on realized that the problem wasn't that Stumpp was changing his gender. It was that he was coming back to work afterward. It was one thing to figure out how the QM department would go on without Mark. It was quite another to figure out how to continue with someone named Maggie in his place. Someone was going to have to explain this delicate situation in Prudential's executive offices, to the company's clients, to the marking and sales representatives who vouched for Stumpp's research.

Bringing it all together was Andrews's job. Throughout the summer and into the fall, Andrews worked his way down a list of people who needed to know, figuring out not just who they would tell in turn, but how they would do it. In a month long thread of calls, meetings, and memos, he, company lawyers, and sales managers drew up a list of 30 clients that relied on Stumpp's research and investment strategies.

They decided that a Prudential customer relationship manager would contact each one to explain who would soon be handling their money. And then Andrews and his group wrote an extended outline with "key communication points." "We wanted our clients and our customers not to hear this from some sort of grapevine," Andrews says. "We wanted to make sure they hear it from us."

In the QM department, though, Stumpp's story was still known only to Scott and another employee, Stacie Mintz. So, after Stumpp left on an unexplained medical leave in January 2002, Scott called the homes of all 35 members in the department. "I need to talk to you about Mark," began each conversation.

On January 8, a two-page memo arrived in the e-mail box of everyone in the department, with a lead-in "From: M. Stumpp; Subject: Me."

The note poked fun at the situation, but also appealed for understanding. And it emphasized that returning to work was something Stumpp had a legal right to do. "This will be new ground for all of us," Stumpp wrote. "However, if September 11 taught us anything, it was that life is far too precious and short. Each of us must strive to be at peace with ourselves." She signed the note "Margaret."

The note leapfrogged around the company, and soon employees started e-mailing back. Many, including some top executives, expressed support. A few of the women offered to help Stumpp pick out clothes.

Some took more convincing. In the weeks before Stumpp's scheduled return date—Monday, February 4—Mintz says it felt like there was a line of coworkers at her door, mostly concerned about how to act when Mark walked in as Margaret. Stumpp, recuperating at home, offered to return at first in men's clothes if it would make people more comfortable. No, his fellow workers replied, if you're Maggie, then come back as Maggie. We're as ready as we'll ever be.

Return to the Office

Maggie Stumpp made it to the fourth floor before nearly everyone else that first morning back. Her coworkers walked in and there she was, joking about the joy of being thin, of having to wear pantyhose, of how hard it had been to find shoes her size.

One of the first trials came a few weeks after Stumpp's return, when they took a call from a longtime client, a labor union whose members' reputations did not jive with her heels and pantyhose. The union officials asked to meet Stumpp to reevaluate her suitability to continue managing their business. The department braced to lose the account.

They met over dinner at a steakhouse. The first few hours were spent discussing the stock market and the economy, smoothed over by a couple of drinks. Gradually, the men's doubts appeared to ease. Prudential kept the account. Inside Prudential, however, there were still some tensions. To ease the uncertainties of some female colleagues, Andrews set aside a small bathroom for her for six months. After that she could use the women's room. Six months and a day after Stumpp returned, a female employee protested Stumpp's presence in the adjoining stall of the women's room.

"Grow up!" Andrews told her, intentionally setting a tone. While the company did not expect all of its employees to accept Stumpp personally, they would be expected to do so professionally. There are inevitable stumbles and awkward moments. "The hardest thing is the pronouns," Scott says. "It just drives me crazy."

Maggie is not denying a life as Mark, but she is eager to move on as Maggie. There are times when the phone in her office rings and the voice asks to speak to Mark. And depending on the nature of the call and her mood, she relishes a certain answer.

"Oh, him," Maggie Stumpp says. "We got rid of him a long time ago."

Case Questions

1. What does this case illustrate about the challenges of valuing cultural diversity?
2. What stand should top management at Prudential take if a large account, such as the union pension fund, threatens to leave if Maggie Stumpp stays in her position as senior managing director?
3. What should be the response of the human resource director if a woman employee complains about Maggie Stumpp using the restroom for female employees?
4. What alternative can you suggest to Maggie Stump saying "Oh him. We got rid of him a long time ago" when an occasional client asks to speak with Mark Stumpp?

Source: Adam Geller, "How a Company Coped When Mark Became Margaret," *The Detroit News*, 24 May 2003.

ENDNOTES

1. Bureau of Labor Statistics data reported in Todd Campbell, "Diversity in Depth," *HR Magazine*, March 2003, p. 152.
2. Jennifer Schramm, "Immigration at Work," *HR Magazine*, April 2003, p. 160.
3. Joan Crockett, "Winning Competitive Advantage through a Diverse Workforce," *HRfocus*, May 1999, p. 9.
4. Study reported in Fay Hansen, "Diversity's Business Case Doesn't Add Up," *Workforce*, April 2003, pp. 28–32.
5. Orlando C. Richard, "Racial Diversity, Business Strategy, and Firm Performance: A Resource-Based View," *Academy of Management Journal*, April 2000, pp. 164–177; Debbe Kennedy, "Boosting Business Success through Diversity," pp. 29–30; *Business: The Ultimate Resource* (Cambridge, MA: Perseus Books Group, 2002), pp. 31–32; Hansen, "Diversity's Business Case," pp. 28–32.
6. Richard, "Racial Diversity," pp. 164–177.
7. Rosabeth Moss Kanter, *The Change Masters* (New York: Simon and Schuster, 1983).
8. Brochure for *Diversity Summit 2002* (Little Falls, NJ:IQPC), p.3.
9. Jacqueline A. Gilbert and John M. Ivancevich, "Valuing Diversity: A Tale of Two Organizations," *Academy of Management Executive*, February 2000, pp. 93–105.
10. Geert Hostede, *Culture's Consequences: International Differences in Work-Related Values* (Beverly Hills, CA: Sage, 1980); updated and expanded in "A Conversation with Geert Hofstede," *Organizational Dynamics* (Spring 1993), pp. 53–61; Jim Kennedy and Anna Everest, "Put Diversity in Context," *Personnel Journal*, September 1991, pp. 50–54.
11. Facts are from Christopher Broads, "Clocking Out: Short Work Hours Undercut Europe in Economic Drive," *The Wall Street Journal*, August 8, 2002, pp. A1, A6; Karl Ritter, "Swedes See Surge in Sick Leave," Associated Press, September 1, 2002; "German Workers Want Shorter Hours," Associated Press, June 26, 2003.
12. Mark F. Peterson, et al, "Role Conflict, Ambiguity, and Overload: A 21-Nation Study," *Academy of Management Journal*, April 1995, pp. 429–452.
13. John Schaubroeck and Simon S. K. Lam, "How Similarity to Peers and Supervisor Influences Organizational Advancement in Different Cultures," *Academy of Management Journal*, December 2002, pp. 1120–1136.
14. Geert Hofstede, "Cultural Constraints in Management Theories," *Academy of Management Executive*, February 1993, pp. 81–94; Hofstede, "The Universal and the Specific in 21st-Century Global Management," *Organizational Dynamics*, Summer 1999, pp. 35–41.
15. Felix C. Brodbeck, Michael Frese, and Mansour Javidan, "Leadership Made in Germany: Low on Compassion, High on Performance," *Academy of Management Executive*, February 2002, pp. 16–30.
16. Arvand V. Phatak, *International Dimensions of Management* (Boston: Kent, 1983), p. 167.
17. Jack Scarborough, *The Origins of Cultural Differences and Their Impact on Management* (Westport, CT: Quorum, 2000).
18. Harry C. Triandis, *Culture and Social Behavior* (New York: McGraw-Hill, 1994), pp. 249–259.
19. The model in Exhibit 16-4 is an integration of Badi G. Foster, Gerald Jackson, William E. Cross, Bailey Jackson, and Rita Hardiman, "Workforce Diversity and Business," *Training and Development Journal*, April 1988, pp. 39–40; and Taylor Cox, "The Multicultural Organization," *Academy of Management Executive*, May 1991, pp. 34–47.
20. Triandis, *Culture and Social Behavior*, pp. 249–259.
21. Quoted in "Discrimination is Brain's Way," *Los Angeles Times*, May 7, 1995.
22. Jennifer Schramm, "Immigration at Work," p. 160.
23. Manfred F. R. Ket De Vries and Elizabeth Florent-Treacy, "Global Leadership from A to Z: Creating High Commitment Organizations," *Organizational Dynamics*, Spring 2002, pp. 295–309.
24. Dianne H. B. Welsch, Fred Luthans, and Steven S. Sommer, "Managing Russian Factory Workers: The Impact of U.S.-based

Behavioral and Participative Techniques," *Academy of Management Journal,* February 1993, pp. 58–79.

25. Simon S. K. Lam, Xiao-Ping Chen, and John Schaubroeck, "Participative Decision Making and Employee Performance in Difficult Cultures: The Moderating Effects of Allocentrism/Idiocentrism and Efficacy," *Academy of Management Journal,* October 2002, pp. 905–914.

26. David Vogel, "Is U.S. Business Obsessed with Ethics?" *Across the Board,* November–December 1993, pp. 58–79.

27. John L. Graham and Roy A. Herberger, Jr., "Negotiators Abroad—Don't Shoot from the Hip," *Harvard Business Review,* July–August 1983, p. 167.

28. Marc Diener, "Culture Shock," *Entrepreneur,* July 2003, p. 77.

29. Catherine Tinsley, "Models of Conflict Resolution in Japanese, German, and American Cultures," *Journal of Applied Psychology,* April 1998, pp. 316–323.

30. Christopher Robert, et al., "Empowerment and Continuous Improvement in the United States, Mexico, Poland, and India: Predicting Fit on the Dimensions of Power Distance and Individualism," *Journal of Applied Psychology,* October 2000, pp. 643–658.

31. R. Roosevelt Thomas, Jr., *Beyond Race and Gender: Unleashing the Power of Your Total Work Force by Managing Diversity* (New York: AMACOM, 1991), p. 25.

32. Gillian Flynn, "The Harsh Reality of Diversity Programs," *Workforce,* December 1998, p. 27.

33. Jerry Langdon, "Minority Executives Benefit from Mentors," Gannett News Service, December 7, 1998. See also Letty C. Hardy, "Mentoring: A Long-Term Approach to Diversity," *HRfocus,* July 1998, p. S11.

34. Triandis, Culture and Social Behavior, p. 263.

35. Carroll Lachnit, "Low-Cost Tips for Successful Inpatriation," *Workforce,* August 2001, pp. 42–47.

36. Marcia Forsberg, "Cultural Training Improves Relations with Asian Clients," *Personnel Journal,* May 1993, pp. 79–89.

37. Gillian Flynn, "White Males See Diversity's Other Side," *Workforce,* February 1999, pp. 52–55.

38. Mildred L. Culp, "New Mentality Compels Business Effectiveness . . . Global Mind-Set: Don't Leave Home without It," WorkWise®, December 6, 1998.

A

360-Degree Survey A formal evaluation of superiors based on input from people who work for and with them, sometimes including customers and suppliers.

Action Learning Learning that occurs while working on real problems, involving the acquisition of new skills, tools, and concepts.

Active Listening Listening for full meaning without making premature judgments or interpretations.

Administrative Management A school of management thought concerned primarily with how organizations should be structured and managed.

Attitude A predisposition to respond that exerts an influence on a person's response to a person, a thing, an idea, or a situation.

Attribution Theory The process by which people ascribe causes to the behavior they perceive.

A-Type Conflict Conflict that focuses on personalized, individually oriented issues.

Avoidance Motivation Rewarding by taking away an uncomfortable consequence.

B

Behavioral Approach to Leadership An attempt to specify how the behavior of effective leaders differs from their less effective counterparts.

Behavioral Approach to Management The belief that specific attention to the workers' needs creates greater satisfaction and productivity.

Behavioral Decision Model An approach to decision making that views managers as having cognitive limitations and acting only in terms of what they perceive in a given situation.

Bounded Rationality The idea that people's limited mental abilities, combined with external influences over which they have little or no control, prevent them from making entirely rational decisions.

Bureaucracy A rational, systematic, and precise form of organization in which rules, regulations, and techniques of control are precisely defined.

Burnout A pattern of emotional, physical, and mental exhaustion in response to chronic job stressors.

C

Casual Time Orientation The perception of time as an unlimited and unending resource, leading to patience.

Centralization The extent to which executives delegate authority to lower organizational units.

Charisma The ability to lead others based on personal charm, magnetism, inspiration, and emotion.

Classical Decision Model An approach to decision making that views the manager's environment as certain and stable and the manager as rational.

Coercive Power Controlling others through fear or threat of punishment.

Cognitive Dissonance The situation in which the pieces of knowledge, information, attitudes, or beliefs held by an individual are contradictory.

Cognitive Learning Theory A theory emphasizing that learning takes place in a complicated manner involving much more than acquiring habits and small skills.

Cognitive Skills Mental ability and knowledge.

Cognitive Style The mental processes used to perceive and make judgments from information.

Collectivism A value emphasizing that the group and society receive top priority.

Communication (or Information) Overload A situation that occurs when people are so overloaded with information that they cannot respond effectively to messages, resulting in stress.

Complexity The number of different job titles and units within an organization.

Concern for Others An emphasis on personal relations and a concern for the welfare of others. Usually measured along a continuum, with materialism at the opposite end.

Conflict The opposition of persons or forces giving rise to some tension.

Confrontation and Problem Solving A method of identifying the true source of conflict and resolving it systematically.

Glossary

Consideration The degree to which the leader creates an environment of emotional support, warmth, friendliness, and trust.

Contingency Approach to Management The viewpoint that there is no one best way to manage people or work but that the best way depends on certain situational factors.

Contingency Theory of Leadership The position that the best style of leadership depends on factors relating to group members and the work setting.

Creative Self-efficacy The belief that one can be creative in a work role.

Creativity The process of developing good ideas that can be put into action.

Cross-Functional Team A work group, composed of workers with different specialties but from about the same organizational level, who come together to accomplish a task.

C-Type Conflict Conflict that focuses on substantive, issue-related differences.

Cultural Sensitivity An awareness of and a willingness to investigate the reasons why people of another culture act as they do.

Cultural Training Training that attempts to help workers understand people from other cultures.

Culture Shock A group of physical and psychological symptoms that can develop when a person is abruptly placed in a foreign culture.

Customer Departmentalization An organizational structure based on customer needs.

Cybernetic Theory of Stress, Coping, and Well-Being in Organizations The view that stress is a discrepancy between an employee's perceived state and desired state.

Decision Criteria The standards of judgment used to evaluate alternatives.

Decision The act of choosing among two or more alternatives in order to solve a problem.

Delphi Technique A group decision-making technique designed to provide group members with one another's ideas and feedback, while avoiding some of the problems associated with interacting groups.

Demographic Diversity Differences in background factors about the workforce that help shape worker attitudes and behavior.

Departmentalization The process of subdividing work into departments.

Difficult Person An individual who creates problems for others, yet has the skill and mental ability to do otherwise.

Disability A physical or mental condition that substantially limits an individual's major life activities.

Diversity Training Training that attempts to bring about workplace harmony by teaching people how to get along better with diverse work associates.

Double-Loop Learning A change in behavior that occurs when people use feedback to confront the validity of the goal or the values implicit in the situation.

Downsizing The laying off of workers to reduce costs and increase efficiency.

Dysfunctional Conflict A situation that occurs when a dispute or disagreement harms the organization.

E-learning A Web-based form of computer-based training.

Emotion A feeling such as anger, fear, joy, or surprise that underlies behavior.

Emotional Intelligence Qualities such as understanding one's own feelings, empathy for others, and the regulation of emotion to enhance living.

Emotional Labor The process of regulating both feelings and expressions to meet organizational goals.

Empowerment The process of sharing power with group members, thereby enhancing their feelings of self-efficacy.

Equity Theory The theory that employee satisfaction and motivation depend on how fairly the employees believe that they are treated in comparison to peers.

Ethics An individual's moral beliefs about what is right and wrong or good and bad.

Ethnocentrism The assumption that the ways of one's culture are the best ways of doing things.

Expectancy Theory The theory that motivation results from deliberate choices to engage in activities in order to achieve worthwhile outcomes.

Expectancy A person's subjective estimate of the probability that a given level of performance will occur.

Experience of Flow Being "in the zone"; total absorption in one's work.

Expert Power The ability to influence others because of one's specialized knowledge, skills, or abilities.

Extinction Weakening or decreasing the frequency of undesirable behavior by removing the reward for such behavior.

Feedback Information about how well someone is doing in achieving goals. Also, messages sent back from the receiver to the sender of information.

Filtering The coloring and altering of information to make it more acceptable to the receiver.

Flat Organization Structure An organization structure with relatively few layers.

Force-Field Theory The theory contending that an organization simultaneously faces forces for change (the driving forces) and forces for maintaining the status quo (the restraining forces).

Formal Communication Channels The official pathways for sending information inside and outside an organization.

Formal Group A group deliberately formed by the organization to accomplish specific tasks and achieve goals.

Formal Organization Structure An official statement of reporting relationships, rules, and regulations.

Formality Attaching considerable importance to tradition, ceremony, social rules, and rank.

Formalization The degree to which expectations regarding the methods of work are specified, committed to writing, and enforced.

Frame of Reference A perspective and vantage point based on past experience.

Functional Conflict A situation that occurs when the interests of the organization are served as a result of a dispute or disagreement.

Functional Departmentalization The grouping of people according to their expertise.

Fundamental Attribution Error The tendency to attribute behavior to internal causes when focusing on someone else's behavior.

g **(general) factor** A major component of intelligence that contributes to problem-solving ability.

Gainsharing A formal program of allowing employees to participate financially in the productivity gains they have achieved.

Goal What a person is trying to accomplish.

Grapevine The major informal communication channel in organizations.

Group Polarization A situation in which post-discussion attitudes tend to be more extreme than pre-discussion attitudes.

Group A collection of people who interact with one another, work toward some common purpose, and perceive themselves as a group.

Groupthink A deterioration of mental efficiency, reality testing, and moral judgment in the interest of group cohesiveness.

Growth Curve Model A model that traces the inevitability of change through a firm's life cycle.

Hawthorne Effect The tendency of people to behave differently when they receive attention because they respond to the demands of the situation.

Heuristics Simplified strategies that become rules of thumb in decision making.

High-context Culture A culture that makes more extensive use of body language.

Horizontal Structure The arrangement of work by teams that are responsible for accomplishing a process.

367

Human Relations Movement An approach to dealing with workers based on the belief that there is an important link among managerial practices, morale, and productivity.

Hybrid (or Mixed) Organization Structure An organization structure that combines two or more types of organization forms into one structure.

Implicit Learning Learning that takes place unconsciously and without an intention to learn.

Individual Differences Variations in how people respond to the same situation based on personal characteristics.

Individualism A mental set in which people see themselves first as individuals and believe that their own interests take priority.

Informal Communication Channels The unofficial network of channels that supplements the formal channels.

Informal Group A group that emerges over time through the interaction of workers, typically to satisfy a social or recreational purpose.

Informal Learning A planned learning that occurs in a setting without a formal classroom, lesson plan, instructor, or examination.

Informal Organization Structure A set of unofficial working relationships that emerges to take care of the events and transactions not covered by the formal structure.

Informality A casual attitude toward tradition, ceremony, social rules, and rank.

Initiating Structure The degree to which a leader establishes structure for group members.

Instrumentality The individual's subjective estimate of the probability that performance will lead to certain outcomes.

Intellectual Capital Knowledge that transforms raw materials and makes them more valuable; it is also a capital asset consisting of intellectual material.

Intelligence The capacity to acquire and apply knowledge, including solving problems.

Intrinsic Motivation A person's beliefs about the extent to which an activity can satisfy his or her needs for competence and self-determination.

Intuition An experience-based way of knowing or reasoning in which weighing and balancing evidence are done automatically.

Job Characteristics Model A method of job design that focuses on the task and interpersonal demands of a job.

Job Crafting The physical and mental changes workers make in the task or relationships aspects of their job.

Job Demands–Job Control Model An explanation of job stress contending that workers experience the most stress when the demands of the job are high yet they have little control over the activity.

Job Enrichment The process of making a job more motivational and satisfying by adding variety, responsibility, and managerial decision making.

Job Satisfaction The amount of pleasure or contentment associated with a job.

Knowledge Management (KM) The systematic sharing of information to achieve advances in innovation, efficiency, and competitive advantage.

Large–Scale Organizational Change The method used to accomplish a major change in the firm's strategy and culture.

Leader-Member Exchange Model The model that recognizes that leaders develop unique working relationships with each group member.

Leadership Grid® A framework for classifying leadership styles that simultaneously examines a leader's concerns for task accomplishment and people.

Leadership Style The relatively consistent pattern of behavior that characterizes a leader.

Leadership The ability to inspire confidence and support among the people on whose competence and commitment performance depends.

Learning Organization An organization that is skilled at creating, acquiring, and transferring knowledge and at modifying behavior to reflect new knowledge and insights.

Learning Style A person's particular way of learning, reflecting the fact that people learn best in different ways.

Learning A relatively permanent change in behavior based on practice or experience.

Legitimate Power Power based on one's formal position within the hierarchy of the organization.

Linguistic Style A person's characteristic speaking pattern, involving the amount of directness used, pacing and pausing, word choice, and the use of jokes, figures of speech, questions, and apologies.

Locus of Control The way in which people look at causation in their lives.

Long-term Orientation In describing national culture, taking a long-range perspective.

Low-context Culture A culture that makes less use of body language.

Machiavellianism A tendency to manipulate others for personal gain.

Machine Bureaucracy An ideal organization that standardizes work processes and is efficient.

Management by Walking Around The process of managers intermingling freely with workers on the shop floor, in the office, and with customers.

Maslow's Hierarchy of Needs A classical theory of motivation that arranges human needs into a pyramid-shaped model, with basic physiological needs at the bottom and self-actualization needs at the top.

Materialism An emphasis on assertiveness and the acquisition of money and material objects. Usually measured along a continuum, with concern for others at the opposite end.

Matrix Organization Structure An organization consisting of a project

structure superimposed on a functional structure.

Mechanistic Organization A primarily hierarchical organization with an emphasis on specialization and control, vertical communication, and heavy reliance on rules, policies, and procedures.

Message A purpose or an idea to be conveyed in a communication event.

Meta-analysis A quantitative or statistical review of the literature on a particular subject; an examination of a range of studies for the purpose of reaching a combined result or best estimate.

Meta-communicate To communicate about your communication to help overcome barriers or resolve a problem.

Micromanagement Supervising group members too closely and second guessing their decisions.

Mixed Signals Communication breakdown resulting from the sending of different messages about the same topic to different audiences.

Modeling Imitation; learning a skill by observing another person performing that skill.

Motivation In a work setting, the process by which behavior is mobilized and sustained in the interest of achieving organizational goals.

Multicultural Manager A manager with the skills and attitudes to relate effectively to and motivate people across race, gender, age, social attitudes, and lifestyles, and to conduct business in a diverse, international environment.

Multicultural Organization An organization that values cultural diversity and is willing to encourage and even capitalize on such diversity.

Multiple Intelligences A theory that proposes that people know and understand the world in distinctly different ways according to the varying degrees to which they possess eight faculties: linguistic, logical-mathematical, musical, spatial, bodily/kinesthetic, intrapersonal, interpersonal, and naturalist.

Need for Achievement The desire to accomplish something difficult for its own sake.

Need for Affiliation The desire to establish and maintain friendly and warm relationships with others.

Need for Power The desire to control other people, to influence their behavior, and to be responsible for them.

Negative Lifestyle Factors Behavior patterns predisposing a person to job stress, including poor exercise and eating habits and heavy consumption of caffeine, alcohol, tobacco, and other drugs.

Network Organization A spherical structure that can rotate self-managing teams and other resources around a common knowledge base.

Network Structure (or Virtual Organization) A temporary association of otherwise independent firms linked by technology to share expenses, employee talents, and access to one another's markets.

Noise Anything that disrupts communication, including the attitude and emotions of the receiver.

Nominal Group Technique (NGT) An approach to developing creative alternatives that requires group members to generate alternative solutions independently.

Non-programmed (or Non-routine) Decision A unique response to a complex problem.

Nonverbal Communication The transmission of messages by means other than words.

Normative Decision Model A contingency viewpoint of leadership that views leadership as a decision-making process in which the leader examines certain situational factors to determine which decision-making style will be most effective.

Open-Door Policy An understanding in which any employee can bring a gripe to the attention of upper-level management without checking with his or her immediate manager.

Operant Conditioning Learning that takes place as a consequence of behavior.

Organic Structure An organization laid out like a network, emphasizing horizontal specialization, extensive use of personal coordination, extensive communication among members, and loose rules, policies, and procedures.

Organigraph A map that provides an overview of a company's functions and the way people organize themselves.

Organization Development (OD) Any strategy, method, or technique for making organizations more effective by bringing about constructive, planned change.

Organization Structure The arrangement of people and tasks to accomplish organizational goals.

Organization A collection of people working together to achieve a common purpose (or simply a big group).

Organizational Behavior Modification (OB Mod) The application of reinforcement theory for motivating people in work settings.

Organizational Behavior The study of human behavior in the workplace, the interaction between people and the organization, and the organization itself.

Organizational Citizenship Behavior Behaviors that express a willingness to work for the good of an organization even without the promise of a specific reward.

Organizational Culture A system of shared values and beliefs that influence worker behavior.

Organizational Design The process of creating a structure that best fits a purpose, strategy, and environment.

Organizational Effectiveness The extent to which an organization is productive and satisfies the demands of its interested parties.

Organizational Politics Informal approaches to gaining power through means other than merit or luck.

Outsource The practice of having work performed by groups outside the organization.

Paradigm A model, framework, viewpoint, perspective, or frame of reference.

Parochialism The assumption that the ways of one's culture are the only way of doing things.

Path–goal Theory of Leadership An explanation of leadership that specifies what the leader must do to achieve high morale and productivity in a given situation.

Perception The various ways in which people interpret things in the outside world and how they act on the basis of these interpretations.

Personality Clash An antagonistic relationship between two people based on differences in personal attributes, preferences, interests, values, and styles.

Personality The persistent and enduring behavior patterns of an individual that are expressed in a wide variety of situations.

Personalized Power The use of power primarily for the sake of personal aggrandizement and gain.

Person–Role Conflict A condition that occurs when the demands made by the organization or a manager clash with the basic values of the individual.

Positive Reinforcement The application of a pleasurable or valued consequence when a person exhibits the desired response.

Power Distance The extent to which employees accept the idea that members of an organization have different levels of power.

Power The potential or ability to influence decisions and control resources.

Problem A discrepancy between the ideal and the real.

Process Consultation An intervention in which the organization development specialist examines the pattern of a work unit's communications.

Procrastinate Delaying to take action without a valid reason.

Product/Service Departmentalization The arrangement of departments according to the products or services they provide.

Professional Bureaucracy An organization composed of a core of highly trained professionals that standardizes skills for coordination.

Programmed (or Routine) Decision A standard response to an uncomplicated problem.

Project A temporary group of specialists working together under one manager to accomplish a fixed objective.

Punishment The presentation of an undesirable consequence for a specific behavior.

Readiness The extent to which a group member has the ability and willingness or confidence to accomplish a specific task.

Reengineering The radical redesign of work to achieve substantial improvements in performance.

Referent Power The ability to influence others that stems from one's desirable traits and characteristics; it is the basis for charisma.

Reinforcement Theory The contention that behavior is determined by its consequences.

Relaxation Response A general-purpose method of learning to relax by oneself, which includes making oneself quiet and comfortable.

Resource Dependence Perspective The need of the organization for a continuing flow of human resources, money, customers, technological inputs, and material to continue to function.

Reward Power Controlling others through rewards or the promise of rewards.

Role Ambiguity A condition in which the job holder receives confused or poorly defined role expectations.

Role Conflict Having to choose between competing demands or expectations.

s (special) factors Components of intelligence that contribute to problem-solving ability.

Satisficing Decision A decision that provides a minimum standard of satisfaction.

Scientific Management The application of scientific methods to increase worker's productivity.

Self-Awareness Insightfully processing feedback about oneself to improve personal effectiveness.

Self-determination Theory The idea that people are motivated when they experience a sense of choice in initiating and regulating their actions.

Self-efficacy The feeling of being an effective and competent person with respect to a task.

Self-managed Work Team A formally recognized group of employees responsible for an entire work process or segment that delivers a product or service to an internal or external customer.

Self-serving Bias An attribution error whereby people tend to attribute their achievements to good inner qualities, whereas they attribute their failure to adverse factors within the environment.

Semantics The varying meanings people attach to words.

Sexual Harassment Unwanted sexually oriented behavior in the workplace that results in discomfort and/or interference with the job.

Shaping Learning through the reinforcement or rewarding of small steps to build to the final or desired behavior.

Short-term Orientation In describing a national culture, a demand for immediate results.

Situational Control The degree to which the leader can control and influence the outcomes of group effort.

Situational Leadership Model The model that matches leadership style to the readiness of group members.

Six Sigma A data-driven method for achieving near-perfect quality with an emphasis on preventing problems.

Social Learning The process of observing the behavior of others, recognizing its consequences, and altering behavior as a result.

Social Loafing Freeloading, or shirking individual responsibility when placed in a group setting and removed from individual accountability.

Social Responsibility The idea that firms have an obligation to society beyond their economic obligations to owners or stockholder and also beyond those prescribed by law or contract.

Socialization The process of coming to understand the values, norms, and customs essential for adapting to an organization.

Socialized Power The use of power to achieve constructive ends.

Stock Option A financial incentive that gives employees the right to purchase a certain number of company shares at a specified price, generally the market price of the stock on the day the option is granted.

Stress The mental and physical condition that results from a perceived threat that cannot be dealt with readily.

Stressor Any force creating the stress reaction.

Subculture A pocket in which the organizational culture differs from the dominant culture, as well as other pockets of subculture.

Substitutes for Leadership Factors in the work environment that provide guidance and incentives to perform, making the leader's role almost superfluous.

Team Efficacy A team's belief that it can successfully perform a specific task.

Team A special type of group in which the members have complementary skills and are committed to a common purpose, a set of performance goals, and an approach to the task.

Teamwork A situation in which there is understanding and commitment to group goals on the part of all team members.

Telecommuting Working at home and sending output electronically to the office.

Territorial Departmentalization An organizational structure in which those responsible for all the activities of a firm in a given geographic area report to one manager.

Territorial Games Also known as turf wars, territorial games refer to behaviors involving the hoarding of information and other resources.

Total Quality Management (TQM) A management system for improving performance throughout an organization by maximizing customer satisfaction, making continual improvements, and relying heavily on employee involvement.

Transformational Leader One who helps organizations and people make positive changes in the way they conduct their activities.

Triarchic Theory of Intelligence The theory that intelligence is composed of three different types of intelligence: analytical, creative, and practical.

Two-factor Theory of Work Motivation Herzberg's theory contending that there are two different sets of job factors. One set can satisfy and motivate people (motivators or satisfiers); the other set can only prevent dissatisfaction (dissatisfiers or hygiene factors).

Uncertainty Avoidance The extent to which people accept the unknown and tolerate risk and unconventional behavior.

Urgent Time Orientation The perception of time as a scarce resource, therefore leading to impatience.

Valence The value a person places on a particular outcome.

Value Judgment An overall opinion of something based on a quick perception of its merit.

Value The importance a person attaches to something that serves as a guide to action.

Virtual Team A group that conducts almost all of its collaborative work via electronic communication rather than face-to-face meetings.

Virtuous Circle The idea that corporate social performance and corporate financial performance feed and reinforce each other.

Wellness Program A formal organization-sponsored activity to help employees stay well and avoid illness.

Whistle Blower An employee who discloses organizational wrongdoing to parties who can take action.

Win–Win The belief that, after conflict has been resolved, both sides should gain something of value.

Work–Family Conflict Conflict that ensues when the individual has to perform multiple roles: worker; spouse; and, often, parent.

Index

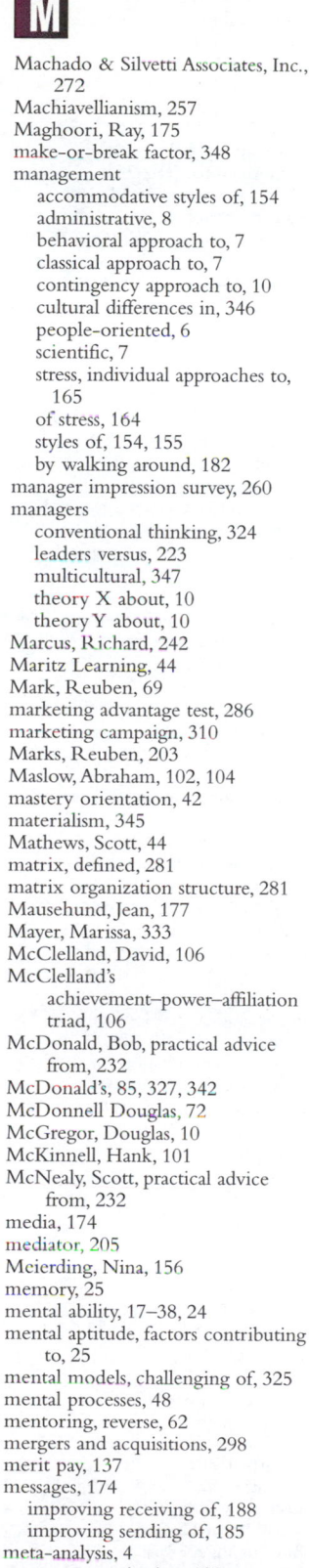